计机构成立五十周年

湖南统计年鉴

2002

HUNAN STATISTICAL YEARBOOK

湖南省统计局 编

Edited by

Statistical Bureau of Hunan Province

中国统计出版社

China Statistics Press

湖湘数典

★国内生产总值（亿元）

Gross Domestic Product(100 million yuan)

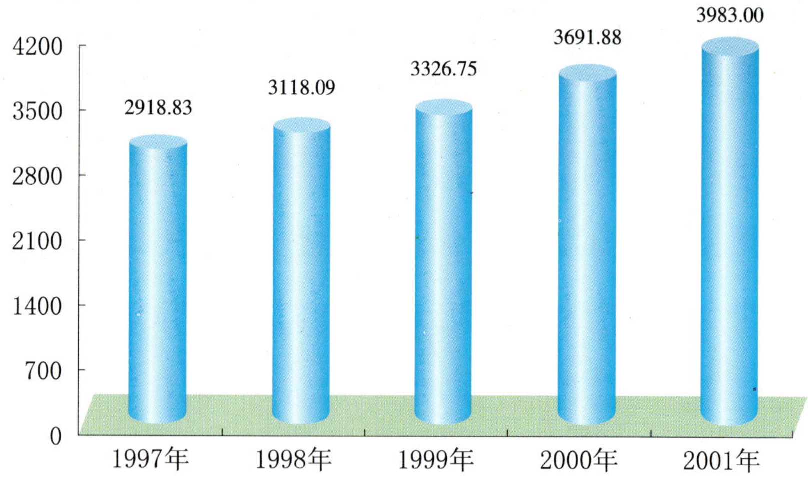

★人均国内生产总值（元）

Per Capita GDP (yuan)

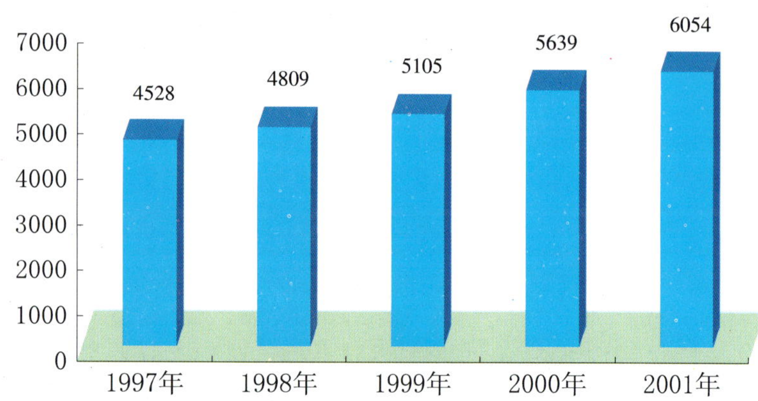

★国内生产总值构成 (%)

Composition of GDP (%)

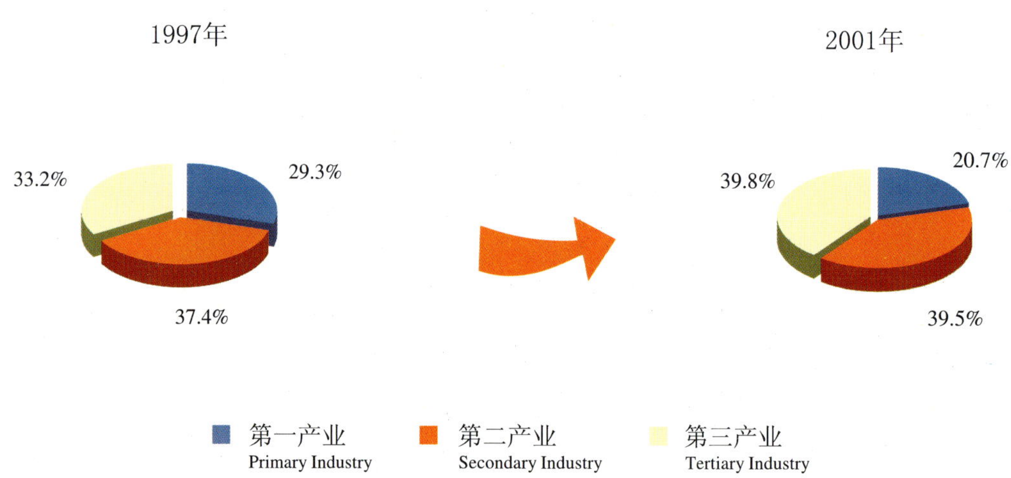

DIGITAL HUNAN

DIGITAL HUNAN

★外贸进出口总额（亿美元）

Total Value of Foreign Trade Imports and Exports (USD 100 million)

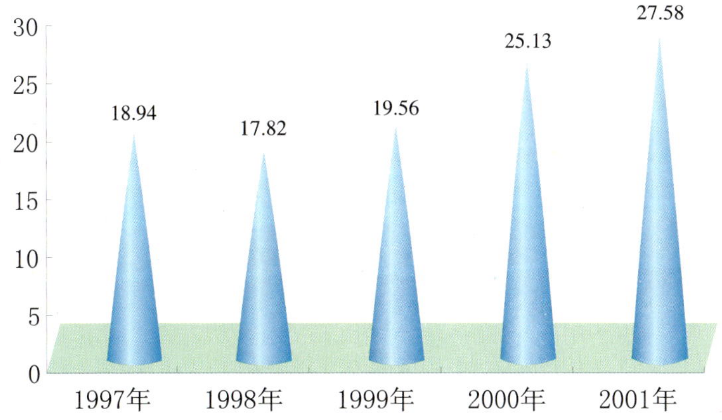

★地方财政收入(亿元)

Local Financial Revenue（100 million yuan）

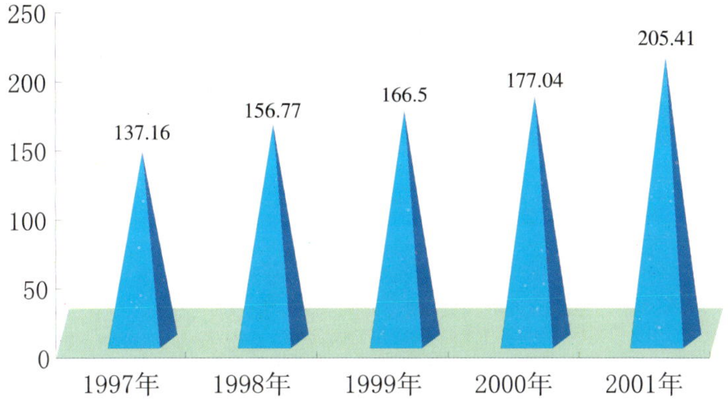

★居民收入（元）

Income of Households(yuan)

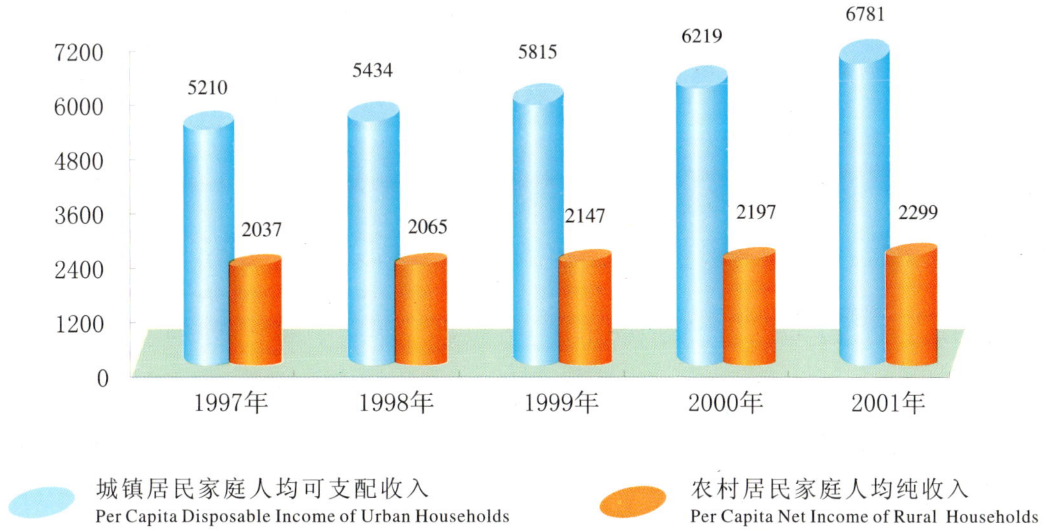

人口与就业

POPULATION AND EMPLOYMENT

指 标		1997	1998	1999	2000	2001	年均增长（%）
年底总人口	（万人）	6465.0	6502.0	6532.0	6562.0	6595.9	0.50
市镇人口	（万人）	1629.0	1684.0	1724.0	1952.2	2031.5	5.68
乡村人口	（万人）	4836.0	4818.0	4808.0	4609.8	4564.3	-1.44
城市化水平	（%）	25.20	25.90	26.39	29.75	30.80	-
从业人员数	（万人）	3560.29	3603.17	3601.39	3577.58	3607.96	0.33
#职工人数	（万人）	597.48	594.16	590.75	580.82	534.22	-2.76
第一产业从业人员	（万人）	1998.59	2002.51	2026.09	2120.98	2078.36	0.98
第二产业从业人员	（万人）	802.25	822.49	839.09	840.52	748.90	-1.71
第三产业从业人员	（万人）	759.45	778.17	736.21	616.08	780.70	0.69

国民经济核算

NATIONAL ECONOMIC ACCOUNTING

指 标		1997	1998	1999	2000	2001	年均增长（%）
国内生产总值	（亿元）	2918.83	3118.09	3326.75	3691.88	3983.00	9.10
第一产业	（亿元）	855.75	828.31	778.25	784.92	825.73	3.63
第二产业	（亿元）	1092.80	1200.86	1297.74	1461.86	1573.00	10.99
第三产业	（亿元）	970.28	1088.92	1250.76	1445.10	1584.27	10.90
人均国内生产总值	（元）	4528	4809	5105	5639	6054	8.51
国内生产总值指数	（上年为100）	110.7	108.5	108.3	109.0	109.0	-

固定资产投资

INVESTMENT IN FIXED ASSETS

指 标		1997	1998	1999	2000	2001	年均增长（%）
全社会固定资产投资	（亿元）	700.73	848.59	943.34	1066.27	1210.63	12.28
国有单位	（亿元）	366.34	457.00	522.95	574.12	618.54	10.51
集体单位	（亿元）	84.48	95.65	95.81	118.80	145.78	12.96
个体经济	（亿元）	195.17	230.15	263.42	281.89	291.55	10.30
基本建设投资	（亿元）	258.01	343.06	368.47	403.96	476.70	13.43
更新改造投资	（亿元）	107.26	115.54	143.30	175.20	198.31	10.54
房地产开发投资	（亿元）	34.02	42.12	55.50	74.83	107.41	21.71
其他投资	（亿元）	289.07	347.87	376.07	412.28	428.21	10.15
房屋建筑竣工面积	（万平方米）	8674.84	11382.54	10094.18	10892.52	10216.65	-0.70
#住宅竣工面积	（万平方米）	7012.41	9639.96	8408.18	9117.54	8344.88	-1.32

财政和金融

PUBLIC FINANCE AND BANKING

指 标		1997	1998	1999	2000	2001	年均增长（%）
地方财政收入	（亿元）	137.16	156.77	166.50	177.04	205.41	9.52
#各项税收	（亿元）	105.75	102.95	105.50	111.57	124.45	7.18
财政支出	（亿元）	230.82	273.64	313.12	347.83	431.70	14.67
#基本建设支出	（亿元）	13.78	28.75	37.66	38.08	39.40	24.20
教育事业费	（亿元）	37.92	39.33	44.54	50.88	65.09	12.89
金融机构年末存款余额	（亿元）	1769.91	2110.71	2539.75	2874.75	3342.91	15.95
金融机构年末贷款余额	（亿元）	2123.00	2274.41	2408.36	2403.38	2787.92	9.50
保险机构保费收入	（亿元）	30.74	34.47	42.29	60.89	56.09	15.48

农业

AGRICULTURE

指 标		1997	1998	1999	2000	2001	年均增长（%）
农林牧渔业总产值	（亿元）	1322.26	1262.46	1200.94	1251.89	1313.22	4.27
农业	（亿元）	660.02	628.98	624.70	633.84	665.70	3.66
林业	（亿元）	47.98	48.20	48.20	51.01	51.88	3.36
牧业	（亿元）	538.15	505.71	458.62	486.13	510.42	4.30
渔业	（亿元）	76.10	79.57	69.42	80.91	85.23	8.44
粮食总产量	（万吨）	2953.28	2818.19	2892.35	2874.97	2700.30	-0.01
猪牛羊肉总产量	（万吨）	404.02	429.03	420.51	436.51	452.12	4.29
水产品总产量	（万吨）	110.76	116.78	124.45	133.21	140.96	7.48

工业

INDUSTRY

指 标		1997	1998	1999	2000	2001	年均增长（%）
工业总产值	（亿元）	3279.53	3593.14	3786.19	4272.00	4508.70	11.65
工业增加值	（亿元）	944.95	1024.30	1096.56	1230.71	1309.50	10.97
发电量	（亿千瓦小时）	345.96	345.69	332.51	354.42	384.35	2.54
钢产量	（万吨）	243.73	270.59	309.02	304.13	441.90	18.46
水泥产量	（万吨）	2209.00	2338.00	2273.85	2395.72	2496.02	1.65

建筑业

CONSTRUCTION

指 标		1997	1998	1999	2000	2001	年均增长（%）
建筑业增加值	（亿元）	147.85	176.56	201.18	231.15	263.50	10.75
建筑施工企业技术装备率	（元/人）	3954	4430	4857	5428	5200	6.98
建筑施工企业动力装备率	（千瓦/人）	4.1	4.2	4.5	4.7	4.4	2.35
人均竣工房屋建筑面积	（平方米/人）	28.1	28.8	32.9	32.5	33.1	1.34

交通运输和邮电

TRANSPORTATION, POSTAL AND TELECOMMUNICATION SERVICES

指 标		1997	1998	1999	2000	2001	年均增长（%）
电气化铁路里程	（公里）	477	595	601	672	1211	28.25
高速公路里程	（公里）	45	172	280	449	585	67.03
旅客运输量	（万人）	79250	79540	87806	87462	92381	3.88
旅客周转量	（亿人公里）	592.16	610.53	676.04	724.06	761.62	7.19
货物运输量	（万吨）	48946	49078	51057	51090	52879	0.96
货物周转量	（亿吨公里）	998.64	978.72	967.36	1074.14	1131.78	1.92
邮电业务总量	（亿元）	52.24	76.00	92.47	140.92	134.16	25.71
电话普及率	（部/百人）	4.12	5.21	6.33	10.69	10.82	24.21

贸易外经和旅游

DOMESTIC TRADE, FOREIGN TRADE, FOREIGN ECONOMIC AND TOURISM

指 标		1997	1998	1999	2000	2001	年均增长（%）
社会消费品零售总额	（亿元）	1041.60	1125.33	1229.21	1364.66	1511.07	9.79
#批发零售贸易业	（亿元）	678.10	718.81	779.99	885.05	985.14	9.61
餐饮业	（亿元）	82.19	97.95	117.18	139.55	161.08	17.76
对外贸易进出口总额	（亿美元）	18.94	17.82	19.56	25.13	27.58	9.36
#出口	（亿美元）	14.48	12.83	12.82	16.53	17.54	6.32
接待境外游客总人数	（万人）	30.16	34.86	38.58	45.40	50.46	17.15
旅游外汇收入	（亿美元）	1.40	1.56	1.85	2.21	2.71	21.56

教育、文化和卫生

EDUCATION, CULTURE AND PUBLIC HEALTH

指 标		1997	1998	1999	2000	2001	年均增长（%）
普通高等学校专任教师	（万人）	1.59	1.65	1.80	2.03	2.39	8.75
普通中学专任教师	（万人）	19.48	20.18	21.24	22.37	23.62	4.77
普通小学专任教师	（万人）	29.95	30.41	30.74	30.64	29.16	-0.47
普通高等学校在校学生	（万人）	14.37	15.67	19.36	25.31	33.13	19.54
普通中学在校学生	（万人）	323.24	336.23	356.05	391.73	425.59	6.87
普通小学在校学生	（万人）	787.13	769.35	721.40	663.93	601.26	-4.73
教育经费总支出	（亿元）	98.97	120.32	137.56	153.12	177.77	15.36
广播人口覆盖率	（%）	78.62	79.11	81.09	81.46	81.62	-
电视人口覆盖率	（%）	87.71	88.16	98.38	91.38	91.70	-
电视节目每周播出时间	（小时）	1734	1820	2170	2338	8224	39.86
医院卫生院个数	（个）	3349	3318	3359	3339	3335	-0.52
医院卫生院床位数	（万张）	13.47	13.43	13.46	13.21	13.43	0.10
卫生技术人员数	（万人）	18.36	19.01	19.53	19.89	19.90	2.39

人民生活与物价

PEOPLE'S LIVELIHOOD AND PRICE INDICES

指 标		1997	1998	1999	2000	2001	年均增长（%）
城镇单位职工年平均工资	（元）	5326	5473	5939	6515	7698	8.58
城镇居民人均可支配收入	（元）	5209.7	5434.3	5815.4	6218.7	6780.6	6.06
城镇居民人均消费性支出	（元）	4317.2	4371.0	4800.0	5218.8	5546.2	6.24
城镇居民人均居住面积	（平方米）	8.66	9.91	10.77	11.75	11.80	7.92
农村居民人均纯收入	（元）	2037.1	2064.9	2147.2	2197.2	2299.5	5.11
农村居民人均消费支出	（元）	1815.8	1889.2	1920.2	1942.9	1990.3	2.76
农村居民人均居住面积	（平方米）	27.37	28.79	29.88	30.92	32.87	4.11
城乡居民人均储蓄存款	（元）	1947.2	2119.1	2585.9	2862.7	3319.3	12.52
居民消费价格总指数	（上年为100）	102.8	100.2	100.5	101.4	99.1	-

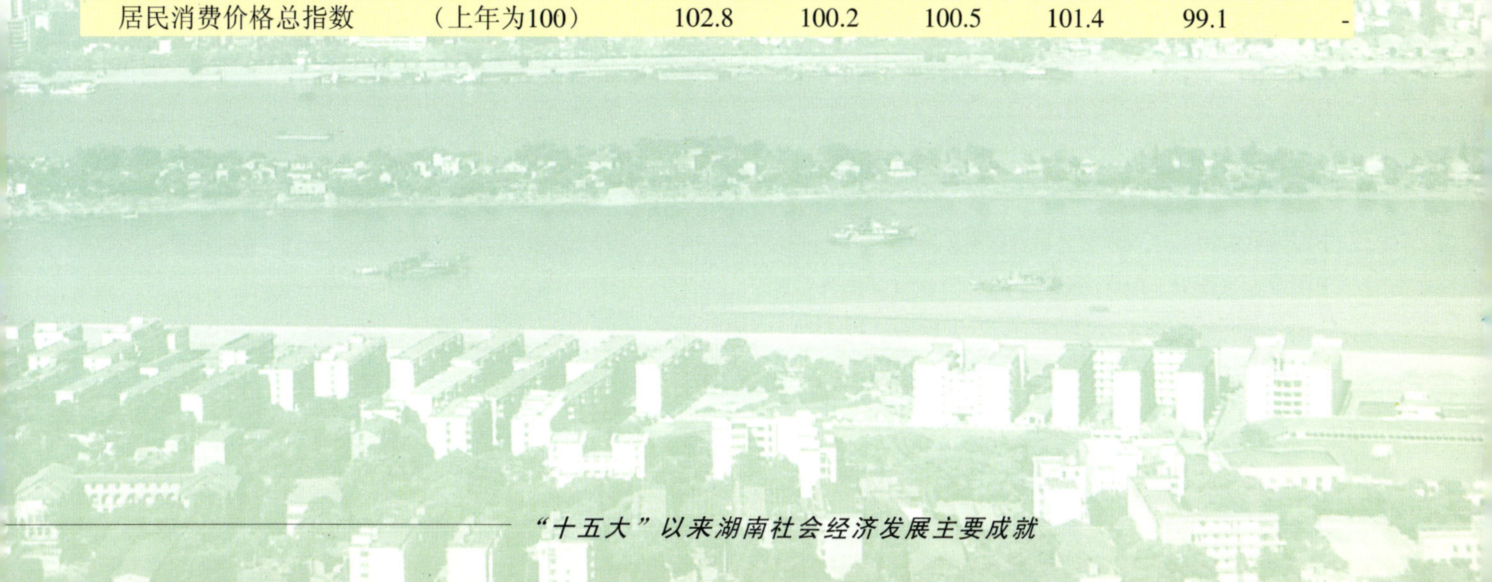

（京）新登字 041 号

图书在版编目(CIP)数据

湖南统计年鉴.2002 / 湖南省统计局　编
北京：中国统计出版社，2002.7
ISBN　7-5037-3765-4
Ⅰ. 湖...
Ⅱ. 湖...
Ⅲ. 社会经济统计－统计资料－湖南省－2002－年鉴
Ⅳ. C832. 64-54
中国版本图书馆 CIP 数据核字(2002)第 033313 号

湖南统计年鉴－2002

作　　者/湖南省统计局
责任编辑/蔡启新　　李生春
E-mail/yearbook@stats.gov.cn
责任校对/李生春
封面设计/宋飞燕
出版发行/中国统计出版社
通信地址/北京市西城区三里河月坛南街 75 号　中国统计出版社
电　　话/（010）63262295
印　　刷/湖南彩印厂　13907491437
经　　销/新华书店
开　　本/297mm/210mm
字　　数/170 万字
印　　张/35
印　　数/2000 册
版　　别/2002 年 7 月第 1 版
版　　次/2002 年 7 月第 1 次印刷
书　　号/ISBN　7-5037-3765-4/F・1342
定　　价/220 元

《湖南统计年鉴--2002》编辑委员会和编辑工作人员

一、编委会

主任委员

马　勇

副主任委员

吴星明　邱运斌　周菊华　张世平　刘志荣
江利国　黎新明　张松青　张光友

委　　员　（以姓氏笔划为序）

马爱霞　王立凯　冯文金　叶扬宗　江金生
刘红旗　刘其祝　刘明亮　刘顺国　刘湘林
陈良米　陈建军　李　波　李平安　李机生
李建平　李绍文　李春喜　邱伯莉　苏寿泉
肖胜利　张少虹　张昭红　林定春　林德勇
欧阳美嫔　周志明　周海俊　贺友斌　赵子荣
高　勇　高群芳　唐素芳　徐　朋　谭蒲辉
戴乐平

二、编辑工作人员

总　编　辑　刘志荣

编辑部主任　高　勇

编辑部副主任　曾斌求　周碧红

责任编辑　蔡启新　李生春

专文特载　戴乐平　曾斌求　彭积龙　周曙东　顾　虹

英文翻译　戴乐平　顾　虹

校　　订　高　勇　李生春　顾　虹

《Hunan Statistical Yearbook -- 2002》 Editorial Board and Staff

编 者 说 明

一、《湖南统计年鉴－2002》是一部全面反映湖南省国民经济和社会发展情况的资料性年刊。收录了全省及各市、州、县2001年经济和社会发展方面的大量统计数据，以及重要历史年份的全省主要统计数据。是一本党政部门、企事业单位、经济研究工作者、教学科研人员及来湘投资者的重要工具书。

二、《湖南统计年鉴－2002》在保持过去历年统计年鉴结构联贯、资料可比的基础上，做了部分补充和调整。首卷为特载《湖南省统计局关于2001年国民经济和社会发展统计公报》。统计资料分19部分，即：1. 综合；2. 国民经济核算；3. 人口就业和职工工资；4. 固定资产投资；5. 财政、金融、保险；6. 物价指数；7. 人民生活；8. 城市建设，环境保护；9. 农业；10. 工业；11. 建筑业；12. 运输、邮电；13. 国内外贸易、对外经济和旅游；14. 教育和科技；15. 文化、体育、卫生；16. 党群、政法和社会福利；17. 企业调查；18. 各市、州、县主要经济和社会统计指标；19. 各省、市、自治区主要经济和社会统计指标。

三、本《年鉴》资料大部分来自年度统计报表，一部分来自抽样调查。各市、州、县主要经济和社会统计指标是根据当年各地的统计年报资料整理的；全国及各省、市、自治区的年度引用数据是根据国家统计局反馈资料加工的；有些专业性很强的指标是由省直有关业务厅局年报提供的；土地面积、森林资源、河流湖泊状况是按照有关部门近年来普查资料整理的。

四、本《年鉴》中价值指标均按当年价格计算，指数均按可比价格计算。如有变化，表后即有说明。本年鉴数据均为电脑合成，由于单位取舍按四舍五入处理产生的计算误差，均未作机械调整。

五、本《年鉴》是按照《中国统计年鉴》的大体框架和规范要求编辑的。统一使用《中国统计年鉴》指标解释，统一采用国际度量衡标准计量单位，统一使用《中国统计年鉴》规范符号。

“...”表示数据不足本表最小单位数；“#”表示其中的主要项；“空格”表示指标数据不详或无该项统计数据；“※”表示表下有注释。

Preface

Ⅰ.《Hunan Statistical Yearbook-2002》is an annual statistical publication, which provides comprehensive data series in 2001, and some selected data series for historically important years at provincial level and local levels of cities, prefecture and counties. There for, it is an important reference book for party and government departments, enterprises and administrations units, economic and scientific research works, teachers and investment units come to Hunan.

Ⅱ.《Hunan statistical Yearbook-2002》has been adjusted and added partly and it maintains the continuity compared with the yearbooks published before. The first special issue is statistical communique on the National Economy and Social Development of Hunan province Statistical Bureau 200 1.

The Statistical figures contains the following 19 parts, 1. General Survey; 2. National Economy Accounting; 3. Population, Employment and Wage; 4. Investment in Fixed Assets; 5. Public Finance, Banking, Insurance; 6. Price Indices; 7. People's Livelihood; 8. Construction of Cities, Environmental Protection; 9. Agriculture; 10. Industry; 11. Construction; 12. Transportation, Post and Telecommunication Services; 13. Domestic Trade, Foreign Trade, Foreign Economy and Tourism; 14. Education and Science; 15. Culture, Sports and Public Health;16.Party and Mass, Politics and Law, Social Welfare; 17. Enterprises Survey; 18. Main Economic and Social Statistics Indicators of Cities, Prefecture and Counties; 19. Main Economic and Social Indicators by Provinces (Municipalities and Autonomous Regions).

Ⅲ. The major data of the book are from annual statistical reports, and some from sampling surveys. Main economic and social statistics indicators of cities, Prefecture and counties are arranged according to their annual statistical reports. Annual data of state, and other provinces, municipalities directly under central government and autonomous regions are quoted from data returned by State Statistical Bureau. Some very specialized indicators are applied by the province directly under administrational annual reports. Area of total land, Forest resources, the condition of rivers and lakes are arranged according to census by the departments concerned in recent years.

Ⅳ. All of the value indicators in this book are calculated by the same year's prices. All of the indices are calculated by the constant price. Explanatory notes are provided behind the list in which if there are changes. Data of the book are composed by computers.

Ⅴ. The book is edited according to the frame and standard of China Statistical Yearbook. The indicator explanatory notes are edited according to China Statistical Yearbook, and the units of measurement are internationally standard measurement units. The notations are standard notations of China Statistical Yearbook.

"…" not large enough to be rounded into the least unit.

"#" of which: major items.

"Space" data not available.

"※"see footnotes below.

目　录

CONTENTS

特载：SPECIAL ISSUE:

一、综合

Chapter 1 General Survey

二、国民经济核算

Chapter 2 National Economic Accounting

三、人口、就业和职工工资

Chapter 3 Population, Employment and Wages of Staff and Workers

四、固定资产投资
Chapter 4 Investment in Fixed Assets

五、财政、金融、保险

Chapter 5 Finance, Banking and Insurance

八、城市建设、环境保护

Chapter 8　Construction of Cities, Environmental Protection

九、农业

Chapter 9　Agriculture

十、工业

Chapter 10 Industry

十一、建筑业

Chapter 11 Construction

十二、交通运输、邮电业

Chapter 12 Transportation, Postal and Telecommunication Services

十三、国内、外贸易、对外经济和旅游

Chapter 13 Domestic Trade,Foreign Trade, Foreign Economy and Tourism

十五、文化、体育、卫生
Chapter 15 Culture, Sports and Public Health

十六、党群、政法和社会福利
Chapter 16 Party and Mass, Politics and Law,Social Welfare

十七、企业调查
Chapter 17 Enterprises Survey

十八、各市、州、县主要经济和社会统计指标

Chapter 18 Main Economic and Social Statistics Indicators of Cities,Perfecture and Counties

十九、各省、市、自治区主要经济和社会统计指标

Chapter 19 Main Economic and Social Statistics Indicators by Provinces,Municipalities and Autonomous Regions

特载：

湖南省统计局
关于2001年国民经济和社会发展统计公报

2002年2月8日

2001年，面对复杂多变的国际经济环境，在省委、省政府的正确领导下，全省人民坚持以“三个代表”重要思想为指导，认真贯彻落实党中央、国务院一系列方针政策，以经济结构调整为主线，大力推进农业产业化、工业化、城市化，国民经济快速健康发展，各项社会事业繁荣稳定，精神文明建设不断加强，人民生活进一步改善。“十五”计划开局良好。

一、综合

全省国民经济综合实力进一步增强。初步测算，全年国内生产总值3983亿元，比上年增长9.0%。其中，第一产业增加值826亿元，增长4.0%；第二产业增加值1570亿元，增长10.0%；第三产业增加值1587亿元，增长10.5 %。人均国内生产总值6054元，增长8.4%。三次产业构成为20.7:39.4:39.9,与上年相比，第一产业下降0.6个百分点，第二产业下降0.2个百分点，第三产业上升0.8个百分点。

市场物价呈小幅下降态势。全年居民消费价格总水平比上年下降0.9%,其中消费品价格下降1.8%,服务项目价格上涨2.5%,涨幅比上年回落11.1个百分点。在居民消费价格中，食品价格下降1.4%，衣着价格下降2.6%，医疗保健及个人用品下降0.2%，娱乐教育文化用品及服务上涨2.1%，其中教育上涨5.4%。工业品出厂价格指数为99.8%,下降0.2%；原材料、燃料、动力购进价格上涨1.1%，涨幅比上年回落5.6个百分点。房地产价格上涨1.6%。

劳动就业工作力度加大。据劳动部门统计，年末全省国有企业下岗职工46.12万人，比上年末下降7.8%,国有企业下岗职工再就业率为11.7%，全年城镇登记失业人员30.34万人，新安置失业人员22万人。全省城镇登记失业率为4.0%。

各项改革稳步推进。国有企业改革继续深化，年初确定的50户大中型企业的建制工作进展顺利，中小企业产权制度改革力度加大，农村改革进一步深化，政府行政审批制度改革取得初步成果，整顿和规范市场经济秩序初见成效。

2001年，我省加大城市基础设施建设投入力度，推进小城镇建设，城市化进程加快。小城镇已发展到1086个，增加31个，城市化水平为30.8%，比上年提高1.05个百分点。

经济和社会发展中存在的主要问题是：国民经济结构性矛盾仍然突出，供给结构还不能适应市场变化；农民和城市低收入群体收入增长缓慢，收入差距继续扩大；经济自主增长内在动力不强；就业和再就业形势依然严峻。

二、农业和农村经济

农业和农村经济继续保持平稳发展。全年农林牧渔业总产值1313.23亿元，增长4.0%。主要农产品产量有升有降。全年粮食总产量2700.3万吨，减少2.4%；棉花19万吨，增加20.3%；油料137.39万吨，减少1.4%；烤烟15.11万吨，减少2.8%；茶叶5.84万吨，增长2.0%；水果186.54万吨，增长23.9%。出栏肉猪6257.54万头，增长3.6%；出栏牛137.73万头，增长4.6%；出栏羊569.15万只，增长9.6%；水产品产量140.96万吨，增长5.8%。全年人工造林7.56万公顷，其中退耕还林2.75万公顷，年末有林地面积达957.95万公顷，活立木蓄积量为3.06亿立方米，立竹14.7亿根，森林覆盖率为52.8%，比上年提高0.4个百分点。

农业结构调整加快，产业化经营效果显现。全省粮食播种面积480.28万公顷，比上年调减22.71万公顷，其中早稻调减15.47万公顷；优质稻面积118.81万公顷，增加15.06万公顷。经济作物中，棉花、麻类、药材种植面积分别达14.94万公顷、4.84万公顷和5.6万公顷，增长2.3%、37.7%和31.9%；蔬菜和果用瓜面积为82.86万公顷和12.89万公顷，分别增长15.0%和22.2%。生猪生产稳步发展，草食牲畜、家禽和名特优水产快速增长，畜牧水产业总产值达到596亿元，比上年增长4.1%，占农林牧渔业总产值比重达45.4%。龙头企业对农村经济的带动和市场辐射能力进一步增强。23家省级龙头企业共连结基地38.6万公顷，年销售收入95亿元，增长26.6%；实现利润7.5亿元，增长38.9%。

农村基础设施建设取得新成效。全省共开工各类水利工程61万处，已完成项目46万处，投入资金29亿元，完成土石方5.1亿立方米，新增灌溉面积1.01万公倾，治理水土流失面积334.4平方公里，解决了53.72万人、47.94万头牲畜的饮水困难。全省农业机械总动力2358万千瓦，增长6.7%。收获机械和农用运输机械呈快速增长态势。

小康建设和扶贫工作进展顺利。2001年，全省共投入扶贫资金12.8亿元，年末贫困人口110万人，比上年减少20万人。全省农村整体进入小康，共计有65个县（市、区）达到小康标准。

三、工业和建筑业

工业生产持续稳定增长。全部工业增加值1309.5亿元，比上年增长9.9%。其中国有工业及年销售收入500万元以上非国有工业（简称规模以上工业）增加值617.93亿元，增长13.8%，增幅比上年提高0.2个百分点。规模以上工业中，轻工业增加值 225.55亿元，增长15.2%；重工业增加值392.38亿元，增长13.1%。国有及国有控股工业增加值增长 12.0%，集体工业增长15.6%，股份合作制工业增长15.8%，股份制工业增长14.7%。

工业结构得到持续调整。2001年，工业企业技术改造力度加大，全年全省完成工业技改投资112.3亿元，增长38.6%。企业技术创新步伐加快。全年完成省级以上新产品开发472项，规模以上企业新产品产值214.5亿元，新产品产值率11.6%。2001年，全省规模以上工业产品产量中，水泥 2496.02万吨，比上年增长6.0%；成品钢材389.01万吨，增长29.6%；十种有色金属89.76万吨，增长8.7%；发电量384.35亿千瓦小时，增长8.5%；化肥146.11万吨，减少0.7%；化学农药4.91万吨，增长6.8%；汽车2.05万辆，增长16.5%；彩色显象管448.65万只，增长20.9%。

企业经济效益继续提高。全年国有工业及年销售收入500万元以上非国有工业盈亏相抵后实现利润51.67亿元，比上年增长48.6%；亏损企业亏损额30.11亿元，下降14.2%；企业亏损面为30.4%，比上年下降4.1个百分点。国有及国有控股工业企业实现利润28.59亿元，增长71.6%；亏损额24.95亿元，下降11.5%；亏损面37.3%，下降8.1个百分点。

建筑业生产稳步发展，效益好转。全社会建筑业增加值260.5亿元，增长10.8%。四级及以上建筑业企业实现利润总额5.41亿元，增长23.2%；税金总额16.88亿元，增长54.7%。施工单位工程个数20646个，减少3.8%，其中投标承包11299个，减少1.0%。房屋建筑施工面积5016.7万平方米，减少1.4%；房屋建筑竣工面积2483.2万平方米，减少4.6%。

四、固定资产投资

固定资产投资快速增长。2001 年全省全社会固定资产投资 1209.27 亿元，增长 13.4%。其中国有及其他经济完成投资 798.42 亿元，增长 16.6%；集体和个人投资 410.85 亿元，增长 7.6%。国有及其他经济类型投资中，基本建设投资 476.71 亿元，增长 18.0%；更新改造投资 198.29 亿元，增长 13.2%；房地产开发投资 106.32 亿元，增长 42.1%。地方项目投资 573.61 亿元，增长 37.0%；中央项目投资 224.81 亿元，下降 9.4%。年内新开工项目 4830 个，增长 14.6%；年内竣工项目 4208 个，增长 2.2%。

投资向基础产业和基础设施倾斜。在国有及其他经济投资中，农业、电力、交通邮电、社会服务、卫生体育、科技等行业投资 444.99 亿元，占 55.7%。其中农林牧渔业投资 5.71 亿元，增长 26.1%；交通投资 152.17 亿元，增长 18.5%；社会服务业投资 94.48 亿元，增长 93.0%；卫生体育和社会福利业投资 17.31 亿元，增长 140.9%；科研和综合技术服务业 3.79 亿元，增长 24.5%；电力、煤气及水的生产和供应业投资 87.72 亿元，与上年基本持平。

重点工程建设成效显著。全省在建重点建设项目 26 个，完成投资 270 亿元，完成年计划的 108%，比上年净增 10 亿元。全部和单项投产项目均已建成。京珠国道主干线耒宜高速公路建成通车；益阳电厂 2 台机组投产发电；株六铁路复线和武广铁路电气化建成通车；永连公路一期工程 99 公里已完成；湘江流域环境治理常德污水厂投产；湖南移动 GSM 六期扫尾和七期扩容全面完成年度计划、联通 CDMA 网络建设已经开通；上瑞高速公路湖南段——潭邵线进展顺利。

全年主要新增生产能力：发电机组 62.1 万千瓦，11 万伏及以上变电设备能力 325.5 万千伏安，输电线路长度 527.86 公里；长途电缆 6154 延长公里，程控交换机 233.89 万线，移动通信基站设备 2161 信道；新扩建万吨级港口码头年吞吐量 6 万吨，新建公路 710.19 公里，其中高速公路 135.37 公里，改建公路 1869 公里；城市自来水日供水量 37.6 万吨，城市污水日处理量 4. 75 万吨，城市道路扩建长度 105.2 公里，扩建面积 464.46 万平方米。

五、国内贸易

2001 年，在国家连续两次增加公务员工资和城镇中低收入阶层居民收入，扩大消费信贷等多种促进消费政策措施的作用下，国内市场商品销售稳中趋活。全年实现社会消费品零售总额 1511.07 亿元，比上年增长 10.7%。其中城市 800.06 亿元，增长 12.7%，农村(县及县以下)711.01 亿元，增长 8.6%。分行业为，批发零售贸易业零售额 985.14 亿元，增长 11.3%；餐饮业 161.08 亿元，增长 15.4%；其他行业 364.85 亿元，增长 7.3%。分经济类型是，公有经济实现零售额 404.85 亿元，增长 2.0%；非公有经济 1106.22 亿元，增长 14.3%。大型市场逐步成为商品交易市场的主体，2001 年，全省亿元市场 101 家，商品成交额 466 亿元，占全省商品交易市场成交额的 54.6%，连锁超市等新型业态发展迅速，2001 年，我省限额以上连锁商业企业 30 家，零售额 20 亿元，增长 2.4 倍。

六、对外经济贸易和旅游业

2001 年，受世界经济增长放慢的影响，我省对外贸易增速有所下降。全年进出口总额为 27.58 亿美元，比上年增长 9.8%。 其中出口 17.54 亿美元，增长 6.1%；进口 10.04 亿美元，增长 16.9%。对外贸易中，一般贸易进出口额为 23.84 亿美元，增长 15.2%；加工贸易进出口额 2.7 亿美元，下降 12.6%。按出口企业性质分，国有企业出口 13.44 亿美元，增长 0.1%；外商投资企业 2.13 亿美元，增长 16.3%；集体企业 1.28 亿美元，增长 44.1%；私营企业 0.69 亿美元，增长 77.9%。出口商品中，机电产品 3.38 亿美元，增长 8.4%；

纺织品及服装3.1亿美元，增长17.4%；未锻造的锌及锌合金1.29亿美元，下降14.9%；烟花、爆竹0.85亿美元，增长4.0%。

利用外资再创新绩。全年协议利用外资13.31亿美元，增长21.7%；实际利用外资11.87亿美元，增长7.1%。其中外商直接投资8.1亿美元，增长18.8%。

对外经济合作大幅增长。全年新签对外承包工程、劳务合作、设计咨询的合同金额2.7亿美元，增长44.3%；营业额2.65亿美元，增长91.4%。

国内国际旅游快速发展。全年共接待国内旅游者4985.06万人次，增长7.2%，国内旅游收入188.09亿元，增长44.1%；接待入境旅游者50.46万人次，增长11.1%；国际旅游创汇2.7亿美元，增长22.2%。实现旅游总收入210亿元，比上年增长41.4%，旅游总收入占全省国内生产总值的5.2%，比上年提高1.2个百分点。旅游业已成为我省重要的支柱产业之一。

七、交通和邮电业

2001年完成全社会货物周转量1132.26亿吨公里，比上年增长5.4%。其中，铁路运输674.62亿吨公里，增长6.7%；公路运输316.03亿吨公里，增长6.1%；水运141.22亿吨公里,减少1.8%；民航0.12亿吨公里，增长9.1%。旅客周转量760.80亿人公里，增长5.1%。其中，铁路411.07亿人公里，增长4.3%；公路337.90亿人公里，增长6.1%；水运3.23亿人公里，减少9.0%；民航8.6亿人公里，增长5.7%。

全年邮电业务总量187.77亿元，比上年增长37.8%。年末全省固定电话用户758.5万户，增长10.9%。电话普及率11.5%，比上年提高0.8个百分点。移动电话、互联网迅速发展。移动电话用户410.38万户，增长73.6%；互联网用户107.2万户，增长88.1%。

八、金融和保险业

金融业不断强化和完善服务功能，对经济的支持力度进一步加大，存贷款大幅增长。年末各项存款余额3342.91亿元，比年初增加471.54亿元。其中企业存款余额873.89亿元，增加111.16亿元；城乡居民储蓄存款余额2183.73亿元，增加311.88亿元。年末各项贷款余额2787.92亿元，比年初增加389.59亿元。其中短期贷款余额1798.73亿元，增加193.56亿元；中长期贷款余额787.52亿元，增加157.51亿元。贷款投放趋向集中，年内工业贷款新增39.6亿元，农业贷款新增36.66亿元，基本建设贷款新增107.64亿元，个人消费贷款余额76.23亿元，增加27.56亿元。但中小企业和农村居民贷款难的问题没有根本好转。

保险事业不断发展。全年保费收入56.22亿元，比上年增长20.5%。其中财产险保费收入16.36亿元，寿险保费收入39.86亿元，分别增长16.9%和22.1%。全年赔付额18.54亿元，增长67.9%。其中财产险赔付7.92亿元，寿险赔付10.62亿元，分别增长10.0%和176.6%。

九、科学技术和教育

科教兴湘进程加快，科研成果显著。长沙软件园列入国家软件园基地，岳麓山大学科技园由国家授牌。全省共取得各类科研成果1008项，其中“选择性沉淀法从钨酸盐溶液中除钼、砷、锑新工艺”、“水稻两用核不育系‘培矮64S’选育及其应用研究”等11项优秀科研成果获国家科技奖励，“基于通用系统理论的决策支持系统的理论与应用”、“汽车覆盖件冲压成型工艺与模具一体化技术与装备”、“高强度超强结合力型泡沫镍”等150项科技成果获省级科技进步奖。全省高新技术产品产值为606亿元，创利税92.38亿元，分别增长21.2%和20.0%。高新技术企业中，年产值过亿元的有70家，过10亿元的有12家。专利工作取得新成绩。全省三种专利申请 4292 项，增长 4.3%；三种专利批准数 2401 项。科技事业进一步繁荣。全省拥有各类科学研究开发机构 321 个，其中自然科学研究机构 174 个，人文社会科学研究机构 3 个，科技情报与文献机构 13 个，省级重点实验室 25 个。全省地方国有单位各类专业技术人员 107.8 万人，在湘“两院”院士达到 41 人。

教育事业稳步发展。2001 年，新批准设置了湘潭大学兴湘学院等 6 所普通高校民办学院。年末全省拥有普通高校 61 所，全年招生 11.73 万人，在校学生 33.13 万人，分别比上年增长 17.3%、16.1%和 30.9%。研究生培养单位 16 个，招收新生 4575 人，在学研究生 10589 人，招生数和在学数分别增长 31.7%和 37.0%。成人高校数 26 所，招生 11.94 万人，在校学生 25.25 万人，招生数和在校人数分别增长 26.4%和 34.0%。中等专业学校 125 所，招生 7.14 万人，增长 12.3%；在校学生 24.09 万人，减少 6.7%。普通中学 4695 所，在校学生 425.59 万人，普通初中入学率为 93.0%，比上年下降 2.9 个百分点，初中在校学生辍学率为 3.4%，比上年下降 1 个百分点。普通小学 29340 所，在校学生 601.26 万人，小学适龄儿童入学率为 97.9%，比上年下降 0.5 个百分点，小学在校学生辍学率为 0.54%，上升 0.13 个百分点。

十、文化卫生和体育

文化产业发展壮大，文化艺术不断繁荣。2001 年，湖南日报和长沙晚报两个报业集团相继组建，全年报纸、杂志和图书出版量分别为 90102.12 万份、9796.98 万册和 24851.11 万册，广播影视业加快发展。2001 年末，全省拥有广播电台 11 座，中短波广播发射台和转播台 25 座，电视台 15 座，一千瓦以上电视发射台和转播台 50 座，电视人口覆盖率为 91.7%，广播人口覆盖率为 81.6%。文化艺术的繁荣丰富了人们的文化生活。花鼓戏《秋天的花鼓》获中宣部“五个一工程”奖，大型舞蹈诗《扎花女》获第三届少数民族文艺汇演创作金奖、演出金奖，影片《毛泽东在 1925》荣获第 21 届电影金鸡奖最佳故事片奖。年末全省共有艺术表演团体 91 个，文化馆 125 个，群众艺术馆 15 个，博物馆、纪念馆 66 个，公共图书馆 115 个，档案馆 199 个。

医疗卫生保健事业不断进步。2001 年末，全省医疗卫生机构 4205 个，卫生技术人员 19.9 万人。全省卫生机构床位数为 14.62 万张，比上年增长 1.9%。全省乡镇卫生院床位数为 2.12 万张，比上年增长 3.2%。农村有医疗点的村占总村数的比重为 92.6%，比上年提高 1.1 个百分点。

体育事业继续发展。2001 年，在重大国际体育比赛中，我省运动员共获世界冠军 3 个，金牌 5 枚，银牌 8 枚，铜牌 1 枚；在全国性体育比赛中获金牌 24 枚，银牌 21.5 枚，铜牌 26.5 枚。在第九届全运会上，我省共获得金牌 19.5 枚，居全国第 7 位。群众体育运动进一步普及，经常参加体育活动的人数占全部人口的 33.5%；体育达标学生占全部学生的 96.0%。

十一、环境保护

环境保护工作取得进展。2001 年，全省共建立了环保监测站 129 个，现有环境监测人员 2107 人，完成环境污染治理项目 331 个，环境污染治理项目投资额 2.71 亿元，增长 14.0%。建成烟尘控制区 157 个，比上年增长 25.6%；环境噪声达标区 126 个，增长 61.5%。年末全省建有自然环境保护区 68 个，其中国家级 8 个，省级 26 个；自然环境保护区面积 80.34 万公顷，比上年增长 4.3%。烟尘控制区面积 495.2 平方千米；噪声达标区面积 267.7 平方千米。城市污水集中处理率、城市生活垃圾无害化处理率、工业用水重复利用率分别为 27.3%、52.1%和 54.0%，比上年提高 9.2、1.6 和 1.9 个百分点。洞庭湖综合治理取得成绩，生态环境逐步改善，通过三年的平垸行洪，湖区面积有所扩大，蓄洪能力有所增强。但部分地区环境污染和生态破坏加剧的趋势仍未得到有效控制。

十二、人口

2001年末，全省总人口为6595.85万人，比上年末增加33.8万人。其中城镇人口2031.52万人，乡村人口4564.33万人。据抽样调查，2001年全省人口出生率为11.8‰，回升了0.35个千分点；死亡率为6.7‰；自然增长率为5.1‰，回升了0.42个千分点。

据第五次人口普查数据推算，2001年，我省0-14岁人口为1404.26万人，占总人口的比重为21.3%；15-64岁人口为4679.09万人，占总人口的比重为70.9%；65岁及以上老年人口为512.5万人，占总人口的比重为7.8%，老年人口比上年增加22.31万人，我省人口老龄化特征更加明显。

十三、人民生活与社会保障

据抽样调查，2001年全省城镇居民人均可支配收入为6780.56元，增长9.0%，考虑价格下降因素，实际增长10.2%。城镇居民人均实际支出6925.54元，增长7.7%，考虑价格因素，实际增长8.9%。城市居民的消费正明显地向住、行、通信、教育、旅游等新的增长点转变。2001年城镇居民人均消费性支出5546.22元，增长6.3%。其中交通及通信消费、旅游消费、教育消费及医疗保健支出的增长分别为20.0%、67.6%、19.9%和21.6%。2001年，农村居民人均可支配收入2264.71元，增加105.71元，增长4.9%，考虑价格因素，实际增长5.4%。农民人均纯收入2299.46元，增加102.3元，增长4.7%。人均可支配收入中，工资性收入840.11元，增加50.37元；家庭经营的第一产业净收入972.97元，增加34.41元；家庭经营的第二、三产业净收入398.87元，增加8.33元；转移性和财产性净收入52.76元，增加12.6元。农民人均生活消费总支出1990.33元，增加47.83元，增长2.5%，考虑价格因素，实际增长3.0%。2001年，我省城乡居民居住条件进一步改善。城市居民人均住房面积11.8平方米，比上年增加0.4平方米；农村居民人均住房面积32.87平方米，比上年增加1.95平方米，其中砖木和钢筋混凝土住房占93.6%，比上年提高0.4个百分点。

社会保障进一步加强。2001年，随着我省社会保障制度建设步伐加快，全省城镇职工参加养老保险的职工人数为452.12万人，减少0.97%；参加养老保险的退休人数147.98万人，增长8.4%；参加失业保险职工人数355万人，增长2.5%；月平均领取失业保险金人数为3.3万人。参加基本医疗保险人数351万人，增长175.7 %；至2001年11月底止，参加基本医疗保险的退休人员48.22万人，增长82.3%；参加大病统筹的职工人数141.38万人，增长110.5%。

注：

1.本公报各项统计数据为初步统计数。

2.公报中国内生产总值、各产业增加值绝对数按现价计算，增长速度按可比价格计算。

STATISTICAL COMMUNIQUE OF HUNAN PROVINCE ON THE 2001 NATIONAL ECONOMIC AND SOCIAL DEVELOPMENT

STATISTICAL BUREAU OF HUNAN PROVINCE

February 8, 2002

In 2001, facing the complex international economic environment, under the correct leadership of Hunan Provincial Party Committee and Government, people all over the province uphold the "Three Represent's" important thought, and conscientiously carried out the important decisions and policies formulated by the Central Party Committee and the State Council, concentrated on economic restructuring, advanced agricultural industrialization, industrialization and urbanization energetically, national economy maintained a trend of rapid and healthy development , the social affairs was prosperous and stable， the construction of spiritual civilization was strengthened continuously and the living standards of people was further improved. The beginning of the " Tenth -Five-Year " program was good.

I General Outlook

The comprehensive strength of the national economy gained further improved. Preliminary statistics indicated that the Gross Domestic Product (GDP) of the province was 398.30 billion yuan, increased by 9.0 percent over the previous year. Of this total, the value-added of the primary industry was 82.6 billion yuan, having increased 4.0 percent; the value-added of the second industry was 157.0 billion yuan, have an increase of 10.0 percent; and that of tertiary industry was 158.7 billion yuan, up by 10.5 percent. The per-capita GDP reached 6054 yuan, up by 8.4 percent. The percentage of the three industries was 20.7:39.4:39.9, comparing with the previous year, the value-added of the primary industry down by 0.6 percentage points, and that of the second industry down 0.2 percentage points as well, the tertiary industry up by 0.8 percentage points.

The price of market appeared a small down. The general level of the residents consumer price for the year had a decrease of 0.9 percent over the previous year, of which， the consumable prices fell by 1.8 percent, the prices for service items went up by 2.5 percent, the range of increase declined 11.1 percentage points over the previous year. Of the consumer price, food price fell by 1.4 percent; clothing fell by 2.6 percent, the price of medical and personal things went down by 0.2 percent, the prices of entertainment and education instrument up by 2.1 percent and the price of education went up 5.4 percent. The index of ex-factory price of industrial products was 99.8 percent, fell by 0.2 percent; the purchasing price for raw material, fuel, and power in industrial enterprises went up by 1.1 percent, the range of increase declined 5.6 percentage point over the previous year. The price of the real estate went up by 1.6 percent.

Work on employment was strengthened. According to statistics from the labor department, by the end of 2001, the number of laid-off workers of state-owned enterprises was 461.2 thousand, a decrease of 7.8 percent as compared with that at the end of 2000. The rate of re-employment of the unemployed people was 11.7 percent,

303.4 thousand registered unemployment in urban, and 220 thousand were settled again. The urban rate of registered unemployment was 4.0 percent all over the province.

Various reforms pushed on steadily. The reforms of the state-owned enterprises continued deepening, The working of establishing modern enterprises system of 50 large-medium enterprises got along very well, the property right reform of small-medium enterprises got further strengthened .The rural reforms became more deepened, the reform in examining and approving system of the governmental administration gained initial fruit, neatening and ruling the order of market economy acquired initial results.

In 2001, Hunan accelerated the pace of urbanization by investing municipal infrastructure facilities and pushing on the construction of towns. The total number of small towns of the whole province reached 1086 and 31 more than last year, the level of urbanization was 30.8 percent, rose by 1.05 percentage points.

Major problems that remained in economy performance and social development included: the structural contradiction was still prominent in national economy, the supply structure couldn't meet the change of social demand; the income of the lower income group in urban and rural areas grew slowly, the gap of income distribution continued to enlarge; the internal power of economic growth was not strong; and the situations of employment and re-employment were still severe.

II **Agriculture and Rural Economy**

There was stable development in agriculture and rural economy. The gross output value of agriculture was 131.32 billion yuan, up by 4.0 percent. The rise and decline existed simultaneously in the output of main agriculture product. The total output of grain amounted to 27,003 thousand tons, decreased by 2.4 percent; the output of cotton amounted to 190 thousand tons; increased by 20.3 percent; the output of oil-bearing seeds was 139,350 thousand tons, decreased by 1.4 percent; flue-cured tobacco 151.10 thousand tons, increased by 2.8 percent; the output of tea reached 58.40 thousand tons, had a increase of 2.0 percent; fruits was 1865.40 thousand tons, grew by 23.9 percent. The number of slaughtered fattened hogs amounted to 62575.40 thousand heads, grew by 3.6 percent; the number of slaughtered beef cattle was 1377.30 thousand heads, up by 23.9 percent; the sheep and goats 5691.5 thousand heads, up by 9.6 percent; the total aquatic products amounted to 1409.6 thousand tons, up by 5.8 percent. The afforestation areas reached 75.6 thousand hectares, of which, returning the farmland to forest reached to 27.5 thousand hectares, by the end of 2001, the area with woodland was 957.95 thousand hectares, the storage of live wood reached to 306 million cubic meters, the number of bamboo was 1.47 billion roots. The forest coverage rate reached 52.8 percent, up by 0.4 percentage points over the previous year.

Structural adjustment for agricultural production was quickened, the effect of industrialization management appeared. The sown areas of grain crops was 4802.8 thousand hectares, decreased by 227.1 thousand hectares over the previous year, of that, the early rice decreased by 154.7 hectares; the areas of the high quality rice 1188.1 thousand hectares, increased by 150.6 thousand hectares. Among the cash crops, the sown areas of cotton, fiber crops, medical herbs were 149.4 thousand hectares, 48.4 thousand hectares and 56 thousand hectares, increased by 2.3 percent, 37.7 percent and 31.9 percent respectively. The sown areas of vegetables and melons were 828.6 thousand hectares and 128.9 thousand hectares, increased by 15.0 percent and 22.2 percent respectively. Hogs production developed steadily. The herbivores, fowls and high quality aquatic product were quickened. The gross output value of animal husbandry and aquatic product reached to 59.6 billion yuan, up by 4.1 percent over previous year, it covered 45.4 percent of that of the whole agriculture. The chief enterprises were more effective on promoting the rural economy and expanding the market. The 23 chief enterprises at province-level connected the base 386 thousand hectares, the sales revenue annually was 9.5 billion yuan, up by 26.5 percent; and realized profits 0.75 billion yuan, grew by 38.9 percent.

The construction of rural infrastructure facilities was strengthened. 610 thousand water conservancy projects were started working in all province, 460 thousand of those projects were finished. 2.9 billion yuan was invested and 0.51 billion earth-stone cubic metres was finished. Newly increased irrigated areas 10.1 thousand hectares, the areas of controlling soil erosion reached to 334.4 square kilometers, the drinking difficulty of 537.2 thousand people and 479.4 thousand livestock have been resolved. The total power of agricultural machinery reached 2.36 million kw, up by 6.7 percent. The machinery for harvesters and transportation grew at fast speed.

The construction of being fairly well and the aid-the poor project were taken smoothly. In 2001, 1.28 billion yuan was spent on the aid-the poor project. At the end of 2001, the population in poverty was 1.1 million, 200 thousand less than the previous year. The whole province had 65 counties(cities、 districts) reached well-off level.

Ⅲ **Industry and Construction**

Industrial production increased steadily. In 2001, the gross value-added of industrial sectors was 130.95 billion yuan, up by 9.9 percent over the previous year. The value-added of the state-owned and state-holding industrial enterprises and those non-states-owned enterprises with an annual sales income over 5 million yuan (referred to as industrial enterprises above designated size hereafter) was 61.79 billion yuan, had an increase of 13.8 percent, up by 0.2 percentage points. Of this total, the value-added of the light industry was 22.56 billion yuan, having increased 15.2 percent, and the heavy industry was 39.24 billion yuan, up by 13.1 percent. The value-added of state-owned and state-holding industrial enterprises grew 12.0 percent; that of collective owned industry was up 15.6 percent; that of share holding cooperative enterprises was up 15.8 percent; that of share holding enterprises was up 14.7 percent.

Industrial structural adjustment made significant progress. In 2001, the technical reconstructions in industrial enterprises were strengthened. The investment of the technical reconstruction in industry reached 11.23 billion yuan, up by 38.6 percent. The technical innovation in industrial enterprises kept fast growth. 472 projects of new products above the province-level had developed, the output value of new products was 21.5 billion yuan, the percentage of new products value accounted to 11.6 percent. In 2001, of all this industry's outputs above designated size, the output of cement reached 24.96 million tons, up by 6.0 percent; steel 3.89 million tons, up by 29.6 percent; ten kinds of non-ferrous metal 897.6 thousand tons, up by 8.7 percent; electricity was 38.435 billion kwh, up by 8.5 percent; fertilizers 1461.1 thousand tons, down by 0.7 percent; chemical pesticide 49.1 thousand tons, up by 6.8 percent; automobiles 20.5 thousand units, up by 16.5 percent; color monitor 4486.5 thousand units, up by 20.9 percent.

The economic efficiency of the enterprises continued improvement. The total profits after balancing out between deficits and surpluses for sated-owned industrial enterprises and for non-state-owned industrial enterprises with an annual sales revenue over 5 million yuan was 5.17 billion yuan, up by 48.6 percent. The loss value of loss-making enterprises was 3.01 billion yuan, down by 14.2 percent. a decline of 4.1 percentage points over the previous year. The total profit from stated-owned and state-controlling industrial enterprises was 2.859 billion yuan, up by 71.6 percent. The loss value was 2.5 billion yuan, down by 11.5 percent. The ratio of loss-making was 37.3 percent, down by 8.1 percentage points.

The construction industry not only developed steadily, but also the efficiency turned better. The total value-added construction industry reached 26.05 billion yuan, up by 10.8 percent. The total profits for construction industry above grade four was 0.54 billion yuan, up by 23.2 percent. The total taxes reached 1.688 billion yuan, up by 54.7 percent. There were 20646 construction enterprises, decreased by 3.8 percent, of which 11299 through tender for the construction, down by 1.0 percent .The floor space of building under construction was 501.67 thousand square meters, down by 1.4 percent. The floor space of buildings completed was 24.83 million square meters, down by 4.6 percent.

Ⅳ Investment in Fixed Assets

Investment in fixed assets increased quickly. In 2001, the investment in fixed assets throughout the province reached 120.93 billion yuan, having increased 13.4 percent. Of which, the investment of state-owned units and other types of units were 79.842 billion yuan, up by 16.6 percent; that of collectives and individuals were 41.09 billion yuan, increased by 7.6 percent. Among the investment of state-owned units and other types of units, the investment in capital construction was 47.67 billion yuan, had an increase of 18.0 percent; the investment in technical updating and transformation reached 19.83 billion yuan, up by 13.2 percent; and that in real estate development was 10.63 billion yuan, grew by 42.1 percent; The investment in the local projects reached 57.36 billion yuan, increased by 37.0 percent; the investment in the government 22.48 billion yuan, down by 9.8 percent. The newly started projects in the year reached 4830, increased by 14.6 percent. The finished projects in the year amounted to 4208, up by 2.2 percent.

The investment leaned toward the primary industries and the infrastructure facilities. Among the investment of stated-owned units and other types of units, the investment on agriculture、electric power、 transportation、 postal and telecommunication、 social services、 health care and sports、 science and technology amounted to 9.45 billion yuan, had an growth of 93.0 percent; and that of health care, sports, social welfare amounted to 379 million yuan, increased by 24.5 percent; electric power, gas and water production and supply reached 8.77 billion yuan, as the same as the previous year.

Key projects constructed smoothly. The key projects under construction all over the province amounted 26, and the total complete investment was 27 billion yuan, or 108 percent of the year plan, increased 1 billion yuan over previous year. The entire and individual projects were finished. Lei-Yi speedway that is one part of the main road of Jin-Zhu national highway was built and opened to traffic; Yiyang Power Plant with two sets were put into production and generated electricity; the second line of Zhu-Liu railway and the electrification of Wu-Guang railway were finished and opened to traffic; the first phase of the project of Yong-Lian highway (99 kilometers) were completed; Changde Sewage Plant constructed for controlling environment pollution in the Xiangjiang River valley was put into production; the annual plan that rounding off of Hunan Mobile GSM in the sixth phase and expanding volume in the seventh phase was finished entirely and the net building of Uninet CDMA was opened; Shang-Rui speedway in Hunan province (Tan-Shao) constructed smoothly.

The newly-increased annual production capacity in 2001 through capital construction projects included: the capacity of power generating sets 621 thousand kw, the electric substation equipment (equal or larger than 110 thousand v) 3255 thousand volt-ampere, the length of transmission line extended 6154 kms, the program controlling exchange 2338.9 thousand lines, the facility of mobile communication base 2161 sign paths; the newly built of grade 10 thousand parts annual 60 thousand tons, and 710.19 kms of newly constructed highways, including 135.37 kms of express highways and 1869 kms of reconstructed highways; the capacity of daily city tap water supply 376 thousand tons; the capacity of daily disposal sewer 47.5 thousand tons, the length of extending city road 105.2 kms, the area of city road extended 4.65 million square meters.

V Domestic Trade

In 2001, with a series of the effective implementation of policies on increasing the wages of official in twice, as well as the residents' income of grade low and medium in urban, and that of expanding consume credit, commodity sales on domestic market were stable and active. The total retail sales of consumer goods reached 151.11 billion yuan, up by 10.7 percent over the previous year. Of this total, the retail sales of consumer goods in urban areas reached 80.01 billion yuan, up by 12.7 percent; the retail sales of consumer goods at and below county level was 71.1 billion yuan, had an increase of 8.6 percent. In terms of different industries, 98.51 billion yuan from wholesale and retail sale trade, an increase of 11.3 percent; 16.11 billion yuan from catering industries, increased by 15.4 percent; 36.49 billion yuan from other industries, up by 7.3 percent. According to the types of economics, 40.485 billion yuan from state-owned units, up by 2.0 percent; 110.62 billion yuan from non-state-owned units, up by 14.3 percent. The large-sized market place have became a main body of the commodities transaction at the market. In 2001, there were 101 units that sales over one hundred million yuan, with 46.6 billion yuan of transaction value, amounted to 54.6 percent of the value of commodities transaction markets all over the province. The new industries, such as general chain super markets developed quickly. In 2001, there were 30 general chain commercial enterprises above designated size with 2 billion yuan of the retail sales, up by 240 percent.

VI Foreign Economic Relations and Tourism

Affected by the slowly growth of world economic, the growth rate of foreign trade in our province was seen to decline. The total volume of export and import in 2001 amounted to 2.76 billion US dollars, up by 9.8 percent, of which, the export value was 1.75 billion US dollars, up by 6.1 percent; the import was 1.01 billion US dollars, up by 16.9 percent. The export of general trade was 2.38 billion US dollars, up by 15.2 percent; the export of processing trade was 0.27 billion US dollars, down by 12.6 percent. By the types of export enterprises, the export of foreign investment enterprises was 0.21 billion US dollars, up by 16.3 percent; and the export of collective owned enterprises was 0.13 billion US dollars, up by 44.1 percent; the export of private enterprises reached 69 million US dollars, grew by 77.9 percent. Of which, the export of machinery and electronic products was 0.34 billion US dollars, up by 8.4 percent; the export of textile and articles was 0.31 billion US dollars, had an increase of 17.4 percent, unwrought zinc and zinc alloys was 0.13 billion US dollars, down by 14.9 percent, fireworks and firecrackers was 0.09 billion US dollars, up by 4.0 percent.

New progress was made again in utilization of foreign capitals. During the year, the contracted foreign capitals reached 1.33 billion US dollars, up 21.7 percent over the previous year, and that of actually utilized 1.19 billion US dollars, up by 7.1 percent, of which, the foreign direct investment was 0.81 billion US dollars, up by 18.8 percent.

Economic cooperation with foreign countries kept high growth. The contracted value of newly signed contract projects, labor services, design and consultancy services reached 0.27 billion US dollars, increased by 44.3 percent. The accomplished business revenue was 0.27 billion US dollars, up 91.4 percent.

Domestic and international tourism maintained fast growth. The year 2001 saw 49.85 million domestic tourists, up by 7.2%. Income from domestic tourism stood at 18.81 billion yuan, had an increase of 44.1 percent, 504.6 thousand tourists from overseas were received, up by 11.1 percent, income of foreign exchange from international tourism reached 0.27 billion yuan, up by 22.2%. The total income of tourism reached 21 billion yuan, up by 41.4 percent, it was equivalent to 5.2 percent of the province' Gross Domestic Product, and increased 1.2 percentage points over the previous year. The tourism had become one of the important mainstay industry in this province.

Ⅶ Transportation, Posts and Telecommunication

In 2001, total volume of cargo transported by various means was 113.23 billion ton-kilometers, up by 5.4 percent over the previous year. Of which, the cargo transportation by railways was 67.46 billion ton-kilometers, increased by 6.7 percent; by highways, 31.60 billion ton-kilometers, up 6.6 percent; by waterways, 14.12 billion ton-kilometers, down by 1.8 percent and by airways, 12 million ton-kilometers, up 9.1 percent. The volume of passenger transportation was 76.08 billion person-kilometers, an increase of 5.1 percent. Of which, passengers carried by railways were 41.11 billion person-kilometers, up 4.3 percent by highways, 33.79 billion person-kilometers, up by 6.1 percent; by waterways 0.32 billion person-kilometers, down by 9.0 percent; by airways, 0.86 billion person-kilometers, up by 5.7 percent.

The business transactions of postal and telecommunication services in 2001 totaled 18.78 billion yuan, up 37.8 percent over the previous year. By the end of 2001,telephone subscribers numbered 7.585 million, up 10.9 percent. There were 11.5 telephones per 100 persons in this province, up 0.8 percentage points. Mobile telephone and internet services developed rapidly. Mobile telephone users numbered 4.11 million, up 73.6 percent; over the previous year internet services users reached 1.07 million, up 88.1 percent.

Ⅷ Banking and Insurance

The service of banking was perfect gradually, and its support to the economy was strengthened. The deposits and loans increased by a wide margin. By the end of 2001,the total amount of the deposit of the banking institutions in the province was 334,291 million yuan, an increase of 47,154 million yuan over the beginning of the year. Of this total, savings of enterprises accounted for 87,389 million yuan, increased by 11,116 million yuan, and the savings deposits by urban and rural residents reached 218,373 million yuan, increased by 31,188 million yuan .The year-end value of loans stood at 278,792 million yuan, an increase of 38,959 million yuan over the beginning og the year .Of this total, the short-term loans accounted for 179,873 million yuan, increased by 19,356 million yuan, and the long-term and medium-term loans accounted for 78,752 million yuan, increased by 15,751 million yuan. The loans were comparatively centered on items of the industry、agriculture、capital construction and consumer credit, its was still increased by 3,960、3,666、10,764 and 2,756 million yuan over the beginning of the year. But it was very hard for small-medium enterprises and rural residents to get loans

The insurance industry gained continuous development. The insurance fee of all the insurance organs of the province reached 5,622 million yuan, up 20.5 percent over the previous year. Of this total, the premium of property insurance was 1,636 million yuan, that of life insurance was 3,986 million yuan, up by 16.9 percent and 22.1 percent respectively. The compensation payment reached 1,854 million yuan, up 69.7 percent, in which the compensation payment for property reached 792 million yuan, having increased 10 percent; the compensation payment for life accidents reached 1,062 million yuan, up 176.6 percent.

Ⅸ Science, Technology and Education

The science and technology kept fast development, and achievements was notable. Changsha Software Garden had become a base of national software research and development, Mount Yue-lu University Garden of Science and Technology was built. The number of the achievement of all sorts of scientific research in 2001 was 1008, among which, 11 excellent items won state sci-tech progress award, 150 items won provincial sci-tech progress a word. The new high-tech enterprises realized output value of 60.6 billion yuan, having produced profit and tax of 9.24 billion yuan, with an increase of 21.2 percent and 20 percent respectively. Among the high-tech enterprises, there were 70 enterprises of output value over 100 million yuan, 12 enterprises of output value over billion yuan. The patent work made new progress. There were 4292 applications for "Three types of patent", increased by 4.3 percent; 2401 applications was examined and certified. Scientific and technological under taking was prosperous. By the end of 2001, there were 321 scientific research institutes, among which, there were 174 institutes for natural scientific research, 3 institutes for social science, 13 institutes for sci-tech intelligence and literature, 25 key labs at the province level. The specialized personnel in local state-owned units by sector reached 1.08 million. The number of academicians in Hunan reached 41.

Education development accelerated in the course of reform and adjustment, in 2001, 6 new civilian colleges were built. There were 61 general universities in Hunan with 331.3 thousand enrolled undergraduate students, including 117.3 thousand new entrants by the end of the year, having increased by 17.3%, 30.9% and 16.1% respectively. There were 16 universities or institutions that offered courses leading to postgraduate degrees, with 10,589 enrolled graduate students, including 4575 new entrants, and 26 institutions of adult higher education, with 252.5 thousand enrolled students, including 119.4 thousand new entrants, having increased 26.4 percent and 34.0 percent. 240.9 thousand students in 125 secondary vocational or technical schools of various types including 71.4

thousand new entrants, and 4,695 ordinary schools whose students amounted to 4,255.9 thousand, the entrance rate of the ordinary junior middle school was 93 percent, having decreased 1 percentage. There were 29,340 ordinary primary schools with 6.01 million students, the enrollment rate of primary-school-age children being 97.9 percent, down 0.5 percentage points over the previous year, the drop-off rate of primary school students was 0.5 percent, up 0.13 percentage points.

X Culture, Public Health and Sports

Cultural industry was strengthened and cultural and art undertaking made rapid progress. In 2001, Hunan Daily Group and Changsha Evening Paper Group were founded, all sorts of newspaper issued 901.02 million copies; magazines, 97.97 million copies; and books, 248.51 million copies. Radio, movie and televisions speed up. By the end of 2001, there were 11 radio broadcasting stations, 25 medium and short wave radio transmitting and relaying stations, 15 TV stations through out Hunan brought radio programs were 81.6 percent of the total population, 50 TV transmitting and relaying stations covered 91.7 percent of the population. The flourish of cultural and art enrich people's life. Huagu opera Huagu in Autumn gained award inaugurated by the State Propaganda Department, dance poem Zha Hua woman gained the gold award of creation and performance of 3th minority nationality theatrical festival, film Mao-Ze dong in 1925 gained the award of the best feature film of the 21th Jin JI festival. By the end of 2001, there were 91 art-performing groups, 125 cultural centers, 15 public artistic centers, 66 museums, 115 public libraries and 199 archives establishment in Hunan.

Continued development was made in public health undertakings. By the end of 2001,there were 4205 health care institutions, with a total of 146.2 thousand beds (including 21.2 thousand beds in the hospital of villages and towns), increased by 1.9 percent, 199 thousand health workers through out province. Rural villages with medical-care stations account of 92.6 percent, up 1.1 percent compared with the previous year.

Vigorous development was scored in sports. In 2001, athletes from Hunan won 3 world champions, 5 gold medals, 8 silver medals and 1 bronze at important international sport games; furthermore, athletes from Hunan won 24 gold medals, 21.5 silver medals and 26.5 bronze at national sport games. In 9th national sport games, athletes from Hunan made a breakthrough by winning 19.5 gold champions, making Hunan at the seventh place. Sports were further popularized among the masses, 33.5 percent of the population often took part in sports activities, 96 percent of students were up to standard of national sports.

XI Environment Protection

The environment protection made progress. By the end of 2001, there were 2107 people working in environment protection agencies in Hunan, and 129 environment monitoring station were in operation. 331 programs of treating environment pollution were finished, 271 million yuan of investment on the treatment of environment protection was realized, grew by 14 percent. 157 smoke-dust control zones were established, increased by 25.6 percent; 126 noise control zones, increased by 61.5 percent. Hunan also had 68 natural protection zones (including 8 nation-level zones and 26 province-level zones); the area of the protection zones reached 803.4

thousand hectares, having increased 4.3 percent. Smoke-dust control zones covering an area of 495.2 square kilometers; noise control zones covering an area of 267.7 square kilometers. The percentage of industrial waste water treated, the percentage of the industrial solid waste treated in cites and the percentage of repeated use of industrial water were 27.3 percent, 52.1 percent and 54 percent respectively, increased 9.2,1.6 and 1.9 percentage points. New achievement was made in overall settlement of Dongting Lake, the ecological environment of the Lake was improved gradually, an areas of the Lake was enlarged and the storage capacity was much more after three-year-level the land and store floodwater. But in some areas, the tendency of environmental pollution and ecological deterioration were still not under control.

XII Population

By the end of 2001, the total population reached 65.96 million in the whole province, and had an increase of 338 thousand over the end of the previous year. Of the total population, those living in cities and towns were 20.32 million, and those living in rural areas were 45.64 million. According to sampling survey, in 2001, the crude birth rate was 11.8 per thousand, rose 0.35 per-thousand-points; the crude death rate was 6.7 per thousand; the natural growth rate was 5.1 per thousand, or 0.42 per-thousand-points higher than that of 2000.

According to the estimate based on the Fifth Census, the population of age 0-14 was 14.04 million and accounted for 21.3 percent of the total population; the population of age 15-64 was 46.79 million and accounted for 70.9 percent; the population of age 65 and over reached 5.13 million, and accounted for 7.8 percent, and increased 223.1 thousand people over the previous year. Hunan is gradually facing an aging population problem.

XIII People's Life and Social Security System

According to the sampling survey, the annual per capita disposable incomes of urban households was 6780.56 yuan in 2001, increased by 9 percent, if the change in price's was taken into consideration, the real increase was 10.2 percent. The annual per capita actual expenditure of urban households was 6925.54 yuan, having increased 7.7 percent, if the change in price's was taken into consideration, the real increase was 8.9 percent. The expenditure of urban households was changing to new growth points such as housing、transportation、telecommunication、education and tourism. The annual per capita consumption expenditures was 5546.22 yuan, a growth of 6.3 percent, in which, the growth rate of expenditure on transportation and telecommunication、 tourism、 education、 medicine and medicine services were 20 percent、 67.6 percent、 19.9 percent and 21.6 percent respectively. The annual per capita disposable incomes of rural households 2264.71 yuan in 2001, increased 105.71 yuan, an increase of 4.9 percent, if the change in price's was taken into consideration, the real increase was 5.4 percent. Per capita net incomes of rural households was 2299.46 yuan, increased 102.3 yuan and an increase of 4.7 percent. Among the peasants' net incomes, the incomes from salary reached 840.11 yuan, increased 50.37 yuan; the net incomes from the primary industry was 972.97 yuan, an increase of 34.41 yuan, and from the secondary and tertiary industry was 398.87 yuan, increased 8.33 yuan; the incomes from transfer and property was 52.76 yuan, an increase of 12.6 yuan. The per capita consumption expenditures of rural households was 1990.33 yuan, increased 47.83 yuan, a growth of

2.5 percent, if the change in price's was taken into consideration, the real growth was 3 percent. In 2001, the housing condition both rural and municipal residents kept further improving. Per capita municipal residents' housing area reached 11.8 square meters and more 0.4 square meters than last year; the rural resident's per capital housing areas reached 32.87 square meters and more 1.95 square meters than last year, the percentage of brick-wood and concrete structure accounted for 93.6 percent, rose 0.4 percentage points.

Social security system was further strengthened. With the improvement of social security system, there were 4.52 million staff and workers participated in the retirement security program by the end of the year and having decreased 0.97 percent over the previous year; and a total of 1.48 million retirees participated in the retirement security program, raised 8.4 percent; some of 3.55 million staff and workers participated in the unemployment insurance program, grew 2.5 percent; and 33 thousand people received their monthly unemployment insurance. There were 3.51 million staff and workers participated in the general health care program, aad a growth of 175.7 percent; by the end of November this year, some of 482.2 thousand retirees participated in the general health care program, increased by 82.3 percent; employers joining the life insurance reached 1.41 million and having increased 110.5 percent.

Notes:

1. All figures in the Communique are preliminary statistics.
2. Figures in value terms on Gross Domestic Product and Value-added of various sectors quoted in the Communique are at current prices, whereas growth rates are calculated at comparable prices.

一、综合

GENERAL SURVEY

资料整理人员：　陈洲艳　刘昕毅　李生春
　　　　　　　　顾　虹　郑红梅　曾晓林

1-1 行政区划

Administrative Division

单位：个 (unit)

年份 Year	市州 Cities and A.P	地州数 Number of Prefecture and A.P	地级市 Number of Cities at Prefectural Level	县级市 Number of Cities at County Level	县数 Number of Counties	市辖区数 Districts Under the Jurisdiction of Cities at Prefectural Level	镇数 Number of Towns	乡数 Number of Township
1978		12	3	7	90	13	154	3295
1980		12	5	9	90	22	155	3321
1981		11	5	9	89	22	185	3331
1982		11	5	11	87	22	196	3340
1983		9	6	10	88	22	230	3340
1984		9	6	12	86	27	513	3090
1985		9	6	14	84	27	544	3011
1986		7	6	16	82	27	581	2895
1987		7	6	18	80	26	585	2903
1988		6	8	17	78	30	596	2889
1989		6	8	17	78	30	621	2807
1990		6	8	18	78	29	628	2801
1991		6	8	18	78	29	639	2784
1992		6	8	19	77	26	663	2773
1993		6	8	20	76	26	748	2689
1994		5	9	20	74	28	769	2658
1995		4	10	19	73	30	899	1406
1996		3	11	17	73	32	950	1360
1997		3	11	18	72	32	979	1327
1998		2	12	17	72	33	1001	1350
1999		1	13	16	72	34	1023	1330
2000		1	13	16	72	34	1055	1310
2001		1	13	16	72	34	1087	1275
长沙市	Changsha City		1	1	3	5	78	40
株洲市	Zhuzhou City		1	1	4	4	68	70
湘潭市	Xiangtan City		1	2	1	2	35	24
衡阳市	Hengyang City		1	2	5	5	110	75
邵阳市	Shaoyang City		1	1	8	3	94	103
岳阳市	Yueyang City		1	2	4	3	98	76
常德市	Changde City		1	1	6	2	100	111
张家界市	Zhangjiajie City		1		2	2	32	62
益阳市	Yiyang City		1	1	3	2	69	59
郴州市	Chenzhou City		1	1	8	2	85	166
永州市	Yongzhou City		1		9	2	108	80
怀化市	Huaihua City		1	1	10	1	88	230
娄底市	Loudi City		1	2	2	1	57	26
湘西土家族苗族自治州	West Hunan Tujia and Miao A.P	1		1	7		65	153

长沙市 Changsha City

芙蓉区(Furong District)、天心区(Tianxin District)、岳麓区(Yuelu District)、开福区(Kaifu District)、雨花区(Yuhua District)
浏阳市(Liuyang City)、长沙县(Changsha County)、望城县(Wangcheng County)、宁乡县(Ningxiang County)

株洲市 Zhuzhou City

荷塘区(Hetang District)、石峰区(Shifeng District)、芦淞区(LouSong District)、天元区(Tianyuan District)、醴陵市(Liling City)
株洲县(Zhuzhou County)、攸县(Youxiang County)、茶陵县(Chaling County)、炎陵县(Yanling County)

湘潭市 Xiangtan City

雨湖区(Yuhu District)、岳塘区(Yuetang District)、湘乡市(Xiangxiang City)、韶山市(Shaoshan City)、湘潭县(Xiangtan County)

衡阳市 Hengyang City

珠晖区(Zhuhui District)、雁峰区（Yanfeng District)、石鼓区(Shigu District)、蒸湘区（Zhengxiang District)
南岳区(Nanyue District)、耒阳市(Leiyang City)、常宁市(Changning City)、衡阳县(Hengyang County)、衡南县(Hengnan County)
衡山县(Hengshan County)、衡东县(Hengdong County)、祁东县(Qidong County)

邵阳市 Shaoyang City

双清区(Shuangqing District)、大祥区(Daxiang District)、北塔区(Beita District)、武冈市(Wugang City)、邵东县(Shaodong County)
新邵县(Xinshao County)、邵阳县(Shaoyang County)、隆回县(Longhui County)、洞口县(Dongkou County)、
新宁县(Xinning County)、绥宁县(Suining County)、城步苗族自治县 (Chengbu Miao Autonomous County)

岳阳市 Yueyang City

岳阳楼区(Yueyanglou District)、云溪区(Yunxi District)、君山区(Junshan District)、汨罗市(Miluo City)、临湘市(Linxiang City)
岳阳县(Yueyang County)、平江县(Pingjiang County)、湘阴县(Xiangyin County)、华容县(Huarong County)

常德市 Changde City

武陵区(Wuling District)、鼎城区(Dingcheng District)、津市市(Jinshi City)、安乡县(Anxiang County)、汉寿县(Huanshou County)
澧县(Li County)、临澧县(Linli County)、桃源县(Taoyuan County)、石门县(Shimen County)

张家界市 Zhangjiajie City

永定区(Yongding District)、武陵源区(Wulingyuan District)、慈利县(Chili County)、桑植县(Shanhzhi County)

益阳市 Yiyang City

资阳区(Ziyang District)、赫山区(Heshan District)、沅江市(Yuanjiang City)、南县(Nan County)、桃江县(Taojiang County)、
安化县(Anhuan County)

郴州市 Chenzhou City

北湖区(Beihu District)、苏仙区(Suxian District)、资兴市(Zixing City)、桂阳县(Guiyang County)、永兴县(Yongxing County)、
宜章县(Yizhang County)、嘉禾县(Jiahe County)、临武县(Linwu County)、汝城县(Rucheng County)、桂东县(Guidong County)、
安仁县(Anren County)

永州市 Yongzhou City

芝山区(Zhishan District)、冷水滩区(Lengshuitan District)、东安县(Dongan County)、道县(Dao County)、
宁远县(Ningyuan County)、江永县(Jiangyong County)、江华瑶族自治县(Jianghua Yao Autonomous County)、
蓝山县(Lanshan County)、新田县(Xintian County)、双牌县(Shuangpai County)、祁阳县(Qiyang County)

怀化市 Huaihua City

鹤城区(Hecheng District)、洪江市(Hongjiang City)、中方县(Zhongfang County)、沅陵县(Yuanling County)、
辰溪县(Shenxi County)、溆浦县(Xupu County)、麻阳苗族自治县(Mayang Miao Autonomous County)、会同县(Huitong County)
新晃侗族自治县(Xinhuang Tong Autonomous County), 芷江侗族自治县(Zhijiang Tong Autonomous County),
靖州苗族侗族自治县(Jinzhou Miao and Tong Autonomous County)、通道侗族自治县(Tongdao Tong Autonomous County)

娄底市 Loudi City

娄星区(Louxing District)、冷水江市(Lengshuijiang City)、涟源市(Lianyuan City)、双峰县(Shuangfeng County)、
新化县(Xinhua County)

湘西土家族苗族自治州 West Hunan Tujia and Miao Autonomous Prefecture

吉首市(Jishou City)、泸溪县(Louxi County)、凤凰县(Fenghuang County)、花垣县(Huayuan County)、保靖县(Baojin County)、
古丈县(Guzhang County)、永顺县(Yongshun County)、龙山县(Longshan County)

1-2 人口和自然资源

Population and Natural Resources

项 目	Item	2001
人口	**Population**	
年底人口数(万人)	Total Population at the Year-end (10 000 persons)	6595.85
人口密度 (人/平方公里)	Density of Population (person/sq.km)	311.42
土地	**Land**	
土地面积 (万平方公里)	Area of Land (10 000 sq.km)	21.18
耕地面积 (万公顷)	Area of Cultivated Land (10 000 hectares)	391.26
气候	**Climate**	
年平均降水量(毫米)	Annual Average Precipitation (mm)	1355.3
年降水总量 (亿立方米)	Annual Total Precipitation (100 million cu.m)	2870
森林	**Forest**	
有林地面积(万公顷)	Area with woodland (10 000 hectares)	957.95
(万亩)	Area of Forest (10 000 mu)	14369.25
森林覆盖率 (%)	Forest Coverage Rate (%)	52.76
林木蓄积量 (万立方米)	Stock Volume of the Forest (10 000 cu.m)	30562.81
水文、水利	**Water**	
5公里以上河流 (条)	Rivers Over 5 km (unit)	5341
5公里以上河流长度 (万公里)	Total Length of Rivers Over 5 km (10 000 km)	9
河川年径流总量 (亿立方米)	Annual Total Flow of Rivers (100 million cu.m)	1839.5
淡水总面积 (万公顷)	Total Area of Fresh Water (10 000 hectares)	135.38
(万亩)	Total Area of Fresh Water (10 000 mu)	2030.7
#已放养面积 (万公顷)	# Cultivated Area (10 000 hectares)	42.25
(万亩)	(10 000 mu)	633.72
天然水资源总量 (亿立方米)	Natural Water Volume (100 million cu.m)	1640.4
地表水资源总量 (亿立方米)	Surface Water Volume (100 million cu.m)	1633.8
地下(浅层)水量 (亿立方米)	Shallow Ground Water Volume (100 million cu.m)	396.7
水力资源蕴藏量 (万千瓦)	Hydropower Resources (10 000 kw)	1532.45
#可开发量	#Developable Resources	1083.84
矿产资源(保有储量)	**Mineral Resources (Ensured Resources)**	
煤 (亿吨)	Coal (100 million ton)	30.2
铁矿石 (亿吨)	Iron Ore (100 million ton)	11.06
磷矿石 (亿吨)	Phosphate Ore (100 million ton)	20.32
盐 (亿吨)	Salt (100 million ton)	36.13

注:1.本表淡水面积、可养殖面积、水力资源蕴藏量均为过去清查数，有待进一步普查和勘测。

2.河川年径流总量=省内各水系年径流量+客水+地下水。

3.2001年耕地面积为国土资源厅统计数据（后同）。

a. Figures in this table, except population, cultivated area and mineral resources were obtained from surveys in previous years, and is subject to further verification.

b. The annual total flow of rivers=annual flow of major rivers in our province + branch water + groundwater.

c. The data of cultivated land in 2000 from Hunan Province Territory Resource Bureau.The same as in the following table.

1-3 土地状况(2001年)

Land Characteristics (2001)

项 目	Item	总面积 Total Area 万公顷 (10000 hectares)	万亩 (10000 mu)	占总面积的% Percentage to Total Area (%)
总面积	**Total Area**	**2118.29**	**31774.35**	**100.0**
按地形分	**By Topographic Feature**			
山地	Mountains	1084.72	16270.80	51.2
盆地	Basins	294.12	4411.73	13.9
平原	Plains	277.86	4167.90	13.1
丘陵	Hills	326.22	4893.28	15.4
水面	Water-face	135.37	2030.64	6.4
按地高分	**By Altitude**			
50米以下	Under 50m	210.65	3159.76	9.9
50-100米	50-100m	235.27	3529.03	11.1
100-300米	100-300m	491.74	7376.09	23.2
300-500米	300-500m	478.36	7175.34	22.6
500-800米	500-800m	390.48	5857.19	18.5
800-1000米	800-1000m	220.58	3308.73	10.4
1000米以上	Above 1000m	91.21	1368.21	4.3
按特征分	**By Land Use**			
耕地	Cultivated Land	391.26	5868.83	18.5
有林地	Woodland	957.95	14369.32	45.2
宜林荒山	Undeveloped Land Usable for Afforestation	16.22	243.30	0.8
疏林	Sparsely Forests	34.47	517.05	1.6
灌木	Shrubbery	141.27	2119.05	6.7
未成林造林地	Afforestation for Undeveloped Forests	31.27	469.05	1.5
淡水总面积	Total Area of Fresh Water	135.38	2030.70	6.4
其他	Others	410.47	6157.05	19.3

注:为使用方便,面积列出万公顷数与万亩数。

Data on area were listed with 10 000 hectares and 10 000 mu for the sake of convenience.

1-4 主要山脉基本情况

Major Mountain Ranges

名称	Name	平均高度(米) Average Height(m)	最高峰(米) Heightest Peak (m)	Heightest Peak
雪峰山	Xuefeng Mountain Range	1500	2021 (城步县二宝顶)	Erbao Peak in Chengbu County
武陵山	Wuling Mountain Range	500--1200	2098.7 (石门县壶瓶山)	Huping Mountain in Shimen County
南岭山脉 (指大庾岭、骑田岭、萌渚岭、都庞岭、越城岭)	Nanling Mountain Range (Dageng Peak,Qitian Peak, Mengzhu Peak, DuPang Peak, Yuecheng Peak)	1000-1500	2009 (道县韭菜岭)	Jiucai Peak in Dao County
幕阜山---罗霄山	Mofu Mountain ---Luoxiao Mountain Range	1000	2052 (炎陵县斗笠顶)	Douli Peak in Yanling County
			2041.1 (桂东县八面山)	Bamian Mountain in Guidong County

1-5 主要河流基本情况

Major Rivers

名称	Item	河长(公里) Length of River (km)	#省内 #In Province	河流条数(条) Number of River (unit)	流域面积(平方公里) Drainage Area (sq.km)	#省内 #In Province	省内年径流量(亿立方米) Annual Flow in Province (100 million cu.m)	水力资源蕴藏量(万千瓦) Hydro-power Resources (10000 kw)	#可开发量 Develop-able Resources
合计	**Total**			**5341**		**211829**	**1623**	**1532.45**	**1083.84**
湘 江	Xiangjiang River	856	670	2157	94660	85383	664.9	470.7	318.29
资 水	Zijiang River	713	630	771	28142	26738	217.4	201.03	147.71
沅 江	Yuanjiang River	1033	568	1491	89163	51066	393.3	537.51	460.21
澧 水	Lishui River	388	388	326	18496	15505	131.2	152.46	137.11
洞庭湖水系	Water System of Dongting Lake			432		27269	157.7	140.2	13.65
鄱阳湖水系	Water System of Poyang Lake			16		683	44.6	3.12	0.58
珠江水系	Water System of Zhujiang River			148		5185	13.9	27.43	6.29

注：1.河流条数指河长5公里以上的河流数,河长共9万公里。

2.资水河长以夫夷水作水源计算。

3.据1986年勘定,洞庭湖面积为2691平方公里。

a. Rivers refer to those which are more than 5 km long, and the total length of the rivers are 90 000 km.

b. The length of Zishui River refers to that of Fuyi River.

c. The figure on the area of Dongting Lake was taken from the survey in 1986.

1-6 主要城市平均气温(2001年)

Monthly Average Temperature of Major Cities(2001)

单位:摄氏度 (℃)

城市	City	1月 January	2月 February	3月 March	4月 April	5月 May	6月 June	7月 July
长沙	Changsha	5.4	7.5	12.7	16.5	22.9	25.7	30.5
株洲	Zhuzhou	5.9	8.0	12.8	16.9	23.2	25.9	30.5
湘潭	Xiangtan	5.7	7.8	12.7	16.7	22.9	25.4	30.2
衡阳	Hengyang	6.6	8.5	13.8	17.1	23.4	26.3	30.5
邵阳	Shaoyang	6.1	7.8	13.0	16.4	22.3	25.2	29.2
岳阳	Yueyang	5.4	7.4	13.1	16.8	23.2	26.4	30.9
常德	Changde	5.7	7.8	13.4	16.8	23.1	26.1	31.0
张家界	Zhangjiajie	6.4	8.4	13.2	16.8	22.2	25.3	29.4
益阳	Yiyang	5.3	7.6	12.8	16.5	22.9	25.8	30.4
郴州	Chenzhou	7.4	9.3	14.6	17.7	23.2	26.2	29.7
永州	Yongzhou	6.7	8.9	14.0	16.9	22.5	25.9	29.1
娄底	Loudi	5.7	7.5	13.0	16.0	21.4	24.8	28.8
怀化	Huaihua	6.0	8.1	13.1	16.7	23.1	25.9	30.1
吉首	Jishou	6.3	7.9	13.0	16.4	21.5	24.7	28.7

城市	City	8月 August	9月 September	10月 October	11月 November	12月 December	全年平均 Annual Average	上年平均 Annual Average Preceding Year
长沙	Changsha	27.4	25.0	19.2	13.3	4.9	17.6	17.2
株洲	Zhuzhou	27.3	25.7	19.9	13.8	5.4	17.9	17.4
湘潭	Xiangtan	27.3	25.2	19.3	13.4	5.2	17.7	17.1
衡阳	Hengyang	27.8	26.4	20.8	15.0	6.2	18.5	17.9
邵阳	Shaoyang	27.0	25.3	19.7	13.5	5.6	17.6	16.9
岳阳	Yueyang	27.7	25.4	19.3	13.9	5.3	17.9	17.5
常德	Changde	27.6	25.4	19.0	13.5	5.3	17.9	17.5
张家界	Zhangjiajie	27.1	25.3	18.9	13.4	6.1	17.7	17.1
益阳	Yiyang	27.3	25.0	18.8	13.1	4.8	17.5	17.2
郴州	Chenzhou	27.3	25.2	20.6	14.7	6.3	18.5	18.1
永州	Yongzhou	26.9	24.9	20.5	14.5	6.3	18.1	17.7
娄底	Loudi	26.8	25.0	18.5	13.3	5.4	17.2	17.4
怀化	Huaihua	27.7	25.9	20.0	14.0	5.6	18.0	16.7
吉首	Jishou	26.5	24.5	18.5	13.1	5.7	17.3	16.7

1-7 主要城市降水量 (2001年)

Monthly Precipitation in Major Cities (2001)

单位:毫米 (millimeter)

城市	City	1月 January	2月 February	3月 March	4月 April	5月 May	6月 June	7月 July
长沙	Changsha	114	71	110.5	265.3	162.5	277.2	73.2
株洲	Zhuzhou	110	69	107	232	125	281	77
湘潭	Xiangtan	101	67	79	207	139	237	40
衡阳	Hengyang	77	63	99	235	181	182	37
邵阳	Shaoyang	58	54	92	188	337	277	55
岳阳	Yueyang	106	40	102	207	94	166	124
常德	Changde	86	35	87	318	87	168	69
张家界	Zhangjiajie	47	26	105.2	169	110	95.2	119.7
益阳	Yiyang	149	65	108	260	99	175	53
郴州	Chenzhou	117	92	122	265	115	305	48
永州	Yongzhou	97	74	105	285	193	174	101
娄底	Loudi	76	45	60	195	213	271	198
怀化	Huaihua	74	69	77	260	196	278	66
吉首	Jishou	46	34	49	105	110	134	125

城市	City	8月 August	9月 September	10月 October	11月 November	12月 December	全年 Annual Total	上年全年 Annual Total Preceding year
长沙	Changsha	146.8	2.5	79.9	80.6	68.1	1451.5	1508
株洲	Zhuzhou	189	16	52	76	82	1416.9	1573
湘潭	Xiangtan	64	9	49	67	72	1130	1500
衡阳	Hengyang	100	8	38	148	72	1239.5	1396
邵阳	Shaoyang	38	2	36	95	52	1286.6	1384
岳阳	Yueyang	121	7	99	59	53	1178.1	1228
常德	Changde	83	9	126	82	45	1195.3	1331
张家界	Zhangjiajie	145.8	0	147	44	31	1039	1158
益阳	Yiyang	129	7	134	86	68	1331.9	1369
郴州	Chenzhou	242	49	59	47	57	1529.2	1728
永州	Yongzhou	115	12	58	54	59	1325.1	1325
娄底	Loudi	117	11	127	76	29	1417	1193
怀化	Huaihua	42	4	48	60	57	1231.1	1398
吉首	Jishou	123	11	166	47	29	979	1076

1-8 主要城市日照时数 (2001年)

Monthly Sunshine Hours in Major Cities (2001)

单位:小时 (hour)

城市	City	1月 January	2月 February	3月 March	4月 April	5月 May	6月 June	7月 July
长沙	Changsha	45.6	31.9	93.5	85.9	177.4	141.6	168.4
株洲	Zhuzhou	43.9	42	84.2	83.8	140.7	136	269
湘潭	Xiangtan	51.9	49.1	102.2	91	177.5	165.3	184.2
衡阳	Hengyang	41.5	54.2	97.6	49.1	148.8	151.2	270.5
邵阳	Shaoyang	54.3	32	105.2	56.4	145.9	122.9	275.9
岳阳	Yueyang	78.9	73.2	144.4	129.8	201.5	183.3	320.2
常德	Changde	86.4	79.1	151	126.8	187	144.8	294.1
张家界	Zhangjiajie	60.9	52.9	105	88.6	134	92	226
益阳	Yiyang	67.2	57	118	93.7	172.4	160	260.3
郴州	Chenzhou	24.8	51.6	95.7	67.1	98.8	122.5	215.8
永州	Yongzhou	43.5	44.2	99.2	44	140.8	156.9	261.1
娄底	Loudi	39.6	41.5	107.8	48.9	133.2	137.5	260.6
怀化	Huaihua	59.7	51.3	103.1	63.2	152.2	143.9	257.7
吉首	Jishou	43.8	33.2	105.3	70.7	132.6	123.5	250.9

城市	City	8月 August	9月 September	10月 October	11月 November	12月 December	全年 Annual Total	上年全年 Annual Total Preceding year
长沙	Changsha	169.7	210.1	133.9	126.9	70.2	1555.1	1296
株洲	Zhuzhou	140.7	134.9	126.7	142.3	71.4	1515.6	1462
湘潭	Xiangtan	177.1	247.6	130.5	150.7	84.2	1711.3	1486
衡阳	Hengyang	131	206.4	98	155	81.6	1484.7	1354
邵阳	Shaoyang	167	189.2	82	149.3	63.3	1443.4	1484
岳阳	Yueyang	241	261	126	176	95	2031.5	1809
常德	Changde	218.9	221	102	157	85	1853.1	1616
张家界	Zhangjiajie	156	169	72	128	58	1340.7	1169
益阳	Yiyang	169	225	121.6	146.9	79.4	1670.5	1447
郴州	Chenzhou	131.9	157.7	82	151.2	59.9	1258.9	1225
永州	Yongzhou	137.7	181.8	83.6	134.5	72.6	1399.9	1429
娄底	Loudi	161	195.2	70.2	123.5	57	1376	1424
怀化	Huaihua	169.6	222	133	145	86	1585.2	1392
吉首	Jishou	149.1	186.2	66.5	131.6	32.1	1325.5	1129

1-9 国民经济和社会发展总量指标

Principal Indicators of National Economy and Social Development

指 标	Item	总量指标 Aggregate Data			
		1995	1999	2000	2001
人口与就业	**Population and Employment**				
人口 (万人)	**Population (10 000 persons)**				
年底总人口	Population at the Year-end	6392	6532	6562.04	6595.85
市镇人口	Urban	1550.99	1724	1952.21	2031.52
乡村人口	Rural	4841.01	4808	4609.84	4564.33
男性人口	Male	3322.27	3389.22	3422.77	3409.72
女性人口	Female	3069.73	3142.68	3139.28	3186.13
就业 (万人)	**Employment (10 000 persons)**				
从业人员数	Employees	3467.31	3601.39	3577.58	3607.96
职工人数	Staff and Workers	597.5	590.75	580.82	534.22
城镇登记失业人员数	Un-employees in Urban	27.4	30.7	27.57	30.34
宏观经济	**Macro-economy**				
国民核算 (亿元)	**National Accounting (100 million yuan)**				
国内主产总值	Gross Domestic Products	2151.43	3326.75	3691.88	3983.00
第一产业	Primary Industry	685.30	778.25	784.92	825.73
第二产业	Secondary Industry	771.55	1297.74	1461.86	1573.00
第三产业	Tertiary Industry	694.58	1250.76	1445.10	1584.27
国内支出总额	Total Domestic Expenditure	2151.43	3326.75	3691.88	3983.00
最终消费	Final Consumption	1396.88	2212.47	2383.27	2553.14
居民消费	Households Consumption	1108.78	1690.66	1782.77	1871.64
政府消费	Government Consumption	228.10	521.81	600.50	681.50
资本形成总额	Gross Capital Formation	756.23	1086.10	1274.94	1426.47
固定资本形成总额	Gross Fixed Capital Formation	534.12	956.10	1082.00	1233.17
存货增加	Changes in Inventory	222.11	130.00	192.94	193.30
固定资产投资 (亿元)	**Investment in Fixed Assets (100 million yuan)**				
全社会固定资产投资总额	Total Investment in Fixed Assets	524.01	943.34	1066.27	1210.63
国有单位	State-owned unit	316.9	522.95	574.12	618.54
集体单位	Collective-owned Unit	39.83	95.81	118.8	145.78
个体经济	Individuals	120.34	263.42	281.89	291.55
财政 (亿元)	**Public Finance (100 million yuan)**				
地方财政收入	Local Government Revenue	108.16	166.5	177.04	205.41
地方财政支出	Local Government Expenditure	173.94	313.12	347.83	431.7
物价总指数 (上年=100)	**Price Index (preceding year=100)**				
商品零售价格总指数	General Retail Price Index	115.5	97.6	99.3	98.8
居民消费价格总指数	General Consumer Price Index	119	100.5	101.4	99.1
农副产品收购价格总指数	General Farm and Sideline Products Purchasing Price Indices	117.2	91.1	96.8	-
农产品生产者价格指数	Producer Price Indices of Farm Products	-	-	-	100.9
利用外资 (万美元)	**Utilization of Foreign Capital (USD 10 000)**				
签订利用外资协议额	Amount of Foreign Capital for Utilization Through Signed Contracts or Agreements	174427	94351	109370	133063
实际利用外资额	Amount of Foreign Capital Actually Utilized	87104	106945	110843	118747

1-9 续表 1

continued

指　标	Item	总量指标 Aggregate Data 1995	1999	2000	2001
产　业	**Industry**				
农业	**Agriculture**				
耕地面积(千公顷)	Cultivated Areas (1 000 hectares)	3249.7	3213.2	3921.6	3912.55
农林牧渔业从业人员(万人)	Number of Persons Engaged in Farming, Forestry, Animal Husbandry and Fishery (10 000 persons)	2114.71	2074.13	2065.92	2058.67
农林牧渔业总产值(亿元)	Gross Output Value of Farming, Forestry, Animal Husbandry and Fishery (100 million yuan)	1046.97	1200.94	1251.89	1313.22
农作物种植业	Planting	543.16	578.46	579.81	611.22
林业	Forestry	42.58	48.2	51.01	51.88
牧业	Animal Husbandry	369.34	458.62	486.13	510.42
副业	Sideline	36.76	46.24	54.03	54.48
渔业	Fishery	54.93	69.42	80.91	85.23
主要农产品产量(万吨)	Output of Major Farm Products (10 000 tons)				
粮食	Grain	2752.09	2892.35	2874.97	2700.3
棉花	Cotton	22.35	17.7	17.13	19
油料	Oil-bearing Crops	112.04	130.17	139.35	137.39
苎麻	Ramie	5.83	3.82	6.62	9.42
黄红麻(熟麻)	Jute and Ambary Hemp	0.36	0.23	0.23	0.19
烤烟	Fluecured Tobacco	7.88	12.4	15.55	16.28
茶叶	Tea	6.14	5.63	5.73	5.84
柑桔	Citrus	101.5	149.66	125.92	154.15
猪牛羊肉	Pork, Beef and Mutton	317.37	420.51	436.51	452.12
水产品	Aquatic Products	85.78	124.45	133.21	140.96
工业	**Industry**				
工业总产值(亿元)	Gross Industrial Output Value (100 million yuan)	2166.66	3786.19	4272	4508.7
主要工业产品产量	Output of Major Industrial Products				
布(亿米)	Cloth (100 million m)	4.89	2.87	3.41	3.05
机制纸及纸板(万吨)	Machine-made Paper and Paperboards (10 000 tons)	94.02	53.04	70.07	77.61
糖(万吨)	Sugar (10 000 tons)	6.31	10.13	4.44	7.19
合成洗涤剂(万吨)	Synthetic Detergents (10 000 tons)	6.05	6.79	8.12	9.27
缝纫机(万架)	Sewing Machine (10 000 sets)	10.03	0.95	1.56	0.94
家用电冰箱(万台)	Household Refrigerators (10 000 sets)	22.28	28.6	44.54	47.79
电视机(万部)	Television Sets (10 000 sets)	24.73	0.28	-	0.87
录放音机(万台)	Video Recorders (10 000 sets)	38.58	105.04	66	1.5
原煤(万吨)	Coal (10 000 tons)	5564.51	1432.87	1490.81	1546.11
发电量(亿千瓦小时)	Electricity (100 million kw.h)	332.94	332.51	354.42	384.35
钢(万吨)	Steel (10 000 tons)	175.6	309.02	304.13	441.9
成品钢材(万吨)	Steel Products (10 000 tons)	154.54	288.79	299.05	389.01
水泥(万吨)	Cement (10 000 tons)	2196.02	2273.85	2395.72	2496.02
独立核算工业企业财务指标	Principal Financial Item of Industrial Enterprises with Independent Accounting Systems				
年底固定资产原价(亿元)	Original Value of Fixed Assets (100 million yuan)	1282.75	1800.18	1947.23	2095.68
年底固定资产净值(亿元)	Net Value of Fixed Assets (100 million yuan)	907.38	1191.85	1268.61	1368.37
利润和税金总额(亿元)	Profits and Taxes (100 million yuan)	90.96	177.04	205.87	235.66

1-9 续表 2 continued

指　标	Item	总量指标 Aggregate Data 1995	1999	2000	2001
建筑业	**Construction**				
建筑业企业人数（万人）	Number of Employed Persons (10 000 persons)	60.97	77.18	76.3	96.73
建筑业总产值（亿元）	Gross Output Value of Construction (100 million yuan)	188.28	333.9	354.29	489.79
施工房屋面积（万平方米）	Floor Space of Buildings Under Construction (10 000 sq.m)	4507	5180.91	5087.93	6259.27
#竣工房屋面积	Floor Space of Buildings Completed	2313	2681.81	2603.03	3204.6
交通运输	**Transportation**				
货运量（万吨）	Freight Traffic (10 000 tons)	49853	51057	51090	50518
铁路	Railways	5017	4456	4676	4965
公路	Highways	41272	43296	42868	41823
水运	Waterways	3531	3178	3406	3572
客运量（万人）	Passenger Traffic (10 000 persons)	71566	87794	87462	92381
铁路	Railways	4135	5010	5233	5202
公路	Highways	65971	81675	81005	85971
水运	Waterways	1375	1002	1094	1063
邮电通信业	**Postal and Telecommunications Services**				
邮电业务总量　（万元）	Total Business Revenue (10 000 yuan)	314794	924733	1409225	1341636.1
函件　（万件）	Number of Letters Delivered (10 000 pieces)	34412	25377	21255	39470
报刊期发数　（万份）	Number of Newspapers and Magazines Distributed (10 000 copies)	1485	1603	1042.72	1022
交换机容量　（万门）	Capacity of Office Telephone Exchanges (10 000 lines)	273.75	585.96	873.2	964.59
城市	Urban Areas	205.65	385.4	504.46	550.39
农村	Rural Areas	68.1	200.56	368.74	414.2
电话机(万部)	Number of Telephone Sets (10 000 units)	163.1	409.93	700.04	711.94
城市	Urban Areas	132.24	279.84	416.57	409.54
农村	Rural Areas	30.86	130.09	283.47	302.4
国内商业（亿元）	**Domestic Trade (100 million yuan)**				
社会消费品零售总额	Total Retail Sales of Consumer Goods	837.41	1229.21	1364.66	1511.07
对外经济贸易和旅游	**Foreign Trade and Tourism**				
进出口总额　（亿美元）	Total Exports and Imports (USD 100 million)	20.17	19.56	25.13	27.58
进口额	Imports	5.66	6.74	8.6	10.04
出口额	Exports	14.51	12.82	16.53	17.54
国际旅游	International Tourism				
来湘旅游人数(万人次)	Tourism to Hunan (10 000 person-times)	17.73	38.58	45.4	50.46
旅游外汇收入(万美元)	Foreign Exchange Earnings from Tourism (USD 10 000)	6499	18546	22106.46	27069.87
金融保险（亿元）	**Finance and Insurance (100 million yuan)**				
商业银行各项存款	Deposits of Commercial Banks	831.35	1665.06	1905.79	2337.87
商业银行各项贷款	Loans of Commercial Banks	944.82	1567.27	1479.94	1799.65
城市信用社各项存款	Deposits of Urban Credit Cooperative	70.68	66.46	40.14	32.7
城市信用社各项贷款	Loans of Urban Credit Cooperative	43.99	39.81	26.03	15.74
农村信用社各项存款	Deposits of Rural Credit Cooperative	320.36	491.35	560.03	633.26
农村信用社各项贷款	Loans of Rural Credit Cooperative	212.88	326.17	372.04	414.45

注:对外贸易中的进出口总额,统一按海关统计数据。

Figures on total imports and exports from foreign trade are obtained from the customs statistics.

1-9 续表 3 continued

指 标	Item	总量指标 Aggregate Data 1995	1999	2000	2001
教育、科技、文化	**Education, Science and Technology, Culture**				
教育	**Education**				
专任教师数(人)	Full-time Teachers (person)				
普通高等学校	Institutions of Higher Education	15307	17990	20317	23878
普通中学	Secondary Schools	189679	212435	223693	236161
小学	Primary Schools	297967	307404	306387	291574
在校学生(万人)	Students Enrollment (10 000 persons)				
普通高等学校	Institutions of Higher Education	13.04	17.99	25.31	33.13
普通中学	Secondary Schools	285.41	356.05	391.73	425.6
小学	Primary Schools	736.65	721.4	663.93	601.26
教育事业费支出(亿元)	Government Expenditures on Education (100 million yuan)	31.58	44.54	50.88	65.09
科技	**Science and Technology**				
各类专业技术人员数(人)	Number of Scientific and Technical Personnel (person)	1033039	1073923	1093367	1103287
科技三项及科学事业费支出(亿元)	Expense on S&T Promotion and Operating Expenses for Sciences (100 million yuan)	2.21	4.4	5.55	7.42
技术市场技术交易成交额(亿元)	Transaction Value in Technical Market (100 million yuan)	5.08	7.15	10.95	11.31
文化	**Culture**				
出版数量	Publications				
图书(万册)	Number of Books (10 000 copies)	33677	30765	24844	23808
杂志(万册)	Number of Magazines (10 000 copies)	7768	12437	10504	10051
报纸(万份)	Number of Newspapers Issue (10 000 copies)	62425	84995	83467	92273
电视节目每周播出时间(小时)	Time for TV Programs Telecasting (hour)	1291	2170	2338	8224
家庭、生活、环境	**Family, People's Livelihood and Environment**				
家庭	**Family**				
家庭总户数(万户)	Total Number of Households (10 000 households)	1785.31	1814.64	1874.87	1884.47
城镇居民平均每户家庭人口(人)	Average Household Size in Urban Areas (person)	3.19	3.08	3.09	3.06
农村居民平均每户常住人口(人)	Average Household Size in Rural Areas (person)	4.19	3.93	3.97	3.93
婚姻(万对)	**Marriages and Divorces (10 000 couples)**				
结婚数	Number of Marriages	43.77	40.52	38.31	36.57
离婚数	Number of Divorces	6.33	5.67	6.45	7.34
居住(平方米/人)	**Housing (sq.m/person)**				
城市居民人均居住面积	Per Capita Floor Space of Urban Residents	7.75	10.77	11.75	11.8
农村居民人均住房面积	Per Capita Floor Space of Rural Residents	25.57	29.88	30.92	32.87

1-9 续表 4 continued

指 标	Item	总量指标 Aggregate Data			
		1995	1999	2000	2001
生活	**People's Livelihood**				
城市居民人均可支配收入(元)	Per Capita Annual Disposable Income of Urban Households(yuan)	4705.2	5815.4	6218.7	6780.6
农村居民人均纯收入(元)	Per Capita Annual Net Income of Rural Households (yuan)	1425.16	2147.18	2197.16	2299.46
城乡储蓄存款余额(亿元)	Outstanding Amount of Saving Deposits in Urban and Rural Areas (100 million yuan)	880.35	1689.12	1874.22	2183.73
工资福利	**Wages and Welfare**				
工资总额(亿元)	Total Wages (100 million yuan)	282.05	349.06	377.19	407.58
职工平均工资(元)	Average Wage of Staff and Workers (yuan)	4797	5939	6515	7698
在岗职工劳保福利费(亿元)	Labour Insurance and Welfare Funds for Staff and Workers on the Job (100 million yuan)	86.81	17.74	-	-
离休、退休、退职人数(万人)	Number of Retired & Resigned Staff and Workers (10 000 persons)	138.23	150.57	153.3	165.26
离退休退职人员劳保福利费(亿元)	Pensions, Labour Insurance and Welfare Funds for Retired Staff and Workers (100 million yuan)	59.28	92.52	103.31	117.2
卫生	**Health Care**				
医院与卫生院(个)	Number of Hospitals (unit)	3879	3359	3339	3335
医生(万人)	Number of Doctors (10 000 persons)	8.46	8.49	8.87	8.95
医院床位数(万张)	Number of Hospital Beds (10 000 units)	13.52	13.46	13.21	13.43
市政建设	**City Construction**				
自来水供应量(亿吨)	Volume of Tap Water Supply (100 million tons)	31.78	28.32	28.24	27.63
排水管道长度(公里)	Length of Sewer Pipelines (km)	2928	4922	3754	3854
城市煤气供气量(万立方米)	Volume of Coal Gas Supply in Urban Areas (10 000 cu.m)	69984	74550	60375	48559
石油液化气用量(万吨)	Volume of Liquefied Petroleum Gas (10 000 tons)	11.65	18.96	20.2	24.76
公共汽车总数(辆)	Total Number of Public Buses (unit)	6871	8891	9083	8616
公交客运总量(万人次)	Total Passenger Traffic of Public Transportation (10 000 person-times)	92334	91835	106227	101835
环境、灾害	**Environment and Disaster**				
治理污染资金使用额(亿元)	Actual Investment in Implementation of the Project for Pollution Treatment (100 million yuan)	3.77	3.37	5.45	6
环境污染事故数(次)	Number of Pollution Accidents (times)	301	168	317	238
环境污染事故罚款金额(万元)	Amount of Reparations and Fines (10 000 yuan)	35	44.41	30.82	29.6
火灾发生数(次)	Number of Fire Disasters (times)	1128	2871	3440	3979
火灾经济损失(万元)	Loss of Fire Accidents (10 000 yuan)	6824	8315	4799	4397.35
交通事故发生数(次)	Number of Traffic Accidents (times)	10361	15337	23938	32504
交通事故经济损失(万元)	Loss of Traffic Accidents (10 000 yuan)	6203	8315	9662	8799.48

1-10 国民经济和社会发展速度指标

Develop Speed of National Economy and Social Development

单位：%　　(%)

指　标	Item	指数 Index (2001为下列年) 2001 as percentage of the following years			年均增长速度 Average Annual Growth Rate	
		1995	1999	2000	1991-1995	1996-2000
人口与就业	**Population and Employment**					
人口	**Population**					
年底总人口	Population at the Year-end	103.19	100.98	100.52	0.78	0.53
市镇人口	Urban	130.98	117.84	104.06	7.52	4.71
乡村人口	Rural	94.28	94.93	99.01	-0.92	-0.97
男性人口	Male	102.63	100.60	99.62	0.76	0.60
女性人口	Female	103.79	101.38	101.49	0.79	0.45
就业	**Employment**					
从业人员数	Employees	104.06	100.18	100.85	1.91	0.63
职工人数	Staff and Workers	89.41	90.43	91.98	1.60	-0.56
城镇登记失业人员数	Un-employees in Urban	110.73	98.83	110.05	11.50	0.12
宏观经济	**Macro-economy**					
国民核算	**National Accounting**					
国内生产总值	Gross Domestic Products	173.23	118.80	109.00	11.00	9.71
第一产业	Primary Industry	126.91	108.07	104.00	5.00	4.06
第二产业	Secondary Industry	195.89	121.99	110.30	15.90	12.17
第三产业	Tertiary Industry	188.82	122.21	110.50	12.30	11.31
国内支出总额	Total Domestic Expenditure	173.23	118.80	109.00	11.00	9.71
最终消费	Final Consumption	156.49	114.05	108.00	5.80	7.70
居民消费	Households Consumption	145.87	109.51	105.70	5.60	6.65
政府消费	Government Consumption	195.85	129.15	115.00	6.80	11.24
资本形成总额	Gross Capital Formation	175.97	122.54	111.30	18.49	9.59
固定资本形成总额	Gross Fixed Capital Formation	224.50	125.43	113.10	18.68	14.70
存货增加	Changes in Inventory	63.19	107.96	100.90	18.17	-8.93
固定资产投资	**Investment in Fixed Assets**					
全社会固定资产投资总额	Total Investment in Fixed Assets	231.03	128.33	113.54	33.40	15.27
国有单位	State-owned unit	195.18	118.28	107.74	34.50	12.62
集体单位	Collective-owned Unit	366.01	152.16	122.71	26.40	24.43
个体经济	Individuals	242.27	110.68	103.43	24.70	18.56
财政	**Pubic Finance**					
地方财政收入	Local Government Revenue	189.91	123.37	116.02	9.1	10.36
地方财政支出	Local Government Expenditure	248.19	137.87	124.11	16.8	14.87
物价总指数(上年=100)	**Price Index (preceding year=100)**					
商品零售价格总指数	General Retail Price Index	98.92	98.12	98.90	13.5	0.02
居民消费价格总指数	General Consumer Price Index	112.05	100.49	99.10	15	2.49
农副产品收购价格总指数	General Farm and Sideline Products Purchasing Price Index	-	-	-	12.6	-4.44
利用外资	**Utilization of Foreign Capital**					
签订利用外资协议额	Amount of Foreign Capital for Utilization Through Signed Contracts or Agreements	76.29	141.03	121.66	46.1	-8.91
实际利用外资额	Amount of Foreign Capital Actually Utilized	136.33	111.04	107.13	29.6	4.94

单位：%　　1-10 续表 1 continued　　(%)

指 标	Item	指数 Index(2001为下列年) 2001 as percentage of the following years) 1995	1999	2000	年均增长速度 Average Annual Growth Rate 1991-1995	1996-2000
产　业	**Industry**					
农业	**Agriculture**					
耕地面积	Cultivated Areas	120.40	121.76	99.77	-0.38	3.83
农林牧渔业从业人员	Number of Persons Engaged in Farming, Forestry, Animal Husbandry and Fishery	97.35	99.25	99.65	-0.95	-0.47
农林牧渔业总产值	Gross Output Value of Farming, Forestry,Animal Husbandry and Fishery	133.63	108.44	103.97	5.90	5.14
农业	Farming	123.36	106.85	103.50	3.14	3.57
林业	Forestry	121.75	107.59	103.20	5.10	3.36
牧业	Animal Husbandry	145.28	108.41	104.30	10.10	6.36
渔业	Fishery	180.84	117.64	105.50	12.40	11.40
主要农产品产量	Output of Major Farm Products					
粮食	Grain	98.12	93.36	93.92	0.40	0.88
棉花	Cotton	85.01	107.34	110.92	13.20	-5.18
油料	Oil-bearing Crops	122.63	105.55	98.59	9.20	4.46
苎麻	Ramie	161.58	246.60	142.30	18.30	2.57
黄红麻(熟麻)	Jute and Ambary Hemp	52.78	82.61	82.61	-28.10	-8.57
烤烟	Fluecured Tobacco	206.60	131.29	104.69	-6.80	14.56
茶叶	Tea	95.11	103.73	101.92	-3.60	-1.37
柑桔	Citrus	151.87	103.00	122.42	16.80	4.41
猪牛羊肉	Pork, Beef and Mutton	142.46	107.52	103.58	10.90	6.58
水产品	Aquatic Products	164.33	113.27	105.82	10.10	9.20
工业	**Industry**					
工业总产值	Gross Industrial Output Value	221.25	121.54	109.40	15.48	15.13
主要工业产品产量	Output of Major Industrial Products					
布	Cloth	62.37	106.27	89.44	1.00	-6.96
机制纸及纸板	Machine-made Paper and Paperboards	82.55	146.32	110.76	7.70	-5.71
糖	Sugar	113.95	70.98	161.94	-1.90	-6.79
合成洗涤剂	Synthetic Detergents	153.22	136.52	114.16	-37.50	6.06
缝纫机	Sewing machine	9.37	98.95	60.26	-8.60	-31.08
家用电冰箱	Household Refrigerators	214.50	167.10	107.30	-2.60	14.86
录放音机	Video Recorders	3.89	1.43	2.27	-7.60	11.34
原煤	Coal	27.79	107.90	103.71	10.50	-23.16
发电量	Electricity	115.44	115.59	108.44	10.60	1.26
钢	Steel	251.65	143.00	145.30	5.20	11.61
成品钢材	Steel Products	251.72	134.70	130.08	5.10	14.11
水泥	Cement	113.66	109.77	104.19	17.00	1.76
独立核算工业企业财务指标	Principal Financial Item of Industrial Enterprises with Independent Accounting Systems					
年底固定资产原价	Original Value of Fixed Assets	163.37	116.42	107.62	21.80	8.71
年底固定资产净值	Net Value of Fixed Assets	150.80	114.81	107.86	22.90	6.93
利润和税金总额	Profits and Taxes	259.08	133.11	114.47	10.00	17.75

指 标	Item	指数 Index(2001为下列年) 2001 as percentage of the following years)			年均增长速度 Average Annual Growth Rate	
		1995	1999	2000	1991-1995	1996-2000
建筑业	**Construction**					
建筑业企业人数	Number of Employed Persons	158.65	125.33	126.78	-	4.59
建筑业总产值	Gross Output Value of Construction	260.14	146.69	138.25	-	13.48
施工房屋面积	Floor Space of Buildings Under Construction	138.88	120.81	123.02	-	2.37
竣工房屋面积	Floor Space of Buildings Completed	138.55	119.49	123.11	-	2.39
交通运输	**Transportation**					
货运量	Freight Traffic	101.33	98.94	98.88	5.70	0.49
铁路	Railways	98.96	111.42	106.18	1.00	-1.40
公路	Highways	101.34	96.60	97.56	6.80	0.76
水运	Waterways	101.16	112.40	104.87	1.90	-0.72
客运量	Passenger Traffic	129.09	105.22	105.62	5.70	4.09
铁路	Railways	125.80	103.83	99.41	3.50	4.82
公路	Highways	130.32	105.26	106.13	6.10	4.19
水运	Waterways	77.31	106.09	97.17	-2.60	-4.47
邮电通信业	**Postal and Telecommunications Services**					
邮电业务总量	Total Business Revenue	426.19	145.08	95.20	47.90	34.96
函件	Number of Letters Delivered	114.70	155.53	185.70	11.40	-9.19
报刊期发数	Number of Newspapers and Magazines Distributed	68.82	63.76	98.01	8.70	-6.83
交换机容量	Capacity of Office Telephone Exchanges	352.36	164.62	110.47	58.30	26.11
城市	Urban Areas	267.63	142.81	109.10	63.20	19.66
农村	Rural Areas	608.22	206.52	112.33	47.50	40.19
电话机	Number of Telephone Sets	436.51	173.67	101.70	59.80	31.38
城市	Urban Areas	309.69	146.35	98.31	62.30	23.64
农村	Rural Areas	979.91	232.45	106.68	51.00	52.73
国内商业	**Domestic Trade**					
社会消费品零售总额	Total Retail Sales of Consumer Goods	180.45	122.93	110.73	23.20	10.26
对外经济贸易和旅游	**Foreign Trade and Tourism**					
进出口总额	Total Exports and Imports	136.74	141.00	109.75	25.40	4.50
进口额	Imports	177.39	148.96	116.74	43.20	8.73
出口额	Exports	120.88	136.82	106.11	21.10	2.64
国际旅游	International Tourism					
来湘旅游人数	Number of Tourism to Hunan	284.60	130.79	111.15	15.80	20.69
旅游外汇收入	Foreign Exchange Earnings from Tourism	416.52	145.96	122.45	45.30	27.74

注:对外贸易中的进出口总额,统一按海关统计数据。

Figures on total imports and exports from foreign trade are obtained from the customs statistics.

单位：%　　1-10 续表 3 continued　　(%)

指　标	Item	指数 Index(2001为下列年) 2001 as percentage of the following years)			年均增长速度 Average Annual Growth Rate	
		1995	1999	2000	1991-1995	1996-2000
金融保险	**Finance and Insurance**					
商业银行各项存款	Deposits of Commercial Banks	281.21	140.41	122.67	21.10	18.05
商业银行各项贷款	Loans of Commercial Banks	190.48	114.83	121.60	15.40	9.39
城市信用社各项存款	Deposits of Urban Credit Cooperative	46.26	49.20	81.46	-	-10.70
城市信用社各项贷款	Loans of Urban Credit Cooperative	35.78	39.54	60.47	-	-9.96
农村信用社各项存款	Deposits of Rural Credit Cooperative	197.67	128.88	113.08	37.30	11.82
农村信用社各项贷款	Loans of Rural Credit Cooperative	194.69	127.07	111.40	38.70	11.81
教育、科技、文化	**Education, Science and Technology, Culture**					
教育	**Education**					
专任教师数	Full-time Teachers					
普通高等学校	Institutions of Higher Education	155.99	132.73	117.53	1.20	5.83
普通中学	Secondary Schools	124.51	111.17	105.57	2.60	3.35
小学	Primary Schools	97.85	94.85	95.17	-0.60	0.56
在校学生	Students Enrollment					
普通高等学校	Institutions of Higher Education	254.06	184.16	130.90	8.10	14.18
普通中学	Secondary Schools	149.12	119.53	108.65	3.30	9.24
小学	Primary Schools	81.62	83.35	90.56	1.20	-2.06
教育事业费支出	Operating Expenses for Education	206.11	146.14	127.93	-	10.01
科技	**Science and Technology**					
各类专业技术人员数	Number of Scientific and Technical Personnel	106.80	102.73	100.91	-	1.14
科技三项及科学事业费支出	Expense on S&T Promotion and Operating Expenses for Sciences	335.75	168.64	133.69	16.60	20.22
技术市场技术交易成交额	Transaction Value in Technical Market	222.64	158.18	103.29	36.00	16.60
文化	**Culture**					
出版数量	Publications					
图书	Number of Books	70.70	77.39	95.83	0.90	-5.90
杂志	Number of Magazines	129.39	80.82	95.69	8.30	6.22
报纸	Number of Newspapers Issue	147.81	108.56	110.55	3.80	5.98
电视节目每周播出时间	Time for TV Programs Telecasting	637.03	378.99	351.75	14.30	12.61
家庭、生活、环境	**Family, People's Livelihood and Environment**					
家庭	**Family**					
家庭总户数	Total Number of Households	105.55	103.85	100.51	2.50	0.98
城镇居民平均每户家庭人口	Average Household Size in Urban Areas	95.92	99.35	99.03	-0.80	-0.63
农村居民平均每户常住人口	Average Household Size in Rural Areas	93.79	100.00	98.99	-0.90	-1.07

单位：%　　1-10 续表 4 continued　　(%)

指 标	Item	指数 Index(2001为下列年) 2001 as percentage of the following years)			年均增长速度 Average Annual Growth Rate	
		1995	1999	2000	1991-1995	1996-2000
婚姻	**Marriages and Divorces**					
结婚数	Number of Marriages	83.55	90.25	95.46	-4.40	-2.63
离婚数	Number of Divorces	115.96	129.45	113.80	11.20	0.38
居住	**Housing**					
城市居民人均居住面积	Per Capita Floor Space of Urban Residents	152.26	109.56	100.43	2.30	8.68
农村居民人均住房面积	Per Capita Floor Space of Rural Residents	128.55	110.01	106.31	2.80	3.87
生活	**People's Livelihood**					
城市居民人均可支配收入	Per Capita Annual Disposable Income of Urban Households	130.10	116.14	110.20	7.50	3.42
农村居民人均纯收入	Per Capita Annual Net Income of Rural Households	140.35	110.13	105.10	3.30	5.96
城乡储蓄存款余额	Outstanding Amount of Saving Deposits in Urban and Rural Areas	248.05	129.28	116.51	31.70	16.31
工资福利	**Wages and Welfare**					
工资总额	Total Wages	144.51	116.77	108.06	4.70	5.99
职工平均工资	Average Wage of Staff and Workers	160.48	129.62	118.16	3.10	3.79
离休、退休、退职职工人数	Number of Retired & Resigned Staff and Workers	119.55	109.76	107.80	6.50	2.09
离退休、退职职工劳保福利费	Pensions, Labour Insurance and Welfare Funds for Retired Staff and Workers	197.71	126.68	113.44	25.60	11.75
卫生	**Health Care**					
医院与卫生院	Number of Hospitals	85.98	99.29	99.88	-1.50	-2.95
医生	Number of Doctors	105.79	105.42	100.90	0.50	0.95
医院床位数	Number of Hospital Beds	99.33	99.78	101.67	0.20	1.18
市政建设	**City Construction**					
自来水供应量	Volume of Tap Water Supply	86.94	97.56	97.84	-0.60	-2.33
排水管道长度	Length of Sewer Pipelines	131.63	78.30	102.66	12.20	5.10
城市煤气供气量	Volume of Coal Gas Supply in Urban Areas	69.39	65.14	80.43	-4.30	-2.91
石油液化气用量	Volume of Liquefied Petroleum Gas	212.53	130.59	122.57	28.50	11.64
公共汽车总数	Total Number of Public Buses	125.40	96.91	94.86	24.00	5.74
公交客运总量	Total Passenger Traffic of Public Transportation	110.29	110.89	95.87	-	2.84
环境、灾害	**Environment and Disaster**					
治理污染资金使用额	Used Value for Pollution Treatment	159.15	178.04	110.09	16.50	7.65
环境污染事故数	Number of Pollution Accidents	79.07	141.67	75.08	7.30	1.04
环境污染事故罚款金额	Amount of Reparations and Fines	84.57	66.65	96.04	1.80	-2.51
火灾发生数	Number of Fire Disasters	352.75	138.59	115.67	-9.20	24.98
火灾经济损失	Loss of Fire Accidents	64.44	52.88	91.63	25.00	-6.80
交通事故发生数	Number of Traffic Accidents	313.71	211.93	135.78	-1.40	18.23
交通事故经济损失	Loss of Traffic Accidents	141.86	105.83	91.07	36.40	9.27

1-11 国民经济和社会发展效益指标

Beneficial Indicators of National Economy and Social Development

指 标	Item	1995	1999	2000	2001
人口与就业	**Population and Employment**				
人口出生率(‰)	Birth Rate (‰)	13.02	11.72	11.45	11.80
人口死亡率(‰)	Death Rate(‰)	7.15	7.12	6.79	6.72
人口自然增长率(‰)	Natural Growth Rate(‰)	5.87	4.60	4.66	5.08
就业者负担人口(人)	Dependency Rate(person)	1.85	1.81	1.83	1.83
城镇登记失业率(%)	Unemployment Rate in Urban Areas (%)	3.80	3.90	3.70	4.00
宏观经济	**Macro Economy**				
全社会劳动生产率(元/年人)	Overall Labor Productivity (yuan/person-year)	6265.45	9235.12	10285.30	11086.15
第一产业	Primary Industry	3304.44	3863.63	3785.40	3932.67
第二产业	Secondary Industry	10373.43	15620.55	17407.10	19793.38
第三产业	Tertiary Industry	11272.90	16518.44	21372.60	22684.60
人均国内生产总值(元)	Per Capita GDP (yuan)	3400.00	5105.00	5639.00	6054.00
全社会固定资产投资相当于国内生产总值(%)	Proportion of Investment in Fixed Assets to GDP (%)	24.36	28.66	28.88	30.39
国有经济项目投产率(%)	Rate of Projects Completed and Put into Use in State-owned Economic (%)	57.20	61.15	62.30	58.30
国有经济固定资产交付使用率(%)	Rate of Fixed Assets Completed and Put into Use in State-owned Economic (%)	64.00	68.47	69.80	56.50
基本建设固定资产交付使用率(%)	Rate of Fixed Assets Completed in Capital Construction and Put into Use (%)	57.64	66.38	68.40	46.80
基本建设项目建成投产率(%)	Rate of Projects Completed in Capital Construction and Put into Use (%)	56.76	60.57	58.40	50.50
地方财政收入相当于国内生产总值(%)	Proportion of Local Government Revenue to GDP (%)	5.03	5.00	4.80	5.12
地方财政支出相当于国内生产总值(%)	Proportion of Local Government Expenditures to GDP (%)	8.08	9.41	9.42	10.84
工农商品综合比价(以1999年为100)(%)	Overall Industrial and Farm Products Price Parity Index (1999=100)(%)	99.60	106.50	102.10	-
实际利用外资相当于签订利用外资额(%)	Proportion of Foreign Capital Actually Used to Total Amount of Foreign Capital for Utilization by Signed Contracts or Agreements (%)	49.94	116.31	101.35	89.24

1-11 续表1 continued

指 标	Item	1995	1999	2000	2001
产 业	**Industry**				
农业人均耕地面积(公顷)	Per Capita Cultivated Land (hectare)	0.0671	0.0493	0.06	0.0593
农业从业者人均耕地面积(公顷)	Cultivated Land per Agricultural Laborer (hectare)	0.154	0.155	0.189	0.1899
农业从业者人均农业总产值(元)	Agricultural Output Value per Agricultural Laborer (yuan)	5038	5790	6048	6367.76
每公顷耕地农业机械总动力(千瓦)	Total Power of Agricultural Machinery per Hectare per Hectare of Cultivated Land (kw)	4.71	6.25	5.63	6.02
每公顷耕地用电量(千瓦小时)	Electric Power Consumption per Hectare of Cultivated Land (kw.h)	1158	1337	1135	1193
每公顷播种面积化肥施用量(公斤)	Chemical Fertilizer Consumption per Hectare of Sown Area (kg)	214	225	228	232.29
每公顷耕地生产的农业产值(元)	Agricultural Output Value per Hectare of Cultivated Land (yuan)	32214	37375	31923	33525.5
每一农业从业者农产品产量	Output of Farm Products per Agricultural Laborer				
粮食(公斤)	Grain (kg)	1326	1394	1388.86	1309.37
棉花(公斤)	Cotton (kg)	10.76	8.53	8.28	9.21
油料(公斤)	Oil-bearing Crops (kg)	53.97	62.76	67.32	66.62
肉类(公斤)	Meat (kg)	152.90	202.76	239.69	250.54
水产品(公斤)	Aquatic Products (kg)	41.53	60.00	64.35	68.35
每公顷播种面积农产品产量	Output of Farm Products per Hectare of Sown Area				
粮食(公斤)	Grain (kg)	5380	5632	5716	5723
棉花(公斤)	Cotton (kg)	1206	1121	1173	1354
油料(公斤)	Oil-bearing Crops (kg)	1258	1392	1490	1505
独立核算工业企业效益	Economic Efficiency of Industrial Enterprises with Independent Accounting Systems				
固定资产利税率(%)	Rate of Per-tax Profits to Fixed Assets (%)	9.7	9.84	10.57	11.25
全部资金利税率(%)	Rate of Per-tax Profits to Total Assets (%)	8.14	8.18	8.76	9.54
产值利税率(%)	Rate of Per-tax Profits to Output Value (%)	9.07	12.53	12.65	13.01
流动资产周转天数(天)	Number of Days of Turnover Circulating Funds (day)	222	256.84	249	244.82
百元销售收入实现利税(元)	Per-tax profits per 100 Yuan Sales Revenue (yuan)	1.42	12.96	13.17	13.87
工业增加值率(%)	Ratio of Value Added to Gross Industrial Output Value (%)	29.43	28.52	28.45	28.87
工业产品销售率(%)	Proportion of Industrial Products Sold (%)	95.04	98.57	99.32	99.2
全员劳动生产率(元／年人)	Overall Labor Productivity (yuan/person-year)	34823	55598	73284.25	89130
建筑业技术装备率(元／人)	Value of Machinery in Construction per Laborer (yuan/person)	4014	4857	5428	5199.5
建筑业动力装备率(千瓦／人)	Power of Machinery per Laborer (kw/person)	4.2	4.5	4.7	4.38
建筑业产值利税率(%)	Ratio of Per-tax Profits to Gross Output Value (%)	3.9	3.6	4.3	5.21
建筑业全员劳动生产率(元／人)	Overall Labor Productivity (yuan/person-year)	36707	43263	46436	56128.62
运输业铁路网密度(公里／万平方公里)	Railway Density in Transportation (km/10000 sq.km)	122.85	136.51	138.07	136.65
运输业公路网密度(公里／万平方公里)	Highway Density in Transportation (km/10000 sq.km)	2792	2852	2872.9	3144.15
城镇百人拥有电话机数(部)	Number of Telephones per 100 persons in Urban (unit)	8.53	16.23	22.66	20.56
农村百人拥有电话机数(部)	Number of Telephones per 100 persons in Rural (unit)	0.64	2.71	6.02	6.59
全省人均消费品零售额(元)	Per Capita Retail Sales of Consumer Goods (yuan)	1319	1882	2084.39	2296.82
进出口总额相当于GDP(%)	Proportion of Total Imports and Exports to GDP (%)		4.87	5.63	5.73
每一来湘旅游客人次支出(美元)	Expenditure per International Tourist in Hunan (USD)	366.55	480.72	486.92	536.46

1-11 续表 2 continued

指 标	Item	1995	1999	2000	2001
教育、科技、文化	**Education, Science and Technology , Culture**				
学龄儿童入学率(%)	Rate of School-age Children Enrollment (%)	98	98.8	98.42	97.9
小学升学率(%)	Rate of Graduates of Primary Schools Entering Junior Secondary Schools(%)	90.6	95.2	97.04	97.89
初中升学率(%)	Rate of Graduates of Junior Secondary Schools Entering Senior Secondary Schools(%)	47.7	47.8	51.15	60.45
学校每一专任教师负担学生人数	Number of Students Supported by Each Fulltime Teacher				
#高等学校(人)	Institutions of Higher Education (person)	8.5	10.8	12.5	13.87
普通中学(人)	Secondary Schools (person)	15.9	16.8	17.5	18.02
小学学校(人)	Primary Schools (person)	24.7	23.5	21.7	20.62
当年教育事业费(亿元)	Operating Expenses for Education (100 million yuan)	31.58	44.54	50.88	65.09
教育事业费相当于国内生产总值(%)	Proportion of Operating Expenses for Education to to GDP (%)	1.47	1.34	1.38	1.63
科技三项及科学事业费相当于国内生产总值(%)	Proportion of Operating Expenses for Sciences and Expenses on S&T Promotion to GDP (%)	0.1	0.13	0.15	0.19
每百万人有电影院(个)	Number of Cinemas per Million Persons	6.06	-	-	-
每百万人有艺术表演团体(个)	Number of Troupes per Million Persons	1.39	1.35	1.39	1.32
每百万人有公共图书馆(个)	Number of Public Libraries per Million Persons	1.83	1.76	1.76	1.74
家庭、生活、环境	**Family , People's Livelihood and Environment**				
离婚率(‰)	Divorce Rate (‰)	2	1.74	1.97	2.23
在岗职工福利相当于工资比例 (%)	Welfare Funds of Staff and Workers as Percentage of Total Wages (%)	30.78	5.32	-	-
离退休职工相当于在岗职工比例(%)	Proportion of the Retired or Resigned to Staff and Workers on the Job (%)	23.1	32.78	34.74	41.13
每万人口中医院卫生院数(个)	Number of Hospitals per 10 000 persons (unit)	0.61	0.51	0.51	0.51
每万人口中医生数(人)	Number of Doctors per 10 000 persons (person)	13.32	12.99	13.52	13.54
每万人口中医院床位数(张)	Number of Hospital Beds per 10 000 persons (unit)	21.28	20.6	20.13	20.36
医院病床使用率(%)	Utilization Rate of Hospital Beds (%)	64.6	48.98	45.59	57.44
城市自来水普及率(%)	Percentage of Households with Access to Tap Water (%)	97.7	97.85	97.5	97.4
城市用气普及率(%)	Percentage of Households with Access to Tap Gas(%)	55.5	75.54	78.35	82.6
人均公共绿地面积(平方米)	Per Capita Public Green Areas (sq.m)	4.3	4.87	5.1	4.55
平均每起火灾经济损失(万元)	Average Loss of per Fire Disaster (10 000 yuan)	6.05	2.19	1.4	1.11
平均每起交通事故经济损失(万元)	Average Loss of per Traffic Accident (10 000 yuan)	0.6	0.54	0.4	0.27
平均每起环境污染事故罚款(万元)	Average Loss of per Pollution Accident (10 000 yuan)	0.12	0.26	0.097	0.124

注:1999-2001年本表的职工都是在岗职工,1998年以前均为全部职工。

Data in 1999-2001 are on-post staff and workers figures, and data prior to 1998 refer to those of all staff and workers.

1-12 国民经济主要比例关系

Main Proportional Relations of National Economy

单位:% (%)

指 标	Item	1995	1999	2000	2001
国内生产总值比例	**Ratio of Gross Domestic Products**				
第一产业	Primary Industry	31.9	23.4	21.3	20.7
第二产业	Secondary Industry	35.9	39.0	39.6	39.5
#工业	# Industry	30.4	33.0	33.3	32.9
建筑业	Construction	5.4	6.0	6.3	6.6
第三产业	Tertiary Industry	32.2	37.6	39.1	39.8
#运输邮电业	# Transportation, Post and Telecommunications	6.2	7.2	7.5	7.4
商业	Commerce	9.8	9.5	9.4	9.6
国内支出总额比例	**Ratio of Gross National Expenditure**				
资本形成总额	Gross Capital Formation	35.2	32.6	34.5	35.8
#固定资本形成总额	#Fixed Capital Formation	70.6	88.0	84.9	86.4
存货增加	Changes in Inventories	29.4	12.0	15.1	13.6
最终消费	Final Consumption Expenditure	64.9	66.5	64.6	64.1
#居民消费	#Resident Consumption	79.4	76.4	74.8	73.3
#农民	#Agricultural Resident' Consumption	60.8	60.4	58.3	56.9
非农业居民	Non-agricultural Resident' Consumption	39.2	39.6	41.7	43.1
政府消费	Government Consumption	20.6	23.6	25.2	26.7
全社会固定资产投资的资金来源比例	**Ratio of Investment in Fixed Assets by Source of Finance**				
国家预算内投资	State Budgetary Appropriation	3.8	7.2	7.2	7.7
国内贷款	Domestic Loans	19.3	16.2	20.0	17.0
债 券	Bunds	0.1	1.0	0.2	0.1
利用外资	Foreign Investment	6.3	3.5	2.1	2.4
自筹投资	Fundraising	52.7	55.9	58.5	62.6
其他投资	Others	17.7	16.3	12.1	10.2
固定资产投资中各行业比例	**Ratio of Investment in Fixed Assets by Sector**				
(国有经济)	(State-owned Economic)				
农 业	Agriculture	0.3	0.5	0.8	1.0
轻工业	Light Industry	6.1	2.6	2.4	0.8
重工业	Heavy Industry	34.2	19.0	21.4	16.2
#能源工业	#Energy	19.4	14.8	15.5	15.4
运输、邮电、仓储业	Transportation, Postal and Telecommunications, Storage	26.0	40.0	42.5	36.5
地方财政收入比例	**Ratio of Local Government Revenue**				
工商税收	Industrial and Commercial Tax	60.5	66.5	54.0	60.6
企业所得税	Income Tax of Enterprises	6.3	7.1	6.8	11.0
国有企业亏损补贴	Subsidies to Loss-suffering State-owned Enterprises	-4.2	-3.3	-2.8	-2.9
地方财政收入相当于国内生产总值	**Proportion of Local Government Revenue to GDP (%)**	5.0	5.0	4.8	5.2

单位：%　　1-12 续表 continued　　(%)

指　标		1995	1999	2000	2001
农业总产值中农林牧副渔比例	**Ratio of Agricultural Output Value**				
农业	Farming	55.4	82.0	50.6	50.7
#种植业	#Planting	51.9	48.2	46.3	46.5
林业	Forestry	4.1	4.0	4.1	4.0
牧业	Animal Husbandry	35.3	8.2	38.8	38.9
渔业	Fishery	5.2	5.8	6.5	6.5
规模工业总产值中轻重工业比例	**Ratio of Gross Output Value of Industrial Enterprises above Designated Size**				
轻工业	Light Industry	-	36.0	34.7	35.0
以农产品为原料	Using Farm Products as Raw Materials	-	74.7	75.3	76.5
以非农产品为原料	Using Non-Farm Products as Raw Materials	-	25.3	24.7	23.5
重工业	Heavy Industry	-	64.0	65.3	65.0
采掘工业	Mining and Quarrying	-	7.6	6.6	6.3
原料工业	Raw Materials Industry	-	54.0	56.0	54.6
加工工业	Manufacturing Industry	-	38.4	37.3	39.1
客运量比例	**Ratio of Total Passenger Traffic**				
铁路	Railways	5.8	5.7	6.0	5.6
公路	Highways	92.2	93.0	92.6	93.1
水运	Waterways	1.9	1.1	1.3	1.2
民用航空	Civil Aviation	0.1	0.1	0.2	0.2
货运量比例	**Ratio of Total Freight Traffic**				
铁路	Railways	10.1	8.7	9.2	9.4
公路	Highways	82.8	84.8	83.9	83.9
水运	Waterways	7.1	6.2	6.7	6.8
货物周转量比例	**Ratio of Total Freight Ton-kilometers**				
铁路	Railways	72.0	64.5	58.9	59.6
公路	Highways	22.6	28.2	27.7	27.9
水运	Waterways	5.4	7.2	13.4	12.5
全社会消费品零售总额比例	**Ratio of Total Retail Sales of Consumer Goods**				
市	City	51.1	50.9	52.0	52.9
县	County	19.9	19.1	18.7	18.4
县以下	Under County Level	29.0	30.0	29.3	28.7
公有经济	Public -Owned Economic	40.5	30.2	29.1	26.8
#国有经济	#State-owned Economic	25.5	17.0	17.1	16.3
非公有经济	Non Public-Owned Economic	59.5	69.8	70.9	73.2

1-13 平均每天主要社会经济活动

Selected Indicators of Average Daily Social and Economic Activities

指　标	Item	1995	1999	2000	2001
全省每天创造的财富	**Daily Production**				
国内生产总值(亿元)	Gross Domestic Product (100 million yuan)	5.89	9.11	10.11	10.91
农业总产值(亿元)	Gross Output Value of Agriculture(100 million yuan)	2.87	3.29	3.43	3.6
地方财政收入(万元)	Local Government Revenue (10 000 yuan)	2963	4562	4850.4	5627.64
布(万米)	Cloth (10 000 m)	134	79	93.42	83.56
机制纸及纸板(吨)	Machine-made Paper and Paperboard (ton)	2576	1453	1919.73	2126.3
原　煤(万吨)	Coal (10 000 tons)	15.25	3.93	4.08	4.24
发电量(万度)	Electricity (10 000 kw.h)	9121	9110	9710.14	10530.1
原油加工量(吨)	Machining Crude Oil (ton)	9500	13062	14422.47	11943.29
钢(吨)	Steel (ton)	4811	8466	8331.51	12106.85
成品钢材(吨)	Steel Products (ton)	4234	7911	8193.15	10657.8
水　泥(万吨)	Cement (10 000 tons)	6.02	6.23	6.56	6.84
粮　食(万吨)	Grain (10 000 tons)	7.54	7.92	7.88	7.4
棉　花(吨)	Cotton (ton)	612	485	469.32	520.55
油　料(吨)	Oil-bearing Crops (ton)	3070	3566	3817.81	3764.11
苎　麻(吨)	Ramie (ton)	160	105	181.37	258.08
烤　烟(吨)	Flue-cured Tobacco (ton)	216	340	426.03	446.03
茶　叶(吨)	Tea (ton)	168	154	156.99	160
柑　桔(吨)	Oranges (ton)	2781	4100	3449.86	4223.39
猪牛羊肉(吨)	Pork, Beef and Mutton (ton)	8695	11521	11959.18	12386.85
水产品(吨)	Aquatic Products (ton)	2364	3410	3649.59	3861.92
对外贸易进出口总额(万美元)	Total Imports and Exports (USD 10 000)	552.6	535.89	688.49	755.62
进口总额(万美元)	#Total Imports (USD 10 000)	155.07	184.66	235.62	275.07
出口总额(万美元)	Total Exports (USD 10 000)	397.53	351.23	452.88	480.55
全省每天消费	**Daily Consumption**				
城乡居民消费总额(亿元)	Resident Consumption (100 million yuan)	3.05	4.64	4.88	5.13
平均每人消费额(元)	Per Capita Consumption (100 million yuan)	4.8	7.11	7.46	7.79
其他经济活动	**Other Daily Economic Activities**				
邮电业务总量(万元)	Business Volume of Postal and Telecommunications Services (10 000 yuan)	862.45	2533.52	3860.89	3675.72
出版图书(万册)	Books Published (10 000 copies)	92.27	84.29	68.07	65.23
出版杂志(万册)	Magazines Published (10 000 copies)	21.28	34.07	28.78	27.54
出版报纸(万份)	Newspaper Published (10 000 copies)	171	232.86	228.68	252.8
邮寄函件(万份)	Post Letters (10 000 pieces)	94.28	82.16	58.23	108.14
全省每天人口变动和婚姻	**Daily Population Changes and Marriages**				
出　生(人)	Births (person)	2266	2097	2054	2121
死　亡(人)	Deaths (person)	1244	1274	1218	1208
结　婚(对)	Marriages (couples)	1199	1110	1050	1002
离　婚(对)	Divorces (couples)	173	155	177	201

1-14 人均主要工农业产品产量

Per Capita Output of Major Agricultural and Industrial Products

指　标	Item	1995	1999	2000	2001
粮食(公斤)	Grain (kg)	439.0	443.8	439.0	410.4
棉花(公斤)	Cotton (kg)	3.6	2.7	2.6	2.9
食用植物油(公斤)	Edible Vegetable Oil (kg)	7.2	8.2	8.6	8.5
甘蔗(公斤)	Sugarcane (kg)	22.5	25.9	17.7	25.3
烤烟(公斤)	Flue-cured Tobacco (kg)	1.2	1.9	2.4	2.3
茶叶(公斤)	Tea (kg)	1.0	0.9	0.9	0.9
水果(公斤)	Fruit (kg)	18.6	26.5	23.0	75.4
#柑桔(公斤)	#Oranges (kg)	16.1	23.0	19.2	23.4
猪牛羊肉(公斤)	Pork, Beef and Mutton (kg)	50.6	64.5	66.7	68.7
#猪肉(公斤)	#Pork (kg)	49.2	61.4	63.3	65.2
禽蛋(公斤)	Poultry Eggs (kg)	7.4	10.7	11.2	11.7
水产品(公斤)	Aquatic Products (kg)	13.7	19.1	20.3	21.4
纱(混合数)(公斤)	Yarn (kg)	2.32	2.14	2.53	2.53
布(混合数)(米)	Cloth (meter)	7.73	4.4	5.19	4.64
针棉织品(折用纱量)(公斤)	Cotton Knitwear (kg)	0.12	0.1	0.1	0.07
丝织品(米)	Silk (meter)	0.04	0.0004	0.0015	…
机制纸及纸板(公斤)	Machine-made Paper and Paperboard (kg)	14.86	9.07	10.68	11.79
自行车(辆／百人)	Bicycles (unit/100 persons)	0.11	…	…	…
合成洗涤剂(公斤)	Synthetic Detergents (kg)	0.95	1.04	1.24	1.41
原盐(公斤)	Salt (kg)	9.43	10.63	11.11	10.43
糖(公斤)	Sugar (kg)	1	1.55	0.68	1.09
卷烟(箱／百人)	Cigarettes (cases/100 persons)	3.95	3.51	3.51	3.71
原煤(吨)	Coal (ton)	0.88	0.22	0.23	0.24
原油加工量(公斤)	Machining Crude Oil (kg)	54.8	72.99	80.22	66.25
发电量(度)	Electricity (kw.h)	526.17	509.05	540.11	584.12
生铁(公斤)	Pig Iron (kg)	31.68	49.74	50.7	63.41
钢(公斤)	Steel (kg)	27.75	47.31	46.35	67.16
钢材(公斤)	Steel Products (kg)	24.42	44.21	45.57	59.12
水泥(吨)	Cement (ton)	0.35	0.35	0.37	0.38
合成氨(公斤)	Synthetic Ammonia (kg)	24.93	27.44	25.49	22.68
农用化肥(折纯量)(公斤)	Chemical Fertilizers (kg)	24.14	24.09	21.6	22.21
#氮肥(公斤)	#Nitrogen Fertilizers (kg)	17.87	19.96	17.21	18.14
农药(原药折纯量)(公斤)	Chemical Pesticide (kg)	0.72	0.94	0.7	0.75

1-15 贫困县市基本情况(2001年)

Basic Statistics on Poverty Counties and Cities (2001)

县 市	Country & City	总人口(万人) Total Population (10 000 persons)	国内生产总值(万元) Gross Domestic Products (10 000 yuan)	农业总产值(万元) Gross Output Value of Agriculture (10 000 yuan)	工业总产值(万元) Gross Output Value of Industry (10 000 yuan)	财政收入(万元) Govern-ment Revenue (10 000 yuan)	粮食产量(万吨) Total Output of Grain (10 000 ton)	农民人均纯收入(元) Per Capita Annual Net Income of Rural Households (yuan)
国家级贫困县	Poverty Counties and Cities at Country Level							
邵阳县	Shaoyang County	95.17	187947	120388	16505	8677	33.56	1073
隆回县	Longhui County	110.92	275362	150859	38989	14122	40.25	1129
城步县	Chengbu County	25.41	65954	37784	24844	4827	9.12	1142
平江县	Pingjiang County	99.18	314011	182203	43217	13336	42.27	1297
桑植县	Shangzhi County	42.83	78155	46461	10435	3900	13.82	1199
安化县	Anhua County	95.11	216851	134975	47265	10273	26.47	1345
汝城县	Nucheng County	36.70	143843	64017	33898	7967	16.04	1446
桂东县	Guidong County	17.09	46116	24036	3680	2928	5.61	1282
新田县	Xintian County	37.19	109125	80818	17129	3877	14.19	1290
江华县	Jianghua County	45.16	131845	90869	22358	5616	15.86	1253
沅陵县	Yuanling County	64.04	279168	98366	76514	9575	22.67	1359
通道县	Tongdao County	21.88	49096	38649	9745	3320	8.09	1272
新化县	Xinhua County	128.86	279240	169868	35874	13553	44.17	1224
泸溪县	Louxi County	27.99	62602	38643	30280	1446	8.04	1129
凤凰县	Fenghuang County	36.92	83520	37689	17191	2838	10.55	1254
花垣县	Huayuan County	27.08	66412	35893	74227	3750	10.21	1150
保靖县	Baojing County	27.80	62410	36637	24430	2272	8.93	1117
古丈县	Guzhang County	13.69	28584	17549	4522	756	3.70	1121
永顺县	Yongsun County	48.28	94518	67204	7189	2655	20.92	1204
龙山县	Longshan County	52.81	128750	78312	47496	3737	18.46	1298
省级贫困县	Poverty Counties and Cities at Province Level							
茶陵县	Chaling County	56.01	217303	137390	23316	9156	33.13	1817
炎陵县	Yanling County	17.66	85678	42213	3616	4409	10.78	1705
新邵县	Xinshao County	72.35	209238	113982	30259	6292	29.72	1449
新宁县	Xinning County	58.70	144901	88286	20108	7565	28.35	1065
石门县	Shimen County	68.45	312701	162073	62231	11906	22.60	1740
永定区	Yongding Distract	41.58	147748	74793	18002	6245	15.91	1587
武陵源区	Wulingyuan Distract	4.47	45128	7390	922	6508	1.36	1758
慈利县	Cili County	67.41	198736	109642	29772	6866	27.10	1636
宜章县	Yizhang County	55.52	236169	98052	51210	13607	23.25	1991
安仁县	Anren County	39.82	123375	103124	22608	7439	26.14	1853
双牌县	Shuangpai County	16.99	66257	38749	23261	3725	6.03	1676
宁远县	Ningyuan County	77.42	187480	128761	13384	6863	24.68	1309
辰溪县	Chenxi County	51.19	120463	66179	33129	6640	16.40	1731
麻阳县	Mayang County	35.93	86211	60738	11958	3817	12.67	1339
新晃县	Xinhuang County	25.36	79459	34971	28381	3440	9.57	1291
芷江县	Zhijiang County	35.27	124539	80302	25442	5544	16.33	1673
涟源市	Lianyuan City	107.09	282408	132936	69411	14099	40.57	1639
吉首市	Jishou City	27.85	191348	43710	116730	8425	4.84	1867

注：工业总产值的综合范围是指全部国有工业企业及年销售收入500万元及以上的非国有工业企业。

Gross output value of industry are calculated with all state-owned and the non-state-owned industrial enterprises with an annual sales income of over 5 million yuan.

1-16 城乡私营企业基本情况(2001年)

Basic Statistics on Private Enterprises in Urban and Rural Areas (2001)

项 目	Item	户 数 (户) Number of Enterprises (unit)	投资者 (人) Employers (person)	雇工人数 (人) Number of Employed Persons (person)	注册资金 (万元) Registered Capital (10000 yuan)
合计	**Total**	30405	84960	476611	2903863
#城镇	Urban	24566	65559	353759	2572495
独资企业	Private-funded Enterprises	6101	6475	97071	238107
合伙企业	Private Partnership Enterprises	3073	12467	61129	116215
有限责任公司	Private Limited Liability Corporations	21206	65725	313024	2444348
股份有限公司	Private Share-holding Corporations Ltd.	25	293	5387	105193

1-17 城乡私营企业生产经营情况(2001年)

Basic Statistics of Production and Operation on Private Enterprises in Urban and Rural Areas (2001)

单位：亿元 (100 million yuan)

项 目	Item	总产值 Total Output Value	#城镇 Urban	销售总额或营业收入 Total Sales	#城镇 Urban	零售额 Retail Sales	#城镇 Urban
合 计	**Total**	**194.61**	**133.75**	**202.60**	**163.51**	**147.14**	**111.67**
农林牧渔业	Farming, Forestry, Animal Husbandry and Fishery	7.71	4.29	7.13	4.47	2.80	1.64
农林牧渔服务业	Farming, Forestry, Animal Husbandry and Fishery Service			0.79	0.62	0.27	0.20
采掘业	Mining and Quarrying	9.90	2.91			2.70	1.18
制造业	Manufacturing	150.66	105.49			42.19	27.44
建筑业	Construction	26.33	21.05			4.64	3.94
交通运输、仓储业	Transport, Storage			9.07	6.88	2.38	1.84
仓储业	Storage			1.40	1.31	1.13	0.90
批发零售贸易、餐饮业	Wholesale and Retail Trades and Catering Services			150.95	122.16	75.06	60.12
餐饮业	Catering Trade			41.97	41.02	22.10	17.86
社会服务业	Social Services			26.01	22.44	12.99	11.54
日用品修理业	Commodity Revamp			0.98	0.73	0.33	0.29
旅馆业	Hotels			1.53	1.27	0.85	0.71
娱乐服务业	Recreational Services			1.18	0.99	1.17	1.05
其他行业	Others			9.45	7.55	4.40	3.96

1-18 城乡个体工商业基本情况(2001年)

Basic Statistics on Individuals and Commerce in Urban and Rural Areas (2001)

金额单位：亿元　　　　　　　　　　　　　　　　　　　　(100 million yuan)

项　目	Item	户数(户) Number of Enterprise (household)	#城镇 Urban	从业人员(人) Number of Employees (person)	#城镇 Urban	注册资金 Registered Capital	#城镇 Urban
合　计	**Total**	**872123**	**481372**	**1886273**	**1043306**	**128.78**	**78.74**
农林牧渔业	Farming, Forestry, Animal Husbandry and Fishery	3309	1014	7906	2071	0.71	0.29
农林牧渔服务业	Services	205	82	563	166	0.03	0.02
采掘业	Mining and Quarrying	1378	269	9391	1471	0.93	0.15
制造业	Manufacturing	91936	44352	237338	113104	17.23	8.92
建筑业	Construction	1234	768	7124	4195	0.69	0.41
交通运输、仓储业	Transport, Storage	99228	41435	170883	73707	25.18	10.23
仓储业	Storage	11959	2901	17219	5394	3.79	0.82
批发零售贸易、餐饮业	Wholesale and Retail Trades and Catering Services	555607	320536	1197319	686224	67.42	47.19
餐饮业	Catering	147313	87340	354620	198232	18.5	12.41
社会服务业	Social Services	108283	67298	224379	143165	13.99	10.27
日用品修理业	Commodity Revamp	23282	10709	41503	20175	1.63	0.95
旅馆业	Hotels	7066	4296	18562	10669	1.43	0.97
娱乐服务业	Recreational Services	12414	8546	28867	19012	2.37	1.78
其他行业	Others	11148	5700	31933	19369	2.63	1.27

项　目	Item	总产值 Total Output Value	#城镇 Urban	销售总额或营业收入 Total Sales	#城镇 Urban	零售额 Retail Sales	#城镇 Urban
合　计	**Total**	**248.02**	**123.01**	**765.70**	**456.93**	**470.84**	**282.96**
农林牧渔业	Farming, Forestry, Animal Husbandry and Fishery	17.13	3.62	8.34	3.13	4.26	1.54
农林牧渔服务业	Services			0.69	0.44	0.31	0.21
采掘业	Mining and Quarrying	17.01	2.67			4.03	1.20
制造业	Manufacturing	190.77	104.42			45.76	23.51
建筑业	Construction	23.11	12.30			4.33	2.71
交通运输、仓储业	Transport, Storage			122.18	52.54	36.67	14.95
仓储业	Storage			20.16	6.56	7.07	1.73
批发零售贸易、餐饮业	Wholesale and Retail Trades and Catering Services			547.04	344.45	326.93	207.16
餐饮业	Catering			167.64	99.08	107.07	60.87
社会服务业	Social Services			77.92	51.02	41.03	28.57
日用品修理业	Commodity Revamp			11.75	6.87	5.85	3.52
旅馆业	Hotels			5.68	3.21	2.40	1.42
娱乐服务业	Recreational Services			12.32	9.81	7.59	5.90
其他行业	Others			10.23	5.79	7.83	3.32

1-19 "三资"企业投资基本情况(2001年)

Basic Statistics on Investment of "Three Types of Capital" Enterprises (2001)

类别	Item	项目数(个) Number of Projects (unit)	合同外资(万美元) Contracted Value (USD 10 000)	实际投资(万美元) Used Value (USD 10 000)	年末实有企业数(个) Number of Registered Enterprises (unit)	#本年新增企业 Newly Increase this Year
总　计	**Total**	**338**	**95327**	**81011**	**2080**	**231**
中外合资企业	Joint-venture Enterprises	103	32389	41373	1172	90
中外合作企业	Cooperation Enterprises	34	20483	7859	212	24
外商独资企业	Enterprises with Sole Foreign Investment	201	42455	31779	695	117
按国民经济行业分组	**By Economic Sector**					
农、林、牧、渔业	Farming, Forestry, Animal Husbandry and Fishery	25	5531	3626	46	9
采掘业	Mining and Quarrying	7	3506	2205	29	3
制造业	Manufacturing	194	48083	41542	1188	130
纺织业	Textiles				60	5
石油加工及炼焦业	Petroleum Processing and Coking				4	
化学原料及化学制品制造业	Raw Chemical Materials and Chemical Products				119	9
普通机械制造业	Ordinary Machinery				38	5
专用设备制造业	Equipment for Special Purposes				42	3
交通运输设备制造业	Transport Equipment				57	5
电气机械及器材制造业	Electric Equipment and Machinery				54	6
电子及通信设备制造业	Electronic and Telecommunications Equipment				70	8
电力、煤气及水的生产和供应业	Production and Supply of Electric Power, Gas and Water	11	11936	4777	27	7
建筑业	Construction	4	3525	1123	80	7
地质勘查业、水利管理业	Geological Prospecting and Water Conservancy				1	
交通运输、仓储及邮电通信业	Transportation, Storage, Postal and Telecommunications Services		139	2020	44	
批发和零售贸易、餐饮业	Wholesales &Retail Trade and Catering Services	14	2882	1482	52	13
房地产业	Real Estate Trade	25	9692	8830	270	20
社会服务业	Social Services	53	7988	13741	318	37
卫生、体育和社会福利业	Health Care, Sports and Social Welfare	1	800		4	1
教育、文艺及广播电影电视业	Education, Culture and Arts, Radio, Film and Television	2	885	925	7	
科学研究和综合技术服务业	Scientific Research and Polytechnical Services	2	360	340	9	3
其他	Others			400	5	1

类 别	Item	项目数 (个) Number of Projects (unit)	合同外资 (万美元) Contracted Value (USD 10 000)	实际投资 (万美元) Used Value (USD 10 000)	年末实有企业数 (个) Number of Registered Enterprises (unit)	#本年新增企业 Newly Increase this Year
按国别(地区)分组	**By Country (Territory)**	**338**	**95327**	**81011**	**2080**	**231**
亚洲	Asian	262	55416	60093	1725	175
香港	Hong Kong	149	39096	39552	1120	92
澳门	Macao	5	838	598	44	3
台湾	Taiwan	74	11980	6929	376	51
日本	Japan	7	3619	1258	57	5
菲律宾	Philippines	5	598	1923	13	4
泰国	Thailand	2	1212	1519	16	1
马来西亚	Malaysia	2	1337	749	28	2
新加坡	Singapore	7	3095	3837	41	7
印度尼西亚	Indonesia				2	
韩国	Republic of Korea	8	-7725	2886	18	6
非洲	Africa	1	20	20	3	
欧洲	Europe	11	19242	8115	82	8
德国	Federal Republic of Germany		9	1390	13	
法国	France	2	439	179	3	1
意大利	Italy	1	77	211	10	
荷兰	Netherlands	3	18148	4927	8	3
英国	United Kingdom	3	515	1121	21	2
挪威	Norway				3	
奥地利	Austria				1	
拉丁美洲	Latin America	10	4681	4204	38	8
维尔京群岛	Virgin Islands	9	4675	4198	30	7
北美洲	North America	46	13309	6988	200	33
加拿大	Canada	5	589	290	31	3
美国	United States	41	12720	6698	168	29
大洋洲	Oceanic	9	2611	1591	29	7
澳大利亚	Australia	7	511	576	24	5
新西兰	New Zealand			233	2	

二、国民经济核算

NATIONAL ECONOMIC ACCOUNTING

资料整理人员：　张雍雍　肖首雄

2-1 总产出

Gross Output

单位：亿元 (100 million yuan)

年份 Year	总产出 Gross Output	第一产业 Primary Industry	第二产业 Secondary Industry	工业 Industry	建筑业 Construction	第三产业 Tertiary Industry	交通运输仓储邮电业 Transportation, Postal and Telecommunications	批发零售贸易餐饮业 Wholesale, Retail Trade and Catering	其他 Other
1952	39.34	23.79	9.09	8.19	0.90	6.46	1.32	2.79	2.35
1955	49.24	25.83	14.47	12.11	2.36	8.94	2.39	4.50	2.05
1960	113.37	27.78	62.58	48.85	13.73	23.01	6.90	8.45	7.66
1965	107.35	42.70	45.55	38.90	6.65	19.10	5.93	5.35	7.82
1970	162.14	58.22	78.40	68.94	9.46	25.52	7.16	7.71	10.65
1975	234.10	76.06	120.60	105.34	15.26	37.44	9.25	11.23	16.96
1978	289.79	81.91	160.32	142.78	17.54	47.56	11.40	14.45	21.71
1979	347.74	109.18	186.04	164.12	21.92	52.52	12.12	16.05	24.35
1980	376.14	111.14	206.57	177.85	28.72	58.43	12.60	17.81	28.02
1981	408.13	126.36	214.61	187.02	27.59	67.16	12.68	19.77	34.71
1982	449.11	142.71	235.37	205.78	29.59	71.03	13.63	22.68	34.72
1983	498.03	158.16	261.66	221.15	40.51	78.21	15.14	22.84	40.23
1984	562.67	171.26	299.00	255.06	43.94	92.41	18.54	28.72	45.15
1985	698.36	198.44	372.89	314.68	58.21	127.03	26.00	40.52	60.51
1986	810.42	222.68	437.15	368.88	68.27	150.59	28.44	48.42	73.73
1987	980.08	253.39	540.92	456.74	84.18	185.77	32.68	58.96	94.13
1988	1239.59	303.01	690.19	581.85	108.34	246.39	43.09	80.03	123.27
1989	1390.89	337.48	768.85	680.09	88.76	284.56	51.37	85.79	147.40
1990	1571.34	397.42	809.86	712.67	97.19	364.06	56.35	136.70	171.01
1991	1777.40	425.58	928.67	803.71	124.96	423.15	70.50	157.16	195.49
1992	2210.80	471.22	1147.44	970.18	177.26	592.14	90.01	232.92	269.21
1993	2863.77	563.47	1610.45	1364.02	246.43	689.85	142.87	289.82	257.16
1994	3942.50	792.90	2075.56	1757.29	318.27	1074.04	227.34	393.00	453.70
1995	4997.42	1046.97	2569.29	2166.66	402.63	1381.16	283.72	506.55	590.89
1996	6178.52	1226.32	3446.08	2936.18	509.90	1506.12	324.74	590.37	591.01
1997	6932.53	1322.26	3842.26	3279.53	562.73	1768.01	375.85	649.63	742.53
1998	7544.08	1262.46	4273.81	3593.14	680.67	2007.81	419.37	705.80	882.64
1999	8122.44	1200.94	4559.96	3786.19	773.77	2361.54	465.98	773.05	1122.51
2000	9210.52	1251.89	5167.95	4272.00	895.95	2790.68	545.15	859.43	1386.10
2001	9966.39	1313.23	5534.70	4508.70	1026.00	3118.46	582.76	949.15	1586.55

注：由于规模以下工业总产值统计调查方法改变，1992年至1998年的国民经济核算数据按国家规定进行了调整，采用时以此年鉴为准。

Since the way of researching on industrial total output value was changed, data on national economy in 1992-1998 were adjusted in accordance with the government regulations.

2-2 总产出构成

Composition of Gross Output

单位：%　　(以总产出为100) (Gross Output=100)　　(%)

年份 Year	总产出 Gross Output	第一产业 Primary Industry	第二产业 Secondary Industry	工业 Industry	建筑业 Construction	第三产业 Tertiary Industry	交通运输仓储邮电业 Transportation,Postal and Telecommunications	批发零售贸易餐饮业 Wholesale, Retail Trade and Catering	其他 Other
1952	100.0	60.5	23.1	20.8	2.3	16.4	3.4	7.1	5.9
1955	100.0	52.5	29.4	24.6	4.8	18.1	4.9	9.1	4.1
1960	100.0	24.5	55.2	43.1	12.1	20.3	6.1	7.5	6.7
1965	100.0	39.8	42.4	36.2	6.2	17.8	5.5	5.0	7.3
1970	100.0	35.9	48.4	42.5	5.9	15.7	4.4	4.8	6.5
1975	100.0	32.5	51.5	45.0	6.5	16.0	4.0	4.8	7.2
1978	100.0	28.3	55.3	49.2	6.1	16.4	3.9	5.0	7.5
1979	100.0	31.4	53.5	47.2	6.3	15.1	3.5	4.6	7.0
1980	100.0	29.5	54.9	47.3	7.6	15.6	3.3	4.7	7.6
1981	100.0	31.0	52.6	45.8	6.8	16.4	3.1	4.8	8.5
1982	100.0	31.8	52.4	45.8	6.6	15.8	3.0	5.0	7.8
1983	100.0	31.8	52.5	44.4	8.1	15.7	3.0	4.6	8.1
1984	100.0	30.4	53.1	45.3	7.8	16.5	3.3	5.1	8.1
1985	100.0	28.4	53.4	45.1	8.3	18.2	3.7	5.8	8.7
1986	100.0	27.5	53.9	45.5	8.4	18.6	3.5	6.0	9.1
1987	100.0	25.9	55.2	46.6	8.6	18.9	3.3	6.0	9.6
1988	100.0	24.4	55.7	47.0	8.7	19.9	3.5	6.5	9.9
1989	100.0	24.3	55.3	48.9	6.4	20.4	3.7	6.2	10.5
1990	100.0	25.3	51.5	45.3	6.2	23.2	3.6	8.7	10.9
1991	100.0	23.9	52.2	45.2	7.0	23.9	4.0	8.8	11.1
1992	100.0	21.3	51.9	43.9	8.0	26.8	4.1	10.5	12.2
1993	100.0	19.7	56.2	47.6	8.6	24.1	5.0	10.1	9.0
1994	100.0	20.1	52.6	44.6	8.0	27.3	5.8	10.0	11.5
1995	100.0	21.0	51.4	43.4	8.0	27.6	5.7	10.1	11.8
1996	100.0	19.8	55.8	47.5	8.3	24.4	5.3	9.6	9.5
1997	100.0	19.1	55.4	47.3	8.1	25.5	5.4	9.4	10.7
1998	100.0	16.7	56.7	47.6	9.1	26.6	5.6	9.4	11.6
1999	100.0	14.8	56.1	46.6	9.5	29.1	5.7	9.5	13.9
2000	100.0	13.6	56.1	46.4	9.7	30.3	5.9	9.3	15.1
2001	100.0	13.2	55.5	45.2	10.3	31.3	5.9	9.5	15.9

2-3 总产出发展速度

Growth Rate of Gross Output

单位：% (以上年为100)(precending year=100) (%)

年份 Year	总产出 Gross Output	第一产业 Primary Industry	第二产业 Secondary Industry	工业 Industry	建筑业 Construction	第三产业 Tertiary Industry	#交通运输仓储邮电业 Transportation,Postal and Telecommunications	#批发零售贸易餐饮业 Wholesale, Retail Trade and Catering
1952	100.0	121.3	151.9	132.3	236.8	100.0	129.3	107.7
1955	115.1	118.5	111.8	105.8	154.5	110.2	118.8	99.5
1960	105.2	84.7	117.1	112.3	140.5	105.3	96.6	109.8
1965	115.5	104.4	126.1	127.9	114.5	112.2	109.6	105.0
1970	124.3	105.0	142.3	144.6	123.3	100.9	116.6	109.1
1975	117.4	104.6	128.4	131.2	111.3	112.9	109.6	106.3
1978	114.8	110.2	117.0	115.6	130.3	115.8	113.2	113.2
1979	110.4	106.3	112.9	112.1	120.0	108.7	106.6	109.5
1980	105.8	98.1	109.8	108.0	123.6	104.8	102.6	104.8
1981	105.6	106.1	103.2	104.0	98.4	112.9	98.8	109.2
1982	108.7	110.1	109.2	109.6	106.3	104.4	108.3	112.8
1983	108.9	105.0	111.4	107.8	137.6	108.2	110.3	107.6
1984	110.7	105.7	112.2	112.6	104.3	115.1	122.3	121.9
1985	114.5	104.9	116.1	116.4	114.3	125.9	140.3	127.0
1986	110.6	105.4	112.1	113.0	106.3	113.6	111.6	114.1
1987	113.3	103.3	116.2	116.9	111.4	117.8	109.2	110.1
1988	111.0	100.5	114.6	115.3	110.0	112.6	118.7	107.8
1989	104.3	105.1	103.1	106.7	76.6	107.2	109.7	90.8
1990	103.9	101.9	104.7	105.0	100.9	103.8	109.4	91.2
1991	109.5	103.9	111.9	111.2	117.3	110.5	112.9	110.4
1992	112.6	103.8	116.3	115.6	121.5	113.6	121.5	132.4
1993	115.3	105.3	119.1	121.0	105.8	116.5	119.6	109.4
1994	113.4	106.4	116.0	116.3	113.8	113.7	110.8	109.0
1995	112.4	110.2	113.6	113.5	114.6	111.3	108.1	111.6
1996	118.9	108.4	126.4	127.5	117.1	108.9	112.7	108.7
1997	113.4	108.3	114.8	115.6	108.1	113.4	113.5	106.7
1998	111.2	101.5	113.3	113.0	116.1	113.0	115.7	111.0
1999	109.8	103.4	109.5	109.3	111.4	115.2	110.1	112.1
2000	111.0	104.3	111.2	111.1	112.4	114.7	119.0	112.0
2001	110.0	104.0	110.0	109.4	113.0	112.8	110.9	111.8

2-4 总产出指数

Indices of Gross Output

单位：%　　(1952 =100)　　(%)

年份 Year	总产出 Gross Output	第一产业 Primary Industry	第二产业 Secondary Industry	工业 Industry	建筑业 Construction	第三产业 Tertiary Industry	#交通运输仓储邮电业 Transportation,Postal and Telecommunications	#批发零售贸易餐饮业 Wholesale, Retail Trade and Catering
1952	100.0	100.0	100.0	100.0	100.0	100.0	100.0	100.0
1955	126.2	108.7	175.7	163.0	283.3	132.4	191.6	147.7
1960	260.8	103.1	773.1	619.0	1514.3	320.5	549.6	261.1
1965	213.6	116.7	541.0	477.6	644.7	248.7	452.9	151.3
1970	341.1	151.4	1015.3	926.6	917.7	350.7	543.7	218.8
1975	494.8	186.5	1573.9	1456.6	1480.3	532.0	702.5	319.8
1978	622.9	209.5	2104.0	1981.4	1716.6	675.6	863.9	410.9
1979	687.6	222.7	2375.4	2220.8	2060.1	734.3	921.0	450.0
1980	727.5	218.4	2608.1	2398.2	2546.6	769.6	944.5	471.5
1981	768.2	231.6	2691.6	2493.0	2504.9	868.8	933.6	514.7
1982	835.1	255.1	2939.3	2732.4	2663.9	907.1	1010.9	580.6
1983	909.4	267.9	3274.3	2946.3	3666.3	981.5	1115.1	624.9
1984	1006.7	283.1	3673.8	3347.1	3825.3	1129.7	1363.9	762.0
1985	1152.7	297.0	4265.3	3894.3	4371.0	1422.2	1913.4	967.7
1986	1274.9	313.2	4781.4	4401.3	4647.3	1615.7	2136.1	1103.8
1987	1444.4	323.5	5556.6	5144.4	5177.6	1903.3	2331.9	1214.8
1988	1603.3	325.2	6367.2	5931.2	5695.4	2143.1	2768.0	1309.6
1989	1672.3	341.8	6564.5	6328.6	4362.7	2297.4	3036.5	1189.1
1990	1737.5	348.3	6873.1	6647.7	4401.9	2384.7	3321.9	1084.5
1991	1902.6	361.9	7691.0	7302.2	5163.4	2635.1	3750.4	1197.3
1992	2142.3	375.6	8944.6	8441.3	6273.6	2993.5	4556.8	1585.2
1993	2470.1	395.5	10653.0	10214.0	6637.4	3487.4	5449.9	1734.2
1994	2801.1	420.8	12357.5	11878.9	7553.4	3965.2	6038.5	1890.3
1995	3148.4	463.7	14038.1	13482.6	8656.2	4413.2	6527.6	2109.6
1996	3743.4	502.7	17744.2	17190.3	10136.4	4806.1	7356.6	2293.1
1997	4245.0	544.4	20370.3	19872.0	10957.4	5450.1	8349.7	2446.7
1998	4720.4	552.6	23079.5	22455.4	12721.5	6158.6	9660.6	2715.8
1999	5183.0	571.4	25272.1	24543.8	14171.8	7094.7	10636.3	3044.4
2000	5753.1	596.0	28102.6	27268.2	15929.1	8137.6	12657.2	3409.7
2001	6328.4	619.8	30912.9	29831.4	17999.9	9179.2	14036.8	3812.0

2-5 国内生产总值

Gross Domestic Product

单位：亿元 (100 million yuan)

年份 Year	国民生产总值 Gross National Product	国内生产总值 Gross Domestic Product	第一产业 Primary Industry	第二产业 Secondary Industry	工业 Industry	建筑业 Construction	第三产业 Tertiary Industry	交通运输仓储邮电业 Transportation,Postal and Telecommunications	批发零售贸易餐饮业 Wholesale, Retail Trade and Catering
1978	146.99	146.99	59.83	59.82	51.94	7.88	27.34	5.91	9.71
1979	178.01	178.01	79.40	68.42	59.23	9.19	30.19	6.47	10.85
1980	191.72	191.72	81.14	76.99	65.31	11.68	33.59	6.77	11.73
1981	209.68	209.68	93.29	77.78	67.19	10.59	38.61	6.93	13.42
1982	232.52	232.52	107.99	82.51	71.31	11.20	42.02	7.61	12.81
1983	257.43	257.43	117.79	93.37	78.84	14.53	46.27	8.16	12.56
1984	287.29	287.29	128.28	104.34	90.79	13.55	54.67	9.30	15.40
1985	349.95	349.95	147.72	127.08	110.05	17.03	75.15	13.23	22.94
1986	397.68	397.68	165.28	143.31	124.30	19.01	89.09	15.00	27.60
1987	469.44	469.44	187.09	172.45	149.67	22.78	109.90	20.13	34.56
1988	584.07	584.07	217.03	221.28	190.40	30.88	145.76	24.12	46.61
1989	640.80	640.80	234.31	238.15	212.21	25.94	168.34	26.81	45.48
1990	744.44	744.44	279.09	249.98	220.69	29.29	215.37	32.27	62.94
1991	833.30	833.30	301.02	281.95	242.96	38.99	250.33	41.68	73.91
1992	986.98	986.98	323.91	337.17	284.66	52.51	325.90	51.29	104.96
1993	1259.55	1259.55	383.68	470.25	398.79	71.46	405.62	72.47	123.71
1994	1666.64	1666.64	532.89	590.29	497.99	92.30	543.46	99.63	167.75
1995	2151.43	2151.43	685.30	771.55	654.76	116.79	694.58	132.39	211.37
1996	2584.98	2584.98	793.98	946.25	808.93	137.32	844.75	168.88	245.95
1997	2918.83	2918.83	855.75	1092.80	944.95	147.85	970.28	195.38	270.12
1998	3118.09	3118.09	828.31	1200.86	1024.30	176.56	1088.92	216.49	291.73
1999	3326.75	3326.75	778.25	1297.74	1096.56	201.18	1250.76	240.40	315.04
2000	3691.88	3691.88	784.92	1461.86	1230.71	231.15	1445.10	277.69	348.10
2001	3983.00	3983.00	825.73	1573.00	1309.50	263.50	1584.27	294.90	382.40

单位：亿元　　　　2-5 续表　continued　　　　（100 million yuan）

年份 Year	金融保险业 Banking and Insurance	房地产业 Real Estate Trade	社会服务业 Social Services	卫生体育和社会福利事业 Health Care, Sports and Social Welfare	教育文化艺术和广播电影电视业 Education, Culture, Arts, Radio, Film and Television	科学研究和综合技术服务业 Scientific Research and Poly-technical Services	国家机关政党机关和社会团体 Government Agencies, Party Agencies, and Social Organiza-tions	其他 Others	人均国内生产总值（元） Per Capita Gross Domestic Product (yuan)
1978	2.55	2.03	0.62	1.05	3.21	0.20	1.86	0.20	286
1979	2.50	2.10	0.68	1.24	3.72	0.28	2.10	0.25	343
1980	2.70	2.32	0.83	1.54	4.46	0.31	2.63	0.30	365
1981	3.60	3.56	0.95	1.72	4.83	0.36	2.89	0.35	394
1982	5.02	3.96	1.06	1.96	5.60	0.39	3.21	0.40	430
1983	5.66	5.18	1.17	2.33	6.40	0.49	3.87	0.45	470
1984	6.53	5.76	1.58	2.58	7.57	0.57	4.88	0.50	519
1985	8.85	7.84	3.34	2.87	9.13	0.68	5.67	0.60	626
1986	12.55	7.93	3.39	3.26	10.80	0.84	6.75	0.97	703
1987	15.94	8.53	3.91	3.84	12.61	0.99	8.14	1.25	818
1988	20.91	9.96	6.55	5.08	17.61	3.99	10.93		999
1989	26.94	11.00	8.73	6.04	21.61	6.07	13.86	1.80	1074
1990	31.01	16.25	10.84	7.98	17.43	7.36	26.51	2.78	1228
1991	38.26	17.73	10.88	9.02	19.14	7.45	29.08	3.18	1357
1992	49.01	20.57	16.52	11.35	23.02	9.41	34.72	5.05	1595
1993	63.47	25.73	18.54	14.08	27.55	10.93	43.96	5.18	2023
1994	73.60	32.30	24.84	20.72	42.37	15.78	59.70	6.77	2656
1995	90.15	40.90	29.39	25.47	55.99	19.86	79.98	9.08	3400
1996	105.14	57.37	33.11	33.84	67.21	8.62	99.78	24.85	4033
1997	119.22	65.75	39.66	40.62	80.27	10.23	119.35	29.68	4528
1998	125.62	75.67	47.05	48.19	97.97	12.07	139.39	34.74	4809
1999	129.76	86.98	66.31	61.50	124.12	14.79	172.20	39.66	5105
2000	140.70	97.14	82.87	77.11	154.16	17.38	203.67	46.28	5639
2001	143.16	108.00	91.98	85.60	170.20	17.90	241.35	48.78	6054

2-6 国内生产总值构成

Composition of GDP

单位：%　　(GDP=100)　　(%)

年份 Year	国内生产总值 Gross Domestic Product	第一产业 Primary Industry	第二产业 Secondary Industry	工业 Industry	建筑业 Construction	第三产业 Tertiary Industry	交通运输仓储邮电业 Transportation,Postal and Telecommunications	批发零售贸易餐饮业 Wholesale, Retail Trade and Catering
1978	100.0	40.7	40.7	35.3	5.4	18.6	4.0	6.6
1979	100.0	44.6	38.4	33.3	5.1	17.0	3.6	6.1
1980	100.0	42.3	40.2	34.1	6.1	17.5	3.5	6.1
1981	100.0	44.5	37.1	32.0	5.1	18.4	3.3	6.4
1982	100.0	46.4	35.5	30.7	4.8	18.1	3.3	5.5
1983	100.0	45.8	36.3	30.6	5.7	17.9	3.2	4.9
1984	100.0	44.7	36.3	31.6	4.7	19.0	3.2	5.4
1985	100.0	42.2	36.3	31.4	4.9	21.5	3.8	6.6
1986	100.0	41.6	36.0	31.3	4.7	22.4	3.8	6.9
1987	100.0	39.9	36.7	31.9	4.8	23.4	4.3	7.4
1988	100.0	37.2	37.9	32.6	5.3	24.9	4.1	8.0
1989	100.0	36.6	37.2	33.1	4.1	26.2	4.2	7.1
1990	100.0	37.5	33.6	29.6	4.0	28.9	4.3	8.5
1991	100.0	36.1	33.8	29.2	4.6	30.1	5.0	8.9
1992	100.0	32.8	34.2	28.8	5.4	33.0	5.2	10.6
1993	100.0	30.5	37.3	31.7	5.6	32.2	5.8	9.8
1994	100.0	32.0	35.4	29.9	5.5	32.6	6.0	10.1
1995	100.0	31.9	35.9	30.4	5.5	32.2	6.2	9.8
1996	100.0	30.7	36.6	31.3	5.3	32.7	6.5	9.5
1997	100.0	29.3	37.4	32.4	5.0	33.3	6.7	9.3
1998	100.0	26.6	38.5	32.9	5.6	34.9	6.9	9.4
1999	100.0	23.4	39.0	33.0	6.0	37.6	7.2	9.5
2000	100.0	21.3	39.6	33.3	6.3	39.1	7.5	9.4
2001	100.0	20.7	39.5	32.9	6.6	39.8	7.4	9.6

单位：%　　2-6 续表 continued　　(%)

年份 Year	金融保险业 Banking and Insurance	房地产业 Real Estate Trade	社会服务业 Social Services	卫生体育和社会福利事业 Health Care, Sports and Social Welfare	教育文化艺术和广播电影电视业 Education, Culture, Arts, Radio, Film and Television	科学研究和综合技术服务业 Scientific Research and Poly-technical Services	国家机关政党机关和社会团体 Government Agencies, Party Agencies, and Social Organizations	其他 Others
1978	1.7	1.4	0.4	0.7	2.2	0.1	1.3	0.2
1979	1.4	1.2	0.4	0.7	2.1	0.2	1.2	0.1
1980	1.4	1.2	0.4	0.8	2.3	0.2	1.4	0.2
1981	1.7	1.7	0.5	0.8	2.3	0.2	1.4	0.1
1982	2.2	1.7	0.5	0.8	2.4	0.2	1.4	0.1
1983	2.2	2.0	0.5	0.9	2.5	0.2	1.5	0.0
1984	2.3	2.0	0.5	0.9	2.6	0.2	1.7	0.2
1985	2.5	2.2	1.0	0.8	2.6	0.2	1.6	0.2
1986	3.2	2.0	0.9	0.8	2.7	0.2	1.7	0.2
1987	3.4	1.8	0.8	0.8	2.7	0.2	1.7	0.3
1988	3.6	1.7	1.1	0.9	3.0	0.7	1.9	0.0
1989	4.2	1.7	1.4	0. 9	3.4	0.9	2.2	0.3
1990	4.2	2.2	1.5	1.1	2.3	1.0	3.6	0.4
1991	4.6	2.1	1.3	1.1	2.3	0.9	3.5	0.4
1992	5.0	2.1	1.7	1.1	2.3	1.0	3.5	0.5
1993	5.0	2.0	1.5	1.1	2.2	0.9	3.5	0.4
1994	4.4	1.9	1.5	1.2	2.5	0.9	3.6	0.5
1995	4.2	1.9	1.4	1.2	2.6	0.9	3.7	0.3
1996	4.1	2.2	1.3	1.3	2.6	0.3	3.9	1.0
1997	4.1	2.3	1.4	1.4	2.8	0.4	4.1	0.8
1998	4.0	2.4	1.5	1.5	3.1	0.4	4.5	1.2
1999	3.9	2.6	2.0	1.8	3.7	0.4	5.2	1.3
2000	3.8	2.6	2.2	2.1	4.2	0.5	5.5	1.3
2001	3.6	2.7	2.3	2.1	4.3	0.4	6.1	1.3

2-7 国内生产总值发展速度

Growth Rate of GDP

单位：%　　(以上年为100)　(precending year=100)　　(%)

年份 Year	国民生产总值 Gross National Product	国内生产总值 Gross Domestic Product	第一产业 Primary Industry	第二产业 Secondary Industry	工业 Industry	建筑业 Construction	第三产业 Tertiary Industry	交通运输仓储邮电业 Transportation, Postal and Telecommunications	批发零售贸易餐饮业 Wholesale, Retail Trade and Catering
1978	116.4	116.4	111.7	121.8	121.6	123.3	115.5	110.7	120.4
1979	109.1	109.1	106.8	111.4	111.3	112.1	109.0	109.3	110.1
1980	105.2	105.2	98.9	111.0	109.7	119.9	105.5	104.5	102.5
1981	105.5	105.5	107.0	100.2	101.4	92.7	113.3	102.6	112.6
1982	109.4	109.4	113.0	106.0	106.1	105.0	107.5	109.6	94.0
1983	109.2	109.2	103.7	116.7	114.8	130.2	108.2	107.2	95.8
1984	109.4	109.4	106.6	109.7	113.0	89.8	115.6	113.9	119.3
1985	112.0	112.0	103.7	113.6	114.3	108.7	127.2	140.6	134.8
1986	108.1	108.1	105.2	107.7	108.5	101.6	114.1	112.6	114.6
1987	109.3	109.3	102.9	112.8	113.3	108.6	114.0	127.1	113.8
1988	108.2	108.2	97.7	115.0	115.3	112.6	112.6	120.4	108.9
1989	103.6	103.6	105.7	101.2	103.0	79.3	105.0	97.3	90.6
1990	104.0	104.0	103.2	104.6	104.5	106.1	103.8	113.7	83.7
1991	107.9	107.9	105.6	108.5	107.4	116.7	110.5	118.6	112.0
1992	111.1	111.1	103.5	117.3	116.8	120.4	114.1	112.8	110.0
1993	112.6	112.6	104.3	118.2	120.0	105.5	116.1	125.2	110.8
1994	110.6	110.6	105.4	115.4	115.9	111.7	110.3	110.6	109.0
1995	110.4	110.4	106.5	113.5	113.4	114.6	110.4	116.3	109.1
1996	112.1	112.1	106.2	116.3	116.8	112.3	112.6	117.8	109.0
1997	110.7	110.7	106.1	113.3	114.3	104.4	111.5	115.0	109.5
1998	108.5	108.5	100.9	111.5	111.2	114.1	111.0	113.4	110.3
1999	108.3	108.3	103.3	109.3	109.0	111.7	110.9	108.0	110.5
2000	109.0	109.0	103.9	110.6	110.5	111.5	110.6	114.5	111.4
2001	109.0	109.0	104.0	110.3	109.9	112.3	110.5	110.2	111.3

单位：%　　2-7 续表 continued　　(%)

年份 Year	金融保险业 Banking and Insurance	房地产业 Real Estate Trade	社会服务业 Social Services	卫生体育和社会福利事业 Health Care, Sports and Social Welfare	教育文化艺术和广播电影电视业 Education, Culture, Arts, Radio, Film and Television	科学研究和综合技术服务业 Scientific Research and Poly-technical Services	国家机关政党机关和社会团体 Government Agencies, Party Agencies, and Social Organizations	其他 Others
1978	115.3	104.0	100.0	113.4	115.8	115.1	116.9	100.0
1979	96.5	101.7	101.9	115.9	113.6	137.9	111.2	125.0
1980	97.8	110.4	104.8	113.5	110.0	103.7	115.3	112.0
1981	131.0	146.4	151.3	110.4	106.6	114.5	108.2	116.7
1982	137.3	110.3	110.2	112.1	114.3	105.8	109.1	111.4
1983	110.1	128.5	128.5	116.0	111.8	124.7	117.7	112.8
1984	111.9	110.0	108.8	107.9	114.9	114.0	122.7	106.6
1985	122.1	128.4	125.9	100.9	109.5	109.0	106.1	110.6
1986	135.3	100.9	97.4	109.4	113.0	118.6	113.7	157.7
1987	114.9	105. 0	99.4	107.0	106.2	107.4	109.8	118.3
1988	104.6	109.5	149.8	107.1	112.6	131．1	108.5	112.4
1989	150.6	86.7	122.5	113.6	117.5	146.3	120.8	101.8
1990	109.0	109.0	104.3	110.2	107.3	108.9	110.4	115.3
1991	115.5	106.1	100.0	107.8	104.9	100.0	106.0	107.6
1992	130.3	110.6	116.7	104.4	106.3	108.7	116.8	107.8
1993	121.3	124.0	107.1	116.8	113.1	108.4	113.3	101.0
1994	105.7	112.0	107.4	117.9	123.2	125.5	109.2	104.6
1995	106.0	114.7	102.4	106.5	104.4	104.4	116.0	116.2
1996	110.6	117.1	107.1	126.3	114.1	117.5	110.3	106.6
1997	110.3	110.2	111.3	112.4	114.9	113.0	111.1	108.1
1998	105.2	113.3	114.0	112.5	115.7	111.7	110.7	111.1
1999	105.1	117.3	121.6	112.8	115.4	112.0	112.0	111.7
2000	106.0	109.2	111.2	111.6	111.4	106.5	109.0	109.6
2001	103.5	109.3	111.5	109.5	108.9	103.9	117.8	105.8

2-8 国内生产总值指数

Gross Domestic Product Indices

单位：% (1978 =100) (%)

年份 Year	国民生产总值 Gross National Product	国内生产总值 Gross Domestic Product	第一产业 Primary Industry	第二产业 Secondary Industry	工业 Industry	建筑业 Construction	第三产业 Tertiary Industry	交通运输仓储邮电业 Transportation,Postal and Telecommunications	批发零售贸易餐饮业 Wholesale, Retail Trade and Catering
1978	100.0	100.0	100.0	100.0	100.0	100.0	100.0	100.0	100.0
1979	109.1	109.1	106.8	111.4	111.3	112.1	109.0	109.3	110.1
1980	114.8	114.8	105.6	123.6	122.1	134.4	115.0	114.2	112.9
1981	121.0	121.0	113.0	123.9	123.8	124.6	130.4	117.2	127.1
1982	132.4	132.4	127.7	131.3	131.4	130.8	140.2	128.4	119.4
1983	144.6	144.6	132.5	153.3	150.8	170.3	151.7	137.7	114.4
1984	158.2	158.2	141.2	168.1	170.4	153.0	175.4	156.8	136.5
1985	177.2	177.2	146.4	191.0	194.7	166.3	223.0	220.5	184.0
1986	191.7	191.7	154.1	205.8	211.3	168.9	254.5	248.3	210.9
1987	209.5	209.5	158.5	232.2	239.4	183.5	290.0	315.6	240.0
1988	226.7	226.7	154.9	267.0	276.1	206.6	326.6	379.9	261.4
1989	234.9	234.9	163.8	270.2	284.3	163.8	342.9	369.1	236.8
1990	244.3	244.3	169.1	282.7	297.1	173.8	355.9	420.3	198.2
1991	263.6	263.6	178.5	306.7	319.1	202.8	393.3	498.5	222.0
1992	292.9	292.9	184.8	359.8	372.7	244.2	448.7	562.3	244.2
1993	329.8	329.8	192.7	425.3	447.2	257.6	520.9	704.0	270.6
1994	364.8	364.8	203.1	490.8	518.3	287.7	574.6	742.0	295.0
1995	402.7	402.7	216.3	557.1	587.8	329.7	634.3	863.3	321.8
1996	451.4	451.4	229.7	647.9	686.6	370.3	714.2	1017.0	350.8
1997	499.7	499.7	243.7	734.1	784.8	386.6	796.3	1169.6	384.1
1998	542.2	542.2	245.9	818.5	872.7	441.1	883.9	1326.3	423.7
1999	587.2	587.2	254.0	894.6	951.2	492.7	980.2	1432.4	468.2
2000	640.0	640.0	263.9	989.4	1051.1	549.4	1084.1	1640.1	521.6
2001	697.6	697.6	274.5	1091.3	1155.2	617.0	1197.9	1807.4	580.5

单位：% 2-8 续表 1 continued (%)

年份 Year	金融保险业 Banking and Insurance	房地产业 Real Estate Trade	社会服务业 Social Services	卫生体育和社会福利事业 Health Care, Sports and Social Welfare	教育文化艺术和广播电影电视业 Education, Culture, Arts, Radio, Film and Television	科学研究和综合技术服务业 Scientific Research and Poly-technical Services	国家机关政党机关和社会团体 Government Agencies, Party Agencies, and Social Organiza-tions	其他 Others
1978	100.0	100.0	100.0	100.0	100.0	100.0	100.0	100.0
1979	96.5	101.7	101.9	115.9	113.6	137.9	111.2	125.0
1980	94.4	112.3	106.8	131.5	125.0	143.0	128.2	140.0
1981	123.6	164.4	161.6	145.2	133.2	163.7	138.7	163.4
1982	169.7	181.3	178.1	162.8	152.3	173.2	151.4	182.0
1983	186.9	233.0	228.8	188.8	170.2	216.0	178.1	205.3
1984	209.1	256.3	248.9	203.8	195.6	246.3	218.6	219.3
1985	255.4	329.1	313.4	205.6	214.2	268.4	231.9	242.5
1986	345.5	332.0	305.0	224.9	242.0	318.4	263.7	382.4
1987	397.0	348.6	303.4	240.7	257.0	341.9	289.5	452.4
1988	415.2	381.7	454.5	257.8	289.4	448.3	314.1	508.5
1989	625.3	331.0	556.8	292.8	340.0	655.8	379.5	517.7
1990	681.6	360.8	580.7	322.7	364.8	714.2	419.0	596.9
1991	787.2	382.8	580.7	347.8	382.7	714.2	444.1	642.3
1992	1025.7	423.4	677.7	363.1	406.8	776.3	518.7	692.4
1993	1244.2	525.0	725.8	424.1	460.1	841.5	587.7	699.3
1994	1315.1	588.0	779.5	500.0	566.8	1056.1	641.8	731.5
1995	1394.0	674.4	798.2	532.5	591.8	1102.6	744.5	850.0
1996	1541.8	789.7	854.9	672.5	675.2	1295.6	821.2	906.1
1997	1700.6	870.2	951.5	755.9	775.8	1464.0	912.4	979.5
1998	1789.0	985.9	1084.7	850.4	897.6	1635.3	1010.0	1088.2
1999	1880.2	1156.5	1319.0	959.3	1035.8	1831.5	1131.2	1215.5
2000	1993.0	1262.9	1466.7	1070.6	1153.9	1950.5	1233.0	1332.2
2001	2062.8	1380.3	1635.4	1172.3	1256.6	2026.6	1452.5	1409.5

年份 Year	国民生产总值 Gross National Product	国内生产总值 Gross Domestic Product	第一产业 Primary Industry	第二产业 Secondary Industry	工业 Industry	建筑业 Construction	第三产业 Tertiary Industry	#交通运输仓储邮电业 Transportation,Postal and Telecommunications	#批发零售贸易餐饮业 Wholesale, Retail Trade and Catering
1952	100.0	100.0	100.0	100.0	100.0	100.0	100.0	100.0	100.0
1955	126.1	126.1	110.3	190.0	165.0	331.5	150.4	192.5	140.2
1960	197.5	197.5	90.4	765.8	671.7	1274.9	292.1	506.9	229.1
1965	170.1	170.1	111.7	558.4	570.3	417.8	186.1	274.9	116.7
1970	247.0	247.0	139.5	1005.8	1057.3	569.4	245.9	363.1	179.7
1975	307.6	307.6	162.4	1325.9	1329.2	1142.5	309.9	449.5	232.0
1978	390.3	390.3	184.3	1903.0	1949.8	1427.7	392.8	538.3	308.6
1979	425.7	425.7	196.8	2119.1	2169.4	1600.1	428.2	588.3	339.8
1980	448.0	448.0	194.6	2352.0	2380.0	1918.7	451.9	614.8	348.3
1981	472.4	472.4	208.3	2357.8	2414.0	1779.3	512.1	630.5	392.2
1982	516.7	516.7	235.4	2498.9	2561.8	1868.4	550.6	690.8	368.7
1983	564.4	564.4	244.2	2917.3	2939.9	2432.2	595.9	740.7	353.2
1984	617.4	617.4	260.2	3198.9	3321.7	2184.7	688.9	843.8	421.4
1985	691.8	691.8	269.9	3634.5	3795.5	2375.4	875.9	1186.1	568.0
1986	748.1	748.1	284.0	3916.1	4119.2	2414.5	999.7	1335.2	650.9
1987	817.8	817.8	292.2	4418.7	4668.6	2622.1	1139.2	1697.3	740.7
1988	884.9	884.9	285.5	5081.5	5382.9	2952.5	1282.7	2043.5	806.6
1989	916.8	916.8	301.8	5142.5	5544.4	2341.3	1346.8	1988.3	730.8
1990	953.1	953.1	311.6	5380.0	5793.9	2484.2	1397.9	2260.7	611.7
1991	1028.4	1028.4	329.0	5837.3	6222.6	2899.1	1544.7	2681.2	685.1
1992	1142.6	1142.6	340.5	6847.2	7268.0	3490.5	1762.5	3024.4	753.6
1993	1286.6	1286.6	355.1	8093.4	8721.6	3682.5	2046.3	3786.5	835.0
1994	1423.0	1423.0	374.3	9339.8	10108.3	4113.4	2257.1	4187.9	910.2
1995	1571.0	1571.0	398.6	10600.7	11462.8	4713.9	2491.8	4870.5	993.0
1996	1761.1	1761.1	423.3	12328.6	13388.6	5293.7	2805.8	5737.4	1082.4
1997	1949.5	1949.5	449.1	13968.3	15303.2	5526.6	3128.5	6598.0	1185.2
1998	2115.2	2115.2	453.1	15574.7	17017.2	6305.9	3472.6	7482.1	1307.3
1999	2290.8	2290.8	468.1	17023.1	18548.7	7043.7	3851.1	8080.7	1444.6
2000	2497.0	2497.0	486.3	18827.5	20496.3	7853.7	4259.3	9252.4	1609.3
2001	2721.7	2721.7	505.8	20766.7	22525.4	8819.7	4706.5	10196.1	1791.2

2-9 国内生产总值构成项目表

Structure of Gross Domestic Product

单位:亿元 (100 million yuan)

指 标	Item	1995	1999	2000	2001
国内生产总值	**Gross Domestic Product**	**2151.43**	**3326.75**	**3691.88**	**3983.00**
劳动者报酬	Compensation of Laborers	1454.72	2076.20	2287.45	2491.25
固定资产折旧	Depreciation of Fixed Assets	233.67	433.88	578.46	600.74
生产税净额	Net Taxes on Production	217.92	420.34	465.18	493.34
营业盈余	Operating Surplus	245.12	396.33	360.79	397.67
第一产业	**Primary Industry**	**685.30**	**778.25**	**784.92**	**825.73**
劳动者报酬	Compensation of Laborers	590.90	686.42	691.52	727.39
固定资产折旧	Depreciation of Fixed Assets	20.59	30.82	31.40	33.56
生产税净额	Net Taxes on Production	15.20	16.00	15.70	15.87
营业盈余	Operating Surplus	58.61	45.01	46.30	48.91
第二产业	**Secondary Industry**	**771.55**	**1297.74**	**1461.86**	**1573.00**
劳动者报酬	Compensation of Laborers	452.91	635.70	712.74	775.86
固定资产折旧	Depreciation of Fixed Assets	101.92	215.25	219.10	232.11
生产税净额	Net Taxes on Production	127.49	292.47	330.10	366.89
营业盈余	Operating Surplus	89.23	154.32	199.92	198.14
#工业增加值	**# Added Value of Industry**	**654.76**	**1096.56**	**1230.71**	**1309.50**
劳动者报酬	Compensation of Laborers	363.34	521.52	578.44	622.01
固定资产折旧	Depreciation of Fixed Assets	94.32	199.61	200.61	210.83
生产税净额	Net Taxes on Production	114.80	269.54	303.98	318.21
营业盈余	Operating Surplus	82.30	105.89	147.68	158.45
#建筑业增加值	**# Added Value of Construction**	**116.79**	**201.18**	**231.15**	**263.50**
劳动者报酬	Compensation of Laborers	89.57	114.18	134.30	153.85
固定资产折旧	Depreciation of Fixed Assets	7.60	15.64	18.49	21.28
生产税净额	Net Taxes on Production	12.69	22.93	26.12	48.68
营业盈余	Operating Surplus	6.93	48.43	52.24	39.69
第三产业	**Tertiary Industry**	**694.58**	**1250.76**	**1445.10**	**1584.27**
劳动者报酬	Compensation of Laborers	410.91	754.08	883.19	988.00
固定资产折旧	Depreciation of Fixed Assets	111.16	187.81	327.96	335.07
生产税净额	Net Taxes on Production	75.23	111.87	119.38	110.58
营业盈余	Operating Surplus	97.28	197.00	114.57	150.62
#交通运输仓储邮电业增加值	**# Added Value of Transport,Storage, Postal and Telecommunications**	**132.39**	**240.40**	**277.69**	**294.90**
劳动者报酬	Compensation of Laborers	90.79	148.46	163.54	160.55
固定资产折旧	Depreciation of Fixed Assets	29.24	89.61	109.73	119.32
生产税净额	Net Taxes on Production	15.96	17.72	20.40	20.74
营业盈余	Operating Surplus	-3.60	-15.39	-15.98	-5.71
#批发零售贸易餐饮业增加值	**# Added Value of Wholesale, Retail Trade and Catering Services**	**211.37**	**315.04**	**348.10**	**382.40**
劳动者报酬	Compensation of Laborers	127.66	191.50	211.32	231.80
固定资产折旧	Depreciation of Fixed Assets	19.76	41.18	45.28	49.57
生产税净额	Net Taxes on Production	37.34	47.28	52.28	57.48
营业盈余	Operating Surplus	26.61	35.08	39.22	43.55

单位：亿元　　2-9 续表 continued　　(100 million yuan)

指 标	Item	1995	1999	2000	2001
#金融保险业增加值	**# Added Value of Finance and Insurance**	**90.15**	**129.76**	**140.7**	**143.16**
劳动者报酬	Compensation of Laborers	16.73	32.38	44.93	61.78
固定资产折旧	Depreciation of Fixed Assets	4.55	9.24	33.04	9.58
生产税净额	Net Taxes on Production	10.63	23.91	13.15	15.39
营业盈余	Operating Surplus	58.24	64.23	49.58	56.41
#房地产业增加值	**# Added Value of Real Estate Trade**	**40.9**	**86.98**	**97.14**	**108**
劳动者报酬	Compensation of Laborers	3.11	5.05	5.9	6.88
固定资产折旧	Depreciation of Fixed Assets	34.21	2.64	84.93	93.63
生产税净额	Net Taxes on Production	1.7	2.5	2.9	3.37
营业盈余	Operating Surplus	1.88	76.79	3.41	4.12
#社会服务业增加值	**# Added Value of Social Services**	**29.39**	**66.31**	**82.87**	**91.98**
劳动者报酬	Compensation of Laborers	10.77	22.68	28.42	37.68
固定资产折旧	Depreciation of Fixed Assets	2.9	5.97	7.46	9.2
生产税净额	Net Taxes on Production	8.74	18.1	27.62	10.34
营业盈余	Operating Surplus	6.98	19.56	19.37	34.76
#卫生体育福利业增加值	**# Added Value of Health Care,Sports and Social Welfare**	**25.47**	**61.5**	**77.11**	**85.6**
劳动者报酬	Compensation of Laborers	21.91	49.26	61.72	68.57
固定资产折旧	Depreciation of Fixed Assets	3.39	7.26	0.54	9.84
生产税净额	Net Taxes on Production	0.04	0.37	9.02	0.6
营业盈余	Operating Surplus	0.13	4.61	5.83	6.59
#教育文艺广播电影电视业增加值	**# Added Value of Education,Culture and Arts,Radio, Film and Television**	**55.99**	**124.12**	**154.16**	**170.2**
劳动者报酬	Compensation of Laborers	47.82	107.98	133.96	147.73
固定资产折旧	Depreciation of Fixed Assets	7.31	13.65	16.96	18.72
生产税净额	Net Taxes on Production	0.16	0.62	0.77	1.02
营业盈余	Operating Surplus	0.7	1.87	2.47	2.73
#科学研究和综合技术服务业增加值	**# Added Value of Scientific Research and Polytechnical Services**	**19.86**	**14.79**	**17.38**	**17.9**
劳动者报酬	Compensation of Laborers	15.92	10.65	12.53	12.91
固定资产折旧	Depreciation of Fixed Assets	2.62	2.03	2.38	2.43
生产税净额	Net Taxes on Production	0.52	0.47	0.54	0.55
营业盈余	Operating Surplus	0.8	1.64	1.93	2.01
#国家政党机关和社会团体增加值	**# Added Value of Government Agencies, Party Agencies and Social Organizations**	**79.98**	**172.2**	**203.67**	**241.35**
劳动者报酬	Compensation of Laborers	73.05	159.8	188.67	223.49
固定资产折旧	Depreciation of Fixed Assets	6.32	11.88	14.26	17.62
生产税净额	Net Taxes on Production	0.14	0.18	0.2	0.24
营业盈余	Operating Surplus	0.47	0.34	0.54	
#其他增加值	**# Added Value of Others**	**9.08**	**39.66**	**46.28**	**48.78**
劳动者报酬	Compensation of Laborers	3.15	26.32	32.2	36.61
固定资产折旧	Depreciation of Fixed Assets	0.86	4.35	4.9	5.16
生产税净额	Net Taxes on Production		0.72	0.98	0.85
营业盈余	Operating Surplus	5.07	8.27	8.2	6.16

2-10 国内生产总值(支出法)

GDP (by Expenditure Approach)

单位:亿元 (100 million yuan)

年份 Year	国内生产总值 GDP by Expenditure Approach	最终消费 Final Consumption Expenditure	居民消费 Household Consumption	农业居民 Agricultural	非农业居民 Non-agricultural	政府消费 Government Consumption
1978	146.99	100.83	93.93	70.87	23.06	6.90
1979	178.01	118.77	109.67	83.37	26.30	9.10
1980	191.72	136.94	125.42	93.15	32.27	11.52
1981	209.68	155.72	142.77	107.33	35.44	12.95
1982	232.52	174.68	159.45	121.93	37.52	15.23
1983	257.43	195.09	178.56	137.91	40.65	16.53
1984	287.29	218.09	199.24	152.95	46.29	18.85
1985	349.95	263.11	240.71	182.85	57.86	22.40
1986	397.68	290.14	265.54	196.12	69.42	24.60
1987	469.44	328.34	298.85	218.93	79.92	29.49
1988	584.07	399.15	364.37	256.19	108.18	34.78
1989	640.80	439.54	393.49	270.81	122.68	46.05
1990	744.44	564.70	454.90	314.05	140.85	109.80
1991	833.30	621.93	500.84	340.27	160.57	121.09
1992	986.98	725.60	582.91	379.23	203.68	142.69
1993	1259.55	885.05	706.55	442.35	264.20	178.50
1994	1666.64	1113.62	883.46	534.34	349.12	230.16
1995	2151.43	1396.88	1108.78	674.09	434.69	288.10
1996	2584.98	1753.27	1409.44	896.48	512.96	343.83
1997	2918.83	1956.22	1540.67	970.95	569.72	415.55
1998	3118.09	2062.84	1601.83	1009.06	592.77	461.01
1999	3326.75	2212.47	1690.66	1021.56	669.10	521.81
2000	3691.88	2383.27	1782.77	1038.80	743.97	600.50
2001	3983.00	2553.14	1871.64	1065.00	806.64	681.50

年份 Year	资本形成总额 Gross Capital Formation	固定资本 Fixed Capital	存货增加 Changes in Inventories	货物和服务净出口 Net Export of Goods&Services	资本形成率(投资率)% Rate of Capital Formation (%)	最终消费率(消费率)% Rate of Final Consumption(%)
1978	42.41	27.68	14.73	3.75	28.9	68.6
1979	41.82	29.81	12.01	17.42	23.5	66.7
1980	40.02	32.76	7.26	14.76	20.9	71.4
1981	41.19	27.95	13.24	12.77	19.6	74.3
1982	50.53	34.07	16.46	7.31	21.7	75.1
1983	56.63	43.89	12.74	5.71	22.0	75.8
1984	59.06	42.15	16.91	10.14	20.6	75.9
1985	92.19	58.14	34.05	-5.35	26.3	75.2
1986	115.02	75.57	39.45	-7.48	28.9	73.0
1987	139.84	91.79	48.05	1.26	29.8	69.9
1988	184.75	114.73	70.02	0.17	31.6	68.3
1989	169.41	83.19	86.22	31.85	26.4	68.6
1990	184.12	122.82	61.30	-4.38	24.7	75.9
1991	224.80	160.49	64.31	-13.43	27.0	74.6
1992	291.04	228.29	62.75	-29.66	29.5	73.5
1993	396.00	330.54	65.46	-21.50	31.4	70.3
1994	553.74	422.61	131.13	-0.72	33.2	66.8
1995	756.23	534.12	222.11	-1.68	35.2	64.9
1996	833.12	678.32	154.80	-1.41	32.2	67.8
1997	947.22	725.73	221.49	15.39	32.5	67.0
1998	1038.75	846.37	192.38	16.50	33.3	66.2
1999	1130.67	956.10	174.57	-16.39	34.0	66.5
2000	1274.94	1082.00	192.94	33.67	34.5	64.6
2001	1426.47	1233.17	193.30	3.39	35.8	64.1

2-11 最终消费构成项目

Compostion of Final Consumption

单位：亿元 (100 million yuan)

年份 Year	最终消费 Final Consumption Expenditure	居民消费 Household Consumption	农业居民 Agricultural Households	自给性消费 Self-Sufficient	商品性消费 Commodity Consumption	文化生活服务 Cultural,Life and Services
1978	100.83	93.93	70.87	46.07	19.35	1.91
1979	118.77	109.67	83.37	47.76	28.51	1.85
1980	136.94	125.42	93.15	50.67	33.72	1.77
1981	155.72	142.77	107.33	53.77	42.82	2.48
1982	174.68	159.45	121.93	62.42	46.58	0.49
1983	195.09	178.56	137.91	62.06	56.82	3.03
1984	218.09	199.24	152.95	69.44	63.17	3.82
1985	263.11	240.71	182.85	81.13	89.85	2.87
1986	290.14	265.54	196.12	82.54	100.88	3.56
1987	328.34	298.85	218.93	85.01	117.40	6.38
1988	399.15	364.37	256.19	89.98	145.58	8.94
1989	439.54	393.49	270.81	90.88	154.75	11.81
1990	564.70	454.90	314.05	136.03	152.46	12.44
1991	621.93	500.84	340.27	145.00	166.39	14.44
1992	725.60	582.91	379.23	153.78	173.94	35.72
1993	885.05	706.55	442.35	173.97	203.25	46.55
1994	1113.62	883.46	534.34	218.72	239.01	54.05
1995	1396.88	1108.78	674.09	256.35	311.44	70.56
1996	1753.27	1409.44	896.48	346.21	367.75	121.20
1997	1956.22	1540.67	970.95	351.51	410.07	147.95
1998	2062.84	1601.83	1009.06	351.60	438.59	148.12
1999	2212.47	1690.66	1021.56	329.30	463.32	147.38
2000	2383.27	1782.77	1038.80	249.05	504.23	187.87
2001	2553.14	1871.64	1065.00	244.43	519.74	194.96

年份 Year	住房及水电消费 Housing Water and Electricity	非农业居民 Non-Agricultural Households	商品性消费 Commodity Consumption	文化生活服务 Cultural Life and Services	住房及水电消费 Housing Water and Electricity	政府消费 Government Consumption
1978	3.54	23.06	20.96	1.59	0.51	6.90
1979	5.25	26.30	23.90	1.82	0.58	9.10
1980	6.99	32.27	29.40	2.19	0.68	11.52
1981	8.26	35.44	32.36	2.34	0.74	12.95
1982	12.44	37.52	34.07	2.59	0.86	15.23
1983	16.00	40.65	37.16	2.56	0.93	16.53
1984	16.52	46.29	42.40	2.83	1.06	18.85
1985	9.00	57.86	51.75	4.77	1.34	22.40
1986	9.14	69.42	61.92	6.29	1.21	24.60
1987	10.14	79.92	70.46	7.64	1.82	29.49
1988	11.69	108.18	97.08	8.95	2.15	34.78
1989	13.37	122.68	109.30	9.82	3.56	46.05
1990	13.12	140.85	125.82	11.06	3.97	109.80
1991	14.44	160.57	142.58	13.50	4.49	121.09
1992	15.79	203.68	169.99	27.59	6.10	142.69
1993	18.58	264.20	221.65	35.39	7.16	178.50
1994	22.56	349.12	282.11	54.49	12.52	230.16
1995	35.74	434.69	362.77	56.61	15.31	288.10
1996	61.32	512.96	418.38	50.01	44.57	343.83
1997	61.42	569.72	439.82	80.04	49.86	415.55
1998	70.75	592.77	441.57	95.24	55.96	461.01
1999	81.56	669.10	467.17	157.55	44.38	521.81
2000	97.65	743.97	509.76	184.77	49.44	600.50
2001	105.87	806.64	533.43	207.97	65.24	681.50

2-12 最终消费发展速度及指数

Growth Rate and Indices of Final Consumption Expenditure

单位:% (%)

年份 Year	以上年为100 (preceding year=100)					以1952年为100 (1952 =100)				
	最终消费 Final Consumption Expenditure	居民消费 Household Consumption	农业居民 Agricultural	非农业居民 Non-Agricultural	政府消费 Government Consumption	最终消费 Final Consumption Expenditure	居民消费 Household Consumption	农业居民 Agricultural	非农业居民 Non-Agricultural	政府消费 Government Consumption
1978	112.5	112.9	111.0	118.7	107.7	258.5	246.2	211.6	490.9	677.9
1979	112.3	110.8	110.3	112.2	131.4	290.3	272.8	233.4	550.8	890.8
1980	108.9	108.5	109.2	106.5	112.8	316.2	296.0	254.8	586.6	1004.8
1981	111.2	111.3	113.0	106.5	109.9	351.6	329.4	288.0	624.8	1104.3
1982	111.8	111.3	113.4	105.0	116.5	393.0	366.6	326.5	656.0	1286.5
1983	107.5	107.7	108.8	104.2	104.7	422.5	394.8	355.3	683.5	1347.0
1984	108.9	108.8	108.3	110.2	110.6	460.1	429.6	384.8	753.3	1489.8
1985	108.3	108.4	107.6	111.3	106.6	498.3	465.7	414.0	838.4	1588.1
1986	104.5	104.5	101.8	113.3	104.3	520.7	486.6	421.5	949.9	1656.4
1987	102.3	102.1	101.2	104.5	104.5	532.7	496.9	426.5	992.6	1730.9
1988	98.3	98.2	95.6	105.4	99.4	523.7	487.9	407.7	1046.2	1720.5
1989	97.7	96.8	97.0	96.2	107.9	511.6	472.3	395.5	1006.5	1856.5
1990	105.9	105.0	101.7	113.8	114.0	541.8	495.9	402.2	1145.4	2116.4
1991	105.4	105.3	104.1	108.0	106.0	571.1	522.2	418.7	1237.0	2243.4
1992	103.9	103.5	101.4	108.3	105.4	593.3	540.5	424.6	1339.7	2364.5
1993	105.3	104.5	100.7	112.2	108.9	624.8	564.8	427.5	1503.1	2575.0
1994	105.8	105.9	100.6	115.5	105.6	661.0	598.1	430.1	1736.1	2719.2
1995	108.6	108.7	109.2	107.8	108.4	717.9	650.2	469.6	1871.5	2947.6
1996	113.8	114.4	120.7	104.4	111.3	817.0	743.8	566.8	1953.8	3280.7
1997	108.0	106.2	105.7	107.3	115.1	882.4	790.0	599.1	2096.4	3776.1
1998	105.6	104.9	105.7	103.4	108.2	931.8	828.7	633.2	2167.7	4085.7
1999	105.7	104.5	101.3	110.5	110.1	984.9	866.0	641.4	2395.3	4498.4
2000	105.6	103.6	100.7	108.7	112.3	1040.1	897.2	645.9	2603.7	5051.7
2001	108.0	105.7	102.7	109.8	115.0	1123.3	948.3	663.3	2858.9	5809.5

2-13 居民消费水平

Household Consumption

年份 Year	按当年价计算 At Current Prices			以上年为100 Preceding Year=100			以1952年为100 1952=100		
	居民消费水平(元) Household Consumption Level (yuan)	农业居民 Agricultural Households	非农业居民 Non-Agricultural Households	居民消费水平(%) Household Consumption Level (yuan)	农业居民 Agricultural Households	非农业居民 Non-Agricultural Households	居民消费水平(%) Household Consumption Level (yuan)	农业居民 Agricultural Households	非农业居民 Non-Agricultural Households
1978	183	154	427	111.7	110.0	115.4	153.4	134.7	252.9
1979	211	181	454	109.6	110.0	104.5	168.2	148.2	264.3
1980	239	201	523	107.3	108.8	100.1	180.4	161.2	264.6
1981	268	229	552	109.9	112.0	102.4	198.3	180.6	270.9
1982	295	257	567	109.5	111.8	101.7	217.2	201.9	275.5
1983	326	287	603	106.2	107.4	102.4	230.6	216.8	282.1
1984	360	317	650	107.7	108.0	104.3	248.4	234.2	294.3
1985	430	379	751	107.3	107.6	102.9	266.5	252.0	302.8
1986	469	404	866	103.3	101.1	108.9	275.3	254.7	329.8
1987	521	446	969	100.7	100.0	101.6	277.2	254.7	335.0
1988	623	514	1256	96.4	94.2	101.0	267.2	239.9	338.4
1989	660	534	1372	100.0	103.6	91.8	267.2	248.6	310.6
1990	750	611	1533	103.6	100.0	111.9	276.9	248.6	347.6
1991	816	654	1714	104.0	102.9	105.9	288.0	255.8	368.1
1992	942	726	2106	102.7	101.1	104.9	295.8	258.6	386.1
1993	1134	849	2598	103.9	100.8	106.6	307.3	260.7	411.6
1994	1408	1027	3260	105.0	100.8	109.6	322.7	262.8	451.1
1995	1752	1294	3884	107.8	109.0	103.2	347.9	286.5	465.5
1996	2199	1710	4395	113.0	119.9	100.1	393.1	343.5	466.0
1997	2390	1851	4746	105.6	105.7	104.3	415.1	363.1	486.0
1998	2471	1921	4813	104.3	105.6	100.8	432.9	383.4	489.9
1999	2594	1945	5290	104.0	101.3	107.6	450.2	388.4	527.1
2000	2723	1981	5705	103.2	100.8	105.5	464.6	391.5	556.1
2001	2845	2037	5974	105.2	103.0	106.0	488.8	403.2	589.5

2-14 按三次产业分的资本形成总额

Total Capital by Type of Industry

单位:亿元 (100 million yuan)

年份 Year	合计 Total 资本形成总额 Gross Capital Formation	固定资本 Fixed Capital	存货增加 Changes in Inventories	第一产业 Primary Industry 资本形成总额 Gross Capital Formation	固定资本 Fixed Capital	存货增加 Changes in Inventories
1978	42.41	27.68	14.73	4.59	3.43	1.16
1979	41.82	29.81	12.01	4.74	3.73	1.01
1980	40.02	32.76	7.26	3.58	3.31	0.27
1981	41.19	27.95	13.24	1.49	1.40	0.09
1982	50.53	34.07	16.46	2.36	1.60	0.76
1983	56.63	43.89	12.74	1.40	1.67	-0.27
1984	59.06	42.15	16.91	4.37	1.56	2.81
1985	92.19	58.14	34.05	2.71	1.45	1.26
1986	115.02	75.57	39.45	6.28	1.51	4.77
1987	139.84	91.79	48.05	6.37	2.48	3.89
1988	184.75	114.73	70.02	5.24	3.56	1.68
1989	169.41	83.19	86.22	13.70	2.41	11.29
1990	184.12	122.82	61.30	7.99	3.45	4.54
1991	224.80	160.49	64.31	12.01	3.91	8.10
1992	291.04	228.29	62.75	15.73	8.45	7.28
1993	396.00	330.54	65.46	32.27	15.73	16.54
1994	553.74	422.61	131.13	83.95	69.37	14.58
1995	756.23	534.12	222.11	150.04	95.46	54.58
1996	833.12	678.32	154.80	78.31	28.64	49.67
1997	947.22	725.73	221.49	126.93	32.15	94.78
1998	1038.75	846.37	192.38	125.17	30.64	94.53
1999	1130.67	956.10	174.57	101.15	29.42	71.73
2000	1274.94	1082.00	192.94	126.50	48.36	78.14
2001	1426.47	1233.17	193.30	132.11	53.94	78.17

年份 Year	第二产业 Secondary Industry 资本形成总额 Gross Capital Formation	固定资本 Fixed Capital	存货增加 Changes in Inventories	第三产业 Tertiary Industry 资本形成总额 Gross Capital Formation	固定资本 Fixed Capital	存货增加 Changes in Inventories
1978	20.15	17.68	2.47	17.67	6.57	11.10
1979	18.85	17.83	1.02	18.23	8.25	9.98
1980	16.23	15.36	0.87	20.21	14.09	6.12
1981	16.25	14.53	1.72	23.45	12.02	11.43
1982	21.84	18.09	3.75	26.33	14.38	11.95
1983	26.11	24.49	1.62	29.12	17.73	12. 39
1984	38.97	23.94	15.03	15.72	16.65	-0.93
1985	38.93	32.73	6.20	50.55	23.96	26.59
1986	58.05	47.08	10.97	50.69	26.98	23.71
1987	69.19	59.48	9.71	64.28	29.83	34.45
1988	92.67	75.03	17.64	86.84	36.14	50.70
1989	101.59	56.24	45.35	54.12	24.54	29.58
1990	110.18	78.61	31.57	65.95	40.76	25.19
1991	116.64	99.02	17.62	96.15	57.56	38.59
1992	132.22	119.42	12.80	143.09	100.42	42.67
1993	185.25	127.78	57.47	178.48	187.03	-8.55
1994	191.33	145.74	45.59	278.46	207.50	70.96
1995	219.99	158.33	61.66	386.20	280.33	105.87
1996	257.01	205.55	51.46	497.80	444.13	53.67
1997	317.18	215.69	101.49	503.11	477.89	25.22
1998	305.60	190.62	114.98	607.98	625.11	-17.13
1999	297.00	216.79	80.21	732.52	709.89	22.63
2000	321.76	232.04	89.72	826.68	801.60	25.08
2001	377.01	286.84	90.17	917.35	892.39	24.96

2-15 国内生产总值(支出法)构成

Composition of GDP (by Expenditure Approach)

单位:% (%)

年份 Year	以国内生产总值为100 GDP=100			以最终消费为100 Final Consumption Expenditure=100		以居民消费为100 Household Consumption=100	
	最终消费 Final Consumption Expenditure	资本形成总额 Gross Capital Formation	货物和服务净出口 Net Export of Good and Services	居民消费 Household Consumption	政府消费 Government Consumption	农业居民 Agricultural Households	非农业居民 Non Agricultural Households
1978	68.6	28.9	2.5	93.2	6.8	75.4	24.6
1979	66.7	23.5	9.8	92.3	7.7	76.0	24.0
1980	71.4	20.9	7.7	91.6	8.4	74.3	25.7
1981	74.3	19.6	6.1	91.7	8.3	75.2	24.8
1982	75.1	21.7	3.2	91.3	8.7	76.5	23.5
1983	75.8	22.0	2.2	91.5	8.5	77.2	22.8
1984	75.9	20.6	3.5	91.4	8.6	76.8	23.2
1985	75.2	26.3	-1.5	91.5	8.5	76.0	24.0
1986	73.0	28.9	-1.9	91.5	8.5	73.9	26.1
1987	69.9	29.8	0.3	91.0	9.0	73.3	26.7
1988	68.3	31.6	0.1	91.3	8.7	70.3	29.7
1989	68.6	26.4	5.0	89.5	10.5	68.8	31.2
1990	75.9	24.7	-0.6	80.6	19.4	69.0	31.0
1991	74.6	27.0	-1.6	80.5	19.5	67.9	32.1
1992	73.5	29.5	-3.0	80.3	19.7	65.1	34.9
1993	70.3	31.4	-1.7	79.8	20.2	62.6	37.4
1994	66.8	33.2	0.0	79.3	20.7	60.5	39.5
1995	64.9	35.2	-0.1	79.4	20.6	60.8	39.2
1996	67.8	32.2	0.0	80.4	19.6	63.6	36.4
1997	67.0	32.5	0.5	78.8	21.2	63.0	37.0
1998	66.2	33.3	0.5	77.7	22.3	63.0	37.0
1999	66.5	34.0	-0.5	76.4	23.6	60.4	39.6
2000	64.6	34.5	0.9	74.8	25.2	58.3	41.7
2001	64.1	35.8	0.1	73.3	26.7	56.9	43.1

2-16 资本形成总额发展速度及指数

Growth Rate and Indices of Gross Capital Formation

单位:%　　(%)

年份 Year	以上年为100 (Preceding year=100) 资本形成总额 Gross Capital Formation	固定资本 Fixed Capital	存货增加 Changes in Inventories	以1952年为100 (1952=100) 资本形成总额 Gross Capital Formation	固定资本 Fixed Capital	存货增加 Changes in Inventories
1952				100.0	100.0	100.0
1955	172.8	84.5	514.0	322.3	170.1	860.5
1960	86.5	106.0	40.0	1351.5	1610.6	762.6
1965	119.4	120.8	114.1	752.8	825.8	631.5
1970	169.6	177.2	149.1	1705.4	1783.3	1751.5
1975	113.5	115.8	99.6	1761.3	2102.2	1014.7
1978	154.2	156.3	148.0	2708.0	2749.5	2992.9
1979	98.0	106.2	75.9	2653.9	2920.0	2270.6
1980	96.1	105.9	58.4	2550.4	3092.3	1327.0
1981	95.8	84.2	176.5	2443.2	2603.7	2342.7
1982	122.7	122.4	123.7	2997.9	3186.9	2898.9
1983	113.5	125.0	75.4	3402.6	3983.6	2186.4
1984	99.6	93.9	130.4	3389.0	3740.6	2850.1
1985	138.0	125.6	185.8	4676.8	4698.2	5295.1
1986	119.7	123.6	110.1	5598.1	5807.0	5828.1
1987	113.7	113.7	113.3	6365.0	6602.6	6602.0
1988	114.1	109.7	127.4	7262.5	7243.0	8409.8
1989	81.2	68.6	113.3	5897.1	4968.7	9525.7
1990	88.1	90.9	86.0	5195.4	4516.6	8192.1
1991	115.4	121.4	103.4	5995.5	5483.2	8470.6
1992	112.3	122.1	89.1	6732.9	6694.9	7547.3
1993	115.8	123.2	91.7	7796.7	8248.2	6920.9
1994	118.7	112.6	144.9	9254.7	9287.5	10028.4
1995	122.0	114.5	147.4	11290.7	10634.2	14781.9
1996	113.7	124.5	85.6	12837.5	13239.6	12653.3
1997	114.2	105.1	148.6	14660.4	13914.8	18802.8
1998	108.7	113.9	94.7	15935.9	15848.9	17806.3
1999	109.6	112.7	99.7	17465.7	17861.7	17752.9
2000	110.1	110.9	107.0	19229.7	19808.6	18995.6
2001	111.3	113.1	100.9	21402.7	22403.5	19166.6

2-17 各市、州全社会总产出及指数(2001年)

Gross Output of Society and Its Indices of Cities and Prefecture (2001)

市州	Cities and Prefecture	总产出(万元) Gross Output (10 000 yuan)	第一产业 Primary Industry	第二产业 Secondary Industry	工业 Industry	建筑业 Construction	第三产业 Tertiary Industry	#交通运输仓储邮电 Transport Postal and Telecommunications	#批发零售贸易餐饮 Wholesale Retail Trade and Catering	总产出指数(以上年为100) Gross Output Indices (preceding year=100)
长沙市	Changsha	18794719	1239986	10198665	7318347	2880318	7356068	820026	3536519	112.1
株洲市	Zhuzhou	8874317	782114	5674136	4940290	733846	2418067	649890	711116	110.8
湘潭市	Xiangtan	5563218	556339	3222115	2800799	421316	1784764	474055	537321	113.5
衡阳市	Hengyang	9102679	1647209	4701993	3844618	857375	2753477	586955	835414	110.9
邵阳市	Shaoyang	5055077	1552200	1805500	1420580	384920	1697377	274991	380885	111.7
岳阳市	Yueyang	10523932	1510835	6621616	5782974	838642	2391481	643735	622621	110.0
常德市	Changde	8922276	1649031	4657291	3797378	859913	2615954	412420	778689	108.2
张家界	Zhangjiajie	1436246	238286	482508	282937	199571	715452	199979	191565	110.7
益阳市	Yiyang	4777633	881034	2182725	1742162	440563	1713874	552488	490976	108.8
郴州市	Chenzhou	5631807	981665	2928330	2210332	717998	1721812	524401	393552	111.8
永州市	Yongzhou	5191323	1327837	2465439	1953055	512384	1398047	386762	465472	109.7
怀化市	Huaihua	4440352	892794	1856526	1468306	388220	1691032	476399	420090	110.7
娄底市	Loudi	4039968	611165	2296361	1777613	518748	1132442	362521	290314	109.1
湘　西	West Hunan	1740801	355637	933027	714628	218399	452137	121936	141946	109.1

2-18 各市、州国内生产总值及构成(2001年)

Gross Domestic Products and Its Composition of Cities and Prefecture (2001)

市州	Cities and Prefecture	国内生产总值(万元) GDP (10 000 yuan)	第一产业 Primary Industry	第二产业 Secondary Industry	工业 Industry	建筑业 Construction	第三产业 Tertiary Industry	#交通运输仓储邮电 Transport Postal and Telecommunications	#批发零售贸易餐饮 Wholesale Retail Trade and Catering	人均国内生产总值(元) Per Capita GDP (yuan)
长沙市	Changsha	7280774	783636	2970933	2179077	791856	3526205	563590	1109818	12443
株洲市	Zhuzhou	3226716	515986	1530467	1315340	215127	1180263	340158	265447	8805
湘潭市	Xiangtan	2382813	341186	1034156	862177	171979	1007471	166160	208406	8509
衡阳市	Hengyang	3862195	1089687	1363531	1135727	227804	1408977	355918	338571	5483
邵阳市	Shaoyang	2432092	931482	633868	490100	143768	866742	115603	197495	3348
岳阳市	Yueyang	4069650	982000	1663645	1437695	225950	1424005	448282	325603	7777
常德市	Changde	3985929	1100375	1548652	1277380	271272	1336902	244851	291331	6692
张家界	Zhangjiajie	667147	151481	141040	90982	50058	374626	103439	96505	4273
益阳市	Yiyang	2100108	563009	632717	489651	143066	904382	262023	213607	4661
郴州市	Chenzhou	2571121	628999	863420	726035	137385	1078702	315847	266535	5661
永州市	Yongzhou	2492887	838696	695239	567143	128096	958952	238826	274987	4404
怀化市	Huaihua	2141565	584056	581120	464654	116466	976389	293938	212986	4415
娄底市	Loudi	1800628	400011	709035	558598	150437	691582	223323	150923	4508
湘　西	West Hunan	718144	227940	251252	196698	54554	238952	50128	60570	2745

2-19 各市、州国内生产总值指数(2001年)

Indices of Gross Domestic Products of Cities and Prefecture(2001)

以上年为100 (preceding year=100)

市州	Cities and Prefecture	国内生产总值 Gross Domestic Products	第一产业 Primary Industry	第二产业 Secondary Industry	工业 Industry	建筑业 Construction	第三产业 Tertiary Industry	#交通运输仓储邮电 Transport Postal and Telecommunications	#批发零售贸易餐饮 Wholesale Retail Trade and Catering	人均国内生产总值 Per Capita GDP
长沙市	Changsha	112.1	104.9	113.1	108.9	127.0	112.9	110.2	112.7	111.6
株洲市	Zhuzhou	110.7	103.8	112.2	111.4	117.9	111.9	112.8	110.8	110.7
湘潭市	Xiangtan	110.7	104.2	112.7	112.5	113.8	111.0	114.4	111.5	110.5
衡阳市	Hengyang	109.2	102.1	112.7	113.1	110.5	111.8	109.0	110.8	108.9
邵阳市	Shaoyang	107.1	102.6	109.4	107.7	115.5	110.5	115.0	110.5	106.0
岳阳市	Yueyang	110.6	106.7	112.4	112.2	114.0	111.4	110.5	112.9	110.1
常德市	Changde	110.6	105.0	111.8	111.7	112.1	114.1	121.3	110.2	110.6
张家界	Zhangjiajie	109.5	102.2	101.9	98.9	108.0	116.2	118.5	113.2	109.0
益阳市	Yiyang	108.5	105.7	108.6	108.7	108.5	110.1	110.3	109.3	108.3
郴州市	Chenzhou	110.6	103.5	114.6	115.4	110.7	112.0	114.6	110.5	110.0
永州市	Yongzhou	108.9	102.7	113.1	114.0	108.8	111.7	112.8	110.9	108.5
怀化市	Huaihua	108.7	103.0	112.1	112.0	112.5	110.3	109.4	109.0	108.1
娄底市	Loudi	108.2	100.5	109.8	105.2	130.9	111.6	114.5	111.2	107.7
湘　西	West Hunan	108.0	102.2	111.0	109.9	114.9	111.1	111.8	106.6	107.4

2-20 各市、州支出法国内生产总值(2001年)

Gross Domestic Expenditures of Cities and Prefecture(2001)

市州	Cities and Prefecture	支出法国内生产总值(万元) GDP by Expenditure Approach (10 000 yuan)	最终消费 Final Comsumption Expenditure	资本形成总额 Gross Capital Formation	货物和服务净出口 Net Export of Goods and Services	投资率(%) Capital Formation Rate (%)	消费率(%) Comsumption Rate (%)
长沙市	Changsha	7280774	3547784	3002536	730454	41.2	48.7
株洲市	Zhuzhou	3226716	1631323	1198981	396412	37.2	50.6
湘潭市	Xiangtan	2382813	1372805	985961	24047	41.4	57.6
衡阳市	Hengyang	3862195	3045066	1200961	-383832	31.1	78.8
邵阳市	Shaoyang	2451496	1969459	493178	-11141	20.1	80.3
岳阳市	Yueyang	4069650	2473718	1550577	45355	38.1	60.8
常德市	Changde	3985929	2441072	1257161	287696	31.5	61.2
张家界	Zhangjiajie	664404	402023	263255	-874	39.6	60.5
益阳市	Yiyang	2100108	1639289	602780	-141961	28.7	78.1
郴州市	Chenzhou	2571121	1719655	876428	-24962	34.1	66.9
永州市	Yongzhou	2492887	1763837	727651	1399	29.2	70.8
怀化市	Huaihua	2141565	1583475	492254	65836	23	73.9
娄底市	Loudi	1800628	1162834	631408	6386	35.1	64.6
湘　西	West Hunan	718144	597433	213023	-92312	29.7	83.2

2-21 各市、州国内生产总值项目构成(2001年)

Item Composition of Gross Domestic Products of Cities and Prefecture(2001)

单位:万元 (10 000 yuan)

市州	Cities and Prefecture	国内生产总值 Gross Domestic Products	劳动者报酬 Compensation of Laborers	固定资产折旧 Depreciation of Fixed Assets	生产税净额 Net Taxes on Production	营业盈余 Operating surplus
长沙市	Changsha	7280774	4156936	908299	967664	1247875
株洲市	Zhuzhou	3226716	1706106	419300	405786	695524
湘潭市	Xiangtan	2382813	1384134	451898	229507	317274
衡阳市	Hengyang	3862195	2434527	627385	431888	368395
邵阳市	Shaoyang	2432092	1648924	294932	197069	291167
岳阳市	Yueyang	4069650	2508270	613641	532340	415399
常德市	Changde	3985929	2286099	595936	726067	377827
张家界	Zhangjiajie	667147	436033	122132	56357	52625
益阳市	Yiyang	2100108	1420098	356666	182098	141246
郴州市	Chenzhou	2571121	1502450	444871	288246	335554
永州市	Yongzhou	2492887	1676891	310830	244775	260391
怀化市	Huaihua	2141565	1244482	265592	194023	437468
娄底市	Loudi	1800628	1230996	283281	113296	173055
湘　西	West Hunan	718144	497597	75834	89633	55080

2-22 各市、州支出法国内生产总值结构(2001年)

Structure of gross Domestic Expenditures of Cities and Prefecture (2001)

单位:万元 (10 000 yuan)

市州	Cities and Prefecture	资本形成总额 Gross Capital Formation				最终消费 Final Consumption Expenditure					
		绝对数 Absolute Figure		比重 Proportion (%)		绝对数 Absolute Figure				比重 Proportion (%)	
		固定资本 Fixed Capital	存货增加 Changes in Inventories	固定资本 Fixed Capital	存货增加 Changes in Inventories	居民消费 Household Consumption	农业居民 Agricultural	非农居民 Non-agricultural	政府消费 Government Consumption	居民消费 Household Consumption	政府消费 Government Consumption
长沙市	Changsha	2482996	519540	82.7	17.3	2667435	1104784	1562651	880349	75.2	24.8
株洲市	Zhuzhou	790512	408469	65.9	34.1	1348215	731669	616546	283108	82.6	17.4
湘潭市	Xiangtan	662263	323698	67.2	32.8	1113292	597490	515802	259513	81.1	18.9
衡阳市	Hengyang	1008676	192285	84.0	16.0	2534150	1737557	796593	510916	83.2	16.8
邵阳市	Shaoyang	393506	99672	79.8	20.2	1739127	1206818	532309	230332	88.3	11.7
岳阳市	Yueyang	1108223	442354	71.5	28.5	2078171	909344	1168827	395547	84.0	16.0
常德市	Changde	849165	407996	67.5	32.5	2160556	1145718	1014838	280516	88.5	11.5
张家界	Zhangjiajie	223471	39784	84.9	15.1	353720	218113	135607	48303	88.0	12.0
益阳市	Yiyang	524364	78416	87.0	13.0	1276246	828293	447953	363043	77.9	22.1
郴州市	Chenzhou	845918	30510	96.5	3.5	1354961	696598	658363	364694	78.8	21.2
永州市	Yongzhou	560355	167296	77.0	23.0	1403943	903648	500295	359894	79.6	20.4
怀化市	Huaihua	367123	125131	74.6	25.4	1303006	793397	509609	280469	82.3	17.7
娄底市	Loudi	615685	15723	97.5	2.5	1108523	655714	452809	54311	95.3	4.7
湘　西	West Hunan	211286	1737	99.2	0.8	405698	246716	158982	191735	67.9	32.1

三、人口、就业与职工工资

POPULATION, EMPLOYMENT AND WAGES OF STAFF AND WORKERS

资料整理人员：　石　梅　　欧阳普

3-1 人口数(年底数)

Population (year-end)

年份 Year	总户数 (万户) Households (10 000 households)	总人口 (万人) Total Population (10 000 persons)	男 Male	女 Female	市镇 Urban	乡村 Rural
1978	1167.53	5165.91	2684.80	2481.11	593.86	4572.05
1980	1197.88	5280.95	2740.40	2540.55	671.05	4609.90
1985	1334.54	5622.49	2928.44	2694.05	915.90	4706.59
1990	1661.65	6110.89	3178.31	2932.58	1072.46	5038.43
1991	1697.69	6166.33	3208.42	2957.91	1147.86	5018.47
1992	1725.72	6207.78	3231.73	2976.05	1217.74	4990.04
1993	1745.47	6245.58	3249.20	2996.38	1205.95	5039.63
1994	1765.67	6302.58	3279.07	3023.51	1356.56	4946.02
1995	1796.19	6392.00	3322.27	3069.73	1550.99	4841.01
1996	1799.97	6428.00	3339.25	3088.75	1606.95	4821.05
1997	1798.83	6465.00	3356.43	3108.57	1629.00	4836.00
1998	1809.00	6502.00	3374.33	3127.67	1684.00	4818.00
1999	1814.64	6532.00	3389.32	3142.68	1724.00	4808.00
2000	1874.87	6562.05	3422.77	3139.28	1952.21	4609.84
2001	1884.47	6595.85	3409.72	3186.13	2031.52	4564.33

注：1995年以前的人口数均为年报数；2000年的人口数根据第五次人口普查有关数据推算，其余各年人口数均根据人口变动抽样调查资料推算。

The data on the total population are collected from the year-reports before 1995.

The data 2000 are estimated on the data collected from fifth population surveys.

The data of other years are estimated on the basis of the data collected from the sample surveys on population changes.

3-2 人口出生率、死亡率、自然增长率

Birth Rate,Death Rate and Natural Growth Rate of Population

单位:‰ (‰)

年份 Year	出生率 Birth Rate	死亡率 Death Rate	自然增长率 Natural Growth Rate
1978	17.40	7.01	10.39
1980	17.68	6.88	10.80
1985	18.16	6.47	11.69
1990	23.93	7.23	16.70
1991	20.50	7.30	13.20
1992	16.70	7.30	9.40
1993	14.08	7.13	6.95
1994	13.88	7.03	6.85
1995	13.02	7.15	5.87
1996	12.81	7.20	5.61
1997	12.59	6.99	5.60
1998	12.31	7.10	5.21
1999	11.72	7.12	4.60
2000	11.45	6.79	4.66
2001	11.80	6.72	5.08

3-3 前四次全国人口普查人口基本情况

Basic Statistics on National Population of Four Censuses

单位：万人 (10 000 persons)

指 标	Item	第一次 1953 First	第二次 1964 Second	第三次 1982 Third	第四次 1990 Fourth
总户数 (万户)	**Total Households (10 000 households)**	836.11	916.20	1233.88	1573.79
家庭户	Family Households			1227.89	1564.88
集体户	Non-Family Households			5.99	8.91
总人口	**Total Population**	3322.69	3718.23	5401.05	6065.80
男性人口	Male	1752.64	1931.70	2805.23	3149.76
女性人口	Female	1570.05	1786.53	2595.82	2916.04
#育龄妇女(15—49岁)	#Women at Childbearing Age (Age 15-49)	750.73	819.43	1301.08	1607.99
各年龄组人口	**Population by Age**				
0—6岁	Age 0-6	669.02	706.05	701.81	869.47
7—14岁	Age 7-14	519.19	768.91	1131.16	826.93
劳动年龄人口	Population within Working Age	1720.75	1878.68	2936.91	3618.26
男60、女55岁以上人口	Males Age 60 and Females Age 55 and Over	319.57	285.00	503.39	628.16
民族人口	**Population by Nationality**				
汉族	Han Nationality	3254.67	3589.80	5180.92	5583.42
少数民族	Minority Nationalities	68.02	128.43	220.13	482.38
15岁以上婚姻人口	**Marital Status of Population Aged 15 and Over**				
未婚	Unmarried			1009.86	1099.89
有配偶	Married			2271.76	2963.86
丧偶	Widowed			262.16	278.87
离婚	Divorced			24.31	26.77
6岁以上文化程度人口	**Population Aged 6 and Over by Educational Level**				
大学本科	University		} 9.77	} 24.56	20.72
大学专科	Three Years College				48.27
中专	Specialized Secondary School		} 40.99	} 353.64	81.82
高中	Senior Secondary School				404.79
初中	Junior Secondary School		160.27	932.53	1370.42
小学	Primary School		1256.03	2325.78	2552.16
不识字或识字很少	Illiterate and Semi-Illiterate		1255.57	1173.52	822.76
#文盲、半文盲人口	#Illiterate and Semi-Illiterate Aged 15 and Over		1255.57	943.97	742.56
在业人口	**Employed Population**			2827.75	3489.74
不在业人口	**Unemployed Population**			740.34	879.65
市镇县人口	**Population of Cities,Towns and Counties**				
市	Cities	134.97	161.31	507.43	765.62
镇	Towns	157.57	160.79	260.00	328.20
县	Counties	3030.15	3396.13	4633.62	4971.98

注：1. 劳动年龄人口指男16-59岁，女16-54岁人口。

2. 各年龄组人口缺15岁人口和年龄不详人口，加总不等于总人口。

3. 由于四次普查所设指标不同，故此表空栏处均表示该年度普查无此调查项目。

4. 1964年人口普查时，6-12岁不在校儿童没有调查其相当的文化程度，故各项文化程度人口加总不等于6周岁及以上人口数。

a.Working age range refers to 16-59 years for men and 16-54 years for women.

b. The sum of the population of the age group is not equal to the total population, because the population aged 15 is not shown and there is population whose true age is unknown.

c. Since the quota in the four population censuses were set differently, the blank space indicates the absence of this item of the year.

d. Data in 1964 excludes the children in school aged from 6-12, thus the sum of the population at all education levels does not equal to the population aged above six.

3-4 第五次全国人口普查机器汇总数据

The Computer Collected Data of National Population of Fifth Censuses

指标	Item	数量 Volume
总户数（万户）	**Number of Households (10 000 households)**	**1800.38**
家庭户	Family Households	1766.21
集体户	Non-Family Households	34.17
总人口（万人）	**Total Population (10 000 persons)**	**6327.42**
家庭户人口	Population of Family Households	6106.15
集体户人口	Population of Non-Family Households	221.27
平均家庭户规模（人/户）	**Average Family Size (person/household)**	**3.46**
总人口中：男性人口（万人）	**In Total: Male (10 000 persons)**	**3299.37**
女性人口（万人）	Female (10 000 persons)	3028.05
性别比	Sex Ratio	108.96
总人口中：汉族人口（万人）	**In Total: Han Nationality (10 000 persons)**	**5686.35**
少数民族人口（万人）	Minority Nationalities (10 000 persons)	641.07
少数民族人口比重（%）	Percentage of Minonrity Nationalities Population (%)	10.13
总人口中：市镇人口（万人）	**In Total: Urban Population (10 000 persons)**	**1915.92**
乡村人口（万人）	Rural Population (10 000 persons)	4524.15
总人口中：0—5岁人口（万人）	**In Total: Age 0-5 (10 000 persons)**	**387.71**
6—14岁人口（万人）	Age 6-14 (10 000 persons)	1012.25
15—64岁人口（万人）	Age 15-64 (10 000 persons)	4454.8
65岁以上人口（万人）	Aged 65 and Over (10 000 persons)	472.66
6周岁及以上人口（万人）	**Population Aged 6 and Over by Educational Level (10 000 persons)**	**5939.70**
未上过学（万人）	Unschool (10 000 persons)	298.22
扫盲班（万人）	Literacy Courses (10 000 persons)	67.69
小学（万人）	Primary School (10 000 persons)	2421.99
初中（万人）	Junior Secondary School (10 000 persons)	2259.38
高中和中专（万人）	Senior and Specialized Secondary School (10 000 persons)	707.25
大专及以上（万人）	College and Over (10 000 persons)	185.17
每十万人口中：小学文化（人）	**Per 100000 Population: Primary School (person)**	**38278**
初中文化（人）	Junior Secondary School (person)	35708
高中和中专（人）	Senior and Specialized Secondary School (person)	11177
大专及以上（人）	College and Over (persons)	2926
文盲、半文盲人口（万人）	**Population of Illiterate and Semi Literate (10 000 persons)**	**294.96**
文盲率（%）	**Illiterate Rate (%)**	**5.99**
普查年度出生率（‰）	**Birth Rate in Census Year（‰）**	**11.45**
普查年度死亡率（‰）	**Death Rate in Census Year（‰）**	**6.79**
普查年度自然增长率（‰）	**Natural Growth Rate in Census Year（‰）**	**4.66**

注：1. 表中的各项数据均按普查登记的口径计算，不包括本省外出的人口，包括外省来本省的人口。

2. 普查年度是指1999年11月1日0时至2000年10月31日24时。

3. 城乡人口是按国家统计局1999年发布的《关于统计上划分城乡的规定（试行）》计算。

a. The data in table are calculated according to the approach of censuses. The data excluded the population of going to other provinces and included the population from other provinces.

b. The censuses year is 1999-11-1 zero o'clock to 2000-10-31 24 o'clock.

c. The urban population and rural population are calculated according to the <regulations concerning plot out urban and rural in the statistical(test run) > promulgated in 1999.

3-5 第五次人口普查各民族人口数

The Number of Population by Nationality of National Population of Fifth Censuses

单位：人 (person)

民族	Nationality	第三次人口普查 Third Censuses	第四次人口普查 Fourth Censuses	第五次人口普查 Fifth Censuses	男性 Male	女性 Female
总人口	**Total**	**54010538**	**60658037**	**63274173**	**32993704**	**30280469**
汉族	Han Nationality	51809228	55834200	56863479	29639115	27224364
蒙古族	Mongolian Nationality	542	1468	15869	5384	10485
回族	Hui Nationality	66952	93583	97368	50412	46956
藏族	Tibet Nationality	95	552	2930	1339	1591
维吾尔族	Uygur Nationality	4448	5794	7939	4148	3791
苗族	Miao Nationality	761171	1568951	1921495	998820	922675
彝族	Yi Nationality	1288	1151	4116	1793	2323
壮族	Zhuang Nationality	14117	20918	23559	12168	11391
布衣族	Bouyei Nationality	471	1227	3173	1241	1932
朝鲜族	Korean Nationality	221	423	2693	1330	1363
满族	Manchu Nationality	2426	5446	8206	4112	4094
侗族	Dong Nationality	317924	749026	842123	448292	393831
瑶族	Yao Nationality	282881	460667	704564	378435	326129
白族	Bai Nationality	155	114843	125597	65371	60226
土家族	Tujia Nationality	745069	1794855	2639534	1376741	1262793
哈尼族	Hani Nationality	45	563	1337	285	1052
哈萨克族	Kazaki Nationality	3	5	110	54	56
傣族	Dai Nationality	43	388	587	102	485
黎族	Li Nationality	2911	689	862	430	432
傈僳族	Li su Nationality	2	47	145	45	100
佤族	Va Nationality	7	658	803	260	543
畲族	She Nationality	18	454	2891	1736	1155
高山族	Gaoshan Nationality	52	107	189	86	103
拉祜族	La hu Nationality	7	309	480	27	453
水族	Shui Nationality	66	213	270	91	179
东乡族	Dongxiang Nationality	8	3	28	13	15
纳西族	Naxi Nationality	35	76	113	60	53
景颇族	Jingpo Nationality	1	42	136	18	118
柯尔克孜族	Kirgiz Nationality	1	9	10	3	7
土族	Tu Nationality	58	110	1097	570	527
达斡尔族	Daur Nationality		3	116	56	60
仫佬族	Mulam Nationality	27	654	719	389	330
羌族	Qiang Nationality	2	11	73	34	39
布朗族	Blang Nationality	1	57	100	9	91
撒拉族	Salar Nationality	3	7	272	126	146
毛南族	Maonan Nationality	8	64	52	20	32
仡佬族	Gelao Nationality	8	83	397	241	156
锡伯族	Xibe Nationality	44	78	93	44	49
阿昌族	Achang Nationality		8	29	1	28
普米族	Pumi Nationality	2	15	22	8	14
塔吉克族	Tajik Nationality	5		105	58	47
怒族	Nu Nationality		2	29	18	11
乌孜别克族	Uzbek Nationality			22	8	14
俄罗斯族	Russian Nationality		5	25	7	18
鄂温克族	Ewenki Nationality			34	17	17
德昂族	Deang Nationality		3	15	6	9
保安族	Bonan Nationality		2	6	4	2
裕固族	Yugur Nationality		1	3	1	2
京族	Jing Nationality	17	24	46	25	21
塔塔尔族	Tatar Nationality		11	16	8	8
独龙族	Dulong Nationality		3	66	36	30
鄂伦春族	Oroqen Nationality		5	8	4	4
赫哲族	Hezhen Nationality			5	3	2
门巴族	Monba Nationality	2	8	7	2	5
珞巴族	Lhoba Nationality		4	15	9	6
基诺族	Jino Nationality		24	13	2	11
其他未识别的民族	Other Unknown Nationality	116	149	172	86	86
外国人加入中国籍	Acquired Chinese Citizenship	58	39	10	1	9

3-6 第五次人口普查分年龄人口数

The Number of Population by Age Group of National Population of Fifth Censuses

年龄别	Age Group	总人口（人） Total Population (person)	市镇 Urban	男性 Male	女性 Female	乡村 Rural	男性 Male	女性 Female
合计	**Total**	**63274173**	**17397837**	**8950694**	**8447143**	**45876336**	**24043010**	**21833326**
0岁组	Age 0	674259	178560	96934	81626	495699	280397	215302
1岁组	Age 1	571994	159539	87284	72255	412455	233211	179244
2岁组	Age 2	676834	172881	93919	78962	503953	282309	221644
3岁组	Age 3	637510	163652	88785	74867	473858	262133	211725
4岁组	Age 4	638640	164278	88921	75357	474362	260146	214216
5岁组	Age 5	677889	174226	93870	80356	503663	274506	229157
6岁组	Age 6	638950	171721	92078	79643	467229	254075	213154
7岁组	Age 7	715554	180687	96748	83939	534867	289946	244921
8岁组	Age 8	826829	189397	101529	87868	637432	345707	291725
9岁组	Age 9	1048815	225668	120166	105502	823147	442949	380198
10岁组	Age 10	1512740	306858	161513	145345	1205882	634673	571209
11岁组	Age 11	1427682	299220	156149	143071	1128462	587166	541296
12岁组	Age 12	1341436	291033	150940	140093	1050403	545480	504923
13岁组	Age 13	1414403	299433	154510	144923	1114970	578041	536929
14岁组	Age 14	1196063	265258	136605	128653	930805	484116	446689
15岁组	Age 15	1105820	274407	137658	136749	831413	437645	393768
16岁组	Age 16	1091168	319081	155989	163092	772087	411936	360151
17岁组	Age 17	1053005	345585	169838	175747	707420	386746	320674
18岁组	Age 18	1211246	410069	207867	202202	801177	435888	365289
19岁组	Age 19	898167	308685	163414	145271	589482	314756	274726
20岁组	Age 20	859088	280230	147743	132487	578858	298798	280060
21岁组	Age 21	879286	288969	151044	137925	590317	304813	285504
22岁组	Age 22	837362	266489	136318	130171	570873	291692	279181
23岁组	Age 23	807703	257717	128516	129201	549986	285643	264343
24岁组	Age 24	984673	301547	147573	153974	683126	356253	326873
25岁组	Age 25	1067972	329369	160812	168557	738603	390004	348599
26岁组	Age 26	1193575	360199	175806	184393	833376	441374	392002
27岁组	Age 27	1166123	354956	176624	178332	811167	433718	377449
28岁组	Age 28	1213608	370952	185539	185413	842656	445047	397609
29岁组	Age 29	1181164	364465	184431	180034	816699	429397	387302
30岁组	Age 30	1439593	433189	218775	214414	1006404	515861	490543
31岁组	Age 31	1324491	391696	199604	192092	932795	479287	453508
32岁组	Age 32	1586224	459791	235891	223900	1126433	581703	544730
33岁组	Age 33	1137483	317139	161544	155595	820344	418553	401791
34岁组	Age 34	1334318	374978	192159	182819	959340	491439	467901
35岁组	Age 35	1357642	396262	205163	191099	961380	495880	465500
36岁组	Age 36	1318544	406460	209803	196657	912084	464247	447837
37岁组	Age 37	1569908	487382	253399	233983	1082526	560040	522486
38岁组	Age 38	1110224	332400	174265	158135	777824	402904	374920
39岁组	Age 39	399639	137660	71071	66589	261979	133247	128732
40岁组	Age 40	649726	214718	112973	101745	435008	228127	206881
41岁组	Age 41	576770	183297	96624	86673	393473	208623	184850
42岁组	Age 42	824537	250184	131971	118213	574353	304175	270178
43岁组	Age 43	989162	286816	149901	136915	702346	372082	330264
44岁组	Age 44	869662	248744	128183	120561	620918	324940	295978
45岁组	Age 45	878989	250196	129326	120870	628793	330586	298207
46岁组	Age 46	936001	267095	137105	129990	668906	348732	320174
47岁组	Age 47	866503	240364	123478	116886	626139	325336	300803
48岁组	Age 48	930458	256912	133188	123724	673546	351237	322309

年龄别	Age Group	总人口（人） Total Population (person)	市镇 Urban	男性 Male	女性 Female	乡村 Rural	男性 Male	女性 Female
49岁组	Age 49	741084	204009	105626	98383	537075	278131	258944
50岁组	Age 50	780839	217497	113685	103812	563342	294447	268895
51岁组	Age 51	774266	208011	109413	98598	566255	303377	262878
52岁组	Age 52	676801	177776	92945	84831	499025	265188	233837
53岁组	Age 53	629733	165649	88972	76677	464084	247810	216274
54岁组	Age 54	552324	144296	77441	66855	408028	214563	193465
55岁组	Age 55	473661	121772	64614	57158	351889	185027	166862
56岁组	Age 56	525573	131763	70207	61556	393810	212871	180939
57岁组	Age 57	450470	114147	59601	54546	336323	181222	155101
58岁组	Age 58	446369	118282	61663	56619	328087	178495	149592
59岁组	Age 59	484338	124320	64779	59541	360018	197833	162185
60岁组	Age 60	486905	129444	67018	62426	357461	194180	163281
61岁组	Age 61	421397	109612	56358	53254	311785	168605	143180
62岁组	Age 62	513574	127941	66278	61663	385633	209306	176327
63岁组	Age 63	479258	115712	60794	54918	363546	194624	168922
64岁组	Age 64	461599	113857	58964	54893	347742	183442	164300
65岁组	Age 65	403166	96851	48810	48041	306315	158589	147726
66岁组	Age 66	398689	94172	48257	45915	304517	156791	147726
67岁组	Age 67	414276	99081	52396	46685	315195	164264	150931
68岁组	Age 68	354864	82618	43023	39595	272246	139123	133123
69岁组	Age 69	319102	75197	40024	35173	243905	123917	119988
70岁组	Age 70	357290	82802	43219	39583	274488	138238	136250
71岁组	Age 71	261475	58223	30077	28146	203252	102021	101231
72岁组	Age 72	298720	65369	33495	31874	233351	116806	116545
73岁组	Age 73	254130	55919	27745	28174	198211	98278	99933
74岁组	Age 74	207753	45900	21936	23964	161853	77910	83943
75岁组	Age 75	209739	44327	21083	23244	165412	79172	86240
76岁组	Age 76	203349	42123	19111	23012	161226	75879	85347
77岁组	Age 77	158550	33149	14867	18282	125401	57916	67485
78岁组	Age 78	147665	32017	13968	18049	115648	52755	62893
79岁组	Age 79	129099	27452	12127	15325	101647	45634	56013
80岁组	Age 80	115865	23839	9858	13981	92026	39668	52358
81岁组	Age 81	85054	17266	7260	10006	67788	29207	38581
82岁组	Age 82	79792	16150	6393	9757	63642	26348	37294
83岁组	Age 83	70786	14790	5731	9059	55996	22577	33419
84岁组	Age 84	57534	12257	4520	7737	45277	17793	27484
85岁组	Age 85	46061	9697	3589	6108	36364	13700	22664
86岁组	Age 86	40954	8912	3151	5761	32042	11737	20305
87岁组	Age 87	29637	6457	2122	4335	23180	8195	14985
88岁组	Age 88	22728	5076	1608	3468	17652	6108	11544
89岁组	Age 89	16613	3688	1168	2520	12925	4422	8503
90岁组	Age 90	12808	2839	916	1923	9969	3309	6660
91岁组	Age 91	7752	1792	549	1243	5960	1997	3963
92岁组	Age 92	6424	1470	463	1007	4954	1635	3319
93岁组	Age 93	4656	1095	347	748	3561	1102	2459
94岁组	Age 94	3285	731	228	503	2554	754	1800
95岁组	Age 95	2595	617	194	423	1978	693	1285
96岁组	Age 96	2125	501	197	304	1624	610	1014
97岁组	Age 97	1674	397	163	234	1277	580	697
98岁组	Age 98	1153	278	111	167	875	360	515
99岁组	Age 99	664	156	55	101	508	165	343
100岁及以上	Age 100+	523	127	29	98	396	72	324

3-7 年末从业人员人数

Number of Employed Persons at the Year-end

单位:万人 (10 000 persons)

年份 Year	从业人员人数 Number of Employed Persons	职工人数 Number of Staff and Workers	国有经济 State-owned Economic Units	城镇集体经济 Urban Collective-owned Economic Units	其他经济类型 Economic Units of Other Types	城镇个体私营企业从业人员 Employees in Urban Private Enterprises and Self-Employed Individuals	农村从业人员 Employees in Rural	其他从业人员 Other Employees
1978	2280.05	363.78	282.06	81.72		0.35	1915.92	
1980	2399.95	409.16	316.80	92.36		1.81	1988.98	
1985	2728.71	475.15	352.73	122.34	0.08	16.19	2237.37	
1990	3158.42	551.03	422.28	128.07	0.68	31.94	2575.45	
1991	3222.43	567.07	435.66	130.35	1.06	32.52	2622.84	
1992	3278.83	579.74	447.88	130.43	1.43	39.93	2659.16	
1993	3345.61	588.87	454.26	126.70	7.91	60.42	2675.75	20.57
1994	3400.29	589.48	459.14	121.57	8.77	106.51	2685.54	18.76
1995	3467.31	597.50	466.00	119.13	12.37	133.86	2717.38	18.57
1996	3514.16	596.84	471.55	114.47	10.82	166.21	2732.35	18.76
1997	3560.29	597.48	471.52	110.48	15.48	200.36	2744.33	18.12
1998	3603.17	594.16	461.65	101.21	31.30	222.46	2772.59	13.96
1999	3601.39	590.75	461.83	96.01	32.91	210.29	2784.00	16.35
2000	3577.58	580.82	456.28	90.33	34.21	148.54	2832.04	16.18
2001	3607.96	534.22	407.55	70.95	55.72	199.76	2856.70	17.28

3-8 按三次产业分的年末从业人员

Employees by Type of Industry at the Year-end

年份 Year	年末从业人员(万人) Employees at the Year-end (10000 persons)	第一产业 Primary Industry	第二产业 Secondary Industry	第三产业 Tertiary Industry	构成(以合计为100) Composition in Percentage (total=100)	第一产业 Primary Industry	第二产业 Secondary Industry	第三产业 Tertiary Industry
1978	2280.05	1788.17	305.37	186.51	100.0	78.4	13.4	8.2
1980	2399.95	1846.46	339.06	214.43	100.0	77.0	14.1	8.9
1985	2728.71	1946.85	458.68	323.18	100.0	71.4	16.8	11.8
1990	3158.42	2176.70	553.83	427.89	100.0	68.9	17.5	13.6
1991	3222.43	2219.82	570.35	432.26	100.0	68.9	17.7	13.4
1992	3278.83	2213.42	613.57	451.84	100.0	67.5	18.7	13.8
1993	3345.61	2140.76	679.22	525.63	100.0	64.0	20.3	15.7
1994	3400.29	2076.14	731.01	593.14	100.0	61.1	21.5	17.4
1995	3467.31	2071.61	756.54	639.16	100.0	59.8	21.8	18.4
1996	3514.16	1994.90	810.38	708.88	100.0	56.8	23.0	20.2
1997	3560.29	1998.59	802.25	759.45	100.0	56.1	22.5	21.4
1998	3603.17	2002.51	822.49	778.17	100.0	55.6	22.8	21.6
1999	3601.39	2026.09	839.09	736.21	100.0	56.3	23.3	20.4
2000	3577.58	2120.98	840.52	616.08	100.0	59.3	23.5	17.2
2001	3607.96	2078.36	748.90	780.70	100.0	57.6	20.8	21.6

3-9 按类型分的年末从业人员

Employees by Type at the Year-end

单位：万人 (10 000 persons)

类 别	Item	2000 合计 Total	2000 #城镇 Urban	2001 合计 Total	2001 #城镇 Urban
从业人员总计	**Total Number of Employed Persons**	**3577.58**	**745.54**	**3607.96**	**751.26**
按就业身份分	**By Status**				
在岗职工	Staff and Workers on the Job	441.32	441.32	401.78	401.78
离开本单位仍保留劳动关系职工	Staff and Workers Left Self Unit and Remind Labor Relations	139.50	139.50	132.44	132.44
私营业主	Private Enterprises Owner	7.06	5.42	8.49	6.55
个体户主	Self-Employed Individuals	95.01	48.55	87.21	48.14
私营企业和个体从业人员	Number of Employees in Private Enterprises and Self-Employed Individuals	171.90	94.57	252.59	145.07
乡镇企业从业人员	Number of Employees in Township Enterprises	242.12		201.90	
农村劳动力	Laborer in Rural	2464.49		2506.27	
其他从业人员	Others	16.18	16.18	17.28	17.28
#再就业的离退休人员	#Retired Persons of Reemployment	0.87		0.86	0.86
按经济类型分	**By Economic Types**				
国有经济	State-owned Economy	467.98	467.98	419.71	419.71
集体经济	Collective-owned Economy	2799.59	92.99	2781.79	73.62
私营经济	Private Enterprises	46.19	33.54	58.66	44.43
个体经济	Self-Employed Individuals	227.78	114.99	289.63	155.33
联营经济	Joint Ownership Enterprises	0.91	0.91	1.12	1.12
股份制经济	Share-holding Corporations Enterprises	24.3	24.3	45.36	45.36
外商投资经济	Enterprises With Foreign Investment	3.16	3.16	2.67	2.67
港、澳、台投资经济	Enterprises With Investment from Hong Kong, Macao and Taiwan	3.07	3.07	3.15	3.15
其他经济类型	Enterprises of Other Types of Ownership	4.6	4.6	5.87	5.87
按国民经济行业分	**By Sector**				
农、林、牧、渔业	Farming,Forestry,Animal Husbandry and Fishery	2126.7	37.13	2083.52	24.85
采掘业	Mining and Quarrying	78.68	25.22	70.94	23.39
制造业	Manufacturing	587.27	200.48	498.54	176.69
电力、煤气及水的生产和供应业	Production and Supply of Electricity,Gas and Water	11.51	11.51	11.98	11.98
建筑业	Construction	163.06	36.72	167.44	36.7
地质勘查业、水利管理业	Geological Prospecting and Water Conservancy	6.27	6.27	5.57	5.57
交通运输、仓储及邮电通信业	Transport,Storage,Post and Telecommunications	98.55	46.9	98.25	43.68
批发和零售贸易、餐饮业	Wholesale and Retail Trade and Catering Services	224.17	160.81	272.75	181.15
金融、保险业	Finance and Insurance	15.08	15.08	15.06	15.06
房地产业	Real Estate Trade	2.79	2.79	5.35	5.35
社会服务业	Social Services	64.94	35.25	175.34	54.9
卫生、体育和社会福利业	Health Care,Sports and Social Welfare	28.57	23.89	28.97	24.33
教育、文化艺术和广播电影电视业	Education,Culture and Arts,Radio,Film and Television	75.12	75.12	71.99	71.99
科学研究和综合技术服务业	Scientific Research and Polytechnical Services	5.84	5.84	5.06	5.06
国家机关、政党机关和社会团体	Government Agencies,Party Agencies and Social Organizations	80.05	55.1	85.95	60.9
其他行业	Others	8.98	7.43	11.25	9.66

3-10 各行业年末从业人员及构成(2001年)

Number of Employees and Its Composition by Sector at the Year-end (2001)

行业	Sector	从业人员 Employees	职工 Staff and Workers	城镇个体私营企业 Urban Private Enterprises and Self-Employed Individuals	农村从业人员 Employees in Rural	其他从业人员 Other Employees
总计(绝对数,万人)	**Total (ABS,10 000 persons)**	3607.96	534.22	199.76	2856.70	17.28
农、林、牧、渔业	Farming,Forestry,Animal Husbandry and Fishery	2083.52	23.35	0.60	2058.67	0.90
采掘业	Mining and Quarrying	70.94	22.53	0.42	47.55	0.44
制造业	Manufacturing	498.54	148.62	25.85	321.85	2.22
电力、煤气及水的生产和供应业	Production and Supply of Electricity, Gas and Water	11.98	11.85			0.13
建筑业	Construction	167.44	28.53	3.87	130.74	4.30
地质勘查水利管理业	Geological Prospecting and Water Conservancy	5.57	5.49			0.08
交通运输仓储邮电通信	Transport,Storage,Post and Telecommunications	98.25	33.69	7.94	54.57	2.05
批发和零售贸易餐饮业	Wholesale and Retail Trade and Catering Services	272.75	59.55	120.44	91.60	1.16
金融、保险业	Finance and Insurance	15.06	12.10			2.96
房地产业	Real Estate Trade	5.35	5.26			0.09
社会服务业	Social Services	175.34	16.86	37.33	120.44	0.71
卫生体育和社会福利业	Health Care,Sports and Social Welfare	28.97	23.98		4.64	0.35
教育文化艺术和广播电影电视业	Education,Culture and Arts,Radio, Film and Television	71.99	71.05			0.94
科研和综合技术服务业	Scientific Research and Polytechnical Services	5.06	4.92			0.14
国家机关、政党机关和社会团体	Government Agencies,Party Agencies and Social Organizations	85.95	60.44		25.05	0.46
其他行业	Others	11.25	6.00	3.31	1.59	0.35
构成(以合计为100)	**Composition in Percentage (total=100)**	100.0	14.8	5.5	79.2	0.5
农、林、牧、渔业	Farming,Forestry,Animal Husbandry and Fishery	100.0	1.1		98.9	
采掘业	Mining and Quarrying	100.0	31.8	0.6	67.0	0.6
制造业	Manufacturing	100.0	29.8	5.2	64.6	0.4
电力、煤气及水的生产和供应业	Production and Supply of Electricity, Gas and Water	100.0	98.9			1.1
建筑业	Construction	100.0	17.0	2.3	78.1	2.6
地质勘查水利管理业	Geological Prospecting and Water Conservancy	100.0	98.6			1.4
交通运输仓储邮电通信	Transport,Storage,Post and Telecommunications	100.0	34.3	8.1	55.5	2.1
批发和零售贸易餐饮业	Wholesale and Retail Trade and Catering Services	100.0	21.8	44.2	33.6	0.4
金融、保险业	Finance and Insurance	100.0	80.3			19.7
房地产业	Real Estate Trade	100.0	98.3			1.7
社会服务业	Social Services	100.0	9.6	21.3	68.7	0.4
卫生体育和社会福利业	Health Care,Sports and Social Welfare	100.0	82.8		16.0	1.2
教育文化艺术和广播电影电视业	Education,Culture and Arts,Radio, Film and Television	100.0	98.7			1.3
科研和综合技术服务业	Scientific Research and Polytechnical Services	100.0	97.2			2.8
国家机关、政党机关和社会团体	Government Agencies,Party Agencies and Social Organizations	100.0	70.3		29.2	0.5
其他行业	Others	100.0	53.4	29.4	14.1	3.1

3-11 年末城乡劳动力资源与分配

Resources and Distribution of Labor Force in Urban and Rural Areas at theYear end

单位:万人 (10 000 persons)

类 别	Item	合计 Total		城 镇 Urban		乡 村 Rural	
		2000	2001	2000	2001	2000	2001
总计	**Total**	**4910.95**	**4894.35**	**1061.75**	**1206.03**	**3849.20**	**3688.32**
经济活动人口	Economy Active Population	3605.15	3638.30	773.11	781.60	2832.04	2856.70
从业人员	Employees	3577.58	3607.96	745.54	751.26	2832.04	2856.70
失业人员	Unemployment	27.57	30.34	27.57	30.34		
非经济活动人口	Non-Economy Active Population	1305.80	1256.05	288.64	424.43	1017.16	831.62

3-12 年末城镇各单位按行业分组的女性从业人员(2001年)

Number of Female Employees by Sector at the Year-end (2001)

单位:万人 (10 000 persons)

行 业	Sector	女性单位从业人员 Number of Female Employed in Units	国有经济 State-owned Economic Units	城镇集体 Urban Collective-owned Economic Units	其他经济 Economic Units of Other Types
总 计	**Total**	**156.08**	**120.71**	**16.10**	**19.27**
农、林、牧、渔业	Farming,Forestry,Animal Husbandry and Fishery	7.65	7.38	0.20	0.07
采掘业	Mining and Quarrying	3.78	3.06	0.22	0.50
制造业	Manufacturing	36.47	19.47	5.91	11.09
电力、煤气及水的生产和供应业	Production and Supply of Electricity,Gas and Water	3.91	3.46	0.06	0.39
建筑业	Construction	4.92	2.88	1.38	0.66
地质勘查业、水利管理业	Geological Prospecting and Water Conservancy	1.08	1.05	0.03	
交通运输、仓储及邮电通信业	Transport,Storage,Post and Telecommunications	8.66	7.13	0.67	0.86
批发和零售贸易、餐饮业	Wholesale and Retail Trade and Catering Services	13.71	7.76	3.37	2.58
金融、保险业	Finance and Insurance	6.68	4.03	1.60	1.05
房地产业	Real Estate Trade	1.26	0.81	0.09	0.36
社会服务业	Social Services	7.62	5.67	0.60	1.35
卫生、体育和社会福利业	Health Care,Sports and Social Welfare	12.99	11.45	1.49	0.05
教育、文化艺术和广播电影电视业	Education,Culture and Arts,Radio,Film and Television	29.42	29.14	0.11	0.17
科学研究和综合技术服务业	Scientific Research and Polytechnical Services	1.59	1.54	0.01	0.04
国家机关、政党机关和社会团体	Government Agencies,Party Agencies and Social Organizations	14.62	14.51	0.09	0.02
其他行业	Others	1.72	1.37	0.27	0.08

3-13 各行业年末在岗职工(2001年)

Total Number of Staff and Workers on the Job by Sector at the Year-end (2001)

单位:万人 (10 000 persons)

行业	Sector	全部在岗职工 Number of Staff and Workers on the Job	国有经济 State-owned Economic Units	城镇集体 Urban Collective-owned Economic Units	其他经济 Economic Units of Other Types
总计	**Total**	**401.78**	**319.59**	**39.61**	**42.58**
农、林、牧、渔业	Farming,Forestry,Animal Husbandry and Fishery	19.58	18.66	0.81	0.11
采掘业	Mining and Quarrying	13.94	11.47	0.49	1.98
制造业	Manufacturing	88.32	49.70	12.20	26.42
电力、煤气及水的生产和供应业	Production and Supply of Electricity, Gas and Water	10.65	9.39	0.17	1.09
建筑业	Construction	21.64	11.78	7.56	2.30
地质勘查业、水利管理业	Geological Prospecting and Water Conservancy	4.15	3.99	0.16	
交通运输、仓储及邮电通信业	Transport,Storage,Post and Telecommunications	26.52	21.80	2.67	2.05
批发和零售贸易、餐饮业	Wholesale and Retail Trade and Catering Services	28.40	17.19	7.00	4.21
金融、保险业	Finance and Insurance	11.44	7.26	3.30	0.88
房地产业	Real Estate Trade	3.08	2.08	0.20	0.80
社会服务业	Social Services	14.45	11.32	1.08	2.05
卫生、体育和社会福利业	Health Care,Sports and Social Welfare	22.87	19.88	2.88	0.11
教育文化艺术和广播电影电视业	Education,Culture and Arts,Radio, Film and Television	69.55	69.09	0.23	0.23
科学研究和综合技术服务业	Scientific Research and Polytechnical Services	4.58	4.46	0.04	0.08
国家机关、政党机关和社会团体	Government Agencies,Party Agencies and Social Organizations	57.97	57.73	0.19	0.05
其他行业	Others	4.64	3.79	0.63	0.22

3-14 城镇个体及私营企业年末从业人员

Employees in Urben Individual and Private Enterprises at the Year-end

单位:万人 (10 000 persons)

指标	Item	1995	1999	2000	2001
合计	**Total**	**133.86**	**210.29**	**148.54**	**199.76**
工业	Industry	19.55	37.33	25.05	26.28
建筑业	Construction	0.76	3.18	3.25	3.87
交通运输仓储业	Transport and Storage	8.95	17.04	9.85	7.94
批发零售餐饮业	Wholesale and Retail Trade and Catering Services	86.69	120.76	88.06	120.44
社会服务业	Social Services	15.18	28.90	19.30	37.33
其它行业	Others	2.73	3.08	3.03	3.90

3-15 城镇新就业人数及登记失业人员

Number of New Employees and Registered Unemployment in Urban Areas

单位：万人 (10 000 persons)

指标	Item	1995	1999	2000	2001
城镇新就业人数合计	**Total Number of New Employees in Urban Areas**	**30.62**	**25.52**	**29.05**	**27.66**
按来源分：	**By Source**				
从城镇招收	Recruitment from Urban	6.85	1.91	2.04	1.95
从农村招收	Recruitment from Rural	4.27	2.16	2.06	2.26
大中专技校毕业生	Graduates of University,College, Specialized Secondary Schools and Technical Secondary Schools	8.69	7.35	6.16	4.13
其他	Others	10.81	14.10	18.79	19.32
按就业去向分：	**By Outlet of New Employees**				
国有经济	State-owned Unit	21.08	13.97	13.11	9.92
城镇集体经济	Urban Collective-owned Unit	4.64	2.19	2.40	1.49
其他经济类型	Units of Other Types of Ownership	1.66	1.76	2.12	3.02
从事个体劳动	Self-Employed Individuals	3.24	7.60	11.42	13.23
城镇登记失业人员	**Number of Registered Unemployment in Urban Areas**	**27.40**	**30.70**	**27.57**	**30.34**
城镇登记失业率(%)	**Rate of Registered Unemployment (%)**	**3.8**	**3.9**	**3.7**	**4.0**

3-16 职业介绍服务机构及劳动力交流情况

Employment Services and Labor Force Exchanges

项 目	Item	2000	2001
职业介绍服务机构(个)	**Number of Employment Services (unit)**	**788**	**788**
#劳动部门办	# Run by Labor Departments	374	508
其他组织办	Run by Other Organization	231	90
公民个人办	Run by Private	183	190
本年登记求职人数(万人次)	**Registered Persons in This Year (10 000 person-times)**	**81.18**	**87.03**
#下岗职工	#Laid-off Workers	18.04	20.70
失业人员	Former Unemployed	26.56	26.09
获得职业资格人员	Persons with Certificates	11.14	18.87
本年介绍成功人数(万人次)	**Number of Persons Actually Employed (10 000 person-times)**	**39.79**	**27.15**
#女性	#Female	21.10	17.48
#下岗职工	#Laid-off Workers	9.48	10.53
失业人员	Former Unemployed	13.43	12.58
获得职业资格人员	Persons with Certificates	5.61	10.52

3-17 职工工资总额及年平均工资

Total Wages and Average Annual Wage of Staff and Workers

年 份 Year	全部职工 Totel Number of Staff and Workers	国有经济 State-owned Economic	城镇集体经济 Urban Collective-owned Economic	其他经济 Economic Units of Other Types
工资总额 (亿元)	Total Wages (100 million yuan)			
1978	20.33	16.29	4.04	
1980	28.73	23.09	5.64	
1981	30.09	24.17	5.92	
1982	32.46	26.13	6.33	
1983	34.48	27.71	6.77	
1984	41.69	32.28	9.41	
1985	49.30	38.36	10.93	0.01
1986	58.80	45.97	12.81	0.02
1987	70.14	55.16	14.94	0.04
1988	87.38	69.78	17.54	0.06
1989	96.78	78.66	18.02	0.10
1990	108.97	88.92	19.91	0.14
1991	119.67	97.57	21.91	0.19
1992	143.69	118.37	24.96	0.36
1993	181.84	148.64	29.51	3.69
1994	238.22	198.56	34.76	4.90
1995	282.05	233.48	41.12	7.45
1996	299.57	251.74	41.59	6.24
1997	314.91	265.53	40.70	8.68
1998	323.76	269.17	35.94	18.65
1999	349.06	293.70	34.55	20.81
2000	377.19	318.62	34.21	24.36
2001	407.58	335.75	29.00	42.83
年平均工资 (元)	Average Annual Wage (yuan)			
1978	563	589	474	
1980	718	746	625	
1981	725	748	643	
1982	750	772	670	
1983	780	803	700	
1984	922	965	800	
1985	1059	1111	912	1270
1986	1220	1281	1043	1078
1987	1400	1470	1190	1483
1988	1688	1777	1407	1966
1989	1836	1945	1475	2125
1990	2014	2141	1593	2089
1991	2152	2278	1727	2361
1992	2526	2686	1966	2852
1993	3142	3324	2379	4970
1994	4104	4388	2910	5762
1995	4797	5082	3525	6259
1996	5100	5412	3724	5897
1997	5326	5683	3736	5733
1998	5473	5849	3585	5994
1999	5939	6385	3627	6403
2000	6515	6999	3800	7217
2001	7698	8295	4146	7825

3-18 职工实际工资总额指数

Total Wage Indices of Staff and Workers

年份 Year	以1978年为100 (1978 =100) 全部职工 Total Number of Staff and Workers	#国有经济 State-owned Units	#城镇集体经济 Urban Collective-owned Units	以上年为100 (preceding year=100) 全部职工 Total Number of Staff and Workers	国有经济 State-owned Units	城镇集体经济 Urban Collective-owned Units	其他经济类型 Units of Other Types of Ownership
1978	100.0	100.0	100.0	106.1	121.5	72.3	
1980	121.4	121.8	120.0	108.6	109.9	101.5	
1985	168.1	163.2	187.5	105.7	106.2	103.9	
1990	213.5	217.4	196.3	111.9	112.3	99.4	139.2
1991	223.1	227.0	205.5	104.5	104.4	104.7	129.1
1992	236.0	242.6	206.3	105.8	106.9	100.4	166.9
1993	255.9	261.1	209.0	108.4	107.5	101.2	878.3
1994	267.3	278.1	196.3	104.5	106.5	93.9	105.9
1995	268.0	276.9	196.6	100.3	99.6	100.1	128.7
1996	265.6	278.6	185.4	99.1	100.6	94.3	78.1
1997	269.6	283.7	175.4	102.3	102.6	95.2	135.3
1998	275.3	285.6	153.8	102.3	100.9	87.9	213.8
1999	298.0	312.9	148.4	107.8	109.1	96.1	111.6
2000	317.9	335.1	145.1	106.7	107.1	97.7	115.6
2001	347.3	357.0	124.3	109.3	106.5	85.7	177.8

3-19 职工年平均工资指数

Average Annual Wage Indices of Staff and Workers

年份 Year	货币工资指数 Indices of Average Money Wage 全部职工 Total Number of Staff and Workers	国有经济 State-owned Units	城镇集体经济 Urban Collective-owned Units	其他经济类型 Units of Other Types of Ownership	实际工资指数 Indices of Average Real Wage 全部职工 Total Number of Staff and Workers	国有经济 State-owned Units	城镇集体经济 Urban Collective-owned Units	其他经济类型 Units of Other Types of Ownership
1978=100								
1990	357.7	363.5	336.1		141.4	143.7	132.9	
1995	852.0	862.7	743.4		164.6	166.7	143.7	
1996	905.9	918.8	785.7		163.3	165.5	141.5	
1997	946.0	964.9	788.2		164.7	168.0	137.2	
1998	972.1	993.0	756.3		168.0	171.7	130.7	
1999	1054.9	1084.0	765.2		183.1	188.1	132.8	
2000	1157.2	1188.3	801.7		198.3	203.6	137.3	
2001	1367.3	1408.3	874.7		236.8	243.9	151.5	
以上年为100	**preceding year=100**							
1990	109.7	110.1	108.0	98.3	109.0	109.4	107.3	97.7
1995	116.9	115.8	121.1	108.6	99.0	98.1	102.5	92.0
1996	106.3	106.5	105.6	94.2	99.2	99.3	98.5	87.9
1997	104.4	105.0	100.3	97.2	101.6	102.1	97.6	94.6
1998	102.8	102.9	96.0	104.6	102.2	102.4	95.5	104.0
1999	108.5	109.2	101.2	106.8	109.0	109.6	101.6	107.3
2000	109.7	109.6	104.8	112.7	108.3	108.2	103.4	111.3
2001	118.2	118.5	109.1	108.4	119.5	119.8	110.3	109.6

3-20 各行业在岗职工工资总额(2001年)

Total Wages of Staff and Workers on the Job by Sector (2001)

单位：万元 (10 000 yuan)

行 业	Sector	工资总额 Total Wage		
		全 省 Total	#国有经济 State-owned Units	#城镇集体经济 Urban Collective-owned Units
总 计	**Total**	**3855286.1**	**3188031.2**	**269410.0**
农、林、牧、渔业	**Farming,Forestry,Animal Husbandry and Fishery**	**108491.0**	**103465.8**	**4344.4**
#农业	#Farming	67300.5	66950.6	346.3
林业	Forestry	9460.5	9231.9	228.6
畜牧业	Animal Husbandry	1835.1	1454.6	
渔业	Fishery	3576.9	3117.7	339.1
农、林、牧、渔服务业	Services	26318.0	22711.0	3430.4
采掘业	**Mining and Quarrying**	**107726.0**	**87999.0**	**3664.6**
制造业	**Manufacturing**	**790331.2**	**480977.2**	**76254.5**
电力煤气及水的生产和供应业	**Production and Supply of Electricity,Gas and Water**	**132195.3**	**111965.2**	**1951.1**
建筑业	**Construction**	**175696.7**	**109186.8**	**48545.1**
#土木工程建筑业	#Civil Engineering	156074.5	95917.9	45326.4
线路、管道和设备安装业	Circuit,Pipelines and Equipment Installation	19289.4	13208.3	3065.2
建筑物的装修装饰业	Buildings Fitting up and Decoration	332.8	60.6	153.5
地质勘查业、水利管理业	**Geological Prospecting and Water Conservancy**	**34074.8**	**32905.1**	**1155.1**
#地质勘查业	#Geological Prospecting	11830.6	11830.6	
水利管理业	Water Conservancy	22244.2	21074.5	1155.1
交通运输、仓储及邮电通信业	**Transport,Storage,Post and Telecommunications**	**317449.6**	**280581.7**	**13689.1**
#铁路运输业	#Transport Railway	116862.5	116191.4	403.4
公路运输业	Transport Highway	30576.0	18703.0	3966.4
水上运输业	Transport Waterway	6537.0	4740.6	1522.0
航空运输业	Air Transport	2716.1	1523.5	
交通运输辅助业	Transport Supporting and Auxiliary Services	66467.1	57543.8	7176.4
其他交通运输业	Other Transport	302.0	85.1	24.3
仓储业	Storage	8496.8	8007.2	366.6
邮电通信业	Post and Telecommunications	85492.1	73787.1	230.0
批发和零售贸易、餐饮业	**Wholesale and Retail Trade and Catering Services**	**221681.0**	**140371.0**	**41027.2**
#食品、饮料、烟草和家庭用品批发业	#Wholesale Trade of Food,Beverages,Tobacco and Household Goods	91558.5	72770.5	11187.1
能源、材料和机械电子设备批发业	Wholesale Trade of Energy,Materials and Electronic Equipment	27432.4	16665.1	1921.0
其他批发业	Other Wholesale Trade	19623.5	12242.6	5832.8
零售业	Retail Trade	73022.7	32766.8	21243.6
商业经纪与代理业	Commercial Brokerage and Agencies	183.2	150.7	5.5
餐饮业	Catering Services	9860.7	5775.3	837.2
金融、保险业	**Finance and Insurance**	**163027.9**	**108689.9**	**39299.1**
#金融业	Finance	152069.7	101171.2	39299.1
保险业	Insurance	10958.2	7518.7	
房地产业	**Real Estate Trade**	**28557.0**	**20373.2**	**1366.0**
#房地产开发与经营业	#Real Estate Development and Operation	14234.0	6621.6	1186.4
房地产管理业	Real Estate Management	13393.4	12897.2	158.2
房地产代理与经纪业	Real Estate Brokerages and Agencies	929.6	854.4	21.4

行业	Sector	工资总额 Total Wage 全省 Total	#国有经济 State-owned Units	#城镇集体经济 Urban Collective-owned Units
社会服务业	**Social Services**	**128259.8**	**100970.0**	**8710.2**
#公共服务业	#Public Facilities Services	66229.8	60808.0	1569.4
居民服务业	Resident Services	6257.5	2927.4	2307.1
旅馆业	Hotels	32340.6	20597.0	2876.2
租赁服务业	Leasing Services	723.7	554.2	44.2
旅游业	Tourism	2689.3	1253.9	155.5
娱乐服务业	Recreational Services	709.8	466.2	30.2
信息、咨询服务业	Information and Consultancy Services	2876.0	2108.9	256.6
计算机应用服务业	Computer Application Services	3036.5	702.9	
其他社会服务业	Other Social Services	13396.6	11551.5	1471.0
卫生、体育和社会福利业	**Health Care,Sports and Social Welfare**	**261552.8**	**240293.4**	**20262.6**
#卫生	#Health Care	251680.0	230768.6	19918.7
体育	Sports	2058.5	2051.0	7.5
社会福利保障业	Social Welfare	7814.3	7473.8	336.4
教育、文化艺术和广播电影电视业	**Education,Culture and Arts,Radio, Film and Television**	**718664.5**	**714583.4**	**1692.1**
#教育	#Education	671037.4	668738.6	1300.8
#普通高等教育	#Regular Institution of Higher Education	93499.8	93499.8	
普通中学	Regular Secondary Schools	262260.6	261175.5	381.7
小学校	Primary Schools	231224.5	230999.2	201.2
文化艺术业	Culture and Arts	22304.7	21877.5	331.4
广播电影电视业	Radio,Film and Television	25322.4	23967.3	59.9
科学研究和综合技术服务业	**Scientific Research and Polytechnical Services**	**58032.8**	**56393.1**	**274.9**
#科学研究	#Scientific Research	15110.4	14870.2	8.5
#自然科学研究	#Natural Scientific Research	13001.9	12761.7	8.5
社会科学研究	Social Scientific Research	990.0	990.0	
其他科学研究	Other Scientific Research	1118.5	1118.5	
综合技术服务业	Polytechnical Services	42922.4	41522.9	266.4
#气象	#Meteorology	2500.8	2497.7	3.1
地震	Seismology	257.1	257.1	
测绘	Survey and Mapping	2143.3	2143.3	
技术监督		6828.3	6711.5	35.4
环境保护	Environmental Protection	3297.6	3227.7	69.9
技术推广和科技交流服务业	Technological Application & Science Technological	5855.8	5529.3	64.4
工程设计业	Engineering Design	21460.8	20641.0	60.9
其他综合技术服务业	Other Polytechnical Services	578.7	515.3	32.7
国家机关、政党机关和社会团体	**Government Agencies,Party Agencies and Social Organizations**	**562475.2**	**560596.0**	**1608.9**
#国家机关	#Government Agencies	534914.7	524891.0	9874.0
政党机关	Party Agencies	30183.5	30183.5	
其他行业	**Others**	**47070.5**	**38680.4**	**5565.1**
#企业管理机构	#Enterprise Management Organizations	39096.4	30744.5	5536.6

3-21 各行业在岗职工年平均工资(2001年)

Average Annual Wage of Staff and Workers on the Job by Sector (2001)

单位：元 (yuan)

行业	Sector	平均工资 Average Wage 全省 Total	#国有经济 State-owned Units	#城镇集体经济 Urban Collective-owned Units
总计	**Total**	**9616**	**9985**	**6876**
农、林、牧、渔业	**Farming,Forestry,Animal Husbandry and Fishery**	**5568**	**5573**	**5323**
#农业	#Farming	5329	5331	4954
林业	Forestry	4707	4729	3948
畜牧业	Animal Husbandry	5471	5136	
渔业	Fishery	5119	5236	3836
农、林、牧、渔服务业	Services	6905	7150	5717
采掘业	**Mining and Quarrying**	**7670**	**7500**	**7054**
制造业	**Manufacturing**	**8732**	**9316**	**6200**
电力煤气及水的生产和供应业	**Production and Supply of Electricity,Gas and Water**	**12477**	**11992**	**11904**
建筑业	**Construction**	**8494**	**9498**	**6955**
#土木工程建筑业	#Civil Engineering	8283	9450	6755
线路、管道和设备安装业	Circuit,Pipelines and Equipment Installation	10780	9864	12917
建筑物的装修装饰业	Buildings Fitting up and Decoration	6525	10632	4767
地质勘查业、水利管理业	**Geological Prospecting and Water Conservancy**	**8183**	**8223**	**7157**
#地质勘查业	#Geological Prospecting	9538	9538	
水利管理业	Water Conservancy	7608	7632	7157
交通运输仓储及邮电通信业	**Transport,Storage,Post and Telecommunications**	**11918**	**12841**	**5069**
#铁路运输业	#Transport Railway	15060	15099	11022
公路运输业	Transport Highway	6159	6104	5085
水上运输业	Transport Waterway	5902	7029	4048
航空运输业	Air Transport	9039	7797	
交通运输辅助业	Transport Supporting and Auxiliary Services	10215	11691	4945
其他交通运输业	Other Transport	10272	16686	5651
仓储业	Storage	8098	8091	8351
邮电通信业	Post and Telecommunications	17382	17143	26744
批发和零售贸易、餐饮业	**Wholesale and Retail Trade and Catering Services**	**7770**	**8115**	**5846**
#食品、饮料、烟草和家庭用品批发业	#Wholesale Trade of Food,Beverages,Tobacco and Household Goods	8215	8573	6312
能源、材料和机械电子设备批发业	Wholesale Trade of Energy,Materials and Electronic Equipment	8702	8291	6371
其他批发业	Other Wholesale Trade	7998	12106	4340
零售业	Retail Trade	7042	6750	6101
商业经纪与代理业	Commercial Brokerage and Agencies	8404	8762	3667
餐饮业	Catering Services	7113	6306	7205
金融、保险业	**Finance and Insurance**	**14333**	**15116**	**11907**
#金融业	Finance	14355	15179	11907
保险业	Insurance	14029	14313	
房地产业	**Real Estate Trade**	**9687**	**10277**	**7159**
#房地产开发与经营业	#Real Estate Development and Operation	8641	8920	7199
房地产管理业	Real Estate Management	11010	11092	6878
房地产代理与经纪业	Real Estate Brokerages and Agencies	11054	11039	7133

单位：元　　　　3-21 续表　continued　　　　(yuan)

行 业	Sector	平均工资 Average Wage 全 省 Total	#国有经济 State-owned Units	#城镇集体经济 Urban Collective-owned Units
社会服务业	**Social Services**	**9002**	**9077**	**7992**
#公共服务业	#Public Facilities Services	9163	9167	6547
居民服务业	Resident Services	11117	11435	12614
旅馆业	Hotels	8158	7870	7597
租赁服务业	Leasing Services	9115	9457	6406
旅游业	Tourism	8438	8337	9256
娱乐服务业	Recreational Services	7287	6948	7366
信息、咨询服务业	Information and Consultancy Services	9887	10711	8120
计算机应用服务业	Computer Application Services	9634	21694	
其他社会服务业	Other Social Services	9626	10388	6415
卫生、体育和社会福利业	**Health Care,Sports and Social Welfare**	**11658**	**12333**	**7123**
#卫生	#Health Care	11693	12407	7076
体育	Sports	12707	12747	6818
社会福利保障业	Social Welfare	10407	10350	11804
教育、文化艺术和广播电影电视业	**Education,Culture and Arts,Radio, Film and Television**	**10425**	**10431**	**8311**
#教育	#Education	10350	10353	9186
#普通高等教育	#Regular Institution of Higher Education	20499	20499	
普通中学	Regular Secondary Schools	10050	10055	7004
小学校	Primary Schools	8517	8516	9911
文化艺术业	Culture and Arts	12220	12434	6070
广播电影电视业	Radio,Film and Television	11145	11120	8095
科学研究和综合技术服务业	**Scientific Research and Polytechnical Services**	**12740**	**12690**	**7594**
#科学研究	#Scientific Research	11872	11817	9444
#自然科学研究	#Natural Scientific Research	11704	11639	9444
社会科学研究	Social Scientific Research	15278	15278	
其他科学研究	Other Scientific Research	11519	11519	
综合技术服务业	Polytechnical Services	13077	13035	7547
#气象	#Meteorology	13066	13125	2818
地震	Seismology	15677	15677	
测绘	Survey and Mapping	11020	11020	
技术监督	Technological Supervision	13041	13149	7696
环境保护	Environmental Protection	11029	11180	6786
技术推广和科技交流服务业	Technological Application & Science Technological	11116	11209	5600
工程设计业	Engineering Design	14542	14285	16459
其他综合技术服务业	Other Polytechnical Services	10580	10941	7976
国家机关、政党机关和社会团体	**Government Agencies,Party Agencies and Social Organizations**	**9839**	**9847**	**8380**
#国家机关	#Government Agencies	10012	9849	85489
政党机关	Party Agencies	9803	9803	
其他行业	**Others**	**10259**	**10409**	**8399**
#企业管理机构	#Enterprise Management Organizations	10597	10898	8374

3-22 离休、退休、退职人员年末人数(2001年)

Number of Retired and Resigned Persons at the Year-end (2001)

单位:万人 (10 000 persons)

项目	Item	合计 Total	离休人员 Retried Veterans	退休人员 Retried Persons	领取定期生活费的退职人员 Number of Resigned Persons Receiving Periodical Living Expenses
总 计	**Total**	**165.26**	**3.91**	**158.47**	**2.88**
企业	Enterprises	119.27	1.98	114.97	2.32
#国有企业	#State-owned Enterprises	93.10	1.75	89.71	1.64
集体企业	Collective-owned Enterprises	23.19	0.18	22.42	0.59
其他企业	Other-owned Enterprises	2.84	0.05	2.71	0.08
事业	Institutions	32.98	1.00	31.61	0.37
机关	Agencies & Organizations	13.01	0.93	11.89	0.19

3-23 离休、退休、退职人员保险福利费用构成情况(2001年)

Composition of Social Insurance and Welfare Funds for Retired and Resigned Persons (2001)

单位：万元 (10 000 yuan)

项目	Item	合计 Total	离休金 Pensions for Retired Veterans	退休金 Pensions for Retired Persons	退职生活费 Resignation Allowances for Living Expenses	医疗卫生费 Expenses for Medical Care	其他 Other
总 计	**Total**	**1171963.9**	**56209.3**	**993365.8**	**8559.8**	**71455.4**	**42373.6**
企业	Enterprises	724661.3	30836.5	625953.5	6437.3	34603.4	26830.6
#国有企业	#State-owned Enterprises	592493.6	28443.7	505581.6	5066.1	28933.3	24468.9
集体企业	Collective-owned Enterprises	108690.1	1779.8	99512.5	1172.8	4199	2026
其他企业	Other-owned Enterprises	22675.6	602.5	20172.3	192.9	1455.7	252.2
事业	Institutions	324157.3	13373.4	274452.6	1501.7	23908.4	10921.2
机关	Agencies & Organizations	123145.3	11999.4	92959.7	620.8	12943.6	4621.8

3-24 企业下岗职工情况(2001年)

Basic Indicators of Staff and Workers off the Job in Enterprises (2001)

单位：万人 (10 000 persons)

项目 Item	总计 Total	国有企业 State-owned Enterprises	#中央企业 Centre Enterprises	城镇集体企业 Urban Collective-owned Enterprises	其他经济类型企业 Enterprises of Other Types of Ownership
上年结转下岗职工人数 Number of Staff and Workers off the Job Carry Forward Last Year	77.08	50.02	3.72	26.41	0.65
本年新增下岗职工人数 Number of Staff and Workers off the Job Newly Increased in This Year	11.40	9.26	0.65	2.14	
本年减少下岗职工人数 Number of Staff and Workers off the Job Decreased in This Year	12.64	10.15	1.24	2.44	0.05
年末实有下岗职工人数 Number of Staff and Workers off the Job at the Year-end	75.85	49.13	3.13	26.12	0.60
#进再就业服务中心人数 #Number of Persons for Enter the Services Center of Reemployment	58.83	48.73	2.94		
#签订协议人数 #Number of persons for Signed Agreements	51.47	47.34	2.94		
#足额领取基本生活费人数 #Number of Persons for Entire Receiving Living Expenses	46.26	44.34			
未足额领取基本生活费人数 Number of Persons Partial Receiving Living Expenses	3.59	2.40			
未领取基本生活费人数 Number of Persons Never Receiving Living Expenses	1.62	0.60			

3-25 离开本单位仍保留劳动关系的职工情况(2001年)

Basic Indicators of Staff and Workers Left Self Unit and Remind Labor Relations (2001)

单位：万人 (10 000 persons)

市州	Cities and Prefecture	合计 Total	国有经济 State Owned Units	中央 Centre Genus	省属 Province Genus	地属 Prefecture Genus	县属 County Genus	城镇集体经济 Urban Collective Owned Units	其他经济类型 Units of Other Types of Ownership
合计	**Total**	**132.44**	**87.96**	**7.84**	**11.50**	**31.45**	**37.17**	**31.34**	**13.14**
长沙市	Changsha City	16.67	9.53	1.16	2.28	4.66	1.43	4.63	2.51
株洲市	Zhuzhou City	12.16	8.01	1.05	1.76	3.08	2.12	2.60	1.55
湘潭市	Xiangtan City	9.32	6.22	0.62	1.74	3.22	0.64	2.34	0.76
衡阳市	Hengyang City	16.30	10.73	0.71	0.71	6.04	3.27	3.58	1.99
邵阳市	Shaoyang City	14.56	9.76	0.09	1.18	4.86	3.63	3.41	1.39
岳阳市	Yueyang City	8.60	6.00	1.20	0.20	1.62	2.98	1.91	0.69
常德市	Changde City	8.19	4.52	0.40	0.28	1.17	2.67	2.51	1.16
张家界市	Zhangjiajie City	1.52	1.04	0.03	0.01	0.06	0.94	0.41	0.07
益阳市	Yiyang City	11.56	8.10	0.24	0.68	2.45	4.73	3.08	0.38
郴州市	Chenzhou City	6.46	4.10	0.44	0.47	1.17	2.02	1.33	1.03
永州市	Yongzhou City	7.34	5.42	0.21	0.23	1.28	3.70	1.34	0.58
怀化市	Huaihua City	7.73	5.15	0.55	0.18	0.56	3.86	1.92	0.66
娄底市	Loudi City	7.84	5.97	0.29	1.76	0.61	3.31	1.60	0.27
湘西自治州	West Hunan A.P	3.45	2.67	0.11	0.02	0.67	1.87	0.68	0.10
其他单位	Other Units	0.74	0.74	0.74					

四、固定资产投资

INVESTMENT IN FIXED ASSETS

资料整理人员：　蒋丽芳　向延华　俞　峰

4-1 全社会固定资产投资

Total Investment in Fixed Assets

指 标	Item	1995	1999	2000	2001	2001年比上年±% Increase Rate in 2001 over 2000 (%)
投资总额（亿元）	**Total Investment (100 million yuan)**	**524.01**	**943.34**	**1066.27**	**1210.63**	**13.5**
按经济类型分	**Grouped by Ownership**					
国有经济	State-Owned Units	316.90	522.95	574.12	618.54	7.7
集体经济	Collective-Owned Units	39.83	95.81	118.80	145.78	22.7
#城镇	# Urban	16.22	15.78	18.77	18.64	-0.7
农村	Rural	23.61	80.03	100.02	127.14	27.1
个体经济	Individuals	120.34	263.42	281.89	291.56	3.4
#城镇	# Urban	13.94	66.01	79.49	86.43	8.7
农村	Rural	106.40	197.41	202.40	205.13	1.3
联营经济	Joint Owned Economic Units	0.85	1.39	1.36	1.42	4.4
股份制经济	Share Holding Economic Units	14.45	32.30	49.80	113.59	128.1
外商投资经济	Foreign Funded Economic Units	23.47	13.00	24.72	17.54	-29.0
港澳台投资经济	Economic Units Funded by Entrepreneurs from Hong Kong,Macao and Taiwan	7.46	11.91	13.69	20.18	47.4
其他经济	Others	0.71	2.56	1.91	2.02	5.8
按管理渠道分	**Grouped by Channel of Management**					
基本建设	Capital Construction	217.52	368.47	403.96	476.7	18.0
更新改造	Innovation	92.02	143.30	175.20	198.31	13.2
房地产开发	Real Estate Development	50.84	55.50	74.83	107.41	43.5
其他投资	Others	163.63	376.07	412.28	428.21	3.9
按资金来源分	**Grouped by Source of Funds**					
国家预算内投资	State Budgetary Appropriation	19.95	68.83	76.49	93.43	22.1
国内贷款	Domestic Loans	101.24	154.20	213.41	206.10	-3.4
债券	Bonds	0.72	9.23	2.34	1.48	-36.9
利用外资	Foreign Investment	32.81	32.93	22.01	29.22	32.7
自筹投资	Fundraising	276.30	532.87	623.37	757.56	21.5
#股票	#Shares	0.61	2.09	4.29	3.75	-12.6
其他资金	Others	92.99	145.28	128.65	122.48	-4.5
按构成分	**Grouped by Use of Funds**					
建筑安装工程	Construction and Installation	363.26	686.38	759.94	829.11	9.1
设备、工器具购置	Purchase of Equipment and Instruments	106.51	162.06	198.68	232.39	17.0
其他费用	Others	54.24	94.90	107.65	149.14	38.5
按隶属关系分	**Grouped by Administrative Relationship**					
中央	Central	142.58	222.02	248.26	225.54	-9.2
地方	Local	364.02	681.92	770.23	917.68	19.1
其他	Others	17.41	39.40	47.79	67.41	41.1
按用途分：住宅	**Grouped by Industry: Residential Buildings**	**180.99**	**306.98**	**297.00**	**242.59**	**-18.3**
房屋建筑面积（万平方米）	**Floor Space of Buildings (10 000 sq.m)**					
施工面积	Floor Space Under Construction	8338.70	12128.41	13170.34	12870.57	-2.3
竣工面积	Floor Space Completed	6360.57	10094.18	10892.52	10216.65	-6.2
#住宅	# Residential Buildings	5115.43	8408.18	9117.54	8344.88	-8.5

4-2 各种分组的全社会固定资产投资及构成(2001年)

Total Investment in Fixed Assets and Its composition (2001)

类别	Item	全省总计 Total	国有 State-owned	#基本建设 Capital Construction	#更新改造 Innovation
绝对数	**Absolute Figure**				
投资总额(亿元)	**Total Investment (100 million yuan)**	**1210.63**	**618.54**	**433.90**	**146.88**
按资金来源分	**Grouped by Source of Funds**				
#国家预算内投资	#State Budgetary Appropriation	93.43	69.34	59.45	9.70
国内贷款	Domestic Loans	206.10	159.89	116.99	37.80
债 券	Bonds	1.48	1.37	1.14	0.05
利用外资	Foreign Investment	29.22	18.68	17.76	1.37
自筹投资	Fundraising	757.56	311.58	198.06	93.49
#股票	#Shares	3.75	1.40	0.11	1.21
其他资金	Others	122.84	57.68	40.50	4.47
按构成分	**Grouped by Use of Funds**				
#建安工程	#Construction and Installation	829.11	409.64	333.93	49.46
设备、工具、器具购置	Purchase of Equipment and Instruments	232.39	127.63	41.22	84.29
其他费用	Others	149.14	81.27	58.76	13.13
按用途分：住宅	**Grouped by Industry:Residential Buildings**	242.59	43.18	28.14	0.47
房屋建筑面积(万平方米)	**Floor Space of Buildings (10 000 sq.m)**				
#施工面积	#Floor Space Under Construction	12870.57	2283.26	1804.22	88.22
竣工面积	Floor Space Completed	10216.65	1094.14	829.35	49.59
#住宅	#Residential Buildings	8344.88	606.58	413.44	4.61
构成(%)	**Percentage(%)**				
投资总额	**Total Investment**	**100.0**	**100.0**	**100.0**	**100.0**
按资金来源分	**Grouped by Source of Funds**				
#国家预算内投资	#State Budgetary Appropriation	7.7	11.2	13.7	6.6
国内贷款	Domestic Loans	17.0	25.8	27.0	25.7
债 券	Bonds	0.1	0.2	0.3	0.0
利用外资	Foreign Investment	2.4	3.0	4.1	0.9
自筹投资	Fundraising	62.6	50.4	45.6	63.7
#股票	#Shares	0.3	0.2	0.0	0.8
其他资金	Others	10.1	9.3	9.3	3.0
按构成分	**Grouped by Use of Funds**				
#建安工程	#Construction and Installation	68.5	66.2	77.0	33.7
设备、工具、器具购置	Purchase of Equipment and Instruments	19.2	20.6	9.5	57.4
其他费用	Others	12.3	13.1	13.5	8.9
按用途分：住宅	Grouped by Industry:Residential Buildings	20.0	7.0	6.5	0.3

注：其他含联营经济、股份制经济、中外合资经营、中外合作经营、外资、与大陆合资经营、与大陆合作经营、港澳台独资等经济。

Other types of ownership refer to the types of ownership of joint-owned economic units, share holding economic units, economic units funded by Chinese and foreign ventures, Chinese-foreign joint ventures, foreign-funded economic units, and the economic units funded by enterpriser from Hong Kong, Macao and Taiwan.

4-2 续表 continued

类别	Item	集体 Collective Owned	#农村 Rural	个体 Individuals	#农村 Rural	其他 Other Types of Ownership
绝对数	**Absolute Figure**					
投资总额(亿元)	**Total Investment (100 million yuan)**	**145.78**	**127.14**	**291.56**	**205.13**	**154.75**
按资金来源分	**Grouped by Source of Funds**					
#国家预算内投资	#State Budgetary Appropriation	22.96	22.90	0.05		1.08
国内贷款	Domestic Loans	10.85	8.02	5.99	2.83	29.37
债　券	Bonds					0.11
利用外资	Foreign Investment	2.35	2.31	0.05		8.14
自筹投资	Fundraising	91.87	81.30	271.67	196.21	82.44
#股票	#Shares					2.35
其他资金	Others	17.75	12.61	13.79	6.09	33.61
按构成分	**Grouped by Use of Funds**					
#建安工程	#Construction and Installation	94.00	79.68	234.07	155.19	91.40
设备、工具、器具购置	Purchase of Equipment and Instruments	38.60	36.93	32.83	31.35	33.33
其他费用	Others	13.18	10.54	24.66	18.59	30.02
按用途分：住宅	**Grouped by Industry:Residential Buildings**	15.20	7.66	150.47	141.34	33.73
房屋建筑面积(万㎡)	**Floor Space of Buildings (10 000 sq.m)**					
#施工面积	#Floor Space Under Construction	1161.77	874.00	8324.53	6352.00	1101.01
竣工面积	Floor Space Completed	912.77	789.00	7808.21	6014.00	401.53
#住宅	#Residential Buildings	292.33	212.00	7187.26	5582.00	258.71
构成(%)	**Percentage (%)**					
投资总额	**Total Investment**	**100.0**	**100.0**	**100.0**	**100.0**	**100.0**
按资金来源分	**Grouped by Source of Funds**					
#国家预算内投资	#State Budgetary Appropriation	15.7	18.0			0.7
国内贷款	Domestic Loans	7.4	6.3	2.1	1.4	19.0
债　券	Bonds					0.1
利用外资	Foreign Investment	1.6	1.8	0.0	0.0	5.3
自筹投资	Fundraising	63.0	63.9	93.2	95.7	53.3
#股票	#Shares					1.5
其他资金	Others	12.2	9.9	4.7	3.0	21.7
按构成分	**Grouped by Use of Funds**					
#建安工程	#Construction and Installation	64.5	62.7	80.3	75.7	59.1
设备、工具、器具购置	Purchase of Equipment and Instruments	26.5	29.0	11.3	15.3	21.5
其他费用	Others	9.0	8.3	8.5	9.1	19.4
按用途分：住宅	**Grouped by Industry:Residential Buildings**	10.4	6.0	51.6	68.9	21.8

4-3 各行业基本建设投资(2001年)

Capital Construction Investment by sector (2001)

单位:万元　　　　(10 000 yuan)

行业	Sector	总计 Total	长沙市 Changsha City	株洲市 Zhuzhou City	湘潭市 Xiangtan City
总计	**Total**	**4766962**	**1228457**	**185159**	**137494**
农林牧渔业	Farming,Forestry, Animal Husbandry and Fishery	55709	9620	4242	3308
采掘业	Mining and Quarrying	6822		400	837
制造业	Manufacturing	115114	31948	8209	7831
电力煤气及水的生产和供应业	Production and Supply of Electricity,Gas and Water	772335	73734	26888	30294
建筑业	Construction	14476	2690	2319	219
地质勘查业、水利管理业	Geological Prospecting and Water Conservancy	271360	30921	6088	3111
交通运输仓储及邮电通信业	Transport,Storage,Post and Telecommunications	1602115	166019	15568	5893
批发和零售贸易、餐饮业	Wholesale and Retail Trade, Catering Services	188558	81375	10173	12132
金融保险业	Finance and Insurance	25936	4799	3273	1495
房地产业	Real Estate Trade	9986			2195
社会服务业	Social Services	894912	476937	66944	38708
卫生体育和社会福利业	Health Care,Sports and Social Welfare	146652	92807	6936	4934
教育文化艺术和广播影电视业	Education,Culture and Arts, Radio,Film and Television	304307	146460	11672	16471
科学研究和综合技术服务业	Scientific Research and Polytechnical Services	19163	15149	1147	403
国家机关，政党机关，社会团体	Government Agencies,Party Agencies,Social Organizations	306373	87116	21300	9663
其他行业	Others	33144	8882		

行业	Sector	衡阳市 Hengyang City	邵阳市 Shaoyang City	岳阳市 Yueyang City	常德市 Changde City
总计	**Total**	**220121**	**140752**	**283781**	**335195**
农林牧渔业	Farming,Forestry, Animal Husbandry and Fishery	2064	40	5603	6108
采掘业	Mining and Quarrying	184	681	1299	426
制造业	Manufacturing	3310	1039	10050	16489
电力煤气及水的生产和供应业	Production and Supply of Electricity,Gas and Water	51568	18952	43997	36088
建筑业	Construction	246	2146	250	203
地质勘查业、水利管理业	Geological Prospecting and Water Conservancy	7264	5935	49299	113783
交通运输仓储及邮电通信业	Transport,Storage,Post and Telecommunications	86546	24449	36400	52651
批发和零售贸易、餐饮业	Wholesale and Retail Trade, Catering Services	4222	4243	18878	10575
金融保险业	Finance and Insurance	115	3132	946	3887
房地产业	Real Estate Trade		1990	4000	428
社会服务业	Social Services	18806	21538	74910	55537
卫生体育和社会福利业	Health Care,Sports and Social Welfare	3843	2222	2522	7074
教育文化艺术和广播影电视业	Education,Culture and Arts, Radio,Film and Television	17110	14285	10002	16120
科学研究和综合技术服务业	Scientific Research and Polytechnical Services	305	493	204	360
国家机关，政党机关，社会团体	Government Agencies,Party Agencies,Social Organizations	21559	27797	25421	13946
其他行业	Others	2979	11810		1520

单位:万元 4-3 续表 continued (10 000 yuan)

行业	Sector	张家界市 Zhangjiajie City	益阳市 Yiyang City	郴州市 Chenzhou City	永州市 Yongzhou City
总计	**Total**	**67921**	**242323**	**282795**	**149950**
农林牧渔业	Farming,Forestry, Animal Husbandry and Fishery	269	3320	7459	1839
采掘业	Mining and Quarrying		720	1170	100
制造业	Manufacturing	674	3519	17983	9757
电力煤气及水的生产和供应业	Production and Supply of Electricity,Gas and Water	12339	98455	96401	39775
建筑业	Construction		2200	218	1722
地质勘查业、水利管理业	Geological Prospecting and Water Conservancy	1547	31086	6176	5334
交通运输仓储及邮电通信业	Transport,Storage,Post and Telecommunications	21427	31866	31940	46890
批发和零售贸易、餐饮业	Wholesale and Retail Trade, Catering Services	2441	5432	18383	6082
金融保险业	Finance and Insurance	190	1822	2609	1639
房地产业	Real Estate Trade		100		
社会服务业	Social Services	16225	24810	44991	10640
卫生体育和社会福利业	Health Care,Sports and Social Welfare		8761	5324	2757
教育文化艺术和广播影电视业	Education,Culture and Arts, Radio,Film and Television	4242	14738	13571	10733
科学研究和综合技术服务业	Scientific Research and Polytechnical Services	50	150	156	190
国家机关，政党机关，社会团体	Government Agencies,Party Agencies,Social Organizations	8517	15024	36414	11148
其他行业	Others		320		1344

行业	Sector	怀化市 Huaihua City	娄底市 Loudi City	湘西自治州 West Hunan A.P	不分地区 Not Classified by Region
总计	**Total**	**151965**	**97488**	**125892**	**1117669**
农林牧渔业	Farming,Forestry, Animal Husbandry and Fishery	284	1698	9855	
采掘业	Mining and Quarrying	616	389		
制造业	Manufacturing	660	1537	2108	
电力煤气及水的生产和供应业	Production and Supply of Electricity,Gas and Water	64961	25476	37359	116048
建筑业	Construction	202	2061		
地质勘查业、水利管理业	Geological Prospecting and Water Conservancy	5119	4410	1287	
交通运输仓储及邮电通信业	Transport,Storage,Post and Telecommunications	20771	31651	28423	1001621
批发和零售贸易、餐饮业	Wholesale and Retail Trade, Catering Services	6313	4796	3513	
金融保险业	Finance and Insurance	1214	620	195	
房地产业	Real Estate Trade	873	400		
社会服务业	Social Services	19382	11299	14185	
卫生体育和社会福利业	Health Care,Sports and Social Welfare	4802	1397	3273	
教育文化艺术和广播影电视业	Education,Culture and Arts, Radio,Film and Television	10683	7344	10876	
科学研究和综合技术服务业	Scientific Research and Polytechnical Services	102		454	
国家机关，政党机关，社会团体	Government Agencies,Party Agencies,Social Organizations	10139	4095	14234	
其他行业	Others	5844	315	130	

4-4 各行业基本建设新增固定资产(2001年)

Newly Increased Fixed Assets through Capital Construction by Sector (2001)

单位:万元 (10 000 yuan)

行业	Sector	总计 Total	长沙市 Changsha City	株洲市 Zhuzhou City	湘潭市 Xiangtan City
总计	**Total**	**2232323**	**446324**	**122117**	**158811**
农林牧渔业	Farming,Forestry, Animal Husbandry and Fishery	28093	2768	2650	3525
采掘业	Mining and Quarrying	4952			1240
制造业	Manufacturing	91962	12117	10542	6521
电力煤气及水的生产和供应业	Production and Supply of Electricity,Gas and Water	307118	19095	23754	42185
建筑业	Construction	7668	1615	349	194
地质勘查业、水利管理业	Geological Prospecting and Water Conservancy	138994	37732	1954	3824
交通运输仓储及邮电通信业	Transport,Storage,Post and Telecommunications	653464	53517	7220	1210
批发和零售贸易、餐饮业	Wholesale and Retail Trade, Catering Services	127479	48175	9273	11861
金融保险业	Finance and Insurance	26405	9323	5273	2044
房地产业	Real Estate Trade	9985			6274
社会服务业	Social Services	274667	69786	24919	50839
卫生体育和社会福利业	Health Care,Sports and Social Welfare	52196	1683	3093	6514
教育文化艺术和广播影电视业	Education,Culture and Arts, Radio,Film and Television	243439	119444	10021	15354
科学研究和综合技术服务业	Scientific Research and Polytechnical Services	6451	3311	1327	128
国家机关，政党机关，社会团体	Government Agencies,Party Agencies,Social Organizations	226211	58758	21742	7098
其他行业	Others	33239	9000		

行业	Sector	衡阳市 Hengyang City	邵阳市 Shaoyang City	岳阳市 Yueyang City	常德市 Changde City
总计	**Total**	**125235**	**117230**	**134316**	**120988**
农林牧渔业	Farming,Forestry, Animal Husbandry and Fishery	2494	60	2891	602
采掘业	Mining and Quarrying		832	1074	
制造业	Manufacturing	3632	513	11521	16225
电力煤气及水的生产和供应业	Production and Supply of Electricity,Gas and Water	41823	39815	15721	22240
建筑业	Construction	126	1110	250	
地质勘查业、水利管理业	Geological Prospecting and Water Conservancy	5777	1201	38464	18053
交通运输仓储及邮电通信业	Transport,Storage,Post and Telecommunications	23893	17014	6785	5322
批发和零售贸易、餐饮业	Wholesale and Retail Trade, Catering Services	1310	2236	13256	4516
金融保险业	Finance and Insurance		1818	480	344
房地产业	Real Estate Trade		1990		878
社会服务业	Social Services	4635	5225	21197	27158
卫生体育和社会福利业	Health Care,Sports and Social Welfare	736	2434	1616	8159
教育文化艺术和广播影电视业	Education,Culture and Arts, Radio,Film and Television	14630	12995	7599	9540
科学研究和综合技术服务业	Scientific Research and Polytechnical Services	340	326		100
国家机关，政党机关，社会团体	Government Agencies,Party Agencies,Social Organizations	24245	14321	13462	7851
其他行业	Others	1594	15340		

单位:万元　　4 -4 续表　continued　　(10 000 yuan)

行业	Sector	张家界市 Zhangjiajie City	益阳市 Yiyang City	郴州市 Chenzhou City	永州市 Yongzhou City
]	**Total**	**33897**	**102256**	**211751**	**76477**
农林牧渔业	Farming,Forestry, Animal Husbandry and Fishery	327	3220	3864	1249
采掘业	Mining and Quarrying			1176	
制造业	Manufacturing		1348	17414	6705
电力煤气及水的生产和供应业	Production and Supply of Electricity,Gas and Water	700	12996	36653	18127
建筑业	Construction			528	1283
地质勘查业、水利管理业	Geological Prospecting and Water Conservancy	812	20666	2762	3452
交通运输仓储及邮电通信业	Transport,Storage,Post and Telecommunications	4702	7926	74729	10388
批发和零售贸易、餐饮业	Wholesale and Retail Trade, Catering Services	995	5941	12943	6134
金融保险业	Finance and Insurance		1822	1384	959
房地产业	Real Estate Trade				
社会服务业	Social Services	10992	9005	17434	12231
卫生体育和社会福利业	Health Care,Sports and Social Welfare		13317	5118	1768
教育文化艺术和广播影电视业	Education,Culture and Arts, Radio,Film and Television	3803	11967	10919	6671
科学研究和综合技术服务业	Scientific Research and Polytechnical Services	50	108	156	
国家机关，政党机关，社会团体	Government Agencies,Party Agencies,Social Organizations	11516	13720	26671	7348
其他行业	Others		220		162

行业	Sector	怀化市 Huaihua City	娄底市 Loudi City	湘西自治州 West Hunan A.P	不分地区 Not Classified by Region
总计	**Total**	**66985**	**35589**	**53489**	**426858**
农林牧渔业	Farming,Forestry, Animal Husbandry and Fishery	186	148	4109	
采掘业	Mining and Quarrying	556	74		
制造业	Manufacturing	1002	1476	2946	
电力煤气及水的生产和供应业	Production and Supply of Electricity,Gas and Water	11856	8506	13647	
建筑业	Construction	406	1807		
地质勘查业、水利管理业	Geological Prospecting and Water Conservancy	1401	2081	815	
交通运输仓储及邮电通信业	Transport,Storage,Post and Telecommunications	5075	4876	3949	426858
批发和零售贸易、餐饮业	Wholesale and Retail Trade, Catering Services	3550	679	6610	
金融保险业	Finance and Insurance	1053	1669	236	
房地产业	Real Estate Trade	843			
社会服务业	Social Services	15379	4256	1611	
卫生体育和社会福利业	Health Care,Sports and Social Welfare	3871	1826	2061	
教育文化艺术和广播影电视业	Education,Culture and Arts, Radio,Film and Television	7716	5268	7512	
科学研究和综合技术服务业	Scientific Research and Polytechnical Services	150		455	
国家机关，政党机关，社会团体	Government Agencies,Party Agencies,Social Organizations	7798	2273	9408	
其他行业	Others	6143	650	130	

4-5 基本建设项目个数、项目投产率(2001年)

Number of Capital Construction Projects, Rate of Projects Put into Use (2001)

市州及行业	Cities, Prefecture and Sector	投资额(亿元) Investment (100 millions yuan)	施工项目(个) Projects under Construction (unit)	全部建成投产项目(个) Projects Completed and Put into Uses (unit)	项目建成投产率(%) Rate of Project Completed and Put into Uses (%)	新增固定资产(亿元) Newly Increase Fixed Assets (100 million yuan)	固定资产交付使用率(%) Rate of Fixed Assets Turn Over to Uses (%)
全省总计	**Total**	**476.70**	**4271**	**2157**	**50.5**	**223.23**	**46.8**
按地市分	**By Region**						
长沙市	Changsha City	122.85	586	272	46.4	44.63	36.3
株洲市	Zhuzhou City	18.52	248	148	59.7	12.21	66
湘潭市	Xiangtan City	13.75	174	85	48.9	15.88	115.5
衡阳市	Hengyang City	22.01	307	174	56.7	12.52	56.9
邵阳市	Shaoyang City	14.08	362	182	50.3	11.72	83.3
岳阳市	Yueyang City	28.38	320	174	54.4	13.43	47.3
常德市	Changde City	33.52	371	136	36.7	12.10	36.1
张家界市	Zhangjiajie City	6.79	133	68	51.1	3.39	49.9
益阳市	Yiyang City	24.23	242	152	62.8	10.23	42.2
郴州市	Chenzhou City	28.28	495	308	62.2	21.18	74.9
永州市	Yongzhou City	15.00	302	124	41.1	7.65	51
怀化市	Huaihua City	15.20	326	152	46.6	6.70	44.1
娄底市	Loudi City	9.75	176	75	42.6	3.56	36.5
湘西自治州	West Hunan A.P	12.59	212	104	49.1	5.35	42.5
不分地区	Not Classified by Region	111.77	17	3	17.6	42.69	38.2
按行业分	**By Sector**						
农林牧渔业	Farming,Forestry, Animal Husbandry and Fishery	5.57	119	60	50.4	2.81	50.4
采掘业	Mining and Quarrying	0.68	31	16	51.6	0.50	72.6
制造业	Manufacturing	11.51	209	119	56.9	9.20	79.9
电力煤气及水的生产和供应业	Production and Supply of Electricity,Gas and Water	77.23	262	101	38.5	30.71	39.8
建筑业	Construction	1.45	40	18	45	0.77	53
地质勘查业、水利管理业	Geological Prospecting and Water Conservancy	27.14	231	111	48.1	13.90	51.2
交通运输、仓储及邮电通信业	Transport,Storage,Post and Telecommunications	160.21	555	218	39.3	65.35	40.8
批发和零售贸易餐饮业	Wholesale and Retail Trade, Catering Services	18.86	300	152	50.7	12.75	67.6
金融保险业	Finance and Insurance	2.59	87	51	58.6	2.64	101.8
房地产业	Real Estate Trade	1.00	22	11	50	1.00	100
社会服务业	Social Services	89.49	526	221	42	27.47	30.7
卫生体育和社会福利业	Health Care,Sports and Social Welfare	14.67	229	104	45.4	5.22	35.6
教育文化艺术和广播影电视业	Education,Culture and Arts,Radio, Film and Television	30.43	795	498	62.6	24.34	80
科学研究和综合技术服务业	Scientific Research and Polytechnical Services	1.92	45	23	51.1	0.65	33.7
国家机关、政党机关和社会团体	Government Agencies,Party Agencies and Social Organizations	30.64	769	431	56	22.62	73.8
其他行业	Others	3.31	51	23	45.1	3.32	100.3

4-6 各种分组的更新改造投资(2001年)

Technical Updates and Innovation Investment by Various Characteristics (2001)

单位:万元 (10 000 yuan)

市州	Cities and Prefecture	投资额 Total Investment	按构成分 Grouped by Use of Funds			按建设性质分 Grouped by Type of Construcyion		
			建安工程 Construction and Installation	设备工器具购置 Purchase of Equipment& Instruments	其他费用 Others	新建 New Construction	扩建 Expansion	改建 Re-construction
全 省	**Total**	**1983099**	**696292**	**1115046**	**171761**	**140863**	**999036**	**740073**
长沙市	Changsha	315499	116480	179155	19864	26932	234463	17651
株洲市	Zhuzhou	206940	74788	119798	12354	45578	102847	50711
湘潭市	Xiangtan	129718	51010	67557	11151	0	45763	78709
衡阳市	Hengyang	137305	45249	84762	7294	5700	20665	107206
邵阳市	Shaoyang	50207	23094	25258	1855	1055	32534	11572
岳阳市	Yueyang	262009	114454	136291	11264	22507	59830	172337
常德市	Changde	114900	35955	68711	10234	2900	36739	57785
张家界市	Zhangjiajie	25472	7861	16783	828	1290	15668	7814
益阳市	Yiyang	46292	13874	29909	2509	829	23080	20141
郴州市	Chenzhou	122825	40509	70807	11509	1234	56700	55605
永州市	Yongzhou	49458	6858	41496	1104	711	28707	13369
怀化市	Huaihua	95928	49248	41595	5085	4935	52016	37973
娄底市	Loudi	98090	51473	42739	3878		31376	66634
湘西	West Hunan	84232	28138	48635	7459	27192	47424	9566
不分地区	Not Classified	244224	37301	141550	65373		211224	33000

市州	Cities and Prefecture	按资金来源分 Grouped by Source of Funds					按隶属关系分 Grouped by Administrative Relationship	
		国家预算内 State Budgetary Appropriation	国内贷款 Domestic Loans	利用外资 Foreign Investment	自筹资金 Fundraising	其他投资 Others	中央项目 Central Projects	地方项目 Local Projects
全 省	**Total**	**99944**	**451053**	**35182**	**1270449**	**74944**	**1006963**	**804145**
长沙市	Changsha	2232	44031	12350	216934	3524	112902	106554
株洲市	Zhuzhou	43405	108192	4485	75932	4491	127688	74085
湘潭市	Xiangtan	14004	9197	1455	96209	6904	29132	95699
衡阳市	Hengyang	3300	17237	1145	102326	12527	39136	88479
邵阳市	Shaoyang	2323	13150	197	20456	4053	10675	38452
岳阳市	Yueyang	14438	39859	6773	142171	12865	167820	79021
常德市	Changde		19343	1430	91256	1300	96701	12873
张家界市	Zhangjiajie	485	8711		26388	1571	5798	13994
益阳市	Yiyang	1300	15923	1935	28541	2148	12461	29496
郴州市	Chenzhou	203	13489	1610	92850	9854	55075	58515
永州市	Yongzhou	311	7000		35103	2929	29136	18860
怀化市	Huaihua	16052	18473		58795	8095	30961	52990
娄底市	Loudi	490	3249		97264	3260	24746	73269
湘西	West Hunan	1401	36255	3802	43412	1423	20508	61858
不分地区	Not Classified		96944		142812		244224	

4-7 更新改造完成投资及新增固定资产(2001年)

Technical Updates and Innovation and Newly increased Fixed Assets (2001)

市州及行业	Cities, Prefecture and Sector	投资额(亿元) Invest-ment (100 millions yuan)	施工项目(个) Projects under Construc-tion (unit)	全部建成投产项目(个) Projects Completed and Put into Uses (unit)	项目建成投产率(%) Rate of Project Completed and Put into Uses (%)	新增固定资产(亿元) Newly Increase Fixed Assets (100 million yuan)	固定资产交付使用率(%) Rate of Fixed Assets Turn Over to Uses (%)
全省总计	**Total**	**198.31**	**2622**	**1779**	**67.8**	**158.93**	**80.1**
按地市分	**By Region**						
长沙市	Changsha City	31.55	133	50	37.6	29.56	93.7
株洲市	Zhuzhou City	20.69	172	107	62.2	13.36	64.5
湘潭市	Xiangtan City	12.97	136	83	61.0	13.22	101.9
衡阳市	Hengyang City	13.73	365	260	71.2	9.82	71.5
邵阳市	Shaoyang City	5.02	334	307	91.9	4.60	91.5
岳阳市	Yueyang City	26.20	198	120	60.6	17.24	65.8
常德市	Changde City	11.49	178	101	56.7	4.57	39.8
张家界市	Zhangjiajie City	2.55	41	23	56.1	1.64	64.4
益阳市	Yiyang City	4.63	60	32	53.3	3.42	73.9
郴州市	Chenzhou City	12.28	403	336	83.4	10.46	85.2
永州市	Yongzhou City	4.95	68	38	55.9	3.63	73.5
怀化市	Huaihua City	9.59	195	106	54.4	6.30	65.7
娄底市	Loudi City	9.81	111	84	75.7	13.44	137.0
湘西自治州	West Hunan A.P	8.42	116	96	82.8	8.59	102.0
不分地区	Not Classified by Region	24.42	112	36	32.1	19.09	78.2
按行业分	**By Sector**						
农林牧渔业	Farming,Forestry, Animal Husbandry and Fishery	0.01	1				
采掘业	Mining and Quarrying	4.17	146	90	61.6	3.15	75.6
制造业	Manufacturing	98.72	1004	567	56.5	81.33	82.4
电力煤气及水的生产和供应业	Production and Supply of Electricity,Gas and Water	10.38	203	142	70.0	4.51	43.5
建筑业	Construction	1.59				1.59	100.0
地质勘查业、水利管理业	Geological Prospecting and Water Conservancy	0.11	8	7	87.5	0.09	85.4
交通运输、仓储及邮电通信业	Transport,Storage,Post and Telecommunications	69.74	1074	850	79.1	58.54	83.9
批发和零售贸易餐饮业	Wholesale and Retail Trade, Catering Services	2.95	58	40	69.0	0.99	33.7
金融保险业	Finance and Insurance	0.14	1	1	100.0	0.14	100.0
房地产业	Real Estate Trade						
社会服务业	Social Services	2.11	29	23	79.3	1.98	93.9
卫生体育和社会福利业	Health Care,Sports and Social Welfare	1.89	19	4	21.1	1.62	85.6
教育文化艺术和广播影电视业	Education,Culture and Arts,Radio, Film and Television	3.82	44	26	59.1	2.25	59.0
科学研究和综合技术服务业	Scientific Research and Polytechnical Services	1.74	12	11	91.7	1.81	103.6
国家机关、政党机关和社会团体	Government Agencies,Party Agencies and Social Organizations	0.75	18	13	72.2	0.73	97.6
其他行业	Others	0.20	5	5	100.0	0.20	100.0

4-8 国有经济固定资产投资及构成

Investment in Fixed Assets and Its Composition of State – Owned Units

年份 Year	固定资产投资总额 Total Investment in Fixed Assets	基本建设 Capital Construction	更新改造 Innovation	房地产开发 Real Estae Development	其他 Others	新增固定资产 Newly Increased Fixed Assets	基本建设 Capital Construction	更新改造 Innovation	房地产开发 Real Estae Development	其他 Others
绝对数(亿元)	**Absolute Figure (100 million yuan)**									
1978	14.71	13.51	1.20			10.56	9.65	0.91		
1980	20.32	15.53	4.79			15.24	11.98	3.26		
1985	43.86	25.58	16.20		2.08	30.66	16.91	12.19		1.56
1986	50.40	28.00	20.17		2.23	33.55	19.33	13.94		0.28
1987	60.98	32.47	25.44		3.07	46.68	25.97	19.88		0.83
1988	72.97	38.03	31.42		3.52	56.80	32.77	20.94		3.09
1989	62.94	37.34	24.28		1.32	43.86	24.50	18.22		1.14
1990	72.01	43.11	25.24	2.14	1.52	47.27	25.68	18.81	1.37	1.41
1991	94.85	56.10	32.45	3.20	3.10	82.36	50.75	27.20	2.19	2.22
1992	149.72	90.89	49.17	7.42	2.24	117.07	75.01	36.25	4.05	1.76
1993	203.17	122.75	61.72	15.12	3.58	125.96	69.83	45.07	7.75	3.31
1994	251.21	162.99	70.63	13.81	3.78	154.80	92.09	51.48	7.66	3.57
1995	316.90	209.70	79.85	21.61	5.74	202.81	117.55	68.57	11.88	4.81
1996	375.27	245.10	104.67	17.50	8.00	269.99	163.23	86.82	13.12	6.82
1997	366.34	238.01	89.42	15.79	23.12	269.20	156.86	93.81	11.16	7.37
1998	457.00	306.81	106.43	17.61	26.15	290.91	192.02	75.06	13.57	10.26
1999	522.95	348.31	127.29	22.17	25.18	348.43	233.99	90.40	17.47	6.57
2000	574.12	376.40	145.29	25.21	27.22	388.40	245.12	117.79	16.38	9.11
2001	618.54	433.90	146.88	25.25	12.51	349.76	203.59	115.39	18.69	12.09
构成(%)	**Composition in Percentage (%)**									
1978	100.0	91.8	8.2			100.0	91.4	8.6		
1980	100.0	76.4	23.6			100.0	78.6	21.4		
1985	100.0	58.3	36.9		4.8	100.0	55.1	39.8		5.1
1986	100.0	55.6	40.0		4.4	100.0	57.6	41.6		0.8
1987	100.0	53.3	41.7		5.0	100.0	55.6	42.6		1.8
1988	100.0	52.1	43.1		4.8	100.0	57.7	36.9		5.4
1989	100.0	59.3	38.6		2.1	100.0	55.7	41.5		2.6
1990	100.0	59.9	35.0	3.0	2.1	100.0	54.3	39.8	2.9	3.0
1991	100.0	59.1	34.2	3.4	3.3	100.0	61.6	33.0	2.7	2.7
1992	100.0	60.7	32.8	5.0	1.5	100.0	64.0	31.0	3.5	1.5
1993	100.0	60.4	30.4	7.4	1.8	100.0	55.4	35.8	6.2	2.6
1994	100.0	64.9	28.1	5.5	1.5	100.0	59.5	33.3	4.9	2.3
1995	100.0	66.2	25.2	6.8	1.8	100.0	58.0	33.8	5.8	2.4
1996	100.0	65.3	27.9	4.7	2.1	100.0	60.4	32.2	4.9	2.5
1997	100.0	65.0	24.4	4.3	6.3	100.0	58.3	34.8	4.1	2.7
1998	100.0	67.1	23.3	3.9	5.7	100.0	66.0	25.8	4.7	3.5
1999	100.0	66.6	24.3	4.2	4.8	100.0	67.2	25.9	5.0	1.9
2000	100.0	65.6	25.3	4.4	4.7	100.0	63.1	30.3	4.2	2.4
2001	100.0	70.1	23.7	4.1	2.0	100.0	58.2	33.0	5.3	3.5

注:自1997年开始,其他投资中含50万元以下项目投资。

The investments beyond 500,000 yuan were included in other types of investment since 1997.

4-9 国有经济各种分组的固定资产投资

Investment in Fixed Assets of State - Owned Units by Various Characteristics

指 标	Item	1995	1999	2000	2001	2001年比上年±% Increase Rate in 2001 over 2000 (%)
投资总额(亿元)	**Total Investment (100 million yuan)**	**316.90**	**522.95**	**574.12**	**618.54**	**7.7**
按资金来源分	**Grouped by Source of Funds**					
国家预算内投资	State Budgetary Appropriation	18.36	64.65	57.21	69.34	21.2
国内贷款	Domestic Loans	77.34	124.13	180.12	159.89	-11.2
债 券	Bonds	0.69	8.11	2.34	1.37	-41.5
利用外资	Foreign Investment	23.18	14.52	13.67	18.68	36.7
自筹投资	Fundraising	144.00	217.72	240.50	311.58	29.6
股票	Shares	0.05	1.29	3.65	1.40	-61.5
其他投资	Others	53.33	93.82	80.28	57.68	-28.2
按隶属关系分	**Grouped by Administrative Relationship**					
中央项目	Central Government Projects	141.13	219.50	246.75	217.45	-11.9
地方项目	Local Projects	175.14	283.29	326.61	399.60	22.3
其 它	Others	0.63	20.16	0.76	1.50	97.9
按构成分	**Grouped by Use of Funds**					
建筑安装工程	Construction and Installation	194.80	367.12	394.25	409.64	3.9
设备、工具、器具购置	Purchase of Equipment and Instruments	81.38	89.72	119.42	127.63	6.9
其他费用	Others	40.72	72.22	60.45	81.27	34.4
按建设性质分	**Grouped by Type of Construction**					
新建	New Construction	125.46	207.96	177.16	229.62	29.6
扩建	Expansion	107.46	191.31	186.39	198.75	6.6
改建	Reconstruction	58.83	97.60	132.98	128.41	-3.4
按国民经济主要行业分	**Grouped by Main Sector**					
农业	Agriculture	0.83	2.70	4.42	4.50	1.9
工业	Industry	127.58	112.84	136.29	144.25	5.8
#能源工业	Energy	61.33	77.41	75.46	88.36	17.1
运输邮电业	Transportation,Postal and Telecommunications Services	82.25	209.18	242.17	227.60	-6.0
新增固定资产(亿元)	**Newly Increased Fixed Assets (100 million yuan)**	**202.81**	**348.43**	**388.40**	**349.76**	**-9.9**
房屋建筑面积(万平方米)	**Floor Space of Buildings (10 000 sq.m)**					
施工面积	Floor Space Under Construction	2631.38	2839.09	2429.83	2283.26	-6.0
竣工面积	Floor Space Completed	1337.96	1630.57	1262.35	1094.14	-13.3
#住宅	# Residential Buildings	747.66	1103.77	718.01	606.58	-15.5

4-10 国有经济各行业固定资产投资(2001年)

Investment in Fixed Assets of State-Owned Units by Sector (2001)

行 业	Sector	固定资产投资额 Investment in Fixed Assets	基本建设 Capital Construction	更新改造 Innovation
绝对数(亿元)	**Absolute Figure (100 million yuan)**			
全省总计	**Total**	**618.54**	**433.9**	**146.88**
农、林、牧、渔业	Farming,Forestry,Animal Husbandry and Fishery	4.50	4.19	0.01
采掘业	Mining and Quarrying	3.51	0.68	2.70
制造业	Manufacturing	61.59	4.17	57.13
电力、煤气及水的生产和供应业	Production and Supply of Electricity,Gas and Water	79.16	68.98	10.08
建筑业	Construction	3.06	1.37	1.59
地质勘查业、水利管理业	Geological Prospecting and Water Conservancy	27.28	26.73	0.10
交通运输、仓储及邮电通信业	Transport,Storage,Post and Telecommunications	230.48	158.33	65.10
批发和零售贸易、餐饮业	Wholesale and Retail Trade and Catering Services	14.30	12.49	1.79
金融、保险业	Finance and Insurance	2.78	2.59	0.14
房地产业	Real Estate Trade	25.76	0.51	
社会服务业	Social Services	81.81	78.70	1.96
卫生、体育和社会福利业	Health Care,Sports and Social Welfare	17.31	14.67	1.89
教育、文化艺术和广播电影电视业	Education,Culture and Arts,Radio,Film and Television	27.89	25.23	1.92
科学研究和综合技术服务业	Scientific Research and Polytechnical Services	3.70	1.92	1.74
国家机关、政党机关和社会团体	Government Agencies,Party Agencies and Social Organizations	32.68	30.60	0.73
其他行业	Others	2.75	2.75	
构成（%）	**Composition in Percentage（%）**			
全省总计	**Total**	**100**	**100**	**100**
农、林、牧、渔业	Farming,Forestry,Animal Husbandry and Fishery	0.7	1.0	
采掘业	Mining and Quarrying	0.6	0.2	1.8
制造业	Manufacturing	10.0	1.0	38.9
电力、煤气及水的生产和供应业	Production and Supply of Electricity,Gas and Water	12.8	15.9	6.9
建筑业	Construction	0.5	0.3	1.1
地质勘查业、水利管理业	Geological Prospecting and Water Conservancy	4.4	6.2	0.1
交通运输、仓储及邮电通信业	Transport,Storage,Post and Telecommunications	37.3	36.5	44.3
批发和零售贸易、餐饮业	Wholesale and Retail Trade and Catering Services	2.3	2.9	1.2
金融、保险业	Finance and Insurance	0.5	0.6	0.1
房地产业	Real Estate Trade	4.2	0.1	
社会服务业	Social Services	13.2	18.1	1.3
卫生、体育和社会福利业	Health Care,Sports and Social Welfare	2.8	3.4	1.3
教育、文化艺术和广播电影电视业	Education,Culture and Arts,Radio,Film and Television	4.5	5.8	1.3
科学研究和综合技术服务业	Scientific Research and Polytechnical Services	0.6	0.4	1.2
国家机关、政党机关和社会团体	Government Agencies,Party Agencies and Social Organizations	5.3	7.1	0.5
其他行业	Others	0.4	0.6	

4-11 国有经济各行业新增固定资产（2001年）

Newly Increased Fixed Assets of State-Owned Units by Sector (2001)

行业	Sector	新增固定资产 Newly Increased Fixed Assets	#基本建设 Capital Construction	#更新改造 Innovation
绝对数(亿元)	**Absolute Figure (100 million yuan)**			
全省总计	**Total**	**349.76**	**203.59**	**115.39**
农、林、牧、渔业	Farming,Forestry,Animal Husbandry and Fishery	2.61	2.53	
采掘业	Mining and Quarrying	2.83	0.5	2.22
制造业	Manufacturing	48.94	3.71	44.93
电力、煤气及水的生产和供应业	Production and Supply of Electricity,Gas and Water	29.32	25.69	3.54
建筑业	Construction	2.32	0.71	1.59
地质勘查业、水利管理业	Geological Prospecting and Water Conservancy	14.41	13.9	0.08
交通运输、仓储及邮电通信业	Transport,Storage,Post and Telecommunications	125.98	64.34	54.57
批发和零售贸易、餐饮业	Wholesale and Retail Trade and Catering Services	10.14	9.25	0.87
金融、保险业	Finance and Insurance	2.82	2.64	0.14
房地产业	Real Estate Trade	19.29	0.6	
社会服务业	Social Services	28.39	25.13	1.88
卫生、体育和社会福利业	Health Care,Sports and Social Welfare	7.62	5.22	1.62
教育、文化艺术和广播电影电视业	Education,Culture and Arts,Radio,Film and Television	24.9	23.11	1.42
科学研究和综合技术服务业	Scientific Research and Polytechnical Services	2.49	0.65	1.81
国家机关、政党机关和社会团体	Government Agencies,Party Agencies and Social Organizations	24.69	22.62	0.73
其他行业	Others	3	3	
构成（%）	**Composition in Percentage (%)**			
全省总计	**Total**	**100**	**100**	**100**
农、林、牧、渔业	Farming,Forestry,Animal Husbandry and Fishery	0.75	1.24	
采掘业	Mining and Quarrying	0.81	0.25	1.92
制造业	Manufacturing	13.99	1.82	38.94
电力、煤气及水的生产和供应业	Production and Supply of Electricity,Gas and Water	8.38	12.62	3.07
建筑业	Construction	0.66	0.35	1.38
地质勘查业、水利管理业	Geological Prospecting and Water Conservancy	4.12	6.83	0.07
交通运输、仓储及邮电通信业	Transport,Storage,Post and Telecommunications	36.02	31.6	47.29
批发和零售贸易、餐饮业	Wholesale and Retail Trade and Catering Services	2.9	4.54	0.75
金融、保险业	Finance and Insurance	0.81	1.3	0.12
房地产业	Real Estate Trade	5.52	0.29	
社会服务业	Social Services	8.12	12.34	1.63
卫生、体育和社会福利业	Health Care,Sports and Social Welfare	2.18	2.56	1.4
教育、文化艺术和广播电影电视业	Education,Culture and Arts,Radio,Film and Television	7.12	11.35	1.23
科学研究和综合技术服务业	Scientific Research and Polytechnical Services	0.71	0.32	1.57
国家机关、政党机关和社会团体	Government Agencies,Party Agencies and Social Organizations	7.06	11.11	0.63
其他行业	Others	0.86	1.47	

4-12 国有经济房屋建设指标(2001年)

Indicators of Building Construction of State – Owned Units(2001)

指 标	Item	合 计 Total	基本建设 Capital Construction	更新改造 Innovation	房地产开发 Real Estate Development	其他固定资产投资 Others
施工房屋面积 (万平方米)	Floor Space of Buildings under Construction (10 000 sq.m)	2283.26	1804.22	88.22	383.44	7.39
住宅	Residential Buildings	1043.6	705.9	5.88	329.57	2.24
竣工房屋面积 (万平方米)	Floor Space Completed (10 000 sq.m)	1094.14	829.35	49.59	210.75	4.44
住宅	Residential Buildings	606.58	413.44	4.61	186.28	2.24
竣工房屋价值 (万元)	Value of Buildings Completed (10 000 yuan)	863273	649025	46189	164705	3354
住宅	Residential Buildings	378852	239543	2578	135721	1010
房屋建筑面积竣工率 (%)	Rate of Floor Space of Buildings Completed (%)	47.92	45.97	56.21	54.96	60.08
住宅	Residential Buildings	58.12	58.57	78.4	56.52	100
竣工房屋单位面积造价 (元/平方米)	Cost of Buildings Completed (yuan/sq.m)	789	782.57	931.42	781.52	755.41
住宅	Residential Buildings	624.57	579.39	559.22	728.59	450.89

4-13 国有经济分地市项目个数、项目投产率及固定资产交付使用率(2001)

Number of Projects, Rate of Projects Put into Use and Rate of Fixed Assets Put into Use of State—Owned Units (2001)

市州	Cities and Prefecture	施工项目个数(个) Number of Projects under Construction (unit)	全投项目个数(个) Number of Projects Completed and Put into Use (unit)	项目投产率(%) Rate of Projects Completed and Put into Use (%)	固定资产交付使用率(%) Rate of Fixed Assets Put into Use (%)
全省总计	**Total**	**6434**	**3750**	**58.3**	**56.5**
长沙市	Changsha	666	325	48.8	48.1
株洲市	Zhuzhou	408	267	65.4	67.7
湘潭市	Xiangtan	250	142	56.8	112.6
衡阳市	Hengyang	616	404	65.6	63.1
邵阳市	Shaoyang	667	470	70.5	84.9
岳阳市	Yueyang	467	279	59.7	57.2
常德市	Changde	504	218	43.3	33.4
张家界市	Zhangjiajie	174	91	52.3	58.6
益阳市	Yiyang	282	173	61.3	49.0
郴州市	Chenzhou	841	608	72.3	75.4
永州市	Yongzhou	374	162	43.3	58.9
怀化市	Huaihua	451	222	49.2	63.4
娄底市	Loudi	298	167	56.0	85.8
湘西自治州	West Hunan	307	183	59.6	60.3
不分地区	Not Classified by Region	129	39	30.2	45.4

注: 施工、全投项目及项目投产率未包括房地产开发统计资料。

The data of projects under construction, projects completed put into use and rate of projects completed put into use excluded information of real estate development.

4-14 国有经济基本建设投资

Investment in Capital Construction of State – Owned Units

类 别	Item	1995	1999	2000	2001
投资总额(亿元)	**Total Investment (100 million yuan)**	**209.70**	**348.31**	**376.40**	**433.90**
按资金来源分	**Grouped by Source of Funds**				
国家预算内投资	State Budgetary Appropriation	17.27	59.27	52.44	59.45
国内贷款	Domestic Loans	48.20	74.38	118.63	116.99
债 券	Bonds	0.59	7.81	2.06	1.14
利用外资	Foreign Investment	15.56	13.70	12.42	17.76
自筹投资	Fundraising	96.72	133.64	147.32	198.06
其他投资	Others	31.36	59.51	43.53	40.50
按隶属关系分	**Grouped by Administrative Relationship**				
中央项目	Central Government Projects	94.05	124.96	142.03	122.78
地方项目	Local Projects	115.45	222.79	234.12	310.44
其 它	Others	0.20	0.56	0.25	0.68
按构成分	**Grouped by Use of Funds**				
建筑安装工程	Construction and Installation	147.49	290.72	286.10	333.93
设备、工器具购置	Purchase of Equipment and Instruments	33.62	24.55	46.90	41.22
其他费用	Others	28.59	33.04	43.39	58.76
按建设性质分	**Grouped by Type of Construction**				
新建	New Construction	101.46	149.39	174.39	220.42
扩建	Expansion	66.01	115.25	93.58	128.97
改建	Reconstruction	19.42	46.52	81.21	58.58
按大中小类型分	**Grouped by Sized**				
大中型项目	Large and Medium Sized	79.74	78.83	54.79	17.05
小型项目	Small Sized	128.81	269.48	320.56	414.93
按行业主要门类分	**Grouped by Main Sector**				
农业	Agriculture	0.71	2.48	3.85	4.19
工业	Industry	73.85	66.17	83.49	73.83
轻工业	Light Industry	7.25	5.98		3.50
重工业	Heavy Industry	66.60	60.19		70.33
#能源工业	Energy Industry	54.75	58.08	72.75	66.71
运输邮电仓储业	Transportation,Postal, Telecommunications and Storage	53.66	127.19	150.90	158.33
新增固定资产 (亿元)	**Newly Increased Fixed Assets (100 million yuan)**	**117.55**	**233.99**	**245.12**	**203.59**
建设项目个数 (个)	**Number of Projects (unit)**				
施工项目	Number of Projects under Construction	5304	4857	4057	4043
大中型项目	Large and Medium Sized	52	43	29	19
全部建成投产项目	Number of Projects Completed and Put into Use	3026	2955	2380	2051
大中型项目	Large and Medium Sized	5	4	8	1
房屋建筑面积 (万㎡)	**Floor Space of Buildings (10 000 sq.m)**				
施工面积	Floor Space Under Construction	1876.10	2259.55	1898.50	1804.22
#住宅	Residential Buildings	897.79	1289.01	861.52	705.90
竣工面积	Floor Space Completed	1023.02	1312.06	984.46	829.35
#住宅	Residential Buildings	541.93	846.60	510.31	413.44

4-15 国有经济基本建设项目计划总投资完成情况

Situation in Completion of Investment in Capital Construction of Projects of Projects of State–Owned Units and Situation Completed

单位：亿元 (100 million yuan)

指 标	Item	1995	1999	2000	2001
基本建设项目	**Capital Construction Projects**				
计划总投资	Panning Gross Investment	726.28	1344.72	1407.95	1578.83
自开始建设至本年底累计完成投资	Accumulative Investment Actually Made Since Starting of Construction up to the Year-end	462.13	769.05	845.87	898.15
本年完成投资	Investment Made in This Year	209.7	348.31	376.4	433.9
本年新开工项目投资	Started Projects This Year	49.52	99.54	137.19	131.2
累计新增固定资产	Accumulative Newly Increased Fixed Assets	195.32	314.92	370.32	262.27
未完工程投资	Investment of Uncompleted Projects	247.28	332.11	434.43	546.73
全部建成尚需投资	Further Investment Required for the Completion of Construction	372.4	607.85	572.14	703.79
未完工程占用率 (%)	Rate of Investment in Projects Uncompleted (%)	117.9	95.35	115.42	126
建设周期（年）	Period to Complete Panning Gross Investment (year)	3.42	3.86	3.74	3.64
基本建设大中型项目	**Large and Medium Capital Construction Projects**				
计划总投资	Panning Gross Investment	430.67	444.11	344.3	187.14
自开始建设至本年底累计完成投资	Accumulative Investment Actually Made Since Starting of Construction up to the Year-end	229.77	300.33	220.73	69.39
本年完成投资	Investment Made in This Year	80.7	78.83	54.79	17.05
本年新开工项目投资	Started projects This Year	1.66	0.56	2.43	2.09
累计新增固定资产	Accumulative Newly Increased Fixed Assets	72.6	124.54	101.86	12.22
未完工程投资	Investment of Uncompleted Projects	144.19	122.2	115.92	56.81
全部建成尚需投资	Further Investment Required for the Completion of Construction	200.9	371.38	123.23	121.23
未完工程占用率（%）	Rate of Investment in Projects Uncompleted (%)	178.7	155	211.57	333.2
建设周期（年）	Period to Complete Panning Gross Investment (year)	4.85	5.63	6.28	10.98

4-16 国有经济重点行业固定资产投资

Investment in Fixed Assets of State—Owned Units in Key Sector

项目	Item	1995	1999	2000	2001
投资额（亿元）	**Investment (100 million yuan)**				
农 业	Agriculture	0.83	2.70	4.42	4.50
轻工业	Light Industry	19.35	13.73	13.70	19.52
重工业	Heavy Industry	108.23	99.11	122.59	124.73
能源工业	Energy Industry	61.33	77.41	88.95	88.36
运输邮电仓储业	Transportation,Postal and Telecommunications, Storage	82.25	209.18	244.10	230.48
构成（%）	**Percentage (%)**				
农 业	Agriculture	0.3	0.5	0.8	0.7
轻工业	Light Industry	6.1	2.6	2.4	3.2
重工业	Heavy Industry	34.2	19.0	21.4	20.2
能源工业	Energy Industry	19.4	14.8	15.5	14.3
运输邮电仓储业	Transportation,Postal and Telecommunications Storage	26.0	40.0	42.5	37.3
基建投资额(亿元)	**Investment in Capital Construction (100 million yuan)**				
农 业	Agriculture	0.71	2.48	3.85	4.19
轻工业	Light Industry	7.25	5.98	5.02	3.5
重工业	Heavy Industry	66.60	60.19	78.47	70.33
能源工业	Energy Industry	54.75	58.08	74.90	66.71
运输邮电仓储业	Transportation,Postal and Telecommunications Storage	53.66	127.19	150.90	158.33
构成（%）	**Percentage (%)**				
农 业	Agriculture	0.3	0.7	1.0	1.0
轻工业	Light Industry	3.5	1.7	1.3	0.8
重工业	Heavy Industry	31.8	17.3	20.8	16.2
能源工业	Energy Industry	26.1	16.7	19.9	15.4
运输邮电仓储业	Transportation,Postal and Telecommunications Storage	25.6	36.5	40.1	36.5

4-17 国有经济按用途分的更新改造投资

Technical Updating and Innovation Investment of State–Owned Units by Purpose

指 标	Item	更改投资（万元） Investment in Innovation (10 000 yuan)			构 成 (%) Percentage (%)		
		1995	2000	2001	1995	2000	2001
总计	**Total**	**798532**	**1452907**	**1468814**	**100.0**	**100.0**	**100.0**
增产	Increase Production	311143	296334	347163	39.0	20.4	23.6
节约能源	Energy Saving	14078	37122	21123	1.8	2.6	1.4
其他节约	Other Saving Measures	2396	10608	4734	0.3	0.7	0.3
增加品种	Increase Production Variety	94837	66931	161570	11.9	4.6	11.0
提高产品质量	Improving Product Quality	79705	176065	120693	10.0	12.1	8.2
三废治理	Treatment of Waste Water, Waste Gas and Solid Wastes	11105	22434	29796	1.4	1.5	2.0
其他	Others	285268	843413	783735	35.6	58.1	53.4
在总计中：住宅	**Residential Buildings**	**24432**	**14829**	**4747**	**3.1**	**1.0**	**0.3**

4-18 基本建设新增生产能力(2001年)

Newly Increased Production Capacity (2001)

生产能力(或效益)名称	Item	合计 Total	国有经济 State-owned Economic	其他经济 Other Types of Ownership
水力发电(万千瓦)	Hydropower (10000kw)	10.78	4.48	6.30
输电线路长度(11万伏及以上)(公里)	Transmission Line (>110000 v) (km)	543.86	543.86	
变电设备(11万伏及以上)(万千伏安)	Electric Substation Equipment (>110000 v)(10000 kva)	351.90	351.90	
水　泥(万吨/年)	Cement (10000 tons/year)	15		15
合成氨(吨/年)	Synthetic Ammonia (ton/year)	100000		100000
输液(万瓶/年)	Drip - feed (10000 bottles/year)	80	80	
摩托车制造(辆/年)	Motor Cycle (unit/year)	100000		100000
新建公路(公里)	Length of New Highways (km)	589.11	587.61	1.50
其中:高速公路(公里)	Expressway	135.37	135.37	
一级公路(公里)	First-class Highway	84.55	84.55	
二级公路(公里)	Second-class Highway	124.35	124.35	
改建公路(公里)	Length of Reconstructed Highways (km)	415.96	393.26	22.70
二级公路(公里)	Second-class Highway	145.48	125.48	20.00
新建独立公路桥梁(延长米)	Newly Built Highway Bridge (extend metre)	3434.28	3434.28	
(座)	(set)	9	9	
新(扩)建港口码头(年吞吐量:万吨)	Newly Built or Expanded Ports (Annual Handling Capacity:10000 tons)	6	6	
(泊位:个)	(Number of Berth : unit)	1	1	
新(扩)建客、货运站(个)	Newly Built or Expanded Passenger and Freight Station	4	4	
(平方米)	(sq.m)	10710	10710	
候机楼(座)	Number of Departure Hall (unit)	1	1	
(平方米)	(sq.m)	11878.00	11878.00	
耕地面积(万亩)	Cultivated Land Area (10000 mu)	0.10	0.10	
造林面积(万亩)	Afforested Area (10000 mu)	30.80	30.80	
水库容量(总库容)(亿立方米)	Reservoir Capacity (100 million m^3)	0.80	0.80	
有效灌溉面积(万亩)	Effective Irrigated Area (10000 mu)	25.23	25.23	
除涝面积(万亩)	Flooded or Water Logged Area Under Control (10000 mu)	2.33	2.33	
粮食仓库(万公斤)	Grain Storehouse (10000 kg)	34353	34353	
(平方米)	(sq.m)	75962	75962	
高等院校:学生席位(个)	Number of Student seat of Universit and College	29535	18535	11000
建筑面积(平方米)	(sq.m)	153842	119828	34014
中等学校:学生席位(个)	Number of Student seat of Regular Secondary School	78414	76934	1480
建筑面积(平方米)	(sq.m)	260325	249225	11100
小学校:学生席位(个)	Number of Student seat of Primary School	29203	28403	800
建筑面积(平方米)	(sq.m)	97631	83415	14216
其他院校:学生席位(个)	Number of Student seat of Other School	7850	7850	
建筑面积(平方米)	(sq.m)	29008	29008	
公共图书馆:藏书量(万册(件))	Collections of Public Library	148	148	
阅览室座席(个)	Seating Capacity of Reading Room	1180	1180	
建筑面积(平方米)	(sq.m)	10438	10438	
医院病床(张)	Number of Hospital Bed	1469	1469	
宾馆、旅馆、招待所客房数 (间)	Number of Hotel Guest-Room	2305	1445	860
(平方米)	(sq.m)	49499	24025	25474
城市自来水供水能力(万吨/日)	Capacity of City Tap Water Supply (10000 tons/day)	30	10	20
城市自来水管道长度(公里)	Length of City Tap Water Pipe (km)	34.15	20.15	14.00
城市公共交通车辆购置(辆)	Purchase of City Bus (unit)	20	20	
城市道路扩建长度(公里)	Length of City Road Extended (km)	85.48	83.71	1.77
城市道路扩建面积(万平方米)	Area of City Road Extended (10000 sq.m)	158.08	154.28	3.80
城市排水管道铺设长度(公里)	Length of Sewer Pipelines (km)	42.93	42.93	
城市永久性桥梁(座)	Number of City Bridge (unit)	4	4	
城市防洪堤长度(公里)	Length of City Embarkment (km)	17.93	17.93	

4-19 更新改造新增生产能力(2001年)

Newly Increased Production Capacity (2001)

生产能力(或效益)名称	Item	合计 Total	国有经济 State-owned Economic	其他经济 Other Types of Ownership
原煤开采(万吨/年)	Loal Mining (10000 tons/year)	25.7	21.5	4.2
人造富铁矿(万吨/年)	Man-made Ferrous Ore (10000 tons/year)	12	12	
水力发电(万千瓦)	Hydropower (10000kw)	1.47	0.62	0.85
变电设备能力(11万伏及以上)(万千伏安)	Electric Substation Equipment (>110000 v)(10000 kva)	31.5	31.5	
水　泥(万吨/年)	Cement (10000 tons/year)	34.5	26.5	8
硫　酸(吨/年)	Sulfuric Acid (ton/year)	155000	95000	60000
合成氨(吨/年)	Synthetic Ammonia (ton/year)	2000	2000	
氮肥(吨/年)	Chemical Fertilizer (ton/year)	2200	2200	
化学农药(吨/年)	Chemical Pesticide (ton/year)	2000		2000
精甲醇(吨/年)	Alcohol Refined (ton/year)	5000	5000	
化学纤维(吨/年)	Chemical Fiber (ton/year)	37000		37000
其中:合成纤维(吨/年)	Synthetic Fiber (ton/year)	30000		30000
棉纺锭(锭)	Cotton Spindles (unit)	1760	960	800
白　酒(万吨/年)	Wine (10000 tons/year)	0.01	0.01	
软饮料(吨/年)	Soft Beverage (ton/year)	8800	800	8000
机制纸浆(万吨/年)	Machine -made Paper Puip (10000 tons/year)	3	3	
机制纸(万吨/年)	Machine -made Paper (10000 tons/year)	5.01	5.01	
日用陶瓷器(万件/年)	Daily -use Ceramics (10000 pcs/year)	120		120
改建公路(公里)	Length of Reconstructed Highways (km)	196.82	196.82	
一级公路(公里)	First-class Highway	12	12	
城市自来水供水能力(万吨/日)	Capacity of City Tap Water Supply (10000 tons/day)	6	6	
城市自来水管道长度(公里)	Length of City Tap Water Pipe (km)	3.4	3.4	
城市公共交通车辆购置(辆)	Purchase of City Bus (unit)	606	606	
城市道路扩建长度(公里)	Length of City Road Extended (km)	10.5	10.5	
城市道路扩建面积(万平方米)	Area of City Road Extended (10000 sq.m)	26	26	

4-20 基本建设大中型、更新改造限额以上及重点项目基本情况(2001年)

Basic Statistics on Investment in Capital Construction of Large and Medium Projects,and Technical Uppdating and Innovation in Above - norm (2001)

项目名称 Item	开工时间(年·月) Starting Date (y.m)	投产时间(年·月) The Date for Put into Use (y.m)	计划总投资(万元) Total Invest-ment Planned (10 000 yuan)	累计完成投资(万元) Accu-mulative Investment Acually Made (10 000 yuan)	本年完成投资(万元) Investment Made this Year (10 000 yuan)
基本建设大中型项目：					
Capital Construction of Large and Medium Projects:					
湘潭市湘江三大桥 Xiangtan Xiang River NO.3 Bridge	1998.06	2001.04	18500	18714	260
湘潭北农大生猪产业化示范工程 Xiangtan demonstrative Pig Iadustrial Project	1998.03	2001.03	10500	5200	1825
湘潭市自来水公司一水厂搬迁 NO.1 Factory Removal Project of Xiangtan Tap Water Corporation	1999.03		11014	6053	2000
湖南五凌水电开发有限责任公司近尾洲水电站 Jinweizhou Hydropower Station of Hunan Wuling Hydropower Development Limited liability Corp	1994.01		59100	59043	16024
耒阳电厂二期 Second Phrase of Leiyang Electric Power Corp.	2001.06		284963	6285	6285
隆回县六都寨灌区灌溉工程 Irrigation Project of Liuduzai Irrigation District in Longhui County	1991.1		37500	26544	2048
湖南巫水流域水利水电开发有限责任公司白云电站 Baiyun Hydropower Station of Hunan Wushui Hydropower and Conservancy Limited Liabitity Corporation	1991.01		43000	42377	811
邵阳市大圳灌区工程 Irrigation Project of Dazhen Irrigation District in Shaoyang City	1965.10		12300	11360	144
岳阳市铁山灌区工程 Irrigation Project of Tieshang Irrigation District in Yueyang City	1977.11		26276	39277	200
岳阳城陵矶粮食专用码头 Yueyang Chenglingji Port for Food Special Purpose	1995.01		20101	19526	891
☆岳阳市洞庭湖大桥 Yueyang Dongting Lake Bridge	1996.12		78689	77901	200

4 -20 续表 1 continued

项目名称 Item	开工时间(年·月) Starting Date (y.m)	投产时间(年·月) The Date for Put into Use (y.m)	计划总投资(万元) Total Investment Planned (10 000 yuan)	累计完成投资(万元) Accumulative Investment Acually Made (10 000 yuan)	本年完成投资(万元) Investment Made this Year (10 000 yuan)
常德恒安纸业有限公司二期工程建设 Second Phrase of Hengan Paper Corp. in Changde	2001.11		20000	525	525
常德市自来水公司第四水厂建设 No. 4 Factory Construction of Changde Tap Water Corporation	1998.12		17025	11700	4500
湖南省澧水公司皂市水库水利枢纽工程 Conservancy Project of Zaoshi Reservoir			311000	14451	12100
常德创元铝业有限公司 Chuangyuan Aluminum Corp. in Changde	2001.11		100000	3000	3000
☆益阳火电厂一期工程 First Phrase of Yiyang Thermal Power Factory Project	1998.12		297160	274819	75911
郴州方舟化工集团扩建20万吨/年复合肥工程 200 Thousand Tons Compound Fertilizer Extension Work of Chenzhou Fangzhou Chemical Group	1999.06	2001.04	18528	14258	3893
宜章县康达水泥厂 Kangda Cement Factory in Yizhang	2001.10		70928	6619	6619
☆湖南省冷水滩虎岩粮库中央直属库扩建工程 Lengshuitang State-owned Food Strorehouse Extension Work	1998.11		5152	5451	441
湖南冷水滩宋家洲水电站 Lengshuitang Songjiazhou Hydropower Station	1993.10		61952	49485	1092
芷江蟒塘溪水利水电开发工程 Zhijiang Mangtangxi Conservancy and Hydropower Development Project	1998.08		53087	41047	12676
☆洪江水电站 Hongjiang Hydropower Station	1998.01		199500	92614	28000
湖南华达机械总厂整体脱险搬迁二期工程 Second Phrase of Hunan Huada Mechanical Factory Removal for Safety	1985.12		11176	12621	185
保靖碗米坡电站 Baojing Wangmipo Hydropower Station	2000.08		203362	30257	20208
广铁集团公司洛湛铁路益娄段 The Yiyang-to-Loudi Section in Luoyang-to-Zhanjiang Railway of Guangzhou Railway Group Corporation	2000.12		186747	82585	71585

4 -20 续表 2 continued

项目名称 Item	开工时间(年·月) Starting Date (y.m)	投产时间(年·月) The Date for Put into Use (y.m)	计划总投资(万元) Total Investment Planned (10 000 yuan)	累计完成投资(万元) Accumulative Investment Acually Made (10 000 yuan)	本年完成投资(万元) Investment Made this Year (10 000 yuan)
更新改造限额以上项目 **Above Normal Innovation Projects**					
湖南省三湘客车集团客车专用底盘制造及装配生产线 Bus Chassis Manufacture and Assembly Line of Hunan Sanxiang Bus Group	1997.08		4992	4361	1261
☆LG曙光增资扩建工程 Extension Work of LG Shuguang Group Corporation	1999.02	2001.08	243600	235504	47584
中汽长电股份有限公司双加二期工程 Second Phrase of Changsha Automobile Electrical Equipment Limited Liability Company	1997.12		19516	6952	1189
株洲硬质合金厂钨钼异型大制品深加工工程 Tungsten and Molybdenum Product Finishing Project of Zhuzhou Rigid Alloy Factory	2000.10		5000	3258	2751
株洲硬质合金厂高性能精密可转位刀片及刀具配套生产线 Blade and Cutter Matching Manufacture Line of Zhuzhou Rigid Alloy Factory	2000.12		21000	16385	14037
中国南方航空动力机械公司WS11航空技改项目 WS11 Air Technical Revolution Project of China South Air Power Machine Company	2001.01		14700	7591	6610
中国南方航空动力机械公司航空发动机转包生产线 Air Engine Manufacture Line of China South Air Power Machine Company	1998.11	2001.12	6300	6620	1649
中国南方航空动力机械公司南方普惠航空发动机 HP Air Engine Project of China South Air Power Machine Company	1999.02		22767	44721	40052
中国南方航空动力机械公司WZ9航空技改项目 WZ9 Air Technical Revolution Project of China South Air Power Machine Company	2001.08		28100	10362	10362
株洲电厂电厂二期工程技改 Second Phrase of Zhuzhou Power Station Technical Revolution Project	2001.06		226426	44721	40052
株洲电力机车研究所城市轨道交通车交流牵引传动与控制国产化 City Tram Control Device Manufacture Localization Project of Zhuzhou Electric Locomotive Institute	1999.12		12970	8000	3000
株洲冶炼厂铅烧结烟气综合治理 Fume Control Project of Zhuzhou Smelting Work	2000.09		15396	14219	8582
湖南南天实业股份有限公司百菌清扩产 Extension Work of Hunan Nantian Limited Company by Shares	1999.01		4819	2606	1264
湘潭电机厂城轨项目 City Track Project of Xiangtang Electric Machine Factory	2000.01		5006	1716	586
湘潭电机厂城轨项目二期 Second City Track Project of Xiangtang Electric Machine Factory	2001.06		5377	323	323
湘潭钢铁公司转炉工程 Steel Converter Project of Xiangtang Steel Limited Group Corporation	1999.01	2001.12	13176	12276	5100

4-20 续表 3

continued

项目名称 Item	开工时间(年.月) Starting Date (y.m)	投产时间(年.月) The Date for Put into Use (y.m)	计划总投资(万元) Total Investment Planned (10 000 yuan)	累计完成投资(万元) Accumulative Investment Acually Made (10 000 yuan)	本年完成投资(万元) Investment Made this Year (10 000 yuan)
湘潭电机集团有限公司093军工程研制保障条件建设 093 Guaranteed Conditions Construction Project of Xiangtang Electric Machine Limited Group Corporation	1998.09		4200	4280	180
湘潭电化集团公司2万吨/年无汞碱电池专用电解二氧化锰 20 Thousang Tons Manganese Peroxide Project of Xiangtang Electrochemical Limited Group Corporation	1999.10	2001.12	17833	16035	5490
湖南铁合金厂有毒铬渣处理工程 Harmful Chromium Waste Disposal Project of Hunan Iron Alloy Factory	1999.12		11403	3754	3020
衡阳有色冶金机械总厂卷取机生产线 Manufacture Line of Hengyang Nonferrous Metals Smelting and Pressing Machine Factory	2000.11		5669	980	480
衡阳南岳油泵油嘴有限公司合营生产喷油泵技改 Technical Revolution Project of Hengyang Pump Limited Corporation	1994.12		17000	15630	130
水口山矿务局污水处理 Waste Water Treatment Project of Shuikoushang Mineral Bureau	1998.11		8235	7314	1396
邵阳市自来水工程西水东调工程 Shaoyang Tap Water From West to East Transferring Project	1995.06		16652	15152	1652
岳阳纸业集团有限公司年产12万吨系列胶印书刊纸工程 120 Tousand Tons Newsprint Paper Project of Yueyang Paper Limited Group Corporation	2000.11		138851	21040	20077
郴州金亚实业有限公司山河电站 Shanghe Power Station of Chenzhou Jinya Limited Company	1996.12	2001.04	5700	6840	134
郴州市碾米机有限公司优质米加工成套设备产业化工程 High Quality Rice Processing Industrial Project of Chenzhou Mill Machine Limited Corporation	1999.11		7800	2500	240
华峰电子集团有限公司华峰三线调整搬迁 The Third Line Removal of Huafeng Electrical Limited Group Corp.	1987.05		5500	5338	4
怀化莱孚铝业有限公司电解铝锭生产 Electrolytic Aluminum Project of Huaihua Laifu Aluminum Limited Corp.	1996.08		23500	23447	2510
涟源钢铁集团有限公司二轧全连移地大修改造 Removal and Repair Project of Lianyuan Steel Limited Group Corp.	2000.03	2001.04	19800	23580	11470
涟源钢铁集团有限公司二号焦炉易地改造 No.2 Furnace Repair Project of Lianyuan Steel Limited Group Corp.	2001.02		33000	8785	8785
涟源钢铁集团有限公司转炉大修改造工程 Steel Converter Repair Project of Lianyuan Steel Limited Group Corp.	1999.10	2001.11	49777	60522	11235
湖南大乘资氮集团三万吨合成氨五万吨尿素填平补齐工程 30 Thousand Tons Synthetic Ammonia and 50 Thousand Tons Urea Project of Hunan Dacheng Group	1998.01		12977	11920	92

项 目 名 称 Item	开 工 时 间 (年.月) Starting Date (y.m)	投 产 时 间 (年.月) The Date for Put into Use (y.m)	计划总投资 (万元) Total Invest-ment Planned (10 000 yuan)	累计完成投资 (万元) Accu-mulative Investment Acually Made (10 000 yuan)	本年完成投资 (万元) Investment Made this Year (10 000 yuan)
重点项目 **Main Projects**					
长沙市第一污水处理厂 Changsha No. 1 Waste Water Treatment Factory	1999.12		26605	14001	5761
长沙市二环线道路工程 Changsha the Second Loop Line Project	1994.12		414318	296822	41342
株洲市城市快速环道一期工程 First Phrase of Zhuzhou City Quick Loop Line Project	1999.02		185357	42246	23422
攸县城关国家粮食储备库 Youxian State-owned Food StoreHouse for Emergency	2000.12	2001.12	1100	1100	650
醴陵市泗汾国家粮食储备库 Liling State-owned Food StoreHouse for Emergency	2000.12	2001.11	1100	1100	539
岳阳君山区高台粮食储备库 Yueyang State-owned Food StoreHouse for Emergency	2000.02		1200	900	544
岳阳市水电局长江干堤加固工程 the Long River Bank Reinforce Project of Yueyang Hydropower Bureau	1998.09		230100	113253	13499
永州市永连公路指挥部 Yongzhou Highway Commanding Department	1998.05		73000	63381	24057
临长高速公路 Expressway from Linxiang to Changsha	2000.06		509174	304705	153857
潭邵高速公路 Expressway from Xiangtang to Shaoyang	2000.07		563278	318421	160774
衡枣高速公路 Expressway from Hengyang to Zaomupu	2000.12		512563	207872	157177
耒宜高速公路 Expressway from Leiyang to Yizhang	1998.11	2001.12	392714	385714	102657

4-21 城镇集体各行业项目个数、投资额及新增固定资产(2001年)

Number of Projects, Investment and Newly Increased Fixed Assets of Urban Collective – Owned Units by Sector (2001)

指 标	Item	施工项目个数(个) Number of Projects under Construction (unit)	全投项目个数(个) Number of Projects Completed and Put into Use (unit)	固定资产投资(万元) Investment in Fixed Assets (10 000 yuan)	新增固定资产(万元) Newly Increased Fixed Assets (10 000 yuan)
总计	**Total**	**260**	**146**	**186359**	**143822**
农林牧渔业	Farming,Forestry,Animal Husbandry and Fishery	5	4	865	1120
采掘业	Mining and Quarrying	16	13	3766	2748
制造业	Manufacturing	91	57	39493	33924
#食品加工业	Food Processing	5	3	3650	3650
食品制造业	Food Production			100	100
纺织业	Textiles	11	11	11220	12220
服装及其他纤维制品制造业	Garments and Other Fiber Products	2		200	0
木材加工及竹、藤、棕、草制品业	Timber Processing, Bamboo, Cane, Palm Fiber and Straw Products	1	1	60	60
家具制造业	Furniture Manufacturing	3	1	2310	107
造纸及纸制品业	Papermaking and Paper Products	1	1	380	380
印刷业、记录媒介复制业	Printing and Record Medium Reproduction	2	1	190	150
化学原料及化学制品制造业	Raw Chemical Materials and Chemical Products	9	5	1814	1543
塑料制品业	Plastic Products	3	1	996	418
非金属矿物制品业	Nonmetal Mineral Products	15	11	2832	2372
黑色金属冶炼及压延加工业	Smelting and Pressing of Ferrous Metals	2	0	276	0
有色金属冶炼业及压延加工业	Smelting and Pressing of Nonferrous Metals	2	2	695	695
金属制品业	Metal Products	2	1	1970	1870
普通机械制造业	Ordinary Machinery	8	4	2346	1966
专用设备制造业	Equipment for Special Purposes	8	6	2933	1330
交通运输设备制造业	Transport Equipment	4	1	913	938
电气机械及器材制造业	Electric Equipment and Machinery	3	2	318	268
电力、煤气及水的生产和供应业	Production and Supply of Electricity, Gas and Water	3		533	65
电力、蒸汽、热水的生产和供应业	Production and Supply of Electricity, Steam and Hot Water	3		533	65
建筑业	Construction	23	7	3587	1416
地质勘查业、水利管理业	Geological Prospecting and Water Conservancy	1	1	150	150
交通运输、仓储及邮电通信业	Transport,Storage,Post and Telecommunications	11	3	4182	920
批发和零售贸易、餐饮业	Wholesale and Retail Trade and Catering Services	38	19	19360	13005
金融、保险业	Finance and Insurance	29	18	4317	2947
房地产业	Real Estate Trade			95409	74224
社会服务业	Social Services	18	9	6186	4419
卫生、体育和社会福利业	Health Care,Sports and Social Welfare	1	1	110	110
教育、文化艺术及广播电影电视业	Education,Culture and Arts,Radio, Film and Television	3	3	3980	3980
科学研究和综合技术服务业	Scientific Research and Polytechnical Services	1	1	100	100
国家机关、政党机关和社会团体	Government Agencies,Party Agencies and Social Organizations	13	6	1424	1489
其他行业	Others	7	4	2897	3205

注:施工、全投项目个数中未含房地产开发项目。

Data on real estate development were not included in the data on construction and fully constructed projects.

4-22 房地产开发情况(2001年)

Real Estate Development (2001)

市州	Cities and Prefecture	开发公司个数(个) Number of Develop-ment Enterprises (unit)	国有经济 State-owned Enterprises	集体经济 Collective-owned Enterprises	外商投资经济 Foreign Funded Enterprises	港澳台投资经济 Funded by Enterpreneurs from Hong Kong, Macao and Taiwan	年平均职工人数(人) Number of Staff and Workers (persons)	房地产开发投资(万元) Investment (10 000 yuan)
全省总计	**Total**	**782**	**215**	**92**	**23**	**70**	**26936**	**1074104**
长沙市	Changsha	231	51	26	11	33	8164	549376
株洲市	Zhuzhou	94	18	12	2	3	2079	76604
湘潭市	Xiangtan	59	23	7	3	3	2192	74646
衡阳市	Hengyang	56	14	12	2	7	3955	67965
邵阳市	Shaoyang	50	18	9		2	952	23442
岳阳市	Yueyang	49	20	5	1	4	2045	66053
常德市	Changde	82	17	6		5	2197	91162
张家界市	Zhangjiajie	11	7	0		1	571	9047
益阳市	Yiyang	46	12	5		2	1353	24227
郴州市	Chenzhou	54	14	6	3	3	1387	45448
永州市	Yongzhou	16	5	1	1	2	618	9271
怀化市	Huaihua	17	9	3		0	695	21222
娄底市	Loudi	16	6			5	714	15346
湘西	West Hunan	1	1				14	295

市州	Cities and Prefecture	经营总收入(万元) Total Revenue (10 000 yuan)	土地转让收入 Land Transferred	商品房屋销售收入 Commercial Houses Sold	房屋出租收入 Houses Leased	其他收入 Others	税金及附加(万元) Taxes and Extra Charges (10 000 yuan)	利润总额(万元) Total Profits (10 000 yuan)
全省总计	**Total**	**665477**	**60049**	**486086**	**9236**	**110106**	**33712**	**-46350**
长沙市	Changsha	329268	45524	233063	2220	48461	16299	-17273
株洲市	Zhuzhou	42900	5687	33137	110	3966	1928	-1053
湘潭市	Xiangtan	48063	838	40595	72	6558	2501	-2777
衡阳市	Hengyang	60217		30224	1421	28572	3916	-14378
邵阳市	Shaoyang	10569	4786	4162	350	1271	391	-11763
岳阳市	Yueyang	40422	2210	31883	1003	5326	1975	239
常德市	Changde	54226	45	46198	2134	5849	2795	-68
张家界市	Zhangjiajie	4933		3389	16	1528	230	311
益阳市	Yiyang	16986	60	15139	581	1206	780	-49
郴州市	Chenzhou	19986	21	19779	85	101	858	-51
永州市	Yongzhou	6410	577	4243	1119	471	362	341
怀化市	Huaihua	21905		19340	125	2440	1045	-368
娄底市	Loudi	9269	301	4934		4034	621	537
湘西	West Hunan	323				323	11	2

4-23 房地产开发统计主要指标(2001年)

Major Statistics Indicators of Real Estate Development (2001)

单位:万元 (10 000 yuan)

指标	Item	合计 Total	国有 State-owned	集体 Colective-owned	其他 Other Types of Ownership
计划总投资	**Panning Gross Investment**	**3835575**	**911429**	**430675**	**2493471**
实际需要的总投资	Gross Investment in Actual Need	3874971	919710	433991	2521270
累计完成投资	Accumulative Investment Completed	2020667	486803	187766	1346098
累计新增固定资产	Accumulative Newly Increased Fixed Assets	1012557	280282	113966	618309
本年底未完工程累计投资	Accumulative Investment of Projects Uncompleted	939486	189927	62669	686890
本年计划投资	Planning Investment in the year	1237599	304561	110927	822111
本年完成投资	Investment Made in This Year	1074104	252448	95409	726247
按构成分:	Group by Form:				
建筑工程	Construction	739197	167426	76611	495160
安装工程	Installation	21639	1706	525	19408
设备、工具器具购置	Purchase of Equipment,Tools and Apparatus	11398	1754	465	9179
按工程用途分:	Group by use of Projects				
住宅	Residential Buildings	598680	144683	61711	392286
办公楼	Business Buildings	34093	3439	2687	27967
商业营业用房	Commercial Buildings	155787	21787	14452	119548
其他	Others	285544	82539	16559	186446
房地产开发企业本年资金来源	Group by Source of Funds	1115246	262214	85071	767961
国内贷款	Domestic Loans	205611	50400	19652	135559
债券	Bond				
自筹资金	Fund Raising	408868	98548	36008	274312
本年土地开发投资	Investment in Development of Land	99797	37349	5366	57082
本年新增固定资产	Newly Increased Fixed Assets	687728	186906	74224	426598
本年施工房屋面积(平方米)	Floor Space of Buildings Under Construction	15846185	3834393	1770149	10241643
#住宅	Residential Buildings	12313757	3295742	1342903	7675112
本年竣工房屋面积(平方米)	Floor Space of Buildings Completed	6488588	2107523	767619	3613446
#住宅	Residential Buildings	5420753	1862840	618083	2939830
本年竣工房屋价值	Value of Buildings Completed	560467	164705	61074	334688
#住宅	Residential Buildings	436738	135721	49208	251809
土地开发面积(平方米)	Area of Land Development	3481760	1722632	292300	1466828
商品房销售额	Total Sales of Commercial House	549356	151531	67432	330393
商品房销售建筑面积(平方米)	Floor Space of Selling Commercial House	4400713	1432330	502943	2465440

4-24 商品房屋销售情况(2001年)

Sales of Commercial House (2001)

市州	Cities and Prefecture	实际销售商品房屋面积(平方米) Floor Space of Selling Commercial House (sq.m)	#住宅 Residential Buildings	个人购买商品房住宅(平方米) Commercial Houses Purchased by Individuals(sq.m)	商品房屋销售额(万元) Total Sales of Commercial House (10 000 yuan)	#住宅 Residential Buildings
全省总计	**Total**	**4400713**	**3922626**	**3315950**	**549356**	**440679**
长沙市	Changsha	1593950	1483077	1228503	290098	257418
株洲市	Zhuzhou	338234	316481	316481	31385	26340
湘潭市	Xiangtan	441765	361902	358168	43173	29273
衡阳市	Hengyang	254391	227176	218244	30148	18393
邵阳市	Shaoyang	55054	48370	40358	4133	3074
岳阳市	Yueyang	409783	349414	187195	37745	27912
常德市	Changde	526354	462018	436368	49762	33473
张家界市	Zhangjiajie	55079	48998	45998	4353	3497
益阳市	Yiyang	195134	151532	104680	15465	8623
郴州市	Chenzhou	207652	185840	185840	18862	14225
永州市	Yongzhou	68236	52269	52269	5068	2670
怀化市	Huaihua	136418	130270	36567	9748	8309
娄底市	Loudi	118663	105279	105279	9416	7472
湘西自治州	West Hunan A.P					

4-25 房地产开发建设房屋建筑面积和造价(2001年)

Floor Space of Building and Cost of Real Estate Development (2001)

市州	Cities and Prefecture	施工房屋面积(平方米) Floor Space of Buildings under Construction (sq.m)	竣工房屋面积(平方米) Floor Space of Buildings Completed (sq.m)	房屋建筑面积竣工率(%) Rate of Floor Space of Buildings Completed (%)	竣工房屋价值(万元) Value of Buildings Completed (10 000 yuan)	竣工房屋造价(元/平方米) Cost of Buildings Completed (yuan/sq.m)
全省总计	**Total**	**15846185**	**6488588**	**40.9**	**560467**	**863.8**
长沙市	Changsha	6293164	2102903	33.4	267642	1272.7
株洲市	Zhuzhou	1531343	790420	51.6	49468	625.8
湘潭市	Xiangtan	1319579	607934	46.1	45000	740.2
衡阳市	Hengyang	1376090	369280	26.8	24755	670.4
邵阳市	Shaoyang	377966	96098	25.4	4985	518.7
岳阳市	Yueyang	1082196	735724	68	51678	702.4
常德市	Changde	1335528	738127	55.3	52622	712.9
张家界市	Zhangjiajie	114365	79477	69.5	4928	620.1
益阳市	Yiyang	559983	247595	44.2	12511	505.3
郴州市	Chenzhou	918263	344772	37.5	24488	710.3
永州市	Yongzhou	153852	61079	39.7	3980	651.6
怀化市	Huaihua	439188	150456	34.3	8970	596.2
娄底市	Loudi	336966	158021	46.9	9117	576.9
湘西自治州	West Hunan A.P	7702	6702	87	323	481.9

4-26 城镇集体单位固定资产投资和房屋建筑面积(2001年)

Investment in Fixed Assets and Floor Space of Buildings of Urban Collective – Owned Units (2001)

市州	Cities and Prefecture	本年完成投资(万元) Investment Completed this Year (10 000 yuan)				房屋建筑面积(万平方米) Floor Space of Building Construction (10 000 sq.m)			
		合计 Total	建筑安装工程 Construction and Installation	设备工具器具购置 Purchase of Equipment and Instruments	其他费用 Others	施工面积 Floor Space under Construction	#住宅 Residential Buildings	竣工面积 Floor Space Completed	#住宅 Residential Buildings
全省总计	**Total**	**186359**	**143200**	**16725**	**26434**	**287.77**	**171.02**	**123.77**	**80.33**
长沙市	Changsha	70817	54574	1517	14726	90.7	41.79	38.25	20.09
株洲市	Zhuzhou	14263	12025	1223	1015	25.97	17.76	17.76	12.01
湘潭市	Xiangtan	12315	6807	3335	2173	11.38	7.05	6.3	4.61
衡阳市	Hengyang	21894	19104	777	2013	50.3	31.98	17.57	11.06
邵阳市	Shaoyang	9933	7188	635	2110	14.13	7.94	6.58	3.91
岳阳市	Yueyang	14515	10541	3327	647	19.76	17.43	11.72	10.65
常德市	Changde	14525	11265	1877	1383	25.64	12.97	5.84	4.65
张家界市	Zhangjiajie	1450	1246	115	89	1.13		0.78	
益阳市	Yiyang	3216	2085	920	211	7.37	5.73	3.93	2.75
郴州市	Chenzhou	13941	10598	1725	1618	14.44	11.34	3.68	2.85
永州市	Yongzhou	2601	1895	676	30	7.05	3.54	1.85	0.74
怀化市	Huaihua	4461	3887	260	314	11.68	8.98	6.48	5.1
娄底市	Loudi	945	852	40	53	6.22	3.61	1.77	1.55
湘　西	Wrst Hunan	1483	1133	298	52	2.01	0.89	1.26	0.35

4-27 国有农林牧渔业基本建设、更新改造投资及新增固定资产

Investment in Capital Construction，Technical Updating and Transformation and Newly Increased Fixed Assets of State-Owned Units of Farming，Forestry，Animal Husbandry，Fishery

单位：万元 (10 000 yuan)

行　业	Sector	固定资产投资总额 Investment of Fixed Assets		新增固定资产 Newly Increased Fixed Assets	
		2000	2001	2000	2001
基本建设	**Investment in Capital Construction**	**38491**	**41873**	**42292**	**25308**
#农业	#Farming	10530	16499	5173	10801
林业	Forestry	11243	15004	10325	7761
畜牧业	Animal Husbandry	4208	3492	5354	1273
渔业	Fishery	413	355	270	233
农林牧渔服务业	Services	12097	6523	21170	5240
更新改造	**Technical Updating and Transformation**	**77**	**72**	**77**	**15**
#农业	#Farming	77		77	
林业	Forestry				
畜牧业	Animal Husbandry				
渔业	Fishery				
农林牧渔服务业	Services		72		15

4-28 国有农林牧渔业投资额施工投产项目和固定资产交付使用率(2001年)

Investment，Projects Put into Operation and Rate of Fixed Assets Turned over to Uses of State—Owned Units of Farming，Forestry，Animal Husbandry，Fishery (2001)

行业	Sector	投资额合计(万元) Total Investment (10 000 yuan)	#住宅 Residential Buildings	施工项目个数(个) Number of Projects Under Construction (unit)	全部建成投产项目个数(个) Projects Completed and Put into Production (unit)	项目投产率(%) Rate of Project Put into Production (%)	固定资产交付使用率(%) Rate of Fixed Assets Turn Over to Uses (%)
总计	**Total**	**44981**	**993**	**119**	**60**	**50.4**	**58.1**
农业	Farming	17209	644	47	27	57.4	66.9
林业	Forestry	17014	70	34	16	47.1	45.6
畜牧业	Animal Husbandry	3733	0	11	2	18.2	36.2
渔业	Fishery	430	90	5	2	40	54.2
农林牧渔服务业	Services	6595	189	22	13	59.1	79.7

4-29 城镇和工矿区私人建房情况(2001年)

Building Construction by Individuals in Cities，Towns and Industrial Mining Areas (2001)

市州	Cities and Prefecture	城镇、工矿区个数(个) Number of Cities, Towns and Industrial Mining Areas (unit)	本年竣工房屋建筑面积(万平方米) Floor Space of Buildings Completed This Year (10000 sq.m)		本年竣工房屋价值(万元) Value of Buildings Completed This Year (10000 yuan)		建房户数(户) Number of Households of Building Construction (household)
			合计 Total	#住宅 Residential Buildings	合计 Total	#住宅 Residential Buildings	
全省总计	**Total**	**1033**	**1681.06**	**1531.41**	**642311**	**580332**	**78800**
长沙市	Changsha	6	109.02	105.27	62933	59974	4018
株洲市	Zhuzhou	67	66.73	65.44	30260	29751	2476
湘潭市	Xiangtan	43	49.70	43.55	16961	14980	2648
衡阳市	Hengyang	107	149.90	141.83	55309	51493	7691
邵阳市	Shaoyang	71	165.30	151.63	66674	61122	8340
岳阳市	Yueyang	93	175.38	170.02	65906	59762	9453
常德市	Changde	101	158.32	151.40	58530	56014	10046
张家界市	Zhangjiajie	55	46.23	44.94	33874	33436	2803
益阳市	Yiyang	60	69.91	59.54	29882	24047	3026
郴州市	Chenzhou	89	117.73	102.32	46632	41148	6123
永州市	Yongzhou	116	284.14	239.60	93609	78233	11968
怀化市	Huaihua	89	45.36	38.02	16002	12882	2425
娄底市	Loudi	72	159.82	138.91	55144	47631	5960
湘西自治州	West Hunan A.P	64	83.52	78.94	10595	9859	1823

4-30 国有工业施工、投资项目及项目投产率(2001年)

Projects Under Construction,Put into Use and Rate of Projects Put into Use of State – Owned Industrial Enterprises (2001)

指 标	Item	施工项目个数(个) Number of Projects Under Construction(unit)	全投项目个数(个) Projects Completed and Put into Production(unit)	项目投产率(%) Rate of Project Put into Production(%)
总 计	**Total**	**1305**	**739**	**56.6**
采掘业	**Mining and Quarrying**	**158**	**93**	**58.9**
煤炭采选业	Coal Mining and Dressing	57	32	56.1
黑色金属矿采选业	Mining and Dressing of Ferrous Metals	9	5	55.6
有色金属矿采选业	Mining and Dressing of Nonferrous Metals	79	51	64.6
非金属矿采选业	Mining and Dressing of Nonmetal Minerals	10	4	40
制造业	**Manufacturing**	**710**	**418**	**58.9**
#食品加工业	Food Processing	14	8	57.1
食品制造业	Food Production	7	7	100
饮料制造业	Beverages	14	5	35.7
烟草加工业	Tobacco	73	28	38.4
纺织业	Textiles	29	19	65.5
服装及其他纤维制品制造业	Garments and Other Fiber Products	1	1	100
木材加工及竹、藤、棕、草制品业	Timber Processing, Bamboo, Cane, Palm Fiber and Straw Products	10	6	60
造纸及纸制品业	Papermaking and Paper Products	27	18	66.7
印刷业、记录媒介的复制	Printing and Record Medium Reproduction	7	2	28.6
石油加工及炼焦业	Petroleum Processing and Coking	25	20	80
化学原料及化学制品制造业	Raw Chemical Materials and Chemical Products	102	59	57.8
医药制造业	Medical and Pharmaceutical Products	15	9	60
化学纤维制造业	Chemical Fiber	1	1	100
橡胶制品业	Rubber Products			50
塑料制品业	Plastic Products	1	1	100
非金属矿物制品业	Nonmetal Mineral Products	65	50	76.9
黑色金属冶炼及压延加工业	Smelting and Pressing of Ferrous Metals	93	80	86
有色金属冶炼及压延加工业	Smelting and Pressing of Nonferrous Metals	60	34	56.7
金属制品业	Metal Products	4	2	50
普通机械制造业	Ordinary Machinery	19	11	57.9
专用设备制造业	Equipment for Special Purposes	33	10	30.3
交通运输设备制造业	Transport Equipment	55	25	45.5
武器弹药制造业	Ammunition Production	13	6	46.2
电气机械及器材制造业	Electric Equipment and Machinery	26	10	38.5
电子及通信设备制造业	Electronic and Telecommunications Equipment	12	3	25
仪器仪表及文化、办公用机械制造业	Instruments, Meters, Cultural and Office Machinery	3	2	66.7
其他制造业	Other Manufacturing			
电力、煤气及水的生产和供应业	**Production and Supply of Electric Power, Gas and Water**	**437**	**228**	**52.2**
电力、蒸汽、热水的生产和供应业	Production and Supply of Electric Power, Steam and Hot Water	354	189	53.4
煤气生产和供应业	Production and Supply of Gas	10	4	40
自来水的生产和供应业	Production and Supply of Tap Water	73	35	47.9

4-31 农村固定资产投资情况

Investment of Fixed Assets in Rural Areas

单位：万元、万平方米 (10 000 yuan, 10 000 sq.m)

		2000年		2001年	
		总计 Total	#非农户 Non Agricultural Household	总计 Total	#非农户 Non Agricultural Household
本年新增固定资产	**Newly Increase Fixed Assets this Year**	**2440362**	**627168**	**2719991**	**849092**
本年固定资产投资完成额	**Completed Investment this Year**	**3024189**	**1000214**	**3322719**	**1271449**
按投资来源分	**Grouped by Source of Funds**				
#国内贷款	Domestic Loans	123884	57542	108535	80233
群众集资	Crowd Raising Funds	167747	167747	186987	126115
国家资金	State Capital	185977	185977	228991	228991
利用外资	Foreign Investment	14848	14848	23145	23145
自筹资金	Fundraising	2510847	574100	2775061	812965
按投资构成分	**Grouped by Use of Funds**				
#建筑工程	Construction	2182393	590647	2277602	727736
#农田水利	Farmland and Water Conservancy	256308	221458	263455	208241
住宅	Residential House	1555387	90796	1489936	76557
安装工程	Installation	55232	51477	71063	69052
设备工器具购置	Purchase of Equipment and Instruments	551228	278494	682780	369255
#生产设备	Equipment for Production	331911	172221	457520	244964
按投资方向分	**Grouped by Direction of Investment**				
#农业	Agriculture	429627	250298	476782	241926
采掘业	Mining and Quarrying	46103	44969	82272	82272
制造业	Manufacturing	174248	163242	348517	335140
电力煤气及水的生产和供应业	Production and Supply of Electric Power, Gas and Water	71240	71240	88840	88155
建筑业	Construction	1589523	31794	93763	91020
交通运输业	Transportation	122260	37344	185645	45101
邮电通讯业	Postal and Telecommunications Services	33075	27011	50245	32660
批发零售贸易业	Wholesale & Retail Trade	33966	30407	51045	50223
社会服务业	Social Services	16916	16511	27266	27080
文化教育事业	Culture and Education	108879	108372	111206	99060
卫生体育社会福利事业	Health Care, Sports and Social Welfare	23501	23501	17783	17560
按具体投资项目分	**Grouped by Item of Investment**				
#住宅	Residential House	1555387	90796	1489936	76557
道路	Roadways	70467	70467	103213	103139
桥梁	Bridges	2337	2337	3508	3508
设备	Equipment	551228	278494	682780	369255
水利	Water Conservancy	256308	221458	263455	208241
本年施工房屋面积	**Floor Space of Buildings Under Construction in Current Year**	**7767**	**941**	**7226**	**874**
#住宅	Residential House	6720	402	6206	235
当年新开工	New Construction in Current Year	6919	617	6787	791
本年竣工房屋面积	**Floor Space of Buildings Completed in Current Year**	**7374**	**673**	**6803**	**789**
#住宅	Residential House	6499	258	5794	212
本年竣工房屋投资完成额	**Investment Made of Building Completed in Current Year**	**1667854**	**209898**	**1657387**	**262502**
#住宅	Residential House	1453207	81966	1380927	70144

五、财政、金融、保险

FINANCE，BANKING AND INSURANCE

资料整理人员：　顾　虹　李生春

5-1 地方财政收支总额

Total Local Government Revenue and Expenditures

单位：亿元 (100 million yuan)

年份 Year / 市州 Cities and Prefecture	总收入(亿元) Total Revenue	#企业收入 Revenue form Enterprises	#各项税收 Taxes Revenue	总支出(亿元) Total Expenditure	#基本建设支出 Expenditure for Capital Construction	#支援农村生产支出及农业事业费 Expenditure for Supporting Agricultural Production and Agricultural Operating Expenses	#文教科学卫生事业费 Operating Expenses for Culture, Education Science and Health Care	#行政管理费 Expenditure for Government Administration
1978	28.98	9.68	17.17	24.46	7.62	3.57	4.33	1.88
1980	29.86	9.58	19.53	23.71	4.86	3.44	6.68	2.66
1981	31.40	9.10	21.49	21.39	3.00	3.07	6.81	2.90
1982	30.33	5.11	24.48	23.26	3.12	2.95	7.91	3.03
1983	29.27	2.25	26.16	25.31	3.48	3.26	8.79	3.58
1984	32.85	2.74	29.12	30.04	4.43	3.21	9.86	4.87
1985	39.19	1.61	36.83	40.09	4.60	4.01	12.53	5.20
1986	47.65	4.08	42.26	54.29	5.80	4.52	14.22	5.54
1987	54.38	4.37	48.36	55.93	4.65	3.09	14.88	6.22
1988	56.54	-0.47	54.25	64.89	5.21	5.88	18.30	6.13
1989	68.86	-1.48	64.88	74.23	5.44	6.91	20.69	6.43
1990	70.07	-3.70	67.33	80.08	5.60	8.17	21.92	6.82
1991	80.52	-0.91	74.14	88.58	6.16	8.81	24.47	7.80
1992	92.78	-0.78	84.90	99.10	6.23	9.86	28.42	11.03
1993	127.56	-0.66	116.31	132.03	7.73	12.89	32.96	13.18
1994	85.89	2.70	65.04	151.49	7.89	13.74	42.54	17.79
1995	108.16	2.74	78.05	173.94	9.65	14.55	47.87	21.46
1996	130.36	2.30	88.00	217.74	13.33	17.09	53.70	24.27
1997	137.16	2.72	105.75	230.82	13.78	17.66	58.75	26.20
1998	156.77	3.63	102.95	273.64	28.75	22.16	61.94	26.88
1999	166.50	6.04	105.50	313.12	37.66	21.49	66.40	29.36
2000	177.04	8.60	111.57	347.83	38.08	22.15	73.55	32.78
2001	205.41	19.35	124.45	431.70	39.40	25.55	91.62	41.42
长沙 Changsha	42.16	4.42	29.86	52.33	3.41	3.07	8.82	5.63
株洲 Zhuzhou	14.51	2.10	8.92	21.00	0.62	1.23	4.47	2.46
湘潭 Xiangtan	7.97	0.82	5.13	14.28	0.09	0.70	2.73	1.36
衡阳 Hengyang	14.02	0.71	6.43	23.69	0.24	1.43	6.80	3.23
邵阳 Shaoyang	10.68	0.45	5.58	23.30	0.07	1.49	6.54	3.64
岳阳 Yueyang	15.10	1.52	8.91	24.81	1.32	1.71	6.07	2.80
常德 Changde	14.56	1.77	7.98	23.35	0.02	1.70	5.83	3.62
张家界 Zhangjiajie	3.01	0.51	1.82	7.60	0.08	0.49	2.10	1.03
益阳 Yiyang	6.80	0.93	3.80	14.73	0.10	1.02	4.64	2.29
郴州 Chenzhou	15.24	0.94	7.97	23.76	0.15	1.90	6.85	2.94
永州 Yongzhou	9.24	0.24	4.93	18.82	0.10	1.08	6.35	2.78
娄底 Loudi	8.04	0.35	4.24	14.55	0.22	0.89	4.01	2.28
怀化 Huaihua	8.62	0.55	5.30	18.25	0.06	1.23	5.27	2.68
湘西 West Hinan	3.52	0.35	2.46	15.87	0.06	1.27	4.38	2.41

5-2 财政收入及构成

Government Revenue and Its Composition

项目	Item	财政收入(万元) Government Revenue (10 000 yuan) 2000	2001	2001年比上年增长% Increase Rate in 2001 over 2000(%)	收入构成(%) Composition (%) 2000	2001
本年地方财政收入合计	**Total Local Government Revenue**	**1770403**	**2054078**	**16.02**	**100.00**	**100.00**
#增值税	#Value Added Tax	260989	293807	12.57	14.74	14.30
营业税	Operating Tax	343357	364410	6.13	19.39	17.74
企业所得税	Income Tax of Enterprises	135892	227791	67.63	7.68	11.09
企业所得税退税	Return for Enterprises' Income Tax	-16040	-2831	-82.35	-0.91	-0.14
个人所得税	Individual Income Tax	114397	186663	63.17	6.46	9.09
资源税	Resources Tax	6002	6663	11.01	0.34	0.32
固定资产投资方向调节税	Tax on the Adjustment of the Investment in the Fixed Assets	9413	1201	-87.24	0.53	0.06
城市维护建设税	Tax on Town Maintenance and Construction	113841	118145	3.78	6.43	5.75
房产税	Tax on Real Estates	44018	44161	0.32	2.49	2.15
印花税	Stamp Tax	12686	13521	6.58	0.72	0.66
城镇土地使用税	Tax on the Use of Urban Land	21589	20684	-4.19	1.22	1.01
土地增值税	Land Value Added Tax	863	860	-0.35	0.05	0.04
车船使用税	Tax on the Use of Vehicles and Ships	4290	4111	-4.17	0.24	0.20
屠宰税	Slaughter Tax	25219	22573	-10.49	1.42	1.10
筵席税	Banquet Tax					
农业税	Agricultural Tax	84512	77836	-7.90	4.77	3.79
农业特产税	Tax on Special Agricultural Products	45314	51579	13.83	2.56	2.51
牧业税	Tax on the Animal Husbandry					
耕地占用税	Tax on Occupancy of Cultivated Land	12656	16968	34.07	0.71	0.83
契税	Contract Tax	16591	21302	28.39	0.94	1.04
国有资产经营收益	State-owned Assets Profits	15266	27669	81.25	0.86	1.35
国有企业计划亏损补贴	Planning Subsidies to Loss-suffering State-owned Enterprises	-49152	-59121	20.28	-2.78	-2.88
行政性收费收入	Income from Administrative Fees	185640	215082	15.86	10.49	10.47
罚没收入	Penalty and Confiscation Income	188953	212715	12.58	10.67	10.36
土地和海域有偿使用收入	Income on the Use of Land and Sea Area	258	431	67.05	0.01	0.02
专项收入	Expert Project Income	68341	71671	4.87	3.86	3.49
其他收入	Other Income	125508	116187	-7.43	7.09	5.66
上划中央"两税"收入	**Income from Two Taxes of Turn in Central Government**	**1448134**	**1563002**	**7.93**		
#增值税	#Value Added Tax	782963	881441	12.58		
消费税	Consumption Tax	665171	681561	2.46		
财政总收入	**Total Government Revenue**	**3218537**	**3617080**	**12.38**		

5-3 地方财政支出及构成

Local Government Expenditure and Its Composition

科 目	Item	财政支出（万元）Government Expenditure (10 000 yuan)		2001年比上年增长% Increases Rate in 2001 over 2000(%)	支出构成（%）Composition (%)	
		2000	2001		2000	2001
地方财政支出合计	**Total Local Government Expenditure**	**3478324**	**4316953**	**24.11**	**100.00**	**100.00**
#基本建设支出	#Expenditure for Capital Construction	380819	394040	3.47	10.95	9.13
企业挖潜改造资金	Expenditure for Innovation Enterprises	86561	97654	12.82	2.49	2.26
地质勘探费	Expenditure for Geological Prospecting	23230	46502	100.18	0.67	1.08
科技三项费用	Expenditure for Science and Technology Promotion	37969	51541	35.74	1.09	1.19
支援农村生产支出	Expenditure for Supporting Agricultural Production	67576	65467	-3.12	1.94	1.52
农业综合开发支出	Expenditure for Comprehensive Development of Agriculture	32433	41131	26.82	0.93	0.95
农林水利气象等部门的事业费	Operating Expenses for Agriculture, Forestry, Water Conservancy and Meteorology	121524	148858	22.49	3.49	3.45
工业交通等部门的事业费	Operating Expenses for Departments of Industry and Transportation	30763	48570	57.88	0.88	1.13
流通部门事业费	Operating Expenses for Department of Commerce	9375	12902	37.62	0.27	0.30
文体广播事业费	Operating Expenses for Departments of Culture,Sport and Broadcasting	90316	107482	19.01	2.60	2.49
教育事业费	Operating Expenses for Education	508830	650949	27.93	14.63	15.08
科学事业费	Operating Expenses for Science	17541	22641	29.07	0.50	0.52
卫生经费	Operating Expenses for Public Health	118790	135138	13.76	3.42	3.13
税务等部门的事业费	Operating Expenses for Department of Revenue,Statistic,Finance and Audit	158395	193434	22.12	4.55	4.48
抚恤和社会福利救济费	Pensions, Social and Relief Funds for Social Welfare	73506	100905	37.27	2.11	2.34
行政事业单位离退休经费	Expenditure for Retired Persons in Administrative Department	200466	243306	21.37	5.76	5.64
社会保障补助支出	Expenditure on Subsidies to Social Security Programs	281159	387483	37.82	8.08	8.98
行政管理费	Expenditure for Government Administration	327797	414152	26.34	9.42	9.59
外交外事支出	Expenditure for Foreign Affairs	1084	1239	14.30	0.03	0.03
城市维护费	Expenditure for City Maintenance	149062	170653	14.48	4.29	3.95
政策性补贴支出	Expenditure for Price Subsidies	127822	205900	61.08	3.67	4.77
支援不发达地区	Expenditure for Supporting Underdeveloped Areas	46802	51379	9.78	1.35	1.19
土地和海域开发建设支出	Expenditure for Developing Land and Sea Area	246	81	-67.07	0.01	0.00
专项支出	Expenditure for Special Items	63254	74347	17.54	1.82	1.72
其他支出	Other Expenditure	523004	651199	24.51	15.04	15.08

5-4 金融机构信贷收支

Credit Income and Expenditures of Financial Institutions

单位：万元 (10 000 yuan)

项目	Item	2000 年末余额 Balance at the Year-end	2000 比年初增减 Increase Over the Year-beginning	2001 年末余额 Balance at the Year-end	2001 比年初增减 Increase Over the Year-beginning
各项存款	**Deposits**	**28747514**	**3349517**	**33429120**	**4715421**
企业存款	Deposits of Enterprises	7631014	1016205	8738857	1111607
活期存款	Demand Deposits	5946293	781039	7086569	1142419
工业存款	Industrial Deposits	1082945	79484		
商业存款	Commercial Deposits	625996	137431		
建筑企业存款	Construction Deposits	388113	55707		
集体企业存款	Deposits of Collective-owned Enterprises	198408	6294		
乡镇企业存款	Deposits of Township Enterprises	29717	1201		
定期存款	Fixed Deposits	1684721	235167	1652288	-30811
财政存款	Treasury Deposits	389227	118195	527973	138532
机关团体存款	Deposits of Government	480961	106651	482957	1964
储蓄存款	Savings Deposits	18742258	1861249	21837281	3118822
活期储蓄	Demand Saving	5589928	1108407	6825710	1239263
定期储蓄	Fixed Saving	13152329	752842	15011571	1879559
农业存款	Agricultural Deposits	566615	102896	653019	86457
信托存款	Trusted Deposits	47871	-16156	45723	-2148
委托存款	Commission Deposits	295600	9856	298195	1630
其他存款	Other Deposits	593969	150620	845115	258556
金融证券	Financial Bonds	139	-547	133	-7
国家投资债券	Government Investment Bonds				
证券业务款项	Funds of Securities Operation	87274	13848		
流通中货币	Currency in Circulation				
所有者权益	Creditors' Equity	-1725424	-520371	-1533691	54637
实收资本	Total Capital Hold	502943	33084	654778	152206
当年结益	Current Retained Profits	-669053	-669030	-519043	-517006
同业往来	Same Trade Current Account	1642408	181587		
同业存放款	Deposits	1483159	196019		
同业拆借	Debit	159249	-14433		
联行存放款	Deposits and Loans of the Joint Bank	46056555	-827240		
省辖往来	Provincial-run Current Account	2063036	834933		
全国联行往来	Nation-run Current Account	785620	-24575		
系统内资金往来	Internal System Funds Current Account	36185080	-2259169		
各项准备	All Plans	113917	5599	191991	77939
应付及暂收款	Payable & Actually Received Funds	671098	-393224	708450	38199
应付利息	Payable Interest	139671	74435	164942	12639
临时存款	Temporary Deposits	304592	70559		
其他	Others	-4212183	-133483	-2361124	-1238451
资金来源总计	**All Sources**	**71685889**	**1746269**	**30434879**	**3647738**

单位：万元　　5-4 续表　continued　　(10 000 yuan)

项目	Item	2000 年末余额 Balance at the Year-end	2000 比年初增减 Increase Over the Year-beginning	2001 年末余额 Balance at the Year-end	2001 比年初增减 Increase Over the Year-beginning
各项贷款	**Loans**	**24033863**	**2819979**	**27879156**	**3895868**
短期贷款	Short-term Loans	16349861	1624519	17724259	1858248
工业贷款	Industry Loans	3847408	-94545	4248030	318637
商业贷款	Commercial Loans	5530555	270293	5589754	-21260
农副产品贷款	Loans of Agricultural and Sideline Products	3369033	211344	3490264	121142
建筑业贷款	Construction Loans	249054	133377	266213	2771
农业贷款	Agricultural Loans	1965535	152039	2332126	366623
乡镇企业贷款	Loans to the Township Enterprises	1219120	134138	1214011	-5099
三资企业贷款	Loans to Sino-foreign Joint Venture and Cooperative Enterprises and Foreign-funded Enterprises	173923	13197	187680	-4625
私营企业及个体贷款	Loans to Private Enterprises and Individuals	95936	-23638	131845	31980
其他短期贷款	Other Short-term Loans	3268330	1039657	3754599	1169222
中期流动资金贷款	Medium-term Circulating Funds of Loans	1169394	383220	1401715	231623
中长期贷款	Medium-term and Long-term Loans	5642616	878641	7875204	1575099
基本建设贷款	Capital Construction	3110240	557542	4238147	1076430
技术改造贷款	Technical Innovation	1096526	149573	1147028	47911
其他中长期贷款	Other Medium-term&Long-term Loans	1435850	171527	2490028	450758
信托贷款	Trusted Loans	78073	5725	135348	11708
融资祖赁	Circulating Funds Tenancy	1563	201	1228	-335
委托贷款	Commission Loans	322953	27120	293088	-32929
逾期类贷款	Overdue Loans	469402	-99447		
国家投资债券贷款	Loans to Nation Investment Bonds	20719	-307		
有价证券及投资	Securities and Investment	782274	184579	1103745	303032
证券业务占款	Purchase of Securities' Operation	72930	36008		
委托投资	Consigned Investment	36475	-40542	23996	-12479
金银占款	Purchase of Gold and Silver	50711	25160	18124	-32588
外汇占款	Purchase of Foreign Exchanges	1752	4901	-382	-1704
库存现金	Vault Cash	458336	-95195	382595	-75457
财政借款	Government Debt				
准备金存款	Deposits of Prepared Funds	1714874	-7562		
存放中央银行特种存款	Special Deposits in the Central Banks	20052	-2613		
存放中央银行财政性存款	Treasury Deposits in the Central Banks	19724	4627		
同业往来	Same Trade Current Account	934157	6919		
存放同业款项	Deposits	631203	25064		
拆放同业	Debit	302954	-18145		
存放联行款项	Deposits and Loans of the Joint Bank	42075976	1797350		
省辖往来	Province-run Current Account	1955913	403850		
全国联行往来	Nation-run Current Account	784374	-60650		
系统内资金往来	Internal System Current Account	32263378	509052		
应收及预付款项	Account Receivable and Advance Payment	1464047	-2987035	1027645	-428934
应收利息	Receivable Interest	649373	39116	379063	-242748
资金运用总计	**All Uses**	**71685889**	**1746269**	**30434879**	**3647738**

5-5 商业银行信贷收支

Credit Income and Expenditures of State Commercial Banks

单位：万元 (10 000 yuan)

项目	Item	2000 年末余额 Balance at the Year-end	2000 比年初增减 Increase Over the Year-beginning	2001 年末余额 Balance at the Year-end	2001 比年初增减 Increase Over the Year-beginning
各项存款	**Deposits**	**19057935**	**2407231**	**23378694**	**3403620**
企业存款	Deposits of Enterprises	6715446	996930	8424645	1074108
活期存款	Demand Deposits	5243158	785332	6878674	1117965
定期存款	Fixed Deposits	1472288	211598	1545971	-43858
机关团体存款	Deposits of Government			457009	56484
储蓄存款	Savings Deposits	11317014	1176325	13594797	2004619
活期储蓄	Demand Saving	3883687	868391	4946642	920413
定期储蓄	Fixed Saving	7433326	307934	8648155	1084206
农业存款	Agricultural Deposits	82276	12427	89913	7420
信托存款	Trusted Deposits				
其他存款	Other Deposits	943200	221550	812330	260989
代理财政性存款	Agent of Government Deposits	29152	5145	49649	20172
发行金融债券	Issuance Financial Bonds	97	28	91	-7
发行政策性金融债券	Policy Financial Bonds				
国家投资债券	Government Investment Bonds				
卖出回购证券	Selling Debits of Buy-return	-8400	54	407000	213900
向中央银行借款	Debit from Central Banks	181541	40326	47105	-142435
同业往来	Same Trade Current Account	592048	40642	1195969	431131
同业存放款	Deposits	591153	40484	1183269	431656
同业拆借	Debit	895	158	12700	-525
委托存款及委托投资基金	Commission Deposits and Commission Investment Funds	-94073	36152	-73714	20556
委托存款	Commission Deposits	-68836	495		
委托投资基金	Commission Investment Funds	-25237	35657		
代理金融机构贷款基金	Loan Funds in Agent of Financial Institutions	16793	-1444	12736	-2317
中央银行委托贷款基金	Commission Loan Funds in Central Banks	15293	-1444	12736	-2317
各项准备	All Plans			111941	67676
其中：贷款呆帐准备金	Plan Funds for Loans			111941	67676
所有者权益	Creditors' Equity	-1367891	-330716	-1146651	198183
实收资本	Total Capital Hold			53367	-1
当年结益	Current Retained Profits	-426102	-426079	-252038	-252061
其他	Others	-1178170	-437324	-3237331	-2663424
资金来源总计	**All Sources**	**17229033**	**1760093**	**21091385**	**1592785**

单位：万元　　　　5-5 续表　continued　　　　(10 000 yuan)

项目	Item	2000 年末余额 Balance at the Year-end	2000 比年初增减 Increase Over the Year-beginning	2001 年末余额 Balance at the Year-end	2001 比年初增减 Increase Over the Year-beginning
各项贷款	**Loans**	**14799419**	**1883508**	**17996473**	**2664220**
短期贷款	Short-term Loans	9347653	1005263	10367631	1319641
工业贷款	Industrial Loans	3779079	-87299	4210938	333627
商业贷款	Commercial Loans	2419919	77275	2380569	-192260
收购贷款	Buying Loans	379310	-5679	334950	-44446
建筑业贷款	Construction Loans	243025	132077	266213	2771
农业贷款	Agricultural Loans	313101	-9917	332237	17193
乡镇企业贷款	Loans to Township Enterprises	254262	11967	250045	-4902
三资企业贷款	Loans to Sino-foreign Joint Venture and Cooperative Enterprises and Foreign-funded Enterprises	173227	13208	187680	-4625
私营企业及个体贷款	Loans to Private Enterprises and Individuals	66145	-10577	116713	31054
贴现	Discount	138652	76398	348674	208690
其他短期贷款	Other Short-term Loans	1960243	802130	2623235	1136783
个人消费贷款	Loans to Personnal Expenditure			91787	41054
中期流动资金贷款	Medium-term Circulating Funds of Loans	1169394	383568	1401715	231623
中长期贷款	Medium-term & Long-term Loans	4120020	513280	5786857	866223
基本建设贷款	Capital Construction	1930329	259198	2392697	392370
技术改造贷款	Technical Innovation	1066488	157146	1105608	36597
其他中长期贷款	Other Medium-term&Long-term Loans	1123203	96937	2288553	437256
个人消费贷款	Loans to Personnal Expenditure			659604	227138
信托贷款	Trusted Loans				
逾期类贷款	Overdue Loans	162352	-18603		
国家投资债券贷款	Loans to Nation Investment Bonds	20719	-307		
有价证券及投资	Securities and Investment	1039711	4563	825568	-593242
应收及预付款	Receivable and Advance Payment			753844	-407857
应收利息	Receivable Interest			283571	-238270
缴存准备金存款	Hand in Deposits of Prepared Funds	898357	-65251	1070169	1767
存放中央银行特种存款	Special Deposits in the Central Banks		-54		
存放中央银行财政性存款	Treasury Deposits in the Central Banks	19401	4485	28488	9087
同业往来	Same Trade Current Account	182662	20142	157812	-49429
存放同业	Deposits	10406	87	12334	1437
拆放同业	Debit	172256	20055	145478	-50866
代理金融机构贷款	Loans from Agent of Financial Institutions	21694	-1825	17351	-2603
代理人行专项贷款	Loans for Special Items from Agent of People's Bank	20194	-1825	17351	-2603
库存现金	Vault Cash	245319	-90069	202782	-53282
外汇占款	Purchase of Foreign Exchanges	1752	4901	-382	-1704
资金运用总计	**All Uses**	**17229033**	**1760093**	**21091385**	**1592785**

5-6 国家银行现金收支分析(2001年)

General Survey of Cash Statistics of State Banks (2001)

单位:万元 (10 000 yuan)

项目	Item	本年累计 Add up this Year	比上年增减额 Increase Over the Year-beginning	比上年增减% Increase Rate in 2001 over 2000 (%)
收入合计	**Total Income**	**81536664**	**16444331**	**25.26**
商品销售收入	Income from Commodity Sales	**7401369**	**639348**	**9.45**
服务业收入	Income from Service Trade	4406291	695595	18.75
税款收入	Income from Taxes	627296	62080	10.98
城乡个体经营收入	Income from Urban and Rural Individual Business	722550	90821	14.38
储蓄存款收入	Income from Saving Deposits	58456955	13299600	29.45
其他金融机构收入	Income from Other Financial Institutions	1021833	21659	2.17
居民归还贷款收入	Income from Repayment of Loans by Residents	275600	42688	18.33
汇兑收入	Income from Remittances	1318965	139611	11.84
有价证券收入	Income from Securities	240428	-103937	-30.18
其他收入	Other Income	7065377	1556866	28.26
#兑换外币收入	#Income from Exchange of Foreign Currencies	8022	-14698	-64.69
支出合计	**Total Expenditure**	**79266651**	**15957788**	**25.21**
工资性支出	Expenditure for Wages	5567711	650202	13.22
#国家工资及奖金支出	#Expenditure for Wages and Bounties of Government	3461292	365035	11.79
国家对个人其他支出	Other Payments to Individuals of Government	1137226	115199	11.27
部队存款支出	Expenditure for Army Deposits	159116	16250	11.37
其他单位工资性支出	Expenditure for Wages of Other Units	810077	153717	23.42
农副产品采购支出	Purchases of Agricultural and Sideline Products	1312879	33823	2.64
工矿及其他产品采购支出	Expenditure for Purchases of Industrial and Mineral Products	1120993	108955	10.77
行政企事业管理费支出	Government and Enterprises Overhead	3835337	404430	11.79
城乡个体经营支出	Expenditure for Individual Business	837961	26423	3.26
储蓄存款支出	Expenditure for Savings Deposits	57128430	12885593	29.12
其他金融机构支出	Expenditure for Other financial Institutions	674639	-4305	-0.63
居民提取贷款支出	Expenditure for Repayment of Loans by Residents	231405	15190	7.03
汇兑支出	Expenditure for Remittances	1505797	452578	42.97
有价证券支出	Expenditure for Securities	177559	15192	9.36
其他支出	Other Expenditure	6873940	1369707	24.88
#兑换外币支出	#Expenditure for Exchange of Foreign Currencies	26016	17038	189.78
附:代发工资	**Supersede Pay Wages**	**1622756**	**-537018**	**-24.86**

5-7 城市信用社信贷收支情况

Credit Income and Expenditures of Urban Credit Cooperative

单位：万元 (10 000 yuan)

项目	Item	2000		2001	
		年末余额 Balance at the Year-end	比年初增减 Increase Over the Year-beginning	年末余额 Balance at the Year-end	比年初增减 Increase Over the Year-beginning
各项存款	**Deposits**	**401442**	**-263113**	**326986**	**-41922**
企业存款	Deposits of Enterprises	71985	-106503	48111	-16106
活期存款	Demand Deposits	58236	-85674	38837	-13254
定期存款	Fixed Deposits	13749	-20829	9274	-2852
城镇储蓄存款	Savings Deposits in Urban	327695	-154022	276658	-27305
活期储蓄	Demand Saving	36806	-50458	20525	-12638
个人定期储蓄存款	Fixed Saving	290889	-103564	256133	-14667
农业存款	Agricultural Deposits				
信托存款	Trusted Deposits				
其他存款	Other Deposits	1762	-2588	2217	1489
代理财政性存款	Agent of Government Deposits	1057	490	4	-1052
发行金融债券	Issuance Financial Bonds				
发行政策性金融债券	Policy Financial Bonds				
国家投资债券	Government Investment Bonds				
卖出回购证券	Selling Debits of Buy-return		-1000		
向中央银行借款	Debit from Central Banks	30102	10534		
同业往来	Same Trade Current Account	23334	-15064	924	-9787
同业存放款	Deposits	2084	-3142		-456
同业拆借	Debit	21250	-11922	924	-9331
委托存款及委托投资基金	Commission Deposits and Commission Investment Funds		-72		
委托存款	Commission Deposits	-1000	-72		
委托投资基金	Commission Investment Funds	1000			
代理金融机构贷款基金	Loan Funds in Agent of Financial Institutions		-293		
中央银行委托贷款基金	Commission Loan Funds in Central Banks		-13		
各项准备	All Plans			1531	-101
其中：贷款呆帐准备金	Plan Funds for Loans			1531	-101
所有者权益	Creditors' Equity	-24096	6311	-1440	7323
实收资本	Total Capital Hold	6755	-9097	21167	15856
当年结益	Current Retained Profits	-13312	-13312	-18274	-16851
其他	Others	-95717	19930	-80382	3907
资金来源总计	**All Sources**	**336122**	**-242277**	**250274**	**-42699**

单位：万元　　　　5-7 续表　continued　　　　(10 000 yuan)

项目	Item	2000		2001	
		年末余额 Balance at the Year-end	比年初增减 Increase Over the Year-beginning	年末余额 Balance at the Year-end	比年初增减 Increase Over the Year-beginning
各项贷款	**Loans**	**260263**	**-137843**	**157411**	**-48172**
短期贷款	Short-term Loans	157885	-87007	136506	-24144
工业贷款	Industrial Loans	17755	-8256	19282	-12139
商业贷款	Commercial Loans	27877	-16640	29312	5412
收购贷款	Buying Loans				
建筑业贷款	Construction Loans		-123		
农业贷款	Agricultural Loans		-20	90	90
乡镇企业贷款	Loans to Township Enterprises	3			
三资企业贷款	Loans to Sino-foreign Joint Venture and Cooperative Enterprises and Foreign-funded Enterprises		-227		
私营企业及个体贷款	Loans to Private Enterprises and Individuals	14117	-16562	15132	926
贴现	Discount		-110	25	25
其他短期贷款	Other Short-term Loans	98133	-45069	72690	-18433
个人消费贷款	Loans to Personnal Expenditure				-80
中期流动资金贷款	Medium-term Circulating Funds of Loans		-348		
中长期贷款	Medium-term & Long-term Loans	24742	10616	20880	-24053
基本建设贷款	Capital Construction	15089	10289	11182	-13999
技术改造贷款	Technical Innovation				
其他中长期贷款	Other Medium-term&Long-term Loans	9653	327	9698	-5348
信托贷款	Trusted Loans				
逾期类贷款	Overdue Loans	77636	-61104		
国家投资债券贷款	Loans to Nation Investment Bonds				
有价证券及投资	Securities and Investment	10058	-29900	6275	-3296
应收及预付款	Receivable and Advance Payment			12005	-5170
应收利息	Receivable Interest			9846	-2236
缴存准备金存款	Hand in Deposits of Prepared Funds	36480	-36558	44755	9937
存放中央银行特种存款	Special Deposits in the Central Banks		-79		
存放中央银行财政性存款	Treasury Deposits in the Central Banks		-181		
同业往来	Same Trade Current Account	23660	-31389	27310	6847
存放同业	Deposits	19260	-25227	26618	9118
拆放同业	Debit	4400	-6162	692	-2271
代理金融机构贷款	Loans from Agent of Financial Institutions		-273		
代理人行专项贷款	Loans for Special Items from Agent People's Bank		-13		
库存现金	Vault Cash	5661	-6054	2518	-2845
外汇占款	Purchase of Foreign Exchanges				
资金运用总计	**All Uses**	**336122**	**-242277**	**250274**	**-42699**

5-8 农村信用社信贷收支情况

Credit Income and Expenditures of Rural Credit Cooperative

单位：万元 (10 000 yuan)

项目	Item	2000		2001	
		年末余额 Balance at the Year-end	比年初增减 Increase Over the Year-beginning	年末余额 Balance at the Year-end	比年初增减 Increase Over the Year-beginning
各项存款	**Deposits**	**5600272**	**686450**	**6332564**	**734062**
企业存款	Deposits of Enterprises	71644	30519	91850	20207
活期存款	Demand Deposits				
定期存款	Fixed Deposits	71644	30519	91850	20207
机关团体存款	Deposits of Government			18079	1081
储蓄存款	Savings Deposits	4991579	559705	5629327	637684
活期储蓄	Demand Saving	1107816	210142	1296450	188476
定期储蓄	Fixed Saving	3883763	349563	4332877	449208
农业存款	Agricultural Deposits	484121	91749	563106	79037
信托存款	Trusted Deposits				
其他存款	Other Deposits	52928	4477	30202	-3947
代理财政性存款	Agent of Government Deposits	1923	1716	3077	1156
发行金融债券	Issuance Financial Bonds	1	-3	1	
发行政策性金融债券	Policy Financial Bonds				
国家投资债券	Government Investment Bonds				
应付及暂收款	Payable and Temporarily Receiving			215751	231
应付及预提利息	Payable and Interset up Front			106741	5995
卖出回购证券	Selling Debits of Buy-return				
向中央银行借款	Debit from Central Banks	124370	42412	254536	130166
同业往来	Same Trade Current Account	148891	38876	223233	74410
同业存放款	Deposits	104623	30782	112672	8066
同业拆借	Debit	44268	8094	110561	66344
委托存款及委托投资基金	Commission Deposits and Commission Investment Funds	-1003	114	536	1442
委托存款	Commission Deposits	-1003	114		
委托投资基金	Commission Investment Funds				
代理金融机构贷款基金	Loan Funds in Agent of Financial Institutions	3280	-2081	6366	3084
中央银行委托贷款基金	Commission Loan Funds in Central Banks	214	188	3150	2936
所有者权益	Creditors' Equity	-446439	-98098	-523761	-79765
实收资本	Total Capital Hold	283653	45419	327397	43771
当年结益	Current Retained Profits	-127325	-127325	-114278	-113641
其他	Others	-284908	-105703	-399316	45964
资金来源总计	**All Sources**	**5146387**	**563683**	**6167383**	**916456**

单位：万元　　5-8 续表　continued　　(10 000 yuan)

项目	Item	2000 年末余额 Balance at the Year-end	2000 比年初增减 Increase Over the Year-beginning	2001 年末余额 Balance at the Year-end	2001 比年初增减 Increase Over the Year-beginning
各项贷款	**Loans**	**3720381**	**458716**	**4144471**	**424093**
短期贷款	Short-term Loans	3602216	485708	4005737	408312
工业贷款	Industrial Loans				
商业贷款	Commercial Loans				
收购贷款	Buying Loans				
建筑业贷款	Construction Loans				
农业贷款	Agricultural Loans	1650405	166983	1999799	349340
乡镇企业贷款	Loans to Township Enterprises	964508	122556	963966	-197
三资企业贷款	Loans to Sino-foreign Joint Venture and Cooperative Enterprises and Foreign-funded Enterprises				
私营企业及个体贷款	Loans to Private Enterprises and Individuals				
贴现	Discount	2224	-747	7987	5763
其他短期贷款	Other Short-term Loans	985079	196916	1041972	59169
中期流动资金贷款	Medium-term Circulating Funds of Loans				
中长期贷款	Medium-term & Long-term Loans	118165	-26992	130747	10018
基本建设贷款	Capital Construction				
技术改造贷款	Technical Innovation				
其他中长期贷款	Other Medium-term&Long-term Loans	118165	-26992	130747	10018
个人消费贷款	Loans to Personnal Expenditure			10914	7493
信托贷款	Trusted Loans				
逾期类贷款	Overdue Loans				
国家投资债券贷款	Loans to Nation Investment Bonds				
有价证券及投资	Securities and Investment	103182	6659	281593	178428
应收及预付款	Receivable and Advance Payment			104147	-5343
应收利息	Receivable Interest			43985	-4587
缴存准备金存款	Hand in Deposits of Prepared Funds	589765	55025	674733	76237
存放中央银行特种存款	Special Deposits in the Central Banks	20052	-2480	26675	6623
存放中央银行财政性存款	Treasury Deposits in the Central Banks	323	323	106	-217
同业往来	Same Trade Current Account	514993	27433	755788	254561
存放同业	Deposits	456120	39883	719471	277117
拆放同业	Debit	58873	-12450	36317	-22556
代理金融机构贷款	Loans from Agent of Financial Institutions	3572	-1887	5021	1449
代理人行专项贷款	Loans for Special Items from Agent of People's Bank	25	-1	50	25
库存现金	Vault Cash	194119	19894	174747	-19376
外汇占款	Purchase of Foreign Exchanges				
资金运用总计	**All Uses**	**5146387**	**563683**	**6167383**	**916456**

5-9 城乡信用社现金统计

Cash Statistics of Urban and Rural Credit Cooperative

单位:万元 (10 000 yuan)

项目	Item	城市信用社 Urban Credit Cooperative		农村信用社 Rural Credit Cooperative	
		2000	2001	2000	2001
收入合计	**Total Income**	**1817545**	**670051**	**16032988**	**19118495**
商品销售收入	Income from Commodity Sales	140447	44307	853008	1033820
服务业收入	Income from Service Trade	68504	16202	541818	692378
税款收入	Income from Taxes	20367	9857	112396	160511
城乡个体经营收入	Income from Urban and Rural Individual Business	91085	19534	1009928	1421806
储蓄存款收入	Income from Saving Deposits	1341398	525846	10995107	12780769
其他金融机构收入	Income from Other Financial Institutions	8286	46	55195	38530
居民归还贷款收入	Income from Repayment of Loans by Residents	51378	14358	1170848	1529602
汇兑收入	Income from Reemittances	1407	775	30191	34473
有价证券收入	Income from Securities	471	2422	4355	17326
其他收入	Other Income	94202	36704	1260142	1409280
#兑换外币收入	#Income from Exchange of Foreign Currencies				
支出合计	**Total Expenditure**	**1736161**	**627056**	**16129426**	**19173521**
投放(+)回笼(-)	Monetary Issues (+) Cash Withdrawn (-)	-81384	-42995	96438	55027
工资性支出	Expenditure for Wages	83354	17022	648919	789837
国家工资及奖金支出	Expenditure for Wages and Bounses of Government	38455	10396	252564	335016
国家对个人其他支出	Other Payments to Individuals of Government	14802	4193	101513	100108
部队存款支出	Expenditure for Army Deposits	736	76	2498	1178
其他单位工资性支出	Expenditure for Wages of Other Units	29361	3357	292344	353535
农副产品采购支出	Purchases of Agricultural and Sideline Products	40926	15094	333607	456182
工矿及其他产品采购支出	Expenditure for Purchases of Dustrial and Mineral Products	41123	18814	209957	215502
行政企事业管理费支出	Government and Enterprises Overhead	93592	27227	281325	355802
城乡个体经营支出	Expenditure for Individual Business	102080	20453	1223947	1552142
储蓄存款支出	Expenditure for Savings Deposits	1226228	476223	10649863	12388949
其他金融机构支出	Expenditure for Other financial Insititutions	7915	219	68069	49142
居民提取贷款支出	Expenditure for Repayment of Loans by Residents	37397	7146	1266373	1717301
汇兑支出	Expenditure for Remittances	100	675	44491	60868
有价证券支出	Expenditure for Securities	1451	2538	3226	5379
其他支出	Other Expenditure	101995	41645	1399649	1582417
#兑换外币支出	#Expenditure for Exchange of Foreign Currencies	17			
附：代发工资	**Supersede Pay Wages**	**6690**	**-**	**13038**	**46263**

5-10 城乡居民年末储蓄存款余额

Outstanding Amount of Saving Deposits in Urban and Rural Households at the Year-end

单位：亿元 (100 million yuan)

市州	Cities and Prefecture	2000 合计 Total	2000 定期 Fixed	2000 活期 Demand	2001 合计 Total	2001 定期 Fixed	2001 活期 Demand
合计	**Total**	**1855.97**	**1302.02**	**553.95**	**2183.73**	**1501.16**	**682.57**
长沙市	Changsha City	373.22	253.42	119.8	444.06	286.77	157.29
株洲市	Zhuzhou City	150.57	105.68	44.89	167.30	113.59	53.71
湘潭市	Xiangtan City	121.42	97.54	23.88	138.21	110.53	27.68
衡阳市	Hengyang City	201.86	146.75	55.11	237.06	170.91	66.15
邵阳市	Shaoyang City	146.28	101.93	44.35	170.99	119.46	51.53
岳阳市	YueYang City	128.28	86.9	41.38	150.20	103.10	47.10
常德市	Changde City	146.46	105.28	41.18	172.80	121.90	50.90
张家界市	Zhangjiajie City	26.79	16.58	10.21	31.00	18.77	12.23
益阳市	Yiyang C ity	95.19	70.1	25.09	111.69	80.58	31.11
郴州市	Chenzhou City	114.58	75.35	39.23	152.82	99.93	52.89
永州市	Yongzhou City	110.23	78.82	31.41	128.70	91.20	37.50
怀化市	Huaihua City	102.69	66.11	36.58	116.79	73.08	43.71
娄底市	Loudi City	98.91	75.04	23.87	115.19	86.08	29.11
湘西自治州	West Hunan A.P	39.49	22.52	16.97	46.31	25.68	20.63

5-11 保险机构与人员

Institutions and Personnel of Insurance System

项 目	Item	1995	1999	2000	2001
保险机构数（个）	Number of Institutions of Insurance System (unit)	173	332	395	407
省级公司	Provincial Branches	3	4	7	10
地市级公司	Prefecture/City Branches	27	46	63	72
县支公司	County Branches	113	282	325	325
年底实有职工人数（人）	Employees at the Year-end (person)	5255	6118	6522	6532

5-12 财产保险业务主要指标（2001年）

Major Indicators of Property Insurance Business (2001)

指标	Item	承保数量（件）Number of Insuance (case)	保险金额（万元）Insurance Value (10 000 yuan)	保费收入（万元）Premiums (10 000 yuan)	赔款件数（件）Number of Indemnity (case)	赔款支出（万元）Indemnity Expenditure (10 000 yuan)
合 计	**Total**	**1407073**	**32415130**	**162961**	**112688**	**81159**
财产险	**Property Insurance**	**1163263**	**29995361**	**153218**	**103932**	**77537**
企业财产险	Enterprises Property Insurance	19564	14771259	35324	15127	15076
家庭财产险	Family Property Insurance	745051	2007405	5148	8398	1745
机动车辆险	Machine Driving Cars Insurance	323787	7440170	95809	77529	53572
飞机及飞机责任险	Airplane Insurance	3	14255	109	-	690
船舶险	Ships Insurance	50	22811	535	204	387
货运险	Freight Transport Insurance	66760	4195436	11161	1918	3774
#进出口货物险	# Exports and Imports Insurance	8147	1184027	3213	159	812
工程及工程责任险	Projects Responsibility Insurance	503	786725	2073	130	845
机器损坏保险	Machine Damage Insurance	369	364435	1812	457	1101
能源保险	Energy Property Insurance	1	36272	41	-	-
其他财产保险	Other Property Insurance	7175	356592	1206	169	167
责任保险	**Liability Insurance**	**240214**	**2180703**	**8024**	**8505**	**2967**
产品责任保险	Products Liability Insurance	160	163681	426	90	146
雇主责任保险	Employer Liability Insurance	30145	969636	4261	4224	1713
公众责任保险	Public Liability Insurance	49768	369577	1229	3222	445
其他责任保险	Other Liability Insurance	160141	677810	2108	969	663
信用保险	**Credit Insurance**	**1468**	**35980**	**283**	**1**	**1**
保证保险	**Guarantee Insurance**	**1883**	**120200**	**458**	**20**	**78**
农业险	**Agriculture Insurance**	**245**	**82885**	**977**	**230**	**577**
其中：种植业保险	Planting Insurance	245	81436	900	185	495
养殖业保险	Cultivation Insurance	-	1449	77	45	82

5-13 人身保险业务主要指标（2001年）

Major Indicators of Life Insurance Business (2001)

单位：万元 (10 000 yuan)

指标	Item	保费收入 Premiums	赔款支出 Indemnity Expenditure	退保金 Withdrawal Amount Insured	年金给付 Annuity Payment	满期给付 Mature Payment	死伤医疗给付 Payment for Death,Injury and Medical Treatment
合 计	**Total**	**397896.55**	**31719.57**	**53639.16**	**31487.07**	**31580.39**	**12369.47**
个人业务	**Personal Business**	**302443.7**	**8551.42**	**36769.85**	**20057.41**	**27976.25**	**10985.85**
人寿保险	Life Insurance	292254.9	1260.48	36757.23	20057.41	27976.25	10985.85
非分红产品	Non Bonus Products	236273.9	165.92	35372.1	20057.41	27976.25	10985.85
定期寿险	Term Life Insurance	657.26	31.3	1856.33	10	10	77
两全寿险	Endowment Life Insurance	76330.7	140.38	15201.29	1634.59	14496.11	3831.7
终身寿险	Whole Life Insurance	127379.4	-16.02	3335.22	12304.18	12121	4902.87
年金	Annuity	31906.55	10.26	14979.26	6108.64	1349.14	2168.28
分红产品	Bonus Products	50564.2	31.26	996.14			
定期寿险	Term Life Insurance	3323.2	17.22	58.66			
两全寿险	Endowment Life Insurance	28078.9	1.82	219.5			
终身寿险	Whole Life Insurance	18354.1	12.22	626.65			
年金	Annuity	808		91.33			
意外伤害保险	Accidence Injury Insurance	2207.22	978.66	0.49			
一年期以内	Within One Year Period	297.92	42.63				
一年期	One Year Period	1909	936.03	0.49			
健康保险	Health Insurance	7981.55	6312.28	12.13			
一年期及以内	One Year Period and Within One Year Period	7323.85	6301.28				
一年期以上	Over One Year Period	657.7	11	12.13			
团体业务	**Group Insurance**	**95452.85**	**23168.15**	**16869.31**	**11429.66**	**3604.14**	**1383.62**
人寿保险	Life Insurance	57312.99	31.63	16733.33	11429.66	3604.14	280.72
非分红产品	Non Bonus Products	49370.96	31.63	16407.91	11353.66	3604.14	280.72
定期寿险	Term Life Insurance	104.71	31.63	19.26		170.65	3
两全寿险	Endowment Life Insurance	127		1250	2161	1949	216
终身寿险	Whole Life Insurance	346.51		5.16	48.64	95.87	2.02
年金	Annuity	48792.74		15133.49	9144.02	1168.32	26.9
分红产品	Bonus Products	6248.3		258	76		
定期寿险	Term Life Insurance						
两全寿险	Endowment Life Insurance						
终身寿险	Whole Life Insurance						
年金	Annuity	6248.3		258	76		
意外伤害保险	Accidence Injury Insurance	34713.23	17841.36	65.33			366.1
一年期以内	Within One Year Period	3567.83	1855.02				366.1
一年期	One Year Period	31145.4	15471				
健康保险	Health Insurance	3426.63	5295.16	70.65			736.82
一年期及以内	One Year Period and Within One Year Period	3382.38	4646.2				736.82
一年期以上	Over One Year Period	44.25	648.96				

六、物价指数

PRICE INDICES

资料整理人员：　彭建霞　谌　滨　龙立珍
刘征宇　蔡红宇

6-1 各种物价总指数

Overall Price Indices

年份 Year	商品零售价格指数 General Retail Price Index	城市居民消费价格指数 Urban Consumer Price Index	农村居民消费价格指数 Rural Consumer Price Index	农产品收购价格指数 General Purchasing Price Index of Farm Products	农村工业品零售价格指数 General Rural Retail Price Index of Industrial Products	农产品成交价格指数 Farm Products Trade Price Index	工农业商品综合比价指数 General Price Parity Index of Industrial and Farm Products
以上年为100	**Preceding year =100**						
1985	111.1	111.9	110.2	111.6	106.1	118.7	95.1
1986	104.8	105.4	105.3	105.7	103.3	104.7	97.7
1987	110.6	111.3	108.8	110.2	109.9	119.3	99.7
1988	125.9	125.7	125.4	123.1	123.6	136.7	100.4
1989	118.1	117.3	119.1	106.8	120.9	110.8	113.2
1990	99.4	100.6	100.2	94.1	99.7	94.1	106.0
1991	104.1	105.1	103.8	94.3	103.1	99.6	109.3
1992	109.5	113.5	107.9	99.1	104.9	107.8	105.9
1993	115.1	117.4	116.4	114.7	114.9	113.9	100.2
1994	124.5	124.8	125.6	144.1	117.2	135.5	81.3
1995	115.5	118.1	119.5	117.2	116.7	125.2	99.6
1996	105.2	107.2	108.2	104.9	105.1	101.1	100.2
1997	100.3	103.0	102.5	95.3	100.4	95.0	105.4
1998	97.9	100.5	100.1	90.4	97.5	91.7	107.9
1999	97.6	99.6	101.4	91.1	97.0	93.7	106.5
2000	99.3	101.3	101.4	96.8	98.8	95.7	102.1
2001	98.8	98.9	99.3	-	-	96.0	-
以1978年为100	**1978 =100**						
1985	137.1	145.2	113.4	190.3	116.2	157.8	61.1
1986	143.7	153.0	119.4	201.1	120.0	165.2	59.7
1987	158.9	170.3	129.9	221.6	131.9	197.1	59.5
1988	200.1	214.1	162.9	272.8	163.0	269.4	59.7
1989	236.3	251.1	194.0	291.4	197.1	298.5	67.6
1990	234.9	252.6	194.4	274.2	196.5	280.9	71.6
1991	244.5	265.5	201.8	258.6	202.6	279.8	78.3
1992	267.7	301.3	217.7	256.3	212.5	301.6	82.9
1993	308.2	353.7	253.4	294.0	244.2	343.5	83.1
1994	383.6	441.4	318.2	423.7	286.2	465.4	67.6
1995	443.1	521.3	380.2	496.6	334.0	582.7	67.3
1996	466.1	558.8	411.4	520.9	351.0	589.1	67.4
1997	467.5	575.6	421.7	496.4	352.4	559.6	71.0
1998	457.7	578.5	422.1	448.7	343.6	513.6	76.6
1999	446.7	576.2	428.0	408.8	333.3	480.9	81.5
2000	443.6	583.7	434.0	395.7	329.3	460.2	83.2
2001	438.3	577.3	431.0	-	-	441.8	-

6-2 零售物价分类指数(2001年)

Overall Retail Indices by Category of Commodities (2001)

类　别	Item	全省 Total Indices		城市 Urban Indices		农村 Rural Indices	
		以上年为100 Preceding year=100	以1978年为100 1978=100	以上年为100 Preceding year=100	以1978年为100 1978=100	以上年为100 Preceding year=100	以1978年为100 1978=100
零售价格总指数	**General Retail Price Indices**	98.8	438.3	98.1	414.4	99.4	393.0
食品类	Food	98.8	605.5	98.6	189.0	99.1	525.5
粮食	Grain	100.6	803.7	99.3	701.1	101.4	560.6
油脂类	Oil or Fat	89.0	452.7	90.2	412.8	88.0	618.1
肉禽蛋	Meal, Poultry and Eggs	99.2	664.8	99.5	670.5	98.9	649.4
水产品	Aquatic Products	98.3	608.4	99.2	602.6	97.4	623.9
鲜菜	Fresh Vegetables	99.2	1520.2	98.7	1403.1	100.1	
干菜	Dried Vegetables	97.4	501.9	97.2	486.6	97.5	525.5
鲜果	Fresh Fruits	97.9	528.4	96.1	508.5	100.2	321.7
干果	Dried Fruits	100.1	458.4	99.2	467.7	101.0	388.7
其他食品类	Other Food	101.3	461.5	102.0	535.3	100.8	378.6
饮食业	Catering Trade	98.6		98.1		99.2	
饮料、烟酒类	Beverages,Tobacco and Liquor	98.3	235.0	98.5	241.0	98.2	185.5
服装、鞋帽类	Garments,Shoes and Hats	98.9	230.3	97.4	231.3	100.2	240.2
纺织品类	Textiles	98.8	303.6	98.2	304.4	99.2	296.7
中、西药品类	Traditional Chinese and Western Medicines	100.5	407.6	99.6	377.2	101.5	450.7
化妆品类	Cosmetics	99.9		100.0		99.8	
书报、杂志类	Newspapers and Magazines	119.6	1719.0	111.5	1523.1	126.8	1995.5
文化体育用品类	Cultural and Sports Goods	98.5	161.9	99.1	159.1	97.6	168.4
日用品类	Articles for Daily Use	98.0	269.4	98.9	246.3	96.9	293.2
家用电器类	Household Appliances	93.5	108.8	92.7	114.9	94.3	104.3
首饰类	Jewelry	88.5		88.0		90.4	
燃料类	Fuels	102.6	569.0	98.2	570.9	107.6	490.5
建筑装璜材料类	Building Decoration Materials	97.8		99.2		96.6	
机电产品类	Mechanical and Electrical Products	93.8		93.7		93.9	

6-3 农业生产资料价格指数(2001年)

Price Indices of Agricultural Means of Production (2001)

类 别	Item	以上年价格为100 Preceding year=100	以1978年价格为100 1978 year=100
总指数	**General Indices**	98.4	392.2
小农具	Small Farm Tools	100.0	452.5
饲料	Forage	98.1	
幼禽家畜	Young Livestock and Fowls	102.6	
大牲畜	Large Animals	107.9	
半机械化农具	Semi-mechanized Farm Tools	99.1	516.6
机械化农具	Mechanized Farm Machinery	97.0	254.0
化肥	Chemical Fertilizer	98.5	316.1
农药及农药械	Pesticide and Its Appliances	97.5	249.5
#化学农药	Chemical Pesticide	97.6	255.4
农药械	Its Appliances	96.9	186.5
农用机油	Oil for Farm Machinery	99.2	1131.5
其他	Others	83.1	318.3

6-4 居民消费价格总指数

Overall Consumer Price Indices

年份 Year	居民消费价格总指数 Overall Consumer Price Indices	城市 Urban	农村 Rural	服务项目价格指数 Services Price Indices
以上年为100	**Preceding year =100**			
1985	110.9	111.9	110.2	106.5
1986	105.3	105.4	105.3	106.7
1987	109.8	111.3	108.8	116.4
1988	125.6	125.7	125.4	125.6
1989	118.2	117.3	119.1	131.3
1990	100.4	100.6	100.2	113.9
1991	104.4	105.1	103.8	106.2
1992	110.7	113.5	107.9	119.1
1993	116.8	117.4	116.4	130.0
1994	125.3	124.8	125.6	125.5
1995	119.0	118.1	119.5	124.8
1996	107.7	107.2	108.2	112.4
1997	102.8	103.0	102.5	112.5
1998	100.2	100.5	100.1	113.4
1999	100.5	99.6	101.4	116.5
2000	101.4	101.3	101.4	113.6
2001	99.1	98.9	99.3	102.5
以1985年为100	**1985 =100**			
1985	100.0	100.0	100.0	100.0
1986	105.3	105.4	105.3	106.7
1987	115.6	117.3	114.6	124.2
1988	145.2	147.5	143.7	156.0
1989	171.6	173.0	171.1	204.9
1990	172.3	174.0	171.4	233.4
1991	179.9	182.9	178.0	247.8
1992	199.2	207.6	192.0	295.1
1993	232.6	243.7	223.5	383.7
1994	291.5	304.1	280.7	481.5
1995	346.9	359.2	335.7	601.0
1996	373.6	385.1	363.2	675.4
1997	384.1	396.7	372.3	759.8
1998	384.9	398.7	372.7	861.7
1999	386.8	397.1	377.9	1003.9
2000	392.2	402.3	383.2	1140.4
2001	388.7	397.9	380.5	1168.9

6-5 居民消费价格分类指数(2001年)

Consumer Price Indices by Category (2001)

类别	Item	全省 Total Indices		城市 Urban Indices		农村 Rural Indices	
		以上年为100 Preceding year=100	以1978年为100 1978=100	以上年为100 Preceding year=100	以1978年为100 1978=100	以上年为100 Preceding year=100	以1978年为100 1978=100
居民消费价格总指数	**General Consumer Price Indices**	99.1	441.6	98.9	577.3	99.3	431.0
食品	Food	98.6	571.0	98.3	625.8	98.9	498.5
粮食	Grain	98.6	793.2	99.1	722.4	96.8	527.0
淀粉及薯类	Starches and Tubers	100.5		99.9		103.0	
干豆类及豆制品	Bear and Its Products	99.7		100.5		97.8	
油脂类	Oil or Fat	91.1	439.6	90.3	402.4	91.5	587.9
肉禽及其制品	Meal,Poultry and Their Products	99.2	701.7	98.9	716.1	99.6	685.2
蛋类	Eggs	107.5		105.7		110.2	
水产品类	Aquatic Products	96.7	590.0	96.2	568.2	97.3	624.9
菜类	Vegetables	95.1	1265.2	95.3	562.8	94.2	
调味品	Flavoring	99.3	341.1	99	1334.2	99.5	361.2
糖类	Carbohydrate	104.4	398.8	104.8	530.5	104.1	386.7
烟草类	Tobacco	100.1	229.6	100.4	337.5	99.9	190.0
酒	Wine	97.1	198.7	98.6	215.9	95.3	176.1
茶和饮料	Tea and Beverages	98.6	201.7	98.5	215.7	98.8	182.6
干鲜瓜果类	Dried and Fresh Melons and Fruits	99.4	535.4	98.1	507.7	102.3	379.4
糕点类	Cake	99.6	492.6	100.4	582.6	98.2	374.8
奶及奶制品	Milk and Its Products	101.2	333.4	101.5	357.8	97.0	292.2
其他食品	Other Food	98.3	210.6	99	433.7	97.7	314.4
饮食业	Catering Trade	100.0		99.2		100.7	
衣着	Clothing	97.4	244.2	96.4	235.8	99.3	248.7
家庭设备、用品	Household Facilities and Article	96.4	165.0	95.8	198.4	98.0	196.9
医疗保健	Medicine and Medical Articles	99.8	428.6	98.9	370.8	100.7	472.1
交通和通信	Means of Transportation&Communication	97.4		98.2		95.9	
娱乐、教育文化用品	Recreation, Education and Culture Articles	102.1	186.6	103.3	178.4	100.5	193.1
居住	Residence	100.0		99.6		100.3	
服务项目	Services	102.5	1127.7	104	1394.8	100.1	1561.8

6-6 十四个调查市县价格指数

Price Indices in 14 Cities and Counties Under Investigation

(以上年价格为100) (preceding year=100)

市县	Cities and counties	居民消费价格指数 Consumer Price Index		商品零售指数 General Retail Price Index		农业生产资料价格指数 Agricultural Means of Production Price Index	
		2000	2001	2000	2001	2000	2001
长沙市	Changsha City	101.7	98.4	100.7	98.2	-	-
株洲市	Zhuzhou City	101.6	99.3	99.8	98.5	-	-
湘潭市	Xiangtan City	101.6	100.4	99.4	99.3	-	-
衡阳市	Hengyang City	100.4	99.1	98.5	98.6	-	-
邵阳市	Shaoyang City	100.9	99.5	99.2	98.2	-	-
岳阳市	Yueyang City	101.3	97.5	98.4	96.6	-	-
常德市	Changde City	101.6	98.1	100.0	97.9	-	-
益阳市	Yiyang City	100.7	99.6	99.7	99.6	-	-
郴州市	Chenzhou City	101.4	97.5	99.4	97.2	-	-
怀化市	Huaihua City	100.2	100.0	99.5	99.6	-	-
耒阳市	Leiyang City	102.2	100.1	99.4	99.7	101.7	97.0
慈利县	Cili County	101.6	99.7	97.2	99.1	97.4	98.9
道 县	Daoxian County	101.8	98.9	99.3	99.5	95.2	97.7
新化县	Xinhua County	100.2	99.2	97.1	98.9	102.9	99.4

6-7 农业生产资料价格指数(2001)

Price Indices of Agricultural Means of Production (2001)

(以上年价格为100) (preceding year=100)

类 别	Item	道县 Dao County	耒阳市 Leiyang City	新化县 Xinhua County	慈利县 Cili County
农业生产资料价格指数	**Price Indices of Agricultural Means of Production**	97.7	97.0	99.4	98.9
小农具	Small Farm Tools	97.1	102.0	100.0	100.3
饲料	Forage	95.2	99.9	101.9	97.0
幼禽家畜	Young Livestock and Fowls	103.6	94.3	101.2	111.3
大牲畜	Large Animals	98.4	-	120.9	107.9
半机械化农具	Semi-mechanized Farm Tools	99.3	99.8	93.6	100.0
机械化农具	Mechanized Farm Machinery	92.9	95.4	99.9	98.9
化肥	Chemical Fertilizer	99.5	97.2	100.4	97.4
农药及农药械	Pesticide and Its Appliances	96.3	101.1	93.5	98.6
农用机油	Oil for Farm Machinery	104.5	96.5	99.8	96.1
其他	Others	76.2	82.4	86.8	88.1

6-8 农产品生产者价格指数（2001年）

Producer Price Indices of Farm Products (2001)

项目	Item	以上年为100 Preceding Year =100	项目	Item	以上年为100 Preceding Year =100
生产者价格总指数	**Overall Producer Price Indices**	100.94	#毛竹（楠竹）	Phyllostachys	97.43
农业产品	**Farming Products**	**101.88**	林产品	Forest Products	94.12
谷物（原粮）	Cereals	111.49	工业用原料	Industry Raw Materials	95.36
小麦	Wheat	98.47	#油桐籽	Tung-oil Seeds	98.89
稻谷	Paddy	112.19	油茶籽	Tea-oil Seeds	95.49
#早籼稻	Early Season Rice	107.76	坚果	Nut	74.49
晚籼稻	Late Season Rice	112.49	其它林产品	Other Forest Products	99.04
其它稻谷	Other Rice	122.90	竹笋干	Dried Bamboo Shoot	99.04
玉米	Maize	99.51	**牧业（畜产品）**	**Animal Husbandry**	**100.54**
薯类	Tubers	103.34	成年役畜、产品畜	Draught Animals and Commodity Animals	100.22
#红薯	Sweet Potato	104.36			
马铃薯	Potatoes	100.63	#役用牛	Draught Cattle	100.22
豆类	Beans	94.58	肉畜（毛重）	Fatstock (gross weight)	100.81
#大豆	Soja	95.37	#猪	Hogs	100.81
绿豆	Mung Bean	89.56	肉牛	Beef Cattle	102.16
油料	Oil-bearing Crops	90.04	山羊	Goat	100.23
#花生	Peanut	74.76	家禽（毛重）	Fowl (gross weight)	99.47
油菜籽	Rapeseed	96.99	#鸡	Hen	98.34
棉花	Cotton	55.72	鸭	Duck	100.63
麻类	Fiber Crops	93.16	其它饲养动物	Other Feeding Animals	101.80
糖料	Sugar	91.95	#兔	Rabbit	101.54
烟叶	Tobacco	85.38	狗	Dog	100.64
中药材	Medicinal herbs	99.37	蛇	Snake	103.78
#金银花	Honeysuckle	99.62	蛋类	Poultry Eggs	99.64
白术	Lagehead Atractylodes	98.68	#鸡蛋	Hens' Egg	99.81
蔬菜	Vegetables	97.67	鸭蛋	Ducks' Egg	99.36
叶菜类	Greenstuff	95.89	奶类	Milk	97.12
瓜菜类	Melon and Fruit	89.63	#牛奶	Cow Milk	97.12
块根、块茎菜类	Tuber	114.86	**渔业产品**	Fishery Products	98.63
茄果菜类	Nightshade	98.46	淡水鱼类	Freshwater Fish	98.28
菜用豆类	Navy Bean	84.46	#青鱼	Mackerel	99.67
水生菜类	Aquicolous Vegetable	95.47	草鱼	Grass Carp	100.33
食用菌（干鲜混合）	Mushroom (dried and fresh)	102.45	鲤鱼	Carp	92.81
水果	Fruits	91.19	鲢鱼	Silver Carp	99.45
柑桔类	Citrus	108.41	鲫鱼	Crucian	97.75
果用瓜	Fruit Melons	78.35	鳙鱼	Bighrad Carp	96.03
其它水果	Other fruits	90.53	其它淡水养殖产品	Other Freshwater Aquatic Products Cultured	100.87
茶叶（干品）	Tea (dried tea)	96.79			
林业产品	**Forestry Products**	**96.62**	#甲鱼	Turtle	100.30
木材	Timber	99.06	黄鳝	Yellow Eel	103.08
竹材	Bamboo	97.43	泥鳅	Loach	99.54

6-9 主要原材料、燃料、动力购进价格指数

Principal Raw and Processed Materials, Fuel, Power Purchasing Price Indices

(以上年为100) (preceding year=100)

类 别	Item	1995	1999	2000	2001
全部原材料	**General Purchasing Price Indices**	**117.58**	**96.2**	**106.7**	**101.1**
#燃料动力类	Fuels and Motive Power	112.18	98.2	108.6	101.5
黑色金属材料类	Ferrous Metals Materials	94.1	95.5	102.8	102.3
有色金属材料类	Nonferrous Metals Materials and Electric Wire	131.2	96.5	113.5	97.5
化工原料类	Chemical Raw Materials	125.14	95.3	115.4	98.7
木材及纸浆类	Logging and Paper Pulp	129.37	99.3	102.0	100.6
建材及非金属矿类	Building and Nonmetal Materials	103.04	96.8	99.3	98.6
其它工业原料及半成品类	Other Industry Raw Materials & Semi-Finished Products	109.59	92.5	100.4	102.1
农副产品类	Farm Products	138.68	93.4	104.5	103.2
纺织原料类	Textile Raw Materials	123.84	96.7	101.8	102.3

6-10 工业品出厂价格指数

Ex–Factory Price Indices of Industrial Products

(以上年价格为100) (preceding year=100)

行业	Sector	1995	1999	2000	2001
全部工业品	**General Industrial Products**	**121.37**	**98.5**	**102.9**	**99.8**
生产资料	Means of Production	118.97	97.8	104.1	99.8
采掘工业	Mining and Quarrying Industry	131.32	96.8	99.4	104.4
原材料工业	Raw Materials Industry	119.1	99.0	108.5	99.3
加工工业	Manufacturing Industry	115.5	97.9	98.2	99.6
生活资料	Means of Subsistence	126.4	99.9	99.1	99.9
食品类	Food	132.56	103.0	98.5	100.7
衣着类	Clothing	121.1	96.1	101.4	98.7
一般日用品	Articles for Daily use	121.94	97.2	98.1	100.1
耐用消费品	Durable Consumer Goods	104.37	99.5	97.4	97.8
按工业部门分:	**by Sector**				
冶金工业	Manufacturing Industry	114.54	91.8	102.6	100.9
电力工业	Power Industry	117.56	104.1	101.4	100.1
煤炭及炼焦工业	Coal Industry	125.83	97.9	97.6	102.8
石油工业	Petroleum Industry	119.57	105.5	140.7	96.8
化学工业	Chemical Industry	133.42	94.9	99.1	99.0
机械工业	Machine Building Industry	105.2	98.6	99.0	98.9
建材工业	Building Materials Industry	101.26	98.7	96.2	100.7
森林工业	Timber Industry	121.06	99.7	101.1	92.5
食品工业	Food Industry		102.1	98.3	101.2
纺织工业	Textile Industry	120.84	97.1	108.3	94.7
缝纫工业	Tailoring Industry	124.18	91.6	93.3	96.8
皮革工业	Leather Industry	119.75	85.4	110.4	109.9
造纸工业	Paper Industry	149.45	96.4	98.8	100.0
文教艺术用品工业	Cultural, Educational & Handicrafts Articles Industry		97.5	98.9	98.5
其他工业	Others	140.51	95.6	107.7	102.3

6-11 主要工业产品分行业出厂价格指数

Major Industrial Products Price Indices by Sector

(以上年为100) (preceding year=100)

行业	Setor	1995	1999	2000	2001
煤炭采选业	Coal Mining and Dressing	127.05	98.2	97.7	102.64
黑色金届矿采选业	Ferrous Metals Mining and Dressing		95.9	87.48	
有色金属矿采选业	Nonferrous Metals Mining and Dressing	103.58	94.7	104.94	110.65
建筑材料及其它非金属矿采选业	Nonmetal Minerals Mining and Dressing	150.33	95.1	88.99	93.65
采盐业	Salt Mining	129.41	102.5	102.69	97.67
木材及竹材采运业	Logging and Transport of Wood and Bamboo	96.91	105.2	101.08	101.62
自来水生产与供应业	Production and supply of Tap Water	113.54	126.6	120.15	102.36
食品制造业	Food Production	152.05	104.6	88.02	102.37
饮料制造业	Beverage Production	153.26	97.8	100.51	101.02
烟草加工业	Tobacco Processing	104.53	101.4	103.4	99.07
饲料工业	Feed Industry	115.4	92	97.97	102.56
纺织业	Textile Industry	138.1	106	107.52	94.73
缝纫业	Garments and other Fiber products	113.21	95.7	94.38	96.84
皮革、毛皮及其制品业	Leather, Furs and Related Products	124.17	83.9	118.27	109.88
木材加工及竹藤棕草制品业	Timber Processing, Bamboo, Cane, Palm Fiber & Straw Products	119.75	102.7	100.08	89.01
家具制造业	Furniture Manufacturing	104.13	94.2	102.14	99.09
造纸及纸制品业	Papermaking and Paper Products	90.66	96.5	98.44	100.03
文教体育用品制造业	Cultural, Educational and Sports Articles	149.45	95.7	97.9	98.52
电力、蒸气、热水生产和供应业	Production and supply of Electric Power		106.5	101.48	99.74
石油加工业	Petroleum Processing and coking	117.56	95.6	137.98	96.76
炼焦、煤气及煤制品业	Production and suppiy of gas	119.57	103.1	98.41	102.29
化学工业	Raw Chemical Materials and Chemical products	106.37	99.1	99.35	99.78
医药工业	Medical and Pharmaceutical products	135.18	98.8	96.71	96.33
化学纤维工业	Chemical Fiber	115.28	95.3	108.43	89.97
橡胶制品业	Rubber Products	146.19	94.2	97.19	100.1
塑料制品业	Plastic Products	125.05	97.2	105.41	102.25
建筑材料及其它非金届矿制品业	Nonmetal Mineral Products	128.57	99.7	97.14	100.65
黑色金属冶炼及压延加工业	Smelting and Pressing of Ferrous Metals	100.94	98.1	101	101.32
有色金后冶炼及压延加工业	Smelting and Pressing of Nonferrous Metals	97.48	102.2	105.8	97.34
金属制品业	Metal Products	128.66	106.1	96.81	99.2
机械工业	Machine Buiding Industry	95.24	99.5	99.61	99.09
交通运输设备制造业	Transportation Equipment Manufacturing	103.86	98.7	99	98.98
电气机械及器材制造业	Electric Machinery and Equipment	104.42	97.8	100.58	99.2
电力及通讯设备制造业	Electronic and Telecommunications Equipment	112.62	105.6	98.71	97.3
仪器仪表及其它计量器具制造业	Instruments, Meters and Calculating Equipment	104.72	95.3	103.53	100.32
工艺美术制造业	Arts and Crafts	99.73	95.8	101.97	

6-12 主要市州房地产价格指数

Real Estate Price Indices of Major Cities

(以上年为100) (preceding year =100)

市	Cities	销售价格指数 Selling Price Indices		租赁价格指数 Venting Price Indices		土地交易价格指数 Transaction Price Indices of Land	
		2000	2001	2000	2001	2000	2001
全 省	Total	101.1	101.9	100.4	99.6	103.4	103.3
长沙市	ChangSha City	99.6	102.1	99.1	102.5	102.7	103.8
株洲市	ZhuZhou City	103.1	101.8	101.8	102.4	101.5	104.9
湘潭市	XiangTan City	98.4	101.5	101.2	100.1	103.4	103.6
岳阳市	YueYang City	99.0	101.5	100.1	99.1	100.6	100.3
郴州市	ChenZhou City	106.1	102.4	94.0	99.8	103.2	102.9
衡阳市	HengYang City	103.2	102.6	103.0	99.1	104.9	104.9
娄底市	LouDI City	99.8	101.9	110.7	97.1	100.2	100.1
邵阳市	ShaoYang City	94.9	99.2	96.7	98.5	106.7	101.4
怀化市	HuaiHua City	101.2	102.5	96.9	98.9	101.5	101.2
常德市	ChangDe City	99.8	101.4	100.7	101.8	104.2	100.5
益阳市	YiYang City	98.8	97.8	102.4	98.7	104.7	102.0
永州市	YongZhou City	99.3	101.2	92.8	99.8	100.2	105.1

注:张家界市、湘西自治州因各种原因数据空缺。

Data of Zhangjiajie city and West Hunan A.P is missing for some reason.

6-13 固定资产投资和建筑业价格指数

Price Indices of Investment in Fixed Assets and Construction

(以上年为100) (preceding year=100)

项 目	Item	1995	1999	2000	2001
固定资产投资价格总指数	**Price Indices of Investment in Fixed Assets**	**109.5**	**100.5**	**102.3**	**100.3**
建筑安装工程	Construction and Installation	110.4	100.6	103.3	101.8
设备、工具、器具购置	Purchase of Equipment,Tools and Instruments	104.7	98.6	99.0	99.1
其他投资	Others	114.7	103.1	101.4	101.1
建筑业价格总指数	**Price Indices of Construction**				
直接费用指数	Direct Costs	110.6	100.3	102.8	102.0
人工费	Manpower	133.4	104.7	105.6	107.4
材料费	Materials	105.6	98.6	101.3	100.8
其他费用指数	Others Costs	109.0	102.6	106.2	100.4
主要材料费用价格指数	**Price Indices of Main Material Costs**				
钢 材	Steel Products	94.3	97.6	103.1	99.3
木 材	Timber	109.3	100.5	95.4	95.2
水 泥	Cement	104.8	96.8	100.6	102.0
地方材料	Local Materials	114.9	101.4	99.5	103.1
其他材料	Others	115.5	98.7	99.7	99.4

七、人民生活

PEOPLE'S LIVELIHOOD

资料整理人员：　梁　可　　杨鸿雁

7-1 人民物质文化生活提高情况

Improvement in People's Material and Cultural Life

指 标	Item	1995	1999	2000	2001
就业	**Employment**				
每一农村劳动力负担人数(人)	Number of Dependents Per Rural Laborer(person)	1.6	1.52	1.46	1.45
每一城镇就业者负担人数(人)	Number of Dependents Per Urban Employee(person)	1.67	1.66	1.71	1.77
城镇失业率(%)	Urban Unemployment Rate (%)	3.8	3.9	3.7	4
收入	**Income**				
农村居民家庭人均可支配收入 (元)	Annual Per Capita Disposable Income of Rural Residents (yuan)	-	-	2159	2264.71
农村居民家庭人均纯收入 (元)	Annual Per Capita Net Income of Rural Residents (yuan)	1425.16	2147.18	2197.16	2299.46
城镇居民家庭人均可支配收入 (元)	Annual Per Capita Disposable Income of Urban Residents(yuan)	4699.2	5815.4	6218.7	6780.6
职工年平均货币工资 (元)	Average Money Wage of Staff and Workers (yuan)	4797	5939	6515	7698
城乡居民年底人均储蓄存款余额 (元)	Per Capita Balance of Saving Deposit in Urban and Rural Residents at Year-end (yuan)	1391.42	2585.92	2862.71	3319.26
全省居民消费水平 (元)	**Consumption Level (yuan)**	**1752**	**2594**	**2723**	**2845**
农民	Peasants Residents	1294	1945	1981	-
非农业居民	Non-agricultural Residents	3884	5290	5705	-
住房 (平方米)	**Per Capita Living Floor Space (sq.m)**				
农村平均每人住房面积	Rural Residents	25.57	29.88	30.92	32.87
城市平均每人居住面积	Urban Residents	7.75	10.77	11.75	11.8
交通	**Traffic**				
农村居民每百户拥有摩托车(辆)	Motor Cycles per 100 Households in Rural (unit)	-	-	10.51	12.41
城镇居民每百户拥有摩托车(辆)	Motor Cycles per 100 Households in Urban (unit)	3.8	13.5	13.2	15.5
城市每万人拥有公共车辆(标台)	Buses per 10 000 persons in Cities (unit)	9.2	10.32	10.43	10.39
城市公用事业	**Public Utilities in Urban Areas**				
自来水普及率 (%)	Rate of Access to Tap Water (%)	97.7	97.85	97.5	97.4
煤气、液化气普及串 (%)	Rate of Access to Gas and Liquefied Gas (%)	55.5	75.54	78.35	82.6
每人拥有公共绿地 (平方米)	Per Capita Green Areas (sq.m)	4.3	4.87	5.1	4.55
文化	**Culture**				
城镇居民每百户有彩色电视机(台)	Color TV Sets per 100 Households in Urban (unit)	86.8	106.7	109.4	112.6
农村居民每百户有电视机(台)	TV Sets per 100 Households in Rural (unit)	65.6	88.25	97.11	100.35
城镇居民每百户有录音机(台)	Tape Recorders per 100 Households in Urban (unit)	67.8	42.67	37.8	36.7
农村居民每百户有收录机(台)	Radio&Recorders per 100 Households in Rural (unit)	25.6	19.4	13.11	12.89
平均每人每年发函件数(件)	Letters per Person per Year (piece)	5.42	3.88	3.25	6
平均每人每年报刊发行数(份)	Newspapers per Person per Year (piece)	11.06	14.95	14.35	15.55
教育	**Education**				
学龄儿童入学率(%)	Enrollment Ratio of School-age Children (%)	98	98.79	98.42	97.9
每万人口有在校大学生数(人)	University Students Enrollment per 10 000 Persons (person)	20.6	29.7	38.7	50.22
卫生	**Public Health**				
每万人口拥有医院病床数(张)	Number of Hospital Beds per 10 000 Persons (unit)	21.28	20.61	20.13	22.17
每万人口拥有医生数(人)	Number of Doctors per 10 000 Persons (person)	13.32	12.99	13.52	13.57

7-2 城 镇 居 民 生 活

Urban Households' Life

年 份 Year	平均每人每年 (元) Average per Person per Year (yuan)					每一就业者负担人数(人) Persons Supported by Per Employee (person)	人均居住面积(平方米) Per Capita Living Floor Space of Residents (sq.m)
	全部收入 Total Income	可支配收入 Disposable Income	指数 (1978年为100) Indices (1978 =100)	消费性支出 Living Expenditure	#食品支出 Food		
1978	323.88	323.9	100.0	289.56	166.10	1.90	3.90
1980	475.92	475.9	125.2	425.52	244.10	1.76	4.30
1985	760.80	760.8	161.8	685.32	366.48	1.88	6.00
1990	1591.45	1591.5	194.5	1294.00	720.30	1.80	6.91
1991	1783.24	1783.2	207.3	1446.00	772.07	1.80	7.07
1992	2172.00	2166.5	221.9	1732.00	881.56	1.76	7.41
1993	2822.00	2816.5	245.8	2194.00	1049.40	1.73	8.14
1994	3893.00	3887.6	271.9	3138.00	1496.80	1.70	7.93
1995	4705.20	4699.2	278.7	3886.00	1898.10	1.67	7.75
1996	5060.00	5052.1	279.2	4098.00	1986.60	1.64	8.06
1997	5248.90	5209.7	280.1	4317.20	1972.80	1.64	8.66
1998	5474.60	5434.3	290.7	4371.00	1907.60	1.62	9.91
1999	5855.70	5815.4	312.2	4800.00	1942.20	1.66	10.77
2000	6261.20	6218.7	328.9	5218.80	1943.70	1.71	11.75
2001	6832.60	6780.6	362.6	5546.20	1943.60	1.77	11.80

注：1991年及以前的可支配收入均系全部收入。

Data on disposable income prior to 1991 refer to those on the total income.

7-3 农 村 居 民 生 活

Rural Households' Life

年 份 Year	平均每人每年 (元) Per Capita Annual (Yuan)					每一劳动力负担人数(人) Number of Dependents Per Laborer (person)	农村人均居住面积(平方米) Per Capita Living Floor Space of Residents (sq.m)
	纯收入 Net Income	纯收入指数 (1978年为100) Index of Net Income (1978=100)	总支出 Gross Expenditure	生活消费支出 Living Expenditure	#食品支出 Food		
1978	142.56	100.0	167.10	140.07	97.93	2.33	10.50
1980	219.72	147.6	236.13	192.95	127.70	2.09	11.15
1985	395.26	239.4	519.85	348.45	219.43	1.69	18.20
1990	545.69	229.4	780.77	504.60	288.32	1.65	22.27
1991	688.91	234.5	1088.06	655.54	408.21	1.67	22.58
1992	739.42	239.2	1116.06	707.29	438.11	1.67	23.12
1993	851.87	244.5	1306.48	816.55	498.95	1.63	24.56
1994	1155.00	257.0	1766.51	1088.73	665.72	1.60	24.23
1995	1425.16	270.4	2203.36	1367.30	823.91	1.60	25.57
1996	1792.25	292.8	2784.64	1736.71	1025.32	1.56	26.88
1997	2037.06	318.9	2853.42	1815.79	1078.00	1.56	27.37
1998	2064.85	326.6	2829.93	1889.18	1107.23	1.54	28.79
1999	2147.18	344.6	2772.35	1920.15	1122.96	1.52	29.88
2000	2197.16	361.1	2964.85	1942.94	1053.37	1.46	30.92
2001	2299.46	379.5	3030.13	1990.33	1053.15	1.45	32.87

7-4 城镇居民家庭基本情况

Basic Indicators of Urban Households

项目	Item	1995	1999	2000	2001
调查户数(户)	**Number of Households Surveyed (household)**	**1000**	**1000**	**1000**	**1000**
平均每户家庭人口(人)	**Average Household Size (person)**	**3.19**	**3.08**	**3.09**	**3.06**
平均每户就业人口(人)	**Average Number of Employees Per Household (person)**	**1.91**	**1.85**	**1.81**	**1.73**
平均每户就业面(包括就业者)(%)	**Percentage of Employed Persons Per Household (%)**	**59.9**	**60.1**	**58.6**	**56.5**
平均每人全部年收入(元)	**Per Capita Annual Income(yuan)**	**4705.2**	**5855.8**	**6261.2**	**6832.6**
可支配收入	Disposable Income	4699.2	5815.4	6218.7	6780.6
国有单位职工工资	Wages of Staff and Workers in State-owned Units	3326.6	3810.0	4040.0	4047.8
集体单位职工工资	Wages of Staff and Workers in Collective-owned Units	295.2	320.1	207.3	233.2
个体经营劳动者收入	Income of Individual Laborers	26.0	52.4	140.1	170.0
被聘用或留用的离退休人员收入	Income of Re-employed Retirees	2.6	-	7.5	-
其他就业者收入	Income of Other Employees	2.3	5.6	14.1	18.0
其他劳动收入	Part-time Income	94.8	102.9	171.6	182.8
财产性收入	Property Income	81.6	153.9	158.8	239.5
转移性收入	Transfer Income	626.5	925.8	1008.1	1254.7
平均每人消费性支出(元)	**Per Capita Annual Living Expenditures for Consumption (yuan)**	**3885.6**	**4799.5**	**5218.8**	**5546.2**
#食品	#Food	1898.1	1942.2	1943.7	1943.6
衣着	Clothing	481.1	512.3	495.2	551.5
家庭设备和日用品	Household Facilities and Daily Articles	370.7	401.4	544.5	460.1
医疗保健	Medicine and Medical Service	108.7	206.1	270.2	328.6
交通和通讯	Transportation and Communications	206.9	321.3	395.6	474.7
娱乐、教育和文化	Recreation, Education and Cultural Service	408.4	697.2	753.8	826.9
居住	Residence	244.3	492.6	576.7	662.4
杂项商品和服务	Miscellaneous Commodities and Services	167.5	226.4	239.1	298.4

7-5 城镇居民可支配收入指数

Indices of Disposable Incomes of Urban Households

年份 Year	以上年为100 preceding year=100		以1978年为100 (1978 =100)	
	货币收入 Money Income	实际收入 Real Income	货币收入 Money Income	实际收入 Real Income
1995	121.0	102.5	1452.6	278.7
1998	104.3	103.8	1677.8	290.7
1999	107.0	107.4	1795.2	312.2
2000	106.9	105.5	1919.9	328.9
2001	109.0	110.2	2092.7	362.6

注:实际收入指数,指扣除价格上涨因素后的指数。

The real income is calculated without the factor of price increase.

7-6 城镇居民调查户基本情况 (2001年)

Basic Indicators of Urban Households From Sample Survey (2001)

项目	Item	居民家庭总平均 Average	按可支配收入高低分组 By Level of Disposable Income 最低收入 Lowest Income	#更低收入 Lower Income	低收入 Low Income
调查户数(户)	Households Surveyed (household)	1000	100	52	100
平均每户家庭人口(人)	Average Household Size (person)	3.06	3.51	3.62	3.27
平均每户就业人口(人)	Average Number of Employees Per Household (person)	1.73	1.54	1.51	1.69
平均每户就业面(%)	Percentage of Employed Persons Per Household (%)	56.5	43.9	41.7	51.7
平均每一就业者负担人数(人)	Number of Persons Supported by Each Employee(person)	1.77	2.28	2.40	1.93
平均每人每年可支配收入(元)	Per Capita Annual Disposable Income(yuan)	6780.6	2448.7	2112.9	3488.2
平均每人每年实际收入(元)	Per Capita Annual Real Income(yuan)	6832.6	2481.8	2140.4	3518.0
平均每人每年消费性支出(元)	Per Capita Annual Living Expenditures for Consumption (yuan)	5546.2	2376.7	2133.6	3205.9
食品	Food	1943.6	1162.8	1048.7	1513.7
#粮食	#Grain	169.3	148.7	136.0	153.2
肉禽及制品	Meat, Poultry and Related Products	439.6	301.8	283.3	391.8
蛋类	Eggs	44.4	33.7	32.0	37.3
水产品类	Aquatic Products	99.0	64.6	56.5	78.5
鲜菜	Fresh Vegetables	178.4	145.6	124.3	153.9
奶及奶制品	Milk and Dairy Products	50.0	18.5	13.1	28.9
衣着	Clothing	551.5	145.3	129.5	259.8
#服装	#Garments	385.0	91.1	85.7	160.8
家庭设备、用品及服务	Household Facilities, Articles and Services	460.1	115.1	54.3	140.8
#耐用消费品	#Durable Consumer Goods	257.1	49.1	4.6	50.1
家庭日用杂品	Household Miscellaneous Commodities	113.3	45.9	37.6	65.0
医疗保健	Medicine and Medical Services	328.6	168.2	137.1	183.0
交通和通讯	Transportation and Communications	474.7	152.9	152.8	214.5
娱乐、教育、文化服务	Recreation,Education and Cultural Services	826.9	258.3	293.5	407.8
#耐用消费品	#Durable Consumer Goods	122.1	8.4	5.2	12.9
教育	Education	567.5	212.6	263.0	332.7
文化娱乐	Culture and Recreation	137.3	37.4	25.3	62.2
居住	Residence	662.4	308.8	269.4	364.1
#房租	#Rent	176.2	114.1	99.2	125.1
水费	Water	40.0	27.3	24.1	32.8
电费	Electricity	121.5	65.3	55.7	74.8
杂项商品和服务	Miscellaneous Commodities and Services	298.4	65.3	48.3	122.3

7-6 续表 continued

项 目	Item	按可支配收入高低分组 By Level of Disposable Income 中等偏下 Lower Middle Income	中等收入 Middle Income	中等偏上 Upper Middle Income	高收入 High Income	最高收入 Highest Income
调查户数（户）	**Households Surveyed (household)**	**200**	**200**	**200**	**100**	**100**
平均每户家庭人口(人)	**Average Household Size (person)**	**3.15**	**3.04**	**2.95**	**2.86**	**2.69**
平均每户就业人口(人)	**Average Number of Employees Per Household (person)**	**1.68**	**1.82**	**1.77**	**1.78**	**1.77**
平均每户就业面(%)	**Percentage of Employed Persons Per Household (%)**	**53.3**	**59.9**	**60.0**	**62.2**	**65.8**
平均每一就业者负担人数（人）	**Number of Persons Supported by Each Employee (person)**	**1.88**	**1.67**	**1.67**	**1.61**	**1.52**
平均每人每年可支配收入（元）	**Per Capita Annual Disposable Income (yuan)**	**4611.9**	**6251.3**	**8245.0**	**10527.4**	**15524.3**
平均每人每年实际收入（元）	**Per Capita Annual Real Income (yuan)**	**4652.5**	**6294.5**	**8303.1**	**10601.1**	**15638.5**
平均每人每年消费性支出（元）	**Per Capita Annual Living Expenditures for Consumption (yuan)**	**4125.3**	**5161.1**	**6767.9**	**8075.3**	**11363.2**
食品	**Food**	**1740.8**	**1966.8**	**2175.0**	**2522.7**	**2784.8**
#粮食	#Grain	174.2	179.4	166.4	177.0	179.6
肉禽及制品	Meat, Poultry and Related Products	428.1	449.2	473.6	501.4	542.6
蛋类	Eggs	45.4	46.6	45.4	53.0	48.0
水产品类	Aquatic Products	88.5	103.5	113.6	111.9	137.3
鲜菜	Fresh Vegetables	179.2	183.3	185.8	192.4	207.3
奶及奶制品	Milk and Dairy Products	39.3	57.5	52.1	80.5	86.7
衣着	**Clothing**	**363.6**	**535.5**	**756.7**	**1026.3**	**957.6**
#服装	#Garments	239.7	372.7	538.7	733.4	701.9
家庭设备、用品及服务	**Household Facilities, Articles and Services**	**243.7**	**328.6**	**569.6**	**637.7**	**1741.3**
#耐用消费品	#Durable Consumer Goods	101.9	159.2	309.5	344.4	1157.8
家庭日用杂品	Household Miscellaneous Commodities	90.9	91.4	138.3	160.7	256.7
医疗保健	**Medicine and Medical Services**	**316.2**	**263.0**	**365.7**	**437.5**	**695.9**
交通和通讯	**Transportation and Communications**	**305.8**	**404.7**	**586.1**	**799.7**	**1175.6**
娱乐、教育、文化服务	**Recreation,Education and Cultural Services**	**557.5**	**846.1**	**1118.2**	**1156.7**	**1676.8**
#耐用消费品	#Durable Consumer Goods	53.7	77.0	184.1	256.9	386.4
教育	Education	412.9	646.9	763.8	675.3	953.4
文化娱乐	Culture and Recreation	90.9	122.2	170.4	224.5	337.0
居住	**Residence**	**458.1**	**589.0**	**801.7**	**1011.8**	**1454.7**
#房租	#Rent	151.2	184.0	214.1	216.2	235.0
水费	Water	36.6	40.1	43.0	50.0	56.5
电费	Electricity	99.7	119.8	143.6	186.0	189.4
杂项商品和服务	**Miscellaneous Commodities and Services**	**139.6**	**227.4**	**424.8**	**482.9**	**876.6**

7-7 城镇居民2001年消费性支出构成

Composition of Consumption Expenditures of urban Households in 2001

单位：%　　　　(%)

项 目	Item	居民家庭总平均 Average	按人均生活费收入分组 By Level of Income 最低收入 Lowest Income	#更低收入 Lower Income	低收入 Low Income	中等偏下 Lower Middle Income
消费性支出	**Expenditure for Consumption**	**100.0**	**100.0**	**100.0**	**100.0**	**100.0**
食品	**Foods**	**35.0**	**48.9**	**49.2**	**47.2**	**42.2**
#粮食	#Grain	3.1	6.3	6.4	4.8	4.2
肉禽及制品	Meat, Poultry and Related Products	7.9	12.7	13.3	12.2	10.4
蛋类	Eggs	0.8	1.4	1.5	1.2	1.1
水产品类	Aquatic Products	1.8	2.7	2.6	2.4	2.1
鲜菜	Fresh Vegetables	3.2	6.1	5.8	4.8	4.3
奶及奶制品	Milk and Dairy Products	0.9	0.8	0.6	0.9	1.0
衣着	**Clothing**	**9.9**	**6.1**	**6.1**	**8.1**	**8.8**
#服装	#Garments	6.9	3.8	4.0	5.0	5.8
家庭设备用品及服务	**Household Facilities, Articles and Services**	**8.3**	**4.8**	**2.5**	**4.4**	**5.9**
#耐用消费品	#Durable Consumer Goods	4.6	2.1	0.2	1.6	2.5
家庭日用杂品	Daily Use Articles	2.0	1.9	1.8	2.0	2.2
医疗保健	**Medicine and Medical Services**	**5.9**	**7.1**	**6.4**	**5.7**	**7.7**
交通和通讯	**Transportation and Telecommunications**	**8.6**	**6.4**	**7.2**	**6.7**	**7.4**
娱乐、教育文化服务	**Recreation,Education and Cultural Services**	**14.9**	**10.9**	**13.8**	**12.7**	**13.5**
#耐用消费品	#Durable Consumer Goods	2.2	0.4	0.2	0.4	1.3
教育	Education	10.2	8.9	12.3	10.4	10.0
文化娱乐	Recreation and Culture	2.5	1.6	1.2	1.9	2.2
居住	**Residence**	**12.0**	**13.0**	**12.6**	**11.4**	**11.1**
#房租	#Rent	3.2	4.8	4.6	3.9	3.7
水费	Water	0.7	1.1	1.1	1.0	0.9
电费	Electricity	2.2	2.7	2.6	2.3	2.4
杂项商品和服务	**Miscellaneous Commodities and Services**	**5.4**	**2.7**	**2.3**	**3.8**	**3.4**

项目	Item	中等收入 Middle Income	中等偏上 Upper Middle Income	高收入 High Income	最高收入 Highest Income
消费性支出	**Expenditure for Consumption**	**100.0**	**100**	**100.0**	**100.0**
食品	**Foods**	**38.1**	**32.1**	**31.2**	**24.5**
#粮食	#Grain	3.5	2.5	2.2	1.6
肉禽及制品	Meat, Poultry and Related Products	8.7	7.0	6.2	4.8
蛋类	Eggs	0.9	0.4	0.7	0.4
水产品类	Aquatic Products	2.0	1.7	1.4	1.2
鲜菜	Fresh Vegetables	3.6	2.7	2.4	1.8
奶及奶制品	Milk and Dairy Products	1.1	0.8	1.0	0.8
衣着	**Clothing**	**10.4**	**11.2**	**12.7**	**8.4**
#服装	#Garments	7.2	8.0	9.1	6.2
家庭设备用品及服务	**Household Facilities,Articles and Services**	**6.4**	**8.0**	**7.9**	**15.3**
#耐用消费品	#Durable Consumer Goods	3.1	4.6	4.3	10.2
家庭日用杂品	Daily Use Articles	1.8	2.0	2.0	2.3
医疗保健	**Medicine and Medical Services**	**5.1**	**5.4**	**5.4**	**6.1**
交通和通讯	**Transportation and Telecommunications**	**7.8**	**8.7**	**10.1**	**10.3**
娱乐、教育文化服务	**Recreation,Education and Cultural Services**	**16.4**	**16.5**	**14.3**	**14.8**
#耐用消费品	#Durable Consumer Goods	1.5	2.7	3.2	3.4
教育	Education	12.5	11.3	8.4	8.4
文化娱乐	Recreation and Culture	2.4	2.5	2.8	3.0
居住	**Residence**	**11.4**	**11.8**	**12.5**	**12.8**
#房租	#Rent	3.6	3.2	2.7	2.1
水费	Water	0.8	0.6	0.6	0.5
电费	Electricity	2.3	2.1	2.3	1.7
杂项商品和服务	**Miscellaneous Commodities and Services**	4.4	6.3	6.0	7.7

7-8 城镇居民平均每人全年购买商品数量(2001年)

Per Capita Annual Purchases of Commodities of Urban Households (2001)

项目	Item	居民家庭总平均 Average	按家庭人均可支配收入分组 By Level of Income 最低收入 Lowest Income	更低收入 Lower Income	低收入 Low Income	中等偏下 Lower Middle Income	中等收入 Middle Income	中等偏上 Upper Middle Income	高收入 High Income	最高收入 Highest Income
粮食 (千克)	Grain (kg)	77.1	78.6	73.7	74.6	82.4	82.5	71.4	71.7	71.4
淀粉及薯类 (千克)	Starches and Tubers (kg)	5.9	5.1	4.5	5.7	6.6	5.9	5.6	6.1	6.0
大豆 (千克)	Soybeans (kg)	0.3	0.2	0.1	0.2	0.4	0.3	0.2	0.4	0.4
豆腐 (千克)	Bean Curd (kg)	3.4	2.9	2.7	3.0	3.6	3.2	3.4	3.8	4.2
食用植物油 (千克)	Edible Vegetable Oil (kg)	7.2	6.5	5.5	6.8	7.4	8.2	7.8	7.3	5.0
食用动物油 (千克)	Edible Animal Oil (kg)	2.2	2.7	2.7	2.0	2.4	2.7	1.9	1.4	0.9
猪肉 (千克)	Pork (kg)	19.5	16.2	14.8	19.7	20.1	20.2	19.2	19.8	21.1
牛肉 (千克)	Beef (kg)	1.6	1.0	0.8	1.1	1.5	1.8	1.8	1.5	2.1
羊肉 (千克)	Mutton (kg)	0.2	0.2	0.1	0.2	0.2	0.2	0.3	0.3	0.3
家禽 (千克)	Poultry (kg)	7.7	4.6	4.7	6.6	7.9	8.4	8.3	8.3	9.5
蛋类 (千克)	Eggs (kg)	7.0	5.6	5.1	6.0	7.3	7.3	7.1	8.2	7.4
鱼 (千克)	Fish (kg)	8.8	6.9	6.0	8.1	8.5	9.3	9.0	9.5	10.1
虾 (千克)	Shrimp (kg)	0.6	0.3	0.4	0.4	0.6	0.7	0.8	0.8	0.7
鲜菜 (千克)	Fresh Vegetables (kg)	105.4	94.0	80.0	94.6	107.4	107.9	106.6	108.1	117.2
食糖 (千克)	Sugar (kg)	1.2	1.1	1.1	0.9	1.4	1.1	1.3	1.5	1.2
糖果 (千克)	Candy (kg)	0.8	0.4	0.4	0.5	0.7	0.8	0.9	0.9	1.5
卷烟 (盒)	Cigarettes (pack)	25.5	17.8	13.4	28.7	30.4	19.8	24.7	28.8	31.4
白酒 (千克)	Liquor (kg)	1.5	0.8	0.7	1.9	1.7	1.8	1.2	1.5	1.6
果酒 (千克)	Fruit Wine (kg)	0.12	0.03	0.04	0.09	0.19	0.06	0.15	0.18	1.24
啤酒 (千克)	Beer (kg)	2.1	1.0	0.8	2.6	2.8	1.7	1.6	2.5	2.3
其他酒 (千克)	Other Liquor (kg)	0.7	0.3	0.5	0.5	0.8	0.8	0.7	0.4	1.8
鲜瓜果 (千克)	Fresh Melons&Fruits (kg)	72.3	43.0	39.3	57.5	67.6	73.0	83.8	90.8	93.1
糕点 (千克)	Cake (kg)	2.4	1.2	1.1	1.8	2.2	2.2	2.9	3.3	3.6
鲜乳品 (千克)	Fresh Dairy Products (kg)	1.9	0.4	0.6	0.8	1.3	2.9	1.7	3.0	3.6
奶粉 (千克)	Milk Powder (kg)	0.9	0.4	0.2	0.5	0.7	1.0	1.1	1.4	1.7
酸奶 (千克)	Sour Milk (kg)	0.8	0.3	0.3	0.7	0.8	0.7	0.8	1.0	1.7
男士服装 (件)	Men's Clothing (piece)	2.4	1.1	0.9	1.6	2.1	2.3	3.1	3.6	3.7
女士服装 (件)	Women's Clothing (piece)	3.7	1.3	1.3	2.2	2.9	3.8	4.7	6.4	5.4
儿童服装 (件)	Children's Clothing (piece)	1.1	0.4	0.4	0.9	1.0	1.0	1.3	1.6	1.6
棉布 (米)	Cotton Cloth (m)	0.11	0.03	0.01	0.19	0.15	0.06	0.13	0.13	0.11
棉化纤混纺 (米)	Cotton/Chemical Fiber Blend Cloth (m)	0.06	0.03	0.02	0.05	0.04	0.04	0.13	0.01	0.13
化纤布 (米)	Chemical Fiber Cloth (m)	0.20	0.09	0.07	0.21	0.19	0.14	0.22	0.30	0.36
呢绒 (米)	Woolen Fabric (m)	0.01	0.01	0.02	-	0.00	0.01	0.04	0.00	0.03
绸缎 (米)	Silk and Satin (m)	0.01	0.01	-	-	0.01	0.00	0.02	0.00	0.02
毛线 (千克)	Knitting Wool (kg)	0.20	0.08	0.06	0.17	0.19	0.25	0.23	0.15	0.24

7-9 城镇居民平均每百户拥有耐用消费品数量（2001年）

Number of Durable Consumer Goods Owned Per 100 Urban Households (2001)

项目	Item	居民家庭总平均 Average	按家庭人均可支配收入分组 最低收入 Lowest Income	更低收入 Lower Income	低收入 Low Income	中等偏下 Lower Middle Income	中等收入 Middle Income	中等偏上 Upper Middle Income	高收入 High Income	最高收入 Highest Income
毛皮大衣(件)	Fur Coat (piece)	51.6	29.0	30.8	33.9	38.4	57.6	56.9	61.5	85.9
呢大衣（件）	Woolen Coat (piece)	147.3	82.7	82.6	102.9	127.7	141.5	167.4	183.3	231.1
毛毯（条）	Woolen Blanket (unit)	142.2	92.1	105.3	101.5	119.4	140.7	163.2	194.1	187.2
沙发（个）	Sofa (unit)	210.0	165.3	146.9	164.5	176.4	201.9	224.3	277.3	287.7
大衣柜（个）	Wardrobe (unit)	99.9	87.2	99.0	81.0	92.5	112.3	106.2	98.3	110.2
写字台（张）	Desk (unit)	102.5	85.2	97.1	97.1	88.8	107.9	111.6	104.8	120.7
摩托车（辆）	Motorcycle (unit)	15.5	15.0	18.8	8.8	12.0	17.9	13.2	20.5	24.8
自行车（辆）	Bicycle (unit)	96.8	72.5	64.0	99.1	101.5	105.7	91.9	91.6	106.7
缝纫机（台）	Sewing Machine (unit)	45.3	42.0	43.0	41.7	42.9	45.9	43.8	52.7	51.5
洗衣机（台）	Washing Machine (unit)	91.0	82.2	80.0	77.1	86.6	91.3	96.3	99.9	102.1
电风扇（台）	Electric Fan (unit)	244.0	219.6	218.7	236.4	235.0	242.7	254.5	258.3	261.1
电冰箱（台）	Refrigerator (unit)	86.2	68.9	68.2	72.1	81.2	86.7	94.6	96.9	98.9
彩色电视机（台）	Color TV Set (unit)	112.6	94.2	93.5	94.9	107.5	106.7	116.3	133.3	142.9
影碟机(台)	Video Disc Player (unit)	48.8	27.7	33.5	39.2	36.1	47.7	57.4	69.0	69.1
录放像机(台)	Video-recorder (unit)	17.7	10.8	8.9	14.2	14.3	16.5	17.1	23.6	32.4
家用电脑(台)	Computer (unit)	15.4	3.8	4.4	3.4	6.7	16.1	16.0	33.2	36.2
组合音响(套)	Hi-Fi Stereo Component System (unit)	29.9	12.8	18.2	21.4	18.9	26.9	39.3	51.7	42.6
录音机(台)	Tape Recorder (unit)	36.7	22.4	24.5	34.2	31.8	37.8	38.6	48.8	45.1
摄像机(台)	Pickup Camera (unit)	1.2	0.8	1.5	0.8	1.5	0.4	1.8	1.2	1.6
照相机(架)	Camera (unit)	33.1	10.5	9.8	18.5	24.6	34.6	35.4	55.6	57.1
钢琴(架)	Piano (unit)	1.0	1.5	1.5	-	0.4	0.9	1.0	2.5	1.7
其它中高档乐器(件)	Other Medium and High Grade Musical Instrument (piece)	7.9	0.8	-	3.4	3.6	8.0	10.3	13.3	17.1
空调机(台)	Air Conditioner (unit)	38.2	13.9	14.8	19.2	21.5	36.9	46.6	63.2	75.3
电炊具(台)	Electric Cooking Appliances (unit)	67.7	27.5	18.5	45.8	45.4	71.9	89.8	98.2	91.5
淋浴热水器（台）	Shower (unit)	60.1	32.6	28.9	35.0	51.3	57.7	72.7	86.5	83.4
脱排油烟机（台）	Smoke Absorber (unit)	31.8	16.0	13.2	18.7	21.3	35.1	40.7	41.5	47.6
吸尘器(台)	Dust Catcher (unit)	4.0	-	-	-	2.4	1.1	7.6	13.4	4.1

7-10 各市县城镇居民家庭生活基本情况(2001年)

Basic Indicators of Urban Households' Life of Cities and Prefecture (2001)

市县	Cities and Counties	平均每户家庭人口(人) Average Household Size (person)	平均每户就业人口(人) Average Number of Employees Per Household (person)	平均每一就业者负担人数(人) Average Number of Persons Supported by Each Employee (person)	平均每人现金收入(元) Per Capita Annual Cash Income (yuan)	平均每人可支配收入(元) Per Capita Annual Disposable Income (yuan)	平均每人消费性支出(元) Per Capita Annual Living Expenditures for Consumption (yuan)	平均每人年存入储蓄数(元) Per Capita Annual Saving Deposits (yuan)
长沙市	Changsha City	3.04	1.74	1.75	10646.5	8650.8	7683.5	902.4
株洲市	Zhuzhou City	3.01	1.82	1.65	9176.3	7886.5	6115.7	865.7
邵阳市	Shaoyang City	3.06	1.90	1.61	7681.7	5756.4	4690.7	762.4
岳阳市	Yueyang City	3.09	1.83	1.69	9308.4	7980.9	5967.0	1129.8
常德市	Changde City	2.92	1.46	2.00	7859.0	6243.7	5145.6	538.6
郴州市	Chenzhou City	2.88	1.67	1.72	7904.3	6385.3	5598.4	884.8
怀化市	Huaihua City	3.06	1.79	1.71	6898.8	5941.5	4253.3	904.1
衡阳市	Hengyang City	3.17	1.67	1.90	6678.9	5888.8	4758.6	1363.6
湘潭市	Xiangtan City	2.96	1.67	1.77	7572.1	6661.1	5332.5	505.7
益阳市	Yiyang City	3.02	1.91	1.58	8347.1	6939.4	5221.4	948.8
永州市	Yongzhou City	3.38	2.18	1.55	5178.1	4874.4	3477.1	1124.5
娄底市	Loudi City	3.22	1.92	1.68	8243.4	6772.4	5334.3	872.2
吉首市	Jishou City	3.56	2.12	1.68	6851.0	5305.0	4759.8	960.7
张家界市	Zhangjiajie City	3.60	1.78	2.02	6831.2	5525.1	4398.0	783.4
资兴市	Zixing City	2.76	1.24	2.23	8452.0	6603.2	4995.4	1325.4
冷水江市	Lengshuijiang City	3.38	2.08	1.63	6857.6	5312.8	4136.8	955.0
津 市	Jinshi City	3.14	1.82	1.73	5051.4	4276.0	3506.5	368.5
道 县	Daoxian County	3.22	1.78	1.81	6318.0	4616.9	2944.1	1325.2
耒阳市	Leiyang City	3.24	1.64	1.98	6975.9	5504.8	4482.2	1389.8
新化县	Xinhua County	3.33	1.85	1.80	6976.9	5364.5	4539.1	609.2
慈利县	Cili County	3.08	1.36	2.26	6815.0	5447.7	3962.8	1006.4
南 县	Nanxian County	2.98	1.76	1.69	6709.0	6126.2	3714.0	402.4
临湘市	Linxiang City	3.32	1.82	1.82	6933.3	5873.1	4092.6	1162.8
溆浦县	Xupu County	3.12	1.77	1.76	5578.3	4854.3	3406.8	678.0
武冈市	Wugang City	3.34	1.92	1.74	5842.3	4808.7	3199.0	899.8
攸 县	Youxian County	3.14	1.82	1.73	5843.2	5035.1	3760.2	829.3
凤凰县	Fenghuang County	4.02	1.40	2.87	3811.4	3309.7	2388.8	256.1

7-11 各市县城镇居民平均每人全年家庭收入来源(2001年)

Per Capita Annual Income in Urban Households of Cities and Counties (2001)

单位:元 (yuan)

市县	Cities and Counties	可支配收入 Disposable Income	实际收入 Real Income	国有单位职工收入 Income of Staff and Workers in State-owned Units	#工资 Wages	集体单位职工收入 Income of Staff and Workers in Collec-tive-owned Units	#工资 Wages	其他经济类型单位职工收入 Income of Staff and Workers in Other Types of Ownership	转移收入 Transfer Income
长沙市	Changsha City	8650.8	8742.5	5536.2	4976.9	350.1	329.7	719.9	1450.5
株洲市	Zhuzhou City	7886.5	7968.4	4858.2	4429.0	198.2	191.4	364.7	1626.7
邵阳市	Shaoyang City	5756.4	5802.3	4159.5	3837.6	71.0	68.7	373.6	990.7
岳阳市	Yueyang City	7980.9	8001.2	5314.8	4880.9	493.8	468.9	22.6	1449.6
常德市	Changde City	6243.7	6267.1	3746.2	3507.2	153.8	148.0	99.2	1348.4
郴州市	Chenzhou City	6385.3	6435.9	4708.7	4502.4	205.9	205.9	-	1050.5
怀化市	Huaihua City	5941.5	5962.7	4664.8	4508.2	66.7	66.7	-	926.6
衡阳市	Hengyang City	5888.8	5944.9	3119.8	2860.4	15.8	15.8	510.8	1628.4
湘潭市	Xiangtan City	6661.1	6709.1	3450.2	3282.1	324.4	317.9	74.1	1894.8
益阳市	Yiyang City	6939.4	7000.8	4167.9	3737.4	186.8	186.8	1027.8	1295.8
永州市	Yongzhou City	4874.4	4883.6	3794.2	3495.2	579.3	567.9	13.4	172.5
娄底市	Loudi City	6772.4	6844.5	4235.4	3597.3	121.0	121.0	79.0	1572.1
吉首市	Jishou City	5305.0	5341.8	3677.3	3408.4	115.2	115.2	-	788.6
张家界市	Zhangjiajie City	5525.1	5653.0	1538.3	1447.4	1227.2	1203.3	-	1298.5
资兴市	Zixing City	6603.2	6635.6	3732.5	3106.0	95.5	95.5	389.6	2065.5
冷水江市	Lengshuijiang City	5312.8	5339.8	4062.9	3561.3	90.3	61.6	-	1077.0
津　市	Jinshi City	4276.0	4341.4	2028.9	2028.9	447.8	443.6	-	1389.6
道　县	Daoxian County	4616.9	4626.4	2773.6	2642.7	264.4	264.4	-	805.3
耒阳市	Leiyang City	5504.8	5525.7	3173.6	2874.2	150.9	147.8	-	1274.9
新化县	Xinhua County	5364.5	5417.1	2934.9	2814.4	472.9	455.6	-	1048.6
慈利县	Cili County	5447.7	5499.8	2591.8	2451.8	390.8	364.7	-	1515.3
南　县	Nanxian County	6126.2	6175.1	4119.8	3870.1	97.8	97.8	-	1499.3
临湘市	Linxiang City	5873.1	5885.2	4383.7	3826.0	119.4	114.6	-	691.0
溆浦县	Xupu County	4854.3	4887.7	3529.3	3061.7	5.1	5.1	-	666.4
武冈市	Wugang City	4808.7	4886.6	2512.6	2178.2	836.9	770.4	74.0	653.8
攸　县	Youxian County	5035.1	5056.8	3118.3	2886.7	472.2	460.4	-	920.1
凤凰县	Fenghuang County	3309.7	3315.9	1285.1	1285.1	378.4	378.4	4.3	1193.0

7-12 城镇居民家庭平均每人全年现金收入和支出

Per Capita Annual Cash Revenue and Expenditures of Urban Household

单位:元 (yuan)

项 目	Item	1995	1999	2000	2001
期初手存现金	**Cash Available at Year-beginning**	**186.0**	**331.2**	**323.3**	**403.8**
可支配收入	**Disposable Income**	**4699.2**	**5815.4**	**6218.7**	**6780.6**
现金收入	**Cash Income**	**5796.5**	**7206.0**	**7732.1**	**8428.1**
实际收入	**Real Income**	**4705.2**	**5855.8**	**6261.2**	**6832.6**
#国有单位职工收入	Income of Staff and Workers in State-owned Units	3548.7	4121.5	4379.5	4387.3
集体经济单位职工收入	Income of Staff and Workers in Collective-owned Units	314.5	331.2	218.3	244.0
其他经济类型单位职工收入	Income of Staff and Workers in Other Types of Ownership	-	134.4	123.8	287.9
个体经营者的净收入	Net Income of Individual Laborers	26.0	52.4	140.1	170.0
个体被雇者收入	Income of Employed Individual Laborers	-	16.1	26.4	44.0
离退休再就业者收入	Income of Re-employed Retirees	2.6	-	7.5	-
其他就业者收入	Income of Other Employees	2.3	5.6	14.1	18.0
其他劳动收入	Part-time Income	94.8	102.9	171.6	182.8
财产性收入	Property Income	81.6	153.9	158.8	239.5
#利息	Interest	59.8	40.8	23.3	28.4
红利	Bonus	18.4	16.1	28.1	41.3
其他财产租金收入	Others	3.3	97.0	107.4	169.8
转移收入	Transfer Income	626.5	925.8	1008.1	1254.7
#离退休金	#Pensions for Retirees	293.7	449.6	568.6	745.9
价格补贴	Price Subsidies	0.5	1.0	-	0.5
赡养收入	Income from Alimony	51.0	57.5	50.9	54.8
赠送收入	Income from Presentation	200.7	318.3	313.2	324.6
亲友搭伙费	Funds from Relatives or Friends Eat Regularly	40.4	22.4	20.4	23.8
记帐补贴	Subsidies of Keep Accounts	22.7	30.6	30.4	39.2
出售财物收入	Income from Sale Property	6.4	21.5	9.1	3.4
其 他	Others	11.2	24.9	15.6	62.5
家庭副业生产收入	Household Sideline Production Income	8.7	12.0	13.0	4.7
储蓄借贷收入	**Debit and Credit Income**	**1091.3**	**1350.2**	**1470.9**	**1595.5**
#提取储蓄存款	Draw Money from Banks	752.7	1014.6	1066.2	1185.0
提取储金会款	Draw Money from Mutual Savings Banks	21.9	18.1	17.0	9.2
借入款	Borrow Money	218.9	186.7	251.1	242.0

7-12 续表 continued

项 目	Item	1995	1999	2000	2001
收回借出款	Draw Back Loans	52.9	50.6	50.1	48.0
收回储蓄性保险本金	Draw Back principal of Insurance Premium	1.8	5.1	3.8	7.6
兑售有价证券	Exchanging Bunds	10.7	6.1	16.3	10.7
赊购	Buy on Tally	1.0	0.4	0.0	0.3
为购置房屋从银行贷款	Asking for Banks Loan for Purchasing Houses	2.7	26.0	26.0	13.7
其他借贷收入	Others	28.7	42.6	40.5	79.0
现金支出	**Cash Expenditures**	**5699.0**	**7168.9**	**7574.7**	**8289.4**
实际支出	**Real Expenditures**	**4795.5**	**6109.6**	**6433.3**	**6925.5**
#消费性支出	# Expenditures for Consumption	3885.6	4799.5	5218.8	5546.2
非消费性支出	Expenditures for Non-consumption	904.5	1305.6	1211.1	1377.6
#贷款利息	#Interest of Loans	0.1	1.3	0.3	0.8
个人所得税	Individual Income Tax	0.6	5.4	8.7	11.1
其他各种税	Other Taxes	0.1	1.1	2.5	2.9
各种非储蓄性保险	Expenditure for Insurance Non-Premium	2.4	4.9	7.6	6.2
赡养支出	Expenditure for Alimony	109.7	172.6	155.5	193.6
赠送支出	Expenditure for Presentation	457.5	827.1	797.3	769.9
购房建房支出	Expenditure for Purchasing or Building Houses	289.7	255.2	187.6	357.2
其他非消费支出	Others	44.5	38.0	51.8	36.0
家庭副业生产支出	Expenditure for Household Sideline Production	5.4	4.5	3.4	1.7
储蓄借贷支出	**Expenditure for Lend Money and Savings**	**903.5**	**1059.3**	**1141.4**	**1363.9**
存入储蓄款	Savings Deposits in Banks	623.9	654.4	693.6	888.1
存入储蓄会款	Savings Deposits in Mutual Savings Banks	17.8	13.8	8.8	6.1
归还借款	Payment of Borrow Money	100.3	102.2	126.6	78.0
借出款	Lend Money	36.8	31.2	25.5	16.5
储蓄性保险支出	Expenditure for Insurance Premium	21.5	95.3	114.3	149.8
购置有价证券	Expenditure for Purchasing Bunds	16.9	23.1	64.8	54.9
预购	Prepaying	6.0	1.7	0.1	-
归还购置住房的银行贷款	Payment of Banks Loan for Purchasing Houses	6.8	10.8	11.0	30.2
其他借贷支出	Others	73.5	126.8	96.9	140.3
期末手存现金	**Cash Now Available (year-end)**	**283.6**	**368.3**	**480.7**	**542.5**

7-13 农村居民家庭基本情况

Basic Indicators of Rural Households

项 目	Item	1995	1999	2000	2001
调查村数（个）	**Number of Villages Surveyed (unit)**	**370**	**383**	**370**	**370**
已通电话村所占比重（%）	Proportion of Villages Provided with Telephone (%)	53.50	82.50	95.70	97.57
已通公路村所占比重（%）	Proportion of Villages Provided with Highways (%)	97.30	98.20	98.60	99.19
调查户数（户）	**Number of Households Surveyed(household)**	**3700**	**3830**	**3700**	**3700**
调查户人口(常住人口)（人）	Number of Residents Surveyed (person)	15493	15058	14694	14544
平均每户常住人口（人）	Average Number of Permanent Residents per Household (person)	4.19	3.93	3.97	3.93
平均每户整半劳动力（人）	Average Number of Able-bodied and Semi-ablebodied Laborers per Household(person)	2.62	2.59	2.72	2.71
平均每个劳动力负担人口(人)	Number of Dependents per Laborer (person)	1.60	1.52	1.46	1.45
每百个常住人口中乡村企业从业人数(人)	Number of Employed Persons in Township Enterprises per 100 Permanent Residents(person)	1.41	1.28	1.13	1.66
每百个常住人口中在外从事其他劳动人数(人)	Number of Employed Outgoing Persons per 100 Permanent Residents(person)	4.77	9.27	11.23	11.97
平均每人经营耕地面积(亩)	Area of Cultivated Land Under Management per Capita (mu)	1.25	1.12	1.09	1.09
平均每人经营山地面积(亩)	Hilly Area Under Management per Capita (mu)	0.58	0.51	0.39	0.38
平均每人经营水面面积(亩)	Water Area Under Management per Capita (mu)	0.04	0.04	0.05	0.04
平均每户年末拥有生产性固定资产原值(元)	Original Value of Productive Fixed Assets per Household at the Year-end (yuan)	1376.34	2533.94	3006.28	3106.38
平均每百个劳动力中：	**In Per 100 Rural Labor Force :**				
文盲或半文盲（人）	Illiterate and Semi-illiterate (person)	6.65	3.67	3.38	3.13
小学程度（人）	Primary School (person)	43.47	36.98	34.00	32.85
初中程度（人）	Junior Secondary School (person)	38.88	47.09	48.88	49.71
高中程度（人）	Senior Secondary School (person)	10.19	10.54	11.47	11.85
中专程度（人）	Specialized Secondary school (person)	0.63	1.37	1.75	1.85
大专以上（人）	College and Higher Level (person)	0.18	0.35	0.52	0.61
按纯收入分组户数占调查户比重(%)	**Percentage of Households Group by per Capita Annual Net Income (%)**				
100元以下	Under 100 Yuan	0.03	0.05	0.00	0.03
100—200元	100—200 Yuan	0.03	0.03	0.03	0.00
200—300元	200—300 Yuan	0.19	0.05	0.05	0.00
300—400元	300—400 Yuan	0.65	0.08	0.11	0.22
400—500元	400—500 Yuan	1.22	0.16	0.46	0.22
500-600元	500—600 Yuan	2.30	0.37	0.97	0.68
600—800元	600—800 Yuan	7.75	1.70	4.65	2.65
800—1000元	800—1000 Yuan	12.11	3.79	3.70	4.35
1000—1200元	1000—1200 Yuan	14.00	7.47	5.78	6.57
1200—1300元	1200—1300 Yuan	8.00	3.99	3.81	3.35
1300—1500元	1300—1500 Yuan	13.95	9.45	7.35	7.24
1500—1700元	1500—1700 Yuan	10.16	10.08	8.84	8.54
1700-2000元	1700-2000 Yuan	11.92	13.79	13.19	12.32
2000-2500元	2000-2500 Yuan	10.54	19.71	19.24	18.78
2500-3000元	2500-3000 Yuan	4.59	12.04	11.81	12.54
3000—3500元	3000—3500 Yuan	1.49	7.13	8.32	7.94
3500-4000元	3500-4000 Yuan	0.49	3.89	4.30	5.43
4000-4500元	4000-4500 Yuan	0.24	2.38	2.68	3.00
4500-5000元	4500-5000 Yuan	0.24	1.54	1.59	2.03
5000元以上	5000 Yuan and Over	0.11	2.30	3.11	4.11

7-14 农村居民主要农、牧产品出售情况

Sales of Major Farming, Animal Husbandry Products per Rural Household

项 目	Item	1995	1999	2000	2001
粮食（公斤／人）	Grain Crops (kg/person)	104.85	119.44	111.59	134.58
棉花（公斤／人）	Cotton (kg/person)	2.74	2.61	2.92	3.26
油料（公斤／人）	Oil-bearing Crops (kg/person)	6.03	7.03	9.26	8.93
麻类（公斤／人）	Fiber Crops (kg/person)	0.60	0.29	0.52	0.82
糖料（公斤／人）	Sugar Crops (kg/person)	7.46	5.37	8.76	4.04
烟叶（公斤／人）	Tobacco (kg/person)	2.00	3.24	5.01	4.43
蔬菜（公斤／人）	Vegetables (kg/person)	24.82	53.66	72.03	76.44
水果（公斤／人）	Fruits (kg/person)	14.77	30.47	33.37	32.55
茶叶（公斤／人）	Tea (kg/person)	0.12	0.23	0.24	0.12
猪肉（公斤／户）	Pork (kg/household)	192.20	224.40	199.61	216.11
羊肉（公斤／户）	Mutton(kg/household)	0.26	0.81	0.07	0.12
家禽（公斤／户）	Poultry(kg/household)	4.43	6.36	9.22	8.84
禽蛋（公斤／户）	Poultry Eggs (kg/household)	4.50	4.11	7.31	5.19
鱼虾（公斤／户）	Aquatic Products (kg/household)	19.79	22.36	25.17	24.80
蜂蜜（公斤／户）	Mel(kg/household)	0.01	0.01	0.02	0.04

7-15 农村居民平均每人总收入及总支出

Per Capita Annual Revenue and Expenditures of Rural Household

单位：元 (yuan)

项 目	Item	1995	1999	2000	2001
平均每人总收入	**Per Capita Gross Income**	**2235.35**	**2982.67**	**3195.13**	**3305.65**
基本收入	Basic Income	2160.40	2883.62	2919.80	3031.58
劳动者报酬收入	Laborers' Remuneration	268.00	695.62	789.74	840.11
在集体组织中得到的	From Collective Organization	35.04	66.54	80.22	85.34
在企业劳动得到的收入	From Enterprises	211.09	550.65	614.05	653.21
在其他单位劳动得到的	From Other Units	21.87	78.44	95.47	101.56
家庭经营收入	From Household Business Operation	1892.40	2187.99	2130.06	2191.47
转移性和财产性收入	Transfer Income and Property Income	74.96	99.05	275.33	274.07
平均每人总支出	**Per Capita Gross Expenditure**	**2203.36**	**2772.35**	**2964.85**	**3030.13**
#家庭经营费用支出	Expenditure for Household Business	669.27	645.82	642.17	665.53
购置生产用固定资产支出	Expenditure for Purchase of Productive Fixed Assets	35.71	46.77	40.54	52.00
缴纳税款	Taxes	39.71	46.55	39.76	39.38
上交集体承包任务	Payments to Collective Units	33.16	21.14	18.15	17.93
集体提留和摊派	Collective Apportion	32.45	58.85	50.42	44.62
生活消费支出	Expenditure for Consumption	1367.30	1920.15	1942.94	1990.33
其他非借贷性支出	Other Non-Lend Expenditure	25.76	33.07	230.87	220.34
寄给、带给在外人口	Post & Bring to Outgoing Person	1.90	1.50	5.47	3.39
赠送农村外部亲友	Giving Non-Rural Friends and Relatives	2.11	4.26	3.74	4.49
其他支出	Other Expenditure	17.79	17.21	17.30	16.20

7-16 农村居民平均每人纯收入来源构成

Source and Condition of per Capita Net Income of Rural Household

单位:元 (yuan)

项 目	Item	1995	1999	2000	2001
平均每人纯收入	**Per Capita Net Income**	**1425.16**	**2147.18**	**2197.16**	**2299.46**
按纯收入来源分	**Grouped by Source of Income**				
基本收入	Basic Income	1363.89	2068.30	2118.84	2211.95
劳动者的报酬收入	Laborer's Remuneration	268.00	695.62	789.74	840.11
在集体组织中得到的	From Collective Organization	35.04	66.54	80.22	85.34
在企业劳动得到的	From Enterprises	211.09	550.65	614.05	653.21
在其他单位劳动得到的	From Other Units	21.87	78.44	95.47	101.56
家庭经营纯收入	Income from Household Business Operation	1095.89	1372.68	1329.10	1371.84
农业收入	Farming	627.31	716.20	605.37	642.07
林业收入	Forestry	14.28	20.15	16.35	13.33
牧业收入	Animal Husbandry	201.30	223.03	247.67	255.43
渔业收入	Fishery	27.12	29.22	34.82	25.71
手工业收入	Handicraft	28.85	39.00	17.06	18.09
采集捕猎收入	Gathering and Hunting	18.38	22.75	17.29	18.34
工业收入	Industry	21.17	40.00	55.97	58.86
建筑业收入	Construction	55.98	115.43	126.02	126.54
运输业收入	Transportation	20.18	36.33	53.50	59.69
商业收入	Commerce	35.70	64.36	78.55	86.39
饮食业收入	Catering Services	2.03	5.40	6.60	7.26
服务业收入	Service Trade	17.43	40.48	47.54	42.06
其他家庭经营收入	Others	26.16	20.64	22.36	18.07
转移性收入和财产性收入	Transfer Income and Property Income	61.27	78.88	78.32	87.51
按纯收入性质分	**Grouped by Type of Income**				
生产性纯收入	Productive Income	1363.89	2027.82	2071.30	2169.89
非生产性纯收入	Non-productive Income	61.27	119.36	125.86	129.54
按现金和实物分	**Grouped by Modality of Income**				
现金纯收入	Net Cash Income	845.35	1392.65	1569.13	1643.62
实物纯收入	Net Income in Kind	579.91	754.53	630.03	655.84

7-17 农民人均纯收入指数

Indices of Net Income of Rural Household Per Capita

年 份 Year	以上年为100 Preceding year=100		以1978年为100 1978 =100	
	按当年价格计算 At Current Year Prices	扣除价格因素 Subtract Price Affection	按当年价格计算 At Current Year Prices	扣除价格因素 Subtract Price Affection
1995	123.4	105.2	999.7	270.4
1998	101.4	102.4	1448.4	326.6
1999	104.0	105.5	1506.3	344.6
2000	102.3	104.8	1540.8	361.1
2001	104.7	105.1	1613.2	379.5

7-18 农村居民家庭平均每人生活消费支出

Per Capita Living Expenditures of Rural Household

单位：元 (yuan)

项目	Item	1995	1999	2000	2001
生活消费支出	**Living Expenditure**	**1367.30**	**1920.15**	**1942.94**	**1190.33**
按消费类别分：	**By Category of Consumption**				
食品	Food	823.91	1122.96	1053.37	1053.15
#主食	Staple Food	322.18	334.20	244.26	253.47
副食	Non-staple Food	362.86	468.73	469.55	449.81
其他食品	Other food	92.12	124.68	122.49	119.82
衣着	Clothing	73.51	82.65	89.78	93.38
居住	Residence	192.42	267.92	251.92	268.72
家庭设备用品及服务	Household Facilities,Articles and Services	68.79	79.73	78.05	80.76
医疗保健	Medicines and Medical Services	35.78	62.13	82.23	95.71
交通通信	Transportation and communications	26.29	60.24	99.38	102.44
文教娱乐用品及服务	Cultural,Educational and Recreational Articles and Services	128.84	207.67	222.50	234.40
其他商品及服务	Other Commodities and Services	17.75	36.86	65.72	61.76
按消费性质分：	**By Source of Consumption**				
货币性消费	**Consumption paid in Money**				
食品	Food	346.51	547.64	590.19	602.69
衣着	Clothing	73.00	82.35	89.61	93.30
居住	Residence	178.16	252.21	240.26	251.79
家庭设备用品及服务	Household Facilities,Articles and Services	68.77	79.56	78.04	80.73
医疗保健	Medicines and Medical Services	35.78	62.13	82.23	95.71
交通通信	Transportation and communications	26.29	60.24	99.38	102.44
文教娱乐用品及服务	Cultural,Educational and Recreational Articles and Services	128.84	207.67	222.50	234.40
其他商品及服务	Other Commodities and Services	17.75	36.86	65.72	61.76
实物性消费	**Consumption in kind**				
食品	Food	477.40	575.32	463.18	450.46
衣着	Clothing	0.51	0.30	0.17	0.08
居住	Residence	14.26	15.71	11.66	16.93
家庭设备用品及服务	Household Facilities,Articles and Services	0.02	0.17	0.01	0.03
医疗保健	Medicines and Medical Services				
交通通信	Transportation and communications				
文教娱乐用品及服务	Cultural,Educational and Recreational Articles and Services				
其他商品及服务	Other Commodities and Services				

7-19 农村居民平均每人现金收入

Per Capita Cash Revenue of Rural Household

单位:元 (yuan)

项 目	Item	1995	1999	2000	2001
平均每人现金收入	**Per Capita Cash Revenue**	**1873.35**	**2662.31**	**2993.86**	**3066.64**
基本收入	Basic Income	1364.70	1975.05	2167.32	2277.93
劳动者报酬收入	Laborers' Remuneration	267.35	695.06	789.54	839.79
在集体组织中得到的	From Collective Organization	34.78	66.07	80.02	85.15
在企业劳动得到的	From Enterprises	210.69	550.61	614.05	653.10
在其他单位劳动得到的	From Other Units	21.87	78.38	95.47	101.54
家庭经营现金收入	Income from Household Business Operation	1097.35	1279.99	1377.78	1438.14
出售产品收入	From Sales Production	857.40	870.51	904.48	952.67
出售种植业产品收入	From Farming Production	276.27	298.01	317.14	335.00
出售牧业产品收入	From Animal Husbandry Production	500.66	471.22	492.42	524.87
工业加工费的现金收入	From Industry Processing	25.56	26.16	58.29	57.60
建筑业的现金收入	From Construction	59.85	118.41	129.35	133.52
运输业的现金收入	From Transportation	34.90	65.23	93.19	90.17
商业的现金收入	From Commerce	44.00	83.13	109.81	114.39
饮食业的现金收入	From Catering Services	3.00	7.42	9.80	10.22
服务业的现金收入	From Service Trade	20.29	47.03	41.19	47.27
其他家庭经营现金收入	Others	52.35	62.09	31.67	32.30
转移性和财产性收入	Transfer Income and Property Income	150.59	230.16	273.42	271.92
储蓄借贷现金收入	Income from Saving and Credit	358.07	457.10	553.12	516.79
银行信用社得到的贷款	From Banks	35.26	32.11	31.83	29.86
借入款	From Lending	204.49	249.17	277.52	249.96
收回借出款	From Getting in Debt	74.14	90.38	126.73	118.99
从银行信用社取回存款	From Taking out Savings	43.34	84.33	96.03	91.97
收回投资款	From Payback	0.82	1.01	0.57	0.22

7-20 农村居民平均每人现金支出

Per Capita Cash Expenditures of Rural Household

单位:元 (yuan)

项 目	Item	1995	1999	2000	2001
平均每人现金支出	**Per Capita Cash Expenditure**	**1832.79**	**2573.30**	**2875.28**	**2949.91**
生产费用支出	Productive Costs	498.56	517.96	563.83	584.64
家庭经营费用支出	Expenditure for Household Business	462.85	471.19	523.29	532.64
种植业生产支出	Expenditure for Farming	184.93	182.97	190.58	190.95
牧业生产支出	Expenditure for Animal Husbandry	198.83	197.49	217.80	227.53
购置生产用固定资产支出	Purchase Fixed Assets	35.71	46.77	40.54	52.00
缴纳税款	Taxes	35.22	43.90	35.26	37.03
上交集体承包任务	Payments to Collective Units	30.07	20.38	18.00	17.74
集体提留和摊派	Collective Apportion	32.45	58.85	49.50	43.34
生活消费支出	Expenditure for Consumption	875.11	1328.65	1467.92	1522.83
其他非借贷性支出	Others Non-lend Expenditure	121.59	215.79	228.81	218.74
寄给、带给在外人口	Post & bring to Outgoing Person	1.63	1.45	5.42	3.26
赠送农村以外亲友	Giving Non-Rural Friends and Relatives	2.10	3.88	3.61	4.36
其他支出	Others	11.32	15.40	15.43	15.30
储蓄借贷现金支出	Expenditure for Savings and Credit	239.79	387.77	511.96	525.59
归还银行信用社贷款	Return Banks' Loans	26.67	25.01	23.53	26.95
借出款	Lending	26.91	49.82	59.23	48.29
归还款	Payback	101.59	143.00	211.46	216.85
存入银行信用社款	Savings	82.70	158.93	213.57	227.62
支出投资款	Investment	1.92	10.50	4.14	5.87

7-21 农村住户平均每户购买商品情况

Per Capita Purchases of Commodities of Rural Household

项 目	Item	2000		2001	
		实物量 Object Volume	金额(元) value (yuan)	实物量 Object Volume	金额(元) Value (yuan)
购买食品	**Purchase of Food**		**1480.66**		**1463.71**
粮食(原粮)(公斤)	Grain (Unprocessed) (kg)	28.35	30.05	30.74	32.49
食用植物油(公斤)	Edible Vegetable Oil (kg)	3.69	26.74	3.28	24.64
动物油(公斤)	Edible Animal Oil (kg)	18.77	130.71	19.47	122.26
蔬菜(公斤)	Vegetables (kg)	33.46	58.98	35.58	58.35
豆制品(公斤)	Bean and Its Products (kg)	9.31	22.30	9.29	22.10
猪肉(公斤)	Pork (kg)	42.52	377.29	45.87	388.91
牛肉(公斤)	Beef (kg)	1.30	13.85	1.24	13.50
羊肉(公斤)	Mutton (kg)	0.32	4.00	0.33	4.27
家禽(公斤)	Poultry (kg)	5.59	49.43	5.28	47.81
鲜蛋(公斤)	Eggs (kg)	5.51	33.64	4.85	29.98
鲜活鱼类(公斤)	Fresh Fish (kg)	13.94	80.95	15.13	86.10
食糖(公斤)	Sugar (kg)	5.21	18.23	4.98	20.08
糕点(公斤)	Cake (kg)	3.45	22.00	3.37	22.29
糖果(公斤)	Candy (kg)	2.56	17.42	2.52	17.15
卷烟(盒)	Cigarette (pack)	104.83	172.38	95.52	163.06
酒(公斤)	Liquor (kg)	16.14	71.57	14.57	63.80
啤酒(公斤)	Beer (kg)	4.30	13.37	4.11	12.92
茶叶(公斤)	Tea (kg)	1.71	4.30	0.28	3.88
水果(公斤)	Fresh Fruits (kg)	31.20	54.61	35.97	59.77
鲜奶(公斤)	Milk (kg)	0.02	0.15	0.03	0.18
奶制品(公斤)	Dairy Products (kg)	0.26	3.20	0.33	4.45
购买衣着和床上用品	**Purchase of Clothing and Bed Articles**		**377.46**		**396.69**
棉布服装(件)	Cotton Clothing (piece)	0.28	5.27	0.28	6.56
化纤布服装(件)	Chemical Fiber Clothing (piece)	5.31	164.42	5.82	181.29
毛料服装(件)	Woolen Fabric Clothing (piece)	0.05	2.61	0.04	2.17
皮料服装(件)	Leather Clothing (piece)	0.03	3.59	0.00	0.02

7-21 续表 continued

项 目	Item	2000 实物量 Object Volume	2000 金额(元) value (yuan)	2001 实物量 Object Volume	2001 金额(元) Value (yuan)
购买文化体育用品	**Purchase of Culture and Sports Goods**		**186.68**		**209.23**
黑白电视机(台)	B&W TV Sets (unit)	0.01	1.86	0.01	1.18
彩色电视机(台)	Color TV Sets (unit)	0.03	47.80	0.03	53.1
收录机(台)	Radio & Type Recorder (unit)		0.50	0.01	1.16
录放象机(台)	Video-recorder (unit)		0.20		
购买建筑材料	**Purchase of Building Materials**		**506.69**		**497.7**
水泥(公斤)	Cement (kg)	396.27	86.28	371.54	83.82
玻璃(平方米)	Glass (sq)	0.44	5.75	0.29	3.61
购买燃料	**Purchase of Fuels**		**120.23**		**134.16**
煤炭(公斤)	Coal (kg)	525.45	103.02	544.34	117.39
购买日用品	**Purchase of Articles for Daily Use**		**489.49**		**461.76**
生活用塑料制品	Plastic Products for Living		3.32		3.39
自行车(辆)	Bicycle (unit)	0.03	5.61	0.03	5.60
缝纫机(架)	Sewing Machine (unit)		0.13		0.09
洗衣机(台)	Washing Machine (unit)	0.01	8.16	0.01	7.63
电风扇(台)	Electric Fan (unit)	0.08	5.19	0.08	4.53
电冰箱(台)	Refrigerator (unit)		7.83	0.01	9.14
摩托车(辆)	Motor Cycle (unit)	0.01	60.16	0.01	54.73
购买药品及医疗用品	**Purchase of Drug and Medical Articles**		**221.99**		**242.98**
药品(元)	Medicine (yuan)		218.76		240.65
购买生产资料	**Purchase of means of production**		**1863.40**		**1921.36**
化肥(公斤)	Chemical Fertilizer (kg)	472.47	363.94	485.92	363.47
饼肥(公斤)	Cake Fertilizer (kg)	4.81	3.63	2.27	1.60
农药(公斤)	Pesticide (kg)	11.00	117.21	12.16	119.23
农用薄膜(公斤)	Farming Pellicle (kg)	0.80	6.28	0.75	5.94
生产用燃料(公斤)	Fuels for Farm Machinery (kg)	116.35	75.49	125.00	72.86
每百户购买商品	**Purchase of Goods per 100 Households**				
汽车(辆)	Motor Vehicles (unit)	0.11	2958.05	0.19	5475.68
小型和手扶拖拉机(台)	Small and Walking Tractors (unit)	0.27	660.27	0.59	1952.57
机动脱粒机(台)	Motorized Threshing Machines (unit)	0.46	226.65	0.66	218.16
胶轮大车(辆)	Carts with Rubber Tires (unit)	0.14	136.57	0.08	22.70
水泵(台)	Pumps (unit)	1.46	453.38	1.51	432.43
役畜(头)	Draught Animals (head)	2.74	2049.92	2.37	1932.89
产品畜(头)	Commodity Animals (head)	2.70	1238.81	3.11	1514.03

7-22 农村居民平均每人全年主要消费品消费量

Per Capita Annual Consumption of Major Consumer Goods of Rural Household

单位：公斤 (kg)

指 标	Item	1995	1999	2000	2001
粮食(原粮)	Grain (Unprocessed)	299.05	294.50	287.45	278.00
小麦	Wheat		2.31	2.25	1.91
稻谷	Rice		282.49	274.86	267.45
玉米	Corn		1.02	1.85	0.87
高粱	Broomcorn		0.16	…	
薯类	Potato		5.43	3.84	2.38
豆类	Legume	1.98	2.29	2.14	1.74
#大豆	Soja		2.09	1.93	1.09
豆制品	Legume Products	2.95	3.07	2.87	2.34
蔬菜	Vegetables	140.14	157.69	156.18	161.47
#鲜菜	Fresh Vegetables		157.39	155.83	161.26
干菜	Dehydrated Vegetable		0.30	0.35	0.21
油脂类	Oil and Fats	7.51	9.40	9.68	9.25
#植物油	Vegetable Oil	3.45	3.60	3.85	3.32
动物油	Animal Oil	4.06	5.80	5.84	5.93
肉禽及其制品	Meat , Poultry and Related Products	14.77	21.35	22.74	23.02
#猪肉	Pork	14.53	17.70	18.27	18.54
牛肉	Beef	0.24	0.34	0.33	0.32
羊肉	Mutton		0.07	0.14	0.11
家禽	Poultry	2.07	2.99	3.70	3.77
肉禽制品	Meat and Poultry 's Products	0.00	0.11	0.13	0.11
蛋类及蛋制品	Eggs and Its Products	2.56	2.75	3.55	3.64
奶和奶制品	Milk and Dairy Products		0.05	0.07	0.09
水产品	Aquatic Products		4.57	4.76	4.98
#鱼类	Fish		4.39	4.47	4.70
虾类	Shrimps,Prawns and Crabs		0.02	0.04	0.04
贝类	Shell-fish		0.01	0.02	0.02
澡类	Algae		0.07	0.06	0.06
其他水产品	Others		0.07	0.16	0.15
糖类	Sugar	1.44	2.00	1.95	1.91
#食糖	Sugar		1.41	1.31	1.27
糖果	Candy		0.58	0.64	0.64
酒和饮料	Liquor and Beverage	6.72	5.80	7.63	6.46
#白酒	Liquor		3.36	3.85	3.55
啤酒	Beer		1.04	1.09	1.05
果酒	Fruit Wine		0.02	0.02	0.01
汽水、可乐	Soda & Cola		0.12	0.12	0.11
茶叶	Tea	0.21	0.21	0.22	0.21
其他饮料	Other Beverages		0.69	0.72	0.69
糕点	Cake		0.96	0.87	0.86
干鲜瓜果类	Melons and Fruits	14.41	23.92	18.76	26.05
坚果及果仁制品	Nuts and Kernels' Products		2.19	1.15	0.89

7-23 农村居民平均每百户年末拥有耐用消费品数量

Year – End Number of Durable Consumer Goods Per 100 Rural Households

品 名	Item	1995	1999	2000	2001
自行车(辆)	Bicycle (unit)	103.68	95.51	80.59	81.49
缝纫机(架)	Sewing Machine(unit)	40.51	41.23	-	-
钟(只)	Clock(unit)	35.95	55.01	-	-
手表(只)	Watch(unit)	134.32	126.53	-	-
电子表(只)	Electronic Watch(unit)	18.57	29.87	-	-
电风扇(台)	Electric Fan(unit)	97.84	138.38	171.11	176.68
洗衣机(台)	Washing Machine(unit)	4.24	8.38	15.94	16.92
电冰箱(台)	Refrigerator(unit)	1.38	3.92	6.84	7.68
摩托车(辆)	Motor Cycle(unit)	0.89	7.91	10.51	12.41
沙发(个)	Sofa(unit)	27.51	38.22	-	-
大衣柜(个)	Wardrobe(unit)	120.49	117.86	-	-
写字台(张)	Writing Desk(unit)	102.59	105.64	-	-
收音机(台)	Radio(unit)	11.14	10.31	-	-
黑白电视机(台)	B&W Television Set(unit)	61.10	70.63	66.78	65.54
彩色电视机(台)	Color Television Set(unit)	4.43	17.62	30.32	34.81
收录机(台)	Type Recorder(unit)	14.51	19.40	13.11	12.89
照相机(架)	Camera(unit)	0.35	0.91	1.59	1.59
录放像机(台)	Video-recorder(unit)	-	0.91	2.43	2.30
组合音响(台)	Hi-Fi Stereo Component System (set)	-	-	5.70	6.73
空调机(台)	Air Conditioner(unit)	-	-	0.11	0.19
抽油烟机(台)	Smoke Absorber(unit)	-	0.08	0.51	0.54
家用计算机(台)	Computer (set)	-	-	0.22	0.38
寻呼机(台)	Beep-Pager (unit)	-	-	7.59	7.81
电话机(台)	Telephone (unit)	-	-	23.13	27.84
移动电话机(台)	Mobile Telephone (unit)	-	-	1.54	4.14

注：无数据项均为当年度无此调查项目。

The item of missing data didn't surveyed at current year.

7-24 农村居民住房情况

Living Conditions of Rural Households

指 标	Item	1995	1999	2000	2001
平均每户年末使用房屋间数(间)	Number of Rooms Per Household at the End of Year(room)	5.20	5.26	5.50	5.60
平均每人新建房屋面积(平方米)	Per Capita Newly Built Floor Space of Houses (sq.m)	0.94	1.24	1.20	1.35
#砖木结构面积(平方米)	#Brick and Wood Structure	0.74	0.59	0.50	0.58
钢筋混凝土面积(平方米)	Concrete Structure	0.18	0.63	0.70	0.76
楼房面积(平方米)	Areas of Floor Space of Multi-floor Building	0.46	0.49	0.99	1.13
平均每人年末住房面积(平方米)	Per Capita Floor Space of Residential Building at the Year-end (sq.m)	25.57	29.88	30.92	32.87
#砖木结构面积(平方米)	Brick and Wood Structure (sq.m)	19.72	20.98	19.76	21.22
钢筋混凝土面积(平方米)	Reinforced Concrete Structure (sq.m)	2.44	6.54	9.05	9.55
年末每间房屋价值(元)	Value Per Room (Yuan)	1197.02	2825.17	3636.51	3798.95

7-25 农村居民拥有生产性固定资产

Production Fixed Assets of Per Capita Rural Household

指 标	Item	1995	1999	2000	2001
按原值计算(每户拥有)	**Group by Original Value (per household)**				
合 计(元)	**Total (yuan)**	**1376.34**	**2533.94**	**3006.28**	**3106.38**
#役畜、产品畜	#Draught Animals & Commodity Animals	335.69	382.48	318.57	335.48
大中型铁木农具	Large(Medium) Ironwood Farm Tools	151.61	277.31	305.8	306.46
农林牧渔机械	Agricultural Machinery	150.87	267.1	281.66	322.36
工业机械	Industrial Machinery	90.48	158.02	167.51	225.33
运输机械	Transportation Machinery	205.46	336.94	601.13	518.14
生产用房	Buildings for Productive Purpose	417.15	1027.61	1112.87	1139.93
其他	Others	25.08	84.49	218.74	258.68
按实物统计(每百户拥有)	**Number of Productive Fixed Assets (per 100 household)**				
#汽车(辆)	#Motor Vehicles (unit)	0.23	0.51	1.03	0.91
大中型拖拉机(台)	Large(Medium) Tractors (unit)	0.07	0.18	0.26	0.03
小型和手扶拖拉机(台)	Mini and Walking Tractors (unit)	2.07	2.56	3.31	3.21
机动脱粒机(台)	Motorized Threshing Machine (unit)	4.33	9.13	16.24	3.74
胶轮大车(辆)	Carts with Rubber Tires (unit)	0.49	1.31	3.86	4.01
胶轮手推车(辆)	Hand Carts with Rubber Tires (unit)	10.04	10.24	-	-
水泵(台)	Water Pumps (unit)	9.83	14.86	15.33	16.53
机动船(条)	Motor boats (unit)	0.08	0.32	-	-
役畜(头)	Draught Animals (head)	31.02	26.18	15.58	23.4
产品畜(头)	Commodity Animals (head)	29.15	25.01	23.47	26.02

7-26 农村小康实现程度(2001年)

Degree of Being Fairly Well – to – Do of Rural (2001)

指 标	Item	全省		
		数 量 Number Value	实现程度 (%) Degree (%)	得分 (分) Score
收入分配	**Income**			
人均纯收入(元)	Per Capita Net Income (yuan)	2299.46	88.27	26.48
基尼系数	Geni Index	0.276	76	3.8
物质生活	**Physical Life**			
恩格尔系数(%)	Engel Index (%)	52.9	71	4.26
每日每人蛋白质摄入量(克)	Per Day Per Capita Amount of Protein Ingestion (g)	78.6	100	9
衣着消费支出(元/人)	Per Capita Expenditure for Clothing (yuan/person)	93.38	42.12	1.26
钢木结构住房比重(%)	Rate of Reinforced Concrete and Brick&Wood Structure (%)	93.61	100	7
精神生活	**Spiritual Life**			
#电视机普及率(台/百户)	Popularity Rate of TV Set (unit/100 households)	100.31	100	6
服务消费支出比重(%)	Proportion of Service Expenditure (%)	20.2	100	6
人口素质	**Population Quality**			
#劳动力平均受教育年限(年)	Labor Force Education Level (year)	8.12	100	5
农村人口平均预期寿命(岁)	Average Rural Popular Anticipate Life (year-old)	69.8	90	3.6
生活环境	**Living Environment**			
#安全卫生水普及率(%)	Popularity Rate of Safe and Hygienic Drinking-water (%)	95	100	3
用电户比重(%)	Proportion of Household Using Electric Power (%)	99.6	100	3
已通公路的行政村比重(%)	Proportion of Motor-able Villages (%)	89.23	100	3
已通电话的行政村比重(%)	Proportion of Villages Having Telecommunication line (%)	89.7	100	2
社会保障与社会安全	**Social Security**			
#五保人口生活有保障比重(%)	Proportion of Five-guaranteed Indemnify (%)	94.6	100	4
万人刑事案件立案件数(件)	Number of Registered Criminal Case Per 10,000 persons (case)	18.3	100	4
综合分值	**Evaluate Results**			**91.4**

八、城市建设、环境保护

CONSTRUCTION OF CITIES AND ENVIRONMENTAL PROTECTION

资料整理人员：　陈洲艳　欧阳鹏举

8-1 城市公用事业基本情况

Basic Statistics for urban Public Utilities

指标名称	Item	1999	2000	2001
城市个数(个)	**Number of Cities (unit)**			
省辖市	Cities Under the Jurisdiction of Province	13	13	13
县级市	Cities at County Level	16	16	16
城市规模	**City Size**			
城市人口(万人)	Population of Cities (10 000 persons)	1164.89	1196.68	1028.12
#非农业人口	#Non-agricultural Population	668.87	691.72	702.02
城市面积(平方公里)	Total Areas of Cities (sq.km)	12716	12733.44	8426.25
#建成区面积	#Developed Areas	743	799.27	847.47
房屋建筑	**Buildings**			
实有房屋建筑面积(万平方米)	Floor Space of Buildings (10 000 sq.m)	26222	25884	-
实有住宅建筑面积(万平方米)	Floor Space of Residential Buildings (10 000 sq.m)	13883	15749	-
实有住宅居住面积(万平方米)	Living Space of Residential Buildings (10 000 sq.m)	7636	8753.51	-
人均居住面积(平方米)	Per Capita Living Space (sq.m)	10.77	11.75	11.8
供水	**Water Supply**			
综合生产能力(万立方米/日)	Production Capacity of Tap Water (10 000 cu.m/day)	1242.26	1162.21	1263.39
#地下水	#Shallow Ground Water	105.28	103.78	101.33
供水管长度(公里)	Length of Water Supply Pipelines (km)	7487	7650	9664.5
供水总量(万立方米)	Total Annual Volume of Water Supply (10 000 cu.m)	283226	282357	276325
#生活用	# For Residential Use	89522	95233	-
#生产用量	# For Production	-	-	157973
公共服务用量	For Republic Services	-	-	18743
家庭用量	For Family Use	-	-	85723
人均日生活用水量(升)	Per Capita Daily Consumption of Tap Water for Residential Use (liter)	289.33	310.87	339.35
用水普及率(%)	Percentage of Population with Access to Tap Water (%)	97.85	97.5	97.4
供煤气、液化石油气	**Coal Gas and Liquefied Petroleum Gas Supply**			
供气总量	Total Gas Supply			
煤气(万立方米)	Coal Gas (10 000 cu.m)	74550	60375	48559.3
#家庭用	#Consumption for Residential Use	23437	28521	7746.66
液化石油气(吨)	Liquefied Petroleum Gas (ton)	189579	202033	247606
#家庭用	#Consumption for Residential Use	175829	189827	223912
煤气管道长度(公里)	Length of Coal Gas Pipelines (km)	953	1116	1155.8
石油液化气管道长度(公里)	Length of Liquefied Petroleum Gas Pipelines (km)	119	216	461.9
用气普及率(%)	Percentage of Population with Access to Gas (%)	75.54	78.35	82.6
公共交通	**Public Traffic**			
运营车辆合计(辆)	Number of Public Transportation Vehicles (unit)	8891	9083	8616
#汽车	#Buses	8891	9083	8616
小公共汽车	Small Buses	5223	5228	4302
折运营标台(标台)	Convert into Standard Unit (unit)	6904	7212	7021
运营线路长度(公里)	Length of Public Transportation Lines (km)	3065	3713	3169
出租汽车总计(辆)	Total of Taxi (unit)	18316	19534	22663
每万人拥有公共交通车辆(标台)	Number of Public Transportation Vehicles (unit) per 10 000 persons (unit)	10.32	10.43	10.39
公交客运总量(万人次)	Number of Passengers Carried (10 000 person-times)	91835	106227	101835.32

指标名称	Item	1999	2000	2001
市政设施	**Municipal Engineering**			
道路长度(公里)	Length of Paved Roads (km)	4739	4739	4836.97
道路面积(万平方米)	Area of Paved Roads (10 000 sq.m)	4742.93	4815.93	6200.13
人行道面积(万平方米)	Area of Sidewalk (10 000 sq.m)	1283.64	1426.82	1713.24
桥梁数(座)	Number of bridges (unit)	598	637	520
#立交桥	#Cloverleaf Junction	80	82	68
路灯(盏)	Number of Street Lights (unit)	110343	115147	119336
排水管道长度(公里)	Length of Sewer Pipelines (km)	4922	3754.31	3854.31
污水排放量(万立方米)	Number Volume of Let Sewage (10 000 cu.m)	223585	165902	119082.73
污水处理厂(座数)	Number of Sewage Disposal Farm (unit)	21	21	13
处理能力(万立方米/日)	Daily Disposal Capacity of Sewage (10 000 cu.m/day)	61.15	61.15	54.4
设施能力(万立方米/日)	Capacity of Engineering (10 000 cu.m/day)	67.6	83.9	129
污水年处理量(万立方米)	Annual Volume of Sewage Treated (10 000 cu.m)	40252	45316	726262
防洪堤长度(公里)	Length of Banks to Prevent or Control Flood (km)	599.47	602.77	528.46
#百年一遇以上	# Befall 100 Years and Over	73.53	107.03	25.73
人均拥有道路(平方米)	Per Capita of Road Areas (sq.m)	7.09	6.96	6.03
排水管密度(公里 / 平方公里)	Density of Drainage Pipelines (km/sq.km)	6.62	4.7	4.55
污水处理率(%)	Rate of Sewage Disposal (%)	18	27.31	22.05
园林绿化	**Parks, Gardens and Green Areas**			
绿化覆盖面积(公顷)	Coverage Space of Green Areas (hectare)	41899	49290	35433.72
#建成区	#Developed Area	21586	22646	23854.02
园林绿地面积(公顷)	Area of Parks,Gardens and Green Areas in Cities (hectare)	26804	44672	30185.38
#建成区	#Developed Area	18337	19450	20592.56
公共绿地面积(公顷)	Public Green Areas (hectare)	3259	3525	4680.93
公园个数(个)	Number of Parks (unit)	112	116	109
公园面积(公顷)	Area of Parks (hectare)	2557.66	2646.41	2547.84
苗圃面积（公顷）	Area of Nursery (hectare)	981.99	1233.54	-
人均公共绿地面积(平方米)	Per Capita Public Green Areas (sq.m)	4.87	5.1	4.55
建成区绿地率(%)	Rate of Green Areas Developed (%)	24.67	24.33	24.3
建成区绿化覆盖率(%)	Coverage Rate of Green Areas Developed (%)	29.04	28.33	28.15
环境卫生	**Environmental Sanitation**			
实际清扫面积(万平方米)	Area Under Cleaning Program (10 000 sq.m)	2973.93	3236.22	3804.61
#机械清扫	Machine Cleaning	296.87	411.77	310.6
生活垃圾清运量(万吨)	Volume of Garbage Disposal (10 000 tons)	316.82	358.46	1048.3
粪便清运量(万吨)	Volume of Excrement and Urine Disposal (10 000 tons)	23.21	24.25	41.3
垃圾无害化处理场(座数)	Number of Factories to Treat Garbage Harmlessly(unit)	12	15	35
#处理能力(吨/日)	Daily Disposal Capacity (ton/day)	3266	4427	10332
垃圾无害处理量(万吨)	Volume of Garbage Harmlessly Treatment (10 000 tons)	140.33	180.91	878.92
粪便无害化处理能力(吨/日)	Capacity of Urine Harmlessly Treatment (ton/day)	567	375	-
粪便无害化处理量(万吨)	Volume of Urine Harmlessly Treatment (10 000 tons)	14.05	8.31	31.78
公共厕所数(座)	Number of Public Lavatories (unit)	2922	3001	2438
#水冲式	# Water Closet	1762	1771	1720
环卫机械总数(台)	Environmental Sanitation Equipment (unit)	1190	1213	1131
年末环卫工人数(人)	Environmental Sanitation Workers at Year-end (person)	11536	11356	17187
垃圾粪便无害化处理率(%)	Ratio of Garbage and Urine Harmlessly Treatment (%)	45.4	51.01	83.84

8-2 城市规模和建设用地(2001年)

Urban Scale and Construction Land (2001)

单位:平方公里 (sq.km)

城市	Cities	城市人口 Population in Cities (10 000 persons)	#非农人口 Non-Agricultural Population	城市面积 Area of City	建成区面积 Developed Areas	建设用地面积 Area of Construction Use Land 居住用地 Living Space	公共设施用地 Public Engineering	道路广场用地 Road and Plaza	绿地 Green Areas
长沙市	Changsha	175.40	143.50	556.33	128.00	37.88	28.33	9.60	8.09
浏阳市	Liuyang	14.80	7.99	37.00	14.00	5.80	3.50	1.17	0.25
株洲市	Zhuzhou	76.02	56.77	462.00	66.22	18.57	6.32	3.21	5.24
醴陵市	Liling	16.92	11.33	47.00	17.10	4.65	2.82	0.90	0.25
湘潭市	Xiangtan	68.15	55.06	278.77	54.16	14.26	5.00	3.56	2.76
湘乡市	Xiangxiang	11.40	7.27	31.00	13.02	5.16	3.28	1.60	1.80
韶山市	Shaoshan	10.35	3.20	70.00	4.60	0.74	0.42	0.50	0.90
衡阳市	Hengyang	90.00	63.00	543.00	64.00	23.00	3.90	9.00	2.20
耒阳市	Leiyang	23.27	12.00	30.00	23.31	6.93	4.86	3.44	2.84
常宁市	Changning	7.19	7.15	24.90	7.95	1.50	1.57	0.87	1.60
邵阳市	Shaoyang	60.00	31.50	423.00	35.60	10.20	5.30	3.90	1.30
武冈市	Wugang	12.50	8.41	40.00	13.00	5.00	1.00	2.00	1.50
岳阳市	Yueyang	52.71	38.78	845.00	60.00	24.60	7.80	6.70	6.40
汨罗市	Miluo	12.50	5.90	20.00	12.50	5.30	1.70	1.10	1.00
临湘市	Linxiang	9.10	7.30	25.00	10.11	2.01	1.00	1.00	1.10
常德市	Changde	132.81	41.46	2749.00	58.12	19.21	9.90	6.45	2.19
津市市	Jinshi	12.91	10.35	68.30	10.78	3.25	1.11	0.87	1.05
张家界市	Zhangjiajie	16.84	11.63	145.88	17.48	3.97	3.98	1.07	0.19
益阳市	Yiyang	38.20	32.00	70.00	38.00	10.25	7.49	3.98	2.56
沅江市	Yuanjiang	10.50	7.15	12.00	9.70	2.80	1.80	0.55	0.30
郴州市	Chenzhou	28.75	24.17	1313.00	25.85	10.72	4.33	1.10	0.85
资兴市	Zixing	12.66	9.14	146.00	17.80	6.20	1.80	3.50	0.10
永州市	Yongzhou	31.30	24.30	71.50	31.76	9.53	4.15	2.90	4.20
娄底市	Loudi	24.51	21.97	53.00	39.00	12.00	6.00	3.10	2.20
冷水江市	Lengshuijiang	12.10	11.35	18.17	17.42	4.67	1.12	0.85	3.51
涟源市	Lianyuan	7.40	5.86	14.70	9.10	2.85	0.80	0.90	0.30
怀化市	Huaihua	31.97	24.15	52.00	27.33	11.25	2.50	2.05	2.06
洪江市	Hongjiang	12.37	6.80	129.70	7.11	2.72	0.59	0.52	0.52
吉首市	Jishou	15.49	12.53	150.00	14.46	5.07	1.41	1.38	0.25

8-3 城市设施水平(2001年)

Indicators of Municipal Public Utilities Level (2001)

城市	Cities	人口密度(人/平方公里) Population Density (person/sq.km)	人均拥有城市维护建设资金(元) Per Capita Funds for Construction and Maintenance (yuan)	人均日生活用水量(升) Per Capita Water Consumption for Residential Use (liter)	用水普及率(%) Percentage of Population with Access to Tap Water (%)	每万人拥有公共交通车辆(标台) Number of Public Transportation Vehicles Per 10000 persons (unit)	用气普及率(%) Percentage of Population with Access to Gas (%)
长沙市	Changsha	3153	1909	322.64	100.00	10.88	92.00
浏阳市	Liuyang	4000	1605	185.91	47.30	2.16	54.05
株洲市	Zhuzhou	1645	862	368.90	74.68	7.60	70.19
醴陵市	Liling	3600	282	141.36	99.88	2.30	47.28
湘潭市	Xiangtan	2445	540	391.76	100.00	6.19	71.46
湘乡市	Xiangxiang	3677	269	138.65	86.84	3.33	92.11
韶山市	Shaoshan	1479	339	138.70	30.92	0.68	18.36
衡阳市	Hengyang	1657	97	668.59	90.00	4.63	7.04
耒阳市	Leiyang	7757	555	104.50	60.16	5.20	12.89
常宁市	Changning	2888	207	155.69	87.62	5.70	47.29
邵阳市	Shaoyang	1418	387	123.56	100.00	4.73	74.80
武冈市	Wugang	3125	246	106.92	98.40	4.00	41.60
岳阳市	Yueyang	624	548	506.52	100.00	11.00	89.60
汨罗市	Miluo	6250	307	169.05	75.20	3.92	83.20
临湘市	Linxiang	3640	92	153.02	90.11	5.38	76.92
常德市	Changde	483	306	489.45	27.90	2.09	27.56
津市市	Jinshi	1890	133	167.89	96.82	24.55	48.72
张家界市	Zhangjiajie	1154	143	287.99	81.24	4.33	37.95
益阳市	Yiyang	5457	555	209.41	85.86	6.23	47.91
沅江市	Yuanjiang	8750	62	134.25	57.14	5.71	50.48
郴州市	Chenzhou	219	436	453.16	82.64	12.14	74.09
资兴市	Zixing	867	127	346.25	100.00	6.71	25.28
永州市	Yongzhou	4378	178	346.50	95.94	8.37	54.92
娄底市	Loudi	4625	410	272.49	98.33	6.04	88.13
冷水江市	Lengshuijiang	6659	204	251.34	95.04	6.69	48.35
涟源市	Lianyuan	5034	129	224.66	94.00	6.62	68.92
怀化市	Huaihua	6148	429	225.57	93.84	10.82	39.41
洪江市	Hongjiang	954	568	102.74	58.21	1.37	33.14
吉首市	Jishou	1033	818	407.02	89.74	6.58	63.65

8-3 续表 continued

城市	Cities	人均拥有道路面积(平方米) Per Capita Area of Paved Roads (sq.m)	排水管道密度(公里/平方公里) Density of Sewer Pipelines (km/sq.km)	污水处理率(%) Ratio of Sewage Treatment (%)	园林绿化 Parks, Gardens and Green Areas: 人均公共绿地面积(平方米) Per Capita Public Green Areas (sq.m)	建成区绿地率(%) Ratio of Green Area in Developed Areas (%)	建成区绿化覆盖率(%) Green Area Coverage Rate in Developed Areas (%)	垃圾无害化处理率(%) Ratio of Garbage Harmlessly Treatment (%)
长沙市	Changsha	6.27	5.06	24.42	5.73	25.87	28.25	78.36
浏阳市	Liuyang	13.90	2.29		1.56	23.57	24.29	100.00
株洲市	Zhuzhou	6.56	5.82	52.88	4.14	31.43	36.90	91.74
醴陵市	Liling	3.90	3.27		3.90	28.36	30.41	100.00
湘潭市	Xiangtan	6.35	6.11		2.89	28.93	34.44	50.00
湘乡市	Xiangxiang	4.02	3.88		2.11	6.91	11.06	
韶山市	Shaoshan	4.73	13.04	64.00	2.61	33.33	35.17	100.00
衡阳市	Hengyang	4.03	4.86		1.78	24.23	27.45	99.85
耒阳市	Leiyang	7.59	8.07		3.33	16.30	19.86	
常宁市	Changning	15.03	8.74		1.11	9.56	29.43	
邵阳市	Shaoyang	4.83	3.37		3.65	17.22	18.79	100.00
武冈市	Wugang	5.18			1.76	9.38	11.38	100.00
岳阳市	Yueyang	7.02	3.76	27.47	7.00	29.98	35.00	100.00
汨罗市	Miluo	7.92	4.64		6.65	15.36	19.84	
临湘市	Linxiang	5.82	2.67		4.18	4.85	5.93	100.00
常德市	Changde	2.95	4.91	46.88	6.36	30.80	37.84	100.00
津市市	Jinshi	5.07	5.47		7.01	20.18	20.50	77.78
张家界市	Zhangjiajie	9.98	2.97		1.52	12.03	13.87	
益阳市	Yiyang	6.44	3.89		4.59	30.68	31.34	81.93
沅江市	Yuanjiang	4.49	1.86		5.40	17.63	19.67	
郴州市	Chenzhou	6.98	5.02		6.68	27.78	38.34	22.27
资兴市	Zixing	5.24	1.91		5.73	15.73	18.60	84.62
永州市	Yongzhou	9.99	4.12		3.87	19.68	26.04	
娄底市	Loudi	11.38	5.31	20.62	4.96	19.79	23.41	
冷水江市	Lengshuijiang	5.91	2.47	34.25	6.88	19.58	20.15	
涟源市	Lianyuan	7.88	3.71		3.86	24.74	27.10	
怀化市	Huaihua	5.88	2.74		4.04	30.15	32.09	52.27
洪江市	Hongjiang	6.06	2.81		4.28	28.41	32.21	78.13
吉首市	Jishou	6.99	3.91		3.48	17.39	19.02	

8-4 城市供水(2001年)

Tap Water Supply in Cities (2001)

城市	Cities	综合生产能力(万立方米/日) Production Capacity of Tap Water (10 000 cu.m/day)	#地下水 Shallow Ground Water	供水管道长度(公里) Length of Water Supply Pipelines (km)	供水总量(万立方米) Total Annual Volume of Water Supply (10 000 cu.m)	#生产用量 For Productive Use	#公共服务用量 For Republic Services	#家庭用量 For Family Use	用水人口(万人) Number of Residents with Access to Tap Water (10 000 persons)
长沙市	Changsha	157.00	2.70	1120	39872	17610	3192	17464	175.40
浏阳市	Liuyang	4.50	1.50	62	735	169	330	145	7.00
株洲市	Zhuzhou	250.70	0.20	604	38575	28741	1841	5803	56.77
醴陵市	Liling	8.50		190.66	1339	429	3	869	16.90
湘潭市	Xiangtan	103.00	50.40	928	51627	41650	3638	6107	68.15
湘乡市	Xiangxiang	5.63	0.03	72.8	1190	646	120	381	9.90
韶山市	Shaoshan	2.50	1.70	248	248	70	42	120	3.20
衡阳市	Hengyang	81.20	13.70	472	29188	8450	944	18823	81.00
耒阳市	Leiyang	6.30	0.25	210.7	700	60	24	510	14.00
常宁市	Changning	3.30	0.10	4.1	658	260	124	234	6.30
邵阳市	Shaoyang	63.00	1.00	405	5653	1445	348	2358	60.00
武冈市	Wugang	8.60	1.40	172	840	220	110	370	12.30
岳阳市	Yueyang	196.72	2.65	580.45	35706	22609	4117	5628	52.71
汨罗市	Miluo	11.30	3.80	68	968	325	26	554	9.40
临湘市	Linxiang	5.50		85		105		458	8.20
常德市	Changde	42.07	3.52	401.79	10633	3198	1209	5410	37.05
津市市	Jinshi	21.00	1.00	90	4400	3510	317	449	12.50
张家界市	Zhangjiajie	12.10		1950	2220	716	10	1428	13.68
益阳市	Yiyang	40.20	1.20	205	4122	1226	358	2149	32.80
沅江市	Yuanjiang	3.00	3.00	27	300	3	27	267	6.00
郴州市	Chenzhou	57.37	8.38	365.1	7863	3853	955	2975	23.76
资兴市	Zixing	9.60	0.70	173	2690	1060	70	1530	12.66
永州市	Yongzhou	32.60	0.80	270	8300	3375	424	3374	30.03
娄底市	Loudi	39.00		220	8394	5525	238	2159	24.10
冷水江市	Lengshuijiang	44.70		169	9322	8221	60	995	11.50
涟源市	Lianyuan	5.00	2.00	55	704	106	38	536	7.00
怀化市	Huaihua	22.60		214.4	5600	3000	130	2340	30.00
洪江市	Hongjiang	9.90		89	810	459	48	222	7.20
吉首市	Jishou	16.50	1.30	212.5	3061	932		2065	13.90

8-5 城市公共交通(2001年)

Public Traffic in Cities (2001)

城市	Cities	公共汽车 Buses						船舶 Vessels		出租汽车数(辆)
		运营车数 合计(辆) Number of Public Transportation Vehicles (unit)	#小公共汽车 Small Buses	标准运营车数(标台) Number of Vehicles Convert into Standard unit (unit)	运营线路网长度(公里) Length of Public Transportation Lines (km)	客运总量(万人次) Number of Passengers Carried (10 000 person-times)	#小公共汽车 Small Buses	运营船数(艘) Number of Passenger Transport Vessels (unit)	客运总量(万人次) Number of Passengers Carried (10 000 person-times)	Number of Taxis (unit)
长沙市	Changsha	2062	759	1909	328	38615	9000			7192
浏阳市	Liuyang	40	20	32	65	500	240			
株洲市	Zhuzhou	624	239	578	297	10448	3162			2059
醴陵市	Liling	98		39	26	2				500
湘潭市	Xiangtan	495	242	422	251	6039	2543	9	21	1150
湘乡市	Xiangxiang	55	55	38	90	245	245			278
韶山市	Shaoshan	18	18	7	11	180	180			38
衡阳市	Hengyang	596	209	417	137	7932	55	4	99	1299
耒阳市	Leiyang	174	170	121	14	1317	1237			590
常宁市	Changning	60	60	41	14	70	70			80
邵阳市	Shaoyang	423	213	284	67	6.82	1.32	3	32	1047
武冈市	Wugang	120	120	50	40	448	448			178
岳阳市	Yueyang	572		580	199	3881				1046
汨罗市	Miluo	90	78	49	43	660	565			60
临湘市	Linxiang	70	70	49		720	720			302
常德市	Changde	307	147	278	144	3089	1116	3	50	1434
律市市	Jinshi	453	453	317	350	940	940			130
张家界市	Zhangjiajie	132	81	73	118	775	526			850
益阳市	Yiyang	290	173	238	152	4145.8	1535.3			740
沅江市	Yuanjiang	75	75	60	106	280	280			
郴州市	Chenzhou	463	261	349	115	5089	2007.4			960
资兴市	Zixing	85	61	85	52	289	220			60
永州市	Yongzhou	427	304	262	198	3670	1785			279
娄底市	Loudi	178	147	148	46	1760	1430			787
冷水江市	Lengshuijiang	116	116	81	42	1203.2	1203.2			101
涟源市	Lianyuan	65	54	49		940	680			278
怀化市	Huaihua	396	95	346	200	6161	700	18	261	630
洪江市	Hongjiang	30	30	17	36	470	385	18	261	95
吉首市	Jishou	102	52	102	28	1959.5	400			500

8-6 城市市政设施(2001年)

Urban Civil Facilities (2001)

城市	Cities	道路长度(公里) Length of Streets (km)	道路面积(万平方米) Area of Streets (10 000 sq.m)	人行道面积(万平方米) Area of Sidewalk (10 000 sq.m)	桥梁数(座) Number of Bridges (unit)	#立交桥 Cloverleaf Junction	路灯盏数(盏) Number of Street Lights (unit)	排水管道长度(公里) Length of Sewer Pipelines (km)	污水年排放量(万立方米) Annual Volume of Sewage Discharged (10 000 cu.m)
长沙市	Changsha	1098.00	1099.61	273.00	71	20	20067	648.00	28142
浏阳市	Liuyang	33.00	205.70	155.00	17		1842	32.00	1454
株洲市	Zhuzhou	425.41	498.49	150.64	45	12	13200	385.37	15149
醴陵市	Liling	68.00	66.00	12.00	28	3	56	56.00	525
湘潭市	Xiangtan	259.00	433.00	95.00	4		9046	331.00	1421
湘乡市	Xiangxiang	32.75	45.78	13.37	4		2640	50.57	3060
韶山市	Shaoshan	40.80	49.00	8.00	9		430	60.00	450
衡阳市	Hengyang	357.55	363.05	62.93	11	5	6979	310.93	1955
耒阳市	Leiyang	102..00	176.70	41.00	3		3523	188.00	1400
常宁市	Changning	76.50	108.10	18.90	8	2	778	69.50	400
邵阳市	Shaoyang	230.96	289.80	130.00	14		4981	120.00	5200
武冈市	Wugang	49.00	64.69	23.00	17		640		720
岳阳市	Yueyang	270.92	370.00	100.77	7	5	6640	225.64	15000
汨罗市	Miluo	49.00	99.00	29.00	12	3	610	58.00	1100
临湘市	Linxiang	52.00	53.00	22.00	5	1	1100	27.00	800
常德市	Changde	282.06	391.58	102.30	23		8948	285.28	7358.73
津市市	Jinshi	79.00	65.40	16.00	4		3101	59.00	3426
张家界市	Zhangjiajie	159.64	168.08	27.18	27		1917	52.00	
益阳市	Yiyang	172.00	246.00	46.00	4		4851	148.00	4020
沅江市	Yuanjiang	44.00	47.10	17.00	8		623	18.00	500
郴州市	Chenzhou	118.03	200.77	53.09	52	3	8509	129.66	3760
资兴市	Zixing	74.60	66.33	29.25	10		1643	34.00	70
永州市	Yongzhou	193.00	312.80	76.20	15	3	2780	131.00	6650
娄底市	Loudi	140.00	279.00	70.00	11		3700	207.00	4947
冷水江市	Lengshuijiang	81.20	71.50	21.61	13	1	1572	43.00	7300
涟源市	Lianyuan	70.55	58.30	9.77	25	2	1183	33.80	842
怀化市	Huaihua	134.00	188.00	45.00	30	2	5590	75.00	2196
洪江市	Hongjiang	60.00	75.00	9.00	4	1	1232	20.00	926
吉首市	Jishou	84.00	108.35	56.23	39	5	1081	56.56	311

城市	Cities	污水处理厂 Sewage Disposal Factory				污水处理设施处理能力(万方/日) Capacity of Engineering (10 000 cu.m/day)	污水年处理量(万方) Annual Volume of Sewage Disposal (10 000 cu.m)	防洪堤长度(公里) Length of Banks to Prevent or Control Flood (km)	
		座数(座) Number of Units (unit)	#生化处理 Biological and Chemical Disposal	处理能力(万立方米/日) Disposal Capacity (10 000 cu.m/day)	#生化处理 Biological and Chemical Disposal				#百年及以上一遇 Befall 100 Years and Over
长沙市	Changsha	2		20.00			6872	127.00	
浏阳市	Liuyang								
株洲市	Zhuzhou	2	1	11.20	10.00	10.80	8011	33.00	
醴陵市	Liling							5.00	5.00
湘潭市	Xiangtan							19.00	5.00
湘乡市	Xiangxiang							10.08	0.30
韶山市	Shaoshan	1	1	1.50	1.50	32.00	288		
衡阳市	Hengyang							92.90	
耒阳市	Leiyang							0.80	
常宁市	Changning								
邵阳市	Shaoyang							7.70	5.50
武冈市	Wugang							16.00	0.30
岳阳市	Yueyang	6	6	3.70	3.70	8.00	4121	12.00	8.00
汨罗市	Miluo							11.00	
临湘市	Linxiang							4.00	
常德市	Changde	1	1	15.00	15.00		3450	103.50	1.00
津市市	Jinshi							16.00	
张家界市	Zhangjiajie							36.08	0.23
益阳市	Yiyang							13.00	
沅江市	Yuanjiang								
郴州市	Chenzhou							9.57	0.40
资兴市	Zixing					70.00			
永州市	Yongzhou								
娄底市	Loudi	1	1	3.00	3.00		1020		
冷水江市	Lengshuijiang					8.20	2500	0.93	
涟源市	Lianyuan								
怀化市	Huaihua							3.70	
洪江市	Hongjiang							7.20	
吉首市	Jishou								

8-7 城市园林绿化(2001年)

Urban Parks, Gardens and Green Areas (2001)

城市	Cities	绿化覆盖面积(公顷) Coverage Space of Green Areas (hectare)	#建成区 Developed Areas	园林绿地面积(公顷) Area of Parks, Gardens and Green Areas (hectare)	#建成区 Developed Areas	公共绿地面积(公顷) Public Green Areas (hectare)	公园个数(个) Number of Parks (unit)	公园面积(公顷) Area of Parks (hectare)
长沙市	Changsha	5846	3616	5541	3311	1005.00	12	716.00
浏阳市	Liuyang	400	340	349	330	23.10	4	11.80
株洲市	Zhuzhou	2443.45	2443.45	2095.91	2080.91	341.86	4	188.75
醴陵市	Liling	520	520	485	485	66.00	1	55.00
湘潭市	Xiangtan	4269	1865	4053	1567	196.70	13	110.40
湘乡市	Xiangxiang	213	144	191	90	24.00	1	10.00
韶山市	Shaoshan	168.8	161.8	156.3	153.3	27.00	4	22.00
衡阳市	Hengyang	1756.69	1756.69	1550.81	1550.81	160.26	9	94.69
耒阳市	Leiyang	493	463	410	380	77.40	4	65.30
常宁市	Changning	289	234	92	76	8.00	1	7.00
邵阳市	Shaoyang	669	669	613	613	219.00	6	89.30
武冈市	Wugang	148	148	122	122	22.00	3	54.00
岳阳市	Yueyang	4644	2100	3233	1798.9	369.00	4	75.20
汨罗市	Miluo	248	248	192	192	83.10	1	66.70
临湘市	Linxiang	1838	60	1820	49	38.00	1	24.00
常德市	Changde	2199.2	2199.2	1790.3	1790.3	844.90	3	65.43
津市市	Jinshi	582	221	575.5	217.5	90.50	3	86.30
张家界市	Zhangjiajie	867.91	242.51	715.5	210.23	25.55	3	9.13
益阳市	Yiyang	1195	1191	1170	1166	175.20	4	151.40
沅江市	Yuanjiang	249.85	190.76	217.55	171	56.70	2	55.23
郴州市	Chenzhou	991	991	718	718	192.00	5	183.00
资兴市	Zixing	331	331	280	280	72.50	3	57.00
永州市	Yongzhou	848	827	640	625	121.00	4	73.00
娄底市	Loudi	933.6	913	798.9	772	121.49	5	86.84
冷水江市	Lengshuijiang	459	351	343	341	83.20	2	52.60
涟源市	Lianyuan	268.78	246.61	225.17	225.17	28.53	2	5.90
怀化市	Huaihua	1560	877	824	824	129.00	2	63.17
洪江市	Hongjiang	230	229	209	202	53.00	1	29.00
吉首市	Jishou	772.44	275	774.44	251.44	53.94	2	39.70

8-8 城市燃气使用情况(2001年)

Urban Coal Gas and Liquefied Petroleum (2001)

城市	Cities	煤气 Coal Gas					
		供气总量 (万立方米) Total Gas Supply (10 000 cu.m)	#家庭用量 Consumption for Residential Use	用气户数 (户) Number of Household with Access to Gas (household)	#家庭用户 Consumption for Residential Use	用气人口 (万人) Population with Access to Gas (10000 persons)	管道长度 (公里) Length of Pipelines (km)
长沙市	Changsha	2358	1721	68729	68026	23.56	148
浏阳市	Liuyang						
株洲市	Zhuzhou	1930.3	1662.66	66330	66231	23.00	290
醴陵市	Liling						
湘潭市	Xiangtan	32601	1593	39173	39150	13.30	424
湘乡市	Xiangxiang						
韶山市	Shaoshan						
衡阳市	Hengyang						
耒阳市	Leiyang						
常宁市	Changning						
邵阳市	Shaoyang	680	680	25000	25000	7.50	116.8
武冈市	Wugang						
岳阳市	Yueyang						
汨罗市	Miluo						
临湘市	Linxiang						
常德市	Changde						
律市市	Jinshi						
张家界市	Zhangjiajie						
益阳市	Yiyang						
沅江市	Yuanjiang						
郴州市	Chenzhou						
资兴市	Zixing						
永州市	Yongzhou						
娄底市	Loudi	1190	1190	44083	44083	16.20	167
冷水江市	Lengshuijiang	9800	900	3300	3200	0.95	10
涟源市	Lianyuan						
怀化市	Huaihua						
洪江市	Hongjiang						
吉首市	Jishou						

城市	Cities	液化石油气 Liquefied Petroleum Gas					
		供气总量 (吨) Total Gas Supply (ton)	#家庭用量 Consumption for Residential Use	用气户数 (户) Number of Household with Access to Gas (household)	#家庭用户 Consumption for Residential Use	用气人口 (万人) Population with Access to Gas (10 000 persons)	管道长度 (公里) Length of Pipelines (km)
长沙市	Changsha	70200	68806	350510	349770	137.80	75
浏阳市	Liuyang	2328	2328	29850	29850	8.00	
株洲市	Zhuzhou	12791	12791	84973	84973	30.36	5.9
醴陵市	Liling	7000	4840	35000	34000	8.00	
湘潭市	Xiangtan	13015	13015	108458	108458	35.40	16
湘乡市	Xiangxiang	2400	2300	36500	35000	10.50	
韶山市	Shaoshan	1480	1335	5115	4800	1.90	
衡阳市	Hengyang	254	126	20710	5690	6.34	127
耒阳市	Leiyang	1020	1020	8640	8640	3.00	
常宁市	Changning	528	432	9838	8638	3.40	
邵阳市	Shaoyang	5200	5200	95000	95000	37.38	
武冈市	Wugang	200	200	1576	1576	5.20	
岳阳市	Yueyang	57000	49000	210000	200000	47.23	80
汨罗市	Miluo	4010	3980	16020	15980	10.40	
临湘市	Linxiang	1300	1300	19300	19300	7.00	
常德市	Changde	22450	18550	110827	100277	36.60	139.5
津市市	Jinshi	1420	1197	17020	17000	6.29	14
张家界市	Zhangjiajie	3340	2190	18292	18249	6.39	
益阳市	Yiyang	7000	6700	52406	52344	18.30	
沅江市	Yuanjiang	700	700	35001	35000	5.30	
郴州市	Chenzhou	10925	6234	61780	5900	21.30	
资兴市	Zixing	1350	1200	10050	9830	3.20	
永州市	Yongzhou	4610	4300	43150	42250	17.19	
娄底市	Loudi	2900	2536	16160	15100	5.40	
冷水江市	Lengshuijiang	1560	1376	17400	16500	4.90	3
涟源市	Lianyuan	212	189	18500	18000	5.10	
怀化市	Huaihua	9048	8767	42500	40800	12.60	1.5
洪江市	Hongjiang	1260	1200	11500	11500	4.10	
吉首市	Jishou	2105	2100	27600	27300	9.86	

8-9 废水、废气、粉尘与工业固体废物排放及处理情况

Statistic on Discharge and Treatment of Waste Water,Waste Gas, Dust and Industrial Residue

指 标	Item	1995	1999	2000	2001
汇总企业数 (个)	**Number of Enterprises Counted (unit)**	**1704**	**3103**	**2891**	**2818**
工业废水	**Industrial Waste Water**				
治理设施数 (套)	Number of Facilities for Treatment (unit)	3849	2955	3034	2846
治理设施设备原价 (万元)	Original Value of Facilities (10 000 yuan)	126649	173603	248232	34993
工业废水排放总量 (万吨)	Total Volume of Industrial Waste Water Discharged (10 000 tons)	145251	126146	112563	107175
工业废水排放达标率 (%)	Percentage of Industrial Waste Water up to the Standards for Discharge (%)	56	58.3	66.09	74.52
工业废水处理量 (万吨)	Volume of Waste Water Treated (10 000 tons)	144893	141629	141641	-
工业废水处理回用量 (万吨)	Volume of Waste Water Recovered After Treatment (10 000 tons)	70462	74090	80701	-
工业废水处理排放达标量 (万吨)	Volume of Treated Waste Water up to the Discharge Standards (10 000 tons)	39719	43625	45647	-
工业废水处理率 (%)	Percentage of Waste Water Treated (%)	83.2	83.14	86.1	-
工业废气、粉尘	**Industrial Waste Gas and Industrial Dust**				
工业废气排放总量 (亿标立方米)	Total Volume of Industrial Waste Gas Discharge (100 million cu.m)	3466	3787	3569	3959
燃料燃烧过程中废气排放量 (亿标立方米)	Volume of Waste Gas in the Process of Fuel Burning (100 million cu.m)	1893	1870	1718	1848
#经过消烟除尘的 (亿标立方米)	#Volume of Gas with Soot&Dust Removed (100 million cu.m)	1720	1674	1529	-
生产工艺过程中废气排放量 (亿标立方米)	Volume of Waste Gas from the Process of Production (100 million cu.m)	1573	1917	1851	2111
#经过净化处理的(亿标立方米)	#Volume of Gas Purified (100 million cu.m)	1182	1648	1658	-
工业粉尘排放量 (万吨)	Volume of Industrial Dust Discharge (10 000 tons)	27.1	78.38	63.97	62.7
工业固体废物	**Industrial Solid Waste**				
工业固体废物产生量 (万吨)	Volume of Solid Wastes Produced (10 000 tons)	1853	1869	2355	2463
工业固体废物处置量 (万吨)	Volume of Solid Wastes Treated (10 000 tons)	474	187.57	137.32	221.47
工业固体废物处置率 (%)	Percentage of Solid Wastes Treated (%)	25.6	10.03	5.83	8.99
工业固体废物贮存量 (万吨)	Volume of Solid Wastes Accumulated (10 000 tons)	717	628.21	534.23	697.47
工业固体废物贮存率 (%)	Percentage of Solid Wastes Accumulated (%)	38.7	33.61	22.69	28.32
工业固体废物综合利用量 (万吨)	Volume of Solid Wastes Utilized (10 000 tons)	767	1049	1106	1531
工业固体废物综合利用率 (%)	Percentage of Solid Wastes Utilized (%)	41.4	56.11	46.96	59.58
工业固体废物排放量 (万吨)	Volume of Solid Wastes Discharged (10 000 tons)	46	58.58	138.82	135.81
历年工业固体废物累计贮存量 (万吨)	Volume of Solid Wastes Accumulated Past Years (10 000 tons)	25840	25628	23294	-
"三废"综合利用产品产值 (万元)	**Output Value of Products Made from Waste Gas, Waste Water and Solid Wastes (10 000 yuan)**	**98301**	**103071**	**116153**	**123434**
"三废"综合利用利润 (万元)	**Profits Obtained from Use of Waste Gas, Waste Water and Solid Wastes (10 000 yuan)**	**25214**	**20635**	**25722.4**	**-**

8-10 工业污染治理情况

Statistics on Treatment of Industrial Pollution

项 目	Item	1995	1999	2000	2001
污染治理资金来源总计(万元)	**All Sources of Funds (10 000 yuan)**	**37656**	**33710.9**	**54470.2**	**60090.6**
#基本建设资金	#Capital Construction	12625	546	3156.6	13053
更新改造资金	Innovation	14035	2696.2	2836	-
综合利用利润留成	Remain Profits Obtained From Utilized	812	2953	2561.3	-
环保补助资金	Subsidy of Environmental Protection	6623	1783.6	1541.7	621.8
贷款	Loans	5174	3607.9	6723.3	2216.3
其 他	Others	3561	22124.2	37651.3	44199.5
污染治理资金使用总计(万元)	**All Uses of Funds (10 000 yuan)**	**37656**	**33710.9**	**54470.2**	**60055.9**
#治理废水	#Treatment of Waste Water	14111	14599.7	22668.2	21306.9
治理废气	Treatment of Waste Gas	17480	13547.5	28223	35583
治理固体废物	Treatment of Solid Wastes	3885	1508.5	2978.8	2834.1
治理噪声	Treatment of Noise Pollution	1384	121.7	149.4	168.7
其 他	Treatment of Other Pollution	796	3933.5	450.8	163.2
污染治理概况	**Situation of Pollution Treatment**				
#本年施工项目总数 (个)	#Number of Projects Under Construction this Year (unit)	1664	581	995	468
本年竣工项目数 (个)	Number of Projects Completed this Year (unit)	1405	491	893	419
#治理废水	#Treatment of Waste Water	499	170	359	161
治理废气	Treatment of Waste Gas	545	232	438	205
治理固体废物	Treatment of Solid Wastes	153	56	62	24
治理噪声	Treatment of Noise Pollution	128	14	16	16
污染情况	**Situation of Pollution**				
#污染事故 (次)	#Pollution Accidents (times)	301	168	317	238
污染赔款总额 (万元)	Amount of Reparations (10 000 yuan)	420	462.51	442.58	473.7
污染罚款总额 (万元)	Amount of Fines (10 000 yuan)	35	44.41	30.82	29.6

注:本表统计范围为有污染的县及县以上工业企业。

Data in this table refer to the data of the enterprises at and above county levels.

8-11 13个地级市及长沙、株洲、湘潭三城市基本情况(2001年)

Basic Statistics on 13 Prefecture-Level Cities and Basic Indicators of Changsha,Zhu zhou and Xiangtan (2001)

指标	Item	13个城市合计 Total on 13 Cities 全市 Cities Total	13个城市合计 #市辖区 Districts	#长沙市 Changsha City 全市 Cities Total	#长沙市 #市辖区 Districts
人口、劳动力及土地面积	**Population,Labor and Land Area**				
年末总人口(万人)	Total Population at the Year-end (10 000 persons)	6312.99	1128.64	587.09	180.77
#非农业人口(万人)	#Non-agricultural Population (10 000 persons)	1381.44	621.13	191.89	148.93
年平均人口(万人)	Annual Average Population (10 000 persons)	6291.46	1111.05	585.14	178.09
暂住人口(一个月以上)(万人)	Temporary Population (10 000 persons)	83.11	48.42	26.01	23.85
年出生人口(人)	Number of Births (person)	582921	99293	53994	13735
年死亡人口(人)	Number of Deaths (person)	325107	47819	31587	5948
年末总户数(万户)	Total Households at the Year-end (10 000 households)	1802.11	351.2	170.38	54.17
年末单位从业人员数(万人)	Number of Employed Persons at the Year-end (10 000 persons)	390.81	179.92	62.47	47.33
#农、林、牧、渔业	#Farming ,Forestry,Animal Husbandry, Fishery	20.17	7.9	1.33	1.09
采掘业	Mining and Quarrying	15.1	1.77	0.74	0.07
制造业	Manufacturing	85.89	55.26	13.88	10.46
电力、煤气及水的生产和供应业	Production and Supply of Electric , Gas & Water	9.71	3.73	0.82	0.55
建筑业	Construction	24.38	16.56	6.38	6.16
地质勘查业、水利管理业	Geological Prospecting and Water Conservancy	4.11	1.36	0.56	0.27
交通运输仓储及邮电通信业	Transport,Storage,Post & Telecommunications	18.44	9.86	3.05	2.15
批发和零售贸易、餐饮业	Wholesales and Retail Trade, Catering Services	28.14	12.58	5.38	4.56
金融、保险业	Banking and Insurance	13.83	6.71	2.14	1.61
房地产业	Real Estate Trade	3.1	1.82	0.73	0.61
社会服务业	Social Services	14.62	9.99	3.9	3.55
卫生、体育和社会福利业	Health Care,Sports and Social Welfare	21.97	7.78	3.37	2.21
教育文化艺术和广播电影电视业	Education,Culture and Art,Radio, Film and Television	67.19	19.82	10.26	6.56
科学研究和综合技术服务业	Scientific Research and Polytechnical Service	4.58	3.67	2.34	2.26
国家机关、政党机关和社会团体	Government Agencies,Party Agencies and Social Organizations	55.42	17.35	6.01	3.77
其他行业	Others	4.24	2.55	1.58	1.45
城镇个体从业人员(万人)	Self-Employed Individual in Urban (10 000 person)	1633343	573282	138855	78710
年末城镇登记失业人员(人)	Unemployed Persons in Urban (person)	337933	163757	47100	47100
土地面积(平方公里)	Land Area (sq.km)	196548	16729	11819	556
#建成区面积(平方公里)	#Developed Areas (sq.km)		648		128
综合经济	**General Survey Economy**				
国内生产总值(万元)	Gross Domestic Product (10 000 yuan)				
现价	Current Price	39013625	15410957	7280774	4688731
第一产业增加值	Primary Industry	8910604	1042659	783636	88015
第二产业增加值	Secondary Industry	14367823	6826803	2970933	1845957
#工业增加值	#Industry	11594559	5392415	2179077	1310662
第三产业增加值	Tertiary Industry	15735198	7541495	3526205	2754759
2000年不变价格	Comparable Price 2000	38705126	15377034	7357302	4709619

指标	Item	13个城市合计 Total on 13 Cities		#长沙市 Changsha City	
		全市 Cities Total	#市辖区 Districts	全市 Cities Total	#市辖区 Districts
农业	**Agriculture**				
农林牧渔业总产值(当年价格)(万元)	Gross Output Value of Farming ,Forestry,Animal Husbandry and Fishery (10 000 yuan)	12776642		1239985	127688
年末实有耕地面积(千公顷)	Cultivated Area at the Year-end (1 000 hectare)	3104		243	
蔬菜产量(万吨)	Output of Vegetable (10 000 tons)	19360600		2878616	
水果产量(吨)	Output of Fruit (ton)	4471169		155922	
猪牛羊肉产量(吨)	Output of Pork ,Beef and Mutton (ton)	5058781		475220	
奶类产量(吨)	Output of Milk (ton)	17882		5683	
水产品产量(吨)	Output of Aquatic Product (ton)	1392377		89965	
工业	**Industry**				
国有及销售收入500万元以上的非 国有)	State-owned and Non State-owned with the Sales Revenue of over 5 Million Yuan				
工业企业数(个)	Number of Industry Enterprises (unit)	4713	1731	744	337
内资企业(个)	Domestic Funded Enterprises (unit)	4479	1616	668	303
港、澳、台商投资企业(个)	Enterprises with Investment from Hong Kong、Macao and Taiwan (unit)	143	62	42	18
外商投资企业(个)	Enterprises with Foreign Investment (unit)	91	53	34	16
工业总产值(万元)	Gross Output Value (10 000 yuan)	17697279	11267281	3700281	2417588
#内资企业	Domestic Funded Enterprises	16321544	10449662	2891919	1987671
港、澳、台商投资企业	Enterprises with Investment from Hong Kong、Macao and Taiwan	572656	254325	308830	86179
外商投资企业	Enterprises with Foreign Investment	803079	563294	499532	343738
从业人员平均人数(万人)	Average Staff and Workers (10 000 persons)	150.49	75.91	23.02	11.78
流动资产年平均余额 (万元)	Annual Average Balance of Circulating Funds (10 000 yuan)	10876504	7793998	2647381	1963285
固定资产净值年平均余额(万元)	Annual Average Balance of Net Value of Fixed Assets (10 000 yuan)	12168109	8383620	2076331	1549756
产品销售收入(万元)	Sales Revenue (10 000 yuan)	16728789	10968722	3538981	2357796
销售税金及附加(万元)	Sales Tax and Extra Charges (10 000 yuan)	859122	770524	356460	339572
本年应交增值税(万元)	Value Added Tax Payable (10 000 yuan)	816134	555917	237311	174156
利润总额(万元)	Total Profits (10 000 yuan)	476368	384592	240180	167179
年销售收入500万元以下的非国有	Non State-owned with the Sales Revenue Under 5 000 Thousand Yuan				
工业企业数(个)	Number of Industrial Enterprise (unit)	371654	56992		
工业总产值(万元)	Gross Output Value (10 000 yuan)	18281576	2844458	2919737	
交通运输、邮电通信电力	**Transportation,Post, Telecommunication and Electric Power**				
铁路客运量(万人)	Railway Passenger Traffic (10 000 persons)	5415.11		1070	
铁路货运量(万吨)	Railway Freight Traffic (10 000 tons)	5426		188	
民用汽车拥有量(辆)	Civil Motor Vehicles Owned (unit)	500006		106614	
#私人汽车拥有量(辆)	#Private Vehicles (unit)	289532		69285	
公路客运量(万人)	Highway Passenger Traffic (10 000 persons)	82296.13		7242	
公路货运量(万吨)	Highway Freight Traffic (10 000 tons)	37210		6668	
水运客运量(万人)	Waterway Passengers Traffic (10 000 persons)	1053.87		44	
水运货运量(万吨)	Waterway Freight Traffic (10 000 tons)	3567		691	

指标	Item	13个城市合计 Total on 13 Cities 全市 Cities Total	13个城市合计 #市辖区 Districts	#长沙市 Changsha City 全市 Cities Total	#长沙市 #市辖区 Districts
民用航空货邮运量(吨)	Freight Traffic by Civil Aviation (ton)	32921		29226	
民用航空客运量(人)	Passengers Traffic by Civil Aviation (person)	2909557		2217088	
年末邮电局(所)数(处)	Number of Postal Offices at the Yearend (unit)	10847	1689	782	184
邮电业务总量(不变价)(亿元)	Total Business Revenue of Postal and Telecommunications Service (100 million yuan)	1596758	781716	499322	350917
本地电话用户(万户)	Number of Native Telephone (10 000 households)	711.12	263.42	126.44	69.67
年末移动电话用户(万户)	Number of Mobile Telephone (10 000 households)	3515856	1904463	981663	657893
全年用电量(万千瓦时)	Consumption Volume of Energy (10 000 kwh)	3417726	1664414	529409	343137
#工业用电	# Used in Industry	2194396	1113981	281711	167959
生活用电	Used in Living	684743	369886	143681	119738
批发零售贸易、餐饮业	**Wholesales,Retail Trade,Catering Services**				
商品销售总额(万元)	Total Sales Value (10 000 yuan)	15919557	9311148	3989545	3698316
社会消费品零售总额(万元)	Total Retail Sales of Consumer Goods (10 000 yuan)	14829033	7348439	3449742	2699311
对外经济活动、国际旅游	**Foreign Trade, International Tourist**				
外国和港澳台在华直接投资	Direct Investment form Foreign, Hong Kong, Macao and Taiwan				
当年新签项目(合同)(个)	Number of Newly-signed Items(Contracts) (item)	332	152	75	29
当年合同利用外资金额(万美元)	Contract Value (10 000 USD)	94337	41744	24980	10883
当年实际使用外资金额(万美元)	Used Value (10 000 USD)	80197	39052	26527	13674
已投产(开业)企业(个)	Number of Enterprises Put into Production (unit)	1637	559	666	100
从业人员人数(人)	Number of Employed Persons (person)	147590	45331	55800	5464
国际旅游者人数(人)	Number of International Tourists (person)	678370		235246	
#外国人	#Foreigner	276586		126531	
港澳台同胞	From Hong Kong,Macao and Taiwan	398257		108715	
国际旅游收入(万美元)	Revenue of International Tourist (10 000 USD)	24539		13500	
固定资产投资	**Investment In Fixed Assets**				
固定资产投资完成额(万元)	Completed Investment in Fixed Assets (10 000 yuan)	9200203	4654083	2798029	1890677
#住宅建设	Residential Buildings	2370692	835995	820739	396061
房地产开发投资完成额(万元)	Investment Completed in Real Estate Development (10 000 yuan)	1073809	827786	549376	403759
#住宅	Residential Buildings	598604	443309	294015	205794
全年新增固定资产(万元)	Newly-added Fixed Assets (10 000 yuan)	5321135	2773459	1107918	828550
本年施工住宅建筑面积(万平方米)	Space of Residential Buildings Started in this Year (10 000 sq.m)	4179.85	1727.93	639.72	565.34
本年竣工住宅建筑面积(万平方米)	Space of Residential Buildings Completed in this Year (10 000 sq.m)	2928.91	952.81	221.75	196.94
商品房屋销售面积(万平方米)	Floor Space of Selling House (10 000 sq.m)	440.09	317	159.4	113.85
#销售给个人	Sell to the Private	374.02	273.17	124.57	91.7
商品房屋销售额(万元)	Total Value of Selling House (10 000 yuan)	549356	424577	290098	222811
#销售给个人	Sell to the Private	444315	347027	214435	167129

指标	Item	13个城市合计 Total on 13 Cities 全市 Cities Total	#市辖区 Districts	#长沙市 Changsha City 全市 Cities Total	#市辖区 Districts
教育、科技、文化、卫生	**Education,Science and Technology, Culture,Health Care**				
学校数(所)	Number of Schools (unit)				
高等学校	Institutions of Higher Education	60	54	29	23
中等专业学校	Secondary Specialized Schools	135	124	48	44
普通中学	Regular Secondary Schools	4514	787	368	91
小学	Primary Schools	27224	3204	1830	246
专任教师数(人)	Number of Full-time Teachers (person)				
高等学校	Institutions of Higher Education	23218	22828	12130	11740
中等专业学校	Secondary Specialized Schools	9378	8726	2460	2283
普通中学	Regular Secondary Schools	228824	48057	23381	6255
小学	Primary Schools	276953	50759	20681	6911
在校学生数	Number of Students Enrollment				
高等学校(人)	Institutions of Higher Education (person)	323460	320514	172567	169621
中等专业学校(人)	Secondary Specialized Schools (person)	237625	211449	77270	70885
普通中学(万人)	Regular Secondary Schools (10 000 persons)	411.57	71.69	41.3	9.95
小学(万人)	Primary Schools (10 000 persons)	569.17	92.61	39.95	11.46
成人高等教育学校在校学生数(人)	Students Enrollment in Adult Education Schools (person)	144758	135183	27658	25862
各类专业技术人员数(万人)	Number of Various Specialized Technical Personnel (10 000 persons)	172.77	71.6	24.89	19.02
#中级技术职称以上人数(万人)	Number of Persons with above Middle Rank Titles for Technical Personnel (10 000 persons)	49.1	24.82	10.2	8.34
从事科技活动人员数(人)	Number of Persons Engaged in Scientific and Technological Activities (person)	129325	83413	34767	32907
剧场、影剧院数(个)	Number of Music Halls and Theaters (unit)	140	55	10	8
公共图书馆图书藏量(千册)	Books Storage in Public Libraries (1 000 copies)	14522	7951	4815	4409
医院、卫生院数(个)	Number of Hospitals (unit)	4089	1108	265	146
医院、卫生院床位数(张)	Number of Beds in Hospitals (sheet)	137112	63047	18906	14789
医生数(人)	Number of Doctors (person)	92380	38423	12310	9267
财政、金融、保险	**Finance and Insurance**				
中央财政预算内收入(万元)	Budgetary Revenue of Central (10 000 yuan)	885032	601489	170221	108219
地方财政预算内收入(万元)	Budgetary Revenue of Local (10 000 yuan)	1744494	838130	460183	346070
地方财政预算内支出(万元)	Budgetary Expenditure of Local (10 000 yuan)	2842911	1306292	553235	385411
#科学事业费支出	Operating Expenses for Science	15038	7888	2303	2086
教育事业费支出	Operating Expenses for Education	515484	134179	58993	28024
年末金融机构存款余额(万元)	All Deposits Balance in Financial Institutions at the Year-end (10 000 yuan)	32031052	18068199	9868500	7967559
#城乡居民储蓄年末余额(万元)	Urban and Rural Savings Deposits Balance at the Year-end (10 000 yuan)	21462496	10617205	4440700	3576237
年末金融机构各项贷款余额(万元)	All Loans Balance in Financial Institutions at the Year-end (10 000 yuan)	24491665	12598149	7782800	6304290
承保额(万元)	Insurance Amount (10 000 yuan)	55804703	23710539	13140069	10180916
保费(万元)	Premiums (10 000 yuan)	530117	272106	123507	96203

指标	Item	13个城市合计 Total on 13 Cities		#长沙市 Changsha City	
		全 市 Cities Total	#市辖区 Districts	全 市 Cities Total	#市辖区 Districts
人民生活	**The People's Living**				
住宅建筑面积 (万平方米)	Total Space of Residential Buildings (10 000 sq.m)		10478.8		3097
住宅使用面积 (万平方米)	Living Space of Residential Buildings (10 000 sq.m)		7922.36		2323
居住人口 (万人)	Resident Population (10 000 persons)		491.24		148.93
在岗职工平均人数 (万人)	Average Persons on the Job (10 000 persons)	389.99	170.76	59.83	44.93
在岗职工工资总额 (万元)	Total Wages of Workers on the Job (10 000 yuan)	3679055	2029837	733898	584165
城镇居民人均可支配收入 (元)	Per Capita Disposable Income in Urban Presidents (yuan)		6781		8704
城镇居民人均消费支出 (元)	Per Capita Living Expenditures for Consumption in Urban Presidents (yuan)		5546		7745
#食品	# Food		1944		2492
衣着用品	Clothing		551		715
家庭设备用品及服务	Household Facilities,Articles and Services		460		672
医疗保健	Medicine and Medical Services		329		394
交通和通信	Transportation and Telecommunication		475		671
娱乐、教育、文化服务	Recreation,Education and Cultural Service		827		1246
居住	Residence		662		1104
杂项商品和服务	Miscellaneous Commodities and Services				
每百户拥有空调机 (台)	Air Conditioner per 100 Households (unit)		38.15		79
每百户拥有电冰箱 (台)	Refrigerator per 100 Households (unit)		86.18		96
每百户拥有洗衣机 (台)	Washing Machine per 100 Households (unit)				
每百户拥有家用电脑 (台)	Personnel Computer Per 100 Households (unit)		15.43		27
居民消费价格指数 (以上年为100)	General Consumer Price Index (preceding year =100)		99.1		98.4
商品零售价格指数 (以上年为100)	General Retail Price Index (preceding year =100)				
职工保险福利费用 (万元)	Social Insurance and Welfare Funds for Staff and Workers (10 000 yuan)	226152	136414		
年末离休、退休、退职人员数 (万人)	Number of Retired and Resigned Persons at the Year-end (10 000 persons)	150.78	79.38	27.12	24.15
离退休、退职人员保险福利费用额 (万元)	Social Insurance and Welfare Funds for Retired and Resigned Persons (10 000 yuan)	1052149	593035	234229	218767
社会福利院数 (个)	Number of Social Welfare Homes (unit)	1563	215	129	15
社会福利院床位数 (张)	Number of Beds in Social Welfare Homes (sheet)	31190	8562	3913	1804
社会治安	**Public Security**				
交通事故件数 (件)	Number of Traffic Accidents (case)	37404	19487	12750	10294
刑事案件发案数 (件)	Number of Criminal Cases (case)	131558	63797	37852	26470
犯罪人数 (人)	Number of Criminals (person)	58577	15402	9343	

8-11 续表5 continued

指标	Item	#株洲市 Zhuzhou City 全市 Cities Total	#市辖区 Districts	#湘潭市 Xiangtan City 全市 Cities Total	#市辖区 Districts
人口、劳动力及土地面积	**Population,Labor and Land Area**				
年末总人口 (万人)	Total Population at the Year-end (10 000 persons)	372.1	76.02	280.47	68.15
#非农业人口 (万人)	#Non-agricultural Population (10 000 persons)	96.14	56.77	77.64	55.06
年平均人口(万人)	Annual Average Population (10 000 persons)	366.44	75.43	280.04	67.64
暂住人口(一个月以上) (万人)	Temporary Population (10 000 persons)	4.67	4.06	0.95	0.78
年出生人口 (人)	Number of Births (person)	34861	6703	25419	6079
年死亡人口 (人)	Number of Deaths (person)	18101	1794	16300	2581
年末总户数 (万户)	Total Households at the Year-end (10 000 households)	101.35	22.83	82.85	20.83
年末单位从业人员数 (万人)	Number of Employed Persons at the Year-end (10 000 persons)	31.53	19.71	25.13	16.2
#农、林、牧、渔业	#Farming ,Forestry,Animal Husbandry, Fishery	0.68	0.36	0.11	0.04
采掘业	Mining and Quarrying	0.45	0.12	0.69	0.27
制造业	Manufacturing	12.7	10.22	10.13	8.23
电力、煤气及水的生产和供应业	Production and Supply of Electric , Gas & Water	0.84	0.52	0.42	0.32
建筑业	Construction	1.9	1.61	2.23	1.38
地质勘查业、水利管理业	Geological Prospecting and Water Conservancy	0.2	0.1	0.17	0.12
交通运输仓储及邮电通信业	Transport,Storage,Post & Telecommunications	1.41	0.78	0.85	0.49
批发和零售贸易、餐饮业	Wholesales and Retail Trade, Catering Services	1.96	0.98	1.33	0.65
金融、保险业	Banking and Insurance	1.27	0.77	0.9	0.63
房地产业	Real Estate Trade	0.15	0.1	0.22	0.19
社会服务业	Social Services	1.26	1.03	0.87	0.64
卫生、体育和社会福利业	Health Care,Sports and Social Welfare	1.27	0.48	1.1	0.52
教育文化艺术和广播电影电视业	Education,Culture and Art,Radio, Film and Television	3.66	0.98	3.33	1.34
科学研究和综合技术服务业	Scientific Research and Polytechnical Service	0.43	0.39	0.12	0.09
国家机关、政党机关和社会团体	Government Agencies,Party Agencies and Social Organizations	3.25	1.49	2.45	1.1
其他行业	Others	0.1	0.04	0.2	0.18
城镇个体从业人员 (万人)	Self-Employed Individual in Urban (10 000 person)	95074	45498	58788	43588
年末城镇登记失业人员 (人)	Unemployed Persons in Urban (person)	21280	19055	9374	8907
土地面积 (平方公里)	Land Area (sq.km)	11272	542	5015	278
#建成区面积 (平方公里)	#Developed Areas (sq.km)		66		53
综合经济	**General Survey Economy**				
国内生产总值 (万元)	Gross Domestic Product (10 000 yuan)				
现价	Current Price	3226716	1616171	2382813	1297993
第一产业增加值	Primary Industry	515986	42258	341186	26042
第二产业增加值	Secondary Industry	1530467	924532	1034156	651687
#工业增加值	#Industry	1315340	807394	862177	552066
第三产业增加值	Tertiary Industry	1180263	649381	1007471	620264
2000年不变价格	Comparable Price 2000	3225044	1607776	2365600	1288653

指标	Item	#株洲市 Zhuzhou City 全市 Cities Total	#市辖区 Districts	#湘潭市 Xiangtan City 全市 Cities Total	#市辖区 Districts
农业	**Agriculture**				
农林牧渔业总产值(当年价格)(万元)	Gross Output Value of Farming ,Forestry,Animal Husbandry and Fishery (10 000 yuan)	782114	66789	556339	46517
年末实有耕地面积(千公顷)	Cultivated Area at the Year-end (1 000 hectare)	160		121	
蔬菜产量(万吨)	Output of Vegetable (10 000 tons)	1166672		880332	
水果产量(吨)	Output of Fruit (ton)	195065		74316	
猪牛羊肉产量(吨)	Output of Pork ,Beef and Mutton (ton)	258861		278620	
奶类产量(吨)	Output of Milk (ton)	455		1860	
水产品产量(吨)	Output of Aquatic Product (ton)	52822		57985	
工业	**Industry**				
国有及销售收入500万元以上的非国有)	State-owned and Non State-owned with the Sales Revenue of over 5 Million Yuan				
工业企业数(个)	Number of Industry Enterprises (unit)	455	210	306	170
内资企业(个)	Domestic Funded Enterprises (unit)	423	195	290	158
港、澳、台商投资企业(个)	Enterprises with Investment from Hong Kong、Macao and Taiwan (unit)	22	11	8	5
外商投资企业(个)	Enterprises with Foreign Investment (unit)	10	4	8	7
工业总产值(亿元)	Gross Output Value (100 million yuan)	2224989	1881148	1315160	999800
#内资企业	Domestic Funded Enterprises	2136840	1833377	1279088	966439
港、澳、台商投资企业	Enterprises with Investment from Hong Kong、Macao and Taiwan	57926	39443	10355	7814
外商投资企业	Enterprises with Foreign Investment	30223	8328	25717	25547
从业人员平均人数(万人)	Average Staff and Workers (10 000 persons)	19.05	12.44	12.79	9.44
流动资产年平均余额(万元)	Annual Average Balance of Circulating Funds (10 000 yuan)	1614352	1431502	964137	770024
固定资产净值年平均余额(万元)	Annual Average Balance of Net Value of Fixed Assets (10 000 yuan)	1273501	1134532	1362753	1164617
产品销售收入(万元)	Sales Revenue (10 000 yuan)	2103122	1796779	1301865	997552
销售税金及附加(万元)	Sales Tax and Extra Charges (10 000 yuan)	23256	18380	10315	6988
本年应交增值税(万元)	Value Added Tax Payable (10 000 yuan)	105004	87757	79456	66193
利润总额(万元)	Total Profits (10 000 yuan)	59004	49639	31596	37566
年销售收入500万元以下的非国有	Non State-owned with the Sales Revenue Under 5 000 Thousand Yuan				
工业企业数(个)	Number of Industrial Enterprise (unit)	36258	5056	11030	2474
工业总产值(万元)	Gross Output Value (10 000 yuan)	1912389	290468	1418100	440037
交通运输、邮电通信电力	**Transportation,Post, Telecommunication and Electric Power**				
铁路客运量(万人)	Railway Passenger Traffic (10 000 persons)	666.42		141.43	
铁路货运量(万吨)	Railway Freight Traffic (10 000 tons)	508		534	
民用汽车拥有量(辆)	Civil Motor Vehicles Owned (unit)	39473		25625	
#私人汽车拥有量(辆)	#Private Vehicles (unit)	17868		15722	
公路客运量(万人)	Highway Passenger Traffic (10 000 persons)	6129		2547	
公路货运量(万吨)	Highway Freight Traffic (10 000 tons)	2892		1961	
水运客运量(万人)	Waterway Passengers Traffic (10 000 persons)	19		2.73	
水运货运量(万吨)	Waterway Freight Traffic (10 000 tons)	331		315	

指标	Item	#株洲市 Zhuzhou City 全市 Cities Total	#株洲市 Zhuzhou City #市辖区 Districts	#湘潭市 Xiangtan City 全市 Cities Total	#湘潭市 Xiangtan City #市辖区 Districts
民用航空货邮运量(吨)	Freight Traffic by Civil Aviation (ton)				
民用航空客运量(人)	Passengers Traffic by Civil Aviation (person)				
年末邮电局(所)数(处)	Number of Postal Offices at the Yearend (unit)	1064	602	476	189
邮电业务总量(不变价)(万元)	Total Business Revenue of Postal and Telecommunications Service (10 000 yuan)	101504	64965	193179	14729
本地电话用户(万户)	Number of Native Telephone (10 000 households)	65.9	31.97	26.16	19.79
年末移动电话用户(万户)	Number of Mobile Telephone (10 000 households)	280606	187334	223007	134222
全年用电量(万千瓦时)	Consumption Volume of Energy (10 000 kwh)	392390	312700	338855	164650
#工业用电	# Used in Industry	300250	255380	251728	133199
生活用电	Used in Living	44380	24290	37066	19073
批发零售贸易、餐饮业	**Wholesales,Retail Trade,Catering Services**				
商品销售总额(万元)	Total Sales Value (10 000 yuan)	1851758	1111055	227186	154286
社会消费品零售总额(万元)	Total Retail Sales of Consumer Goods (10 000 yuan)	1235633	676698	770180	434679
对外经济活动、国际旅游	**Foreign Trade, International Tourist**				
外国和港澳台在华直接投资	Direct Investment form Foreign, Hong Kong, Macao and Taiwan				
当年新签项目(合同)(个)	Number of Newly-signed Items(Contracts) (item)	25	22	15	13
当年合同利用外资金额(万美元)	Contract Value (10 000 USD)	8794	4404	4062	3430
当年实际使用外资金额(万美元)	Used Value (10 000 USD)	6224	2742	4052	2798
已投产(开业)企业(个)	Number of Enterprises Put into Production (unit)	85	57	80	75
从业人员人数(人)	Number of Employed Persons (person)	24000	15000	4487	1184
国际旅游者人数(人)	Number of International Tourists (person)	2693		9996	
#外国人	#Foreigner	1556		3295	
港澳台同胞	From Hong Kong,Macao and Taiwan	1137		6701	
国际旅游收入(万美元)	Revenue of International Tourist (10 000 USD)	87		356	
固定资产投资	**Investment In Fixed Assets**				
固定资产投资完成额(万元)	Completed Investment in Fixed Assets (10 000 yuan)	434052	351240	370206	305596
#住宅建设	Residential Buildings	32517	18678	113404	51305
房地产开发投资完成额(万元)	Investment Completed in Real Estate Development (10 000 yuan)	76604	43819	74646	66802
#住宅	Residential Buildings	53519	30581	40110	36302
全年新增固定资产(万元)	Newly-added Fixed Assets (10 000 yuan)	404297	296318	376868	316145
本年施工住宅建筑面积(万平方米)	Space of Residential Buildings Started in this Year (10 000 sq.m)	197.87	148.61	195.45	129.2
本年竣工住宅建筑面积(万平方米)	Space of Residential Buildings Completed in this Year (10 000 sq.m)	124.68	88.1	91.49	66.48
商品房屋销售面积(万平方米)	Floor Space of Selling House (10 000 sq.m)	33.82	16.73	44.18	40.32
#销售给个人	Sell to the Private	33.5	16.66	42.14	38.77
商品房屋销售额(万元)	Total Value of Selling House (10 000 yuan)	31385	17248	43173	40482
#销售给个人	Sell to the Private	31135	17136	39704	37433

指标	Item	#株洲市 Zhuzhou City 全 市 Cities Total	#市辖区 Districts	#湘潭市 Xiangtan City 全 市 Cities Total	#市辖区 Districts
教育、科技、文化、卫生	**Education,Science and Technology, Culture,Health Care**				
学校数 (所)	Number of Schools (unit)				
高等学校	Institutions of Higher Education	5	5	5	5
中等专业学校	Secondary Specialized Schools	10	10	11	10
普通中学	Regular Secondary Schools	233	48	239	46
小学	Primary Schools	1386	93	961	110
专任教师数 (人)	Number of Full-time Teachers (person)				
高等学校	Institutions of Higher Education	1870	1870	2802	2802
中等专业学校	Secondary Specialized Schools	836	836	759	759
普通中学	Regular Secondary Schools	13796	2857	11354	2163
小学	Primary Schools	13754	2587	11152	2668
在校学生数	Number of Students Enrollment				
高等学校 (人)	Institutions of Higher Education (person)	23025	23025	41072	41072
中等专业学校 (人)	Secondary Specialized Schools (person)	23687	23687	13728	13728
普通中学 (万人)	Regular Secondary Schools (10 000 persons)	26.27	5.2	20.39	4.02
小学 (万人)	Primary Schools (10 000 persons)	31.3	5.76	23.47	4.67
成人高等教育学校在校学生数 (人)	Students Enrollment in Adult Education Schools (person)	24482	24482	14683	14683
各类专业技术人员数 (万人)	Number of Various Specialized Technical Personnel (10 000 persons)	16.68	9.01	6.78	4.54
#中级技术职称以上人数 (万人)	Number of Persons with above Middle Rank Titles for Technical Personnel (10 000 persons)	5.09	3.18	2.78	1.88
从事科技活动人员数 (人)	Number of Persons Engaged in Scientific and Technological Activities (person)	18060	17175	12036	9889
剧场、影剧院数 (个)	Number of Music Halls and Theaters (unit)	6	3	4	3
公共图书馆图书藏量 (千册)	Books Storage in Public Libraries (1 000 copies)	906	413	797	477
医院、卫生院数 (个)	Number of Hospitals (unit)	187	80	117	44
医院、卫生院床位数 (张)	Number of Beds in Hospitals (sheet)	9844	6787	7307	4463
医生数 (人)	Number of Doctors (person)	5592	3448	4994	2592
财政、金融、保险	**Finance and Insurance**				
中央财政预算内收入 (万元)	Budgetary Revenue of Central (10 000 yuan)	75428	52388	34022	23869
地方财政预算内收入 (万元)	Budgetary Revenue of Local (10 000 yuan)	151572	98761	79698	50187
地方财政预算内支出 (万元)	Budgetary Expenditure of Local (10 000 yuan)	219888	135171	141932	88609
#科学事业费支出	Operating Expenses for Science	647	596	472	385
教育事业费支出	Operating Expenses for Education	31242	10553	18848	6374
年末金融机构存款余额 (万元)	All Deposits Balance in Financial Institutions at the Year-end (10 000 yuan)	2419400	1782957	1827311	1315077
#城乡居民储蓄年末余额 (万元)	Urban and Rural Savings Deposits Balance at the Year-end (10 000 yuan)	1725900	1199174	1382120	951923
年末金融机构各项贷款余额 (万元)	All Loans Balance in Financial Institutions at the Year-end (10 000 yuan)	1639700	1237514	1217374	892813
承保额 (万元)	Insurance Amount (10 000 yuan)	2103755	1759665	4845134	3301959
保费 (万元)	Premiums (10000 yuan)	48337	32520	36327	24888

8-11 续表 9 continued

指标	Item	#株洲市 Zhuzhou City 全市 Cities Total	#株洲市 Zhuzhou City #市辖区 Districts	#湘潭市 Xiangtan City 全市 Cities Total	#湘潭市 Xiangtan City #市辖区 Districts
人民生活	**The People's Living**				
住宅建筑面积 (万平方米)	Total Space of Residential Buildings (10 000 sq.m)		1378.2		
住宅使用面积 (万平方米)	Living Space of Residential Buildings (10 000 sq.m)		1033.65		
居住人口 (万人)	Resident Population (10 000 persons)		57.29		
在岗职工平均人数 (万人)	Average Persons on the Job (10 000 persons)	31.13	19.5	24.97	16.28
在岗职工工资总额 (万元)	Total Wages of Workers on the Job (10 000 yuan)	327981	228878	243759	166144
城镇居民人均可支配收入 (元)	Per Capita Disposable Income in Urban Presidents (yuan)		7886		6662
城镇居民人均消费支出 (元)	Per Capita Living Expenditures for Consumption in Urban Presidents (yuan)		6116		5333
#食品	# Food		2229		1922
衣着用品	Clothing		529		456
家庭设备用品及服务	Household Facilities,Articles and Services		424		379
医疗保健	Medicine and Medical Services		341		378
交通和通信	Transportation and Telecommunication		694		593
娱乐、教育、文化服务	Recreation,Education and Cultural Service		891		724
居住	Residence		651		601
杂项商品和服务	Miscellaneous Commodities and Services				
每百户拥有空调机 (台)	Air Conditioner per 100 Households (unit)		48		51
每百户拥有电冰箱 (台)	Refrigerator per 100 Households (unit)		94		94
每百户拥有洗衣机 (台)	Washing Machine per 100 Households (unit)				
每百户拥有家用电脑 (台)	Personnel Computer Per 100 Households (unit)		20		17
居民消费价格指数 (以上年为100)	General Consumer Price Index (preceding year =100)		99.3		100.4
商品零售价格指数 (以上年为100)	General Retail Price Index (preceding year =100)				
职工保险福利费用 (万元)	Social Insurance and Welfare Funds for Staff and Workers (10 000 yuan)			36964	30920
年末离休、退休、退职人员数 (万人)	Number of Retired and Resigned Persons at the Year-end (10 000 persons)	14.08	9.44	12.12	9.15
离退休、退职人员保险福利费用额 (万元)	Social Insurance and Welfare Funds for Retired and Resigned Persons (10 000 yuan)	104053	70339	78250	60540
社会福利院数 (个)	Number of Social Welfare Homes (unit)	85	19	147	6
社会福利院床位数 (张)	Number of Beds in Social Welfare Homes (sheet)	1792	725	2496	613
社会治安	**Public Security**				
交通事故件数 (件)	Number of Traffic Accidents (case)	3335	2349	3602	1605
刑事案件发案数 (件)	Number of Criminal Cases (case)	18656	9848	9409	6015
犯罪人数 (人)	Number of Criminals (person)	15253	5950	2040	810

九、农业

AGRICULTURE

资料整理人员：王晓华　刘昕毅　龙立珍
张吉世　唐建新　熊　军

9-1 农村基层组织与劳动力

Grassroots Units and Labor Force of Rural Areas

指 标	Item	1995	1999	2000	2001
农村基层组织	**Grassroots Units of Rural Areas**				
#乡(镇)个数 (个)	Number of Township (Town Governments) (unit)	2321	2353	2353	2358
#乡个数	Number of Township	1406	1330	1314	1286
#民族乡	Number of National Township	101	104	104	103
镇个数	Number of Town Governments	899	1023	1039	1072
村(居)民委员会个数 (万个)	Number of Villagers(Residential) Committees (10 000 units)	4.97	4.99	5.01	5.01
#村民委员会 (万个)	Number of Villagers Committees (10 000 units)	4.77	4.75	4.75	4.74
#村民小组 (万个)	Number of Villagers Groups (10 000 units)	48.33	47.98	47.51	46.35
乡村户数、人口、劳动力	**Rural Households、Population、Laborers**				
#乡村户数 (万户)	Number of Rural Households (10 000 households)	1428.5	1440.49	1444	1455.39
#农业户	Agricultural Households	1371.63	1364.26	1362.38	1367.51
非农业户	Non- Agricultural Households	56.87	76.23	81.62	87.88
乡村人口 (万人)	Rural Population (10 000 persons)	5322.32	5355.14	5386.21	5413.75
#农业人口	Agricultural Population	5086.24	5095.91	5106.54	5109.08
乡村从业人员数 (万人)	Number of Rural Laborers (10 000 persons)	2756.07	2810.08	2850.93	2877.58
按性别分:	By sex:				
#男劳力	Male	1502.98	1524.91	1545.29	1560.42
女劳力	Female	1253.09	1285.17	1305.64	1317.16
按国民经济行业分:	By Nationality Economy Sector:				
#农林牧渔业劳动力	Farming ,Forestry,Animal Husbandry and Fishery Laborers	2114.71	2074.13	2065.92	2058.67
工业劳动力	Industry Laborers	169.78	180.9	191.6	194.96
建筑业劳动力	Construction Laborers	98.89	117.44	126.34	130.74
交通运输、仓储、邮电通信业劳动力	Transportation,Storage,Post and Telecommunications Laborers	38.48	47.06	51.65	54.57
批发零售贸易业餐饮业劳动力	Wholesale,Retail and Catering Trades Laborers	59.55	77.26	85.11	91.6
其他非农行业劳动力	Other Non-Agricultural Trades Laborers	271.04	313.29	330.31	347.04
农村社会基础设施	**Country Society Basic Establishment**				
#自来水受益村数 (万个)	Villages Tap Water Benefited (10 000 units)	0.76	1.09	1.17	1.24
通汽车村数 (万个)	Villages Car Available (10 000 units)	4.14	4.33	4.41	4.44
通电话村数 (万个)	Villages Telephone Available (10 000 units)	2.5	3.33	4.05	4.26

注:乡村劳动力未包括国有农场劳动力。

Rural laborers not included laborers in State-owned farm.

9-2 农业基本情况

Basic Indicators of Agriculture

年 份 Year	农林牧渔业劳动力（万人） Number of Laborers (10 000 persons)	年末实有耕地面积（万公顷） Cultivated Areas (yearend) (10 000 hectares)	当年减少耕地面积（万公顷） Decrease in Cultivated Area by Cause (10 000 hectares)	农作物播种面积（万公顷） Total Sown Areas (10 000 hectares)	#粮食作物 Grain Corps	#经济作物 Economical Crops	造林面积（万公顷） Afforestation Areas (10 000 hectares)
1980	1764.83	342.48		790.95	545.13	58.45	24.52
1985	1908.43	334.17		747.71	516.14	72.94	34.40
1990	2133.07	331.23	1.16	795.18	536.56	98.99	37.59
1991	2174.96	331.02	0.92	804.02	536.52	110.42	37.17
1992	2169.74	329.59	1.93	796.08	524.36	118.17	37.75
1993	2101.88	327.31	2.81	765.39	468.84	108.94	27.83
1994	2041.28	325.84	2.40	773.05	507.74	116.58	13.44
1995	2114.71	324.97	1.83	784.04	511.56	125.01	10.95
1996	2089.33	323.94	1.86	792.74	513.39	131.00	5.29
1997	2074.12	323.01	1.66	800.90	515.53	136.64	4.29
1998	2074.51	321.87	1.64	793.63	507.48	131.03	2.86
1999	2074.13	321.32	1.30	802.77	513.52	127.81	2.74
2000	2065.92	392.16	1.18	800.21	502.99	129.30	5.15
2001	2058.67	391.26	1.73	793.17	480.28	130.54	7.56

注：从2000年起，耕地面积为国土资源厅统计数据(后同)。

The data of cultivated land from Hunan Province Territory Resource Bureau since 2000.The same as in the following table.

9-3 农业生产条件

Condition of Agricultural Production

年份 Year	农业机械总动力（万千瓦） Total Power of Agricultural Machinery (10 000 kw)	有效灌溉面积（千公顷） Effective Irrigated Area (1000 hectares)	化肥施用量（万吨） Consumption of Chemical Fertilizers (10 000 tons)	农村用电量（万度） Electricity Consumed in Rural Areas (10 000 kwh)	每公顷面积产量（公斤） Yield per hectare (kg) 粮食 Grain Crops	棉花 Cotton	油料 Oil-bearing Crops
1980	588.99	2742.73	361.04	96674	3900	540	570
1985	892.02	2771.18	369.64	150648	4875	990	1005
1990	1209.17	2676.22	126.09	233704	5025	1020	990
1991	1270.52	2612.7	138.66	257705	5100	1110	1035
1992	1284.37	2681.09	146.18	277089	5115	1215	1065
1993	1374.35	2676.11	148.15	304442	5210	1225	1130
1994	t459.07	2675.09	159.41	330408	5253	1139	1280
1995	1532.54	2680.03	167.91	376414	5380	1206	1258
1996	1616.29	2630.42	167.08	389147	5262	1090	1252
1997	1692.84	2672.38	175.39	416758	5581	1448	1352
1998	1825.57	2675.14	179.93	420064	5553	969	1323
1999	2006.97	2665.4	180.87	429687	5632	1121	1391
2000	2209.74	2677.46	182.15	445291	5716	1173	1490
2001	2358.02	2676.35	184.25	467348	5723	1354	1505

注:化肥施用量1989年及以前均为实物量,1990年及以后为折纯量。

Data of consumption of fertilizers refer to the consumption in quantity prior to 1989, and the consumption in purity in and after 1990.

9-4 农林牧渔业总产值、指数及构成

Indices and Composition of Gross Output Value Agriculture

年 份 Year	农林牧渔业总产值 Gross Output Value	农业 Farming	种植业 Planting	副业 Sideline Occupations	林业 Forestry	牧业 Animal Husbandry	渔业 Fishery
总产值(按当年价格计算，亿元) Gross Output Value (by current prices) (100 million yuan)							
1990	397.42	241.21	219.17	22.04	25.89	117.22	17.10
1995	1046.97	579.92	543.16	36.76	42.58	369.54	54.93
1996	1226.32	649.38	608.71	40.67	45.71	40.82	70.41
1997	1322.26	660.02	618.52	41.50	47.98	538.15	76.10
1998	1262.46	628.98	582.78	46.20	48.20	505.71	79.57
1999	1200.94	624.70	578.46	46.24	48.20	458.62	69.42
2000	1251.89	633.84	579.81	54.03	51.01	486.13	80.91
2001	1313.23	665.70	611.22	-	51.88	510.42	85.23
指数(按可比价格计算，%) Indices(by comparable prices ,%)							
以上年为100 preceding year=100							
1990	105.1	101.3	100.3	111.0	97.4	103.4	103.0
1995	108.8	104.3	104.2	106.1	102.3	115.4	121.4
1996	108.4	103.2	102.1	111.8	103.2	115.0	120.7
1997	108.3	108.1	108.3	106.9	101.5	109.2	110.4
1998	101.5	98.7	97.1	111.2	102.4	104.1	107.1
1999	103.4	105.0	105.3	102.5	105.5	100.2	107.8
2000	104.3	103.2	103.1	105.0	104.3	103.9	111.5
2001	104.0	103.5	103.8	-	103.2	104.3	105.5
以1978年为100 1978 = 100							
1990	166.2	169.3	136.2	499.9	119.5	239.0	447.8
1995	221.3	203.4	156.5	672.5	153.0	387.5	803.6
1996	239.9	209.9	159.8	751.9	157.9	445.6	969.9
1997	259.8	226.9	173.1	803.8	160.3	486.6	1070.8
1998	263.7	224.0	168.1	893.8	164.1	506.6	1146.8
1999	272.7	235.2	177.0	916.1	173.1	507.6	1236.3
2000	284.4	242.7	182.5	961.9	180.5	527.4	1378.5
2001	295.8	251.2	189.4	-	186.3	550.1	1454.3
构成(按当年价格计算，%) Composition (by current prices, %)							
1990	100.0	60.7	55.1	5.6	5.5	29.5	4.3
1995	100.0	55.4	51.9	3.5	4.1	35.3	5.2
1996	100.0	53.0	49.7	3.3	3.7	37.6	5.7
1997	100.0	49.9	46.8	3.1	3.6	40.7	5.8
1998	100.0	49.9	46.2	3.7	3.8	40.0	6.3
1999	100.0	52.0	48.2	3.8	4.0	38.2	5.8
2000	100.0	50.6	46.3	4.3	4.1	38.8	6.5
2001	100.0	50.7	46.5	-	4.0	38.9	6.5

9-5 农林牧渔业分项总产值

Gross Output Value of Farming, Forestry, Animal Husbandry, and Fishery by Branch

单位：万元 (10 000 yuan)

指　标	Item	1995	1999	2000	2001
农林牧渔业总产值	**Gross Output Value Agriculture**	**10469668**	**12009410**	**12518889**	**13132278**
农业产值	**Farming**	**5797398**	**6244566**	**6338419**	**6656995**
#种植业产值	Planting	5431607	5784571	5798130	6112199
主产品产值	Main Products	5243811	5590615	5611359	5948364
粮食	Grain	3294234	3161770	2924594	2839425
#谷物	Cereal	3091628	2943070	2685380	2575690
豆类	Beans	99487	111951	132671	143751
薯类	Tubers	103119	106749	106543	119984
经济作物	Economical Crops	787085	727216	807393	807393
#油料	Oil-bearing Crops	263862	308189	275756	264573
棉花	Cotton	297491	155382	188196	193116
麻类	Fiber Crops	64295	20080	55710	71145
甘蔗	Sugarcane	53275	38748	46341	69890
烟叶	Tobacco	63751	118104	134943	132555
药材类	Medicinal Herbs	34946	72277	86350	119837
其它经济作物	Other Economical Crops	9465	14436	20097	20097
蔬菜、瓜类	Vegetables,Melons	908003	1419547	1540506	1831902
茶、桑、果	Tea,Mulberry,Fruits	185602	173935	212390	212390
青饲料、绿肥作物	Succulence,Green Manure Crops	21515	37599	34689	34689
#饲料作物	Foodstuff Crops	8720	8966	8754	8754
其他农作物	Other Crops	47372	70548	91787	91787
副产品产值	Sideline Products	187796	193956	186771	163835
粮食作物副产品	Grain Crops	166212	174183	163987	163987
#谷物副产品	Cereal	133538	144670	138174	138174
经济作物副产品	Economical Crops	21584	19773	22784	22784
其他农业	Other Farming	365791	459995	540289	544796
采集野生植物	Gathering of Wild Plants	179040	175638	237659	225221
农民家庭兼营商品性工业	Commodity- Industrial Running by Rural Households	186751	284357	302630	319575
林业产值	**Forestry**	**425811**	**482058**	**510087**	**518783**
营林造林	Afforestation and its Added-value	62673	47594	56483	74259
林产品	Forest Products	113066	171307	191048	169054
村及村以下竹木采伐	Lumbering in Village and Lower Levels	250072	263157	262556	275470
牧业产值	**Animal Husbandry**	**3697156**	**4588602**	**4861290**	**5104234**
牲畜	Livestock	3077117	3528686	3791694	3950554
大牲畜繁殖增长增重	Breeding of Large Domestic Animals	56603	75922	81128	88297
#牛	Cattle	56425	75642	80780	87969
#马	Horses	142	233	301	282
#驴	Donkeys	27	31	24	23
#骡	Mules	9	16	23	23
猪	Hogs	3003188	3403272	3650394	3796219
羊	Sheep and Goats	16610	48755	60098	65908
其它	Others	716	737	74	130
家禽的饲养	Poultry Raising	285273	495992	518936	573130
活的畜禽产品	Live Livestock and Poultry Products	312357	529715	510308	534240
捕猎	Hunting	1785	2429	3342	4312
其它动物饲养	Other Animal Feeding	20624	31780	37010	41998
渔业产值	**Fishery**	**549303**	**694184**	**809093**	**852266**

9-6 农村非农行业总产值

Gross Output Value of Non – Agriculture of rural Areas

单位：万元 (10 000 yuan)

指 标	Item	1995	1999	2000	2001
非农行业总产值	**Gross Output Value of Non-Agriculture**	**19093139**	**45523170**	**47976577**	**39999369**
农村工业总产值	**Gross Industrial Output Value of Rural Areas**	**11839597**	**28421942**	**29678442**	**22996299**
#乡办工业总产值	Gross Industrial Output Value of Townships	3428787	6425493	6599866	5570179
村办工业总产值	Gross Industrial Output Value of Villages	2508439	4289916	4542582	3760431
村以下办工业总产值	Gross Industrial Output Value of Villages Lower Levels	5902371	17706533	18535994	13665689
农村建筑业总产值	**Gross Constructional Output Value of Rural Areas**	**2579874**	**6573871**	**6902456**	**6325388**
#建筑安装工程产值	Output Value of Construction Installation Projects	2432136	6103943	6419770	5892877
#兴建房屋产值	Output Value of House Building	1952781	4703191	4898662	4418284
农田水利工程产值	Output Value of Irrigation and Water Conservancy Works	214335	739042	804368	802438
其他建筑安装工程产值	Output Value of Other Construction Installation Projects	265020	661710	716741	672154
其他基本建设产值	Output Value of Other Basic Constructions	147738	469928	482686	432511
#开垦荒地产值	Output Value of Reclaim Wastelands	12285	28657	34649	64882
农村运输业总产值	**Gross Output Value of Transportation of Rural**	**2048346**	**4097361**	**4370090**	**4091113**
#乡办运输企业货运产值	Output Value of Goods Transportation of Township's Transportation Enterprise	58449	127740	119054	117081
村办运输企业货运产值	Output Value of Goods Transportation of Villages' Transportation Enterprise	58593	142417	167748	149204
村以下办运输企业货运产值	Output Value of Goods Transportation of Villages Lower Levels' Transportation Enterprise	1931304	3827204	4083288	3824829
农村批发零售贸易业、餐饮业总产值	**Gross Output Value of Wholesale, Retail and Catering Trades**	**2625322**	**6429996**	**7025588**	**6586569**
#批发零售贸易业产值	Output Value of Wholesale, Retail and Trades	2049540	4720454	5108046	4739215
#农村供销社产值	Rural Supply and Marketing Cooperative	408598	672569	617597	575450
餐饮业产值	Output Value of Catering	575782	1709542	1917543	1847354
#农村供销社产值	Rural Supply and Marketing Cooperative	36576	95311	86757	79528

9-7 农林牧渔业增加值(2001年)

Added - Value of Farming, Forestry, Animal Husbandry, and Fishery (2001)

单位：万元 (10 000 yuan)

指 标	Item	总产值 Gross Output Value	中间消耗 Material Consump-tion	中间物质消耗 Middle Material Consump-tion	中间非物质部门劳务支出 Middle Non-material Department Service Payout	增加值 Added Value
合计	**Total**	**13132278**	**4874523**	**4512108**	**362415**	**8257755**
农业	Farming	6656995	1709469	1519570	189899	4947526
种植业	Planting	6112199	1628448	1462198	166250	4483751
其他农业	Other Farming	544796	81021	57372	23649	463776
#农民家庭兼营商品性工业	Commodity- Industrial Running by Rural Households	319575	79894	56574	23320	239681
林业	Forestry	518783	101146	81117	20029	417637
牧业	Animal Husbandry	5104234	2755853	2632266	123587	2348381
渔业	Fishery	852266	308055	279155	28900	544211

9-8 农林牧渔业商品产值

Commodity Output Value of Farming, Forestry, Animal Husbandry and Fishery

单位：万元 (10 000 yuan)

指标	Item	1995	1999	2000	2001
农林牧渔业商品产值	**Commodity Output Value of Farming, Forestry,Animal Husbandry and Fishery**	**5929723**	**6936161**	**7470917**	**7951563**
农业商品产值	**Commodity Output Value of Farming**	**2365786**	**2739002**	**2944930**	**3243266**
#种植业产值	Planting	2149569	2414393	2591899	2872713
#主产品商品产值	Main Products	2135196	2398724	2578234	2855015
#粮食	Grain	1009237	1064627	1018854	1004790
#谷物	Cereal	929822	970878	911890	879147
豆类	Beans	46553	58048	70760	81729
薯类	Tubers	32862	35701	36204	43914
经济作物	Economical Crops	604208	534929	628882	711532
#油料	Oil-bearing Crops	144797	174096	158647	164231
棉花	Cotton	258578	125621	163704	170007
麻类	Fiber Crops	60695	17682	50896	64750
甘蔗	Sugarcane	40558	28177	34458	60996
烟叶	Tobacco	59876	106180	121022	117579
药材类	Medicinal Materials	32394	72277	86350	119837
其它经济作物	Other Economical Crops	7310	10896	13805	14132
蔬菜、瓜类	Vegetables,Melons	326384	606171	690379	849361
茶、桑、果	Tea,Mulberry,Fruits	150399	130567	156930	179428
青饲料、绿肥作物	Succulence,Green Manure Crops	2894	1024	1555	5098
#饲料作物	Foodstuff Crops	477	394	401	657
其他农作物	Other Crops	42074	61406	81634	104806
副产品产值	Sideline Products	14373	15669	13665	17698
#粮食作物副产品	Grain Crops	13713	14640	12653	16918
#谷物副产品	Cereal	11201	12692	10846	14773
经济作物副产品	Economical Crops	660	1029	1012	780
其他农业	Other Farming	216217	324609	353031	370553
#采集野生植物	Gathering of Wild Plants	29466	40252	50401	50978
农民家庭营商品性工业	Commodity Industry Run by Rural Household	186751	284357	302630	319575
林业商品产值	**Commodity Output Value of Forestry**	**256430**	**301554**	**323311**	**335478**
#林产品	Forest Products	69392	105748	123072	121314
村及村以下竹木采伐	Lumbering in Village and Lower Levels	187038	188750	189808	200130
牧业商品产值	**Commodity Output Value of Animal Husbandry**	**2880398**	**3375799**	**3610516**	**3727382**
#牲畜	Livestock	2498637	2714923	2912441	2955334
#大牲畜繁殖增长增重	Breeding of Large Domestic Animals	18868	33510	39315	41492
#牛	Cattle	18812	33413	39191	41390
马	Horses	35	84	114	93
驴	Donkeys	16	9	8	5
骡	Mules	5	4	2	4
猪	Hogs	2467121	2644761	2829765	2862703
羊	Sheep and Goats	11994	36332	43307	51056
其他	Others	654	320	54	83
家禽的饲养	Poultry Raising	175047	332580	375910	410409
活的畜禽产品	Live Livestock and Poultry Products	187468	301461	289700	325843
捕猎	Hunting	1291	1663	2738	3118
其它动物饲养	Other Animal Feeding	17955	25172	29727	32678
渔业产值	**Commodity Output Value of Fishery**	**427109**	**519806**	**592160**	**645438**

9-9 耕地面积

Cultivated Areas

单位：千公顷 (1 000 hectares)

指 标	Item	1995	1999	2000	2001
年初实有耕地面积	**Actual Cultivated Areas (Year Beginning)**	**3258.43**	**3218.70**	**3926.52**	**3921.60**
年内增加耕地面积	**Increased Cultivated Areas (Year During)**	**9.60**	**7.52**	**6.85**	**8.22**
开荒	Reclaim Wastelands	3.27	4.05	4.37	5.03
围垦	Reclaim Land from Marshes	0.22	0.07		
废弃地利用	Wastelands Using	0.84	1.52		
其他	Others	5.27	1.88		
年内减少耕地面积	**Decrease in Cultivated Area by Cause**	**18.33**	**13.01**	**11.77**	**17.27**
国家建设占地	Capital Construction of the Government	3.49	5.63	4.59	5.82
乡村集体建设占地	Village Collective Construction	1.17	1.20	1.16	1.29
农民建房占地	Peasant Housing Construction	0.83	0.85	1.14	1.06
农业结构调整占地	Agricultural Structure Adjust Construction	5.17	2.91		
#改园地	Altered Garden Plots	1.80	0.79		
改林地	Altered Forest Lands	0.60	0.98		
改牧地	Altered Grazing Lands		0.03		
改渔塘	Altered Fish Ponds	1.38	0.66		
灾害毁地	Destroyed Lands by Disaster	5.65	1.55		
年末实有耕地面积	**Cultivated Areas(Year-end)**	**3249.70**	**3213.21**	**3921.60**	**3912.55**
水田	Paddy Fields	2562.88	2532.20	2962.79	2959.90
旱地	Dry Fields	686.82	681.01	958.81	952.65
#水浇地	Irrigated Lands	71.82	88.44		
#国有单位耕地面积	Cultivated Areas of State-owned Unit	77.61	76.55		

9-10 农田基本建设

Capital Construction On Farmland

单位：千公顷 (1 000 hectares)

指 标	Item	1995	1999	2000	2001
农田有效灌溉面积	Effective Irrigated Areas on Farmland	2680.03	2678.27	2677.46	2676.35
#当年实灌	Actual Irrigated Areas That Year	2514.22	2472.44	2491.81	2496.65
旱涝保收面积	Areas Ensure Stable Yields Despite Drought or Water Logging	2185.66	2192.24	2191.02	2205.39
易涝面积	Area Liable to Flooding or Water Logging	523.97	523.98	526.05	526.05
除涝面积	Flooded or Waterlogged Area Under Control	450.31	454.59	454.74	456.50
机电排灌面积	Mechanical and Electrical Irrigated and Drainage Areas	1268.12	1166.98	1163.26	1164.29
#机电灌溉面积	Mechanical and Electrical Irrigated Areas	1131.20	1032.5	1028.43	1029.75
机灌	Mechanical Irrigation	287.89	225.76	215.78	216.73
电灌	Electrical Irrigation	843.31	806.74	812.65	813.02
固定站	Fixed Stations	851.91	790.33	800.29	824.43
流动机	Mobile Stations	252.10	218.18	201.72	205.32
喷滴灌	Sprinkling and Drip Irrigation	27.19	23.99	26.42	25.89
纯排面积	Simple Irrigated Areas	136.92	134.48	134.83	134.54
水轮泵灌溉面积	Turbine Pump Irrigated Areas	88.75	83.33	83.16	82.87

9-11 农村主要能源及物资消耗

Consumption of Major Energy and Materials of Rural Areas

指 标	Item	1995	1999	2000	2001
农村电气化情况	**Electric Situation of Rural Areas**				
农村用电量(万度)	Electricity Consumed in Rural Areas (10000 kwh)	376414.6	429687.09	445290.53	467347.6
年末乡办水电站个数(个)	Number of Hydropower Station in Rural Areas at the Yearend (unit)	1001	1002	1086	1049
装机容量(千瓦)	Capacity of Power Generating Sets (kw)	296535	315209	327843	330423
发电量(万度)	Generated Energy (10000 kwh)	84929.08	97255.78	109998.37	110693.00
村及村以下办水电站个数(个)	Number of Water Power Stations of Village and Lower Levels (unit)	5030	3925	3423	3129
装机容量(千瓦)	Capacity of Power Generating Sets (kw)	85314	90546	92073	87118
发电量(万度)	Generated Energy (10000 kwh)	24215.4	27603.12	30556.95	28699.74
农用化肥施用量	**Consumption of Agricultural Chemical Fertilizer**				
按实物量计算(吨)	Calculated at Actual Quantity in Natural Form (ton)	6675850	6888156	6954529	6933887
#氮肥(吨)	Nitrogenous Fertilizer (ton)	3884940	3869985	3906876	3862813
#尿素	Carbide	1046434	1089273	1115457	1140628
氨水	Ammonia	16238	8571	7450	7361
碳氨	Carbon Ammonia	2779832	2729158	2714051	2678983
磷肥(吨)	Phosphate Fertilizer (ton)	1808072	1780552	1777537	1757300
钾肥(吨)	Potash Fertilizer (ton)	523057	610634	600221	611626
复合肥(吨)	Compound Fertilizer (ton)	459781	626985	669895	701148
每亩播种面积施用量(公斤)	Consumption of Per-mu Sown Areas (kg)	56	57.2	57.9	58.3
按折纯量计算(吨)	Calculated at Quantity of 100% Content (ton)	1679135	1808715	1821508	1842457
#氮肥(吨)	Nitrogenous Fertilizer (ton)	964796	980235	980845	986014
#尿素	Carbide	479852	495834	507306	517521
氨水	Ammonia	2398	1074	949	932
碳氨	Carbon Ammonia	473162	457443	455329	447902
磷肥(吨)	Phosphate Fertilizer (ton)	246327	244547	242760	239579
钾肥(吨)	Potash Fertilizer (ton)	261629	303809	298514	303984
复合肥(吨)	Compound Fertilizer (ton)	206383	280124	299389	312880
农用薄膜使用量(吨)	**Consumption of Agricultural Films (ton)**	**30493**	**39161**	**40446**	**43011**
#地膜使用量(吨)	Consumption of Ground Films (ton)	22385	24692	25309	27663
地膜覆盖面积(公顷)	Ground Film Covered Areas (hectare)	244240	306481	313340	349343
农药使用量(吨)	**Consumption of Pesticide (ton)**	**73605**	**83444**	**85611**	**85591**
农用柴油使用量(吨)	**Consumption of Agricultural Diesel Oil (ton)**	**211741**	**217294**	**224315**	**247428**

9-12 农业机械年末拥有量

Year – End Possession of Agriculture Machinery

指 标	Item	1995	1999	2000	2001
农业机械总动力合计(千瓦)	**Total Power of Agricultural Machinery (kw)**	**15325431**	**20069727**	**22097435**	**23580223**
柴油发动机(千瓦)	Diesel Engines (kw)	9941749	13788474	15719714	16928064
汽油发动机(千瓦)	Gasoline Engines (kw)	1798702	2177971	2310250	2266035
电动机(千瓦)	Electric motor (kw)	3495999	4002149	3959172	4258519
其他机械(千瓦)	Other Machinery (kw)	88981	101133	108299	127605
耕作机械	**Machinery for Plough**				
大中型拖拉机 (混合台)	Large and Medium Tractors (mixed unit)	5323	7092	15149	18395
(千瓦)	(kw)	202238	268031	381244	450534
#轮式拖拉机 (混合台)	Wheeled Tractors (mixed unit)	3057	3483	5012	6501
(千瓦)	(kw)	87339	94498	122689	150811
小型及手扶拖拉机 (混合台)	Mini and Walking Tractors (mixed unit)	198013	211647	209271	205585
(千瓦)	(kw)	1748573	1938174	1916099	1899036
#小四轮拖拉机 (台)	Mini Four-wheel Tractors (unit)	3632	11245	17828	23611
(千瓦)	(kw)	45380	146989	206373	264405
耕整机 (台)	Tillage Machinery (unit)	319022	460571	536557	593159
(千瓦)	(kw)	1098449	1642269		1970833
机耕(滚)船 (艘)	Wet-field Tractors (unit)	18043	37081	40778	48341
(千瓦)	(kw)	74031	159190		170261
大中型拖拉机配套农具 (部)	Necessary Farm Tools for Large and Medium Tractors (unit)	1266	5233	6428	5151
#机引犁 (部)	Mechanical Ploughs (unit)	456	1805		
机引耙 (部)	Mechanical Harrows (unit)	419	1484		
小型拖拉机配套农具 (部)	Necessary Farm Tools for Mini Tractors (unit)	34535	62822	63865	48793
#机引犁 (部)	Mechanical Ploughs (unit)	9433	22146		
机引耙 (部)	Mechanical Harrows (unit)	7859	16296		
农用排灌机械	**Machinery for Agricultural Drainage and Irrigation**				
农用排灌动力机械 (台)	Motor Machinery for Agricultural Drainage and Irrigation (unit)	681085	1053374	1158134	1220879
(千瓦)	(kw)	3855312	5205325	5664559	5891642
#柴油机 (台)	Diesel Engines (unit)	447655	660147	742261	786497
(千瓦)	(kw)	1999958	3015268	3508951	3686890
电动机 (台)	Electric Motors (unit)	226255	367597	404862	421942
(千瓦)	(kw)	1759757	2007491	2116140	2163060
汽油机 (台)	Gasoline Engines (unit)	2078	19205	11011	12440
(千瓦)	(kw)	5542	99446	39468	41692
#农用水泵 (台)	Pumps (unit)	694948	1081157	1208900	1273184
喷灌机械 (套)	Machinery for Sprinkling Irrigation (unit)	14131	9021	9672	8192

指 标	Item	1995	1999	2000	2001
收获机械	**Machinery for Harvesters**				
联合收获机（台）	Machinery for Combine Harvesters (unit)	18	1335	3049	4925
（千瓦）	(kw)	622	15228	43837	85867
动力打稻机(台)	Motorized Rice Harvesters (unit)	193395	918086		
畜牧机械	**Machinery for Animal Husbandry**				
饲料粉碎机(台)	Fodder Grinders (unit)	59116	127171	132399	133717
牧草收割机(台)	Herbage Harvesters (unit)	36	84	82	97
渔业机械	**Machinery for Fishery**				
渔用机动船（艘）	Motorized Fishing Boats (unit)	9173	12350	12216	13457
（吨）	(ton)	22170	23057	26788	27608
（千瓦）	(kw)	37657	55843	57491	63770
池塘增氧机(台)	Machinery for Pond Oxygen Increase (unit)	2543	11434		
池渠清淤机(台)	Cleaners for Ponds and Canals (unit)	189	811		
农产品加工机械	**Machinery for Agriculture Products Processing**				
农产品加工动力机械（千瓦）	Motorized Machinery for Agriculture Products Processing (kw)	2841140	3237426	3525247	3657373
#柴油机动力(千瓦)	Diesel Engines Power (kw)	1568405	1765476	2006630	2057474
碾米机(部)	Rice Mills (unit)	288210	402135		
压面机(部)	Noodles Pressers (unit)	31463	23945		
弹轧花机(部)	Cotton Gin (unit)	22803	16413		
榨油机(部)	Oil Pressers (unit)	24167	29504		
淀粉加工机械（指磨粉机、磨浆机)(部)	Machinery for Starch Processing (Powder-Milling Machines, Liquid-Milling Machines) (unit)	27310	97827		
揉茶机(部)	Machinery for Tea Kneading (unit)	15850	16413		
运输机械	**Machinery for Transport**				
农用载重汽车（辆）	Trucks for Agricultural use (unit)	56207	66135	69479	73028
（千瓦）	(kw)	4466599	5112523	5504159	5770143
#柴油汽车(辆)	Diesel Trucks (unit)	34319	42442	45730	49925
（千瓦）	(kw)	2624466	3297132	3666220	3984472
机动运输船(艘)	Motorized Transport Ships (unit)	17434	20850	19743	20750
（吨）	(ton)	229423	249786	275220	273046
（千瓦）	(kw)	167463	213090	223778	235805
农用运输车(辆)	Transport Trucks for Agriculture Use (unit)	55352	52391	83944	87492
（千瓦）	(kw)	925013	1265436	1602332	1727609
其他农用机械	**Other Machinery for Agriculture Use**				
推土机(台)	Bulldozers (unit)	1982	3621	3688	4112
（千瓦）	(kw)	112965	205192	216591	242673

9-13 农作物生产情况(2001年)

Basic Indicators of Farm Corp Production (2001)

指标	Item	播种面积 (千公顷) Sown Area (1 000 hectares)	单产 (公斤/公顷) Per Unit Area Yield (kg/hectare)	总产量 (吨) Total Output (ton)
农作物总播种面积	**Total Sown Area**	**7931.71**	**-**	**-**
粮食作物	**Grain Crops**	**4802.81**	**5622**	**27003000**
#谷物	Cereal	4116.99	6015	24762000
#稻谷	Rice	3691.61	6309	23289000
#早稻	Early Season Rice	1361.11	5754	7832000
#杂交稻	Hybrid Rice	602.5	6080	3663000
优质稻	High Quality Rice	489.64	5533	2709000
中稻与一季晚稻	Middle Season Rice and Late Rice of One-season	707.41	6763	4784000
#杂交稻	Hybrid Rice	595.92	6828	4069000
优质稻	High Quality Rice	173.6	6797	1180000
晚稻	Late Season Rice	1623.09	6576	10673000
#杂交稻	Hybrid Rice	1265.29	6636	8396000
优质稻	High Quality Rice	524.86	6175	3241000
小麦	Wheat	110.02	1945	214000
玉米	Corn	269.79	4266	1151000
高粱	Sorghum	11.89	3028	36000
其他谷物	Other Cereal	33.68	2138	72000
#大麦	Barley	11.01	2271	25000
豆类	Soybeans	294.16	2084	613000
#大豆	Beans	203.58	2220	452000
杂豆	Mixed Beans	90.58	1777	161000
#绿豆	Mung Beans	24.89	1808	45000
薯类(按折粮薯类计算)	Tubers(Converted into Grain)	391.66	4157	1628000
#红薯	Sweet Potatoes	292.97	4482	1313000
#夏红薯	Summer Sweet Potatoes	132.67	4605	611000
马铃薯	Potatoes	98.69	3192	315000
油料	**Oil-bearing Crops**	**912.93**	**1505**	**1373939**
#花生果	Peanuts	144.41	2062	297753
油菜籽	Rapeseeds	757.21	1406	1064422
芝麻	Sesame	7.4	1057	7819
向日葵	Sunflower	0.3	980	294
其他油料	Other Oil-bearing Crops	3.61	1011	3651
棉花	**Cotton**	**149.44**	**1271**	**190000**
麻类	**Fiber Crops**	**48.39**	**2030**	**98222**
#黄、红麻	Jute and Ambary Hemp	0.72	2586	1862
苎麻	Ramie	47.04	2002	94178
甘蔗	**Sugarcane**	**30.14**	**55211**	**1664054**
烟叶	**Tobacco**	**85.72**	**1899**	**162776**
#烤烟	Flue-cured Tobacco	77.11	1960	151134
晒(土)烟	Sun-cured Tobacco	8.61	1352	11642
药材	**Medicinal Herbs**	**55.96**		
蔬菜瓜类	**Vegetables,Melons**	**958.86**		
#蔬菜(包括菜用瓜)	Vegetables(include Snake Melons)	828.58	23937	19833604
果用瓜	Fruit Melons	130.28	23890	3112360
其他作物:	**Other Crops**			
#青饲料	Succulence	215.13		
绿肥	Green Manure	594.72		
#草籽留种	Grass-seed Stock	30.66		

9-14 主要农产品产量

Output of Major Farm Products

单位：万吨 (10 000 tons)

年份 year	粮食 Grain	#小麦 Wheat	#稻谷 Rice	棉花 Cotton	油料 Oil-bearing	甘蔗 Sugarcane	茶叶 Tea	水果 Fruit
1990	2692.67	28.56	2517.26	12.01	72.22	127.76	7.39	56.61
1995	2752.09	31.02	2515.34	22.35	112.04	141.52	6.14	272.14
1996	2820.62	30.42	2559.03	18.96	118.12	129.17	5.49	271.88
1997	2953.28	32.11	2668.20	25.57	129.26	174.53	5.55	329.43
1998	2818.19	28.33	2516.30	19.25	120.74	188.41	5.85	307.37
1999	2892.35	25.19	2549.10	17.70	130.17	168.47	5.63	384.47
2000	2874.97	23.31	2528.08	17.13	139.35	115.85	5.73	382.50
2001	2700.30	21.40	2328.90	19.00	137.39	166.41	5.84	496.32

9-15 林业情况

Basic Indicators of Forestry

面积单位：千公顷 (1 000 hectares)

指　标	Item	1995	1999	2000	2001
当年造林面积总计	**Total Afforestation Areas of the Current Year**	**109.47**	**27.44**	**51.54**	**75.63**
#工程造林	Engineering Afforestation	42.20	15.29	24.37	
竹林	Bamboo Forest	3.85	3.5	2.18	3.95
按主要林种用途分	**By the Use of Main Forestry**				
用材林	Timber Forest	59.03	11.98	22.21	20.43
#速生丰产林	Quick and High Yield Forest	24.02	4.69	10.74	9.12
经济林	Economic Forest	34.1	8.94	12.07	10.82
防护林	Shelter-forest	14.92	6.28	17.13	44.11
薪炭林	Charcoal Forest	1.14	0.1	0.01	
特种用途林	Special Use Forest	0.28	0.14	0.12	0.27
迹地更新面积	Slash Reforestation Areas	43.64	29.98	31.82	30.63
封山育林面积	Close Hillsides to Facilitate Afforestation Areas	3262.33	2918.81	121.83	2077.75
#本年新封	New Closed Areas of the Current Year	215.63	209.9	99.72	905.24
零星(四旁)植树(万株)	Oddly (all around) Tree Planting (10 000 roots)	19083.36	13923.1	27187	16202
林木种子采集量(吨)	Forestry Seed Collection (ton)	440.26	705	678	560
育苗面积	Grow Seedlings Areas	1.00	4.04	2.85	8.1
#本年新育面积	New Grow Seedlings Areas of the Current Year	2.72	2.73	1.78	3.02
幼林抚育实际面积	Actual Areas of Young Growth Fostering	431.35	239.65	205.03	
幼林抚育作业面积	Operative Areas of Young Growth Fostering	566.71	325.28	274.27	458.4
成林抚育面积	Mature Timber Fostering Areas	254.18	220.8	346.20	146.89
#中幼林抚育面积	Areas of Middle and Young Growth Fostering	168.90	148.97	301.77	107.77
低产林改造面积	Low Yield Timber Remaking Areas	63.69	333.24	219.51	97.26
抚育改造出材量(万方)	Fostering and Remaking Yields (10 000 cu.m)	85.34	58.33	27	28.00
#中幼林改造出材量	Middle and Young Growth Remaking Yields	63.45	43.48	26	20.00
年末实有母树林面积	**Actual Mother Woods Areas at the Yearend**	**24.14**	**12.44**	**9.22**	**2.74**
年末实有种子园面积	**Actual Seed Garden Areas at the Yearend**	**123.1**	**2.65**	**3.03**	**2.07**

9-16 林产品产量(2001年)

Output of Major Forestry Products (2001)

名称	Item	数量 Number	名称	Item	数量 Number
生 漆(公斤)	Lacquer (kg)	83000	白果(公斤)	Ginkgo (kg)	364000
油桐籽(吨)	Tung-oil Seeds (ton)	40616	杏仁(公斤)	Almond (kg)	24000
油茶籽(吨)	Tea-oil Seeds (ton)	336216	肉桂(公斤)	Cinnamon (kg)	87000
乌桕籽(吨)	Tallow Tree Seeds (ton)	1389	黄柏(公斤)	Golden Cypress (kg)	790000
五倍子(吨)	Gall (ton)	1193	杜仲(公斤)	Gutta-percha (kg)	115000
棕 片(吨)	Palm Leaf (ton)	8077	白蜡(公斤)	Inesctwax (kg)	37000
松 脂(吨)	Pine Resin (ton)	19971	杂木棍(万根)	Mixed Cardstock (10 000 roots)	11446.5
竹笋干(吨)	Bamboo Shoots (ton)	16516	桎木条(吨)	Wood Lath (ton)	39751
核 桃(吨)	Walnuts (ton)	2842	小杂竹(吨)	Small Mixed Bamboo (ton)	113506
板 栗(吨)	Chestnuts (ton)	21168	楠竹尾(吨)	Tails of Phyllostachys Pubescens (ton)	104955
紫 胶(吨)	Shellacs (ton)	15	村及村以下竹木采伐量	Logging Volume of Timber and Bamboo in Village and Lower Level	-
山苍子(吨)	Fructus Litseae (ton)	15236	#木材采伐量(万方)	Woods Cuts (10 000 cu.m)	397.23
香 菇(公斤)	Mushroom (kg)	-	竹材(万根)	Bamboo (10 000 roots)	11647.91
花 椒(公斤)	Prickly Ashes (kg)	163000	#楠竹(万根)	Phyllostachys Pubescens (10 000 roots)	7335.27
黑木耳(公斤)	Black An Edible Fungus (kg)	-	篙竹(万根)	Pole-bamboo (10 000 roots)	1962.08
八 角(公斤)	Anise(kg)	31000			

9-17 茶叶、水果生产情况(2001年)

Output of Tea and Fruit (2001)

单位：吨 (ton)

名称	Item	数量 Number	名称	Item	数量 Number
茶叶产量	**Output of Tea**	**58435**	水果产量	**Output of Fruits**	**4963243**
红毛茶、	Black Tea and	10887	柑 桔	Citrus	1541503
红碎茶原料	It's Raw Material	-	柚 子	Pomeloes	46865
绿毛茶	Green Tea	28886	桃 子	Peaches	63923
乌龙毛茶	Oolong Tea	149	李 子	Plums	69443
紧压茶原料	Raw Material of Impacted Tea	9158	梨	Pears	55348
			葡 萄	Grapes	24218
其他茶	Other tea	9355	红 枣	Red Chinese Dates	14847
			柿 子	Fresh Persimmons	6684
			枇 杷	Loquates	2942
			其他水果	Other Fruits	3137470

9-18 畜牧业主要产品产量

Output of Major Animal Husbandry Products

名 称	Item	1999	2000	2001
当年出栏猪头数 (万头)	Number of Slaughtered Fattened Pigs of the Current Year (10 000 heads)	6060.04	6299.70	6495.78
出栏肉猪	Slaughtered Fattened Hogs	5811.87	6042.18	6257.54
出口中仔猪	Exported Middle Piglets	248.18	257.52	238.24
出售和自宰肉用牛 (万头)	Beef Slaughtered by Peasants Themselves & Sold (10 000 heads)	122.1	131.63	137.73
出售和自宰肉用羊 (万头)	Mutton Slaughtered by Peasants Themselves & Sold (10 000 heads)	463.13	519.23	569.15
出售和自宰肉用驴 (匹)	Donkey Slaughtered by Peasants Themselves & Sold (head)	433	483	496
出售和自宰肉用骡 (匹)	Mule Slaughtered by Peasants Themselves & Sold (head)	48	263	234
马 (匹)	Horses (head)	2995	883	771
家禽 (万羽)	Poultry (10 000 piece)	38444.54	41855.42	44903.53
兔(万只)	Rabbits (10 000 heads)	85.21	93.92	105.71
当年肉类总产量 (吨)	Total Output of Meat (ton)	4792545	4961622	5166968
猪肉产量	Output of Pork	4001059	4146788	4289639
#肉猪产量	Output of Hogs	3946343	4091543	4238208
出口中仔猪产量	Exported Middle Piglets Output	54716	55245	51431
牛肉产量	Beef Output	133387	138606	144323
羊肉产量	Mutton Output	71169	79737	87266
驴肉产量	Meat of Donkey	42	39	51
骡肉产量	Meat of Mule	6	29	26
马肉产量	Meat of Horse	49	91	79
禽肉产量	Meat of Poultry	586200	595096	636851
兔肉产量	Meat of Rabbits	1197	1236	1351
牛奶产量 (吨)	Cow Milk Output (ton)	8526	10552	18462
羊毛产量 (吨)	Wool Output (ton)	20	21	2
山羊毛	Goat Wool	16	18	
绵羊毛	Sheep Wool	4	3	2
蜂蜜产量 (吨)	Honey Output (ton)	4813	5308	7663
蜂蜡产量 (公斤)	Beeswax Output (kg)	138102	114870	144243
禽蛋产量 (吨)	Poultry Eggs Output (ton)	697458	734890	768126
兔毛产量 (吨)	Rabbit Wool Output (ton)	6	7	2
蚕茧产量 (吨)	Silkworm Cocoons (ton)	478	453	509
#桑蚕茧 (吨)	Mulberry Silkworm Cocoons (ton)	475	450	509

9-19 畜牧业年末存栏情况(2001年)

Year - end Animals in Stock (2001)

项 目	Item	合计 Total	能繁母畜 Breeding Dams	当年生仔畜 Young Animals Be Born in the Current Year
大牲畜总头数 (头)	Number of Large Animals (head)	5260959		
#从事劳役的 (头)	Draught Animals (head)	3819337		
牛(头)	Cattle and Buffaloes (head)	5224266		
耕牛	Farm Cattle	5031205		
#从事劳役	Draught Animals	3805649		
黄牛	Ox	3219330	1349181	603335
水牛	Buffaloes	1990128	799398	320819
菜牛	Beef Cattle	178253		
乳牛	Dairy Cattle	14808	10775	2553
马 (匹)	Horses (head)	29826	6303	2126
驴 (匹)	Donkeys (head)	2218	544	223
骡 (匹)	Mules (head)	4649		183
生猪 (万头)	Hogs (10 000 heads)	3770.44	315.5	
羊 (万只)	Goats and Sheep (10 000 heads)	518.33	220.52	
山羊	Goats	518.14	220.47	
绵羊	Sheep	0.19	0.05	

9-20 主要牲畜存栏和水产品产量

Number of Livestock and Output of Aquatic Products

年 份 Year	年底大牲畜头数(万头) Large Animals (year-end) (10 000 heads)	#耕牛 Farm Cattle	年底猪头数 (万头) Hogs(year-end) (10 000 heads)	年底羊只数 (万只) Sheep and Goats (year-end) (10 000 heads)	猪牛羊肉 (万吨) Pork,Beef, and Mutton (10 000 tons)	水产品 (万吨) Aquatic Products (10 000 tons)
1990	400.65	398.24	2798.27	66.46	189.47	53.01
1995	432.65	428.86	3391.10	214.76	317.36	86.27
1996	471.78	462.38	3545.55	390.23	366.46	98.25
1997	496.54	480.99	3632.01	461.31	404.02	110.76
1998	504.02	493.89	3692.24	449.75	429.03	116.78
1999	511.39	500.51	3567.53	466.93	420.56	124.45
2000	522.85	510.29	3694.56	501.27	436.51	133.21
2001	526.10	503.12	3770.44	518.33	452.12	140.96

9-21 渔业生产情况 (2001年)

Basic Indicators of Fishery Production (2001)

名称	Item	数量 Number
水产品总产量 (吨)	**Total Aquatic Products (ton)**	**1409648**
淡水产品捕捞产量 (吨)	**Freshwater Aquatic Products Caught (ton)**	**156497**
#鱼类	Fish	134883
虾蟹类	Shrimps,Prawns and Crabs	9066
贝类	Shellfish	10743
其他	Others	1805
淡水产品养殖产量 (吨)	**Freshwater Aquatic Products Cultured (ton)**	**1253151**
#鱼类	Fish	1214533
虾蟹类	Shrimps,Prawns and Crabs	14264
贝类	Shellfish	14283
其他	Others	10071
淡水产品中:珍珠产量(公斤)	**Freshwater Aquatic Products:Pearl Products (kg)**	**186968**
淡水养殖面积合计 (千公顷)	**Total Freshwater Cultured Area (1 000 hectares)**	**422.48**
#池塘养殖	Pond Cultivated	**221.4**
#渔业专用塘	Fishery Ponds for Special Use	130.37
湖泊养殖	Lake Cultivated	55.08
#粗养	Extensive Cultivated	36.92
河沟养殖	Brook Cultivated	18.61
水库养殖	Reservoir Cultivated	106.23
#粗养	Extensive Cultivated	52.58
其他养殖	Other Cultivated	21.16
附：稻田养殖	**Enclose: Paddy Cultivated**	**202.2**
#鱼种池面积	Areas of (fish) Fry Ponds	16.88
成鱼面积	Growth Fish Areas	133.34

9-22 按全省人口平均的主要农产品产量

Per Capita Output of Major Farm Products

单位：公斤/人 (kg/person)

产品名称	Item	1995	1999	2000	2001
粮食	Grain	439	444	439	410.4
#稻谷	Rice	399	391	386	354
杂粮	Coarse Cereals	7.5	21.4	21.4	19.1
棉花	Cotton	3.6	2.7	2.6	2.9
食用植物油 (包括料折油及茶油)	Edible Vegetable Oil (Include Material Converted to Oil and Tea-seed Oil)	7.2	8.2	8.6	8.5
甘蔗	Sugarcane	22.5	25.9	17.7	25.3
烤烟	Tobacco	1.2	1.9	2.4	2.3
茶叶	Tea	1.0	0.9	0.9	0.9
水果	Fruit	18.6	26.5	23.0	75.4
#柑桔	Citrus	16.1	23.0	19.2	23.4
猪牛羊肉	Pork,Beef and Mutton	50.6	64.5	66.7	68.7
#猪肉	Pork	49.2	61.4	63.3	65.2
禽蛋	Poultry Eggs	7.4	10.7	11.2	11.7
水产品	Aquatic Products	13.7	19.1	20.3	21.4

9-23 自然灾害情况

Statistics on Natural Disaster

名称	Item	1999	2000	2001
受灾面积合计 (千公顷)	**Total Areas Covered (1 000 hectares)**	**2001.56**	**3170.11**	**3774.75**
旱 灾 (千公顷)	Drought (1 000 hectares)	302.51	649.71	1015.67
水 灾 (千公顷)	Flood (1 000 hectares)	1374.79	292.76	426.8
风雹灾 (公顷)	Windstorm (hectares)	204.80		34.78
病 虫 (千公顷)	Plant Diseases and Insect Pests (1 000 hectares)	101.89	1871.07	2232.89
霜 冻 (公顷)	Frost (hectares)	15.47		
其 他 (公顷)	Others (hectares)	2.10	356.57	64.61
成灾面积 (千公顷)	**Areas Affected (1 000 hectares)**	**1286.66**	**759.23**	**795.07**
旱 灾 (千公顷)	Drought (1 000 hectares)	195.26	231.44	396.8
水 灾 (千公顷)	Flood (1 000 hectares)	868.42	128.06	207.02
风雹灾 (公顷)	Windstorm (hectare)	140.96		13.44
霜 冻 (公顷)	Frost (hectare)	9.59		
病虫 (千公顷)	Plant Diseases and Insect Pests (1 000 hectares)	72.13	222.43	152.16
其他 (千公顷)	Others (1 000 hectares)	0.30	177.30	25.65
因灾减产粮食 (万吨)	**Grains Reduced of Disaster (10 000 tons)**	**332.82**	**112.68**	**148.05**
死亡人数 (人)	**Number of Dead Population (person)**	**173**	**176**	**202**
死亡大牲畜 (头)	**Dead Large Animals (head)**	**183237**	**59689**	**82800**
倒塌房屋 (间)	**Collapsed Houses (unit)**	**279195**	**149806**	**174900**
损坏房屋 (间)	**Destroyed Houses (unit)**	**866152**	**436459**	**573700**
成灾人口合计 (人)	**Total Population Affected (person)**	**18437687**	**22237689**	**23480000**
因灾缺粮数量 (吨)	**Grains Quantities Shorted of Disaster (ton)**	**914380**	**1568465**	**192000**
因灾缺粮人口 (人)	**Population of Grains Shorted of Disaster (person)**	**8538437**	**9374555**	**6800000**
因灾经济损失合计 (万元)	**Total Economic Loss of Disaster (10 000 yuan)**	**1650396**	**1081796**	**940000**
#水灾损失 (万元)	Flood Loss (10 000 yuan)	1429909	662662	450000

9-24 乡镇集体企业财务评价指标

Appraise Indicators on Finance of Township and Village – Collective Enterprises

指 标	Item	1995	1999	2000	2001
基本情况	**Basic Status**				
#汇总企业数(个)	Number of Enterprises (unit)	117152	89037	83162	66289
#盈利企业数(个)	Number of Payoff Enterprises (unit)	112076	86014	80482	64709
占汇总企业数比例(%)	Percentage of Total Enterprises (%)	95.67	96.60	96.78	97.62
净利润总额(万元)	Net Profits (10 000 yuan)	448758	770209	765432	320256
亏损企业数(个)	Number of Loss-made Enterprises (unit)	5076	3023	2668	1580
占汇总企业数比例(%)	Percentage of Total Enterprises (%)	4.33	3.40	3.21	2.38
亏损总额(万元)	Total Loss Value (10 000 yuan)	60475	33474	28383	21643
本期职工平均人数(人)	Average of Staff and Workers (person)	2677388	2491773	2407926	1997619
工资总额(万元)	Total Wages (10 000 yuan)	896359	1260304	1253807	1121395
本期人均工资(元/人)	Per Capita Wages (yuan/person)	3348	5058	5207	5614
期末固定资产原值(万元)	Original Value of Fixed Assets (10 000 yuan)	2164342	3395387	3582622	3606600
银行借款余额(万元)	Balance of Loans (10 000 yuan)	990412	1040878	1027672	962053
#短期银行借款	Short-term Loans	530300	553628	554308	514102
长期银行借款	Long-term Loans	460112	487250	473364	447951
营业收入增长率(%)	**Increase Rate of Business Revenue (%)**	**33.74**	**0.42**	**1.68**	**1.70**
#本期营业收入(万元)	Business Revenue in Current Year (10 000 yuan)	8018082	1443	14677802	10631397
上年同期营业收入(万元)	Business Revenue in Preceding Year (10 000 yuan)	5995212	14375798	14435600	10453825
净利润增长率(%)	**Increase Rate of Net Profits (%)**	**36.46**	**5.67**	**1.78**	**5.35**
#本期净利润额(万元)	Net Profits in Current Year (10 000 yuan)	388283	725950	738908	298613
上年同期净利润总额(万元)	Net Profits in Preceding Year (10 000 yuan)	284549	687016	725950	283456
税金增长率(%)	**Increase Rate of Taxes (%)**	**30.13**	**1.03**	**1.68**	**5.2**
#本期税金总额(万元)	Total Taxes in Current Year (10 000 yuan)	423276	515920	487580	404797
上年同期税金总额(万元)	Total Taxes in Preceding Year (10 000 yuan)	325273	510682	495920	384797
资本金增长率(%)	**Increase Rate of Capital (%)**	**27.40**	**6.50**	**0.44**	**9.53**
#本期末资本金总额(万元)	Total Capital at this Yearend (10 000 yuan)	1191314	1904630	1913069	2091395
上年期末资本金总额(万元)	Total Capital at Last Yearend (10 000 yuan)	935088	1788347	1904630	1909464
应收款项与应付款项差额 逆差用"-"号表示)(万元)	**Balance of Receivables and Account Payable** ("-" Indicates Deficit) (10 000 yuan)	**208855**	**204995**	**228525**	**237764**
#本期末应收款项总额(万元)	Total Receivables at this Yearend (10 000 yuan)	1034127	1254883	1292843	1308084
本期末应付款项总额(万元)	Total Account Payable at Last Year (10 000 yuan)	825272	1049888	1064318	1070320
营业收入利润率(%)	**Rate of Profits to Business Revenue (%)**	**5.57**	**5.63**	**5.51**	**3.25**
#营业利润(万元)	Business Profits (10 000 yuan)	446646	813192	808364	345604
营业收入(万元)	Business Revenue (10 000 yuan)	8018082	1443	14677802	10631397
总资产报酬率(%)	**Rate of Recompense to Total Capital (%)**	**16.58**	**18.65**	**18.10**	**8.68**
#利润总额+利息支出(万元)	Total Profits + Interset Expenses (10 000 yuan)	618045	952396	939329	435753
平均资产总额(万元)	Average Capital (10 000 yuan)	3728477	5105795	5190204	5020537

9-24 续表 continued

指 标	Item	1995	1999	2000	2001
资本收益率 (%)	**Rate of Lucre to Capital (%)**	**32.59**	**38.12**	**38.62**	**14.28**
#净利润 (万元)	Net Profits (10 000 yuan)	388283	725950	738908	298613
实收资本 (万元)	Capital Hold (10 000 yuan)	1191314	1904630	1913069	2091395
资本保值增值率 (%)	**Rate of Capital Maintenance and Appreciation (%)**	**123.80**	**108.33**	**103.70**	**106.89**
#期末所有者权益 (万元)	Creditors' Equity at the Yearend (10 000 yuan)	1393685	2194410	2275656	2430302
期初所有者权益 (万元)	Creditors' Equity at the Year-begin (10 000 yuan)	1125749	2025717	2194410	2273752
资产负债率(%)	**Assets-Liability Ratio (%)**	**66.14**	**60.09**	**59.54**	**56.55**
#负债总额 (万元)	Total Liabilities at The Yearend (10 000 yuan)	2722836	3304348	3349203	3162853
资产总额 (万元)	Total Assets (10 000 yuan)	4116521	5498758	5624859	5593155
流动比率 (%)	**Rate of Circulating Funds to Liquid Liabilities (%)**	**108.64**	**107.29**	**108.66**	**111.38**
#流动资产 (万元)	Circulating Funds (10 000 yuan)	2218723	2674607	2731304	2665426
流动负债 (万元)	Liquid Liabilities (10 000 yuan)	2042239	2492907	2513728	2392988
速动比率 (%)	**Rate of Swift Circulating Funds to Liquid Liabilities (%)**	**68.42**	**69.07**	**70.62**	**73.82**
#速动资产 (万元)	Swift Circulating Funds (10 000 yuan)	1397340	1721954	1775217	1766526
流动负债 (万元)	Liquid Liabilities (10 000 yuan)	2042239	2492907	2513728	2392988
应收帐款周转率 (次)	**Ratio of Turnover of Receivables (time)**	**12.26**	**16.68**	**18.24**	**13.3**
#营业收入 (万元)	Business Revenue (10 000 yuan)	8018082	14435600	8877478	10631397
平均应收帐款余额 (万元)	Average Balance of Receivables (10 000 yuan)	653755	865522	486609	799372
存货周转率 (次)	**Ratio of Turnover of Inventory (time)**	**7.26**	**11.75**	**12.80**	**10.29**
#产品销售成本 (万元)	Cost of Sales (10 000 yuan)	3988826	7251637	7423855	5373191
平均存货成本 (万元)	Average Cost of Inventory (10 000 yuan)	549202	617365	579874	522305
社会贡献率 (%)	**Ratio of Social Contribute (%)**	**52.73**	**54.10**	**52.42**	**40.52**
#企业社会贡献总额 (万元)	Total Value of Social Contribute (10 000 yuan)	1966177	2762053	2720849	2034437
平均资产总额 (万元)	Average of Assets (10 000 yuan)	3728477	5105795	5190204	5020537
社会积累率 (%)	**Ratio of Social Accumulate(%)**	**22.31**	**18.68**	**17.92**	**19.9**
#上交国家财政总额 (万元)	Total Value of Turn in Government (10 000 yuan)	438639	515920	487580	404797
企业社会贡献总额 (万元)	Total Value of Social Contribute (10 000 yuan)	1966177	2762053	2720849	2034437
产品销售率 (%)	**Sales Rate of Industrial Products (%)**	**88.90**	**95.00**	**95.69**	**95.78**
#工业销售产值 (万元)	Sales Revenue (10 000 yuan)	5445083	9061329	9154170	6538004
工业总产值 (现行价格) (万元)	Output Value of Industrial (current price) (10 000 yuan)	6125106	9534858	9566481	6825872
固定资产折旧率 (%)	**Ratio of Fixed Assets Depreciation (%)**	**7.38**	**7.54**	**6.98**	**6.18**
#本期固定资产折旧额 (万元)	Fixed Assets Depreciation this Year (10 000 yuan)	147346	236447	228598	204860
固定资产原值平均余额 (万元)	Average Balanceof Original Value of Fixed Assets (10 000 yuan)	1995908	3136182	3275201	3315818
人均利税 (元/人)	**Per Capita Taxes and Profits (yuan/person)**	**3031**	**5000**	**5094**	**3391**
#利税总额 (万元)	Total Taxes and Profits (10 000 yuan)	811559	1241870	1226488	677344
全部职工平均人数 (人)	Average Number of Staff and Workers (person)	2677388	2491773	2407926	1997619

9-25 洞庭湖区主要社会经济指标

Major Economic Indicators and Social Indicatiors on The DongTing Lake Area

指标	Item	2000	2001
总户数（万户）	Total Number of Households (10 000 households)	445.30	450.25
总人口（万人）	Total Number of Population (10 000 persons)	1504.30	1502.40
#乡村人口（万人）	Number of Rural Population (10 000 persons)	1213.70	1228.20
乡村从业人员数（万人）	Employment of Rural Population (10 000 persons)	634.76	645.83
#农林牧渔业（万人）	Farming,Forestry,Animal Husbandry,Fishery (10 000 persons)	457.18	457.71
有效灌溉面积（千公顷）	Effective Irrigated Area (1 000 hectares)	863.13	876.82
国内生产总值（亿元）	Gross Domestic Products (100 million yuan)	981.39	1080.60
#第一产业增加值（亿元）	Added-Value of First Industry (100 million yuan)	260.21	276.23
第二产业增加值（亿元）	Added-Value of Second Industry (100 million yuan)	394.52	418.31
第三产业增加值（亿元）	Added-Value of Third Industry (100 million yuan)	326.66	386.06
农业机械总动力（万千瓦）	Total Power of Major Agriculture Machinery (10 000 kw)	785.00	744.30
农作物总播种面积（千公顷）	Total Sown Area of Crops (1 000 hectares)	2380.14	2350.80
粮食作物播种面积（千公顷）	Sown Area of Grain Crops (1 000 hectares)	1330.21	1215.81
#稻谷（千公顷）	Paddy (1 000 hectares)	1165.77	1057.13
玉米（千公顷）	Corn (1 000 hectares)	40.77	36.22
油料播种面积（千公顷）	Sown Area of Oils-bearing (1 000 hectares)	375.15	362.35
棉花播种面积（千公顷）	Sown Area of Cotton (1 000 hectares)	115.83	118.80
粮食总产量（万吨）	Total Output of Grain (10 000 tons)	778.63	707.68
#稻谷（万吨）	Paddy (10 000 tons)	720.06	652.82
玉米（万吨）	Corn (10 000 tons)	19.15	17.27
油料产量（万吨）	Output of Oils-bearing (10 000 tons)	57.18	55.21
棉花产量（万吨）	Output of Cotton (10 000 tons)	13.49	16.52
肉类总产量（万吨）	Total Output of Meat (10 000 tons)	127.02	133.33
水产品总产量（万吨）	Total Output of Aquatic Products (10 000 tons)	66.70	70.77
水果产量（万吨）	Output of Fruits (10 000 tons)	33.95	154.02
地方财政收入（亿元）	Local Government Revenue (100 million yuan)	24.42	28.04
国有及年销售收入500万元及以上的非国有工业企业总产值(亿元)	Gross Output Value of State-owned Industrial Enterprises and Non State-owned Industrial Enterprises with an Annual Sales Income of Over 5 Million yuan (100 million yuan)	554.55	662.11
普通中学在校学生数（人）	Student Enrollment in General Secondary Schools (person)	897821	1004420
小学在校学生人数（人）	Student Enrollment in Primary Schools (person)	1417139	1267109
医院、卫生院床位数（张）	Hospital Beds (unit)	26203	26584
医院、卫生院技术人员数(人)	Medical Technical Personnel in Hospitals (person)	42438	42073

十、工业

INDUSTRY

资料整理人员：　殷智敏　唐 颖　彭 蕾

10-1 独立核算工业企业各种分组的主要生产指标(2001年)

Major Production Indicators of Industrial Enterprises with Independent Accounting Systems by Various Characteristics (2001)

单位:亿元 (100 million yuan)

指标	Item	企业单位数(个) Number of Enterprises (unit)	#亏损企业 Loss-making Enterprises	工业总产值(现价) Gross Industrial Output Value (current price)	工业增加值(生产法) Value Added of Industry (by producing)
总计	**Total**	**4961**	**1506**	**1811.22**	**606.54**
按登记注册类型:	**Grouped by Registration**				
内资企业	Internal-invested Enterprises	4722	1439	1664.07	563.49
国有企业	State-owned Enterprises	1758	768	705.42	304.03
中央企业	Central Enterprises	100	50	297.22	174.27
地方企业	Local Enterprises	1658	718	408.20	129.76
集体企业	Collective-owned Enterprises	1110	273	202.73	55.55
股份合作企业	Enterprises Cooperated by Joint-stock	269	63	42.16	11.35
联营企业	Cooperative Enterprises	42	12	7.26	2.03
有限责任公司	Limited Liability Company	441	133	266.53	71.04
股份有限公司	Company Limited by Shares	208	50	275.68	75.73
私营企业	Individual-owned Enterprises	875	139	160.80	42.69
其他企业	Enterprises of Other Types of Ownership	19	1	3.49	1.07
港、澳、台投资经济	Enterprises Funded by Entrepreneurs From Hong Kong,Macao and Taiwan	146	42	57.60	15.55
外商投资经济	Enterprises funded by Foreigners	93	25	89.55	27.50
按经济组织类型:	**Grouped by Ownership**				
独资企业	Enterprises Owned by a Sole Investor	3302	1103	986.51	380.42
合作、合伙企业	Enterprises of Partnership	502	101	81.97	23.05
股份有限公司	Company Limited by Shares	282	62	304.21	84.48
有限责任公司	Limited Liability Company	875	240	438.53	118.59
国有控股企业	**State-owned or Controlling Share Hold Enterprises**	**2117**	**879**	**1135.60**	**416.88**
农村工业	**Rural Industry**	**570**	**95**	**117.85**	**32.51**
轻工业	**Enterprises of Light Industry**	**1992**	**586**	**633.45**	**251.84**
以农产品为原料	Using Farm Products as Raw Materials	1308	375	484.87	207.83
以非农产品为原料	Using Non-Farm Products as Raw Materials	684	211	148.57	44.01
重工业	**Enterprises of Heavy Industry**	**2969**	**920**	**1177.77**	**354.69**
采掘工业	Mining and Quarrying	400	93	73.65	24.40
原料工业	Raw Materials Industry	1151	382	643.41	211.27
加工工业	Manufacturing Industry	1418	445	460.71	119.02
按企业规模分:	**Grouped by Size of Enterprises**				
特大型企业	Supper Largest Enterprise	5	1	163.33	51.09
大一型企业	The First Rank of the Large Enterprises	75	16	535.64	213.32
大二型企业	The Second Rank of the Large Enterprises	154	56	237.82	83.89
中一型企业	The First Rank of the Medium-sized Enterprises	114	49	76.39	26.62
中二型企业	The Second Rank of the Medium-sized Enterprises	263	106	99.98	31.07
小型企业	Small Enterprises	4350	1278	698.06	200.55

注：本表综合范围为全部国有工业企业及年产品销售收入500万元及以上的非国有工业企业。

All state-owned and the non-state-owned industrial enterprises with an annual sales income of over 5 million yuan.

单位:亿元　　10-1 续表 1　continued　　(100 million yuan)

指标	Item	企业单位数(个) Number of Enterprises (unit)	#亏损企业 Loss-making Enterprises	工业总产值(现价) Gross Industrial Output Value (current price)	工业增加值(生产法) Value Added of Industry (by producing)
按行业划分:	**Grouped by Sector**				
煤炭采选业	Coal Mining and Dressing	182	54	35.70	12.40
黑色金属矿采选业	Ferrous Metals Mining and Dressing	20	4	2.33	0.72
有色金属矿采选业	Nonferrous Metals Mining and Dressing	127	15	21.53	7.28
非金属矿采选业	Nonmetal Minerals Mining and Dressing	63	12	13.82	4.30
其他矿采选业	Other Types of Mining and Dressing				
木材及竹材采运业	Logging and Transport of Timber and Bamboo	13	8	0.94	0.30
食品加工业	Food Processing	358	112	96.40	26.83
食品制造业	Food Manufacturing	113	25	22.16	5.83
饮料制造业	Beverage Manufacturing	103	30	30.81	12.20
烟草加工业	Tobacco Processing	16	6	149.19	109.03
纺织业	Textile Industry	188	73	50.97	13.75
服装及其他纤维制品制造业	Garments and Other Fiber Products	59	14	10.30	2.69
皮革、毛皮、羽绒及其制品业	Leather,Furs,Down and Related Products	64	16	16.20	3.81
木材加工及竹、藤、棕、草制品业	Timber Processing,Bamboo,Cane, Palm Fiber and Straw Products	123	15	20.71	5.85
家具制造业	Furniture Manufacturing	29	1	10.36	2.73
造纸及纸制品业	Paper making and Paper Products	177	42	51.87	15.34
印刷业、记录媒介的复制	Printing and Record Medium Reproduction	113	35	18.84	7.83
文教体育用品制造业	Cultural,Educational and Sports Goods	16	3	1.14	0.26
石油加工及炼焦业	Petroleum Processing and Coking	11	5	137.50	30.48
化学原料及化学制品制造业	Raw Chemical Materials and Chemical Products	396	122	142.94	36.04
医药制造业	Medical and Pharmaceutical Products	101	28	32.83	11.12
化学纤维制造业	Chemical Fiber	17	5	16.57	2.74
橡胶制品业	Rubber Products	45	15	10.63	2.67
塑料制品业	Plastic Products	96	28	14.74	4.03
非金属矿物制品业	Nonmetal Mineral Products	667	258	113.04	32.74
黑色金属冶炼及压延加工业	Smelting and Pressing of Ferrous Metals	129	42	126.26	42.68
有色金属冶炼及压延加工业	Smelting and Pressing of NonFerrous Metals	178	22	125.14	30.02
金属制品业	Metal Products	161	41	26.25	6.52
普通机械制造业	Ordinary Machinery	245	87	42.66	11.39
专用设备制造业	Special Purpose Equipment	165	56	44.69	15.40
交通运输设备制造业	Transport Equipment	186	67	126.67	30.91
电气机械及器材制造业	Electric Equipment and Machinery	184	51	63.76	15.57
电子及通信设备制造业	Electronic and Telecommunications Equipment	73	24	53.31	11.79
仪器仪表及文化、办公用机械制造业	Instruments,Meters,Cultural and Office Machinery	35	18	13.13	3.83
其他制造业	Other Types of Manufacturing	152	26	18.52	6.16
电力、蒸汽、热水的生产和供应业	Production and Supply of Electric Power, Steam and Hot Water	228	86	120.20	71.43
煤气生产和供应业	Production and Supply of Gas	7	7	4.52	0.41
自来水的生产和供应业	Production and Supply of Tap Water	112	47	12.88	6.67

指标	Item	工业中间投入 Industrial Inter-mediate Input	本年应付工资 Wages Payable in This Year	本年应付福利费 Welfarisms Payable in This Year	全部从业人员年均人数(万人) Average Number of Employees (10 000 persons)
总计	**Total**	**1301.09**	**134.06**	**19.89**	**155.20**
按登记注册类型:	**Grouped by Registration**				
内资企业	Internal-invested Enterprises	1189.87	128.35	19.08	149.32
国有企业	State-owned Enterprises	454.28	68.45	10.03	73.69
中央企业	Central Enterprises	152.61	19.37	2.74	13.52
地方企业	Local Enterprises	301.67	49.08	7.29	60.17
集体企业	Collective-owned Enterprises	152.81	12.82	1.82	21.67
股份合作企业	Enterprises Cooperated by Joint-stock	32.23	2.97	0.39	4.94
联营企业	Cooperative Enterprises	5.50	0.45	0.06	0.79
有限责任公司	Limited Liability Company	208.37	21.92	4.03	24.07
股份有限公司	Company Limited by Shares	210.67	12.68	1.75	10.74
私营企业	Individual-owned Enterprises	123.45	8.92	0.99	13.16
其他企业	Enterprises of Other Types of Ownership	2.56	0.14	0.01	0.26
港、澳、台投资经济	Enterprises Funded by Entrepreneurs From Hong Kong, Macao and Taiwan	44.26	2.36	0.36	2.80
外商投资经济	Enterprises funded by Foreigners	66.96	3.35	0.45	3.08
按经济组织类型:	**Grouped by Ownership**				
独资企业	Enterprises Owned by a Sole Investor	667.18	85.20	12.35	101.36
合作、合伙企业	Enterprises of Partnership	61.43	4.93	0.60	8.52
股份有限公司	Company Limited by Shares	231.87	13.91	1.92	12.69
有限责任公司	Limited Liability Company	340.61	30.02	5.02	32.63
国有控股企业	**State-owned or Controlling Share Hold Enterprises**	**790.17**	**96.16**	**14.81**	**100.83**
农村工业	**Rural Industry**	**88.38**	**6.36**	**0.81**	**11.07**
轻工业	**Enterprises of Light Industry**	**416.26**	**35.79**	**4.78**	**47.24**
以农产品为原料	Using Farm Products as Raw Materials	304.65	22.99	3.19	28.61
以非农产品为原料	Using Non-Farm Products as Raw Materials	111.62	12.80	1.59	18.63
重工业	**Enterprises of Heavy Industry**	**884.82**	**98.27**	**15.11**	**107.96**
采掘工业	Mining and Quarrying	52.61	12.84	2.58	19.60
原料工业	Raw Materials Industry	474.01	45.76	6.51	42.81
加工工业	Manufacturing Industry	358.20	39.67	6.02	45.55
按企业规模分:	**Grouped by Size of Enterprises**				
特大型企业	Supper Largest Enterprise	123.04	10.54	1.46	7.10
大一型企业	The First Rank of the Large Enterprises	357.91	32.55	4.35	25.56
大二型企业	The Second Rank of the Large Enterprises	168.39	23.27	4.46	22.98
中一型企业	The First Rank of the Medium-sized Enterprises	53.70	7.03	1.32	8.09
中二型企业	The Second Rank of the Medium-sized Enterprises	74.22	10.19	1.59	13.02
小型企业	Small Enterprises	523.83	50.48	6.71	78.45

单位:亿元 10-1 续表 3 continued (100 million yuan)

指标	Item	工业中间投人 Industrial Inter-mediate Input	本年应付工资 Wages Payable in This Year	本年应付福利费 welfarisms Payable in This Year	全部从业人员年均人数(万人) Average Number of Employees (10 000 persons)
按行业划分:	**Grouped by Sector**				
煤炭采选业	Coal Mining and Dressing	25.41	8.60	1.66	13.52
黑色金属矿采选业	Ferrous Metals Mining and Dressing	1.70	0.26	0.03	0.36
有色金属矿采选业	Nonferrous Metals Mining and Dressing	15.09	3.12	0.76	3.52
非金属矿采选业	Nonmetal Minerals Mining and Dressing	10.05	1.15	0.18	1.77
其他矿采选业	Other Types of Mining and Dressing				
木材及竹材采运业	Logging and Transport of Timber and Bamboo	0.67	0.18	0.02	0.44
食品加工业	Food Processing	70.47	2.52	0.35	3.88
食品制造业	Food Manufacturing	17.07	1.20	0.16	1.95
饮料制造业	Beverage Manufacturing	20.36	1.75	0.24	2.39
烟草加工业	Tobacco Processing	57.25	4.36	0.58	1.81
纺织业	Textile Industry	38.55	4.64	0.61	7.91
服装及其他纤维制品制造业	Garments and Other Fiber Products	7.87	0.88	0.12	1.28
皮革、毛皮、羽绒及其制品业	Leather, Furs, Down and Related Products	12.68	0.70	0.21	1.05
木材加工及竹、藤、棕、草制品业	Timber Processing, Bamboo, Cane, Palm Fiber and Straw Products	15.46	1.40	0.12	2.04
家具制造业	Furniture Manufacturing	7.78	0.42	0.07	0.54
造纸及纸制品业	Paper making and Paper Products	38.87	3.03	0.42	3.74
印刷业、记录媒介的复制	Printing and Record Medium Reproduction	12.25	1.32	0.19	1.55
文教体育用品制造业	Cultural,Educational and Sports Goods	0.95	0.07	0.01	0.13
石油加工及炼焦业	Petroleum Processing and Coking	112.77	3.63	0.53	2.10
化学原料及化学制品制造业	Raw Chemical Materials and Chemical Products	111.52	11.08	1.57	12.63
医药制造业	Medical and Pharmaceutical Products	23.95	2.19	0.31	2.31
化学纤维制造业	Chemical Fiber	14.46	1.03	0.14	1.22
橡胶制品业	Rubber Products	8.34	0.88	0.09	1.39
塑料制品业	Plastic Products	11.14	0.86	0.12	1.34
非金属矿物制品业	Nonmetal Mineral Products	85.77	11.65	1.55	20.28
黑色金属冶炼及压延加工业	Smelting and Pressing of Ferrous Metals	92.48	10.98	1.41	9.40
有色金属冶炼及压延加工业	Smelting and Pressing of Non Ferrous Metals	100.60	7.91	1.16	6.92
金属制品业	Metal Products	20.44	1.77	0.22	2.44
普通机械制造业	Ordinary Machinery	33.21	5.08	0.67	6.85
专用设备制造业	Special Purpose Equipment	31.91	5.36	1.13	5.98
交通运输设备制造业	Transport Equipment	99.94	10.27	1.37	8.50
电气机械及器材制造业	Electric Equipment and Machinery	50.50	4.64	0.69	5.17
电子及通信设备制造业	Electronic and Telecommunications Equipment	43.92	2.02	0.30	2.01
仪器仪表及文化、办公用机械制造业	Instruments, Meters, Cultural and Office Machinery	9.95	1.19	0.15	1.00
其他制造业	Other Types of Manufacturing	13.38	1.77	0.22	3.98
电力、蒸汽、热水的生产和供应业	Production and Supply of Electric Power, Steam and Hot Water	64.19	11.11	1.84	8.55
煤气生产和供应业	Production and Supply of Gas	4.15	0.36	0.05	0.34
自来水的生产和供应业	Production and Supply of Tap Water	6.95	2.43	0.33	2.16

10-2 独立核算工业企业各种分组的资本金与资产(2001年)

Capital Fund and Fixed Assets of Industrial Enterprises with Independent Accounting Systems by Various Characteristics (2001)

单位:亿元　　(100 million yuan)

指标	Item	流动资产年均余额 Annual Average Balance of Circulating Funds	实收资本 Total Capital Hold	流动资产合计 Total Circulating Funds	固定资产 Fixed Assets 原价合计 Original Value	固定资产 Fixed Assets 净值余额 Annual Average Balance of Net Value
总计	**Total**	**1155.51**	**674.74**	**1171.36**	**2095.68**	**1314.77**
按登记注册类型:	**Grouped by Registration**					
内资企业	Internal-invested Enterprises	1077.47	601.78	1091.52	1958.15	1232.51
国有企业	State-owned Enterprises	556.03	284.92	573.10	1210.30	756.35
中央企业	Central Enterprises	221.69	95.47	230.44	553.89	332.47
地方企业	Local Enterprises	334.34	189.45	342.66	656.41	423.88
集体企业	Collective-owned Enterprises	65.15	38.10	64.70	82.33	52.87
股份合作企业	Enterprises Cooperated by Joint-stock	14.44	12.16	14.50	23.29	15.91
联营企业	Cooperative Enterprises	2.81	2.04	2.82	4.68	3.05
有限责任公司	Limited Liability Company	209.76	127.67	190.99	353.38	226.23
股份有限公司	Company Limited by Shares	174.01	97.74	188.80	225.75	134.51
私营企业	Individual-owned Enterprises	54.28	38.33	55.73	57.15	42.64
其他企业	Enterprises of Other Types of Ownership	0.99	0.82	0.88	1.27	0.95
港、澳、台投资经济	Enterprises Funded by Entrepreneurs From Hong Kong,Macao and Taiwan	27.49	22.45	29.60	32.42	22.56
外商投资经济	Enterprises funded by Foreigners	50.55	50.51	50.24	105.11	59.70
按经济组织类型:	**Grouped by Ownership**					
独资企业	Enterprises Owned by a Sole Investor	643.58	342.84	660.56	1321.45	830.66
合作、合伙企业	Enterprises of Partnership	26.53	21.49	25.98	40.16	27.55
股份有限公司	Company Limited by Shares	183.11	106.52	198.83	239.82	144.02
有限责任公司	Limited Liability Company	302.29	203.89	285.99	494.25	312.54
国有控股企业	**State-owned or Controlling Share Hold Enterprises**	**886.26**	**475.74**	**895.79**	**1704.19**	**1055.99**
农村工业	**Rural Industry**	**28.33**	**19.48**	**28.52**	**39.36**	**26.80**
轻工业	**Enterprises of Light Industry**	**362.69**	**212.59**	**371.18**	**433.38**	**281.46**
以农产品为原料	Using Farm Products as Raw Materials	267.02	142.28	276.51	285.63	182.05
以非农产品为原料	Using Non-Farm Products as Raw Materials	95.67	70.31	94.67	147.75	99.41
重工业	**Enterprises of Heavy Industry**	**792.82**	**462.15**	**800.18**	**1662.30**	**1033.31**
采掘工业	Mining and Quarrying	46.38	34.39	44.06	75.89	46.43
原料工业	Raw Materials Industry	386.92	206.14	369.47	1091.90	679.31
加工工业	Manufacturing Industry	359.52	221.62	386.65	494.51	307.57
按企业规模分:	**Grouped by Size of Enterprises**					
特大型企业	Supper Largest Enterprise	91.43	41.28	93.28	212.41	134.46
大一型企业	The First Rank of the Large Enterprises	379.15	217.53	371.44	656.22	385.20
大二型企业	The Second Rank of the Large Enterprises	214.74	110.48	222.53	390.43	232.33
中一型企业	The First Rank of the Medium-sized Enterprises	73.11	29.84	73.46	129.11	83.39
中二型企业	The Second Rank of the Medium-sized Enterprises	81.69	39.58	86.45	139.06	89.85
小型企业	Small Enterprises	315.39	236.03	324.20	568.45	389.54

单位:亿元 10-2 续表 1 continued (100 million yuan)

指标	Item	流动资产年均余额 Annual Average Balance of Circulating Funds	实收资本 Total Capital Hold	流动资产合计 Total Circulating Funds	固定资产 Fixed Assets 原价合计 Original Value	固定资产 Fixed Assets 净值余额 Annual Average Balance of Net Value
按行业划分:	**Grouped by Sector**					
煤炭采选业	Coal Mining and Dressing	29.42	20.80	27.78	45.56	27.56
黑色金属矿采选业	Ferrous Metals Mining and Dressing	1.61	0.99	1.56	2.50	1.52
有色金属矿采选业	Nonferrous Metals Mining and Dressing	10.32	8.69	9.81	19.68	11.91
非金属矿采选业	Nonmetal Minerals Mining and Dressing	6.12	3.50	5.83	10.64	6.08
其他矿采选业	Other Types of Mining and Dressing					
木材及竹材采运业	Logging and Transport of Timber and Bamboo	1.21	1.33	1.22	1.92	1.45
食品加工业	Food Processing	42.19	24.25	42.97	45.07	31.98
食品制造业	Food Manufacturing	8.91	6.61	8.90	11.67	8.24
饮料制造业	Beverage Manufacturing	34.87	16.97	34.70	29.52	20.99
烟草加工业	Tobacco Processing	84.34	34.10	87.41	76.33	41.85
纺织业	Textile Industry	27.55	15.67	29.40	38.58	24.44
服装及其他纤维制品制造业	Garments and Other Fiber Products	3.54	1.88	3.64	3.45	2.62
皮革毛皮羽绒及其制品业	Leather,Furs,Down and Related Products	5.52	1.88	5.56	5.22	3.85
木材加工及竹、藤、棕、草制品业	Timber Processing,Bamboo,Cane, Palm Fiber and Straw Products	6.19	10.11	6.11	17.77	14.16
家具制造业	Furniture Manufacturing	1.71	0.97	1.78	1.43	1.05
造纸及纸制品业	Paper making and Paper Products	26.43	21.65	30.95	39.91	24.95
印刷业、记录媒介的复制	Printing and Record Medium Reproduction	9.89	6.78	10.59	15.86	9.77
文教体育用品制造业	Cultural,Educational and Sports Goods	0.99	0.28	1.02	0.61	0.46
石油加工及炼焦业	Petroleum Processing and Coking	53.89	8.95	49.28	101.37	62.03
化学原料及化学制品制造业	Raw Chemical Materials and Chemical Products	81.39	73.11	92.75	199.79	121.15
医药制造业	Medical and Pharmaceutical Products	28.06	14.55	27.40	24.18	17.12
化学纤维制造业	Chemical Fiber	9.90	7.07	8.06	25.55	17.39
橡胶制品业	Rubber Products	6.40	3.42	6.75	7.13	4.69
塑料制品业	Plastic Product3	8.33	7.29	9.08	12.64	8.31
非金属矿物制品业	Nonmetal Mineral Products	66.09	47.55	66.47	133.71	87.62
黑色金属冶炼及压延加工业	Smelting and Pressing of Ferrous Metals	68.56	30.66	73.18	165.27	104.81
有色金属冶炼及压延加工业	Smelting and Pressing of Non-Ferrous Metals	55.50	40.30	54.29	81.39	51.92
金属制品业	Metal Products	11.82	7.71	12.50	15.01	9.33
普通机械制造业	Ordinary Machinery	42.27	25.20	50.09	56.56	35.40
专用设备制造业	Special Purpose Equipment	49.43	22.09	50.28	43.81	27.26
交通运输设备制造业	Transport Equipment	104.21	53.10	109.50	102.57	65.52
电气机械及器材制造业	Electric Equipment and Machinery	51.01	29.44	52.52	49.33	29.64
电子及通信设备制造业	Electronic and Telecommunications Equipment	38.89	31.86	37.32	56.02	40.18
仪器仪表及文化、办公用机械制造业	Instruments,Meters,Cultural and Office Machinery	13.64	8.20	14.38	10.56	6.89
其他制造业	Other Types of Manufacturing	6.13	3.20	6.23	4.19	2.93
电力、蒸汽、热水的生产和供应业	Production and Supply of Electric Power, Steam and Hot Water	135.23	58.19	115.98	568.79	344.18
煤气生产和供应业	Production and Supply of Gas	1.64	3.41	1.80	4.69	3.52
自来水的生产和供应业	Production and Supply of Tap Water	11.42	17.97	11.56	44.70	30.41

指标	Item	累计折旧 Add up Depreciation of Fixed Assets	#本年折旧 Depreciation of this Year	流动负债 Total Liquid Liabilities	长期负债 Long-term Liabilities	所有者权益 Creditors Equity
总计	**Total**	**727.31**	**90.38**	**1223.78**	**709.48**	**996.06**
按登记注册类型:	**Grouped by Registration**					
内资企业	Internal-invested Enterprises	677.86	83.32	1136.29	695.42	909.35
国有企业	State-owned Enterprises	425.45	51.98	647.22	480.97	436.70
中央企业	Central Enterprises	197.36	26.42	196.09	298.00	167.02
地方企业	Local Enterprises	228.09	25.56	451.13	182.97	269.68
集体企业	Collective-owned Enterprises	29.62	3.43	69.91	23.46	40.05
股份合作企业	Enterprises Cooperated by Joint-stock	7.02	0.97	14.57	6.15	14.25
联营企业	Cooperative Enterprises	1.67	0.24	3.37	1.30	2.10
有限责任公司	Limited Liability Company	113.88	14.12	204.84	134.22	185.65
股份有限公司	Company Limited by Shares	86.65	9.72	150.97	39.44	169.02
私营企业	Individual-owned Enterprises	13.23	2.81	44.69	9.59	60.59
其他企业	Enterprises of Other Types of Ownership	0.34	0.05	0.72	0.29	0.97
港、澳、台投资经济	Enterprises Funded by Entrepreneurs From Hong Kong,Macao and Taiwan	10.22	1.80	27.76	3.46	26.63
外商投资经济	Enterprises funded by Foreigners	39.23	5.26	59.73	10.60	60.08
按经济组织类型:	**Grouped by Ownership**					
独资企业	Enterprises Owned by a Sole Investor	462.93	56.95	735.93	508.41	503.39
合作、合伙企业	Enterprises of Partnership	12.52	1.81	25.71	9.99	24.99
股份有限公司	Company Limited by Shares	90.67	10.47	159.38	41.37	182.86
有限责任公司	Limited Liability Company	161.19	21.15	302.76	149.71	284.82
国有控股企业	**State-owned or Controlling Share Hold Enterprises**	**601.52**	**72.00**	**945.90**	**627.08**	**729.15**
农村工业	**Rural Industry**	**11.96**	**1.88**	**26.27**	**10.59**	**24.89**
轻工业	**Enterprises of Light Industry**	**148.38**	**19.77**	**340.67**	**99.19**	**353.21**
以农产品为原料	Using Farm Products as Raw Materials	102.19	13.00	239.85	61.07	258.57
以非农产品为原料	Using Non-Farm Products as Raw Materials	46.19	6.77	100.82	38.12	94.64
重工业	**Enterprises of Heavy Industry**	**578.93**	**70.61**	**883.11**	**610.30**	**642.85**
采掘工业	Mining and Quarrying	26.69	2.68	47.94	17.89	41.81
原料工业	Raw Materials Industry	378.28	50.79	420.06	489.56	320.39
加工工业	Manufacturing Industry	173.96	17.14	415.11	102.85	280.65
按企业规模分:	**Grouped by Size of Enterprises**					
特大型企业	Supper Largest Enterprise	68.11	12.82	111.20	60.21	98.21
大一型企业	The First Rank of the Large Enterprises	263.36	29.67	335.29	181.34	384.18
大二型企业	The Second Rank of the Large Enterprises	139.13	15.40	222.49	164.52	150.08
中一型企业	The First Rank of the Medium-sized Enterprises	39.40	5.57	90.34	49.72	45.82
中二型企业	The Second Rank of the Medium-sized Enterprises	47.74	5.39	96.20	55.89	53.58
小型企业	Small Enterprises	169.57	21.53	368.26	197.80	264.19

单位:亿元　　10-2 续表 3 continued　　(100 million yuan)

指标	Item	累计折旧 Add up Depreciation of Fixed Assets	#本年折旧 Depreciation of this Year	流动负债 Total Liquid Liabilities	长期负债 Long-term Liabilities	所有者权益 Creditors Equity
按行业划分:	**Grouped by Sector**					
煤炭采选业	Coal Mining and Dressing	15.75	1.51	28.96	10.14	26.53
黑色金属矿采选业	Ferrous Metals Mining and Dressing	0.96	0.06	1.89	0.48	1.06
有色金属矿采选业	Nonferrous Metals Mining and Dressing	7.23	0.92	10.59	5.50	9.49
非金属矿采选业	Nonmetal Minerals Mining and Dressing	4.30	0.36	6.31	2.17	5.44
其他矿采选业	Other Types of Mining and Dressing					
木材及竹材采运业	Logging and Transport of Timber and Bamboo	0.57	0.05	1.91	0.56	1.41
食品加工业	Food Processing	12.00	1.18	41.14	7.30	43.34
食品制造业	Food Manufacturing	3.81	0.39	9.63	2.54	7.61
饮料制造业	Beverage Manufacturing	8.90	1.40	32.32	8.10	29.31
烟草加工业	Tobacco Processing	35.65	5.26	52.43	10.54	98.11
纺织业	Textile Industry	13.45	1.16	36.65	11.57	14.81
服装及其他纤维制品制造业	Garments and Other Fiber Products	0.80	0.16	4.28	0.71	2.34
皮革毛皮羽绒及其制品业	Leather,Furs,Down and Related Products	1.40	0.13	7.78	1.37	1.40
木材加工及竹、藤、棕、草制品业	Timber Processing,Bamboo,Cane, Palm Fiber and Straw Products	3.22	0.60	7.40	4.99	10.67
家具制造业	Furniture Manufacturing	0.50	0.08	1.12	0.37	1.33
造纸及纸制品业	Paper making and Paper Products	13.62	1.83	26.35	12.12	30.85
印刷业、记录媒介的复制	Printing and Record Medium Reproduction	6.33	0.88	10.50	1.74	10.96
文教体育用品制造业	Cultural,Educational and Sports Goods	0.16	0.01	1.24	0.21	0.13
石油加工及炼焦业	Petroleum Processing and Coking	38.23	5.28	56.08	29.54	30.02
化学原料及化学制品制造业	Raw Chemical Materials and Chemical Products	79.85	7.11	108.20	42.42	84.10
医药制造业	Medical and Pharmaceutical Products	6.47	1.18	23.82	6.75	24.08
化学纤维制造业	Chemical Fiber	8.14	1.42	9.57	10.21	9.02
橡胶制品业	Rubber Products	2.67	0.28	7.16	0.82	4.12
塑料制品业	Plastic Products	3.95	0.41	11.50	2.94	7.68
非金属矿物制品业	Nonmetal Mineral Products	46.48	4.46	85.41	41.75	57.83
黑色金属冶炼及压延加工业	Smelting and Pressing of Ferrous Metals	56.74	9.93	88.82	33.17	82.12
有色金属冶炼及压延加工业	Smelting and Pressing of NonFerrous Metals	28.69	4.11	60.73	22.56	49.01
金属制品业	Metal Products	4.39	0.62	14.63	3.99	8.14
普通机械制造业	Ordinary Machinery	21.16	1.58	54.96	14.95	31.38
专用设备制造业	Special Purpose Equipment	16.71	1.63	48.84	7.66	29.76
交通运输设备制造业	Transport Equipment	35.19	3.72	107.06	20.86	73.86
电气机械及器材制造业	Electric Equipment and Machinery	18.06	1.91	48.00	9.76	37.59
电子及通信设备制造业	Electronic and Telecommunications Equipment	11.22	2.33	49.01	12.58	38.25
仪器仪表及文化、办公用机械制造业	Instruments,Meters,Cultural and Office Machinery	3.35	0.44	13.95	2.55	7.95
其他制造业	Other Types of Manufacturing	1.27	0.18	6.48	0.56	3.31
电力、蒸汽、热水的生产和供应业	Production and Supply of Electric Power, Steam and Hot Water	194.80	25.17	116.36	350.64	84.91
煤气生产和供应业	Production and Supply of Gas	0.95	0.12	2.25	0.95	2.80
自来水的生产和供应业	Production and Supply of Tap Water	13.30	1.93	10.84	10.38	30.81

10-3 独立核算工业企业各种分组的主要财务指标(2001年)

Major Financial Industrial Enterprises with Independent Accounting Systems by Various Characteristics (2001)

单位:亿元 (100 million yuan)

指标	Item	产品销售收入 Sales Revenue	销售费用 Cost of Sales	销售税金及附加 Sales Tax and Extra Charges	销售利润 Sales Profit
总计	**Total**	**1699.15**	**69.53**	**88.18**	**215.78**
按登记注册类型:	**Grouped by Registration**				
内资企业	Internal-invested Enterprises	1565.28	63.05	87.38	195.97
国有企业	State-owned Enterprises	679.27	19.48	71.63	106.60
中央企业	Central Enterprises	292.95	6.95	66.98	54.02
地方企业	Local Enterprises	386.32	12.53	4.65	52.58
集体企业	Collective-owned Enterprises	179.44	8.11	2.75	13.47
股份合作企业	Enterprises Cooperated by Joint-stock	36.66	1.47	0.41	3.39
联营企业	Cooperative Enterprises	7.11	0.34	0.07	0.42
有限责任公司	Limited Liability Company	249.48	10.07	3.94	31.29
股份有限公司	Company Limited by Shares	263.06	13.71	6.20	26.12
私营企业	Individual-owned Enterprises	147.37	9.77	2.34	14.43
其他企业	Enterprises of Other Types of Ownership	2.89	0.10	0.04	0.25
港、澳、台投资经济	Enterprises Funded by Entrepreneurs From Hong Kong,Macao and Taiwan	50.77	2.71	0.37	6.85
外商投资经济	Enterprises funded by Foreigners	83.10	3.77	0.43	12.96
按经济组织类型:	**Grouped by Ownership**				
独资企业	Enterprises Owned by a Sole Investor	930.12	31.07	75.59	126.18
合作、合伙企业	Enterprises of Partnership	71.49	2.88	0.88	5.76
股份有限公司	Company Limited by Shares	290.05	15.40	6.52	30.74
有限责任公司	Limited Liability Company	407.49	20.18	5.19	53.10
国有控股企业	**State-owned or Controlling Share Hold Enterprises**	**1090.22**	**36.54**	**80.32**	**148.93**
农村工业	**Rural Industry**	**107.24**	**5.58**	**1.51**	**8.07**
轻工业	**Enterprises of Light Industry**	**581.34**	**30.69**	**72.64**	**71.17**
以农产品为原料	Using Farm Products as Raw Materials	449.86	21.15	70.36	53.54
以非农产品为原料	Using Non-Farm Products as Raw Materials	131.48	9.54	2.28	17.63
重工业	**Enterprises of Heavy Industry**	**1117.82**	**38.84**	**15.53**	**144.61**
采掘工业	Mining and Quarrying	70.50	2.82	1.06	9.13
原料工业	Raw Materials Industry	623.28	14.15	10.70	77.30
加工工业	Manufacturing Industry	424.04	21.87	3.77	58.18
按企业规模分:	**Grouped by Size of Enterprises**				
特大型企业	Supper Largest Enterprise	161.24	2.02	2.45	19.34
大一型企业	The First Rank of the Large Enterprises	518.01	16.48	65.37	65.85
大二型企业	The Second Rank of the Large Enterprises	231.68	9.23	8.15	43.90
中一型企业	The First Rank of the Medium-sized Enterprises	74.61	5.90	1.87	8.59
中二型企业	The Second Rank of the Medium-sized Enterprises	89.58	4.54	1.86	12.53
小型企业	Small Enterprises	624.03	31.36	8.48	65.57

单位:亿元　　10-3 续表 1　continued　　(100 million yuan)

指标	Item	产品销售收入 Sales Revenue	销售费用 Cost of Sales	销售税金及附加 Sales Tax and Extra Charges	销售利润 Sales Profit
按行业划分:	**Grouped by Sector**				
煤炭采选业	Coal Mining and Dressing	33.81	1.30	0.56	5.42
黑色金属矿采选业	Ferrous Metals Mining and Dressing	2.18	0.10	0.02	0.14
有色金属矿采选业	Nonferrous Metals Mining and Dressing	21.87	0.74	0.21	2.72
非金属矿采选业	Nonmetal Minerals Mining and Dressing	12.60	0.69	0.29	1.17
其他矿采选业	Other Types of Mining and Dressing				
木材及竹材采运业	Logging and Transport of Timber and Bamboo	0.97	0.06	0.07	0.26
食品加工业	Food Processing	90.69	5.42	0.88	6.39
食品制造业	Food Manufacturing	17.69	1.55	0.18	1.94
饮料制造业	Beverage Manufacturing	26.30	2.43	1.83	4.79
烟草加工业	Tobacco Processing	149.10	2.96	66.15	22.46
纺织业	Textile Industry	42.23	1.57	0.30	2.62
服装及其他纤维制品制造业	Garments and Other Fiber Products	9.29	0.74	0.15	0.87
皮革、毛皮、羽绒及其制品业	Leather,Furs,Down and Related Products	14.44	0.38	0.08	0.59
木材加工及竹、藤、棕、草制品业	Timber Processing,Bamboo,Cane, Palm Fiber and Straw Products	18.98	0.83	0.19	1.07
家具制造业	Furniture Manufacturing	10.51	0.48	0.10	0.66
造纸及纸制品业	Paper making and Paper Products	48.21	1.67	0.31	4.82
印刷业、记录媒介的复制	Printing and Record Medium Reproduction	17.19	0.34	0.07	4.71
文教体育用品制造业	Cultural,Educational and Sports Goods	1.15	0.11	0.01	0.15
石油加工及炼焦业	Petroleum Processing and Coking	123.08	0.70	6.33	3.22
化学原料及化学制品制造业	Raw Chemical Materials and Chemical Products	133.45	5.55	0.89	11.92
医药制造业	Medical and Pharmaceutical Products	25.99	4.99	0.33	6.30
化学纤维制造业	Chemical Fiber	16.60	0.36	0.07	1.07
橡胶制品业	Rubber Products	9.49	0.35	0.06	1.04
塑料制品业	Plastic Products	11.57	0.41	0.08	1.28
非金属矿物制品业	Nonmetal Mineral Products	102.66	6.34	1.45	9.32
黑色金属冶炼及压延加工业	Smelting and Pressing of Ferrous Metals	127.36	2.08	0.97	15.77
有色金属冶炼及压延加工业	Smelting and Pressing of Non Ferrous Metals	118.11	2.62	0.74	11.06
金属制品业	Metal Products	23.46	1.00	0.30	2.01
普通机械制造业	Ordinary Machinery	38.26	2.37	0.33	5.62
专用设备制造业	Special Purpose Equipment	40.66	2.57	0.56	9.02
交通运输设备制造业	Transport Equipment	117.92	5.60	1.62	16.06
电气机械及器材制造业	Electric Equipment and Machinery	56.80	5.35	0.29	9.03
电子及通信设备制造业	Electronic and Telecommunications Equipment	51.10	3.06	0.14	6.53
仪器仪表及文化、办公用机械制造业	Instruments,Meters,Cultural and Office Machinery	11.46	0.72	0.05	2.88
其他制造业	Other Types of Manufacturing	15.70	0.82	1.21	1.24
电力、蒸汽、热水的生产和供应业	Production and Supply of Electric Power, Steam and Hot Water	130.95	2.56	1.20	35.92
煤气生产和供应业	Production and Supply of Gas	4.40	0.10	0.00	-0.31
自来水的生产和供应业	Production and Supply of Tap Water	11.95	0.42	0.12	3.35

单位:亿元　　10-3 续表 2　continued　　(100 million yuan)

指标	Item	管理费用 Overhead Expenses	财务费用 Financial Expenses	利润总额 Total Profits	利税总额 Total Per-tax Profits	应付利润 Profits Payable
总计	**Total**	**142.87**	**42.57**	**51.42**	**235.66**	**10.56**
按登记注册类型:	**Grouped by Registration**					
内资企业	Internal-invested Enterprises	134.93	38.49	42.51	218.99	6.37
国有企业	State-owned Enterprises	73.82	19.58	18.41	142.86	1.68
中央企业	Central Enterprises	25.95	7.24	16.84	113.49	0.55
地方企业	Local Enterprises	47.87	12.34	1.57	29.37	1.13
集体企业	Collective-owned Enterprises	8.77	2.95	3.10	11.46	0.61
股份合作企业	Enterprises Cooperated by Joint-stock	2.37	0.63	0.80	2.63	0.25
联营企业	Cooperative Enterprises	0.45	0.09	0.09	0.39	0.01
有限责任公司	Limited Liability Company	26.14	7.92	1.45	18.23	0.78
股份有限公司	Company Limited by Shares	16.81	5.60	12.43	29.34	1.67
私营企业	Individual-owned Enterprises	6.46	1.70	6.12	13.79	1.35
其他企业	Enterprises of Other Types of Ownership	0.11	0.02	0.11	0.29	0.02
港、澳、台投资经济	Enterprises Funded by Entrepreneurs From Hong Kong,Macao and Taiwan	2.97	0.74	3.89	6.43	2.61
外商投资经济	Enterprises funded by Foreigners	4.97	3.34	5.02	10.24	1.58
按经济组织类型:	**Grouped by Ownership**					
独资企业	Enterprises Owned by a Sole Investor	85.27	23.38	23.89	160.46	2.98
合作、合伙企业	Enterprises of Partnership	3.91	1.06	1.61	4.97	0.45
股份有限公司	Company Limited by Shares	18.34	5.84	15.53	34.16	3.78
有限责任公司	Limited Liability Company	35.35	12.29	10.39	36.07	3.35
国有控股企业	**State-owned or Controlling Share Hold Enterprises**	**110.51**	**29.73**	**26.19**	**177.84**	**3.81**
农村工业	**Rural Industry**	**3.68**	**1.53**	**3.55**	**8.11**	**0.45**
轻工业	**Enterprises of Light Industry**	**39.19**	**8.33**	**29.06**	**136.09**	**6.27**
以农产品为原料	Using Farm Products as Raw Materials	26.70	5.69	24.87	122.59	4.38
以非农产品为原料	Using Non-Farm Products as Raw Materials	12.49	2.64	4.19	13.50	1.89
重工业	**Enterprises of Heavy Industry**	**103.68**	**34.24**	**22.36**	**99.57**	**4.30**
采掘工业	Mining and Quarrying	9.58	1.40	0.47	4.89	0.33
原料工业	Raw Materials Industry	45.80	20.74	13.81	66.38	1.46
加工工业	Manufacturing Industry	48.30	12.10	8.08	28.30	2.51
按企业规模分:	**Grouped by Size of Enterprises**					
特大型企业	Supper Largest Enterprise	12.15	4.19	3.64	16.88	0.05
大一型企业	The First Rank of the Large Enterprises	40.66	12.57	23.73	124.67	3.90
大二型企业	The Second Rank of the Large Enterprises	26.90	6.05	9.91	32.53	1.00
中一型企业	The First Rank of the Medium-sized Enterprises	8.46	1.86	0.14	5.93	1.03
中二型企业	The Second Rank of the Medium-sized Enterprises	11.34	2.78	-0.03	7.14	0.23
小型企业	Small Enterprises	43.36	15.12	14.03	48.51	4.35

单位:亿元　　10-3 续表 3　continued　　(100 million yuan)

指标	Item	管理费用 Overhead Expenses	财务费用 Financial Expenses	利润总额 Total Profits	利税总额 Total Per-tax Profits	应付利润 Profits Payable
按行业划分:	**Grouped by Sector**					
煤炭采选业	Coal Mining and Dressing	6.12	0.69	0.16	2.84	0.17
黑色金属矿采选业	Ferrous Metals Mining and Dressing	0.21	0.04	0.02	0.13	0.00
有色金属矿采选业	Nonferrous Metals Mining and Dressing	2.62	0.45	0.26	1.31	0.13
非金属矿采选业	Nonmetal Minerals Mining and Dressing	0.82	0.24	0.14	0.97	0.02
其他矿采选业	Other Types of Mining and Dressing					
木材及竹材采运业	Logging and Transport of Timber and Bamboo	0.28	0.06	-0.09	0.02	0.00
食品加工业	Food Processing	3.88	1.09	2.45	4.22	0.18
食品制造业	Food Manufacturing	1.21	0.23	0.70	1.62	0.36
饮料制造业	Beverage Manufacturing	2.69	0.63	1.70	5.29	1.38
烟草加工业	Tobacco Processing	8.29	0.87	13.81	97.05	0.09
纺织业	Textile Industry	2.77	0.69	-0.42	1.10	0.10
服装及其他纤维制品制造业	Garments and Other Fiber Products	0.53	0.15	0.26	0.67	0.01
皮革毛皮羽绒及其制品业	Leather,Furs,Down and Related Products	0.30	0.22	-0.22	0.16	0.02
木材加工及竹、藤、棕、草制品业	Timber Processing,Bamboo,Cane, Palm Fiber and Straw Products	0.87	0.18	0.37	1.16	0.03
家具制造业	Furniture Manufacturing	0.61	0.10	0.42	0.67	0.05
造纸及纸制品业	Paper making and Paper Products	2.75	0.81	2.01	4.54	0.10
印刷业、记录媒介的复制	Printing and Record Medium Reproduction	1.42	0.25	3.35	4.65	1.66
文教体育用品制造业	Cultural,Educational and Sports Goods	0.13	0.01	0.11	0.19	0.00
石油加工及炼焦业	Petroleum Processing and Coking	5.95	2.61	-2.79	9.29	0.00
化学原料及化学制品制造业	Raw Chemical Materials and Chemical Products	14.07	2.87	1.18	6.69	0.51
医药制造业	Medical and Pharmaceutical Products	3.37	0.73	2.11	4.66	0.88
化学纤维制造业	Chemical Fiber	0.97	-0.05	0.34	1.04	0.29
橡胶制品业	Rubber Products	0.99	0.18	-0.06	0.39	-0.03
塑料制品业	Plastic Products	0.85	0.19	0.34	0.84	0.00
非金属矿物制品业	Nonmetal Mineral Products	9.20	2.82	-0.56	6.35	0.24
黑色金属冶炼及压延加工业	Smelting and Pressing of Ferrous Metals	8.59	2.91	4.85	14.72	0.10
有色金属冶炼及压延加工业	Smelting and Pressing of Non Ferrous Metals	7.62	2.33	4.41	10.61	0.11
金属制品业	Metal Products	1.55	0.48	0.12	1.14	0.07
普通机械制造业	Ordinary Machinery	5.56	1.44	-0.84	1.42	0.16
专用设备制造业	Special Purpose Equipment	6.06	1.07	2.24	5.43	0.24
交通运输设备制造业	Transport Equipment	12.53	3.25	1.70	7.47	0.76
电气机械及器材制造业	Electric Equipment and Machinery	5.76	1.44	2.18	4.77	0.85
电子及通信设备制造业	Electronic and Telecommunications Equipment	4.03	1.78	1.79	4.32	0.95
仪器仪表及文化、办公用机械制造业	Instruments,Meters,Cultural and Office Machinery	2.29	0.43	0.73	1.42	0.03
其他制造业	Other Types of Manufacturing	0.73	0.17	0.47	2.70	0.15
电力、蒸汽、热水的生产和供应业	Production and Supply of Electric Power, Steam and Hot Water	11.28	10.09	8.56	25.18	0.84
煤气生产和供应业	Production and Supply of Gas	0.28	0.02	-0.20	-0.15	0.00
自来水的生产和供应业	Production and Supply of Tap Water	2.92	0.53	0.14	1.00	0.13

10-4 各市、州独立核算工业主要经济指标(2001年)

Major Ecomomic Indicators of Industrial Enterprises with Independent Accounting Systems by Region (2001)

单位：亿元 (100 million yuan)

指标	Item	全省总计 Total	长沙市 Changsha City	株洲市 Zhuzhou City	湘潭市 Xiangtan City	衡阳市 Hengyang City
企业单位数 (个)	Number of Enterprises (unit)	4961	744	455	306	353
#亏损企业	#Loss-making Enterprises	1506	230	143	109	119
工业总产值(现价)	Gross Industrial Output Value	1811.22	370.32	222.69	131.52	140.19
工业增加值(生产法)	Value Added of Industry	606.54	132.84	64.33	40.93	41.12
工业销售产值	Industrial Sales Value	1788.02	363.93	216.99	130.38	140.26
实收资本	Total Capital Hold	674.74	155.29	89.59	52.15	54.08
#外商资本	#Foreign Capital	29.96	17.31	4.05	1.47	1.27
工业中间投入	Industrial Input	1301.09	261.21	168.87	98.56	104.64
全部从业人员年平均人数 (万人)	Annual Average Number of Obtain Employees (10 000 persons)	155.20	23.02	19.05	12.79	16.14
流动资产	Liquid Assets	1171.36	274.22	161.99	96.81	85.14
#存货	#Inventory	373.15	91.77	50.19	33.81	30.82
产成品	Products	133.14	31.46	18.76	9.80	12.29
流动资产年平均余额	Annual Average Balance of Circulating Funds	1155.51	264.74	161.44	96.41	82.07
固定资产	Fixed Assets	1521.05	241.64	142.87	149.74	116.77
固定资产原价合计	Original Value of Fixed Assets	2095.68	315.37	207.25	213.37	165.08
#生产经营用固定资产	#Production and Operating Fixed Assets	1771.15	259.75	179.16	185.78	136.80
累计折旧	Add up Depreciation of Fixed Assets	727.31	101.71	78.37	71.45	57.03
#本年折旧	#Depreciation of the Year	90.38	13.84	8.20	10.39	6.78
固定资产净值年平均余额	Annual Average Balance of Net Value of Fixed Assets	1314.77	207.63	127.35	136.28	103.10
无形及递延资产	Invisible and Deferred Assets	117.63	31.30	13.89	7.17	9.42
资产总计	Total Assets	2978.07	589.19	342.86	259.80	220.02
流动负债合计	Total Liquid Liabilities	1223.78	255.10	155.99	120.02	98.31
长期负债	Long-term Liabilities	709.48	77.75	60.32	56.62	48.82
所有者权益	Creditors Equity	996.06	256.34	123.29	83.16	71.79
产品销售收入	Sales Revenue	1699.15	353.90	210.50	130.19	128.51
产品销售费用	Cost of Sales	69.53	20.42	9.26	3.87	4.27
产品销售税金及附加	Sales Tax and Extra Charges	88.18	35.65	2.33	1.03	1.44
产品销售利润	Sales Profit	215.78	57.90	27.57	18.11	16.68
管理费用	Administrative Expense	142.87	29.67	20.44	11.75	12.10
利息支出	Interest	40.90	6.12	4.09	4.38	3.21
营业利润	Operating Profit	39.19	24.52	3.97	2.71	1.89
利润总额	Total Profit	51.42	24.02	5.90	3.16	2.46
利税总额	Total of Profit and Tax	235.66	83.40	18.73	12.14	9.45
应交所得税	Income Tax Payable	15.09	5.60	2.26	0.83	0.65
应付利润	Profit Payable	10.56	5.71	0.64	0.10	0.46
本年应付工资总额	Total Wages Payable of the Year	134.06	22.39	19.50	12.14	12.68
本年应付福利费	Fringe Benefits Payable of the Year	19.89	3.66	2.77	1.71	1.57
工业增加值率 (%)	Ratio of Added Value to Gross Output Value (%)	28.87	31.09	22.30	25.56	26.74
每百元固定资产原价实现利税 (元)	Per-tax Profits per 100 yuan of Original Volue of Fixed Assets (yuan)	11.25	26.45	9.04	5.69	5.72
每百元销售收入实现利税 (元)	Per-tax Profits per 100 yuan of Sales Revenue (yuan)	13.87	23.57	8.90	9.32	7.35
流动资金周转天数 (天)	Days of Turnover Circulating Funds (day)	244.82	269.30	276.10	266.59	229.91
全部资金利税率 (%)	Ratio of Per-tax Profits to Total Capital (%)	9.54	17.66	6.49	5.22	5.10
产值利税率 (%)	Ratio of Per-tax Profits to Output Value (%)	13.01	22.52	8.41	9.23	6.74
全员劳动生产率(元/人年)	Overall Labor Productivity (yuan/person-year)	89130	138871	96635	85254	70124

注：本表统计范围为全部独立核算国有及年产品销售收入500万元及以上的非国有工业企业。

All state-owned and the non-state-owned industrial enterprises with an annual sales income of over 5 million yuan.

单位：亿元　　10-4 续表 1 continued　　(100 million yuan)

指标	Item	邵阳市 Shaoyang City	岳阳市 Yueyang City	常德市 Changde City	张家界市 Zhangjiajie City	益阳市 Yiyang City
企业单位数 (个)	Number of Enterprises (unit)	400	420	340	53	378
#亏损企业	#Loss-making Enterprises	121	94	118	31	118
工业总产值(现价)	Gross Industrial Output Value	60.50	314.27	150.42	7.93	53.72
工业增加值(生产法)	Value Added of Industry	20.11	88.23	70.66	3.09	14.53
工业销售产值	Industrial Sales Value	59.94	315.36	149.34	7.87	52.66
实收资本	Total Capital Hold	20.40	73.73	53.23	4.69	20.41
#外商资本	#Foreign Capital	0.08	2.02	0.67	0.64	0.38
工业中间投入	Industrial Input	43.12	236.86	89.73	5.26	41.51
全部从业人员年平均人数 (万人)	Annual Average Number of Obtain Employees (10 000 persons)	9.15	14.60	9.50	0.98	7.02
流动资产	Liquid Assets	37.33	140.72	88.24	4.45	39.08
#存货	#Inventory	12.22	39.14	32.41	0.71	13.35
产成品	Products	4.68	17.85	7.22	0.25	6.44
流动资产年平均余额	Annual Average Balance of Circulating Funds	34.80	124.92	85.05	4.34	58.00
固定资产	Fixed Assets	54.15	192.96	114.76	17.75	66.25
固定资产原价合计	Original Value of Fixed Assets	71.19	294.62	146.01	21.79	91.22
#生产经营用固定资产	#Production and Operating Fixed Assets	56.19	279.56	106.51	19.08	72.31
累计折旧	Add up Depreciation of Fixed Assets	23.96	120.12	48.38	4.56	29.01
#本年折旧	#Depreciation of the Year	2.54	12.36	6.74	0.75	2.58
固定资产净值年平均余额	Annual Average Balance of Net Value of Fixed Assets	43.79	171.81	95.96	15.70	54.81
无形及递延资产	Invisible and Deferred Assets	2.53	15.69	8.21	0.37	3.58
资产总计	Total Assets	96.82	369.58	220.45	23.00	120.87
流动负债合计	Total Liquid Liabilities	50.67	144.59	80.31	5.10	49.46
长期负债	Long-term Liabilities	19.73	78.96	56.38	12.72	50.01
所有者权益	Creditors Equity	25.47	116.76	83.76	5.12	21.40
产品销售收入	Sales Revenue	54.57	286.83	138.15	6.46	43.97
产品销售费用	Cost of Sales	2.03	9.47	4.98	0.12	1.77
产品销售税金及附加	Sales Tax and Extra Charges	1.08	7.83	25.41	0.05	0.53
产品销售利润	Sales Profit	5.03	18.49	19.46	0.32	4.12
管理费用	Administrative Expense	5.12	18.25	8.95	0.72	3.77
利息支出	Interest	0.85	6.15	3.17	0.53	1.15
营业利润	Operating Profit	-0.82	-5.00	7.63	-0.99	-0.66
利润总额	Total Profit	-0.10	2.00	6.79	-0.90	-0.52
利税总额	Total of Profit and Tax	3.70	20.65	41.95	-0.43	2.30
应交所得税	Income Tax Payable	0.08	0.88	2.43	0.14	0.15
应付利润	Profit Payable	0.24	0.38	0.89	0.03	0.13
本年应付工资总额	Total Wages Payable of the Year	6.12	13.56	8.23	0.76	4.71
本年应付福利费	Fringe Benefits Payable of the Year	0.89	1.70	1.50	0.10	0.66
工业增加值率 (%)	Ratio of Added Value to Gross Output Value (%)	29.95	25.13	41.45	34.88	24.42
每百元固定资产原价实现利税 (元)	Per-tax Profits per 100 yuan of Original Volue of Fixed Assets (yuan)	5.20	7.01	28.73	-1.97	2.52
每百元销售收入实现利税 (元)	Per-tax Profits per 100 yuan of Sales Revenue (yuan)	6.78	7.20	30.37	-6.66	5.23
流动资金周转天数 (天)	Days of Turnover Circulating Funds (day)	229.58	156.79	221.63	241.86	474.87
全部资金利税率 (%)	Ratio of Per-tax Profits to Total Capital (%)	4.71	6.96	23.18	-2.15	2.04
产值利税率 (%)	Ratio of Per-tax Profits to Output Value (%)	6.12	6.57	27.89	-5.42	4.28
全员劳动生产率(元/人年)	Overall Labor Productivity (yuan/person-year)	52481	136753	94368	46837	68746

单位：亿元　　10-4 续表 2　continued　　(100 million yuan)

指标	Item	郴州市 Chenzhou City	永州市 Yongzhou City	怀化市 Huaihua City	娄底市 Loudi City	湘西州 West Hunan A.P
企业单位数　(个)	Number of Enterprises (unit)	405	308	324	227	248
#亏损企业	#Loss-making Enterprises	48	95	106	101	73
工业总产值(现价)	Gross Industrial Output Value	91.29	72.70	61.36	95.11	39.21
工业增加值(生产法)	Value Added of Industry	33.28	22.75	27.41	32.30	14.97
工业销售产值	Industrial Sales Value	91.02	67.52	61.07	93.56	38.12
实收资本	Total Capital Hold	48.72	24.98	24.39	36.17	16.92
#外商资本	#Foreign Capital	0.19	0.83	0.91	0.06	0.07
工业中间投入	Industrial Input	63.62	53.14	38.58	69.16	26.83
全部从业人员年平均人数　(万人)	Annual Average Number of Obtain Employees (10 000 persons)	10.75	7.13	7.37	13.28	4.41
流动资产	Liquid Assets	50.90	50.18	34.91	61.55	45.84
#存货	#Inventory	13.81	18.47	6.96	17.78	11.73
产成品	Products	5.14	7.86	3.00	5.65	2.75
流动资产年平均余额	Annual Average Balance of Circulating Funds	54.06	47.28	32.90	61.49	48.01
固定资产	Fixed Assets	95.11	56.62	121.05	103.28	48.09
固定资产原价合计	Original Value of Fixed Assets	124.52	72.34	167.77	151.20	53.94
#生产经营用固定资产	#Production and Operating Fixed Assets	107.26	56.03	140.96	131.31	40.45
累计折旧	Add up Depreciation of Fixed Assets	42.26	22.47	51.26	64.16	12.58
#本年折旧	#Depreciation of the Year	5.78	2.86	7.45	8.35	1.75
固定资产净值年平均余额	Annual Average Balance of Net Value of Fixed Assets	79.87	44.63	108.41	84.14	41.29
无形及递延资产	Invisible and Deferred Assets	3.29	3.80	3.59	6.54	8.25
资产总计	Total Assets	159.78	113.94	168.94	181.95	110.86
流动负债合计	Total Liquid Liabilities	53.79	54.43	37.44	68.38	50.19
长期负债	Long-term Liabilities	45.41	29.44	95.26	52.47	25.61
所有者权益	Creditors Equity	59.54	29.79	32.04	55.42	32.17
产品销售收入	Sales Revenue	96.60	63.16	55.51	92.86	37.94
产品销售费用	Cost of Sales	5.57	2.15	2.11	2.41	1.10
产品销售税金及附加	Sales Tax and Extra Charges	4.56	4.06	1.12	1.01	2.08
产品销售利润	Sales Profit	10.64	9.06	11.61	11.51	5.29
管理费用	Administrative Expense	8.28	6.04	5.30	9.13	3.34
利息支出	Interest	2.11	1.72	4.55	1.75	1.13
营业利润	Operating Profit	0.47	1.95	1.68	0.87	0.99
利润总额	Total Profit	1.14	2.13	2.73	1.56	1.05
利税总额	Total of Profit and Tax	11.29	9.37	8.49	8.92	5.71
应交所得税	Income Tax Payable	0.65	0.11	0.24	0.39	0.70
应付利润	Profit Payable	0.74	0.15	0.46	0.05	0.59
本年应付工资总额	Total Wages Payable of the Year	9.84	4.67	5.57	10.79	3.09
本年应付福利费	Welfare Funds Payable of the Year	1.79	0.72	0.80	1.49	0.52
工业增加值率　(%)	Ratio of Added Value to Gross Output Value (%)	32.67	26.86	39.59	28.17	34.07
每百元固定资产原价实现利税 (元)	Per-tax Profits per 100 yuan of Original Volue of Fixed Assets (yuan)	9.07	12.95	5.06	5.90	10.59
每百元销售收入实现利税　(元)	Per-tax Profits per 100 yuan of Sales Revenue (yuan)	11.69	14.84	15.29	9.61	15.05
流动资金周转天数 (天)	Days of Turnover Circulating Funds (day)	201.47	269.49	213.37	238.38	455.55
全部资金利税率　(%)	Ratio of Per-tax Profits to Total Capital (%)	8.43	10.19	6.01	6.13	6.39
产值利税率　(%)	Ratio of Per-tax Profits to Output Value (%)	12.37	12.89	13.84	9.38	14.56
全员劳动生产率(元/人年)	Overall Labor Productivity (yuan/person-year)	63367	88555	58318	47123	68707

10-5 国有及国有控股独立核算工业企业主要指标(2001年)

单位:亿元 (100 million yuan)

指标	Item	企业单位数(个) Number of Enterprises (unit)	#亏损企业 Loss-making Enterprises	工业总产值(现价) Gross Industrial Output Value (current price)
总计	**Total**	**2117**	**879**	**1135.60**
在总计中:轻工业	Light Industry	819	328	327.88
重工业	Heavy Industry	1298	551	807.72
在总计中:特大型企业	Supper Largest Enterprises	4	1	138.04
大一型企业	The First Rank of the Large Enterprises	68	16	489.46
大二型企业	The Second Rank of the Large Enterprises	134	51	206.58
中一型企业	The First Rank of the Medium-sized Enterprises	97	45	63.43
中二型企业	The Second Rank of the Medium-sized Enterprises	191	81	66.97
小型企业	Small Enterprises	1623	685	171.12
煤炭采选业	Coal Mining and Dressing	101	47	23.20
黑色金属矿采选业	Ferrous Metals Mining and Dressing	5	2	0.96
有色金属矿采选业	Nonferrous Metals Mining and Dressing	35	9	7.58
非金属矿采选业	Nonmetal Minerals Mining and Dressing	22	8	3.53
木材及竹材采运业	Logging and Transport of Timber and Bamboo	13	8	0.94
食品加工业	Food Processing	207	81	35.43
食品制造业	Food Manufacturing	45	13	4.56
饮料制造业	Beverage Manufacturing	52	21	14.20
烟草加工业	Tobacco Processing	14	5	148.57
纺织业	Textile Industry	72	33	21.30
服装及其他纤维制品制造业	Garments and Other Fiber Products	12	7	1.20
皮革、毛皮、羽绒及其制品业	Leather,Furs,Down and Related Products	12	4	1.20
木材加工及竹、藤、棕、草制品业	Timber Processing,Bamboo,Cane, Palm Fiber and Straw Products	16	6	3.48
造纸及纸制品业	Paper making and Paper Products	44	15	27.09
印刷业、记录媒介的复制	Printing and Record Medium Reproduction	80	30	9.02
文教体育用品制造业	Cultural,Educational and Sports Goods	8	3	0.06
石油加工及炼焦业	Petroleum Processing and Coking	6	4	136.94
化学原料及化学制品制造业	Raw Chemical Materials and Chemical Products	184	72	96.38
医药制造业	Medical and Pharmaceutical Products	42	15	18.92
化学纤维制造业	Chemical Fiber	10	4	12.43
橡胶制品业	Rubber Products	13	5	4.57
塑料制品业	Plastic Products	23	6	3.48
非金属矿物制品业	Nonmetal Mineral Products	207	89	43.90
黑色金属冶炼及压延加工业	Smelting and Pressing of Ferrous Metals	40	16	108.26
有色金属冶炼及压延加工业	Smelting and Pressing of Non Ferrous Metals	42	9	81.55
金属制品业	Metal Products	36	15	6.13
普通机械制造业	Ordinary Machinery	118	59	24.09
专用设备制造业	Special Purpose Equipment	103	50	25.94
交通运输设备制造业	Transport Equipment	96	48	103.26
电气机械及器材制造业	Electric Equipment and Machinery	60	25	20.13
电子及通信设备制造业	Electronic and Telecommunications Equipment	36	15	13.60
仪器仪表及文化、办公用机械制造业	Instruments,Meters,Cultural and Office Machinery	20	12	9.18
其他制造业	Other Types of Manufacturing	10	3	0.22
电力、蒸汽、热水的生产和供应业	Production and Supply of Electric Power, Steam and Hot Water	210	82	99.09
煤气生产和供应业	Production and Supply of Gas	5	5	1.14
自来水的生产和供应业	Production and Supply of Tap Water	108	47	12.16

Major Indicators of State - Owned and State-owned Share-holding Industrial Enterprises with Independent Accounting Systems (2001)

单位:亿元 (100 million yuan)

工业增加值(生产法) Value Added of Industry (by producing)	工业中间投入 Industrial Inter-mediate Input	本年应付工资 Wages Payable in This Year	本年应付福利费 Welfare Funds Payable in This Year	全部从业人员年均人数(万人) Average Number of Employees (10000 persons)	固定资产净值年均余额 Annual Average Balance of Net Value of Fixed Assets	流动负债 Total Liquid Liabilities	长期负债 Long-term Liabilities	所有者权益 Creditors' Equity
416.88	**790.17**	**96.16**	**14.81**	**100.83**	**1055.99**	**945.90**	**627.08**	**729.15**
165.04	188.26	20.62	2.92	22.82	194.02	232.94	79.36	233.39
251.84	601.91	75.54	11.89	78.01	861.97	712.96	547.72	495.76
46.39	101.29	10.04	1.39	6.73	107.60	85.23	52.84	81.93
194.41	327.40	30.82	4.17	24.82	345.14	308.18	163.97	353.17
74.85	144.81	21.27	4.18	20.81	216.94	201.95	159.83	125.76
22.39	44.23	6.25	1.16	7.29	79.17	80.87	48.04	41.01
20.70	49.89	7.68	1.17	10.05	77.56	80.24	53.14	34.15
58.14	122.55	20.10	2.74	31.13	229.58	189.43	149.26	93.13
8.82	15.99	6.80	1.43	11.05	23.04	26.10	9.38	21.10
0.33	0.67	0.13	0.02	0.15	1.18	1.53	0.42	0.67
3.17	4.85	2.10	0.60	2.27	8.61	7.24	4.01	5.94
1.38	2.46	0.64	0.08	0.88	4.71	4.92	1.65	3.49
0.30	0.67	0.18	0.02	0.44	1.45	1.91	0.56	1.41
10.96	24.88	1.22	0.17	2.15	19.57	30.09	5.29	28.43
1.24	3.53	0.30	0.03	0.54	2.62	4.41	1.54	1.23
6.31	8.98	1.12	0.15	1.50	12.99	24.71	6.24	18.94
108.84	56.81	4.34	0.58	1.78	41.64	52.07	10.46	97.86
5.64	16.38	2.84	0.40	4.27	15.71	22.22	9.28	3.79
0.39	0.86	0.23	0.03	0.30	0.64	1.37	0.30	0.26
0.38	0.86	0.12	0.12	0.19	1.08	2.98	0.72	-1.34
1.18	2.52	0.35	0.05	0.47	9.38	4.31	2.72	6.24
8.40	20.15	1.84	0.29	2.02	16.37	17.98	10.55	19.75
3.19	6.34	0.92	0.13	1.09	6.04	6.92	1.26	5.17
0.01	0.05	0.01	0.00	0.05	0.27	1.00	0.10	-0.32
30.42	112.26	3.61	0.53	2.07	61.90	55.74	29.53	29.85
23.54	75.78	8.68	1.17	9.33	104.37	91.73	37.21	63.84
6.00	14.26	1.49	0.21	1.44	12.88	16.56	5.43	14.12
1.47	11.53	0.86	0.13	0.98	15.27	8.54	8.84	6.69
1.31	3.42	0.51	0.04	0.77	3.04	5.00	0.51	2.07
1.10	2.50	0.24	0.03	0.41	3.89	3.89	1.76	1.69
12.69	34.03	5.75	0.80	9.08	55.94	58.39	27.83	38.67
37.76	78.75	9.88	1.27	7.89	100.44	83.03	31.67	77.43
19.38	66.26	6.23	0.91	4.75	38.41	46.54	19.42	35.87
1.62	4.76	0.65	0.10	0.80	4.86	8.14	2.10	2.96
6.09	19.09	3.26	0.40	4.73	25.63	43.51	13.30	16.82
8.63	18.78	3.89	0.90	4.78	22.81	39.12	6.61	22.87
25.38	81.07	8.46	1.14	6.70	56.17	94.84	19.08	61.08
5.08	15.56	2.67	0.43	2.93	18.59	28.54	6.73	14.12
3.42	10.65	0.98	0.11	1.08	10.66	14.84	4.40	18.07
2.67	6.95	0.99	0.14	0.79	5.69	9.29	2.14	6.97
0.10	0.13	0.06	0.01	0.08	0.33	0.47	0.03	0.24
60.54	51.50	9.83	1.69	7.97	306.42	97.41	330.77	67.17
0.08	1.10	0.31	0.04	0.31	3.40	1.98	0.95	2.35
6.30	6.55	2.41	0.32	2.13	28.32	8.93	10.21	29.27

单位:亿元 10-5 续表 continued (100 million yuan)

指标	Item	流动资产年均余额 Annual Average Balance of Circulating Funds	实收资本 Total Capital Hold	流动资产合计 Total Circulating Funds
总计	**Total**	**886.26**	**475.74**	**895.79**
在总计中：轻工业	Light Industry	245.33	128.25	249.13
重工业	Heavy Industry	640.93	347.49	646.66
在总计中：特大型企业	Supper Largest Enterprises	78.36	25.86	80.89
大一型企业	The First Rank of the Large Enterprises	352.32	202.98	343.71
大二型企业	The Second Rank of the Large Enterprises	194.96	94.10	200.64
中一型企业	The First Rank of the Medium-sized Enterprises	64.25	26.49	64.11
中二型企业	The Second Rank of the Medium-sized Enterprises	63.96	29.63	68.42
小型企业	Small Enterprises	132.41	96.68	138.02
煤炭采选业	Coal Mining and Dressing	25.27	16.46	25.11
黑色金属矿采选业	Ferrous Metals Mining and Dressing	1.23	0.73	1.24
有色金属矿采选业	Nonferrous Metals Mining and Dressing	6.14	5.85	5.94
非金属矿采选业	Nonmetal Minerals Mining and Dressing	4.25	2.29	4.08
木材及竹材采运业	Logging and Transport of Timber and Bamboo	1.21	1.33	1.22
食品加工业	Food Processing	30.25	15.55	30.79
食品制造业	Food Manufacturing	3.41	1.77	3.37
饮料制造业	Beverage Manufacturing	25.75	8.00	26.55
烟草加工业	Tobacco Processing	84.13	33.90	86.94
纺织业	Textile Industry	15.35	8.00	16.02
服装及其他纤维制品制造业	Garments and Other Fiber Products	0.89	0.24	0.95
皮革、毛皮、羽绒及其制品业	Leather,Furs,Down and Related Products	1.04	0.24	1.08
木材加工及竹、藤、棕、草制品业	Timber Processing,Bamboo,Cane, Palm Fiber and Straw Products	2.87	6.11	2.78
造纸及纸制品业	Paper making and Paper Products	17.37	13.51	19.80
印刷业、记录媒介的复制	Printing and Record Medium Reproduction	5.18	4.69	5.60
文教体育用品制造业	Cultural,Educational and Sports Goods	0.44	0.09	0.44
石油加工及炼焦业	Petroleum Processing and Coking	53.69	8.75	49.05
化学原料及化学制品制造业	Raw Chemical Materials and Chemical Products	62.91	59.78	74.31
医药制造业	Medical and Pharmaceutical Products	18.25	7.93	17.07
化学纤维制造业	Chemical Fiber	8.68	5.19	6.86
橡胶制品业	Rubber Products	4.13	1.97	4.39
塑料制品业	Plastic Products	2.51	1.83	2.70
非金属矿物制品业	Nonmetal Mineral Products	44.91	29.85	45.37
黑色金属冶炼及压延加工业	Smelting and Pressing of Ferrous Metals	62.69	26.19	67.31
有色金属冶炼及压延加工业	Smelting and Pressing of Non Ferrous Metals	40.97	29.87	39.58
金属制品业	Metal Products	5.70	3.67	6.04
普通机械制造业	Ordinary Machinery	29.96	15.91	37.10
专用设备制造业	Special Purpose Equipment	38.91	16.28	39.59
交通运输设备制造业	Transport Equipment	91.27	41.94	95.73
电气机械及器材制造业	Electric Equipment and Machinery	24.64	12.34	25.06
电子及通信设备制造业	Electronic and Telecommunications Equipment	17.03	14.00	16.00
仪器仪表及文化、办公用机械制造业	Instruments,Meters,Cultural and Office Machinery	9.88	7.03	9.80
其他制造业	Other Types of Manufacturing	0.31	0.23	0.33
电力、蒸汽、热水的生产和供应业	Production and Supply of Electric Power, Steam and Hot Water	122.16	48.95	102.52
煤气生产和供应业	Production and Supply of Gas	1.14	2.92	1.31
自来水的生产和供应业	Production and Supply of Tap Water	10.85	17.44	11.08

单位:亿元　　10-5 续表 continued　　(100 million yuan)

固定资产原价合计 Original Value of Fixed Assets	累计折旧 Add up Depreciation of Fixed Assets	#本年折旧 Depreciation of this Year	产品销售收入 Sales Revenue	#销售税金及附加 Sales Tax and Extra Charges	#销售利润 Sales Profits	利润总额 Total Profits	利税总额 Total Profits and Tax	应付利润 Profits Payable
1704.19	**601.52**	**72.00**	**1090.22**	**80.32**	**148.93**	**26.19**	**177.84**	**3.81**
305.27	110.15	13.58	312.44	68.48	44.21	16.86	110.68	1.71
1398.92	491.37	58.42	777.78	11.84	104.72	9.33	67.16	2.10
174.01	63.32	11.13	135.09	2.45	17.12	3.58	15.67	0.04
583.34	228.08	25.86	475.02	64.72	56.38	18.99	116.05	1.82
364.19	129.83	13.91	203.76	7.92	39.05	7.93	28.92	0.88
121.64	36.14	5.03	61.89	1.80	5.98	-1.20	3.78	0.18
118.83	40.24	4.39	58.89	1.64	7.80	-1.74	3.52	0.06
342.18	103.91	11.68	155.57	1.79	22.60	-1.37	9.90	0.83
40.77	14.35	1.24	21.43	0.18	3.97	-0.68	1.11	
2.01	0.81	0.04	0.88		0.06	-0.01	0.03	
15.04	6.24	0.73	8.72	0.07	1.49	-0.19	0.32	
8.33	3.48	0.26	3.48	0.13	0.65	-0.14	0.31	
1.92	0.57	0.05	0.97	0.07	0.26	-0.09	0.02	
27.63	6.70	0.58	35.47	0.11	3.05	1.12	1.64	0.04
3.68	1.15	0.09	3.83	0.02	0.46	0.09	0.31	0.14
17.44	5.99	0.61	11.31	1.39	2.51	0.53	3.00	0.46
76.00	35.52	5.24	148.90	66.15	22.42	13.82	97.04	0.08
24.87	9.26	0.72	16.91	0.09	1.21	-0.46	0.28	0.06
0.92	0.28	0.03	1.08	0.01	0.12	0.01	0.06	
1.54	0.45	0.01	0.85		0.01	-0.47	-0.43	
11.57	2.14	0.38	3.23	0.03	0.24	0.05	0.30	
27.78	9.79	1.11	25.96	0.15	2.99	1.05	2.65	0.01
9.91	3.84	0.40	7.66	0.04	1.75	0.95	1.51	0.07
0.35	0.08		0.10		0.01	-0.03	-0.02	
101.19	38.19	5.26	122.53	6.32	3.20	-2.78	9.28	
176.06	73.03	5.82	91.66	0.56	7.55	-0.25	3.24	0.05
18.14	5.07	0.83	15.59	0.15	3.34	0.86	2.36	0.41
22.21	7.13	1.17	12.65	0.06	0.72	0.10	0.73	0.29
4.74	1.84	0.14	4.13	0.02	0.42	-0.27	-0.09	
4.97	1.43	0.11	2.86	0.01	0.33	0.10	0.23	
84.81	29.81	2.48	41.06	0.42	4.93	-1.08	2.16	0.05
158.86	54.90	9.63	110.36	0.73	14.89	4.66	13.65	
64.00	23.58	3.21	78.85	0.40	7.40	3.13	7.60	0.06
7.81	2.28	0.30	5.52	0.04	0.68	-0.30	-0.01	0.03
41.34	15.58	1.07	22.10	0.13	3.30	-1.09	0.13	0.04
37.39	14.81	1.06	23.08	0.37	4.85	-0.25	1.59	0.16
88.84	30.25	3.07	97.06	1.29	13.72	1.50	5.98	0.60
30.74	12.10	1.24	19.53	0.09	3.55	-0.32	0.29	0.03
14.08	5.37	0.45	11.67	0.06	1.87	0.58	1.10	0.24
8.85	2.82	0.32	8.08	0.04	1.84	0.20	0.67	0.02
0.58	0.24	0.01	0.22		0.05	0.01	0.02	0.00
500.24	161.52	21.80	108.98	1.06	29.66	6.32	20.32	0.82
4.46	0.87	0.10	1.02		-0.26	-0.11	-0.07	
42.38	13.02	1.81	11.25	0.10	3.02	-0.02	0.79	0.13

10-6 独立核算工业企业各种分组的主要经济效益指标(2001年)

Major Economic Indicators of Industrial Enterprises with Independent Accounting Systems (2001)

指标	Item	工业增加值率(%) Ratio of Value Added to Gross Industrial Output Value (%)	每百元固定资产原价实现的利税(元) Per-tax Profits per 100 Yuan of Original Value of Fixed Assets (yuan)	每百元销售收入实现的利税(元) Per-tax Profits per 100 Yuan of Sales Revenue (yuan)	流动资金周转天数(天) Number of Days of Turnover Circulating Funds (day)
总计	**Total**	**28.87**	**11.25**	**13.87**	**245**
按登记注册类型:	**Grouped by Registration**				
内资企业	Internal-invested Enterprises	29.15	11.18	13.99	248
国有企业	State-owned Enterprises	35.40	11.80	21.03	295
中央企业	Central Enterprises	50.62	20.49	38.74	272
地方企业	Local Enterprises	25.22	4.47	7.60	312
集体经济	Collective-owned Enterprises	25.35	13.93	6.39	131
股份合作企业	Enterprises Cooperated by Joint-stock	24.63	11.29	7.17	142
联营企业	Cooperative Enterprises	24.97	8.33	5.48	142
有限责任公司	Limited Liability Company	23.08	5.16	7.31	303
股份有限公司	Company Limited by Shares	24.18	13.00	11.15	238
私营企业	Individual-owned Enterprises	24.22	24.13	9.36	133
其他企业	Enterprises of Other Types of Ownership	28.31	22.83	10.03	123
港、澳、台投资经济	Enterprises Funded by Entrepreneurs From Hong Kong,Macao and Taiwan	23.68	19.80	12.65	195
外商投资经济	Enterprises funded by Foreigners	26.90	9.74	12.32	219
按经济组织类型:	**Grouped by Ownership**				
独资企业	Enterprises Owned by a Sole Investor	32.66	12.14	17.25	249
合作、合伙企业	Enterprises of Partnership	25.99	12.38	6.95	134
股份有限公司	Company Limited by Shares	24.47	14.24	11.78	227
有限责任公司	Limited Liability Company	23.61	7.30	8.85	267
国有控股企业	**State-owned or Controlling Share Hold Enterprises**	**30.76**	**10.44**	**16.31**	**293**
农村工业	**Rural Industry**	**25.45**	**20.60**	**7.56**	**95**
按轻重工业分:	**Grouped by Light and Heavy Industry**				
轻工业	Enterprises of Light Industry	35.53	31.40	23.41	225
以农产品为原料	Using Farm Products as Raw Materials	38.29	42.92	27.25	214
以非农产品为原料	Using Non-Farm Products as Raw Materials	26.52	9.14	10.27	262
重工业	Enterprises of Heavy Industry	25.47	5.99	8.91	255
采掘工业	Mining and Quarrying	30.22	6.44	6.94	237
原料工业	Raw Materials Industry	26.77	6.08	10.65	223
加工工业	Manufacturing Industry	22.78	5.72	6.67	305
按企业规模分:	**Grouped by Size of Enterprises**				
特大型企业	Supper Largest Enterprise	24.88	7.95	10.47	204
大一型企业	The First Rank of the Large Enterprises	32.62	19.00	24.07	264
大二型企业	The Second Rank of the Large Enterprises	30.38	8.33	14.04	334
中一型企业	The First Rank of the Medium-sized Enterprises	31.12	4.59	7.95	353
中二型企业	The Second Rank of the Medium-sized Enterprises	27.66	5.13	7.97	328
小型企业	Small Enterprises	26.12	8.53	7.77	182

10-6 续表 1 continued

指标	Item	工业增加值率(%) Ratio of Value Added to Gross Industrial Output Value (%)	每百元固定资产原价实现的利税(元) Per-tax Profits per 100 Yuan of Original Value of Fixed Assets (yuan)	每百元销售收入实现的利税(元) Per-tax Profits per 100 Yuan of Sales Revenue (yuan)	流动资金周转天数(天) Number of Days of Turnover Circulating Funds (day)
按行业划分:	**Grouped by Sector**				
煤炭采选业	Coal Mining and Dressing	31.10	6.23	8.40	313
黑色金属矿采选业	Ferrous Metals Mining and Dressing	27.59	5.20	5.96	266
有色金属矿采选业	Nonferrous Metals Mining and Dressing	30.86	6.66	5.99	170
非金属矿采选业	Nonmetal Minerals Mining and Dressing	29.07	9.12	7.70	175
其他矿采选业	Other Types of Mining and Dressing				
木材及竹材采运业	Logging and Transport of Timber and Bamboo	30.00	1.04	2.06	449
食品加工业	Food Processing	26.55	9.36	4.65	167
食品制造业	Food Manufacturing	23.85	13.88	9.16	181
饮料制造业	Beverage Manufacturing	35.87	17.92	20.11	477
烟草加工业	Tobacco Processing	62.46	127.15	65.09	204
纺织业	Textile Industry	24.45	2.85	2.60	235
服装及其他纤维制品制造业	Garments and Other Fiber Products	24.06	19.42	7.21	137
皮革、毛皮、羽绒及其制品业	Leather,Furs,Downand Related Products	21.17	3.07	1.11	138
木材加工及竹、藤、棕、草制品业	Timber Processing,Bamboo,Cane, Palm Fiber and Straw Products	26.26	6.53	6.11	117
家具制造业	Furniture Manufacturing	24.91	46.85	6.37	59
造纸及纸制品业	Paper making and Paper Products	25.82	11.38	9.42	197
印刷业、记录媒介的复制	Printing and Record Medium Reproduction	35.70	29.32	27.05	207
文教体育用品制造业	Cultural,Educational and Sports Goods	20.80	31.15	16.52	310
石油加工及炼焦业	Petroleum Processing and Coking	19.21	9.16	7.55	158
化学原料及化学制品制造业	Raw Chemical Materials and Chemical Products	22.53	3.35	5.01	220
医药制造业	Medical and Pharmaceutical Products	30.11	19.27	17.93	389
化学纤维制造业	Chemical Fiber	14.00	4.07	6.27	215
橡胶制品业	Rubber Products	22.74	5.47	4.11	243
塑料制品业	Plastic Products	24.74	6.65	7.26	259
非金属矿物制品业	Nonmetal Mineral Products	26.14	4.75	6.19	232
黑色金属冶炼及压延加工业	Smelting and Pressing of Ferrous Metals	26.32	8.91	11.56	194
有色金属冶炼及压延加工业	Smelting and Pressing of NonFerrous Metals	16.98	13.04	8.98	169
金属制品业	Metal Products	22.54	7.59	4.86	181
普通机械制造业	Ordinary Machinery	23.68	2.51	3.71	398
专用设备制造业	Special Purpose Equipment	29.96	12.39	13.35	438
交通运输设备制造业	Transport Equipment	20.81	7.28	6.33	318
电气机械及器材制造业	Electric Equipment and Machinery	21.89	9.67	8.40	323
电子及通信设备制造业	Electronic and Telecommunications Equipment	19.19	7.71	8.45	274
仪器仪表及文化、办公用机械制造业	Instruments,Meters,Culturaland Office Machinery	25.57	13.45	12.39	428
其他制造业	Other Types of Manufacturing	29.66	64.44	17.20	141
电力、蒸汽、热水的生产和供应业	Production and Supply of Electric Power, Steam and Hot Water	50.94	4.43	19.23	372
煤气生产和供应业	Production and Supply of Gas	7.99	-3.20	-3.41	134
自来水的生产和供应业	Production and Supply of Tap Water	48.69	2.24	8.37	344

10-6 续表 2 continued

指标	Item	全部资金利税率(%) Ratio of Per-tax Profits to Total Capital (%)	产值利税率(%) Ratio of Per-tax Profits to Gross Output Value (%)	全员劳动生产率(元/人·年) Overall Labor Productivity (yuan/person·year)
总计	**Total**	**9.54**	**13.01**	**89130**
按登记注册类型:	**Grouped by Registration**			
内资企业	Internal-invested Enterprises	9.48	13.16	82408
国有企业	State-owned Enterprises	10.89	20.25	66100
中央企业	Central Enterprises	20.48	38.19	121626
地方企业	Local Enterprises	3.87	7.20	53603
集体经济	Collective-owned Enterprises	9.72	5.66	71500
股份合作企业	Enterprises Cooperated by Joint-stock	8.67	6.24	67328
联营企业	Cooperative Enterprises	6.66	5.37	80253
有限责任公司	Limited Liability Company	4.18	6.84	91961
股份有限公司	Company Limited by Shares	9.51	10.64	185704
私营企业	Individual-owned Enterprises	14.23	8.58	95597
其他企业	Enterprises of Other Types of Ownership	14.95	8.31	98462
港、澳、台投资经济	Enterprises Funded by Entrepreneurs From Hong Kong,Macao and Taiwan	12.83	11.15	164093
外商投资经济	Enterprises funded by Foreigners	9.29	11.43	346364
按经济组织类型:	**Grouped by Ownership**			
独资企业	Enterprises Owned by a Sole Investor	10.88	16.27	69362
合作、合伙企业	Enterprises of Partnership	9.19	6.06	75047
股份有限公司	Company Limited by Shares	10.44	11.23	174823
有限责任公司	Limited Liability Company	5.87	8.23	120852
国有控股企业	**State-owned or Controlling Share Hold Enterprises**	**9.16**	**15.66**	**81172**
农村工业	**Rural Industry**	**14.71**	**6.88**	**81039**
按轻重工业分:	**Grouped by Light and Heavy Industry**			
轻工业	Enterprises of Light Industry	21.13	21.48	97487
以农产品为原料	Using Farm Products as Raw Materials	27.30	25.28	117309
以非农产品为原料	Using Non-Farm Products as Raw Materials	6.92	9.09	67048
重工业	Enterprises of Heavy Industry	5.45	8.45	85474
采掘工业	Mining and Quarrying	5.27	6.64	25276
原料工业	Raw Materials Industry	6.23	10.32	96148
加工工业	Manufacturing Industry	4.24	6.14	101344
按企业规模分:	**Grouped by Size of Enterprises**			
特大型企业	Supper Largest Enterprise	7.47	10.33	219296
大一型企业	The First Rank of the Large Enterprises	16.31	23.27	136483
大二型企业	The Second Rank of the Large Enterprises	7.28	13.68	82889
中一型企业	The First Rank of the Medium-sized Enterprises	3.79	7.76	74611
中二型企业	The Second Rank of the Medium-sized Enterprises	4.16	7.14	67089
小型企业	Small Enterprises	6.88	6.95	68905

10-6 续表 3 continued

指标	Item	全部资金利税率(%) Ratio of Per-tax Profits to Total Capital (%)	产值利税率(%) Ratio of Per-tax Profits to Gross Output Value (%)	全员劳动生产率(元/人·年) Overall Labor Productivity (yuan/person·year)
按行业划分:	**Grouped by Sector**			
煤炭采选业	Coal Mining and Dressing	4.98	7.96	14615
黑色金属矿采选业	Ferrous Metals Mining and Dressing	4.15	5.58	53611
有色金属矿采选业	Nonferrous Metals Mining and Dressing	5.89	6.08	47443
非金属矿采选业	Nonmetal Minerals Mining and Dressing	7.95	7.02	59831
其他矿采选业	Other Types of Mining and Dressing			
木材及竹材采运业	Logging and Transport of Timber and Bamboo	0.75	2.13	20227
食品加工业	Food Processing	5.69	4.38	179330
食品制造业	Food Manufacturing	9.45	7.31	87436
饮料制造业	Beverage Manufacturing	9.47	17.17	96360
烟草加工业	Tobacco Processing	76.91	65.05	359227
纺织业	Textile Industry	2.12	2.16	57181
服装及其他纤维制品制造业	Garments and Other Fiber Products	10.88	6.50	64531
皮革、毛皮、羽绒及其制品业	Leather,Furs,Downand Related Products	1.71	0.99	126571
木材加工及竹、藤、棕、草制品业	Timber Processing,Bamboo,Cane, Palm Fiber and Straw Products	5.70	5.60	82892
家具制造业	Furniture Manufacturing	24.28	6.47	144259
造纸及纸制品业	Paper making and Paper Products	8.84	8.75	114332
印刷业、记录媒介的复制	Printing and Record Medium Reproduction	23.65	24.68	94968
文教体育用品制造业	Cultural,Educational and Sports Goods	13.10	16.67	70769
石油加工及炼焦业	Petroleum Processing and Coking	8.01	6.76	277810
化学原料及化学制品制造业	Raw Chemical Materials and Chemical Products	3.30	4.68	101710
医药制造业	Medical and Pharmaceutical Products	10.31	14.19	162641
化学纤维制造业	Chemical Fiber	3.81	6.28	151639
橡胶制品业	Rubber Products	3.52	3.67	64820
塑料制品业	Plastic Products	5.05	5.70	93657
非金属矿物制品业	Nonmetal Mineral Products	4.13	5.62	45015
黑色金属冶炼及压延加工业	Smelting and Pressing of Ferrous Metals	8.49	11.66	97830
有色金属冶炼及压延加工业	Smelting and Pressing of NonFerrous Metals	9.88	8.48	144032
金属制品业	Metal Products	5.39	4.34	84877
普通机械制造业	Ordinary Machinery	1.83	3.33	59343
专用设备制造业	Special Purpose Equipment	7.08	12.15	68629
交通运输设备制造业	Transport Equipment	4.40	5.90	135600
电气机械及器材制造业	Electric Equipment and Machinery	5.91	7.48	107834
电子及通信设备制造业	Electronic and Telecommunications Equipment	5.46	8.10	455174
仪器仪表及文化、办公用机械制造业	Instruments,Meters,Culturaland Office Machinery	6.92	10.81	122400
其他制造业	Other Types of Manufacturing	29.80	14.58	36432
电力、蒸汽、热水的生产和供应业	Production and Supply of Electric Power, Steam and Hot Water	5.25	20.95	59766
煤气生产和供应业	Production and Supply of Gas	-2.91	-3.32	97353
自来水的生产和供应业	Production and Supply of Tap Water	2.39	7.76	20093

10-7 独立核算国有及国有控股工业企业

主要经济效益指标(2001年)

Major Economic Benefit Indicators of State – Owned and State – Owned Share – Holding Industrial Enterprises (2001)

单位：%　　　　(%)

指标	Item	工业增加值率 Ratio of Added to Gross Industrial Output Value	总资产贡献率 Ratio of Total Assets to Industrial Output Value	总资产负债率 Assets-Liability Ratio	成本费用利润率 Ratio of Profits to Cost
总计	**Total**	**30.76**	**9.00**	**68.93**	**2.62**
按登记注册类型：	**Grouped by Registration**				
内资企业	Internal-invested Enterprises	30.74	8.96	69.17	2.48
国有企业	State-owned Enterprises	35.40	10.32	72.31	3.10
中央企业	Central Enterprises	50.62	19.31	74.74	8.20
地方企业	Local Enterprises	25.22	4.36	70.55	0.40
集体经济	Collective-owned Enterprises	25.00	4.43	87.60	-1.12
股份合作企业	Enterprises Cooperated by Joint-stock	29.39	4.58	50.43	4.28
联营企业	Cooperative Enterprises	24.66	14.15	62.41	2.71
有限责任公司	Limited Liability Company	22.17	4.59	65.42	-0.17
股份有限公司	Company Limited by Shares	22.52	7.84	58.70	3.19
私营企业	Individual-owned Enterprises		0.00		
港、澳、台投资经济	Enterprises Funded by Entrepreneurs From Hong Kong,Macao and Taiwan	23.32	5.67	49.82	3.14
外商投资经济	Enterprises funded by Foreigners	37.97	19.31	34.30	23.04
按经济组织类型：	**Grouped by Ownership**				
独资企业	Enterprises Owned by a Sole Investor	35.37	10.31	72.33	3.08
合作、合伙企业	Enterprises of Partnership	26.17	6.96	54.49	3.50
股份有限公司	Company Limited by Shares	22.56	7.85	58.53	3.21
有限责任公司	Limited Liability Company	22.80	4.98	64.45	0.60
按轻重工业分：	**Grouped by Light and Heavy Industry**				
轻工业	Light Industry	44.10	21.54	57.51	7.30
以农产品为原料	Using Farm Products as Raw Materials	47.10	27.60	55.01	9.35
以非农产品为原料	Using Non-Farm Products as Raw Materials	27.40	3.71	65.03	-0.52
重工业	Heavy Industry	25.68	5.17	72.42	1.21
采掘工业	Mining and Quarrying	33.87	2.34	64.59	-3.28
原料工业	Raw Materials Industry	26.89	6.52	75.92	2.08
加工工业	Manufacturing Industry	22.41	3.33	67.52	0.29
按企业规模分：	**Grouped by Size of Enterprises**				
特大型企业	Supper Largest Enterprise	26.38	12.20	62.76	2.76
大一型企业	The First Rank of the Large Enterprises	32.25	14.59	58.73	4.72
大二型企业	The Second Rank of the Large Enterprises	31.11	6.93	74.57	4.25
中一型企业	The First Rank of the Medium-sized Enterprises	31.78	3.08	76.00	-1.90
中二型企业	The Second Rank of the Medium-sized Enterprises	27.69	3.49	79.87	-2.88
小型企业	Small Enterprises	30.50	3.85	78.63	-0.86

单位：%　　10-7 续表 1　　(%)

指标	Item	工业增加值率 Ratio of Added to Gross Industrial Output Value	总资产贡献率 Ratio of Total Assets to Industrial Output Value	总资产负债率 Assets-Liability Ratio	成本费用利润率 Ratio of Profits to Cost
按行业划分：	**Grouped by Sector**				
煤炭采选业	Coal Mining and Dressing	33.52	2.50	62.85	-2.94
黑色金属矿采选业	Ferrous Metals Mining and Dressing	29.73	2.27	74.43	-0.97
有色金属矿采选业	Nonferrous Metals Mining and Dressing	37.43	3.10	65.61	-2.01
非金属矿采选业	Nonmetal Minerals Mining and Dressing	34.07	4.16	65.31	-3.99
木材及竹材采运业	Logging and Transport of Timber and Bamboo	30.00	1.71	63.40	-9.28
食品加工业	Food Processing	29.57	3.40	55.83	3.20
食品制造业	Food Manufacturing	24.46	4.35	82.92	2.40
饮料制造业	Beverage Manufacturing	41.35	6.98	62.07	5.45
烟草加工业	Tobacco Processing	62.59	64.20	39.12	19.90
纺织业	Textile Industry	23.89	1.64	89.37	-2.61
服装及其他纤维制品制造业	Garments and Other Fiber Products	29.10	4.71	86.53	0.91
皮革、毛皮、羽绒及其制品业	Leather,Furs,Down and Related Products	29.46	-15.80	156.78	-48.45
木材加工及竹、藤、棕、草制品业	Timber Processing,Bamboo,Cane, Palm Fiber and Straw Products	29.72	2.18	52.98	1.47
造纸及纸制品业	Paper making and Paper Products	26.52	7.31	59.11	4.16
印刷业、记录媒介的复制	Printing and Record Medium Reproduction	29.95	12.83	61.29	13.69
文教体育用品制造业	Cultural,Educational and Sports Goods	14.29	-2.23	141.03	-23.08
石油加工及炼焦业	Petroleum Processing and Coking	19.25	9.40	76.74	-2.29
化学原料及化学制品制造业	Raw Chemical Materials and Chemical Products	21.63	2.54	69.60	-0.26
医药制造业	Medical and Pharmaceutical Products	27.87	7.31	61.67	5.84
化学纤维制造业	Chemical Fiber	9.77	4.59	73.89	0.79
橡胶制品业	Rubber Products	25.44	0.12	72.60	-6.11
塑料制品业	Plastic Products	27.50	3.26	78.11	3.57
非金属矿物制品业	Nonmetal Mineral Products	25.29	2.88	69.09	-2.50
黑色金属冶炼及压延加工业	Smelting and Pressing of Ferrous Metals	26.57	8.61	59.76	4.42
有色金属冶炼及压延加工业	Smelting and Pressing of Non Ferrous Metals	15.06	9.70	64.88	3.98
金属制品业	Metal Products	23.44	1.75	77.58	-5.14
普通机械制造业	Ordinary Machinery	22.26	1.60	77.15	-4.64
专用设备制造业	Special Purpose Equipment	28.65	3.30	67.11	-1.08
交通运输设备制造业	Transport Equipment	20.92	5.23	65.66	1.57
电气机械及器材制造业	Electric Equipment and Machinery	22.52	2.53	71.70	-1.61
电子及通信设备制造业	Electronic and Telecommunications Equipment	21.91	2.43	51.57	4.82
仪器仪表及文化、办公用机械制造业	Instruments,Meters,Culturaland Office Machinery	25.48	5.68	62.12	2.38
其他制造业	Other Types of Manufacturing	43.48	4.11	68.49	4.55
电力、蒸汽、热水的生产和供应业	Production and Supply of Electric Power,Steam and Hot Water	52.45	5.92	86.45	6.61
煤气生产和供应业	Production and Supply of Gas	6.11	-0.75	55.49	-7.14
自来水的生产和供应业	Production and Supply of Tap Water	48.88	2.55	39.55	-0.18

指标	Item	产品销售率(%) Proportion of Products Sold (%)	流动资金周转次数(次) Number of Times of Annual of Turnover Circulating Funds (time)	全员劳动生产率(元/人年) Overall Labor Productivity (yuan/person-year)
总计	**Total**	**99.20**	**1.23**	**81172**
按登记注册类型:	**Grouped by Registration**			
内资企业	Internal-invested Enterprises	99.20	1.23	80648
国有企业	State-owned Enterprises	98.91	1.22	66099
中央企业	Central Enterprises	99.24	1.32	121626
地方企业	Local Enterprises	98.66	1.16	53600
集体经济	Collective-owned Enterprises	96.15	5.87	60750
股份合作企业	Enterprises Cooperated by Joint-stock	95.65	1.57	66786
联营企业	Cooperative Enterprises	100.00	3.25	143043
有限责任公司	Limited Liability Company	98.44	1.06	90278
股份有限公司	Company Limited by Shares	100.98	1.43	204466
私营企业	Individual-owned Enterprises			
港、澳、台投资经济	Enterprises Funded by Entrepreneurs From Hong Kong,Macao and Taiwan	99.06	1.26	126250
外商投资经济	Enterprises funded by Foreigners	98.77	1.58	186944
按经济组织类型:	**Grouped by Ownership**			
独资企业	Enterprises Owned by a Sole Investor	98.90	1.23	66070
合作、合伙企业	Enterprises of Partnership	98.20	2.32	103269
股份有限公司	Company Limited by Shares	100.98	1.44	204460
有限责任公司	Limited Liability Company	98.48	1.07	92647
按轻重工业分:	**Grouped by Light and Heavy Industry**			
轻工业	Light Industry	99.43	1.27	98467
以农产品为原料	Using Farm Products as Raw Materials	99.65	1.33	118024
以非农产品为原料	Using Non-Farm Products as Raw Materials	98.25	1.02	60860
重工业	Heavy Industry	99.10	1.21	76102
采掘工业	Mining and Quarrying	101.52	0.92	13505
原料工业	Raw Materials Industry	100.43	1.46	94009
加工工业	Manufacturing Industry	96.54	0.95	86707
按企业规模分:	**Grouped by Size of Enterprises**			
特大型企业	Supper Largest Enterprise	100.83	1.72	145164
大一型企业	The First Rank of the Large Enterprises	100.25	1.35	126632
大二型企业	The Second Rank of the Large Enterprises	97.26	1.05	78789
中一型企业	The First Rank of the Medium-sized Enterprises	98.75	0.96	67270
中二型企业	The Second Rank of the Medium-sized Enterprises	97.85	0.92	59920
小型企业	Small Enterprises	97.93	1.17	42853

10-7 续表 3 continued

指标	Item	产品销售率(%) Proportion of Products Sold (%)	流动资金周转次数(次) Number of Times of Annual of Turnover Circulating Funds (time)	全员劳动生产率(元/人年) Overall Labor Productivity (yuan/person-year)
按行业划分:	**Grouped by Sector**			
煤炭采选业	Coal Mining and Dressing	102.80	0.85	9466
黑色金属矿采选业	Ferrous Metals Mining and Dressing	101.04	0.72	58667
有色金属矿采选业	Nonferrous Metals Mining and Dressing	97.89	1.42	27093
非金属矿采选业	Nonmetal Minerals Mining and Dressing	101.70	0.82	32841
木材及竹材采运业	Logging and Transport of Timber and Bamboo	104.26	0.80	20227
食品加工业	Food Processing	100.42	1.17	118698
食品制造业	Food Manufacturing	98.68	1.12	65000
饮料制造业	Beverage Manufacturing	96.69	0.44	70667
烟草加工业	Tobacco Processing	100.03	1.77	362360
纺织业	Textile Industry	95.54	1.10	51382
服装及其他纤维制品制造业	Garments and Other Fiber Products	103.33	1.21	35667
皮革、毛皮、羽绒及其制品业	Leather,Furs,Down and Related Products	97.50	0.82	67368
木材加工及竹、藤、棕、草制品业	Timber Processing,Bamboo,Cane, Palm Fiber and Straw Products	95.69	1.13	76596
造纸及纸制品业	Paper making and Paper Products	100.04	1.49	116089
印刷业、记录媒介的复制	Printing and Record Medium Reproduction	97.89	1.48	63303
文教体育用品制造业	Cultural,Educational and Sports Goods	83.33	0.23	10000
石油加工及炼焦业	Petroleum Processing and Coking	103.02	2.28	279807
化学原料及化学制品制造业	Raw Chemical Materials and Chemical Products	99.79	1.46	97170
医药制造业	Medical and Pharmaceutical Products	99.31	0.85	180972
化学纤维制造业	Chemical Fiber	101.85	1.46	157245
橡胶制品业	Rubber Products	100.66	1.00	56234
塑料制品业	Plastic Products	96.84	1.14	91707
非金属矿物制品业	Nonmetal Mineral Products	97.18	0.91	42181
黑色金属冶炼及压延加工业	Smelting and Pressing of Ferrous Metals	99.46	1.76	98251
有色金属冶炼及压延加工业	Smelting and Pressing of Non Ferrous Metals	99.18	1.92	139137
金属制品业	Metal Products	98.04	0.97	66000
普通机械制造业	Ordinary Machinery	98.38	0.74	52854
专用设备制造业	Special Purpose Equipment	97.80	0.59	54477
交通运输设备制造业	Transport Equipment	92.79	1.06	144269
电气机械及器材制造业	Electric Equipment and Machinery	98.46	0.79	67474
电子及通信设备制造业	Electronic and Telecommunications Equipment	98.97	0.69	200926
仪器仪表及文化、办公用机械制造业	Instruments,Meters,Culturaland Office Machinery	101.74	0.82	114684
其他制造业	Other Types of Manufacturing	104.55	0.71	27500
电力、蒸汽、热水的生产和供应业	Production and Supply of Electric Power,Steam and Hot Water	100.10	0.89	44429
煤气生产和供应业	Production and Supply of Gas	97.37	0.89	18387
自来水的生产和供应业	Production and Supply of Tap Water	96.05	1.04	17746

10-8 工业产品产量

Output of Industrial Products

产品	Item	1995	1999	2000	2001
化学纤维 (万吨)	Chemical Fiber (10 000 tons)	4.8	6.28	7.79	6.97
纱(混合数) (万吨)	Yarn (10 000 tons)	14.66	13.95	16.63	16.67
纯棉纱 (万吨)	Pure Cotton Yarn (10 000 tons)	9.04	-	-	-
布(混合数) (亿米)	Cloth (100 million m)	4.89	2.87	3.41	3.05
纯棉布 (亿米)	Pure Cotton Cloth (100 million m)	2.04	0.57	0.7	0.49
针棉织品(折用纱量) (万吨)	Cotton Knitwear (10 000 tons)	0.75	0.67	0.65	0.64
毛巾 (万条)	Towel (10 000 cartons)	8633	5106	5394	5304
袜子 (万双)	Socks (10 000 pairs)	3895	-	-	-
服装 (万件)	Clothes (10 000 pieces)	6861	1042	1151	2094
毛线 (吨)	Knitting Wool (ton)	1407	770.02	1242	1466.94
呢绒 (万米)	Woden Piece Goods (10 000 m)	3	7	-	-
麻袋 (万条)	Gunny-bag (10 000 cartons)	1371	620.11	339.75	165.97
丝(不包括土丝) (吨)	Silk (tons)	95	-	-	-
丝织品 (万米)	Silk Fabrics (10 000 m)	274	2.53	10	-
机制纸浆 (万吨)	Machine_made Paper Pulp (10 000 tons)	62.01	17.01	31.9	34.94
机制纸及纸板 (万吨)	Machine_made Paper and Paper boards (10 000 tons)	94.02	53.04	70.07	77.61
缝纫机 (万架)	Sewing Machine (10 000 units)	10.03	0.95	1.56	0.94
自行车 (万辆)	Bike (10 000 units)	6.67	-	-	-
手表 (万只)	Watch (10 000 units)	94.42	-	-	-
日用搪瓷制品 (吨)	Household enamel Product (ton)	3036	3275.8	3187.7	3062
日用陶瓷器 (亿件)	Household Ceramics (100 million units)	10.64	11.12	9.28	9.61
日用精铝制品 (吨)	Household Aluminium Product (10 000 tons)	1590	1580.9	2479.5	979
日用玻璃制品 (万吨)	Household Glass Product (10 000 tons)	14.35	6.62	5.4	4.16
保温瓶 (万个)	Vacuum Flask (10 000 units)	973.59	1250.2	1300.69	1330
自来水笔 (万支)	Pen (10 000 units)	1102.16	30	-	94
圆珠笔 (万支)	Ball-point pen (10 000 units)	632.58	-	-	-
灯泡 (万只)	Lamp bulb (10 000 units)	12157	8927	12961	10511
合成洗涤剂 (万吨)	Synthetic Detergents (10 000 tons)	6.05	6.79	8.12	9027
肥皂 (万吨)	Soap (10 000 tons)	2.9	1.2	1.1	0.67
牙膏 (万支)	Toothpaste (10 000 units)	3510.15	2642.08	2299.61	2179.67
火柴 (万件)	Match (10 000 units)	99.65	47	46.03	40.21
干电池 (亿只)	Dry Cell (100 million units)	2.61	0.77	0.57	0.31
大米 (万吨)	Rice (10 000 tons)	892	91.68	102.4	97.46
原盐 (万吨)	Salt (10 000 tons)	59.72	69.44	72.93	68.64
糖 (万吨)	Sugar (10 000 tons)	6.31	10.13	4.44	7.19
卷烟 (万箱)	Cigarettes (10 000 cases)	249.88	229.39	230.43	244.22
罐头 (万吨)	Canned Food (10 000 tons)	5.6	3.48	4.21	5.4
软饮料 (万吨)	Soft Drinks (10 000 tons)	7.69	7.65	12.4	16.36

注:1999至2001年产品产量统计口径为全部国有及年产品销售收入500万元以上的非国有工业企业。

Data of product output in 1999-2001 refer to those from all state-owned and the non-state-owned industrial enterprises with an annual sales income of over 5 million yuan.

10-8 续表 1 continued

产品	Item	1995	1999	2000	2001
饮料酒 (万吨)	Liquor (10 000 tons)	47.17	30.06	30.21	30.68
白酒(商品量) (万吨)	Spirit (10 000 tons)	20.57	4.87	3.76	2.67
啤酒 (万吨)	Beer (10 000 tons)	25.48	25.14	26.42	27.98
乳制品 (吨)	Dairy Products (tons)	2074	4370	5577	7182
味精 (吨)	Aginomoto (ton)	4500	4010	4452	3764
食用植物油 (万吨)	Edible Vegetable Oil (10 000 tons)	33.11	11.06	20.14	19.89
化学原料药(24大类) (吨)	Chemical Medicine (ton)	7444	2228.49	1964.76	1525.02
中成药 (吨)	Traditional Chinese Medicine (10 000 tons)	13984	9726.75	11744.53	11118.31
配混合饲料 (万吨)	Fixed-Forage (10 000 tons)	201.86	148.89	163.62	186.77
塑料制品 (万吨)	Plastics Products (10 000 tons)	16.95	7.05	7.29	8.28
皮鞋 (万双)	Leather Shoe (10 000 units)	2851	297.47	429.49	421.43
胶鞋 (万双)	Rubber Overshoes (10 000 units)	6293	2646.43	2782.89	2842
家用电冰箱 (万台)	Household Refrigerators (10 000 units)	22.28	28.6	44.54	47.79
电风扇 (万台)	Electric Fans (10 000 units)	40.16	6.72	4.64	12.83
房间空气调节器 (台)	Air Conditioners (unit)	25144	48284	34696	17214
收音机 (万台)	Radio (10 000 units)	16.64	-	-	-
收录放机 (万台)	Radio Cassette Player (10 000 units)	38.58	105.24	66	1.5
电视机 (万台)	Television Sets (10 000 units)	24.73	0.28	-	0.87
原煤 (万吨)	Coal (10 000 tons)	5564.51	1432.87	1490.81	1546.1
烟煤 (万吨)	Bituminous Coal (10 000 tons)	1760.34	754.52	778.2	691.64
无烟煤 (万吨)	No-Bituminous Coal (10 000 tons)	3801.18	678.35	712.05	854.07
原油加工量 (万吨)	Crude Process (10 000 tons)	346.75	476.76	526.42	435.93
汽油 (万吨)	Gasoline (10 000 tons)	90.38	107.41	120.19	108.65
柴油 (万吨)	Diesel oil (10 000 tons)	104.36	196.21	215.53	192.33
发电量 (亿千瓦小时)	Electricity (100 million kwh)	332.94	332.51	354.42	384.35
水电 (亿千瓦小时)	Hydro-power (100 million kwh)	157.97	165.38	191.15	195.27
火电 (亿千瓦小时)	Thermal Power (100 million kwh)	174.86	167.14	163.27	189.07
生铁 (万吨)	Pig Iron (10 000 tons)	200.46	324.93	332.72	417.26
钢 (万吨)	Steel (10 000 tons)	175.6	309.02	304.13	441.9
成品钢材 (万吨)	Steel Products (10 000 tons)	154.54	288.79	299.05	389.01
铁道用钢材 (万吨)	Railway Steel (10 000 tons)	0.97	1.52	1.41	1.65
普通大型钢材 (万吨)	Ordinary Large Rolled Stell (10 000 tons)	1.83	1.47	2.26	2.43
普通中型钢材 (万吨)	Ordinary Medium Rolled Stell (10 000 tons)	18.15	27.66	46.67	73.57
普通小型钢材 (万吨)	Ordinary Small Rolled Stell (10 000 tons)	48.39	81.71	72.91	102.76
优质型钢材 (万吨)	High Quality Section Steel (10 000 tons)	13.69	13.76	12.11	12.79
线材 (万吨)	Wire Rod (10 000 tons)	51.94	106.76	97.24	120.99
钢带 (万吨)	Steel Band (10 000 ton)	0.23	25.53	31.76	34.87
无缝钢管 (万吨)	Seamless Steel Pipe (10 000 tons)	14.91	27.02	31.63	37.74
焊接钢管 (万吨)	Welding Steel Pipe (10 000 tons)	1.18	1.28	2.17	1.68

产品	Item	1995	1999	2000	2001
机制焦炭 (万吨)	Machine made Coke (10 000 tons)	185.82	207.58	207	200.23
煤气 (亿立方米)	Coal Gas (100 millions cm)	34.78	3.35	3.2	3.23
铁矿石(成品矿) (万吨)	Iron Mineral (10 000 tons)	101.3	19.4	4.27	4.31
水泥 (万吨)	Cement (10 000 tons)	2196.02	2273.85	2395.72	2496.02
平板玻璃 (万重量箱)	Plate Glass (10 000 weight cases)	861.43	710.36	735.34	857.93
硫酸(折100%) (万吨)	Sulfuric Acid (10 000 tons)	99.32	121.08	128.17	141.27
纯碱 (万吨)	Sode Ash (10 000 tons)	10.8	10.05	13.03	12.47
烧碱(折100%) (万吨)	Caustic Soda (10 000 tons)	21.46	18.73	20.96	21.53
合成氨 (万吨)	Synthetic Ammonia (10 000 tons)	157.77	179.26	167.3	149.23
农用化肥(折纯量) (万吨)	Chemical Fertilizer (10 000 tons)	152.78	157.35	141.74	146.11
氮肥	Nitrogen Fertilizers (10 000 tons)	113.05	130.39	112.9	119.37
磷肥	Phosphate Fertilizers (10 000 tons)	39.49	26.06	27.57	25.7
化学农药(原药折纯量) (万吨)	Chemical Pesticide (10 000 tons)	4.53	6.11	4.58	4.91
电石 (万吨)	Calcium Carbide (10 000 ton)	12.16	10.09	10.44	11.03
塑料树脂及共聚物 (万吨)	Plastics (10 000 tons)	5.86	17.2	23.1	19.77
合成橡胶 (万吨)	Synthetic Rubber (10 000 tons)	3.42	7.87	9.83	11.17
轮胎外胎 (万条)	Tires (10 000 units)	56.92	50.91	6.74	6.18
矿山设备 (吨)	Mining Equipment (ton)	15952	10726.8	9911.6	9149.1
起重设备 (吨)	Jack-up Eguiprent (ton)	39383	14043.27	14810.2	27068.64
冶炼设备 (吨)	Smelt Equipment (ton)	6001	1802	4540	3016
化工设备 (吨)	Equipment for Chemical Industry (ton)	8972	4471.86	4292.64	4254
发电设备 (万千瓦)	Power Generating Equipment (10 000 kw)	18.2	14.41	9.92	5.62
交流电动机 (万千瓦)	AC Electric Motor (10 000 kw)	217.59	138.11	137.59	179.84
变压器 (万千伏安)	Transformer (10 000 kva)	420.69	402.21	494.96	822.58
泵 (万台)	Pump (10 000 units)	51.78	15.97	14.24	14.8
金属切削机床 (台)	Metal-cutting Machine Tools (unit)	3297	865	907	1367
锻压机械 (吨)	Forging and Pressing Equipment (ton)	1195(台)	1588	1577	1628
汽车 (辆)	Motor Vehicles (unit)	9895	10566	17614	20514
摩托车 (辆)	Motorcycles (unit)	233744	186535	142452	116358
轴承 (万套)	Bearing (10 000 sets)	4394	5341	1940.13	1546.97
小型拖拉机 (万台)	Small Tractor (10 000 units)	2.97	0.75	0.45	0.33
内燃机 (万千瓦)	Internal Combustion Engines (10 000 kw)	566	238.28	175.94	140.26
工矿电机车 (辆)	Industrial and Mineral Electric Locomotive (unit)	344	-	-	-
铁路机车 (万千瓦)	Railway Locomotive (10 000 KW)	124(台)	83.88	68.96	123.76
铁路货车 (辆)	Railway Freight wagons (unit)	4771	2207	3486	3957
民用钢质船舶 (综合吨)	Civil Plate ship (ton)	502	11040	13541	10733
工业锅炉 (蒸吨)	Industrial Boiler (ton)	1861	2118	2976	3616.85

10-9 按全省人口平均的主要产品产量

Per Capita Output of Major Industrial Products

产品	Item	1995	1999	2000	2001
化学纤维（公斤/人）	Chemical Fiber (kg / person)	0.76	0.96	1.19	1.06
纱(混合数)（公斤/人）	Yarn (kg / person)	2.32	2.14	2.53	2.53
纯棉纱（公斤/人）	Pure Cotton Yarn (kg / person)	1.43			
布(混合数)（米/人）	Cloth (m / person)	7.73	4.4	5.19	4.64
针棉织品(折用纱量)（公斤/人）	Cotton Knitwear (kg / person)	0.12	0.1	0.1	0.07
丝织品(不包括土丝织品)（米/人）	Silk Fabrics (m/ person)	0.04	0.0004	0.0015	
机制纸及纸板（公斤/人）	Machine-made Paper and Paperboards (kg/person)	14.86	9.07	10.68	11.79
缝纫机（架/百人）	Sewing Machine (unit / 100 persons)	0.16	0.01	0.02	0.01
自行车（辆/百人）	Bicycle (unit / 100 persons)	0.11			
手表（只/百人）	Watch (leather / 100 persons)	1.49			
日用陶瓷器（件/人）	Household Ceramics (piece / person)	16.82	17.02	14.14	14.60
日用精铝制品（公斤/百人）	Household Aluminium Products (kg/100 persons)	2.51	2.42	3.78	1.49
合成洗涤剂（公斤/人）	Synthetic Detergents (kg / person)	0.95	1.04	1.24	1.41
原盐（公斤/人）	Salt (kg / person)	9.43	10.63	11.11	10.43
糖（公斤/人）	Sugar (kg / person)	1	1.55	0.68	1.09
卷烟（箱/百人）	Cigarette (case /100 persons)	3.95	3.51	3.51	3.71
家用电冰箱（台/百人）	Household Refrigerators (unit / 100 persons)	0.35	0.44	0.68	0.73
电视机（台/百人）	Television (unit / 100 persons)	0.39	0.04		
原煤（吨 / 人）	Coal (ton / person)	0.88	0.22	0.23	0.24
原油加工量（公斤/人）	Processing Output of Crude Oil (kg / person)	54.8	72.99	80.22	66.25
发电量（千瓦小时/人）	Electricity (kwh / person)	526.17	509.05	540.11	584.12
生铁（公斤/人）	Pig Iron (kg / person)	31.68	49.74	50.7	63.41
钢（公斤/人）	Steel (kg / person)	27.75	47.31	46.35	67.16
成品钢材（公斤/人）	Steel Products (kg / person)	24.42	44.21	45.57	59.12
水泥（吨/人）	Cement (ton / person)	0.35	0.35	0.37	0.38
平板玻璃（重量箱/人）	Plate Glass (weight case / person)	0.14	0.11	0.11	0.13
硫酸(折100)（公斤/人）	Sulfuric Acid (kg / person)	15.69	18.54	19.53	21.47
纯碱（公斤/人）	Soda Ash (kg / person)	1.71	1.54	1.99	1.90
烧碱(折100)（公斤/人）	Caustic Soda (kg / person)	3.39	2.87	3.19	3.27
合成氨（公斤/人）	Synthetic Ammonia (kg / person)	24.93	27.44	25.49	22.68
农用化肥(折纯量)（公斤/人）	Chemical Fertilizer (kg / person)	24.14	24.09	21.6	22.21
氮肥（公斤/人）	Nitrogen Fertilizer (kg / person)	17.87	19.96	17.21	18.14
磷肥（公斤/人）	Phosphate Fertilizer (kg / person)	6.24	3.99	4.2	3.91
化学农药(原药折纯量)（公斤/人）	Chemical Pesticide (kg / person)	0.72	0.94	0.7	0.75
塑料树脂及共聚物（公斤/人）	Plastics (kg / person)	0.93	2.63	3.52	3.00
合成橡胶（公斤/人）	Synthetic Rubber (kg/person)	0.54	1.2	1.5	1.70
汽车（辆/万人）	Motor Vehicles (unit/10 000 persons)	1.56	1.62	2.68	3.12
摩托车（辆/万人）	Motorcycles (unit/10 000 persons)	36.94	28.56	21.72	17.68

10-10 各市、州主要工业产品产量(2001年)

Output of Major Industrial Products (2001)

市州	City and Autonomic Prefect	纱(万吨) Yarn (10 000 tons)	布(亿米) Cloth (100 million meters)	针棉织品(折用纱线)(万吨) Cotton Knitwear (10 000 tons)	机制纸及纸板(万吨) Machine-made Paper and Paperboard (10 000 tons)	缝纫机(万架) Sartorius (10 000 units)	日用陶瓷器(亿件) Household Ceramics (100 million pieces)	灯泡(万只) Lighting Service (10 000 units)
长沙市	Changsha City	1.74	0.11	0.4	3.29	-	0.77	-
株洲市	Zhuzhou City	0.45	-	0.14	0.67	-	5.58	2050
湘潭市	Xiangtan City	1.33	0.82	-	1.5	0.45	0.17	-
衡阳市	Hengyang City	0.68	0.1	-	2.65	-	1.26	5392
邵阳市	Shaoyang City	0.69	0.12	-	14.11	-	-	-
岳阳市	Yueyang City	2.09	0.07	-	20	-	0.12	
常德市	Changde City	4.26	0.55	-	12.75	0.49	-	2820
张家界市	Zhangjiajie City	-	0.01	0.07	0.13	-	-	-
益阳市	Yiyang City	1.87	0.11	-	7.73	-	0.51	249.7
郴州市	Chenzhou City	0.48	0.12	-	6.02	-	0.03	-
永州市	Yongzhou City	0.72	0.34	-	3.87	-	0.27	-
娄底市	Loudi City	0.49	-	-	0.28	-	0.19	-
怀化市	Huaihua City	1.24	0.51	-	4.52	-	0.52	-
湘西自治州	West Hunan A.P	0.44	0.18	0.03	0.11	-	0.19	-

市州	City and Autonomic Prefect	糖(万吨) Sugar (10 000 tons)	卷烟(万箱) Cigarettes (10 000 cases)	化学原料药(吨) Chemical Medicine (ton)	食用植物油(万吨) Edible Vegetable Oil (10 000 tons)	配混合饲料(万吨) Mixed Fodder (10 000 tons)	钢(万吨) Steel (10 000 tons)	生铁(万吨) Pig Iron (10 000 tons)
长沙市	Changsha City	-	92.12	701.24	0.1	9.27	0.08	-
株洲市	Zhuzhou City	-	-	81	0.15	35.01	3.81	-
湘潭市	Xiangtan City	-	-	-	0.02	4.75	201.98	206.84
衡阳市	Hengyang City	-	4.99	38	0.6	5.67	24.69	1.32
邵阳市	Shaoyang City	-	4.45	48	-	9.43	-	1.61
岳阳市	Yueyang City	2.44	-	477.78	9.88	92.86	-	-
常德市	Changde City	1.41	74.84	77	6.2	6.29	0.04	-
张家界市	Zhangjiajie City	-	-	-	0.34	0.82	-	-
益阳市	Yiyang City	3.34	-	-	1.36	5.27	0.3	-
郴州市	Chenzhou City	-	28.19	-	-	3.31	-	3.55
永州市	Yongzhou City	-	25.61	-	0.14	3.76	-	7.62
娄底市	Loudi City	-	-	-	-	2.25	208.82	196.31
怀化市	Huaihua City	-	6.01	92	0.21	7.22	2.18	-
湘西自治州	West Hunan A.P	-	8	10	0.89	0.85	-	-

市州	City and Autonomic Prefect	原煤(万吨) Coal (10 000 tons)	发电量(亿千瓦时) Electricity (100 million kw.h)	#水电 Hydro-power	成品钢材(万吨) Steel Products (10 000 tons)	水泥(万吨) Cement (10 000 tons)	平板玻璃(万重量箱) Plate Class (10 000 weight cases)	硫酸(万吨) Sulfuric Acid (10 000 tons)	烧碱(万吨) Caustic Sode (10 000 tons)
长沙市	Changsha City	165.87	0.66	0.66	2.53	327.31	-	10.37	-
株洲市	Zhuzhou City	56.44	16.96	2.74	3.23	112.69	402.07	49.76	9.66
湘潭市	Xiangtan City	47.84	34.47	1.27	152.82	243.69	-	1.59	0.62
衡阳市	Hengyang City	293.77	27.07	5.18	38.23	123.1	-	33.57	3.15
邵阳市	Shaoyang City	126.9	9.19	6.65	0.27	156.83	68.97	1.17	-
岳阳市	Yueyang City	-	45.47	0.76	-	66.18	-	0.05	4.68
常德市	Changde City	83.77	37.6	12.21	-	331	29.76	7.49	-
张家界市	Zhangjiajie City	23.44	10.01	9.58	-	47.42	-	-	-
益阳市	Yiyang City	7.15	31.74	24.3	2.45	193.75	-	0.74	-
郴州市	Chenzhou City	411.41	39.31	30.67	0.71	261.5	329.26	13.76	1.87
永州市	Yongzhou City	22.18	17.13	16.93	4.74	248.73	0.1	1.05	-
娄底市	Loudi City	250.44	28.54	1.36	183.19	197.09	27.76	7.07	1.02
怀化市	Huaihua City	46.74	80.79	78.04	0.65	137.73	-	1.84	0.39
湘西自治州	West Hunan A.P	10.14	5.11	4.92	0.19	49	-	12.81	0.15

市州	City and Autonomic Prefect	化学农药(原药)(万吨) Chemical Pesticide (10 000 tons)	化学肥料(折纯量)(万吨) Chemical Fertilizers (10 000 tons)	氮肥 Nitrogen Fertilizers	磷肥 Phosphate Fertilizers	电石(万吨) Calcium Carbide (10 000 tons)	塑料树脂及共聚物(吨) Plastics (ton)	矿山设备(吨) Mining Equipment (ton)	金属切削机床(台) Metal-Cutting Machine Tools (unit)
长沙市	Changsha City	0.51	5.12	2.67	2.45	-	-	2464	1063
株洲市	Zhuzhou City	0.79	12.45	9.52	2.94	3.43	36467	-	-
湘潭市	Xiangtan City	0.65	1.75	1.75	-	0.03	120	795	-
衡阳市	Hengyang City	1.1	16.17	13.55	2.54	-	-	3588	-
邵阳市	Shaoyang City	-	6.72	5.86	0.86	-	-	-	-
岳阳市	Yueyang City	0.82	43.28	42.96	0.32	-	146598	-	-
常德市	Changde City	0.1	12.97	8.69	4.28	-	-	1137	-
张家界市	Zhangjiajie City	-	1.09	1.04	0.05	-	-	-	-
益阳市	Yiyang City	0.57	3.9	3.43	0.47	-	-	-	288
郴州市	Chenzhou City	0.17	11.87	8.44	2.56	1.49	14530	803	16
永州市	Yongzhou City	0.05	7.64	4.12	3.52	-	-	-	-
娄底市	Loudi City	0.09	15.64	14.49	1.15	-	-	282.1	-
怀化市	Huaihua City	0.06	5.81	2.86	2.86	6.08	-	80	-
湘西自治州	West Hunan A.P	-	1.7	-	1.7	-	-	-	-

10-11 大中型工业企业主要指标及在工业中的地位(2001年)

指标	Item	企业单位数(个) Number of Enterprises (unit)	在工业中的地位 Status in Industry (%)	工业总产值(现价)(亿元) Gross Industrial Output Value (current price) (100 million yuan)	在工业中的地位 Status in Industry (%)
总计	**Total**	**611**	**12.32**	**1113.16**	**61.46**
按登记注册类型:	**Grouped by Registration**				
国有企业	State-owned Enterprises	353	20.08	582.17	82.53
集体企业	Collective-owned Enterprises	31	2.79	12.25	6.04
股份合作企业	Enterprises Cooperated by Joint-stock	13	4.83	4.94	11.72
有限责任公司	Limited Liability Company	106	24.04	206.44	77.46
股份有限公司	Company Limited by Shares	70	33.65	220.06	79.82
港、澳、台投资企业	Enterprises Funded by Entrepreneurs From Hong Kong,Macao and Taiwan	8	5.48	10.65	18.49
外商投资企业	Enterprises funded by Foreigners	15	16.13	55.22	61.66
按经济组织类型:	**Grouped by Ownership**				
独资企业	Enterprises Owned by a Sole Investor	393	11.90	601.09	60.93
合作、合伙企业	Enterprises of Partnership	15	2.99	8.82	10.76
股份有限公司	Company Limited by Shares	74	26.24	226.23	74.37
有限责任公司	Limited Liability Company	129	14.74	277.02	63.17
按轻重工业分:	**Grouped by Light and Heavy Industry**				
轻工业	Light Industry	192	9.64	331.42	52.32
重工业	Heavy Industry	419	14.11	781.73	66.37
按行业划分:	**Grouped by Sector**				
煤炭采选业	Coal Mining and Dressing	13	7.14	15.44	43.25
黑色金属矿采选业	Ferrous Metals Mining and Dressing	3	15.00	0.86	36.91
有色金属矿采选业	Nonferrous Metals Mining and Dressing	11	8.66	5.29	24.57
非金属矿采选业	Nonmetal Minerals Mining and Dressing	5	7.94	2.74	19.83
木材及竹材采运业	Logging and Transport of Timber and Bamboo	2	15.38	0.50	53.19
食品加工业	Food Processing	18	5.03	34.22	35.50
食品制造业	Food Manufacturing	9	7.96	4.76	21.48
饮料制造业	Beverage Manufacturing	13	12.62	13.29	43.14

Main Indicators of Large and Medium – Sized Enterprises and Status in Industry (2001)

10-11 续表 1 continued

工业增加值(生产法)(亿元) Value Added of Industry (by production) (100 million yuan)	在工业中的地位 Status in Industry (%)	全部从业人员年平均人数(万人) Average Number of Employees (10000 persons)	在工业中的地位 Status in Industry (%)	固定资产原价合计(亿元) Original Value of Fixed Assets (100 million yuan)	在工业中的地位 Status in Industry (%)	利税总额(亿元) Total Pre-tax Profits (100 million yuan)	在工业中的地位 Status in Industry (%)
405.99	**66.94**	**76.75**	**49.45**	**1527.23**	**72.88**	**187.15**	**79.42**
260.88	85.81	47.04	63.83	919.45	75.97	138.20	96.74
3.70	6.66	1.87	8.63	10.98	13.33	0.57	4.97
0.99	8.72	0.54	10.93	4.51	19.36	0.27	10.27
54.69	76.98	17.91	74.41	298.74	84.54	14.12	77.45
57.54	75.98	7.23	67.38	195.06	86.41	21.57	73.52
3.78	24.31	0.26	9.25	7.29	22.49	2.41	37.54
18.20	66.18	1.18	38.31	81.43	77.47	7.19	70.21
266.31	70.01	49.20	48.54	933.19	70.62	139.16	86.73
2.48	10.76	0.66	7.75	6.55	16.31	0.30	6.04
60.83	72.01	7.47	58.87	199.06	83.00	23.86	69.85
76.37	64.40	19.42	59.50	388.44	78.59	23.82	66.04
170.56	67.73	16.57	35.08	268.91	62.05	118.80	87.30
235.43	66.38	60.18	55.74	1258.32	75.70	68.35	68.65
5.56	44.84	7.16	52.96	29.40	64.53	0.71	25.00
0.26	36.11	0.14	38.89	1.97	78.80	0.03	23.08
2.31	31.73	1.37	38.92	11.81	60.01	0.28	21.37
1.14	26.51	0.54	30.51	6.43	60.43	0.36	37.11
0.14	46.67	0.22	50.00	0.86	44.79	0.00	0.00
10.98	40.92	0.92	23.71	17.29	38.36	2.62	62.09
1.11	19.04	0.50	25.64	3.88	33.25	0.32	19.75
6.80	55.74	1.11	46.44	16.00	54.20	3.22	60.87

指标	Item	企业单位数(个) Number of Enterprises (unit)	在工业中的地位 Status in Industry (%)	工业总产值(现价)(亿元) Gross Industrial Output Value (current price) (100 million yuan)	在工业中的地位 Status in Industry (%)
烟草加工业	Tabacco Processing	12	75.00	147.92	99.15
纺织业	Textile Industry	20	10.64	13.44	26.37
服装及其他纤维制品制造业	Garments and Other Fiber Products	5	8.47	1.52	14.76
皮革、毛皮、羽绒及其制品业	Leather,Furs,Down and Related Products	2	3.13	0.66	4.07
木材加工及竹、藤、棕、草制品业	Timber Processing,Bamboo,Cane, Palm Fiber and Straw Products	4	3.25	2.39	11.54
造纸及纸制品业	Paper making and Paper Products	19	10.73	28.77	55.47
印刷业、记录媒介的复制	Printing and Record Medium Reproduction	17	15.04	13.35	70.86
石油加工及炼焦业	Petroleum Processing and Coking	4	36.36	135.74	98.72
化学原料及化学制品制造业	Raw Chemical Materials and Chemical Products	85	21.46	95.90	67.09
医药制造业	Medical and Pharmaceutial Products	16	15.84	17.30	52.70
化学纤维制造业	Chemical Fiber	6	35.29	14.77	89.14
橡胶制品业	Rubber Products	5	11.11	4.10	38.57
塑料制品业	Plastic Products	9	9.38	3.77	25.58
非金属矿物制品业	Nonmetal Mineral Products	55	8.26	31.50	28.14
黑色金属冶炼及压延加工业	Smelting and Pressing of Ferrous Metals	15	11.63	104.21	82.54
有色金属冶炼及压延加工业	Smelting and Pressing of NonFerrous Metals	21	11.80	89.36	71.41
金属制品业	Metal Products	6	3.73	3.34	12.72
普通机械制造业	Ordinary Machinery	47	19.18	22.12	51.85
专用设备制造业	Special Purpose Equipment	37	22.42	16.47	36.85
交通运输设备制造业	Transport Equipment	33	17.74	102.18	80.67
电气机械及器材制造业	Electric Equipment and Machinery	35	19.02	33.76	52.95
电子及通信设备制造业	Electronic and Telecommunications Equipment	15	20.55	40.72	76.38
仪器仪表及文化、办公用机械制造业	Instruments,Meters,Cultural and Office Machinery	9	25.71	8.04	61.23
其他制造业	Other Types of Manufacturing				
电力、蒸汽、热水的生产和供应业	Production and Supply of Electric Power, Steam and Hot Water	41	17.98	85.98	71.53
自来水的生产和供应业	Production and Supply of Tap Water	11	9.82	7.95	61.72

10-11 续表 3 continued

工业增加值(生产法)(亿元) Value Added of Industry (by production) (100 million yuan)	在工业中的地位 Status in Industry (%)	全部从业人员年平均人数(万人) Average Number of Employees (10 000 persons)	在工业中的地位 Status in Industry (%)	固定资产原价合计(亿元) Original Value of Fixed Assets (100 million yuan)	在工业中的地位 Status in Industry (%)	利税总额(亿元) Total Pre-tax Profits (100 million yuan)	在工业中的地位 Status in Industry (%)
108.50	99.51	1.73	95.58	75.05	98.32	96.81	99.75
4.15	30.18	2.46	31.10	15.35	39.79	0.51	46.36
0.46	17.10	0.22	17.19	0.92	26.67	0.07	10.45
0.23	6.04	0.14	13.33	0.57	10.92	-0.41	-256.25
0.81	13.85	0.24	11.76	9.08	51.10	0.29	25.00
9.00	58.67	1.78	47.59	27.61	69.18	3.20	70.48
6.14	78.42	0.73	47.10	10.46	65.95	4.20	90.32
30.26	99.28	2.00	95.24	100.37	99.01	9.21	99.14
23.87	66.23	7.88	62.39	167.77	83.97	4.75	71.00
6.44	57.91	1.25	54.11	16.86	69.73	2.91	62.45
2.22	81.02	1.01	82.79	23.91	93.58	0.94	90.38
1.22	45.69	0.59	42.45	4.04	56.66	0.17	43.59
1.02	25.31	0.25	18.66	6.04	47.78	0.26	30.95
9.13	28.12	5.92	29.21	65.98	49.35	1.70	26.81
36.58	85.71	7.36	78.30	154.17	93.28	13.43	91.24
20.63	68.72	4.85	70.09	66.33	81.50	7.89	74.36
0.91	13.96	0.35	14.34	4.06	27.05	0.02	1.75
6.10	53.56	4.04	58.98	37.06	65.52	0.33	23.24
5.27	34.22	3.68	61.54	31.46	71.81	-0.03	-0.55
25.61	82.85	6.00	70.59	82.56	80.49	6.62	88.62
9.42	60.50	2.94	56.87	35.15	71.25	3.02	63.31
8.84	74.98	1.33	66.17	50.11	89.45	3.31	76.62
2.39	62.40	0.62	62.00	6.95	65.81	0.51	35.92
51.41	71.97	4.20	49.12	400.64	70.44	19.20	76.25
4.52	67.77	0.86	39.81	28.00	62.64	0.81	81.00

10-12 工业企业能源购进、消费及库存(2001年)

Energy Purchase,Consumption and Stock of Industry (2001)

指标	Item	年初库存 Stock at the Beginning of the Year	购进量实物量 Total Purchase	消费量合计 Total Consumption	#生产消费 For Production	#原材料 Material Use	年末库存 Stock at the End of the Year
能源合计 (吨标准煤)	**Total Energy (ton of SCE)**	**1818596**	**39976443**	**46423426**	**45443168**	**5646357**	**1495607**
原煤 (吨)	Raw Coal (ton)	1567961	26779036	27679522	27473835	5722577	1189628
洗精煤 (吨)	Cleaned Coal (ton)	118464	2568123	2675203	2674943		63751
其他洗煤 (吨)	Other Washed Coal (ton)	1273	13904	14834	14318		443
型煤 (吨)	Briquettes (ton)						
焦炭 (吨)	Coke (ton)	143085	1780002	3195976	3175589	1111124	126602
其他焦化产品 (吨)	Other Coking Products (ton)	474	13579	13996	13996		87
焦炉煤气 (万立方米)	Coke Oven Gas (10 000 cu.m)		173	59355	56764		
高炉煤气 (万立方米)	High Oven Gas (10 000 cu.m)		26195	701140	701140		
其他煤气 (万立方米)	Other Coal Gas (10 000 cu.m)	8	11410	38631	38493		6
天然气 (万立方米)	Natural Gas (10 000 cu.m)						
原油 (吨)	Crude Oil (ton)	214054	4318290	4357896	4357896		165294
汽油 (吨)	Gasoline (ton)	8453	46452	47212	31315	6037	11107
煤油 (吨)	Kerosene (ton)	1626	5176	5432	5230	81	7317
柴油 (吨)	Diesel Oil (ton)	35827	117344	117672	102360	4149	46956
燃料油 (吨)	Fuel Oil (ton)	28934	238109	290855	290414	6865	49762
液化石油气 (吨)	Liquefied Petroleum Gas (ton)	3583	300851	368206	366061	207602	1295
炼厂干气 (吨)	Refinery Gas (ton)		26526	134872	134872		
其他石油制品 (吨)	Other Petroleum Products (ton)	30121	210266	423011	423007	86445	33819
热力 (百万千焦)	Heat (million kilo-joule)		8485602	35697244	35169115		
电力 (万度)	Electricity (10 thousand kwh)		2359899	2565741	2452477		
其他燃料 (吨标准煤)	Other Fuel (ton of SCE)	49819	399417	404330	403109	42	49271

注:本表统计范围为全部国有工业企业及年产品销售收入500万元及以上的非国有工业企业。

All state-owned and the non-state-owned industrial enterprises with annual sales income of over 5 million yuan.

10-13 主要能源按工业行业分组消费量(2001年)

Consumption of Energy and Its Main Varieties by Sector (2001)

单位：吨 (ton)

指标	Item	原煤（吨）Raw Coal (ton)	洗精煤（吨）Cleaned Coal (ton)	其他洗煤（吨）Other Washed Coal (ton)	型煤（吨）Briquettes (ton)	焦炭（吨）Coke (ton)
煤炭采选业	Coal Mining and Dressing	2129274	149361	100		3160
黑色金属矿采选业	Ferrous Metals Mining and Dressing	4344				32616
有色金属矿采选业	Nonferrous Metals Mining and Dressing	56793	1737			247
非金属矿采选业	Nonmetal Minerals Mining and Dressing	302036				55
其他矿采选业	Other Types of Mining and Dressing					
木材及竹材采运业	Logging and Transport of Timber and Bamboo	108				
食品加工业	Food Processing	177434				170
食品制造业	Food Manufacturing	87799				
饮料制造业	Beverage Manufacturing	114613				272
烟草加工业	Tobacco Processing	105512		4931		
纺织业	Textile Industry	280923				
服装及其他纤维制品制造业	Garments and Other Fiber Products	5732				46
皮革毛皮羽绒及其制品业	Leather,Furs,Down and Related Products	21390				186
木材加工及竹、藤、棕、草制品业	Timber Processing,Bamboo,Cane, Palm Fiber and Straw Products	230407				170
家具制造业	Furniture Manufacturing	1004				
造纸及纸制品业	Paper making and Paper Products	1137488				1470
印刷业、记录媒介的复制	Printing and Record Medium Reproduction	4968				
文教体育用品制造业	Cultural,Educational and Sports Goods	1043				
石油加工及炼焦业	Petroleum Processing and Coking	957686	361395			
化学原料及化学制品制造业	Raw Chemical Materials and Chemical Products	5159366	17079	3417		115017
医药制造业	Medical and Pharmaceutical Products	149401				
化学纤维制造业	Chemical Fiber	281438				48318
橡胶制品业	Rubber Products	61063		1000		
塑料制品业	Plastic Products	22412				
非金属矿物制品业	Nonmetal Mineral Products	5241325	4089	4962		12754
黑色金属冶炼及压延加工业	Smelting and Pressing of Ferrous Metals	889750	1960191			2538065
有色金属冶炼及压延加工业	Smelting and Pressing of Non-Ferrous Metals	675859	1614	234		353905
金属制品业	Metal Products	46331	104			21825
普通机械制造业	Ordinary Machinery	39854	211			24384
专用设备制造业	Special Purpose Equipment	28185	258			8788
交通运输设备制造业	Transport Equipment	58442	28			7888
电气机械及器材制造业	Electric Equipment and Machinery	72139	25	190		2832
电子及通信设备制造业	Electronic and Telecommunications Equipment	30526				476
仪器仪表及文化、办公用机械制造业	Instruments,Meters,Cultural and Office Machinery	6673				
其他制造业	Other Types of Manufacturing	28168				
电力、蒸汽、热水的生产和供应业	Production and Supply of Electric Power, Steam and Hot Water	9206609				3697
煤气生产和供应业	Production and Supply of Gas	48959	179111			19222
自来水的生产和供应业	Production and Supply of Tap Water	667				

注：本表统计范围为全部国有工业企业及年产品销售收入500万元及以上的非国有工业企业。

All state-owned and the non-state-owned industrial enterprises with annual sales income of over 5 million yuan.

单位：吨　　　　　　　　　　　　　10-13 续表1　continued　　　　　　　　　　　　　（ton）

指标	Item	其他焦化产品 (吨) Other Coking Products (ton)	焦炉煤气 (万立方) Coke Oven Gas (10 000 cu.m)	高炉煤气 (万立方) High Oven Gas (10 000 cu.m)	其他煤气 (万立方) Other Coal Gas (10 000 cu.m)	天然气 (万立方) Natural Gas (10 000 cu.m)
煤炭采选业	Coal Mining and Dressing					
黑色金属矿采选业	Ferrous Metals Mining and Dressing					
有色金属矿采选业	Nonferrous Metals Mining and Dressing					
非金属矿采选业	Nonmetal Minerals Mining and Dressing					
其他矿采选业	Other Types of Mining and Dressing					
木材及竹材采运业	Logging and Transport of Timber and Bamboo					
食品加工业	Food Processing					
食品制造业	Food Manufacturing					
饮料制造业	Beverage Manufacturing					
烟草加工业	Tobacco Processing					
纺织业	Textile Industry					
服装及其他纤维制品制造业	Garments and Other Fiber Products					
皮革毛皮羽绒及其制品业	Leather,Furs,Down and Related Products					
木材加工及竹、藤、棕、草制品业	Timber Processing,Bamboo,Cane, Palm Fiber and Straw Products					
家具制造业	Furniture Manufacturing					
造纸及纸制品业	Paper making and Paper Products					
印刷业、记录媒介的复制	Printing and Record Medium Reproduction					
文教体育用品制造业	Cultural,Educational and Sports Goods					
石油加工及炼焦业	Petroleum Processing and Coking					
化学原料及化学制品制造业	Raw Chemical Materials and Chemical Products	13996				
医药制造业	Medical and Pharmaceutical Products					
化学纤维制造业	Chemical Fiber					
橡胶制品业	Rubber Products					
塑料制品业	Plastic Products					
非金属矿物制品业	Nonmetal Mineral Products			21098		
黑色金属冶炼及压延加工业	Smelting and Pressing of Ferrous Metals		55570	680042	2663	
有色金属冶炼及压延加工业	Smelting and Pressing of Non-Ferrous Metals				35794	
金属制品业	Metal Products					
普通机械制造业	Ordinary Machinery					
专用设备制造业	Special Purpose Equipment					
交通运输设备制造业	Transport Equipment					
电气机械及器材制造业	Electric Equipment and Machinery					
电子及通信设备制造业	Electronic and Telecommunications Equipment				174	
仪器仪表及文化、办公用机械制造业	Instruments,Meters,Cultural and Office Machinery					
其他制造业	Other Types of Manufacturing					
电力、蒸汽、热水的生产和供应业	Production and Supply of Electric Power, Steam and Hot Water					
煤气生产和供应业	Production and Supply of Gas		3785			
自来水的生产和供应业	Production and Supply of Tap Water					

单位：吨　　　　10-13 续表 2　continued　　　　（ton）

原油（吨） Crude Oil (ton)	汽油（吨） Gasoline (ton)	煤油（吨） Kerosene (ton)	柴油（吨） Diesel Oil (ton)	燃料油（吨） Fuel Oil (ton)	液化石油气（吨） Liquefied Petroleum Gas (ton)	其他石油制品（吨） Other Petroleum Products (ton)	热力（百万千焦） Heat (million kilo-joule)	电力（万度） Electricity (10 000 kwh)	其他燃料（吨标准煤） Other Fuel (ton of SCE)
	2169	19	2277	3				137933	
	246		501					9452	
	1495	177	1965	130				32018	128
	549		2546				2908906	13788	
		20							
	82		11					206	
	2651	176	1781	834	2267	16	83	16716	25
	398	5	502	3757	2023		162481	9918	
	493		1257	4530	405			8775	
	506		8988		240			11311	
	598	105	1231	30	88		184277	53061	40
	246		421	54				3307	
	138	1	110				11110	3634	
	173	30	565					13873	
	217		183					538	
	1675	21	2612	775	1478		3483567	90637	4411
	639	4	376	4	12	33		7176	
	24							362	
4357896	41		844	64890	140056	217534	6733753	95062	363776
	8911	360	14785	38811	208926	204940	11250424	466647	31450
	973	1	590	603	6		5639	15489	
	463	9	578	4176			3137195	45605	
	1141	11	207	1			552304	8796	96
	325		2042	2120	90	1	1557	7849	112
	3642	1871	13992	92357	4640	6		303708	989
	2988	232	5058	53326			5006229	375976	10
	2886	253	8090	6575	12		2065984	382491	1441
	517	36	671		7			21049	
	1500	365	2676	363	14	13		25240	1817
	1379	57	1739	4	35	22		20175	
	3298	1574	5314	5239	50	17	10203	38170	1
	1561	15	2245	6881	348	407	117343	25781	
	325	26	8776		1550			31352	
	229	7	24	9				4579	
	442	2	247			1		2153	34
	2806	11	23351	5383		15		217457	
	198		161		5958			6784	
	823	4	322				505	49941	

十一、建筑业

CONSTRUCTION

资料整理人员：　孙　靖

11-1 建筑企业概况

General Survey of Construction Enterprises

指标	Item	1998	1999	2000	2001
总产值（万元）	**Gross Output Value of Construction (10 000 yuan)**	**3273222**	**3338963**	**3542866**	**4897879**
#国有企业	State owned Enterprises	1408906	1462023	1581149	1849867
集体企业	Collective owned Enterprises	1689683	1631890	1509253	1473883
股份合作企业	Cooperative Enterprises	48568	67388	49773	88884
联营企业	Joint Ownership Enterprises	3798	3705	20538	25156
有限责任公司	Limited Liability Corporations	30973	61489	152616	835981
股份有限公司	Share-holding Corporations Ltd.	76618	84584	174020	389794
私营企业	Private Enterprises	13836	20845	41503	211184
其他企业	Others Enterprises		592	566	1975
港澳台商投资企业	Funded by Entrepreneurs from Hong kong,Macao and Taiwan	690	6447	13448	21155
外商投资企业	Enterprises with Foreign Investment	150			
#土木工程	Output Value of Civil Engineering	3043747	3090705	3239377	4576149
#房屋建筑	Building	2421717	2458636	2511859	3446087
矿山建筑	Mines	9120	12520	10769	10204
铁路公路隧道桥梁	Railways,Highways,Tunnels and Bridges	399352	446919	507173	847154
线路管道设备安装	Output Value of Pipes,Lines and Equipment Installation	217575	231881	291745	296123
#设备安装	Equipment Installation	168146	165258	143047	121411
建筑物装修、装饰	Output Value of Building Decoration	11900	16377	11745	25607
增加值（万元）	**Value Aded of construction (10 000 yuan)**	**876333**	**909692**	**967249**	**1307738**
#本年内提取的固定资产折旧	Depreciation of Fixed Assets Of the Year	61815	70743	77163	92710
应付工资	Wages Payable	458869	473493	490810	606021
应付福利费	Welfare Expenses Payable	49148	45698	42946	60940
管理费用中的劳动待业保险费	Labor and Unemployment Insurance in Management Expenses	21992	24473	28358	37760
工程结算税金及附加	Taxes and Extra Charges on Project Settlement Accounts	88216	96048	101064	158977
工程结算利润	Profits of Project Setlement Accounts	219431	218999	250524	341678
管理费用中的税金	Taxes in Management Enpenses	8139	7740	8007	9652
#国有企业	State owned Enterprises	377181	398138	428924	459865
集体企业	Collective owned Enterprises	459562	443665	412859	408047
股份合作企业	Cooperative Enterprises	9138	20374	14906	27628
联营企业	Joint Ownership Enterprises	981	884	6498	7410
有限责任公司	Limited Liability Corporations	7764	17992	63649	233063
股份有限公司	Share-holding Corporations Ltd.	17899	20288	44109	107564
私营企业	Private Enterprises	3555	6000	10393	60650
其他企业	Others Enterprises		75	98	534
港澳台商投资企业	Funded by Entrepreneurs from Hong kong,Macao and Taiwan	190	2276	5813	2977
外商投资企业	Enterprises with Foreign Investment	63			

11-1 续表 1 continued

指标	Item	1998	1999	2000	2001
实收资本 (万元)	**Capital Stock (10 000 yuan)**	**812325**	**883248**	**1004829**	**1521243**
#国有企业	State owned Enterprises	278854	304078	337826	481956
集体企业	Collective owned Enterprises	479365	493793	488259	502047
股份合作企业	Cooperative Enterprises	12563	23113	17883	32150
联营企业	Joint Ownership Enterprises	882	1496	5754	7000
有限责任公司	Limited Liability Corporations	11280	18519	48338	255107
股份有限公司	Share-holding Corporations Ltd.	21817	30152	69068	178893
私营企业	Private Enterprises	7414	9599	30891	59966
其他企业	Others Enterprises		120	100	334
港澳台商投资企业	Funded by Entrepreneurs from Hong kong,Macao and Taiwan	100	2378	6710	3790
外商投资企业	Enterprises with Foreign Investment	50			
资产合计 (万元)	**Total Assets (10 000 yuan)**	**3193807**	**3350854**	**3552544**	**4478393**
#流动资产	Circulating Funds	2109855	2157576	2311307	2835012
#固定资产	Fixed Assets	896622	985884	1032597	1326687
#专项工程	Special Projects	49357	59815	34894	43056
#无形及递延资产	Intangible and Deferred Assets	36414	41677	43736	138502
#国有企业	State owned Enterprises	1708994	1806664	1807419	1953296
集体企业	Collective owned Enterprises	1352191	1331745	1301816	1198775
服份合作企业	Cooperative Enterprises	27432	53002	43725	68947
联营企业	Joint Ownership Enterprises	2748	2240	11063	12668
有限责任公司	Limited Liability Corporations	30161	53348	138182	689782
股份有限公司	Share-holding Corporations Ltd.	55358	73105	182134	352124
私营企业	Private Enterprises	15924	25022	58761	186398
其他企业	Others Enterprises		140	155	1448
港澳台商投资企业	Funded by Entrepreneurs from Hong kong,Macao and Taiwan	588	5588	9287	14955
外商投资企业	Enterprises with Foreign Investment	411			
负债合计 (万元)	**Total Liabilities (10 000 yuan)**	**2127183**	**2228799**	**2287791**	2642947
#流动负债	Liquid Liabilities	1850786	1996057	2064425	2426394
长期负债	Long-term Liabilities	276397	232742	223366	216553
#国有企业	State owned Enterprises	1301068	1385649	1355446	1367100
集体企业	Collective owned Enterprises	753755	728096	697271	591717
股份合作企业	Cooperative Enterprises	12822	26359	21781	34298
联营企业	Joint Ownership Enterprises	1579	720	4977	4057
有限责任公司	Limited Liability Corporations	18156	32526	82412	380900
股份有限公司	Share-holding Corporations Ltd.	31243	38423	103449	143555
私营企业	Private Enterprises	7865	14015	19869	109171
其他企业	Others Enterprises		10	50	1032
港澳台商投资企业	Funded by Entrepreneurs from Hong kong,Macao and Taiwan	336	3001	2535	11117
外商投资企业	Enterprises with Foreign Investment	359			
所有者权益 (万元)	**Creditors' Equity (10 000 yuan)**	**1066624**	**1122055**	**1264753**	**1835445**
#国有企业	State owned Enterprises	407926	421015	451973	586196
集体企业	Collective owned Enterprises	598437	603648	604545	607058
股份合作企业	Cooperative Enterprises	14611	26643	21945	34649
联营企业	Joint Ownership Enterprises	1169	1519	6086	8611
有限责任公司	Limited Liability Corporations	12005	20821	55770	308882
股份有限公司	Share-holding Corporations Ltd.	24115	34682	78685	208568
私营企业	Private Enterprises	8059	11007	38893	77227
其他企业	Others Enterprises		129	105	416
港澳台商投资企业	Funded by Entrepreneurs from Hong kong,Macao and Taiwan	251	2591	6752	3838
外商投资企业	Enterprises with Foreign Investment	50			

11-1 续表 2 continued

指标	Item	1998	1999	2000	2001
企业总收入 (万元)	**Total Income of Enterprises (10 000 yuan)**	**2887205**	**3034630**	**3061339**	**4647297**
#工程结算收入	Revenue of Project Settlement accounts	2776163	2917896	3049291	4517943
工程结算成本	Costs of Project Settlement Accounts	2468515	2602849	2697703	4017288
工程结算利润	Profits of Project Setlement Accounts	219431	218999	250524	341678
其他业务收入	Revenue from Other Business	111042	116734	112048	129354
其他业务利润	Profit from Other Business	11943	19908	28626	23325
#国有企业	State owned Enterprises	1326256	1423768	1476206	1750730
集体企业	Collective owned Enterprises	1433382	1398811	1281118	1354172
股份合作企业	Cooperative Enterprises	29101	60094	47570	82441
联营企业	Joint Ownership Enterprises	3660	3705	17549	30623
有限责任公司	Limited Liability Corporations	26682	53087	133184	848990
股份有限公司	Share-holding Corporations Ltd.	53694	72103	152984	390089
私营企业	Private Enterprises	13398	16137	38906	167863
其他企业	Others Enterprises		478	374	1643
港澳台商投资企业	Funded by Entrepreneurs from Hong Kong,Macao and Taiwan	690	6447	13448	20746
外商投资企业	Enterprises with Foreign Investment	342			
利税总额合计 (万元)	**Total pre-tax Profits (10 000 yuan)**	**115841**	**120981**	**152949**	**255109**
#利润总额	Total Profits	19488	17193	43878	86481
工程结算税金及附加	Taxes and Extra Charges on Project Settlement Accounts	88216	96048	101064	158977
管理费用中的税金	Taxes in Management Enpenses	8139	·7740	8007	9651
产值利税率(%)	Ratio of Pretax Profits to Output Value(%)	3.5	3.6	4.3	5.2
资产利税率(%)	Ratio of tax Profits to Assets	3.9	3.9	4.7	5.7
#国有企业	State owned Enterprises	21288	17567	42940	64225
集体企业	Collective owned Enterprises	87156	89394	82842	86750
股份合作企业	Cooperative Enterprises	1787	4263	3077	5519
联营企业	Joint Ownership Enterprises	254	125	1146	1609
有限责任公司	Limited Liability Corporations	1265	3469	7781	51887
股份有限公司	Share-holding Corporations Ltd.	3337	4707	11236	19853
私营企业	Private Enterprises	733	876	2585	20794
其他企业	Others Enterprises		8	14	68
港澳台商投资企业	Funded by Entrepreneurs from Hong kong,Macao and Taiwan	68	572	1344	804
外商投资企业	Enterprises with Foreign Investment	-47			
利润总额合计 (万元)	**Total Profits (10 000 yuan)**	**19488**	**17193**	**43878**	**86481**
#国有企业	State owned Enterprises	-14144	-20129	2640	13035
集体企业	Collective owned Enterprises	31020	32216	29367	32813
股份合作企业	Cooperative Enterprises	786	2139	1437	2529
联营企业	Joint Ownership Enterprises	146	10	444	840
有限责任公司	Limited Liability Corporations	48	282	2627	22872
股份有限公司	Share-holding Corporations Ltd.	1420	2099	5540	8805
私营企业	Private Enterprises	221	216	1024	5259
其他企业	Others Enterprises		-9		6
港澳台商投资企业	Funded by Entrepreneurs from Hong kong,Macao and Taiwan	51	369	799	322
外商投资企业	Enterprises with Foreign Investment	-60			
工程结算利润总计 (万元)	**Profits of Project Setlement Accounts (10 000 yuan)**	**219431**	**218999**	**250524**	**341678**
#国有企业	State owned Enterprises	101539	97201	118218	125675
集体企业	Collective owned Enterprises	108970	106389	98208	95478
股份合作企业	Cooperative Enterprises	1627	4223	4060	5883
联营企业	Joint Ownership Enterprises	362	170	1864	1973
有限责任公司	Limited Liability Corporations	1748	3836	11112	70462
股份有限公司	Share-holding Corporations Ltd.	4222	4958	11382	26552
私营企业	Private Enterprises	875	1520	3186	14067
其他企业	Others Enterprises		40	42	133
港澳台商投资企业	Funded by Entrepreneurs from Hong kong,Macao and Taiwan	83	665	2453	1455
外商投资企业	Enterprises with Foreign Investment	5			

11-2 建筑施工企业个数和平均人数

Number of Construction Enterprises and Its Average Annual Staff and Workers

年 份 Year	总 计 Total	国有经济 State-owned	集体经济 Collective-owned	其他经济 Others owned	建筑业活动单位 Active unit
施工企业个数(个) Number of Enterprises (unit)					
1995	1283	216	1023	3	41
1996	1811	278	1347	31	155
1997	1748	296	1425	27	…
1998	1840	317	1407	116	…
1999	1812	317	1335	160	…
2000	1812	313	1241	258	…
2001	1628	305	829	494	…
施工企业人数(万人) Staff and Workers (10 000 persons)					
1995	61.33	22.29	38.52	0.16	0.36
1996	78.88	24.32	50.72	0.9	2.94
1997	81.22	25.08	55.37	0.77	…
1998	82.72	24.93	53.2	4.59	…
1999	77.18	22.98	47.19	7.01	…
2000	76.3	22.66	41.98	11.66	…
2001	97	25	39	33	

注：建筑施工企业均指资质等级四级及以上的建筑企业，下同。

Construction enterprises refer to the fourth and higher grade construction enterprises.The same as in the following table.

11-3 建筑施工企业固定资产、流动资产及利润(2001年)

Fixed AssetsCirculating Funds and Profits of Construction Enterprises (2001)

指 标	Item	总 计 Total	国有经济 State-owned	集体经济 Collective-owned	其他经济 other owned
年末固定资产原值 (万元)	Original Value Fixed Assets at the Yearend (10 000 yuan)	1802232	808752	486341	507139
年末固定资产净值 (万元)	Net Value of Fixed Assets at the Yearend (10 000 yuan)	1259312	517544	364456	377312
流动资产年末合计 (万元)	Circulating Funds at the Yearend (10 000 yuan)	2835012	1273709	693473	867830
利润总额(万元)	Total Profits (10 000 yuan)	86481	13035	32813	40633
利税总额 (万元)	Total Pre-tax Profits (10 000 yuan)	255109	64225	86750	104134
资金利润率(元／百元)	Ratio of Fund to Profits (yuan/100 yuan)	1.93	0.67	2.74	3.06
产值利润率 (%)	Ratio of Profit to Gross Output Value (%)	1.77	0.70	2.23	2.58
产值利税率 (%)	Ratio of Pre-tax Profit to Output Value (%)	5.21	3.47	5.89	6.62

注:本表不包括建筑业活动单位。

Enterprises engaged in construction were excluded.

11-4 建筑施工企业工程质量(2001年)

Quality of Construction Works of Construction Enterprises (2001)

指 标	Item	总 计 Total	国 有 State-owned	集 体 Collective-owned	其他经济 Others owned
竣工产值 (万元)	Output Value Completed (10 000 yuan)	3234410	1134170	1039374	1060866
验收鉴定的单位工程 (个)	Number of Projects Completed (unit)	14121	3723	6034	4364
#优良品	#High Quality	5026	1780	1515	1731
验收鉴定的单位工程优良品率(%)	Percentage of High Quality Projects Has Passed Test (%)	35.59	47.81	25.11	39.67
验收鉴定的房屋建筑竣工面积 (万平方米)	Floor Space of Buildings Completed That Has Passed Test (10 000 sq.m)	3204.60	575.96	1548.82	1079.82
#优良品	#High Quality	1408.39	357.69	542.93	507.77
验收鉴定的房屋建筑竣工面积优良品率 (%)	Percentage of Floor Space of High Quality Buildings Has Passed Test (%)	43.95	62.10	35.05	47.02

11-5 建筑施工企业技术装备情况(2001年)

Technical Equipments of Local Construction Enterprises (2001)

指 标	Item	总 计 Total	国 有 State-owned	集 体 Collective-owned	其他经济 Others owned
年底自有机械设备(台)	Number of Machinery and Equipment Owned at the Year-end (set)	327530	79990	147689	99851
年底自有机械设备净值(万元)	Net Value of Machinery and Equipment Owned at the Year-end (10 000 yuan)	502945	210661	141555	150729
技术装备率(期末)(元/人)	Value of Machines Per Laborer (yuan/person)	5199.50	8424.52	3643.02	4585.99
动力装备率(期末)(千瓦/人)	Power of Machines per Laborer (kw/person)	4.38	6.79	3.60	3.47

11-6 建筑施工企业劳动生产率(2001年)

Labor Productivity of Construction Enterprises (2001)

单位：元/人 (yuan/person)

指 标	Item	总 计 Total	国 有 State-owned	集 体 Collective-owned	其他经济 Others owned
按施工产值计算的劳动生产率	Overall Labor Productivity in Terms of Total Output Value	56128.62	73977.80	37931.43	47893.50
按增加值计算的劳动生产率	Overall Labor Productivity in Terms of Added-Value	13519.54	18390.41	10501.38	13381.87
人均竣工面积 (平方米/人)	Floor Space of Buildings Completed per Laborer (sq.m/person)	33.13	23.03	39.86	32.85

11-7 国有建筑企业主要经济指标

Major Economic Indicators on State – Owned Construction Enterprises

指 标	Item	1995	1999	2000	2001
国有建筑施工企业	**State-owned**				
施工产值 (亿元)	Output Value of Projects (100 million yuan)	106.70	146.20	158.11	184.99
全员劳动生产率 (元/人)	Overall Labor Productivity (yuan/person)	47871	63610	69792	79318
计算劳动生产率的平均人数 (万人)	Average Number of Staff and Workers by Calculating Labor Productivity (10 000 person)	22.29	22.98	22.66	23.32
房屋建筑施工面积 (万平方米)	Floor Space of Buildings Under Construction (10 000 sq.m)	1094.53	1333.50	1287.31	1459.86
房屋建筑竣工面积 (万平方米)	Floor Space of Buildings Completed (10 000 sq.m)	361.18	561.10	580.12	575.96
#住宅	Residential Buildings	156.74	341.10		
地方国有建筑施工企业	**Local State-owned**				
施工产值 (亿元)	Output Value of Projects (100 million yuan)	47.44	83.96	92.10	120.96
全员劳动生产率(元／人)	Overall Labor Productivity (yuan/person)	36328	54050	59094	71891
计算劳动生产率的平均人数 (万人)	Average Number of Staff and Workers by Calculating Labor Productivity (10 000 person)	13.06	15.53	15.59	16.83
房屋建筑施工面积 (万平方米)	Floor Space of Buildings Under Construction (10 000 sq.m)	760.60	1092.40	1036.99	1199.90
房屋建筑竣工面积 (万平方米)	Floor Space of Buildings Completed (10 000 sq.m)	278.22	469.70	481.60	518.98
#住宅	Residential Buildings	121.85	297.60		

11-8 建筑业总产值和增加值(2001年)

Gross Output Value and Added - Valueof Construction Enterprises (2001)

单位：万元 (10 000 yuan)

指 标	Item	总 计 Total	国 有 State-owned	集 体 Collective-owned	其他经济 Others owned
建筑业总产值(施工产值)	**Gross Output Value of Construction (Output Value of Projects)**	**4897879**	**1849867**	**1473883**	**1574129**
建筑安装	Construction and Installation	4725276	1796352	1412824	1516100
房屋构筑物修理	Repair of Buildings and Structures	111897	14408	55023	42466
非标准设备制造	Manufactured non-standard equipment	60706	39107	6036	15563
增加值	**Value Aded of construction**	**1307738**	**459865**	**408047**	**439826**
本年提取折旧	Depreciation of Fixed Assets Of the Year	92710	46042	22649	24019
应付工资	Wages Payable	606021	187914	213136	204971
应付福利费	Welfare Expenses Payable	60940	22309	19124	19507
管理费用中劳动待业保险费	Labor and Unemployment Insurance in Management Expenses	37760	26735	3723	7302
工程结算税金及附加	Taxes and Extra Charges on Project Settlement Accounts	158977	47643	50335	60999
管理费用中：税金	Taxes in Management Enpenses	9652	3547	3602	2503
工程结算利润	Profits of Project Setlement Accounts	341678	125675	95478	120525

11-9 房屋建筑面积

Floor Space of Building Construction

单位:万平方米 (10 000 sq.m)

年份 Year 市州 Cities and Prefecture		房屋建筑面积 Floor Space of Building Construction		国有经济 State-owned		集体经济 Collective-owned	
		施工面积 Floor Space Under Construction	竣工面积 Floor Space Completed	施工面积 Floor Space Under Construction	竣工面积 Floor Space Completed	施工面积 Floor Space Under Construction	竣工面积 Floor Space Completed
1990		1159.10	558.70	572.40	233.50	586.70	325.20
1991		1282.70	653.20	577.20	269.50	705.50	383.70
1992		1554.00	711.30	699.40	279.80	854.60	431.50
1993		1869.50	802.20	867.90	334.60	1001.60	467.60
1994		2081.50	868.30	1011.10	378.40	1068.40	489.30
1995		4507.41	2313.70	1094.50	361.20	3223.05	1835.33
1996		4662.00	2393.05	1285.16	467.04	3333.59	1898.28
1997		4719.57	2279.89	1236.68	465.95	3444.90	1783.44
1998		5067.56	2382.33	1397.64	530.70	3373.22	1701.44
1999		5180.91	2681.81	1333.55	561.10	3417.60	1900.54
2000		5087.93	2603.08	1287.31	580.12	3017.81	1634.32
2001		6259.27	3204.60	1459.86	575.96	2734.12	1548.82
长沙	Changsha	1673.41	750.58	472.36	151.30	405.44	207.45
株洲	Zhuzhou	393.86	189.93	84.93	26.21	135.93	86.55
湘潭	Xiangtan	556.28	336.83	108.68	57.71	293.51	197.77
衡阳	Hengyang	909.77	386.26	213.67	58.19	535.45	248.42
邵阳	Shaoyang	403.65	194.24	120.33	46.40	262.34	134.65
岳阳	Yueyang	465.89	337.43	51.78	34.19	230.62	171.90
常德	Changde	412.51	226.15	39.36	18.65	122.09	71.37
张家界	Zhangjiajie	51.74	28.65	6.37	6.28	14.68	7.42
益阳	Yiyang	350.65	172.97	23.12	6.82	107.89	47.15
郴州	Chenzhou	297.96	157.26	115.90	55.93	167.57	96.50
永州	Yongzhou	218.52	115.89	49.02	25.58	169.50	90.31
怀化	Huaihua	192.35	91.81	71.07	33.11	78.17	36.95
娄底	Loudi	226.37	153.93	85.34	47.77	141.03	106.15
湘西自治州	West Hunan	106.30	62.67	17.93	7.82	69.90	46.23

注：1995年及以后各年为资质等级四级及以上企业数据。

Data on construction enterprises in and after 1995 refer to those of the fourth and higher grade construction enterprises.

11-10 建筑业企业分行业生产指标(2001年)

指标	Item	土木工程建筑业 Civil Engineering	房屋建筑业 Building	矿山建筑业 Mines
企业个数 (个)	**Number of Enterprises (unit)**	**1466**	**1298**	**5**
建筑业总产值 (万元)	**Gross Output Value of Construction (10 000 yuan)**	**4576149**	**3446087**	**10204**
#建筑工程	Construction Projects	4244122	3180366	9615
安装工程	Installation Projects	178577	134476	549
房屋构筑物修理	Repair of Buildings and Structures	107209	104847	
非标准设备制造	Manufactured non-standard Equipment	46242	26399	40
竣工产值 (万元)	**Output Value Completed (10000 yuan)**	**3009476**	**2270745**	**7189**
单位工程施工个数 (个)	**Number of Projects in Operation (unit)**	**19896**	**16869**	**79**
#本年新开工个数	Number of Projects Started in Current Year	12523	10692	51
#投标承包个数	Number of Bidding Projects	12354	10390	58
#本年新开工	Started in Current Year	8336	7117	33
单位工程竣工个数 (个)	**Number of Projects Completed (unit)**	**12432**	**10546**	**57**
#优良工程个数	High Quality	4207	3233	24
房屋建筑施工面积 (万平方米)	**Floor Space of Buildings Under Construction (10 000 sq.m)**	**6203**	**6085**	**3**
#本年新开工面积	Floor Space of Buildings Started in Current Year	3632	3557	2
#投标承包的面积	Floor Space of Bidding Buildings	4252	4162	2
#本年新开工	#Started in Current Year	2726	2663	1
房屋建筑竣工面积 (万平方米)	**Floor Space of Buildings Completed (10 000 sq.m)**	**3183**	**3128**	**1**
#优良工程面积	#High Quality	1404	1382	1
自有机械设备年末总台数 (台)	**Total Number of Machinery and Equipment Owned at the Yearend (unit)**	**307606**	**272747**	**1047**
自有机械设备年末总功率 (万千瓦)	**Total Power of Machinery and Equipment Owned at the Yearend (10 000 kw)**	**407**	**292**	**3**
#施工机械功率	#Power of Construction Machines	331	235	2
自有机械设备净值 (万元)	**Net Value of Machinery and Equipment Owned (10 000 yuan)**	**482268**	**315195**	**3003**
计算建筑业劳动生产率的平均人数 (万人)	**Average of Staff and Workers by Calculating Construction Labor Productivity (10 000 persons)**	**83**	**72**	

Production Indicators of Construction Enterprises by Sector (2001)

11-10 续表 continued

铁路公路隧道桥梁建筑业 Railways, Highways, Tunnels and Bridges	堤坝电站码头建筑业 Dykes and dams, Electric Station and Wharf	其他土木工程建筑业 Other Civil Engineering	线路管道设备安装业 Pipes,Lines and Equipment Installation	线路管道安装业 Pipes and Lines Installation	设备安装业 Equipment Installation	建筑物装修装饰业 Building Decoration
80	**35**	**48**	**98**	**34**	**64**	**64**
847154	**252539**	**20165**	**296123**	**174711**	**121411**	**25607**
839171	197630	17340	94733	60064	34670	20844
7606	35025	921	185611	103288	82323	1389
327	312	1723	1314	385	929	3374
50	19572	181	14464	10975	3489	
447331	**266309**	**17902**	**205076**	**123209**	**81867**	**19858**
1954	**548**	**446**	**2315**	**1253**	**1062**	**51**
1107	310	363	1553	926	627	45
1363	437	106	978	568	410	18
889	247	50	763	445	318	1
1084	**363**	**382**	**1650**	**942**	**708**	**39**
662	174	114	810	525	285	9
92	**4**	**19**	**50**	**29**	**21**	**6**
57	2	14	35	20	15	4
72	2	14	31	13	18	
51	2	9	22	8	14	
38	**3**	**13**	**15**	**12**	**3**	**7**
18	2	1	4	3	1	
17196	**14324**	**2292**	**17285**	**10714**	**6571**	**2639**
56	**51**	**5**	**15**	**10**	**5**	**2**
48	41	5	10	6	4	2
105530	**53666**	**4874**	**18096**	**9629**	**8467**	**2581**
7	**3**	**1**	**4**	**2**	**2**	

11-11 国有、集体建筑企业生产指标(2001年)

Production Indicators of State – Owned and Collective – Owned Construction Enterprises (2001)

指标	Item	总计 Total	一、二级企业 The First &Second Grade Enterprise	国有经济 State-Owned	中央 Central	地方 Local	集体经济 Collective Owned
企业个数(个)	Number of Enterprises (unit)	1628	415	305	47	258	829
建筑业总产值(万元)	Gross Output Value of Construction (10 000 yuan)	4897879	3280956	1849867	640250	1209617	1473883
#建筑工程	Construction projects	4359699	2940375	1610560	496870	1113690	1322537
安装工程	Installation projects	365577	236704	185792	116333	69459	90287
房屋构筑物修理	Repair of Buildings and Structures	111897	54579	14408	1560	12848	55023
非标准设备制造	Manufactured Non-standard Equipment	60706	49298	39107	25487	13620	6036
竣工产值(万元)	Output Value Completed(10 000 yuan)	3234410	2017957	1134170	454961	679209	1039374
工程施工个数(个)	Number of Projects in Operation(unit)	22262	10255	6325	2630	3695	9150
#本年新开工	Started in Current Year	14121	6201	3861	1530	2331	5929
#投标承包个数	Number of Bidding Projects	13350	7032	3815	1635	2180	5084
#本年新开工	Started in Current Year	9100	4458	2434	1002	1432	3554
工程竣工个数(个)	Number of Projects Completed(unit)	14121	5858	3723	1486	2237	6034
#优良工程个数	High Quality	5026	3092	1780	1171	609	1515
房屋建筑施工面积(万平方米)	Floor Space of Buildings Under Construction (10 000 sq.m)	6259	3162	1460	260	1200	2734
#本年新开工面积	Floor Space of Buildings Started in Current Year	3672	1738	787	125	662	1632
#投标承包的面积	Floor Space of Bidding Buildings	4283	2352	1035	151	884	1840
#本年新开工	Started in Current Year	2748	1434	635	92	543	1182
房屋建筑竣工面积(万平方米)	Floor Space of Buildings Completed (10 000 sq.m)	3205	1330	576	57	519	1549
#优良工程面积	High Quality	1408	814	358	45	313	543
自有机械设备年末总台数(台)	Number of Machinery and Equipment Owned at the Yearend (unit)	327530	149323	79990	18877	61113	147689
自有机械设备年末总功率(万千瓦)	Power of Machinery and Equipment Owned at the Yearend (10 000 kw)	424	256	170	63	107	140
#施工机械功率	Power of Construction Machines	343	206	130	47	83	118
自有机械设备净值(万元)	Net Value of Machinery and Equipment Owned (10 000 yuan)	502945	336489	210661	56437	154224	141555
计算建筑业劳动生产率的平均人数(万人)	Average of Staff and Workers by Calculating Construction Labor Productivity (10 000 persons)	87	47	23	6	17	35

11-12 十强建筑施工企业排序(2001年)

Top 10 in Construction Enterprises (2001)

完成施工产值前10名企业

Top 10 in Output Value of Projects under Construction

湖南省公路桥梁建设总公司
Hunan Road & Bridge Corporation

中国水利水电第八工程局
NO.8 Hydropower Construction(Grop)

中国建筑第五工程局第三建筑安装公司
NO.5 Construction Company of China Construction Fifth Engineering Bureau

湖南顺天建筑有限公司
Hunan Shuntian Construction Ltd. Company

中国有色第二十三冶金建设公司
NO.23 Construction Grop of China National Non-ferrous metal industry Grop

湖南省第六工程公司
Hunan No.6 Construction Engineering Company

岳阳市公路桥梁基建总公司
Yueyang Municipal Road & Bridge Capital Construction Company

湖南省送变电建设公司
Hunan Electric power Transmission and Substation Construction Company

衡阳公路桥梁建设有限公司
Hengyang Road & Bridge Company

湖南省怀化公路桥梁建设总公司
Huaihua Road & Bridge Compang Hunan

实现利税总额前10名企业

Top 10 in Total Per-tax Profits

中国水利水电第八工程局
NO.8 Hydropower Construction(Grop)

湖南顺天建筑有限公司
Hunan Shuntian Construction Ltd. Company

湖南省公路桥梁建设总公司
Hunan Road & Bridge Corporation

湖南常德公路工程总公司
Changde Road Construction Engineering Company Hunan

湖南移动通信工程有限公司
Hunan Mobile Communication Engineering Ltd. Company

衡阳公路桥梁建设有限公司
Hengyang Road & Bridge Ltd. Company

湖南高岭建设集团股份有限公司
High Ridge Building Group Cor. Ltd.

中铁五局集团机械化工程有限责任公司（原铁道部第五工程局机械筑路工程处）
The Mechanization Engineering Construction Co. Ltd. Under China Railway Fifth Bureau Group

长沙市市政工程公司
Changsha Municipal Engineering Company

湖南省第六工程公司
Hunan No.6 Construction Engineering Company

十二、交通运输、邮电

TRANSPORTATION，POSTAL AND TELECOMMUNICATION SERVICES

资料整理人员：　刘华娟　杨　耒

12-1 运输线路基本情况

Basic Statistics on Transportation Routes

单位：公里 (km)

指标	Item	1995	1999	2000	2001
铁路营业里程	**Lengh of Railways in Operation**	**2602**	**2891.29**	**2924.33**	**2894.4**
地方铁路	Lengh of Local Railway	329	344.7	379.5	349.5
复线里程	Double-Track	642	1032.73	1836.16	1281.6
自动闭塞里程	Automatic Switching	627	716.3	1750.52	2253.4
电气化线路里程	Lengh of Electrified Railway	349	600.92	671.99	1211
内燃机牵引线路里程	Lengh of Diesel Engine	2191	2290.47	3086	1057.9
无缝线路里程	Lengh of Seamless Track	173	794.3	869.49	951.1
公路线路里程	**Lengh of Highways**	**59125**	**60416**	**60848**	**66593**
有路面里程	Paved Highways	58191	59485	59923	64821
#高级次高级路面	High and Secondary Grade	1317	17096	18349	20587
无路面里程	Non-Paved Highway	934	931	925	1772
等级公路	Expressway and Class Ⅰ to Ⅳ Highway	30383	32766	33380	36800
高速	Expressway		280	449	585
一级	First Class	109	204	239	335
二级	Second Class	122	3457	3761	4705
等外路	Highway Below Class Ⅳ	28742	27650	27468	29793
内河航道	**Lengh of Navigable Inland Waterway**	**10050**	**10065**	**10041**	**10041**
民用航空航线(条)	**Civil Aviation Routes (line)**	**17**	**20**	**24**	**25**
#国际航线(条)	Interational Routes (line)	1			1
管道线路里程	**Lengh Of Petroleum And Gas Pipeline**		**163.5**	**163.5**	**164**

12-2 铁路机车拥有量

Number of Railway Locomotives

指标	Item	1995	1999	2000	2001
中央铁路	**Central Railway**				
蒸汽机车（台）	Steam Locomotives (unit)	152	—	—	16
内燃机车（台）	Diesel Locomotives (unit)	413	552	529	376
客　车　（辆）	Passenger Coaches (unit)	1329	1742	1335	1443
电力机车(辆)	Electric Locomotives (unit)	34	120	120	296
地方铁路(窄轨)	**Local Railway Locomotives (narrow gauge)**				
蒸汽机车(台)	Steam Locomotives (unit)	35	15	15	15
内燃机车(台)	Diesel Locomotives (unit)	10	10	12	12
客　车(辆)	Passenger Coaches (unit)	37	21	27	27
货　车(辆)	Freight Cars (unit)	558	322	339	303

12-3 民用车辆、船舶拥有量

Number of Civil Motor Vehicles and Civil Transport Vessels

指标	Item	全省 总计 Total	交通部门合计 Total of Traffic Department	营业性 Business	个体 Individual	非营业性 Non-Business	非交通部门 Non-Traffic Department
公路	**Highway**						
民用汽车 (辆)	Civil Motor Vehicles (unit)	504344	210606	199767	136203	10839	293738
载货汽车 (辆)	Trucks Vehicles (unit)	243935	146387	136378	101482	10009	96718
载重量 (吨位)	General Trucks (ton)	827096	499479	454438	325796	45041	313309
载客汽车 (辆)	Passenger Vehicles (unit)	251620	64219	63389	34721	830	188231
载客量 (客位)	Passenger Vehicles Seats (seat)	2839015	946635	930035	449909	16600	1908980
特种车 (辆)	Special Motor Vehicles (unit)	3188					
轮胎式拖拉机 (辆)	Type Tractor (unit)	177516	109907	109907	109627		67609
摩托车 (辆)	Motors (unit)	1062201					
其他机动车 (辆)	Other Motor Vehicles (unit)	62103	37707	37707	37288		
载货挂车 (辆)	Truck Trailer (unit)	2463	136378	136378			
水运	**Waterway**						
货船 (艘)	Cargoboat (unit)	7164	7164	7164	5650		
净载重量 (吨位)	Net Haulage Capacity (ton)	511888	265721	265721	265721		
客货船 (艘)	Passenger And Cargo Vessel (unit)	4	4	4			
净载重量 (吨位)	Net Haulage Capacity (ton)	50	50	50			
载客量 (客位)	Passenger Capacity (seat)	662	662	662			
客船 (艘)	Passenger Ship (unit)	2228	2228	2228			
载客量 (客位)	Passenger Capacity (seat)	66714	66714	66714	53386		
拖船 (艘)	Drawing (unit)	142	142	142	12		
功率 (千瓦)	Power (kw)	20195	20195	20195	912		
驳船 (艘)	Barges (unit)	397	397	397	36		
净载重量 (吨位)	Net Haulage Capacity (ton)	105833	105833	105833	2476		

12-4 旅客运量和旅客周转量

Passenger Traffic and Turnover Volume of Passenger Traffic

年份 Year	合计 Total	铁路 Railway	中央 Central	地方 Local	公路 Highway	水运 Waterway	民用航空 Civil Aviation
客运量(万人)	Total Passenger Traffic (10 000 persons)						
1980	32776	3434	3271	163	27590	1750	2
1981	33546	3723	3520	203	27871	1950	2
1982	37286	3898	3677	221	31380	2006	2
1983	40380	4117	3895	222	33955	2306	2
1984	43333	4368	4154	214	36497	2466	2
1985	48666	4686	4461	225	41520	2458	2
1986	50903	4368	4159	209	44464	2066	5
1987	53600	4586	4397	189	47071	1935	8
1988	56236	4937	4739	198	49182	2109	8
1989	54084	4357	4205	152	47865	1855	7
1990	54161	3474	3389	85	49112	1568	7
1991	54710	3514	3437	77	49566	1621	9
1992	52641	3638	3564	74	47366	1615	22
1993	55896	4022	3949	73	50252	1562	60
1994	64757	4176	4105	71	59028	1481	72
1995	71566	4135	4083	52	65971	1375	85
1996	76377	3892	3846	46	71087	1298	100
1997	79250	4488	4444	44	73233	1357	172
1998	79540	4497	4469	28	73681	1260	102
1999	87806	5022	5000	22	81675	1002	107
2000	87462	5233	5216	17	81005	1094	130
2001	92381	5202	5188	14	85971	1063	145
周转量(亿人公里)	Total Passenger-kilometers (100 million passenger-km)						
1980	133.68	65.47	65.12	0.35	62.90	5.25	0.06
1981	149.19	73.21	72.80	0.41	70.20	5.71	0.07
1982	159.66	78.05	77.61	0.44	75.62	5.92	0.07
1983	179.81	90.95	90.51	0.44	82.10	6.69	0.07
1984	204.68	104.85	104.42	0.43	93.08	6.68	0.07
1985	254.53	132.78	132.32	0.46	114.95	6.72	0.08
1986	275.38	140.09	139.65	0.44	128.68	6.38	0.23
1987	310.57	161.86	161.45	0.41	142.66	5.74	0.31
1988	354.23	191.21	190.79	0.42	156.57	6.11	0.34
1989	350.34	181.09	180.78	0.31	163.48	5.38	0.39
1990	339.86	162.32	162.17	0.15	172.73	4.25	0.56
1991	378.20	189.29	189.16	0.13	184.27	3.94	0.70
1992	435.19	228.39	228.24	0.15	200.09	4.87	1.84
1993	490.26	270.82	270.68	0.14	209.34	4.58	5.52
1994	539.02	291.44	291.29	0.15	237.00	3.90	6.68
1995	555.13	301.60	301.49	0.11	242.46	3.66	7.41
1996	538.29	262.99	262.89	0.10	263.48	3.45	8.37
1997	592.16	305.06	304.97	0.09	274.68	3.69	8.73
1998	610.53	319.67	319.61	0.06	279.69	3.49	7.68
1999	676.04	353.87	353.83	0.04	310.69	3.76	7.72
2000	724.06	394.00	393.96	0.04	318.37	3.55	8.14
2001	761.62	410.65	410.62	0.03	337.90	3.23	9.84

12-5 货物运量和货物周转量

Freight Traffic and Turnover Volume of Freight Traffic

年份 Year	合计 Total	铁路 Railway	中央 Central	地方 Local	公路 Highway	水运 Waterway	民用航空 Civil Aviation
货运量(万吨)	Total Freight Traffic (10 000 tons)						
1980	23650	3778	3594	184	16576	3261	
1981	24633	3573	3408	165	18067	2955	
1982	26951	3783	3616	167	20054	3076	
1983	29100	3876	3710	166	22095	3089	
1984	31800	3977	3826	151	24655	3128	
1985	32902	4218	402	126	35699	2945	
1986	34902	4346	4213	133	27140	3372	
1987	35747	4485	4354	131	27525	3693	
1988	39020	4522	4401	121	30922	3531	
1989	37842	4731	4567	164	29453	3671	
1990	37708	4771	4597	174	29679	3217	
1991	41219	4777	4614	163	33224	3177	
1992	42548	4906	4787	119	33788	3821	
1993	46040	4982	4886	96	37582	3441	1
1994	48413	4929	4841	88	39912	3536	1
1995	49853	5017	4904	113	41272	3531	1
1996	50420	4893	4830	63	42191	3301	1
1997	48946	4535	4495	40	41340	3034	2
1998	49078	4408	4360	48	41610	2990	1
1999	51057	4456	4424	32	43296	3178	1
2000	51090	4676	4628	48	42868	3406	2
2001	52879	4965	4913	52	44340	3572	2
周转量(亿吨公里)	Total Freight Ton-kilometers (100 million ton-km)						
1980	331.43	272.42	271.02	1.4	33.95	24.98	
1981	340.22	274.11	272.87	1.24	39.57	26.54	
1982	359.71	286.44	285.24	1.2	43.83	29.35	
1983	388.55	302.28	301.1	1.18	50.56	35.61	
1984	435.78	335.83	334.83	1	59.7	40.15	
1985	512.03	392.52	391.73	0.79	75.55	43.86	
1986	582.44	438.71	437.83	0.88	91.91	51.72	
1987	637.6	481.87	480.96	0.91	103.91	51.66	
1988	690.6	504.58	503.74	0.84	134.16	51.76	
1989	730.4	544.44	543.57	0.87	129.58	56.29	
1990	774.81	590.33	589.44	0.89	137.02	47.37	
1991	830.64	621.98	621.18	0.8	164.42	44.15	
1992	901.85	656.29	655.5	0.79	191.53	53.95	
1993	951.77	683.1	682.49	0.61	209.85	58.66	0.07
1994	1003.38	720.46	719.87	0.59	221.78	60.98	0.07
1995	1043.59	751.84	751.24	0.6	235.52	56.06	0.09
1996	1029.25	728.91	728.46	0.45	240.13	60.1	0.11
1997	998.64	690.8	690.47	0.33	244.86	62.78	0.12
1998	978.72	652.98	652.66	0.32	256.56	68.92	0.09
1999	967.36	624.14	623.89	0.25	272.71	70.08	0.11
2000	1074.14	632.12	631.94	0.18	297.79	143.76	0.11
2001	1131.78	674.39	674.25	0.14	316.03	141.22	0.14

12-6 公路、水上客货运输量部门构成情况(2001年)

Composition of Passenger and Freight Traffic by Sectors (2001)

指标	Item	合计 Total	国有经济 State-Owned	个体经济 Self-employed Individual
公路运输	**Highway Transportation**			
客运量 (万人)	Passenger Traffic (10 000 persons)	85971	14613	54349
旅客周转量 (亿人公里)	Passenger Kilometers (100 million persons-km)	337.90	133.00	133.45
货运量 (万吨)	Freight Traffic (10 000 tons)	41823	331	23126
货物周转量 (亿吨公里)	Total Freight Ton-kilometers (100 million ton-km)	316.03	2.77	177.27
水上运输	**Waterway Transportation**			
客运量 (万人)	Passenger Traffic (10 000 persons)	1063	287	776
旅客周转量 (万人公里)	Passenger Kilometersc (10 000 persons-km)	32291	2900	17884
货运量 (万吨)	Freight Traffic (10 000 tons)	3572	221	2690
货物周转量 (万吨公里)	Total Freight Ton-kilometers (10 000 ton-km)	1412198	1096101	237462

12-7 交通运输邮电通信业在岗职工人数

Number of Staff and Workers on Job of Transportation and Postal and Telecommunication

行业	Sector	职工人数 (人) Staff and Workers (person)			
		1995	1999	2000	2001
铁路运输业	Railway Transportation	111585	73414	89844	88410
公路运输业	Highway Transportation	63506	66731	37900	49565
水上运输业	Waterway Transportation	11001	16075	3371	12170
航空运输业	Civil Aviation Transportation	1091	2249	1185	3008
交通运输辅助业	Transpotation Subsidiary	39921	65720	42316	65260
其他运输业	Other Transportation	80	269	50	330
邮电通信业	Telecommunications	44994	49905	44757	52555

12-8 内河航运主要港口概况(2001年)

Major Indicators of Major Ports in Navigable Inland Waterways (2001)

港口名称	Port Name	码头长度 (米) Length of Quay Line (m)	泊位个数 (个) Number of Berths (unit)	货物吞吐量 (万吨) Freight Thruput (10 000 tons)	旅客吞吐量 (万人) Passenger Thruput (10 000 persons)
株洲港	Zhuzhou Port	4789	70	205.55	6
衡阳港	Hengyang Port	1215	46	196.6	
岳阳港	Yueyang Port	3523	69	212.27	118.67
城陵矶港	Chenglingji Port	1573	22	541.13	11.98

12-9 邮电通信网

Postal and Telecommunications Services Network

年 份 Year	邮政局、所 (处) Post Offices	邮路及农村投递线路 总长度(万公里) Lengh of Postal Routes and Rural Delivery Routes (10000 km)	长话电路 (路) Long Distance Telephone Lines (line)	电报电路 (路) Telegram Lines (line)
1995	3210	29.45	24621	428
1997	14676	30.73	49349	398
1998	15867	31.55	77015	361
1999	9145	31.63	68815	427
2000	3598	33.83	84334	17
2001	3081	33.9	92970	-

注：邮政局、所1999年以前数据为邮电局、所数。

Data of post and telecommunication offices prior to 1999 refer to those of numbers.

12-10 邮电通信企业主要财务指标

Main Financial Indicators of Postal and Telecommunications Enterprises

单位：万元 (10 000 yuan)

指 标	Item	合计 Total		中央邮电 Central Enterprises		地方邮电 Local Enterprises	
		2000	2001	2000	2001	2000	2001
业务收入	Business Revenue	1004319.57	1169846.7	893967.57	1169846.7	110352	-
业务支出	Business Defray	755058.01	886783.6	672373.01	886783.6	82685	-
营业外损益净额	Blance Of Revenue And Expenditures	-23787.88	-17041.6	-23231.88	-17041.6	-556	-
税金及附加费	Taxes And Surcharges	29702.05	39639.6	25066.05	39639.6	4636	-
收支差额	Total Balance	-103508.44	-22209.3	-83410.44	-22209.3	-20098	-

12-11 邮电通信水平

Development of Postal and Telecommunications Services

指 标	Item	1995	1999	2000	2001
平均每人每年发函件数 (件)	Annual Average Number of Letters Mailes Per Capita (piece)	5.42	4.59	3.24	6.01
平均每百人每年订报刊数 (份)	Annual Average Number of Newspaper and Magazine Subscribers Per 100 Persons (copy)	2338	1541	1270	1283
平均每万人拥有电话机部数(部)	Telephones Per 100 Persons (line)	256.74	631.19	1066.8	1150
设有邮政局所乡(镇)的比重(%)	Percentage of Townships With Post and Telecommunications Offices (%)	83.7	82.36	81.3	79.35
通邮路的乡(镇)比重 (%)	Percentage Of Townships With Post Offices (%)	100	100	100	100
通电话的乡(镇)比重 (%)	Percentage of Townships with Telephone Communication (%)	99.6	100	100	100
进入长话自动网的乡(镇)比重 (%)	Percentage of Townships with Connected Autoexchang Net of Long Distance Call (%)	-	100	100	100
县以上城市装有自动电话交换机比重(%)	Percentage of Above County Fited Autoexchang of Telephone (%)	100	100	100	100

12-12 邮电业务量(2001年)

Volume of Postal and Telecommunications Services (2001)

市州	Cities and Prefecture	邮电业务总量(万元) Revenue From Postal and Telecommunication (10 000 yuan)	函件(万件) Letters (10 000 pieces)	报刊期发数(万份) Parcels (10 000 copies)	电报(万份) Express Mail (10 000 copies)	长途电话(万次) Long Distance Telephone Calls (10 000 times)	市内电话(万户) Urban Telephone (10 000 households)	农村电话(万户) Rural Telephone (10 000 households)
合计	**Total**	**1341636.13**	**39470**	**1021.93**	**82.36**	**48921**	**409.6**	**302.5**
长沙市	Changsha	322043.50	13902	140.57	7.28	11369	75.6	40.8
株洲市	Zhuzhou	104985.61	2117	62.51	3.12	3248	42.1	21.9
湘潭市	Xiangtan	71583.58	2430	36.59	2.16	2746	25.2	17.1
衡阳市	Hengyang	111538.64	2455	112.60	7.46	4543	39.3	23.6
邵阳市	Shaoyang	91094.72	1867	137.90	5.44	2971	27.1	27.4
岳阳市	Yueyang	102909.98	3112	89.96	19.48	3139	36.3	23.7
常德市	Changde	114462.00	2156	118.13	4.45	4425	36.7	38.7
张家界市	Zhangjiajie	33410.06	1366	20.83	1.61	978	8.8	6.5
益阳市	Yiyang	74570.56	1631	49.39	6.35	2977	20.0	25.9
郴州市	Chenzhou	87389.97	1823	61.24	4.72	2733	21.3	21.6
永州市	Yongzhou	66514.40	1457	51.07	4.94	2451	22.2	19.4
怀化市	Huaihua	67892.39	2316	44.56	7.64	3254	25.6	14.0
娄底市	Loudi	57479.35	1677	51.80	3.33	2742	18.1	15.2
湘西自治州	West Hunan A.P	35761.37	1161	44.78	4.38	1345	11.3	6.7

12-13 邮电通信工具拥有量

Telecommunications Facilties

年份 Year	市话交换机容量(门) Urban Switch Boards Capacity(line)	农话交换机容量(门) Rural Switch Boards Capacity(line)	电话机(部) Telephones (set)	城市电话 Urban	农村电话 Rural
1980	67992	58081	74265	47089	27176
1985	108108	64816	91649	65537	26112
1990	177502	97496	156675	117418	39257
1991	267155	112352	200214	151299	48915
1992	424386	142578	326382	255934	70448
1993	791685	193605	599733	501930	97803
1994	1387209	363546	1055547	889262	166285
1995	2056510	680974	1630988	1322387	308601
1996	2670499	914843	2348882	1864761	484121
1997	2985936	1124934	2652809	1989519	663290
1998	3153675	1342864	3380281	2465380	914901
1999	3854041	2005630	4122927	2802859	1320068
2000	5044640	3687398	7000439	4165693	2834746
2001	5503935	4142000	7119407	4095397	3024010

十三、国内、外贸易
对外经济和旅游

DOMESTIC TRADE，FOREIGN TRADE，
FOREIGN ECONOMY AND TOURISM

资料整理人员：　王忠好　唐双全　曾晓林　郭文峰

13-1 国内贸易基本情况

Basic Statistics on Domestic Trade

项 目	Item	1995	1999	2000	2001
社会消费品零售总额 (亿元)	**Total Retail Sales of Consumer Goods (100 million yuan)**	**837.41**	**1229.21**	**1364.66**	**1511.07**
按地区分	**By Location**				
市	City	428.29	625.77	710.06	800.06
县	Country	166.31	235.09	255.10	278.01
县以下	Under Country Lever	242.81	368.35	399.50	433.00
按经济类型	**By Ownership**				
公有经济	Public -Owned Economic	339.29	371.17	396.77	404.85
国有经济	Stats-Owned Economic	213.73	209.20	232.88	246.17
集体经济	Collective-Owned Economic	117.49	160.79	-	-
非公有经济	Non Public-Owned Economic	498.12	858.04	967.89	1106.21
私营经济	Prvite Economic	13.26	78.47	-	-
个体经济	Individual Economic	326.58	575.54	-	-
按行业分	**By Sector**				
批发零售贸易业	Wholesales and Retail Sales Trade	554.88	779.99	885.05	985.14
餐饮业	Catering Trade	54.63	117.18	139.55	161.08
制造业	Manufacturing	53.24	70.68	69.76	77.93
其他行业	Others	174.66	261.36	270.30	286.92
农民对非农业居民零售	Retail Sales of Peasantry to Non-peasantry	149.63	228.15	243.15	257.58
商品交易市场个数(个)	**Number of Free Markets (unit)**	**3905**	**3629**	**3682**	**3691**
城市	Urban Areas	834	990	1095	1122
乡村	Rural Areas	3071	2639	2587	2569
市场贸易成交额(亿元)	**Transaction Value of Free Markets (100 million yuan)**	**453.43**	**800.72**	**880.93**	**855.74**
按城乡分:	**By Urban or Rural Areas:**				
城市	Urban Areas	230.91	451.20	484.07	466.73
乡村	Rural Areas	222.52	349.52	396.86	389.01
按商品类别分:	**By Types of Goods:**				
粮食类	Grain	22.95	38.25	38.69	42.19
油脂油料类	Oils	14.30	22.68	25.07	23.47
棉烟麻类	Cotton, Tobacco and Hemp	2.32	5.84	6.63	5.80
肉食禽蛋类	Meat,Poultry and Eggs	126.57	176.94	192.53	184.04
水产品类	Aquatic Products	31.38	60.60	68.28	68.38
蔬菜类	Vegetables	42.85	84.99	97.86	99.78
干鲜果类	Dried and Fresh Fruits	33.27	90.53	103.05	99.03
大牲畜类	Large Domeestic Animals	6.26	8.77	10.31	8.74
家畜类	Domeestic Animals	15.93	17.80	18.71	19.16
工业品类	Industrial Products	109.27	256.53	277.02	269.66
其他类	Others	20.61	37.80	42.80	35.51
成交额为社会消费品零售总额(%)	**Proportion of Transaction Value of Free Markets to Total Retail Sales of Consumer Goods(%)**	**54.10**	**65.10**	**64.60**	**56.60**

13-2 限额以上批发零售贸易、餐饮业基本情况(2001年)

Basic Statistics on Gross Value of Purchases, Sales and Inventory of Wholesale and Retail Trade (2001)

指标	Item	法人单位(个) Number of Corporation Unit	产业活动单位(个) Number of Active Units (unit)	从业人数(人) Persons Engaged (person)
总 计	**Total**	**842**	**975**	**152341**
批发业	**Wholesale Trades**	**469**	**512**	**74543**
内资企业	Domestic Funded Enterprises	469	512	74543
国有企业	State-owned Enterprises	289	317	46494
集体企业	Collective-owned Enterprises	57	59	10551
股份合作企业	Cooperative Enterprises	5	6	488
联营企业	Joint Ownership Enterprises	1	1	28
国有与集体联营企业	Joint State-collective Enterprises	1	1	28
有限责任公司	Limited Liability Corporations	39	46	5315
国有独资企业	State-funded Corporations	6	12	1007
其他有限责任公司	Other Limited Liability Corporations	33	34	4308
股份有限公司	Share-holding Corporations Ltd.	59	63	10602
私营企业	Private Enterprises	19	20	1065
私营有限责任公司	Private Limited Liability Corporations	15	16	795
零售业	**Retail Sale Trades**	**284**	**310**	**56260**
内资企业	Domestic Funded Enterprises	281	305	54156
国有企业	State-owned Enterprises	173	178	23814
集体企业	Collective-owned Enterprises	28	32	5198
股份合作企业	Cooperative Enterprises	6	7	814
联营企业	Joint Ownership Enterprises	1	1	14
集体联营企业	Collective Joint Ownership Enterprises			
有限责任公司	Limited Liability Corporations	23	30	5475
国有独资企业	State-funded Corporations			
其他有限责任公司	Other Limited Liability Corporations	23	30	5475
股份有限公司	Share-holding Corporations Ltd.	28	34	14991
私营企业	Private Enterprises	22	23	3850
私营有限责任公司	Private Limited Liability Corporations	15	16	3042
外商投资企业	Enterprises with Foreign Investment	1	3	1332
中外合资经营企业	Joint-venture Enterprises	1	3	1332
餐饮业	**Catering Trades**	**89**	**153**	**21538**
内资企业	Domestic Funded Enterprises	81	128	18762
国有企业	State-owned Enterprises	34	63	10251
集体企业	Collective-owned Enterprises	5	7	711
联营企业	Joint Ownership Enterprises	1	1	141
国有联营企业	Collective Joint Ownership Enterprises			
有限责任公司	Limited Liability Corporations	13	18	2609
国有独资企业	State-funded Corporations			
其他有限责任公司	Other Limited Liability Corporations	13	18	2609
股份有限公司	Share-holding Corporations Ltd..	5	7	1483
私营企业	Private Enterprises	19	23	2047
私营有限责任公司	Private Limited Liability Corporations	6	7	623
港、澳、台商投资企业	Enterprises with Investment from Hongkong,Macro and Taiwan	4	9	1507
合资经营企业(港或澳、台资)	Joint-venture Enterprises (with Funds from HongKong,Macao and Taiwan)	3	7	1241
合作经营企业(港或澳、台资)	Cooperative Enterprises (with Funds from HongKong,Macao and Taiwan)	0	1	116
外商投资企业	Enterprises with Foreign Investment	4	16	1269
中外合资经营企业	Joint-venture Enterprises	1	1	262
中外合作经营企业	Cooperative Enterprises	1	7	390
外资企业	Enterprises with Sole Foreign Investment	2	8	617

13-3 限额以上批发零售贸易业商品销售总额(2001年)

Gross Value of Purchases, Sales and Inventory of Sizes Wholesale and Retail Trade (2001)

单位：亿元 (100 million yuan)

项 目	Item	销售总额 Total Sales	批 发 Wholesale Trade	零 售 Retial Trade
总 计	**Total**	**786.71**	**620.87**	**165.84**
按国民经济行业分组	**By Sector**			
食品、饮料、烟草批发业	Wholesale of Food,Beverages and Tobaccos	221.35	216.79	4.56
粮食、食用油批发业	Wholesale of Grain and Edible Oil	21.39	20.92	0.47
烟草及其制品批发业	Wholesale of Tobaccos	174.16	173.32	0.84
棉、麻、土畜产品批发业	Wholesale of Cotton,Ambery and Animal Products	14.73	14.56	0.17
纺织品、服装和鞋帽批发业	Wholesale of Textiles,Garments, Shoes and Hats	23.91	23.89	0.01
日用百货批发业	Wholesale of Daily Consumer Goods	11.33	10.39	0.93
日用杂品批发业	Wholesale of Daily Sundry Articles	1.54	1.54	0.00
五金、交电、化工批发业	Wholesale of Hardware,Transport, Electric and Chemical Products	13.67	12.75	0.92
药品及医疗器械批发业	Wholesale of Medicines and Medical Appliances	43.43	26.70	16.73
能源批发业	Wholesale of Energy Products	196.08	169.43	26.65
石油及制品批发业	Wholesale of Petroleum and Related Products	195.58	168.93	26.64
煤炭及制品批发业	Wholesale of Coal and Related Products	0.50	0.50	0.00
化工材料批发业	Wholesale of Chemical Materials	3.70	3.63	0.06
建筑材料批发业	Wholesale of Building Materials	2.43	2.43	0.00
矿产品批发业	Wholesale of Mineral Products	0.51	0.51	0.00
金属材料批发业	Wholesale of Metal Materials	33.25	31.36	1.89
机械、电子设备批发业	Wholesale of Machinery and Electronic Equipment	27.79	26.11	1.68
汽车、摩托车及零配件批发业	Wholesale of Motor Vehicles, Motorcycles and Parts	32.42	16.69	15.73
汽车批发业	Wholesale of Motor Vehicles	30.77	15.04	15.73
再生物资回收批发业	Wholesale of Recycled Materials	1.63	1.62	0.01
工艺美术批发业	Wholesale of Arts and Handicraft Products	8.70	8.70	0.00
图书报刊批发业	Wholesale of Books,Newspapers and Magazines	14.25	11.87	2.39
农业生产资料批发业	Wholesale of Means of Agricultural Production	18.59	17.40	1.19
其他类未包括的批发业	Other Wholesale not Classified Elsewhere	1.33	1.30	0.03
食品、饮料和烟草零售业	Retail of Food,Beverages and Tobaccos	9.79	1.99	7.80
粮油食品零售业	Retail of Grain and Edible Oil	3.73	0.82	2.91
副食品零售业	Retail of Non-staple Food	2.66	0.08	2.58
日用百货零售业	Retail of Daily Consumer Goods	66.18	9.97	56.21
百货零售业	Retail of Consumer Goods	64.33	9.27	55.06
文化体育用品零售业	Retail of Cultural and Sports Goods	0.59	0.08	0.51
纺织品、服装和鞋帽零售业	Retail of Textiles,Garments,Shoes and Hats	1.18	0.27	0.91
日用杂品零售业	Retail of Daily Sundry Articles	0.44	0.00	0.44
五金、交电、化工零售业	Retail of Hardware,Transport, Electric and Chemical Products	4.09	1.38	2.72
药品及医疗器械零售业	Retail of Medicines and Medical Appliances	6.52	1.54	4.98
图书报刊零售业	Retail of Books,Newspapers and Magazines	11.53	0.81	10.72
其他零售业	Other Retail Trades	16.07	6.96	9.11
汽车、摩托车及其零配件	Retail of Motor Vehicles, Motorcycles and Parts	1.93	0.07	1.85

13-4 限额以上批发零售贸易业商品购进、销售、库存总额(2001年)

Total Value of Purchases Sales and Inventory of Above – Norm Wholesale and Retail Sales Trade (2001)

单位：亿元 (100 million yuan)

指标	Item	商品购进总额 Total Purchases	商品销售总额 Total Sales	批发 Wholesale Trade	零售 Retail Trade	年末库存总额 Inventory Year-end
总计	**Total**	**729.39**	**786.71**	**620.87**	**165.84**	**109.45**
国有及国有控股	State-owned Enterprises (including enterprises with controlling share hold by the state)	539.64	588.19	522.71	65.48	55.95
按登记注册类型分组	**By Status of Registration**					
内资企业	Domestic Funded Enterprises	723.17	780.59	620.82	159.78	109.07
国有企业	State-owned Enterprises	377.61	417.34	350.75	66.59	51.04
集体企业	Collective-owned Enterprises	46.99	45.53	35.81	9.72	31.60
股份合作企业	Cooperative Enterprises	2.86	2.63	1.14	1.49	0.29
联营企业	Joint Ownership Enterprises	0.87	0.90	0.77	0.12	0.01
集体联营企业	Collective Joint Ownership Enterprises					
国有与集体联营	Joint State-collective Enterprises	0.77	0.77	0.77		0.01
有限责任公司	Limited Liability Corporations	39.05	41.46	28.34	13.12	8.15
国有独资企业	State-funded Corporations	3.45	5.10	4.97	0.13	0.53
其他有限责任公司	Other Limited Liability Corporations	35.61	36.36	23.38	12.99	7.61
股份有限公司	Share-holding Corporations Ltd.	233.11	249.73	187.82	61.91	15.01
私营企业	Private Enterprises	22.68	23.00	16.17	6.83	2.97
私营有限责任公司	Private Limited Liability Corporations	20.39	21.09	15.11	5.98	2.31
外商投资企业	Enterprises with Foreign Investment	5.64	5.53		5.53	0.36
中外合资经营企业	Joint-venture Enterprises	5.64	5.53		5.53	0.36
按国民经济行业分组	**By Sector**					
食品饮料、烟草批发业	Wholesale of Food,Beverages and Tobaccos	195.88	221.35	216.79	4.56	27.61
粮食、食用油批发	Wholesale of Grain and Edible Oil	20.55	21.39	20.92	0.47	12.05
烟草及其制品批发	Wholesale of Tobaccos	152.77	174.16	173.32	0.84	12.26
棉、麻、土畜产品批发业	Wholesale of Cotton,Ambery and Animal Products	17.96	14.73	14.56	0.17	27.10
纺织品、服装和鞋帽批发业	Wholesale of Textiles,Garments, Shoes and Hats	22.61	23.91	23.89	0.01	1.73
日用百货批发业	Wholesale of Daily Consumer Goods	10.95	11.33	10.39	0.93	1.10
日用杂品批发业	Wholesale of Daily Sundry Articles	1.46	1.54	1.54		0.01
五金交电、化工批发业	Wholesale of Hardware,Transport, Electric and Chemical Products	14.24	13.67	12.75	0.92	6.21
药品及医疗器械批发业	Wholesale of Medicines and Medical Appliances	39.36	43.43	26.70	16.73	10.66

指标	Item	商品购进总额 Total Purchases	商品销售总额 Total Sales	批发 Wholesale Trade	零售 Retail Trade	年末库存总额 Inventory Year-end
能源批发业	Wholesale of Energy Products	183.14	196.08	169.43	26.65	6.93
石油及制品批发业	Wholesale of Petroleum and Related Products	182.58	195.58	168.93	26.64	6.87
煤炭及制品批发业	Wholesale of Coal and Related Products	0.55	0.50	0.50	0.00	0.06
化工材料批发业	Wholesale of Chemical Materials	3.60	3.70	3.63	0.06	0.26
建筑材料批发业	Wholesale of Building Materials	2.40	2.43	2.43	0.00	0.25
矿产品批发业	Wholesale of Mineral Products	0.53	0.51	0.51	0.00	0.18
金属材料批发业	Wholesale of Metal Materials	29.63	33.25	31.36	1.89	2.26
机械、电子设备批发业	Wholesale of Machinery and Electronic Equipment	26.05	27.79	26.11	1.68	2.39
汽车、摩托车及零配件批发业	Wholesale of Motor Vehicles, Motorcycles and Parts	30.67	32.42	16.69	15.73	2.12
汽车批发业	Wholesale of Motor Vehicles	29.15	30.77	15.04	15.73	2.00
再生物资回收批发业	Wholesale of Recycled Materials	1.54	1.63	1.63	0.01	0.15
工艺美术批发业	Wholesale of Arts and Handicraft Products	8.64	8.70	8.70	0.00	0.32
图书报刊批发业	Wholesale of Books,Newspapers and Magazines	15.40	14.25	11.87	2.39	3.72
农业生产资料批发业	Wholesale of Means of Agricultural Production	15.93	18.59	17.40	1.19	2.32
其他类未包括的批发业	Other Wholesale not Classified Elsewhere	1.28	1.33	1.30	0.03	0.06
食品饮料和烟草零售业	Retail of Food,Beverages and Tobaccos	8.26	9.79	1.99	7.80	1.34
粮油食品零售业	Retail of Grain and Edible Oil	2.44	3.73	0.82	2.91	0.40
副食品零售业	Retail of Non-staple Food	2.60	2.66	0.08	2.58	0.43
日用百货零售业	Retail of Daily Consumer Goods	59.33	66.18	9.97	56.21	6.78
百货零售业	Retail of Consumer Goods	57.79	64.33	9.27	55.06	6.20
文化体育用品零售业	Retail of Cultural and Sports Goods	0.52	0.59	0.08	0.51	0.34
纺织品、服装和鞋帽零售业	Retail of Textiles,Garments, Shoes and Hats	1.08	1.18	0.27	0.91	0.13
日用杂品零售业	Retail of Daily Sundry Articles	2.46	0.44	0.00	0.44	0.28
五金、交电、化工零售业	Retail of Hardware,Transport, Electric and Chemical Products	3.75	4.09	1.38	2.72	1.02
药品及医疗器械零售业	Retail of Medicines and Medical Appliances	5.81	6.52	1.54	4.98	1.18
图书报刊零售业	Retail of Books,Newspapers and Magazines	12.37	11.53	0.81	10.72	2.46
其他零售业	Other Retail Trades	14.83	16.07	6.96	9.11	0.84
汽车、摩托车及其零配件零售业	Retail of Motor Vehicles, Motorcycles and Parts	1.75	1.93	0.07	1.85	0.12

13-5 限额以上批发零售贸易企业商品销售数量

Total Value of Wholesale in Above-Norm Wholesale and Retail Trade

指标	Item	合计 Total		批发 Wholesale Trade		零售 Retail Trade	
		2000	2001	2000	2001	2000	2001
粮食(吨)	Grain (ton)	420492	470595	312401	367885	108091	102710
(千元)	(1 000 yuan)	541387	667904	369426	472408	171961	195496
食用植物油(吨)	Edible Vegetable Oil (ton)	47275	43490	36368	32356	10907	11134
(千元)	(1 000 yuan)	319562	244790	240183	178314	79379	66476
食糖(吨)	Sugar (ton)	41064	19584	34003	17872	7061	1712
(千元)	(1 000 yuan)	130542	76332	105630	68898	24912	7434
棉花(吨)	Cotton (ton)	131517	106742	131400	106717	117	25
(千元)	(1 000 yuan)	1397444	1135196	1395358	1134932	2086	264
电视机(台)	Television (unit)	269215	260713	51682	42201	217533	218512
(千元)	(1 000 yuan)	638305	532203	105604	65245	532701	466958
组合音响(台)	Hi-Fi Stereo Component System (unit)	16151	14472	561	1085	15590	13387
(千元)	(1 000 yuan)	26135	20891	613	478	25522	20413
摄像机(台)	Pickup Camera (unit)	867	872	32	0	835	872
(千元)	(1 000 yuan)	6661	6958	197	0	6464	6958
录像机(台)	Video Recorder (unit)	692	906	94	0	598	906
(千元)	(1 000 yuan)	573	756	99	0	474	756
影碟机(台)	Video Disc Player (unit)	47949	53891	3542	1755	44407	52136
(千元)	(1 000 yuan)	45762	43160	2394	1171	43368	41989
家用电冰箱(台)	Household Refrigerator (unit)	234423	195214	114842	85465	119581	109749
(千元)	(1 000 yuan)	472897	362844	210189	135411	262708	227433
家用洗衣机(台)	Household Washing Machine (unit)	261414	170761	139104	52127	122310	118634
(千元)	(1 000 yuan)	314802	206418	138223	53697	176579	152721
房间空调器(台)	Room Air Conditioner (unit)	292902	255838	182253	146563	110649	109275
(千元)	(1 000 yuan)	1191904	852227	721888	476293	470016	375934
微波炉(台)	Micro-oven (unit)	117253	157467	53153	81454	64100	76013
(千元)	(1 000 yuan)	101067	99529	46401	51806	54666	47723
微型计算机(台)	Personal Computer (unit)	11687	45607	10742	33495	945	12112
(千元)	(1 000 yuan)	114980	387286	107420	287887	7560	99399

13 - 5 续表 continued

指标	Item	合计 Total 2000	合计 Total 2001	批发 Wholesale Trade 2000	批发 Wholesale Trade 2001	零售 Retail Trade 2000	零售 Retail Trade 2001
普通电话机(台)	Telephone (unit)	206214	135929		14711	206214	121218
(千元)	(1 000 yuan)	23730	17199		1386	23730	15813
移动电话机(台)	Hand Telephone (unit)	13748	9788	1536	310	12212	9478
(千元)	(1 000 yuan)	27668	18795	3996	608	23672	18187
寻呼机(台)	Beep-Pager (unit)	16693	12243			16693	12243
(千元)	(1 000 yuan)	4377	1985			4377	1985
煤炭(吨)	Coal (ton)	407286	197768	271243	92427	136043	105341
(千元)	(1 000 yuan)	67533	35261	50003	21392	17530	13869
木材(立方米)	Wood (cu.m)	10992	2398	10992	2398		
(千元)	(1 000 yuan)	13545	5346	13545	5346		
汽油(吨)	Gasoline (ton)	1174543	1288831	872716	852358	301827	436473
(千元)	(1 000 yuan)	4009171	4264529	2930181	2746333	1078990	1518196
柴油(吨)	Diesel (ton)	2148278	2467149	1635552	1951289	512726	515860
(千元)	(1 000 yuan)	6801003	7374605	5150375	5733293	1650628	1641312
化学肥料(吨)	Chemical Fertilizers (ton)	1914363	1317834	1914363	1317834		
农用薄膜(吨)	Farming Pellicle (ton)	1251	1222	1251	1222		
(千元)	(1 000 yuan)	10002	4464	10002	4464		
化学农药(吨)	Chemical Pesticide (ton)	36577	32029	36577	32029		
(千元)	(1 000 yuan)	474826	249120	474826	249120		
钢材(吨)	Steel (ton)	694507	785906	664910	760293	29597	25613
(千元)	(1 000 yuan)	1891991	1633482	1813413	1566871	78578	66611
铜(吨)	Copper (ton)	7207	2944	7207	2944		
(千元)	(1 000 yuan)	134656	48399	134656	48399		
铝(吨)	Aluminum (ton)	9594	4777	9594	4777		
(千元)	(1 000 yuan)	152648	69367	152648	69367		
水泥(吨)	Cement (ton)	196309	110027	185902	98974	10407	11053
(千元)	(1 000 yuan)	49551	25811	46856	22935	2695	2876
汽车(辆)	Motor Vehicles (unit)	41443	22769	31015	10321	10428	12448
#轿车(辆)	Car (unit)	14716	8835	11358	3619	3358	5216
(千元)	(1 000 yuan)	1750123	1526907	1151451	545301	598672	981606
摩托车(辆)	Motor (unit)	19137	11472	8051	5118	11086	6354
(千元)	(1 000 yuan)	101157	55919	39022	22770	62135	33149
拖拉机(辆)	Tractors (unit)	637	801	637	801		
(千元)	(1 000 yuan)	5722	12770	5722	12770		

13-6 限额以上批发零售贸易企业财务状况(2001年)

单位：万元

项目	Item	合计 Total	内资企业 Domestic Funded Enterprises	国有企业 State-owned Enterprises	集体企业 Collective Owned Enterprises	股份合作企业 Cooperative Enterprises
流动资产合计	Total Circulating Funds	3144446	3133864.1	1751666.2	633527.6	11050.5
存货	Inventories	1013533.1	1011015.5	482115.7	308029.2	2193.4
长期投资	Long-term Investment	296899.9	296094.1	202359.6	9262.1	479.6
固定资产合计	Total Fixed Assets	1245337.9	1188573.1	662148.9	79594.2	8634.7
固定资产原价	Original Value of Fixed Assets	1359686.8	1308143	711291.7	108296.8	8805.3
生产经营用	For Production	1044604	993421.1	514905.1	73362.1	2176.7
累计折旧	Total Depreciation	305482.7	297259.4	177732	33611.9	942.1
本年折旧	Depreciation This Year	47739.5	45931.6	25166.4	2355.9	149.7
无形及递延资产合计	Total Intangible and Deferred Asstes	161293.9	138372	80687.7	5468	443.8
无形资产	Intangible Assets	99441.5	83118.8	61238.2	3733.9	378.3
资产总计	**Total Assets**	**5189583.4**	**5098447**	**2766521.3**	**752961.8**	**20651.8**
流动负债合计	Total Liquid Liabilities	3656532.7	3617405.1	2040901	808165.7	14341.3
长期负债合计	Total Long-term Liabilities	484170.4	470481.7	279734.1	90246.6	1265.9
负债合计	**Total Liabilities**	**4442929.1**	**4390112.8**	**2400311**	**899967.1**	**15617.4**
所有者权益合计	**Total Creditors Equity**	**746654.3**	**708334.2**	**366210.3**	**-147005.3**	**5034.4**
实收资本	Capitals Hold	645297	599143	279393.4	58345.2	5021.9
国家资本	State Capital	397025.6	387094.8	245717.2	6799.5	232
外商资本	Foreign Capital	33723.2				
商品销售收入	Total Sales Revenue	7017891.1	6967826.6	3768369.3	399170	24016.1
商品销售收入净额	Net Sales Revenue	6962936.6	6912917.8	3724634	397143.7	19986.8
商品销售成本	Cost of Sales	6365358.9	6325470.7	3383644.9	374793.3	17401.9
经营费用	Management Cost	249149.9	247550.6	130008.9	16060.6	1488
运杂装卸费	Freight Incidental Expenses	39040.8	38997.5	21663.1	4535.8	26.9
商品销售税金及附加费	Sales Tax and Extra Changes	13213.4	13230.8	7038	453.1	66.5
商品销售利润	Total Profits	335214.4	326665.7	203942.2	5836.7	1030.4
代购代销收入	Income from Buy on Sb and Sell Goods on a Commission Basis	3039.9	3039.9	1502.6	73.2	
主营业务利润	Major Business Profits	338254.3	329705.6	205444.8	5909.9	1030.4
其他业务利润	Other Business Profits	27066.7	24526.6	13269.7	2351.8	70.6
管理费用	Overhead Expenses	261648.1	252736.9	158185.2	17200.4	813.6
税金	Taxes	7689.4	7689.2	4992.3	761.9	24.4
财产保险费	Premiums of Property Insurance	3680.7	3535.8	2252	264	7.4
劳动、待业保险费	Premiums of Labor Insurance	21399.4	21352.1	13698.9	1835.6	14.1
财务费用	Financial Expenses	57208.1	54737.6	32406.8	5506.2	214.8
利息支出	Expenses for Interest	53153.6	51172.2	29667.6	4530.8	58.9
营业利润	Operating Profits	49006.6	49170.6	27119.7	-10642.4	131.4
补贴收入	Subsidies	22809.2	22809.2	19944.5	2517.4	76.6
利润总额	Total Profits	64060	64224	41178.9	-9060.9	195.5
应交所得税	Income Tax Payable	34089.4	34089.4	21430.1	179.6	7.1
应付利润	Profits Payable	18075.6	18075.6	8706.4	166	
本年应付工资总额	Total Wages Payable this Year	135112.5	133331.3	75075.3	10405.6	769
主营业务应付工资	In Major Business	126024.1	124242.9	69145.7	9692.1	761.6
本年应付福利费总额	Welfare Expenses Payable this Year	18969.7	18747.4	11078.3	1381.3	84.3
主营业务应付福利费	In Major Business	17057.1	16834.8	9720.5	1306.6	84.3
本年应缴增值税额	Value-added Tax Payable	85045	84308.3	48779	3197	232.5
本年进项增值税额	Value-added Tax from Buying	918532.1	917242.9	453536.9	32890.2	2573.1
本年销项增值税额	Value-added Tax from Selling	946214.3	944188.4	455459.6	32753.2	2852

Financial Affairs of Above – Norm Wholesale and Retail Trade Enterprises (2001)

(10 000 yuan)

					批发业				零售业
				外商投资		#食品饮料烟草	#五金交电化工	#农业生产资料	
联营企业 Joint Ownership Enterprises	有限公司 Limitied Liability Corporation	股份公司 Share-holding Corporation Ltd.	私营企业 Private Enterprises	Foreign Investment	Wholesale Trade	Food, Beverages Tobaccos	Hardware, Transport Electric Chemical	Means of Agricultural Production	Retail Trade
1310	145818.1	532722.8	57768.9	8237.4	2718458	855847.8	229762.6	97744.9	425988
105.3	43438.9	149992.6	25140.4	2438	885535.3	309210.1	54953.1	18505.4	127997.8
	20662.9	62515.5	814.4	805.8	246812.9	45069.1	92846.3	874.1	50087
371.5	43937.1	368495.2	25391.5	43948.1	752854.3	304857.6	30055.4	22298.5	492483.6
433.1	47583.8	402113.1	29619.2	51162.9	840388.3	321153.2	36363.4	26960.3	519298.5
210.1	39431.2	335706.7	27629.2	51162.9	619685	230306	30391.3	19117.7	424919
61.6	9727.1	70900.7	4284	7230.3	209680.7	78649.7	10354.5	7050.5	95802
7.6	2065.8	14918.5	1267.7	1807.9	29284.8	12178.9	616.7	331.9	18454.7
25.1	9375.4	41092.9	1279.1	22762.8	96150.5	20041.7	7986.5	1516.3	65143.4
25.1	6788.3	10640	315	16171	68066.2	18017.3	4487.6	743.9	31375.3
1707.1	**221540.9**	**1247971.8**	**87092.3**	**75816.1**	**4118978.8**	**1260165.2**	**360801**	**123472.7**	**1070604.6**
1756.1	128887.3	556679.7	66674	28579.1	3046052.6	780868.3	371370.4	103347.9	610480.1
	11108.8	86034.8	2091.5	12038.7	396395.6	172095.6	34534.4	4207.6	87774.8
1756.2	**145991.2**	**855862.5**	**70607.4**	**40617.8**	**3714294.7**	**968482.4**	**406143**	**108158.7**	**728634.4**
-49.1	**75549.7**	**392109.3**	**16484.9**	**35198.3**	**404684.1**	**291682.8**	**-45342**	**15314**	**341970.2**
271.7	49253.5	186143.3	20714	42154	449804.4	122513.8	13703.7	16400.1	195492.6
107.4	28036.7	106202		8430.8	314563.9	104627.1	12814	1916.3	82461.7
				33723.2					33723.2
7371	375957.9	2192232.6	200709.7	44826	5985888.4	2040840	125676.9	181780.7	1032002.7
7371	375241.4	2188324.1	200216.8	44826	5947806.3	2034512.9	125676.9	181780.7	1015130.3
6801.2	335753.4	2019394.4	187681.6	35542.7	5508339.6	1812642.5	114625.9	171899.4	857019.3
401.9	24335.9	66620.5	8634.8	1517.3	192457.1	75089	10550.5	5533.9	56692.8
153.9	1453.3	9933.9	1230.6	34.9	34193.1	10608.8	513.6	2521.6	4847.7
2.7	864.7	4521.3	284.5		8751.7	4531.6	288.7	118.3	4461.7
165.2	14287.4	97787.9	3615.9	7766	238257.9	142249.8	211.8	4229.1	96956.5
	1405.3	35.2	23.6		3000.5	383	1359	73.2	39.4
165.2	15692.7	97823.1	3639.5	7766	241258.4	142632.8	1570.8	4302.3	96995.9
	3473	3994.8	1366.7	2029	14496	4531.7	795.4	293.1	12570.7
152.1	16593.1	55278.2	4514.3	7601.4	180865.8	88974.1	4991.4	4673.7	80782.3
	369.7	1440.3	100.6		5274.5	2588.1	62.4	91.7	2414.9
2.1	89.8	856.2	64.3	144.9	2725.3	1478.6	15.2	68.8	955.4
7.2	1195	4436.4	164.9	47	15673	7203.2	270.5	413.8	5726.4
60.8	1024.5	14258.6	1265.9	2140.8	39243.8	20799.7	1332.1	1722	17964.3
63.4	819.2	14872.7	1159.6	1977.6	38715.2	19773.5	1373.4	1564.5	14438.4
-47.7	1409.5	31952	-751.9	52.8	37185.5	38181.9	-3990.6	-1809.9	11821.1
	107.5	161.9	1.3		20952.5	17941.3		1425.8	1856.7
-47.7	2403.1	30694.3	-1139.2	52.8	51895.6	50970.9	-4506	-985.1	12164.4
2.6	2239.9	9708.3	521.8		27819.1	18530.7	182.5	17.8	6270.3
8.9	648.5	7913.3	632.5		11158.8	7542.7	0	66.7	6916.8
86	12569	29806.9	4619.5	1491.1	90972.6	35474.2	2979.8	2168.3	44139.9
86	11805.7	28194.2	4557.6	1491.1	85380.1	33538.6	2787.1	2055.1	40644
8.4	1935.3	3695.3	564.5	185.4	13074.4	5340.1	385.6	278.6	5895.3
8.4	1744.4	3515.5	455.1	185.4	11539.8	4614.8	359.2	260.5	5517.3
18.9	7241.1	23485.6	1354.2	540.4	63683.1	34654.7	1939.4	126.8	21361.9
1116.4	48448	348947.1	29731.2	656.4	793689.4	247353.5	19785.8	1849.2	124842.7
1135.3	54103.6	366818.1	31066.6	1196.8	802557.1	279549	18168.9	1971.9	143657.2

13-7 限额以上餐饮企业财务状况(2001年)

单位：万元

项目	Item	合计 Total	内资企业 Domestic Funded Enterprise	国有企业 State-owned Enterprises	集体企业 Collective-Owned Enterprises	股份合作企业 Cooperative Enterprises
流动资产合计	Total Circulating Funds	34220.9	27364	14739	896.2	1220.5
存货	Inventories	4664.1	3590.6	2046.9	54.1	142.8
长期投资	Long-term Investment	393.1	93.1	51		
固定资产合计	Total Fixed Assets	109639.6	69904.6	51127.7	1359.3	984.4
固定资产原价	Original Value of Fixed Assets	123093.6	77945.1	56813.1	1872.3	857.7
生产经营用	For Production	67560.7	59183.8	39363.5	1551.8	856.2
累计折旧	Total Depreciation	23664.7	17471.8	9974	513	97.2
本年折旧	Depreciation This Year	3682	2290	1426.5	172.8	9.4
无形及递延资产合计	Total Intangible and Deferred Asstes	5873.5	3406.1	1270.7	306.9	
无形资产	Intangible Assets	799.6	613.5	30.7	185.5	
资产总计	**Total Assets**	**155232.3**	**102237**	**68596.2**	**2562.7**	**2204.9**
流动负债合计	Total Liquid Liabilities	64458	40656.9	25072.8	1862.5	377.3
长期负债合计	Total Long-term Liabilities	31337.9	17575.5	16031.1	159.6	231.7
负债合计	**Total Liabilities**	**97665.5**	**60098.6**	**42216.5**	**2204.4**	**1180.2**
所有者权益合计	**Total Creditors Equity**	**57566.8**	**42138.4**	**26379.7**	**358.3**	**1024.7**
实收资本	Capitals Hold	57859.3	42207.3	25452.9	497.9	1010.1
国家资本	State Capital	21241.8	19987.8	19146		150
港澳台资本	HongKong,Macao and Taiwan	2106.1				
外商资本	Foreign Capital	2088.8				
营业收入	Operating Revenue	86073.4	61769.5	25798.7	3585.7	2477.7
营业成本	Operating Cost	43745.8	33822.3	13860.3	2004.1	1519.2
营业费用	Expenses for Operating	24784.5	17283.6	7804.3	1068.8	691.6
营业税金及附加费	Tax and Extra Changes	4642.9	3403.6	1254.5	207.6	138.4
经营利润	Management Profits	12900.2	7260	2879.6	305.2	128.5
管理费用	Overhead Expenses	11344.7	7248.3	4065.8	251.2	166.8
税金	Taxes	468	388.7	110.4	0.3	4
财务保险费	Premiums of Property Insurance	49.7	29.5	12.3	1.1	
劳动、待业保险费	Premiums of Labor Insurance	351.9	341.5	241.6	2.8	
财务费用	Financial Expenses	3042.6	1139.5	410.5	8.2	14.4
利息支出	Expenses for Interest	2398.1	503.4	379.4		7
营业利润	Operating Profits	-1487.1	-1127.8	-1596.7	45.8	-52.7
利润总额	Total Profits	-1992.7	-1407.9	-1413.3	49.4	-26.2
应交所得税	Income Tax Payable	840.5	298.8	209.2	0.6	
应付利润	Profits Payable	1316	243.5	56.2		
本年应付工资总额	Total Wages Payable this Year	10047.1	7686.1	3465.4	406.3	133.7
主营业务应付工资	In Major Business	9509	7280.1	3276	406.3	109.1
本年应付福利费总额	Welfare Expenses Payable this Year	1134.7	994.4	445.5	28.9	18
主营业务应付福利费	In Major Business	1049	915	416.8	28.9	14.9

Financial Affairs of Above – Norm Catering Enterprises (2001)

(10 000 yuan)

联营企业 Joint Ownership Enterprises	有限公司 Limitied Liability Corporation	股份公司 Share holding Corporation Ltd.	私营企业 Private Enterprises	港澳台 Enterprises With Investment from HongKong Macao and Taiwan	外商投资 Foreign Investment	正餐 Dinner	快餐 Snack	其他餐饮业 Others
137	7858.1	685.3	1827.9	2496.3	4360.6	27913.8	4210.2	2096.9
41	467.2	55.2	783.4	490.6	582.9	3922.3	665.8	76
	42.1			300		393.1		
88	13951.9	230.9	2162.4	35123.3	4611.7	103526.8	4693.9	1418.9
88	15298.4	312.9	2702.7	39961.6	5186.9	115793.2	5820.4	1480
88	14600.3	140.2	2583.8	3248.8	5128.1	60349.4	5731.3	1480
	6251.1	82	554.5	5108.8	1084.1	21748.7	1528.3	387.7
	435.2	32.7	213.4	1154.6	237.4	3367	254	61
	421.8	750.9	655.8	186.1	2281.3	2754.9	2481.2	637.4
	119	221.3	57	186.1		740.1	2.5	57
225	**22313.6**	**1685.8**	**4648.8**	**39404.1**	**13591.2**	**137091.1**	**13723**	**4418.2**
247	10680.5	932.4	1484.4	17554.6	6246.5	57201.4	5731.1	1525.5
	565.3	0.3	587.5	13762.4		31027.9		310
247	**11245.8**	**932.8**	**2071.9**	**31317.3**	**6249.6**	**90098.8**	**5731.2**	**1835.5**
-22	**11067.8**	**753**	**2576.9**	**8086.8**	**7341.6**	**46992.3**	**7991.8**	**2582.7**
	11839.7	532.9	2873.8	10929.8	4722.2	51772.6	4889.2	1197.5
	560.4	71.4	60	1254		20723.7	440.6	77.5
				2106.1		2106.1		
					2088.8	348.1	1740.7	
734	14800.1	4198.7	10174.6	4884	19419.9	59595.4	20973.7	5504.3
416	7729.6	2578.4	5714.7	997.3	8926.2	30898.2	9869.3	2978.3
277	4254.8	1160.4	2026.7	1633.6	5867.3	17346.1	6083.4	1355
52	934	230.3	586.8	264.8	974.5	3364.5	1050.8	227.6
-11	1881.7	229.6	1846.4	1988.3	3651.9	7986.6	3970.2	943.4
	1687.2	256.5	820.8	2709.8	1386.6	9067.8	1662	614.9
	202.1		71.9	71.9	7.4	458	8.4	1.6
	14.5		1.6	18.3	1.9	46.9	0.4	2.4
	87.3		9.8	2.8	7.6	277.4	4.8	69.7
	649	7.8	49.6	1833	70.1	2976.4	79.7	-13.5
	113.9		3.1	1830.7	64	2313.5	83.5	1.1
-11	-454.5	-34.7	976	-2554.5	2195.2	-4057.6	2228.5	342
-11	-382.7	-11.3	387.2	-2479.2	1894.4	-4190.4	1804.9	392.8
12	21.5	4.2	51.3		541.7	150.9	573	116.6
	37.2		150.1		1072.5	199.3	1116.7	
96	1908.3	607.6	1068.8	874.6	1486.4	7786.8	1666.7	593.6
96	1757.1	607.6	1028	799.6	1429.3	7338.6	1628.2	542.2
3	243.3	91.6	164.1	72.7	67.6	971.9	89.9	72.9
3	218	91.6	141.8	71.8	62.2	895.2	87	66.8

13-8 国有商业和供销合作社农业生产资料销售量

Sales of Agricultural Product Goods of State – Owned Trade and Supply and Marketing Cooperative

年 份 Year	化学肥料 (万吨) Chemical Fertilizers (10 000 tons)	化学农药 (万吨) Chemical Pesticide (10 000 tons)	大中型拖拉机 (台) Large and Medium Tractors (unit)	手扶拖拉机 (万台) Walking Agricultural Tractors (10 000 units)	农用动力机械 Power of Agricultural Machinery	
					(万台) (10 000 units)	(万千瓦) (10 000 kw)
1985	358.42	6.45	99	1.73	4.33	48.26
1990	508.76	4.45	45	1.30	8.28	42.57
1991	570.34	5.22	257	2.17	9.65	49.90
1992	539.68	4.00	147	2.23	7.61	44.89
1993	420.11	3.85	251	1.57	6.50	40.21
1994	332.48	3.67	216	2.10	8.03	46.39
1995	404.67	4.10	194	2.24	10.25	55.89
1996	408.31	3.81	118	1.04	10.65	49.07
1997	393.41	4.40	91	0.58	10.60	43.18
1998	365.31	3.79	114	0.35	11.15	47.37
1999	297.18	3.57	164	0.31	11.72	30.00
2000	245.60	3.60	93	0.14	7.40	24.50
2001	202.77	3.91	57	0.13	4.85	16.78

13-9 限额以上贸易、餐饮企业增加值

Added Value of Above - Norm Large and Medium - Sized Trade and Catering Enterprise

单位：万元 (10 000 yuan)

指 标	Item	1995	1999	2000	2001
批发零售贸易业	**Wholesales and Retail Trade**				
增加值合计	Total Value-added	303223.8	286172.5	301523.7	385100.0
本年提取固定资产折旧	Depreciation this Year	34489.9	42040.9	42314.5	47739.5
本年应付工资总额	Total Wages Payable this Year	193776.9	181613.2	116876.2	135112.5
本年应付福利费总额	Welfare Expenses Payable this Year	21237.4	35691.7	16174.6	18969.7
劳动就业保险费	Premiums of Labor Insurance	14721.7	23229.2	21812.7	21399.4
商品销售税金及附加	Sales Tax and Extra Changes	15250.8	11216.4	11327.3	13213.4
利润总额	Total Profits	-5638.0	-91972.7	22575.7	64060.0
管理费用中税金	Taxes in Overhead Expenses	7254.1	14322.6	7610.0	7689.4
餐饮业	**Catering Trade**				
增加值合计	Total Value-added	5590.4	12466.8	12391.6	19100.0
本年提取固定资产折旧	Depreciation this Year	999.5	3751.6	2347.3	3682.0
本年应付工资总额	Total Wages Payable this Year	2930.8	6663.0	9371.4	10047.1
本年应付福利费总额	Welfare Expenses Payable this Year	459.0	860.8	783.8	1134.7
劳动就业保险费	Premiums of Labor Insurance	179.4	643.2	579.0	351.9
商品销售税金及附加	Sales Tax and Extra Changes	1314.7	2787.7	2968.2	4642.9
利润总额	Total Profits	88.5	-2797.5	-3010.5	-1992.7
管理费用中税金额	Taxes in Overhead Expenses	72.9	558.0	132.0	468.0

13-10 对外经济贸易和旅游概况

A Surrey on Foreign Trade and Tourists

指标	Item	1995	1999	2000	2001
进出口总额 (亿美元)	**Total Imports And Exports (USD 100 million)**	**20.17**	**19.56**	**25.13**	**27.58**
出口总额	Total Exports	14.51	12.82	16.53	17.54
进口总额	Total Imports	5.66	6.74	8.6	10.04
进出口差额	Balance	8.85	6.08	7.93	7.5
对外签订利用外资协议项目 (个)	**Number of Projects for Utilization of Foreign Capital in the Signed Agreements & Contracts (unit)**	**726**	**335**	**336**	**356**
对外借款	Foreign Loans	15	14	16	18
外商直接投资	Foreign Direct Investments	574	321	320	338
外商其他投资	Other Foreign Investments	137			
对外签订利用外资协议金额 (亿美元)	**Total Amount of Foreign Capital to Be Utilized in the Signed Agreements & Contracts (USD 100 million)**	**17.44**	**9.19**	**10.94**	**13.3**
对外借款	Foreign Loans	3.7	3.5	3.37	3.47
外商直接投资	Foreign Direct Investments	13.54	5.02	6.67	9.53
外商其他投资	Other Foreign Investments	0.2	0.68	0.9	0.3
实际利用外资 (亿美元)	**Total Amount of Foreign Capital Actually Used (USD 100 million)**	**8.71**	**10.7**	**11.08**	**11.87**
对外借款	Foreign Loans	3.7	3.5	3.37	3.47
外商直接投资	Foreign Direct Investments	4.88	6.54	6.82	8.1
外商其他投资	Other Foreign Investments	0.13	0.66	0.89	0.3
外商投资企业基本情况	**Registered Foreign-funded Enterprises**				
年底登记户数 (户)	Number of Registered Enterprises (unit)		2513	2316	2080
投资总额 (亿美元)	Total Investment (USD 100 million)		72.14	73.06	65.67
注册资本 (亿美元)	Registered Capital (USD 100 million)		44.23	43.38	37.7
#外方	#Capital from Foreign Partners		26.6	26.51	23.13
对外经济合作合同金额 (亿美元)	**Contracted Value of Economic Cooperation With Foreign Countries & Territories (USD 100 million)**	**0.41**	**1.26**	**1.87**	**2.7**
对外承包工程	Contracted Projects		0.69	1.49	2.27
对外劳务合作	Labor Services		0.4	0.34	0.36
设计咨询	Design Consultation		0.17	0.04	0.07
国际旅游人数 (万人)	**Total Number of International Tourists (10 000 persons)**	**17.73**	**38.58**	**45.4**	**50.46**
外国人	Foreigners	7.18	13.48	15.79	18.85
华侨	Overseas Chinese	0.29	0.44		
港澳台同胞	Compatriots from HongKong, Macao and Taiwan	10.26	24.65	29.61	31.61
旅游外汇收入总额 (亿美元)	**Foreign Exchange Earnings from International Tourism (USD 100 million)**		**1.85**	**2.21**	**2.71**
涉外饭店(个)	Total Number of Tourist Hotels		183	212	270

注:外贸进出口资料是海关口径。

Data of total exports and imports were in accordance with the customs statistics.

13-11 长沙海关进出口商品总值

Total Value of Imports and Exports(Changsha Customs Statistics)

单位：万美元 (USD 10 000)

项 目	Item	1995	1999	2000	2001
进出口总值	**Imports & Exports**	**201664**	**195604**	**251259**	**275841**
#出口	Exports	145101	128210	165309	175400
进口	Imports	56563	67394	85951	100441
进出口差额	**Balance**	**88538**	**60815**	**79358**	**74959**

13-12 长沙海关进出口商品主要产销国别(地区)总值

Value of Imports and Exports by Main Producer and Sales Countries(Regions) (Changsha Customs Statistics)

单位：万美元 (USD 10 000)

国家 (地区)	Country (Region)	2000		2001		比上年(+、-)% Increase Rate over 2000	
		进口 Imports	出口 Exports	进口 Imports	出口 Exporst	进口 Imports	出口 Exports
合 计	**Total**	**85951**	**165309**	**100441**	**175400**	**16.9**	**6.1**
香 港	Hong Kong	2505	22487	3894	25061	55.5	11.4
日 本	Japan	17367	15924	18277	18063	5.2	13.4
菲律宾	Philippines	93	1061	61	1143	-34.9	7.7
新加坡	Singapore	212	6351	209	6498	-1.3	2.3
韩 国	Republic of Korea	18226	13263	20826	10865	14.3	-18.1
台湾省	Taiwan ,China	4527	6884	4710	5766	4	-16.2
英 国	United Kingdom	5643	3663	3912	4300	-30.7	17.4
德 国	Germany	4357	9158	7805	7692	79.2	-16
法 国	France	1561	1380	1615	1493	3.5	8.1
意大利	Italy	2572	3659	3172	3299	23.3	-9.8
荷 兰	Netherlands	544	7191	775	7498	42.6	4.3
俄罗斯	Russia	259	1623	328	3313	26.9	104.1
加拿大	Canada	1944	3368	2956	3971	52	17.9
美 国	United States	8021	23962	8759	26138	9.2	9.1
澳大利亚	Australia	4173	2012	3521	1914	-15.6	-4.9
沙特阿拉伯	Saudi Arabia		1000	302	1182		18.2
阿联酋	United Arab Emirates		1732		2163		24.9
比利时	Belgium	181	1172	339	1158	87.5	-1.2
西班牙	Spain	128	1848	189	2100	47.7	13.6
马来西亚	Malaysia	645	1410	1131	1721	75.2	22.1

13-13 进出口商品机电电子产品情况

Import and Export Value of Machinery and Electrical Products

单位：万美元 (USD 10 000)

指标	Item	2000		2001		比上年(+、-)% Increase Rate in 2001 Over 2000	
		进口 Imports	出口 Exports	进口 Imports	出口 Exports	进口 Imports	出口 Exports
机电产品	**Mechanical & Electrical Products**	**51461**	**31040**	**53271**	**33702**	**3.5**	**8.6**
金属制品	Metal and Related Products	929	8405	877	9434	-5.5	12.2
机电仪器产品及设备	Machinery and Electrical Instruments and Equipment	50532	22635	52394	24268	3.7	7.2
机械及设备	Machinery and Equipment	22231	6057	22735	7053	2.3	16.4
电器及电子产品	Electrical Products	16209	11285	13440	10440	-17.1	-7.5
运输工具	facilities of Transportation	7104	4072	7658	4679	7.8	14.9
仪器仪表	Instruments and Meters	3239	498	4250	454	31.2	-8.8
其他	Others	1749	723	4311	1642	146.5	127

注：由于商品名称及编码协调制度的变化，引起与历史数据不一致，以本年度提供资料为准。

Since a new commodity catalogue has been used,there were different data from previous years,Please refer to this year's statistics.

13-14 长沙海关进出口商品贸易方式

Value of Imports and Exports by Trade Ways (Changsha Customs Statistics)

单位：万美元 (USD 10 000)

贸易方式	Trade Ways	2000		2001	
		进 口 Imports	出 口 Exports	进 口 Imports	出 口 Exports
一般贸易	Original Trade	63134	143837	80736	157677
国家间、国际组织无偿援助和赠送的物资	Assistant Goods from International Organization	94	18	121	22
华侨、港、澳同胞、外籍华人捐赠物资	Assistant Goods from Overseas Chinese, Compatriots from Hongkong, Macao and Taiwan	5		9	
补偿贸易	Compensation Trade				
来料加工装配贸易	Processing and Assembly Trade Provided with Raw Material	4897	7101	2964	4586
进料加工贸易	Processing Trade of Imported Material	4560	14319	6450	12983
寄售、代销贸易	Consign and Commission Trade				
边境小额贸易	Frontier Small Value Trade		5		
加工贸易进口的设备	Processing and Assembling Import Equipment Provided with Material				
对外承包工程出口货物	Constructed Projects in Foreign Countries				
租赁贸易	International Lease		7		117
外商投资企业作为投资进口的设备、物品	Imported Equipment and Materials as Investment of Foreign Investment Enterprises	12259		9489	
出料加工贸易	Processing Trade of Exported Material				
易货贸易	Barter				
免税外汇商品	Tax Free Foreign Exchange Commodities				
保税仓库进出境货物	Import & export Commodities in Protective Tariff Zone	841	10	489	3
其它贸易	Others Trade	160	11	184	11

13-15 长沙海关主要出口商品总值

Major Exports Commodities in Value (Changsha Customs Statistics)

单位：万美元 (USD 10 000)

商品名称	Name of Commodities	1995	1999	2000	2001
活猪(种猪除外)	Live Hogs (excluded seed hogs)	5507	5045	4709	4305
鲜、冻猪肉	Fresh Frozen Pork	1408	960	999	881
水海产品	Aquatic Products		1398	23	33
谷物及谷物粉	Cereals and Cereals Flour		1122	1862	397
大米	Rice		1113	1846	375
鲜、干水果	Vegetables , Fruit & Nuts , Fresh or Dried		457	165	122
茶叶	Tea	1711	1794	1310	1602
烤烟	Flue-cured Tobacco		409	400	277
黏土及其耐火矿物	Clay and Other Refractory Minerals		601	1099	1484
天然石墨	Nutural Graphite		596	1091	1474
仲钨酸铵	Tungstates	1476	727	597	476
氧化锌及过氧化锌	Zinc Oxide and Zinc Peroxide		611	1146	623
医药品	Medical and Pharmaceutical Products	3011	2495	1730	2124
烟花、爆竹	Fireworks and Firecrackers	3640	7598	8186	8518
松香及树脂酸	Resin and Resin Acids		438	354	426
家用或装饰用木制品	Woodwork for Family and Decorating		429	555	765
纺织纱线、织物及制品	Textile Yarn,Textile and Related Products		10575	13344	15859
亚麻及苎麻纱线	Flax and Ramine Yarn		1088	1278	1158
棉纺机织物	Cotton Textile Machine Woven		2905	3604	4681
其他棉纺机织物	Other Cotton Textile Machine Woven		2842	3541	4614
亚麻及苎麻机织物	Flax and Ramine Machine Woven	3195	2425	2612	2978
棉浴巾	Cotton Bath Towels	638	487	708	1242
家用陶瓷器皿	Porcelain and Pottery Ware for Household Use	7358	5772	7184	7920
钢材	Rolled Steel		1119	3121	3769
未锻造的锌及锌合金	Unwrought Zinc and Zinc Alloys	3324	11705	15099	12855
未锻造的锡及锡合金	Unwrought Tin and Tin Alloys	1425	466	527	223
未锻造的锑	Unwrought Antimony	721	480	781	
朱锻造的锰	Unwrought Manganese	3450	4110	5524	8444
手用或机用工具	Hand Tools and Tools for Machines	4771	2355	2452	1964
轴承	Bearings	871	968	891	827
印刷电路	Electrocircuit of Presswork		856	1234	1192
通断及保护电器装置及零件	Eletrical Apparatus for Switching or Protecting Electrical Circults	638	437	440	660
汽车零件	Parts of Motor Vehicles		536	965	1175
摩托车	Motorcycles		698	1543	2525
船舶	Ships		455	201	69
旅行用品及箱包	Travel Goods		1100	1333	1211
服装及衣着附件	Articles of Apparel & Clothing Accessories	15555	8394	13027	15165
织物制服装	Garments with Textile	11029	6522	9536	9786
非针织钩编织物服装	Garmens with Non-Kniting or Crocheting		3778	5403	5342
针织或钩编的服装	Garments with Knitting or Crocheting		2744	4133	4444
皮革服装	Leather Garments	2617	1109	2322	3964
鞋类	Footware	5223	2434	4436	4171
鞋	Shoes		2390	4266	4115
以橡胶或塑料制的鞋	Shoes with Rubber or Plastic Materials		1216	2311	2459
橡胶或塑料底纺织材料为面的鞋	Shoes with Tread of Rubber or Plastic Materials and Surface of Textile Materials		914	1441	1108
塑料制品	Plastic Articles		612	770	848

注: 1.本表由长沙海关整理提供;

2.部分指标由于编码变动或指标编码范围变动,引起与历史数据不一致,以本年度提供资料为准。

a.Data were obtained from Changsha Customs.

b.Since a new commodity catalogue has been used, there were different data from previous years. Please refer to this year's statistics.

13-16 长沙海关主要进口商品总值

Major Imports Commodities in Value (Changsha Customs Statistics)

单位：万美元 (USD 10 000)

商品名称	Name of Commodities	1995	1999	2000	2001
食用植物油	Edible Vegetable Oil	810	412	129	91
豆油及其分离品	Bean Oil and Related Separate Articles		220	42	
饲料用鱼粉	Flours and Meals of Fish for Animal Food	691	461	1600	1046
原木	Logs		616	240	482
纸浆	Paper Pulp		513	451	2459
二醋酸纤维丝束	Two of Cellulose Diacetate		1345	992	1181
铁矿砂	Iron Ore	2375	3274	5079	8903
铬矿砂	Chromium Ores		536	823	343
成品油	Petroleum Products Refined	121	280	34	32
乙二醇	Ethylenc Glycol		502	463	1022
对苯二甲醇	Telephthalic Acid		658	1106	1817
初级形状的塑料	Primary Plastic		381	569	450
农药	Pesticides		223	112	
纸及纸板(未切成形的)	Paper and Paperboard	1019	542	717	874
无机物涂布纸	Papers with Mineral Coat		431	687	789
棉机织物	Cotton Textile Machine Woven		869	970	602
针织或钩编织物	Kniting or Crocheting		301	363	341
钢材	Rolled Steels	1118	3278	3805	4016
钢铁板材	Steel-Board		3114	3608	3874
钢铁制标准紧固件	Nails ,Bolts ,etc		1839	520	261
未锻造的铜及铜材	Unwrought Copper and Rolled Copper		461	588	499
铜材	Rolled Copper		426	513	456
活塞式内燃机的零件	Accessories of Gas Engine with Piston		1912	421	335
液泵及液体提升机	Liquid Pump and Machine with Liquid Exaltation		470	249	468
机械提升搬运装卸设备及零件	Portage ,Load and Unload Equipments and Accessories with Machine Exaltation		369	366	277
建筑及采矿用机械	Machinery for Counstruction and Mining	588	400	456	970
制造纸及纸制品用机械	Paper and Pulp Mill Machinery		250	110	172
印刷、装订机械	Printing and Binding Machinery	966	749	601	1050
金属加工机床	Machine Tools for Processing Metals	2511	1211	833	1258
烟草加工机械	Machine Tools for Processing Tobacco	3780	581	294	1059
模型及金属铸造用型箱	Models and Patterns	319	335	165	521
阀门	Valves		298	203	96
自动数据处理设备及其部件	Automatic Data Processing Equipments and Accessories		4124	2952	930
数字式自动数据处理设备	Digital Automatic Data Processing Equipment		2740	1495	336
输入或输出部件	Accessories of I/O Equipments		1285	921	508
有线电话或电报交换机	Lineate Telephones or Telegram Exchanges		1490	356	
有线电话电报设备的零附件	Accessories of Lineate Telephones and Telegrams		832	454	480
电视显像管	Kinescope		724	104	2
彩色显像管	Color Kinescope	526	724	104	2
集成电路及微电子组件	Integrated Circuit and Microelectronics Device		1031	1052	1105
汽车零件	Parts of Motor Vehicles		2118	6374	6809
医疗仪器及器械	Medical Instruments and Appliances	733	1111	1014	2041
计量检测分析自动仪器及器具	Measuring and Checking		1176	1718	1583
印刷品	Pressworks		494	477	186
塑料制品	Articles of Plastics		360	297	272

13-17 长沙海关进出口商品分地区情况(2001年)

Import and Expert Value by Region(Changsha Customs Statistics) (2001)

市州	Cities and Prefecture	进出口总值 万美元 Total Exports and Imports (USD 10 000)	出 口 Exports	进 口 Imports	比上年增减 (%) Increase Rate in 2001 Over 2000 (%)
总 计	**Total**	**275841**	**175400**	**100441**	**9.8**
长沙	Changsha City	165091	104811	60280	0.4
株洲	Zhuzhou City	42098	33396	8702	14.6
湘潭	Xiangtan City	18274	7081	11193	30.1
衡阳	Hengyang City	9357	6519	2838	36.8
邵阳	Shaoyang City	1308	1203	105	52.1
岳阳	Yueyang City	6358	1656	4702	-10.3
常德	Changde City	4869	2512	2357	78.7
张家界	Zhangjiajie City	26	15	11	-66.7
益阳	Yiyang City	2878	1713	1165	88.7
郴州	Chenzhou City	4073	3887	186	64.8
娄底	Loudi City	7107	4099	3008	23.5
永州	Yongzhou City	4913	217	4696	48
怀化	Huaihua City	2098	1499	599	179.7
湘西自治州	West Hunan A.P	7392	6794	598	59.5

13-18 利用外资概况

Utilization of Foreign Capital

项 目	Item	1995	1999	2000	2001
利用外资签订合同项目(个)	**Number of Projects for Utilization of Foreign Capital in the Signed Agreements & Contracts (case)**	**726**	**335**	**336**	**356**
对外借款	Foreign Loans	15	14	16	18
外商直接投资	Foreign Direct Investments	574	321	320	338
外商其他投资	Other Foreign Investments	137			
协议利用外资合同金额(万美元)	**Total Amount of Foreign Capital to be Utilized in the Signed Agreement & Contracts (USD 10 000)**	**174427**	**91949**	**109370**	**133063**
对外借款	Foreign Loans	37000	35000	33700	34700
外商直接投资额	Foreign Direct Investments	135462	50198	66709	95327
外商其他投资额	Other Foreign Investments	1965	6751	8961	3036
实际利用外资金额(万美元)	**Total Amount of Foreign Capital Actually Used (USD 10 000)**	**87104**	**106945**	**110843**	**118747**
对外借款	Foreign Loans	37000	35000	33700	34700
外商直接投资额	Foreign Direct Investments	48802	65374	68182	81011
外商其他投资额	Other Foreign Investments	1302	6571	8961	3036

13-19 外商直接投资签订合同情况(分国别、地区) (2001年)

Basic Statisics on Signed Contracts of Direct Foreign Investment(by Country or Region) (2001)

国别(地区)	Countries (Region)	项目(合同)个数 Number of Projects (case)	合同外资金额 Contract Value (USD 10 000)	实际外资金额 Used Value (USD 10 000)
总 计	**Total**	**338**	**95327**	**81011**
香港(地区)	Hongkong	149	39096	39552
澳门(地区)	Macro	5	838	598
台湾(地区)	Taiwan	74	11980	6929
菲律宾	Philippines	5	598	1923
泰 国	Thailand	2	1212	1519
马来西亚	Malaysia	2	1337	749
新加坡	Singapore	7	3095	3837
日 本	Japan	7	3619	1258
德 国	Germany		9	1390
意大利	Italy	1	77	211
英 国	United Kingdom	3	515	1121
加拿大	Canada	5	589	290
美 国	United States	41	12720	6698
澳大利亚	Australia	7	511	576
维尔京群岛	Virgin Islands	9	4675	4198

13-20 外商直接投资分地区情况 (2001年)

Foreign Direct Investment by Region (2001)

市州	Cities and Prefecture	项目个数(个) Number of Projects (case)	合同外资额(万美元) Agreement Amount (USD 10 000)	实际利用(万美元) Actually Used Amount (USD 10 000)	比上年增减(%) Increase Rate in 2001 Over 2000(%)
总 计	**Total**	**338**	**95327**	**81011**	**18.8**
长沙市	Changsha City	75	24980	26527	49.8
株洲市	Zhuzhou City	25	8794	6224	34.5
湘潭市	Xiangtan City	15	4026	4052	14.1
衡阳市	Hengyang City	78	12858	8980	-27.3
邵阳市	Shaoyang City	9	3765	2867	-3.2
岳阳市	Yueyang City	19	9521	8118	22
常德市	Changde City	27	5035	4770	18.1
张家界市	Zhangjiajie City	9	1928	1203	213.3
益阳市	Yiyang City	14	2248	2776	25.8
郴州市	Chenzhou City	35	16170	9426	39.6
永州市	Yongzhou City	7	499	1379	-52.3
怀化市	Huaihua City	9	1905	1029	6
娄底市	Loudi City	10	2572	2846	19.8
湘西自治州	West Hunan A.P	6	1026	814	14.2

13-21 对外承包工程、劳务合作和设计咨询

Contracted Projects, Labor Service Cooperation, Designs Consultation with Foreign Countries

项 目	Item	1995	1999	2000	2001
对外承包工程、劳务合作和设计咨询合同 (个)	Number of Contracts (case)	86	653	1096	1101
对外承包工程、劳务合作和设计咨询合同金额 (万美元)	Contracted Value (USD 10 000)	4092	12571	18707	27000
实际完成营业额 (万美元)	Value of Businness Fulfilled (USD 10 000)	3451	12220	13845	26500
年末在外人数 (人)	Number of Abroad Person at Year-end (person)	1102	3912	4318	6200
全年派出人次 (人次)	Number of Delegation Person-times All-year (person-time)	515	2062	2280	3163

13-22 国际旅游人数和人天数

Number of International Tourists and Days of Tourism

项 目	Item	1995	1999	2000	2001
接待国际旅游人数合计 (人次)	**Total of International Tourist Arrivals (person-time)**	**177303**	**385830**	**454008**	**504554**
#外国人	Foreigners	71800	134837	157899	188485
华侨	Overseas Chinese	2883	4448	-	-
港澳台同胞	Compatriots From Hongkong,Macao and Taiwan	102620	246545	296109	316069
#台胞	Compatriots from Taiwan	50020	142802	172731	180004
国际旅游人天数合计 (人天)	**Total of International Tourist Arrivals (person-day)**	**496900**	**1195185**	**1443640**	**1728126**
#外国人	Foreigners	201200	561225	596216	640849
华侨	Overseas Chinese	8801	12923	-	-
港澳台同胞	Compatriots From Hongkong,Macao and Taiwan	286899	621037	847424	1087277
#台胞	Compatriots from Taiwan	140001	297292	465221	666015

注：从2000年起，华侨并入外国人统计。

Overseas chinese are bring into foreigners since 2000.

13-23 旅游外汇收人

Foreign Exchange Earnings Through Tourism

项 目	Item	1995	1999	2000	2001
旅游外汇收入合计 (万美元)	**Total (10 000 USD)**	**6499.45**	**18545.75**	**22106.46**	**27069.87**
#商品性收入	Commodity Income	1520.87	5899.84	6742.47	8120.96
#商品销售收入	Shopping	669.44	3885.11	4598.14	5738.81
饮食销售收入	Food-Beverage	851.43	2014.73	2144.33	2382.15
劳务性收入	Service Income	4978.58	12645.91	15363.99	18948.91
#旅行社、旅游业务费收入	Travel Agencies	440.00	732.33	1260.07	1678.34
宿费	Hotel Accommodation	2092.82	2620.91	2542.24	3546.15
长途交通费	Long-distance Transportation	1488.37	4846.20	6875.11	8933.06
#民航	Civil Aviaton	1345.39	3918.36	5283.44	6009.51
铁道	Railway	64.99	391.23	397.92	189.49
公路	Highway	77.99	471.94	641.09	1191.07
市内交通费	Local Transportation	194.99	579.58	442.13	595.54
邮政电讯费	Postal and Communication	422.46	841.65	1326.39	1218.14
文化娱乐费	Culture and Enterainment	129.99	1372.18	1237.96	1353.49
其他	Others	209.95	1653.06	1680.09	1624.19

13-24 接待外国人按国别分组

Number of Foreign Tourists by Country

单位：人次 (person-time)

国 别	Country	1995	1999	2000	2001
外国人合计	**Total**	**71800**	**134837**	**157899**	**188485**
#日 本	Japan	16789	24024	25006	32549
菲律宾	Philippines	762	5325	1707	936
新加坡	Singapore	6692	7993	11813	8927
泰 国	Thailand	1028	5037	5431	3083
印度尼西亚	Indonesia	1247	2305	1181	2474
美 国	United States	13425	20977	18942	31264
加拿大	Canada	1934	8973	9611	10793
德 国	Germany	4172	5091	5519	4087
英 国	United Kingdom	2566	4736	5318	2707
法 国	France	1182	1989	1529	2256
意大利	Italy	936	2504	1132	1408
俄罗斯	Russia	384	1976	1030	1025
澳大利亚	Australia	1468	3999	5103	2474
新西兰	New Zealand	451	1207	575	321
其 他	Others	18764	38701	64002	84181

13-25 旅游业基本情况

Basic Statistics of Tourism

项 目	Item	1995	1999	2000	2001
接待旅游总人数 (万人)	**Number of Tourists (10 000 persons)**		**4338.58**	**4695.4**	**5035.52**
#接待海外游客	International Tourists	17.73	38.58	45.4	50.46
#接待国内游客	Domestic Tourists		4300	4650	4985.06
旅游业总收入 (人民币亿元)	**Income of Tourism (100 million yuan)**		**120.31**	**148.8**	**210.4**
#旅游创汇(亿美元)	Earnings from International Tourism (USD 100 million)	0.65	1.85	2.21	2.71
#国内旅游收入 (人民币亿元)	Earnings from Domestic Tourism (RMB 100 million yuan)		105	130.46	188.09

13-26 各市州接待游客人数

Number of Tourists by Cities and Prefeture

市州	Cities and Rrefeture	2000		2001	
		接待国内游客(万人次) Domestic Tourists (10 000 person-times)	接待境外游客(人次) Foreign Tourists (person-times)	接待国内游客(万人次) Domestic Tourists (10 000 person-times)	接待境外游客(人次) Foreign Tourists (person-times)
合 计	**Total**	**4650**	**454008**	**4985.06**	**504554**
长沙市	Changsha City	1950	161789	1527.54	228585
株洲市	Zhuzhou City	220	6873	236.15	4892
湘潭市	Xiangtan City	240	8509	283.29	6618
衡阳市	Hengyang City	430	13056	729.32	9114
邵阳市	Shaoyang City	100	3048	154	3847
岳阳市	Yueyang City	410	39259	258.23	11194
常德市	Changde City	230	13715	361.86	7475
益阳市	Yiyang City	50	3335	151.81	782
郴州市	Chenzhou City	270	28694	270.12	8513
张家界市	Zhangjiajie City	430	161380	442.46	216516
永州市	Yongzhou City	65	1472	60.33	44
怀化市	Huaihua City	90	4749	152.14	104
娄底市	Loudi City	65	1822	141.5	2520
湘西自治州	West Hunan A.P	100	6307	216.3	4350

十四、教育、科技

EDUCATION，SCIENCE AND TECHNOLOGY

资料整理人员：　陈洲艳　阳小林

14-1 各级学校单位数及教职工数

Number of Schools and School Staff

年 份 Year	普通高等学校 Regular Institution of Higher Education	普通中等专业学校 Secondary Schools	职业中学 Vocational Secondary Schools	技工学校 Technical Schools	普通中学 Regular Secondary Schools	普通小学 Primary Schools	特殊教育学校 Special Education Schools	幼儿园 Kinder-gartens
单位数(所)	Number of Schools (unit)							
1995	49	150	567	161	4863	44105	54	2226
1999	52	157	611	167	4502	37143	58	4448
2000	52	144	539	167	4505	34521	57	5473
2001	61	125	434	167	4695	29340	59	1333
教职工数(人)	Number of Teachers and Staff (person)							
1995	39519	22869	20128	12159	217690	317871	932	53360
1999	42409	23658	24775	10644	248658	325706	3052	39678
2000	46642	21078	22375	10050	259989	324199	1203	39790
2001	53119	17137	21542	10003	276672	309106	1201	28017
专任教师数(人)	Number of Full-time Teachers(person)							
1995	15307	10559	13915	5936	179120	297964	642	46894
1999	17990	11934	17632	6239	212435	307404	860	34725
2000	20317	10775	15795	6117	223693	306387	918	33928
2001	23878	9036	14395	6069	236161	291574	905	20307

注：本表高等学校含3所部属院校，不含军事院校、分院校和大专班。

Regular institutions of higher education includes three institutions managed by the national ministry, excluding military institutions, branches and specialized subject class.

14-2 各级学校在校学生、招生及毕业生数

Student Enrollment, New Student Enrollment and Graduates

单位：人 (person)

年 份 Year	普通高等学校 Regular Institution of Higher Education	普通中等专业学校 Secondary Schools	职业中学 Vocational Secondary Schools	技工学校 Technical Schools	普通中学 Regular Secondary Schools	高中 Senior Secondary Schools	初中 Junior Secondary Schools	普通小学 Primary Schools	特殊教育学校 Special Education	幼儿园 Kinder-gartens
在校学生数	Student Enrollment									
1995	123053	186108	199292	81876	2854079	387275	2466804	7366539	6819	1315962
1999	193553	272556	227864	49124	3560453	531887	3028566	7213955	22804	643161
2000	253084	258342	213898	51237	3917326	625719	3291607	6639289	12179	628744
2001	331301	240910	198813	60193	4255858	752579	3503279	6012579	14635	600570
招生数	New Student Enrollment									
1995	40612	66334	87510	37752	1111674	150502	961172	1376311	299	1227103
1999	77237	81239	87924	22098	1367856	207529	1160327	790897	4198	583649
2000	101020	63625	93447	26683	1518734	260515	1258219	717496	2090	583324
2001	117299	71374	100209	32509	1648254	323625	1324629	723570	2194	530097
毕业生数	Graduates									
1995	32931	32999	47841	34988	717670	106976	610694	1066707	317	-
1999	39688	65341	69394	24589	982024	133018	849006	1223723	2366	-
2000	42428	73076	68800	20479	1000980	145587	855393	1302004	1138	-
2001	49703	80906	59447	19011	1034231	168166	866065	1357129	1273	-

14-3 研 究 生

Number of Postgraduates

单位：人 (person)

年 份	招生数 New Student Enrollment	毕业生数 Graduates	在学人数 Student Enrollment
1980	77		347
1985	1104	296	2016
1986	950	377	2583
1987	874	666	2771
1988	769	1067	2538
1989	600	862	2311
1990	705	812	2165
1991	687	783	2035
1992	734	543	2168
1993	911	668	2357
1994	1209	630	2864
1995	1209	710	3307
1996	1400	876	3775
1997	1383	1087	4027
1998	1723	1131	4552
1999	2380	1394	5585
2000	3475	1311	7729
2001	4575	1639	10589

14-4 普通高等学校分科在校学生、招生及毕业生数

Student Enrollment, New Student Enrollment and Graduates of General Institutions of Higher Education by Field of Study

单位：人 (person)

项目	Item	在校学生数 Student Enrollment		招收学生数 New Student Enrollment		毕业生数 Graduates	
		2000	2001	2000	2001	2000	2001
合 计	**Total**	**253084**	**331301**	**101020**	**117299**	**42428**	**49703**
哲 学	Philosophy	248	206	57	54	35	30
经济学	Economics	34503	15489	14304	5771	6210	1912
法 学	Law	13062	22842	6213	8391	1327	3544
教育学	Education	10201	14992	4352	4984	1779	2386
文 学	Literature	42927	56446	17293	20577	7692	9329
历史学	History	2521	1824	816	510	634	461
理 学	Science	23881	34232	8798	11529	4959	6317
工 学	Engineering	98518	110730	39066	38731	15675	16003
农 学	Agriculture	6643	6972	2389	2262	1404	1146
医 学	Medicine	20580	27585	7732	9445	2713	3286
管理学	Administration		39983		15045		5293

14-5 普通中等专业学校分科在校学生、招生及毕业生数

Student Enrollment, New Student Enrollment and Graduates In General Specialized Secondary Schools by Field of Study

单位：人　　(person)

年 份 Year	合 计 Total	中等技术学校 Secondary Technical Schools	工 业 Industry	农 业 Agriculture	林 业 Forestry	医 药 Health
在校学生数	**Student Enrollment**					
1995	186108	150986	58698	29716	1631	20233
1998	259242	220458	92826	40645	2301	25785
1999	272556	233114	97707	41650	2691	27076
2000	258342	223425	91667	34960	2154	34552
2001	240910	210062	82376	29385	1136	36886
招生数	**New Student Enrollment**					
1995	66337	52220	19769	10393	542	6520
1998	88733	75090	30195	12932	816	8829
1999	81239	70043	27537	11602	977	8703
2000	63625	53290	20327	7838	412	8653
2001	71374	61033	21125	9724	0	9462
毕业生数	**Graduates**					
1995	32999	21919	7996	3730	294	4072
1998	65053	51010	18025	9960	641	6263
1999	65341	54811	20194	11101	621	7211
2000	73076	58488	24543	11517	592	3144
2001	80906	67782	27553	11458	967	7987

年 份 Year	财 经 Economics and Finance	政 法 Politics and Law	体 育 Physical Culture	艺 术 Art	其 他 Others	中等师范学校 Secondary Teacher Training Schools
在校学生数	**Student Enrollment**					
1995	28978	3065	1180	2360	5105	35122
1998	34619	7065	2063	4412	10742	38784
1999	37552	7839	2415	4914	11270	39442
2000	35023	7121	2258	4892	10798	34917
2001	38909	5808	2185	3586	9791	30848
招生数	**New Student Enrollment**					
1995	9970	1135	383	772	2736	14114
1998	12699	2959	718	1658	4214	13713
1999	12783	2034	863	1747	3797	11196
2000	9852	1998	654	1422	2134	10335
2001	14569	1100	834	1160	3059	10341
毕业生数	**Graduates**					
1995	409	500	155	238	835	11080
1998	10215	2145	352	728	2681	14043
1999	9664	1281	463	1057	3219	10530
2000	11498	2652	690	1318	2534	14588
2001	12740	2417	685	1203	2772	13124

14-6 普通中学、小学按城乡和主办部门分组的情况（2001年）

Basic Statistics on General Secondary Schools, Primary Schools by Urban and Rural Area and by Department (2001)

单位：人 (person)

类别	Item	合计 Total	按城乡分 By Urban and Rural Areas 城市 Urban Areas	县镇 Counties and Towns	农村 Rural Areas	按主办部门分 By Departments 教育部门和集体办 Schools Run by Educational Departments	其他部门和民办 Schools Run by Other Departments
普通中学	**Regular Secondary Schools**						
学校数(所)	Number of Schools(unit)	4695	603	1345	2747	4210	485
教职工数	Number of Staff and Teachers	276672	47394	102026	127252	257677	18995
#专任教师数	#Full-time Teachers	236161	36593	85045	114523	221779	14382
招生数	New Student Enrollment	1648254	242978	607037	798239	1541930	106324
毕业生数	Number of Graduates	1034231	151744	365259	517228	990888	43343
在校学生数	Student Enrollment	4255858	628153	1535634	2092071	4004752	251106
普通中学中：高中	**Senior Secondary Schools**						
学校数(所)	Number of Schools(unit)	294	52	161	81	254	40
专任教师数	Full-time Teachers	43706					
招生数	New Student Enrollment	323625	93115	175087	55423	290867	32758
毕业生数	Number of Graduates	168166	53063	87069	28034	155485	12681
在校学生数	Student Enrollment	752579	223801	401011	127767	678343	74236
普通中学中：初中	**Junior Secondary Schools**						
学校数(所)	Number of Schools(unit)	3449	203	915	2331	3294	155
专任教师数	Full-time Teachers	192455					
招生数	New Student Enrollment	1324629	149863	431950	742816	1251063	73566
毕业生数	Number of Graduates	866065	98681	278190	489194	835403	30662
在校学生数	Student Enrollment	3503279	404352	1134623	1964304	3326409	176870
小 学	**Primary Schools**						
学校数(所)	Number of Schools(unit)	29340	1043	2676	25621	28796	544
教职工数	Number of Staff and Teachers	309106	37023	61421	210662	294896	14210
#专任教师数	#Full-time Teachers	291574	33065	56707	201802	279507	12067
招生数	New Student Enrollment	723570	93286	129847	500437	686684	36886
毕业生数	Number of Graduates	1357129	125764	283189	948176	1316250	40879
在校学生数	Student Enrollment	6012579	642265	1143752	4226562	5771377	241202

14-7 普通高等学校、中等专业学校教职工

Staff and Workers in General Institutions of Higher Education and Specialized Secondary Schools

单位：人 (person)

类 别	Item	高等学校 General Institutions of Higher Education			中等专业学校 Specialized Secondary Schools		
		1999	2000	2001	1999	2000	2001
教职工	**Staff and Teachers**	**42409**	**46642**	**53119**	**23658**	**21078**	**17137**
#校部教职工	#Staff and Workers	35998	39745	45982	22009	19755	16120
#专任教师	#Full-time Teachers	17990	20317	23878	11934	10775	9036
教辅人员	Auxiliary Teaching Staff	4432	5137	6144	2230	1903	1500
行政人员	Administrative Personnel	7188	7561	8584	4224	3826	3036
工勤人员	Logistics Personnel	6388	6730	7376	3621	3251	2548

14-8 普通高等学校分科专任教师(2001年)

Full – Time Teachers in General Institutions of Higher Education by Field of Study (2001)

单位：人 (person)

类 别	Item	合 计 Total	正高级 Professors	副高级 Asso. Professors	中 级 Lecturers	初 级 Assistants	无职称 Instructors
合 计	**Total**	**23878**	**2112**	**7411**	**8431**	**4344**	**1580**
哲 学	Philosophy	839	68	276	336	117	42
经济学	Economics	1473	129	447	584	230	83
法 学	Law	942	70	268	347	186	71
教育学	Education	2223	88	672	815	482	166
文 学	Literature	4658	295	1145	1723	1059	436
历史学	History	290	46	90	113	27	14
理 学	Science	3741	330	1365	1241	596	209
工 学	Engineering	6582	696	2114	2259	1145	368
农 学	Agriculture	717	113	308	231	48	17
医 学	Medicine	1765	236	532	522	344	131
管理学	Adminstration	648	41	194	260	110	43

14-9 各类普通中等专业学校专任教师

Full-Time Teachers in General Specialized Secondary Schools by Type of School

单位：人 (person)

类 别	Item	1995	1999	2000	2001
总 计	**Total**	**10559**	**11934**	**21078**	**17137**
中等技术学校	**Secondary Technical Schools**	**8533**	**9788**	**17631**	**14213**
工业学校	Industry	3769	3892	7231	5478
农业学校	Agriculture	1413	1875	3496	2775
林业学校	Forestry	102	108	217	
医药学校	Health	1160	1308	2173	2164
财经学校	Economics and Finance	1409	1824	3180	2510
政法学校	Politics and Law	105	118	254	198
体育学校	Physical Culture	133	236	364	359
艺术学校	Art	215	254	422	441
其 他	Others	227	173	294	288
中等师范学校	**Secondary Teacher Training Schools**	**2026**	**2146**	**3447**	**2924**

14-10 各级学校在校女学生和女教师

Number of Females Students and Teachers by Level of School

类 别	Item	1995	1999	2000	2001
女学生(万人)	**Number of Female Students (10 000 persons)**	**500.38**	**539.74**	**531.25**	**519.19**
普通高等学校	Regular Institutions of Higher Education	4.1	6.96	9.58	13.04
普通中等专业学校	Regular Specialized Secondary Schools	8.14	15.48	15.06	13.77
普通中学	Regular Secondary Schools	126.28	161.22	179.12	198.06
职业中学	Vocational Secondary Schools	9.95	10.66	9.68	9.69
普通小学	Primary Schools	351.91	345.43	317.81	284.63
女学生占全部学生(%)	**Percentage of Female Students to Total Students(%)**	**46.61**	**47.06**	**47.09**	**47.03**
普通高等学校	Regular Institutions of Higher Education	31.44	35.97	37.85	39.35
普通中等专业学校	Regular Specialized Secondary Schools	43.75	56.8	58.29	57.16
普通中学	Regular Secondary Schools	44.25	45.28	45.73	46.54
职业中学	Vocational Secondary Schools	49.93	46.77	45.26	48.74
普通小学	Primary Schools	47.77	47.88	47.87	47.34
女教师(万人)	**Number of Female Teachers (10 000 persons)**	**20.59**	**23.97**	**24.79**	**28.66**
普通高等学校	Regular Institutions of Higher Education	0.45	0.6	0.69	2.16
普通中等专业学校	Regular Specialized Secondary Schools	0.39	0.48	0.43	0.71
普通中学	Regular Secondary Schools	5.54	7.49	8.13	9.9
职业中学	Vocational Secondary Schools	0.45	0.66	0.59	0.82
普通小学	Primary Schools	13.76	14.75	14.95	15.07
女教师占全部教师(%)	**Percentage of Female Teachers to Total Teachers(%)**	**39.83**	**42.24**	**42.97**	**42.31**
普通高等学校	Regular Institutions of Higher Education	29.57	33.17	33.96	40.64
普通中等专业学校	Regular Specialized Secondary Schools	37.22	40.27	39.9	41.19
普通中学	Regular Secondary Schools	30.91	28.73	36.34	35.77
职业中学	Vocational Secondary Schools	32.21	37.24	37.35	38.1
普通小学	Primary Schools	46.18	47.98	48.79	48.76

14-11 平均每万人口中在校学生

Student Enrollment Per l0,000 Population

项目	Item	1995	1999	2000	2001
各类普通学校在校学生占全省人口 (%)	**Students as Percentage of Total Population (%)**	**16.9**	**17.67**	**17.24**	**17.28**
平均每万人口中在校学生(人)	**Student Enrollment Per l0 000 Population (person)**				
普通高等学校	Regular Institutions of Higher Education	20.6	29.7	38.7	50.2
中等学校	Regular Secondary Schools	512	630.7	670.3	711.9
普通小学	Primary Schools	1164.2	1106.7	1014.4	911.6

注: 1.本表未包括技工学校在校学生。

2.各类普通学校在校学生数包括普通高校、普通中专、职业中学、普通中小学的在校学生数。

a. Secondary schools excludes schools for skilled workers.

b. The number of student enrollment refers to that of students enrolled in regular institutions of higher education, specialized secondary schools, vocational schools, regular secondary schools and primary schools.

14-12 民办(私立)学校情况

Statistics on Private Schools

单位：人 (person)

项目	Item	1995	1999	2000	2001
普通中学	**Regular Secondary Schools**				
学校数(所)	Number of Schools(unit)	80	139	166	251
教职工数	Staff and Teachers	1145	3263	4845	9301
专任教师数	Full-time Teachers	790	2246	3367	6567
毕业生数	Graduates	2773	4669	9035	18274
招生数	New Student Enrollment	6570	26774	43333	66519
在校学生数	Student Enrollment	16287	50641	90112	146984
普通小学	**Primary Schools**				
学校数(所)	Number of Schools(unit)	42	203	213	261
教职工数	Staff and Teachers	466	2203	2451	4074
专任教师数	Full-time Teachers	274	1489	1713	2914
毕业生数	Graduates	129	1634	6183	7820
招生数	New Student Enrollment	935	5535	5572	8919
在校学生数	Student Enrollment	3287	40646	45911	59962

14-13 各类学校代课教师及临时工人数

Provisional Teachers and Temporary Workers by Type of School

单位：人 (person)

项 目	Item	1995	1999	2000	2001
普通中学	**Regular Secondary Schools**				
代课教师	Provisional Teachers	6440	2593	2803	4626
临时工	Temporary Workers	2275	1564	1248	-
兼任教师	Part-time Teachers	357	440	674	1267
职业中学	**Vocational Secondary Schools**				
代课教师	Provisional Teachers	623	194	247	510
临时工	Temporary Workers	678	227	196	-
兼任教师	Part-time Teachers	1417	1283	941	1190
技工学校	**Various Technical Schools**				
兼职教师	Part-time Teachers	649	1233	1301	1103
普通小学	**Primary Schools**				
代课教师	Provisional Teachers	33072	15718	9118	8697
临时工	Temporary Workers	2688	2415	1374	-
兼任教师	Part-time Teachers	146	71	118	1157

14-14 平均每一教职工负担学生

Student/ Staff and Worker Ratio

单位：人 (person)

项目	Item	1995	1999	2000	2001
平均每一教职工负担的学生	**Student - Teacher Ratio**				
普通高等学校	Regular Institutions of Higher Education	3.3	4.7	5.5	6.2
普通中等专业学校	Regular Specialized Secondary Schools	8.1	11.5	12	14.1
普通中学	Regular Secondary Schools	13.1	14.3	15.1	15.4
普通小学	Primary Schools	23.2	22.1	20.5	19.5
平均每一专任教师负担的学生	**Student - Full-time Teacher Ratio**				
普通高等学校	Regular Institutions of Higher Education	8.5	10.8	12.5	13.9
普通中等专业学校	Regular Specialized Secondary Schools	17.6	22.8	23.97	26.7
普通中学	Regular Secondary Schools	15.9	16.8	17.5	18
普通小学	Primary Schools	24.7	23.5	21.7	20.6

14-15 初中和小学毕业生升学率及学龄儿童入学率

Percentage of Graduates of Junior Middle Schools and Primary Schools Entering Higher Level Schools,Percentage of School - Age Children Enrolled

项目	Item	1995	1999	2000	2001
初 中	**Junior Middle Schools**				
毕业生数（万人）	Number of Graduates (10 000 persons)	61.32	85.27	85.77	86.61
高级中等学校招生数（万人）	New Student Enrollment of Senior Secondary Schools (10 000 persons)	29.24	40.44	43.87	52.36
升学率 (%)	Percentage of Graduates (%)	47.7	47.4	51.15	60.45
小 学	**Primary Schools**				
毕业生数 (万人)	Number of Graduates (10 000 persons)	106.67	122.37	130.2	135.7
初级中等学校招生数 (万人)	New Student Enrollment of Junior Secondary Schools (10 000 persons)	96.66	116.49	126.34	132.85
升学率 (%)	Percentage of Graduates(%)	90.6	95.2	97.04	97.89
学龄儿童(万人)	**School-age Children (10 000 persons)**	**705.3**	**701.68**	**645.08**	**566.87**
已入学学龄儿童 (万人)	School-age Children Enrolled in Schools (10 000 persons)	691.49	693.19	634.9	554.99
入学率 (%)	Enrollment Rate (%)	98	98.8	98.4	97.9

注：1. 高级中等学校招生数包括中专招收初中毕业生数、普通高中和职业高中的招生数、技工学校的招生数；

2. 初级中等学校招生数包括普通初中和职业初中招生数。初中毕业生包括普通初中和职业初中毕业生。

a. The number of new student enrollment in senior school includes that of students in specialized secondary schools, regular secondary schools and vocational schools and the technical schools.

b. The number of new student enrollment in junior school includes that of students in regular junior schools, and junior vocational schools.

14-16 幼儿园基本情况

Basic Statistics on Kindergartens

项目	Item	1995	1999	2000	2001
幼儿园个数（所）	Number of Kindergartens (unit)	2226	4448	5473	1333
班数 (个)	Number of Classes (unit)	42809	29577	29896	25903
在园幼儿数 (万人)	Student Enrollment (10 000 persons)	131.6	64.32	62.87	60.06
教职工数（万人）	Number of Staff and Teachers (10 000 persons)	5.34	3.97	3.98	1.61
#教师	#Teachers	4.52	3.47	3.39	0.98

14-17 各级成人学校基本情况（2001年）

Statistics on Other Adult Education (2001)

单位：人 (person)

项目	Item	学校数（所）Number of Schools (unit)	毕业生数 Graduates	招生数 New Student Enroll-ment	在校学生 Student Enroll-ment	教职工数 Staff and Teachers	#专任教师 Full-time Teachers
总　计	**Total**	**5504**	**269230**	**313627**	**483131**	**24947**	**11096**
成人高等教育	**Adult Education Schools**	**26**	**50281**	**119414**	**255643**	**7632**	**3670**
广播电视大学	Radio and TV Universities	1	10152	13610	37553	1160	511
职工大学	Schools of Higher Education for Staff	19	6300	13701	25825	4237	2164
管理干部学院	Colleges for Management Cadres	1	2149	1672	4168	591	298
教育学院	Pedagogical Colleges	5	1057	5054	9468	323	179
普通高校函授部、夜大学、成人脱产班	Correspondence Department or Evening Universities Run by Institution of Higher Education		30623	85377	178629	1321	518
成人中等教育	**Secondary Schools for Adults**	**452**	**63427**	**62311**	**85988**	**8502**	**4761**
成人中等专业学校	Specialized Secondary Schools for Adults	176	25081	27598	50974	6181	3710
广播电视中专	Radio and TV Specialized Secondary Schools	5	2454	2207	3388	199	93
职工中专	Specialized Secondary Schools for Staff	39	8879	5725	12923	1426	811
干部中专	Specialized Secondary Schools for Cadres	10	760	672	1757	325	170
农民中专	Specialized Secondary Schools for Peasants	28	2682	5285	9608	1423	970
函授中等专业学校	Correspondence Specialized Secondary Schools						
教师进修	Teacher Training Schools	94	10306	13709	23298	2808	1666
成人中学	Secondary Schools for Adults	276	38346	34713	35014	2321	1051
职工中学	Secondary Schools for Staff	48	5548	5540	7492	965	493
农民中学	Secondary Schools for Peasants	228	32798	29173	27522	1356	558
成人初等教育	**Primary Schools for Adults**	**5026**	**155522**	**131902**	**141500**	**8813**	**2665**
职工初等学校	Primary Schools for Staff	41	3603	2857	4813	134	67
农民初等学校	Primary Schools for Peasants	4985	151919	129045	136687	8679	2598
#扫盲班	#Literacy Courses	1505	59450	34097	30644	3634	646

14-18 特殊教育学校基本情况(2001年)

Basic Statistics on Schools for Special Education (2001)

单位：人 (person)

项目	Item	学校数（所）Number of Schools (unit)	毕业生数 Graduates	招生数 New Student Enroll-ment	在校学生 Student Enroll-ment	教职工数 Staff and Teachers	#专任教师 Full-time Teachers
总 计	**Total**	**59**	**1273**	**2194**	**14635**	**1201**	**905**
盲聋哑学校	Blind, Deaf and Deaf-mute Schools	52			6554		
弱智儿童学校	Mentally Retarded Schools	7			8081		

14-19 成人其他教育

Statistics on Other Adult Education

(person)

项 目	Item	在校学生数 Student Enrollment 2000	2001	结业学生数 Student Completed Course 2000	2001
高等学校	**Adults Education Schools**	**14924**	**14152**	**69973**	**96081**
证书教育	Certificate Education	192	2160	7493	7436
岗位培训班	Station Training Classes	4701	11706	51027	88582
#资格培训班	#Competency Training	2176	8768	23980	61121
适应培训班	Adaptation Training	2525	2938	27047	27461
其他	Others	10031	286	11453	63
中等学校	**Secondary Schools for Adults**	**74434**	**32087**	**69977**	**71218**
单科班	Single Subject Classes	5417	2393	1480	3236
专业证书班	Specialized Certificate Classes	11339	9796	8110	16119
岗位培训	Station Training Classes	25502	18725	48578	51083
#资格培训班	#Competency Training	11844	10003	26059	24061
适应培训班	Adaptation Training	11459	8575	21757	25341
工人技术培训班	Technical Training Classes for Staff	2199	147	762	1681
农村技术培训班	Technical Training Classes for Peasants	381	313	1570	288
文化补习班	Culture Remediation	378	133	163	269
其 他	Others	17759	727	10076	223
成人技术培训学校	**Technical Training Schools for Adults**	**1670909**	**1620692**	**2418036**	**1942787**
职工技术培训学校	Technical Training Schools for Staff	78418	67290	87617	74204
农民技术培训学校	Technical Training Schools for Peasants	1592491	1553402	2330419	1868583
#县办	#Schools Run by Counties	17087	17613	16990	12326

14-20 教育经费总支出情况

Statistics on the Expenses of Educational Funds

单位：万元 (10 000 yuan)

年份 Year	合计 Total	国家财政性教育经费 Government Appropriation for Education	#预算内教育经费 Budgetary	社会团体和公民个人办学经费 Funds of Social Organizations and Citizens for Running Schools	社会捐资和集资办学经费 Donations and Fund-Raising for Running Schools	学费和杂费 Tuition and Miscellaneous Fee	其他教育经费 Other Educational Funds
1996	870239.3	565019.8	374125.3	10502.8	70612.5	143251.6	80852.6
1997	989732.7	636639.5	428334.2	8013.5	91738.1	162014.4	91327.2
1998	1203245.1	710268.5	504295.0	10144.0	72342.6	253321.0	157169.0
1999	1375585.6	797469.8	573878.4	18527.2	71829.1	321773.5	165986.0
2000	1531180.5	862111.2	629976.6	27231.8	42117.6	403493.9	196226.0
2001	1777653.0	1009760.9	766718.4	35535.9	41326.2	471246.5	219783.5

14-21 各类专业技术人员

Various Specialized Technical Personnel

单位：人　　(person)

项 目	Item	合计 Total 2000	合计 Total 2001	国有 States-owned 2000	国有 States-owned 2001	集体 Collective-owned 2000	集体 Collective-owned 2001
总 计	**Total**	**1093367**	**1103287**	**1054299**	**1071697**	**39068**	**31590**
#高级职称	Senior	42638	45258	42257	44896	381	362
中级职称	Secondary	377576	390053	368574	382595	9002	7458
#女性	Female	412366	435712	404342	425307	12956	10405
#自然科学	Natural Sciences	892838	913161	877622	900986	15216	12175
#社会及人文科学	Social Sciences and Humanities	200529	190126	176677	170711	23852	19415

注：此表未包括国家机关与人民团体中的专业技术人员；集体单位含供销社系统。

Technicians from government offices and mass organizations were excluded. Supply and marketing cooperatives were included in the collective-owned units.

14-22 地方国有单位各行业自然科学技术人员(2001年)

Natural Scientific and Technical Personnel in Local State-Owned Units by Sector (2001)

单位：人　　(person)

行 业	Sector	自然科学技术人员 Natural Scientific and Technical Personnel	工程技术人员 Engineering Personnel	农业技术人员 Agricultural Personnel	科学研究人员 Scientific Research Personnel	卫生技术人员 Health Care Personnel	教学人员 Teaching Personnel
合 计	**Total**	**900986**	**142087**	**26269**	**4725**	**144048**	**583857**
农林牧渔业	Farming,Forestry,Animal Husbandry and Fishery	41749	15526	24472	49	580	1122
工 业	Industry	65508	48743	248	38	7818	8661
地质勘探和水利管理业	Geological Prospecting and Water Conservancy	14912	13883	231	14	298	486
建筑业	Construction	14609	13010	2	0	995	602
运输邮电业	Transportation,Postal and Telecommunications	10304	9100	22	4	586	592
商业、饮食业	Wholesale and Retail Trade, Catering Trade	4584	2556	181	24	1646	177
房地产、社会服务业	Real Estate, Social Services	18335	15724	228	40	1394	949
卫生、体育和社会福利事业	Health Care,Sports and Social Welfare	129635	920	19	50	127410	1236
教育、文化和广播电影电视业	Education,Culture and Arts, Radio, Film and TV	578429	5769	327	1626	1915	568792
科学研究和综合技术服务业	Scientific Research and Polytechnical Services	14265	9767	335	2874	787	502
金融保险业	Banking and Insurance	356	220	22	1	33	80
其他行业	Others	8300	6869	182	5	586	658

14-23 地方集体单位各行业自然科学技术人员 (2001年)

Natural Scientific and Technical Personnel in Local Collective-Owned Units by Sector (2001)

单位：人 (person)

行业	Sector	自然科学技术人员 Natural Scientific and Technical Personnel	工程技术人员 Engineering Personnel	农业技术人员 Agricultural Personnel	科学研究人员 Scientific Research Personnel	卫生技术人员 Health Care Personnel	教学人员 Teaching Personnel
合计	**Total**	**12175**	**5460**	**543**	**47**	**5300**	**825**
农林牧渔水利	Farming,Forestry,Animal Husbandry and Fishery,Water Conservancy	263	92	167			4
工业、建筑房地产业	Industry, Construction,Real Estate	4203	3880	3	5	209	106
商业、饮食业	Wholesale and Retail Trade, Catering	1028	532	353		59	84
文化教育卫生科研	Culture, Education,Health Care, Scientific Research	5587	23	2	40	4932	590
其他行业	Others	1094	933	18	2	100	41
合计中：女性	**Female in Total**	**3918**	**794**	**71**	**23**	**2714**	**316**

14-24 地方国有单位各行业社会、人文科学专业人员 (2001年)

Specialized Personnel Engaged in Society and Humane Studies in Local State – Owned Units by Sector (2001)

单位：人 (person)

行业	Sector	社会、人文科学专业人员 Specialized Personnel Engaged in Society and Humane Studies	经济、会计、统计人员 Economic Financial Accounting Statistician	翻译图书档案文博新闻出版播音人员 Translating Archives Publishing Broadcasting	工艺美术体育人员 Craft Physical Culture	律师公证人员 Lawyer	政工人员 Political Workers
合计	**Total**	**170711**	**123568**	**14159**	**6442**	**814**	**25728**
农林牧渔业	Farming,Forestry,Animal Husbandry and Fishery	10055	8061	147	19	11	1817
工业	Industry	43948	32408	1262	374	83	9821
地质勘探和水利管理业	Geological Prospecting and Water Conservancy	3916	2722	196	4	7	987
建筑业	Construction	6053	4664	117	8	11	1253
运输邮电业	Transportation,Postal and Telecommunications	14225	10821	232	28	19	3125
商业、饮食业	Wholesale and Retail Trade,Catering	24165	21760	214	71	16	2104
房地产、社会服务业	Real Estate, Social Services	22550	17570	742	136	530	3572
卫生、体育、福利业	Health Care,Sports,Social Welfare	6902	5092	582	862	3	363
教育、文化、广电业	Education,Culture and Arts, Radio, Film and TV	21622	6254	9816	4576	58	918
科研和技术服务业	Scientific Research and Polytechnical Services	4423	3226	525	223	23	426
金融保险业	Banking and Insurance	3349	3236	17	1	17	78
其他行业	Others	9503	7754	309	140	36	1264

14-25 地方集体单位各行业社会、人文科学专业人员

Specialized Personnel Engaged in Society and Humane Studies in Local Collective-Owned Units by Sector

单位：人 (person)

行 业	Sector	1995	1999	2000	2001
合 计	**Total**	**18403**	**30414**	**23852**	**19415**
农林牧渔业	Farming,Forestry,Animal Husbandry and Fishery	326	1203	1697	580
工业运输房地产业	Industrial, Transportation and Real Estate	12131	6974	5411	3732
商业饮食业	Wholesale and Retail Trade, Catering	3789	18416	14132	11561
文化教育卫生科研	Culture, Education,Health Care,Scientific Research	482	614	667	358
其他行业	Others	1675	3207	1945	3184
合计中：女性	**Female in Total**	**7316**	**10635**	**8024**	**6487**

注：从1999年起，集体单位包含供销社系统。 Supply and marketing cooperatives were included in the collective-owned units since 1999.

14-26 自然科学研究获奖成果

Number of Achievements in Natural Scientific Research

单位：项 (item)

项 目	Item	1995	1999	2000	2001
省科技进步奖	Provincial Scientific Technological Progress Prize	329	308	360	150
国家科学技术进步奖	National Scientific Technological Progress Prize	19	17	13	14
国家批准授予的发明奖	National Invention Prize	6	4		1
国家自然科学奖	National Natural Sciences Prize			1	

14-27 科技成果情况(2001年)

Statistics on Achievements of Science and Technology (2001)

单位:项 (item)

项 目	Item	合 计 Total	科研院所 Research Institutions	大专院校 Universities and Colleges	工矿企业 Industrial and Mining Enterprises	其 他 Others
项目基本情况	**Basic Statistics on Items**					
登记项目数	Number of Registered Items	1008	159	208	417	224
#鉴定项目数	# Number of Appraised Items	757	87	169	380	121
奖励项目数	Number of Prized Items	202	33	68	48	53
项目计划管理情况	**Statistics of Items Planned Management**					
国家计划项目	National Plan Items	167	33	27	90	17
省部计划项目	Provincial Plan Items	308	80	65	70	93
计划外项目	Non-plan Items	385	28	69	250	38
成果水平	**Level of Achievements**					
国际首创或领先	Originate and Keep Ahead at International	44	7	8	13	16
国际先进	International Advanced Level	179	20	41	110	8
国内首创或领先	Originate and Keep Ahead at National	378	73	65	199	41
国内先进	Domestically Advanced Level	228	30	45	85	68
其他	Others	31	11	2	3	15
成果应用领域	**Field of Achievements Using**					
工业、交通、邮电、建筑、地质	Industrial, Transportation, Postal, Construction and Geologic	465	90	100	244	31
农林牧渔	Farming,Forestry,Animal Husbandry and Fishery	89	27	10	30	22
卫生体育和社会福利	Health Care,Sports,Social Welfare	110	6	16	24	64
商业、金融、文教	Commerce, Finance, Culture and Education	95	5	14	58	18
科研和综合技术服务	Scientific Research and Polytechnical Services	37	3	12	17	5
其它行业	Others	64	10	9	37	8

14-28 三种专利申请与批准项数

Three Types of Patent Applications Examined and Certified

单位：项 (item)

项 目	Item	申请数 Applications Examined		批准数 Applications Granted	
		2000	2001	2000	2001
总 计	**Total**	**4117**	**4293**	**2555**	**2401**
按种类分	**By Types:**				
发 明	Creation and Inventions	814	907	197	166
实用新型	Utility Models	2465	2571	1759	1730
外观设计	Designs	838	815	599	505
按申请人类别分	**By Proposer:**				
个 人	Personal	3258	3413	1933	1855
大专院校	Universities and Colleges	83	83	27	33
科研单位	Research Institutions	77	23	60	41
工矿企业	Industrial and Mining Enterprises	681	750	516	452
机关团体	Agencies and Organizations	18	24	19	20

14-29 各类技术合同签订及执行情况(2001年)

Statistics on Contracts Signed and Performed (2001)

项 目	Item	合同数(项) Number of Contracts (item)	合同金额(万元) Contracted Value (10 000 yuan)	#技术交易额 Value of Technical Trade
总 计	**Total**	**22761**	**293887**	**184998**
技术开发合同	Contracts of Technical Development	5104	122288	74728
技术转让合同	Contracts of Technical Alienation	3235	47273	32366
技术服务合同	Contracts of Technical Services	10334	101366	65559
技术咨询合同	Contracts of Technical Consultative	4088	22960	12345

14-30 各级科技计划项目进入技术市场情况(2001年)

Statitics on Different Levels of Scientific Plan Items Put into Technical Markets (2001)

开发类别	Item	合计 Total	国家部门计划 Country Level	省级计划 Province Level	市州县计划 Prefectures and County level
项目个数合计(项)	**Total (Item)**	**7144**	**805**	**2158**	**4181**
#科研机构	Research Institutions	1135	130	365	640
大专院校	Universities and Colleges	1387	192	567	628
工矿企业	Industrial and Mining Enterprises	1738	169	417	1152
技术贸易机构	Institutions of Technical Trade	1954	284	751	919
个人及个人合伙	Personal and Partnership	621	30	58	533
其他	Others	309	-	-	309
金额合计(万元)	**Total (10 000 yuan)**	**113118.4**	**23549.8**	**29343.2**	**60225.4**
#科研机构	Research Institutions	31368.5	9413.6	9937	12017.9
大专院校	Universities and Colleges	11172	4232.2	2539.8	4400
工矿企业	Industrial and Mining Enterprises	37890	4311.2	12683.8	20895
技术贸易机构	Institutions of Technical Trade	20199.6	5092.8	3169.6	11937.2
个人及个人合伙	Personal and Partnership	6132.2	500	1013	4619.2
其他	Others	6356.1	-	-	6356.1

14-31 高新技术产品情况(2001年)

Basic Statistics on High-tech Products (2001)

项目	Item	企业单位数（个）Number of Enterprises (unit)	高新技术产品总产值（万元）Gross Output Value of High-tech Products (10 000 yuan)	高新技术产品增加值（万元）Value Increment of High-tech Products (10 000 yuan)
合计	**Total**	**1256**	**5933628**	**1851458**
#高新技术企业	# High ang New Technology Enterprises	637	3829424	1231230
按市州分：	**By Region:**			
长沙市	Changsha City	649	2448063	781361
株洲市	Zhuzhou City	120	1011729	316072
湘潭市	Xiangtan City	95	609610	203319
衡阳市	Hengyang City	113	354574	90471
邵阳市	Shaoyang City	12	24974	8907
岳阳市	Yueyang City	39	639216	171318
常德市	Changde City	54	143881	62285
张家界市	Zhangjiajie City	2	4642	1160
益阳市	Yiyang City	26	102293	23280
郴州市	Chenzhou City	75	165726	50531
永州市	Yongzhou City	19	266681	66702
怀化市	Huaihua City	10	31883	16678
娄底市	Loudi City	30	51164	12688
湘西自治州	West Hunan A.P	12	79192	46685
长沙高新技术开发区	Changsha High-tech Development District	582	2188070	713400
株洲高新技术开发区	Zhuzhou High-tech Development District	75	639635	219778
湘潭高新技术开发区	Xiangtan High-tech Development District	43	181838	54047
衡阳高新技术开发区	Hengyang High-tech Development District	33	160231	41297
岳阳高新技术开发区	Yueyang High-tech Development District	17	309400	112452
按登记注册类型分：	**By Registration Status**			
国有企业	State-owned Enterprises	250	1575849	500141
集体企业	Collective-owned Enterprises	110	108619	30408
股份合作企业	Cooperative Enterprises	52	81862	23121
股份制企业	Share-holding Corporations	267	2590162	757942
外商及港澳台投资企业	Enterprises with Investment from Foreign、Hong Kong、Macao and Taiwan	119	824678	297548
其他企业	Other Enterprises	458	752459	242298
按企业规模分：	**By Size:**			
大中型工业企业	Large and medium-sized Enterprises	213	3601662	1096086
按高新技术领域分：	**By High-tech Fields:**			
电子与信息	Electron and Information	277	724100	246421
生物医药技术	Medicine and Biotechnology	193	921506	311483
新材料	New Materials	327	1904556	532848
光机电一体化	Optical and Mechatronics	253	1448114	436146
新能源、高效节能	New Energy Resources,Energy Saving	37	180110	82132
环境保护	Environmental Protection	13	26538	9387
航空航天	Avigation and Spaceflight	1	2108	795
地球、空间及海洋工程	Earth,Airspace and Ocean			
其他企业	Other Enterprises	155	726596	232246

项目	Item	高新技术产品销售收入（万元）Sales Revenue of High-tech Products (10 000 yuan)	#出口收入 Exports Revenue	高新技术产品利税总额（万元）Peofits and Tax of High-tech Products (10 000 yuan)	#利润总额 Total of Profit and Tax
合计	**Total**	**6010503**	**424213**	**852837**	**484231**
#高新技术企业	# High ang New Technology Enterprises	3999258	246730	530034	292290
按市州分：	**By Region:**				
长沙市	Changsha City	2711284	127374	382752	215326
株洲市	Zhuzhou City	1000559	136605	120604	61535
湘潭市	Xiangtan City	609150	47550	84374	49464
衡阳市	Hengyang City	325662	38368	42788	25001
邵阳市	Shaoyang City	23862	1207	3712	1104
岳阳市	Yueyang City	576927	11946	102683	74364
常德市	Changde City	132416	2894	19897	9619
张家界市	Zhangjiajie City	4622	100	617	537
益阳市	Yiyang City	82360	13548	6065	1396
郴州市	Chenzhou City	153622	32831	15973	8450
永州市	Yongzhou City	250658	4428	35790	19914
怀化市	Huaihua City	20155	654	5428	1981
娄底市	Loudi City	48067	3401	5896	2327
湘西自治州	West Hunan A.P	71159	3307	26258	13213
长沙高新技术开发区	Changsha High-tech Development District	2468192	122082	337732	196062
株洲高新技术开发区	Zhuzhou High-tech Development District	617120	78299	57542	31427
湘潭高新技术开发区	Xiangtan High-tech Development District	176120	5498	16413	1775
衡阳高新技术开发区	Hengyang High-tech Development District	148704	14337	25609	16788
岳阳高新技术开发区	Yueyang High-tech Development District	298068	2603	70903	53397
按登记注册类型分：	**By Registration Status**				
国有企业	State-owned Enterprises	1547030	142068	199578	97273
集体企业	Collective-owned Enterprises	95840	9247	13029	7196
股份合作企业	Cooperative Enterprises	66317	2148	7156	4036
股份制企业	Share-holding Corporations	2658042	121198	401485	247074
外商及港澳台投资企业	Enterprises with Investment from Foreign 、Hong Kong、 Macao and Taiwan	861821	117099	111816	60039
其他企业	Other Enterprises	781453	32453	119773	68613
按企业规模分：	**By Size:**				
大中型工业企业	Large and medium-sized Enterprises	3751759	269207	465161	248932
按高新技术领域分：	**By High-tech Fields:**				
电子与信息	Electron and Information	779702	64088	97522	55017
生物医药技术	Medicine and Biotechnology	907637	16882	144043	75703
新材料	New Materials	1871581	210946	222974	132260
光机电一体化	Optical and Mechatronics	1370454	52078	176959	92209
新能源、高效节能	New Energy Resources,Energy Saving	170565	2021	33434	18108
环境保护	Environmental Protection	24934	1735	3658	2698
航空航天	Avigation and Spaceflight	2037		20	292
地球、空间及海洋工程	Earth,Airspace and Ocean				
其他企业	Other Enterprises	883593	76463	174227	107944

14-32 大中型工业企业科技活动情况（2001）

Basic Statistics on Scientific and Technological Actives in Large and Medium-Sized Industrial Enterprises (2001)

指　　标	Item	合　计 Total	#国有 State-owned	大型 Large	中型 Medium
大中型工业企业个数（个）	Large and Medium-Sized Industrial Enterprises (unit)	613	364	233	380
#有科技活动的企业个数	# Number of Units Having S&T Activities	348	194	178	170
企业科技活动人员（人）	Number of S&T Personnel of Enterprises(person)	42677	26182	34429	8248
#全时人员	Personnel	20274	12276	16104	4170
#具有高、中级职称	Senior and Medium	19908	13364	17016	2892
#研究与实验发展人员	R&D Employee	18377	11379	14568	3809
#工程技术人员	Technical Employee				
企业办科技机构数（个）	Number of Institutions for S&T in Enterprises (unit)	238	121	154	84
企业办科研机构科技活动人员（人）	Number of Persons of Institutions for S&T in Enterprises (person)	12264	6071	10208	2056
#具有高、中级职称	Senior and Medium	5777	3218	4938	839
#博士毕业	Doctor	70	21	48	22
#硕士毕业	Master	564	371	502	62
#本科毕业	University	5059	2640	4394	665
#研究与实验发展人员	R&D Personnel	5693	3253	4673	1020
当年科技活动经费筹集总额（万元）	Funds of S&T Activities this Year (10 000 yuan)	207482	112483	179431	28051
#企业自筹	#Self-raised	164233	86676	143772	20461
金融机构贷款	Bank Loans	20210	13412	16284	3926
来自政府部门资金	Government Allocation	16952	9127	14010	2942
来自事业单位的资金	From Enterprises Allocation	196	196	169	27
来自国外的资金	From Foreign Investment				
其他资金	Other Investment	5892	3074	5197	695
当年科技活动经费支出总额（万元）	Expenditure for S&T Activities this Year (10 000 yuan)	186650	103655	161110	25540
#内部支出	#Intramural Expenditure	165623	92633	141974	23649
#研究与发展经费	#R&D	89060	51744	75562	13499
基础研究	Fundamental Research	611	268	552	60
应用研究	Applied Research	5708	3125	4388	1320
实验发展	Experimental Development	82741	48351	70622	12119
#新产品开发经费	#New Products Development	68040	30507	56643	11396
#劳务费	#Labor Expenditures	51929	30813	43995	7934
#原材料费	#Raw and Processed Materials Expenditures	47146	28649	39214	7932
新产品产值（万元）	Gross Output Value of New Products (10 000 yuan)	1227301	621373	1151277	76024
新产品销售收入（万元）	Sales Revenue of New Products (10 000 yuan)	1188038	604220	1096944	91094
#出口	#Exported	66512	35593	58224	8288
新产品销售利润（万元）	Sales Profits of New Products (10 000 yuan)	172153	80944	159477	12675
科技活动项目个数（项）	Number of Projects for S&T (item)	2762	1667	2222	540
#新产品开发	#New Products Development	1115	607	785	330
#研究与实验发展	#Research and Experimental Development	1515	855	1196	319
科技活动项目参加人员（人）	Personnel of Projects for S&T Activities (person)	25956	15880	20637	5319
科技活动项目经费支出总额（万元）	Expenditures of Projects fo S&T Activities (10 000 yuan)	136965	77487	117803	19162
专利申请数（件）	Patent Applications (item)	334	104	268	66
拥有发明专利数（件）	Applications of Inventions (item)	230	63	203	27

14-33 大中型工业企业科技活动人员与经费情况（2001）

Basic Statistics on S&T Personnel and Funds of S&T Activities in Large and Medium-Sized Industrial Enterprises (2001)

类别	Item	企业科技活动人员（人）S&T Personnel in Enterprises (person)	#高中级职称人员 Senior and Medium	当年科技活动经费筹集总额（万元）Funds of S&T Activities this Year (10 000 yuan)	当年科技活动经费支出总额（万元）Expenditure for S&T Activities this Year (10 000 yuan)	#新产品开发 New Products Development
总　计	**Total**	**42677**	**19908**	**207482**	**165623**	**68040**
按市州分：	**By Region:**					
长沙市	Changsha City	7662	3082	38024	37793	17351
株洲市	Zhuzhou City	8294	5228	38346	30106	12374
湘潭市	Xiangtan City	8291	3628	43553	29903	15405
衡阳市	Hengyang City	4485	1759	21056	16984	4840
邵阳市	Shaoyang City	1353	529	8937	8083	682
岳阳市	Yueyang City	3903	1758	13898	11939	2088
常德市	Changde City	1895	898	12202	10855	5108
张家界市	Zhangjiajie City	17	4	21	21	21
益阳市	Yiyang City	1128	427	2108	1805	1309
郴州市	Chenzhou City	1562	760	4205	3473	1488
永州市	Yongzhou City	933	217	8186	4636	4400
怀化市	Huaihua City	994	382	2487	1960	1031
娄底市	Loudi City	1693	1134	12857	6568	1524
湘西自治州	West Hunan A.P	467	102	1603	1497	421
按企业规模分组：	**By Size:**					
大型企业	Large	34429	17016	179431	141974	56643
中型企业	Medium	8248	2892	28051	23649	11396
按登记注册类型分组：	**By Registration Status:**					
内资企业	Domestic-Funded Enterprises	42073	19735	204528	162649	66778
国有	State-owned Enterprises	26182	13364	112483	92633	30507
集体	Collective-owned Enterprises	568	294	3358	2739	2001
股份合作	Cooperative Enterprises	139	42	221	245	134
国有联营	State Joint Ownership Enterprises	151	2	268	268	268
集体联营	Collective Joint Ownership Enterprises					
国有与集体联营	Joint State-collective Enterprises					
其他联营	Other Joint Ownership Enterprises					
国有独资公司	State-funded Corporations	5401	1820	23293	19308	9898
其他有限责任公司	Other Limited Liability Corporations	3667	1567	24813	12524	6007
股份有限公司	Share-holding Corporations Ltd.	5444	2461	35419	30512	15539
私营独资	Private-funded Enterprises					
私营合伙	Private Partnership Enterprises					
私营有限责任公司	Private Limited Liability Corporations	481	177	4503	4285	2327
私营股份有限公司	Private Share-holding Corporations Ltd.	40	8	170	126	98
其他内资	Other Enterprises					
港澳台商投资	Enterprises With Investment from Hong Kong, Macao and Taiwan	136	64	620	640	397
外商投资	Enterprises With Foreign Investment	468	109	2334	2334	865

类别	Item	企业科技活动人员（人）S&T Personnel in Enterprises (person)	#高中级职称人员 Senior and Medium	当年科技活动经费筹集总额（万元）Funds of S&T Activities this Year (10 000 yuan)	当年科技活动经费支出总额（万元）Expenditure for S&T Activities this Year (10 000 yuan)	#新产品开发 New Products Development
按工业行业大类分组：	**By Industrial Branch:**					
煤炭采选业	Coal Mining and Dressing	857	454	1459	1369	150
石油和天然气开采业	Petroleum and Natural Gas Extraction					
黑色金属矿采选业	Ferrous Metals Mining and dressing	3	1	22	22	
有色金属矿采选业	Nonferrous Metals Mining and dressing	840	357	1379	1105	207
非金属矿采选业	Nonmetals Mining and dressing	71	35	344	343	
其他矿采选业	Others Minerals Mining and dressing					
木材及竹材采运业	Logging and Transport of Timber and Bamboo					
食品加工业	Food Processing	548	211	3436	2519	1479
食品制造业	Food Production	70	31	187	143	115
饮料制造业	Beverages Production	517	208	2059	2000	783
烟草加工业	Tobacco Processing	458	183	7440	7434	3071
纺织业	Textiles Industry	1018	227	2678	2570	507
服装及其他纤维制品制造业	Garments and Other Fiber Products	20	4	178	158	158
皮革毛皮羽绒及其制品业	Leather,Furs,Down and Related Products	14	4	27	46	46
木材加工及竹、藤、棕、草制品业	Timber Processing,Bamboo,Cane, Palm Fiber and Straw Products	54	44	89	135	
家具制造业	Furniture Manufacturing					
造纸及纸制品业	Papermaking and Paper Products	905	672	3442	3158	165
印刷业、记录媒介的复制	Printing and Record Medium Reproduction	82	20	426	426	150
文教体育用品制造业	Stationery,Educational and Sports Goods					
石油加工及炼焦业	Petroleum Refining and Coking	554	155	3527	2610	1008
化学原料及化学制品制造业	Raw Chemical Materials and Chemical Products	3858	1593	21013	18619	8767
医药制造业	Medical and Pharmaceutical Products	1402	491	6742	3415	1914
化学纤维制造业	Chemical Fiber	612	353	14700	4559	4391
橡胶制品业	Rubber Products	166	106	1628	1603	1302
塑料制品业	Plastic Products	143	68	722	698	646
非金属矿物制品业	Nonmetal Mineral Products	1022	370	3046	2713	628
黑色金属冶炼及压延加工业	Smelting and Pressing of Ferrous Metals	4097	1951	28566	21683	7399
有色金属冶炼及压延加工业	Smelting and Pressing of Nonferrous Metals	2993	1542	10593	8453	2110
金属制品业	Metal Products	190	78	1762	1354	1266
普通机械制造业	Ordinary Machinery	3433	1467	4823	5034	1738
专用设备制造业	Special Purposes Equipment	2150	1110	11585	9840	2367
交通运输设备制造业	Transport Equipment	7509	3956	31972	27376	9337
电气机械及器材制造业	Electric Equipment and Machinery	2746	1429	10350	9790	4347
电子及通信设备制造业	Electric and Telecommunications Equipment	1386	532	8439	7801	5386
仪器仪表及文化办公用机械制造业	Instruments,Meters,Cultural and Clerical Machinery	654	487	8724	5670	5487
其他制造业	Other Manufacturing	2102	631	4915	4444	2403
电力、蒸汽、热水的生产和供应业	Production and Supply of Power,Steam and Hot Water	2169	1119	10473	8511	716
煤气生产和供应业	Production and Supply of Gas					
自来水的生产和供应业	Production and Supply of Tap water	34	19	737	23	

14-34 大中型工业企业办科技机构情况（2001）

Basic Statistics on Institutions for Scientific and Technological in Large and Medium-Sized Industrial Enterprises (2001)

类别	Item	企业办科技机构（个）Number of Institutions for S&T in Enterprises (unit)	企业办科技机构人员（人）Number of Personnel in Institutions for S&T in Enterprises (person)	#高中级职称人员 Senior and Medium	#博士 Doctor	#硕士 Master
总计	**Total**	**238**	**12264**	**5777**	**70**	**564**
按市州分：	**By Region**					
长沙市	Changsha City	51	2545	1328	24	127
株洲市	Zhuzhou City	45	2710	1375	31	319
湘潭市	Xiangtan City	29	2315	964		9
衡阳市	Hengyang City	20	1167	522	1	17
邵阳市	Shaoyang City	7	230	133		1
岳阳市	Yueyang City	8	678	425	6	26
常德市	Changde City	22	797	351	6	38
张家界市	Zhangjiajie City	1	17	4		
益阳市	Yiyang City	11	248	125		
郴州市	Chenzhou City	10	233	98		5
永州市	Yongzhou City	13	402	81		8
怀化市	Huaihua City	7	312	77	1	3
娄底市	Loudi City	10	377	217		10
湘西自治州	West Hunan A.P	4	233	77	1	1
按企业规模分组	**By Size**					
大型企业	Large	154	10208	4938	48	502
中型企业	Medium	84	2056	839	22	62
按登记注册类型分组	**By Registration Status**					
内资企业	Domestic-Funded Enterprises	234	12164	5750	70	564
国有	State-owned Enterprises	121	6071	3218	21	371
集体	Collective-owned Enterprises	5	187	92	2	8
股份合作	Cooperative Enterprises	4	30	7		
国有联营	State Joint Ownership Enterprises					
集体联营	Collective Joint Ownership Enterprises					
国有与集体联营	Joint State-collective Enterprises					
其他联营	Other Joint Ownership Enterprises					
国有独资公司	State-funded Corporations	25	1948	677	1	29
其他有限责任公司	Other Limited Liability Corporations	32	1681	657	1	8
股份有限公司	Share-holding Corporations Ltd.	44	2196	1061	39	138
私营独资	Private-funded Enterprises					
私营合伙	Private Partnership Enterprises					
私营有限责任公司	Private Limited Liability Corporations	3	51	38	6	10
私营股份有限公司	Private Share-holding Corporations Ltd.					
其他内资	Other Enterprises					
港澳台商投资	Enterprises With Investment from Hong Kong, Macao and Taiwan	2	29	14		
外商投资	Enterprises With Foreign Investment	2	71	13		

类 别	Item	企业办科技机构（个）Number of Institutions for S&T in Enterprises (unit)	企业办科技机构人员（人）Number of Personnel in Institutions for S&T in Enterprises (person)	#高中级职称人员 Senior and Medium	#博士 Doctor	#硕士 Master
按工业行业大类分组	**By Industrial Branch**					
煤炭采选业	Coal Mining and Dressing	1	12	9	1	3
石油和天然气开采业	Petroleum and Natural Gas Extraction					
黑色金属矿采选业	Ferrous Metals Mining and dressing					
有色金属矿采选业	Nonferrous Metals Mining and dressing	5	100	39		3
非金属矿采选业	Nonmetals Mining and dressing	1	10	4		
其他矿采选业	Others Minerals Mining and dressing					
木材及竹材采运业	Logging and Transport of Timber and Bamboo					
食品加工业	Food Processing	5	286	98	17	21
食品制造业	Food Production					
饮料制造业	Beverages Production	6	239	96	1	
烟草加工业	Tobacco Processing	6	454	167	4	33
纺织业	Textiles Industry	3	73	54		
服装及其他纤维制品制造业	Garments and Other Fiber Products					
皮革毛皮羽绒及其制品业	Leather,Furs,Down and Related Products	1	14	4		
木材加工及竹、藤、棕、草制品业	Timber Processing,Bamboo,Cane, Palm Fiber and Straw Products					
家具制造业	Furniture Manufacturing					
造纸及纸制品业	Papermaking and Paper Products	4	114	57		
印刷业、记录媒介的复制	Printing and Record Medium Reproduction	2	82	20		2
文教体育用品制造业	Stationery,Educational and Sports Goods					
石油加工及炼焦业	Petroleum Refining and Coking	2	149	67	1	7
化学原料及化学制品制造业	Raw Chemical Materials and Chemical Products	30	1498	754	4	64
医药制造业	Medical and Pharmaceutical Products	12	327	125	2	15
化学纤维制造业	Chemical Fiber	4	454	172	2	9
橡胶制品业	Rubber Products	1	65	25	4	3
塑料制品业	Plastic Products	5	136	56	1	
非金属矿物制品业	Nonmetal Mineral Products	8	455	130		11
黑色金属冶炼及压延加工业	Smelting and Pressing of Ferrous Metals	6	316	186		11
有色金属冶炼及压延加工业	Smelting and Pressing of Nonferrous Metals	12	552	271	4	11
金属制品业	Metal Products					
普通机械制造业	Ordinary Machinery	23	1413	623	1	12
专用设备制造业	Special Purposes Equipment	18	700	452		4
交通运输设备制造业	Transport Equipment	30	1617	702	5	254
电气机械及器材制造业	Electric Equipment and Machinery	14	1136	533	8	20
电子及通信设备制造业	Electric and Telecommunications Equipment	5	223	100	5	10
仪器仪表及文化办公用机械制造业	Instruments,Meters,Cultural and Clerical Machinery	7	634	453	8	54
其他制造业	Other Manufacturing	8	611	267		2
电力、蒸汽、热水的生产和供应业	Production and Supply of Power,Steam and Hot Water	18	582	304	2	14
煤气生产和供应业	Production and Supply of Gas					
自来水的生产和供应业	Production and Supply of Tap water	1	12	9		1

14-35 大中型工业企业科技活动新产品情况（2001）

Basic Statistics on New Products in Large and Medium-Sized Industrial Enterprises (2001)

类 别	Item	新产品产值（万元）Gross Output Value of New Products (10 000 yuan)	新产品销售收入（万元）Sales Revenue of New Products (10 000 yuan)	新产品销售利润（万元）Sales Profits of New Products (10 000 yuan)	专利申请数（件）Total Applications (item)	拥有发明专利数（件）Total Applications of Inventions (item)
总 计	**Total**	**1227301**	**1188038**	**172153**	**334**	**230**
按市州分：	**By Region**					
长沙市	Changsha City	297420	301981	44225	73	90
株洲市	Zhuzhou City	173271	166718	38123	82	26
湘潭市	Xiangtan City	207289	202475	28090	15	9
衡阳市	Hengyang City	160549	129458	14643	14	10
邵阳市	Shaoyang City	8760	8348	1960	2	3
岳阳市	Yueyang City	65241	83390	20087	82	39
常德市	Changde City	152339	143301	11671	9	4
张家界市	Zhangjiajie City	341	172	52		
益阳市	Yiyang City	19713	17509	766	13	1
郴州市	Chenzhou City	18892	17670	2711	1	
永州市	Yongzhou City	93715	88359	7544	2	11
怀化市	Huaihua City	3476	2099	534	12	17
娄底市	Loudi City	26296	24889	1747	29	12
湘西自治州	West Hunan A.P		1669			8
按企业规模分组	**By Size**					
大型企业	Large	1151277	1096944	159477	268	203
中型企业	Medium	76024	91094	12675	66	27
按登记注册类型分组	**By Registration Status**					
内资企业	Domestic-Funded Enterprises	1194711	1161365	167279	331	228
国有	State-owned Enterprises	621373	604220	80944	104	63
集体	Collective-owned Enterprises	22144	20749	2690	1	1
股份合作	Cooperative Enterprises	3592	2771	19	1	1
国有联营	State Joint Ownership Enterprises					
集体联营	Collective Joint Ownership Enterprises					
国有与集体联营	Joint State-collective Enterprises					
其他联营	Other Joint Ownership Enterprises					
国有独资公司	State-funded Corporations	183511	170916	15445	31	38
其他有限责任公司	Other Limited Liability Corporations	51028	31808	5943	11	7
股份有限公司	Share-holding Corporations Ltd.	205988	223391	46957	160	79
私营独资	Private-funded Enterprises					
私营合伙	Private Partnership Enterprises					
私营有限责任公司	Private Limited Liability Corporations	106927	107372	15281	11	39
私营股份有限公司	Private Share-holding Corporations Ltd.	149	140		12	
其他内资	Other Enterprises					
港澳台商投资	Enterprises With Investment from Hong Kong, Macao and Taiwan	12571	12192	823	3	2
外商投资	Enterprises With Foreign Investment	20019	14481	4051		

14-35 续表 continued

类别	Item	新产品产值（万元）Gross Output Value of New Products (10 000 yuan)	新产品销售收入（万元）Sales Revenue of New Products (10 000 yuan)	新产品销售利润（万元）Sales Profits of New Products (10 000 yuan)	专利申请数（件）Total Applications (item)	拥有发明专利数（件）Total Applications of Inventions (item)
按工业行业大类分组	**By Industrial Branch**					
煤炭采选业	Coal Mining and Dressing	118	118			
石油和天然气开采业	Petroleum and Natural Gas Extraction					
黑色金属矿采选业	Ferrous Metals Mining and dressing					
有色金属矿采选业	Nonferrous Metals Mining and dressing				1	
非金属矿采选业	Nonmetals Mining and dressing					
其他矿采选业	Others Minerals Mining and dressing					
木材及竹材采运业	Logging and Transport of Timber and Bamboo					
食品加工业	Food Processing	26186	27246	16128	2	1
食品制造业	Food Production	149	140		12	
饮料制造业	Beverages Production	13344	6864	1154		9
烟草加工业	Tobacco Processing	119530	115731	9262	4	11
纺织业	Textiles Industry	20461	20831	380	3	
服装及其他纤维制品制造业	Garments and Other Fiber Products	2299	2299	351		
皮革毛皮羽绒及其制品业	Leather,Furs,Down and Related Products	1712	1712	107	2	1
木材加工及竹、藤、棕、草制品业	Timber Processing,Bamboo,Cane, Palm Fiber and Straw Products					
家具制造业	Furniture Manufacturing					
造纸及纸制品业	Papermaking and Paper Products	26763	22854	9827	4	
印刷业、记录媒介的复制	Printing and Record Medium Reproduction	3981	3981	796		1
文教体育用品制造业	Stationery,Educational and Sports Goods					
石油加工及炼焦业	Petroleum Refining and Coking	8006	8000	4919	16	17
化学原料及化学制品制造业	Raw Chemical Materials and Chemical Products	71484	66974	712	87	22
医药制造业	Medical and Pharmaceutical Products	18929	16089	5084	9	20
化学纤维制造业	Chemical Fiber	35610	30590	2500		
橡胶制品业	Rubber Products	2650	2565	586	9	4
塑料制品业	Plastic Products	10801	9489	1233		
非金属矿物制品业	Nonmetal Mineral Products	24902	18833	2884	13	1
黑色金属冶炼及压延加工业	Smelting and Pressing of Ferrous Metals	158470	174948	15851	28	10
有色金属冶炼及压延加工业	Smelting and Pressing of Nonferrous Metals	96838	81618	8235	25	25
金属制品业	Metal Products	7161	7263	1289	1	1
普通机械制造业	Ordinary Machinery	36406	54577	8176	20	10
专用设备制造业	Special Purposes Equipment	19371	15247	3200	2	6
交通运输设备制造业	Transport Equipment	244861	233099	29959	20	11
电气机械及器材制造业	Electric Equipment and Machinery	162238	155750	21825	17	45
电子及通信设备制造业	Electric and Telecommunications Equipment	75783	66854	12482	23	20
仪器仪表及文化办公用机械制造业	Instruments,Meters,Cultural and Clerical Machinery	9638	8584	1520	21	1
其他制造业	Other Manufacturing	29613	26127	6612	8	11
电力、蒸汽、热水的生产和供应业	Production and Supply of Power,Steam and Hot Water		9657	676	7	3
煤气生产和供应业	Production and Supply of Gas					
自来水的生产和供应业	Production and Supply of Tap water					

14-36 大中型工业企业科技活动项目情况（2001）

Basic Statistics on Projects for Scientific and Technological Activies in Large and Medium-Sized Industrial Enterprises (2001)

类　别	Item	科技活动项目数（项）Projects for S&T Activities (item)	#新产品开发 New Products R&D	参与项目人员（人）Personnel of Projects (person)	#高中级职称人员 Senior and Medium	项目经费支出（万元）Expenditure of Projects (10 000 yuan)
总　计	**Total**	**2762**	**1115**	**25956**	**13176**	**136965**
按市州分：	**By Region**					
长沙市	Changsha City	550	249	5096	2250	30960
株洲市	Zhuzhou City	552	250	4786	2888	25561
湘潭市	Xiangtan City	371	114	4081	2377	23585
衡阳市	Hengyang City	411	137	3526	1288	16945
邵阳市	Shaoyang City	87	56	598	302	5855
岳阳市	Yueyang City	259	56	2119	1212	10234
常德市	Changde City	73	56	1265	629	7014
张家界市	Zhangjiajie City	8	8	17	4	21
益阳市	Yiyang City	53	36	651	309	1805
郴州市	Chenzhou City	144	21	1311	658	3343
永州市	Yongzhou City	59	52	582	183	3307
怀化市	Huaihua City	40	31	401	113	1331
娄底市	Loudi City	149	47	1316	874	6230
湘西自治州	West Hunan A.P	6	2	207	89	775
按企业规模分组	**By Size**					
大型企业	Large	2222	785	20637	11060	117803
中型企业	Medium	540	330	5319	2116	19162
按登记注册类型分组	**By Registration Status**					
内资企业	Domestic-Funded Enterprises	2743	1101	25589	13091	135038
国有	State-owned Enterprises	1667	607	15880	8962	77487
集体	Collective-owned Enterprises	77	59	461	256	2243
股份合作	Cooperative Enterprises	14	9	104	34	221
国有联营	State Joint Ownership Enterprises	2	2	151	2	268
集体联营	Collective Joint Ownership Enterprises					
国有与集体联营	Joint State-collective Enterprises					
其他联营	Other Joint Ownership Enterprises					
国有独资公司	State-funded Corporations	363	153	2786	1165	16079
其他有限责任公司	Other Limited Liability Corporations	183	69	2445	957	8322
股份有限公司	Share-holding Corporations Ltd.	386	176	3249	1535	26268
私营独资	Private-funded Enterprises					
私营合伙	Private Partnership Enterprises					
私营有限责任公司	Private Limited Liability Corporations	39	20	473	172	4023
私营股份有限公司	Private Share-holding Corporations Ltd.	12	6	40	8	126
其他内资	Other Enterprises					
港澳台商投资	Enterprises With Investment from Hong Kong, Macao and Taiwan	11	9	115	54	622
外商投资	Enterprises With Foreign Investment	8	5	252	31	1305

类别	Item	科技活动项目数（项） Projects for S&T Activities (item)	#新产品开发 New Products R&D	参与项目人员（人） Personnel of Projects (person)	#高中级职称人员 Senior and Medium	项目经费支出（万元） Expenditure of Projects (10 000 yuan)
按工业行业大类分组	**By Industrial Branch**					
煤炭采选业	Coal Mining and Dressing	132	8	714	425	1346
石油和天然气开采业	Petroleum and Natural Gas Extraction					
黑色金属矿采选业	Ferrous Metals Mining and dressing	1		3	1	22
有色金属矿采选业	Nonferrous Metals Mining and dressing	37	2	512	197	1066
非金属矿采选业	Nonmetals Mining and dressing	3		35	9	317
其他矿采选业	Others Minerals Mining and dressing					
木材及竹材采运业	Logging and Transport of Timber and Bamboo					
食品加工业	Food Processing	28	20	360	109	2167
食品制造业	Food Production	14	8	70	31	143
饮料制造业	Beverages Production	49	22	432	197	1351
烟草加工业	Tobacco Processing	42	9	231	112	5064
纺织业	Textiles Industry	22	12	364	154	2482
服装及其他纤维制品制造业	Garments and Other Fiber Products	4	4	20	4	158
皮革毛皮羽绒及其制品业	Leather,Furs,Down and Related Products	3	3	14	4	46
木材加工及竹、藤、棕、草制品业	Timber Processing,Bamboo,Cane, Palm Fiber and Straw Products	2		30	21	85
家具制造业	Furniture Manufacturing					
造纸及纸制品业	Papermaking and Paper Products	74	6	869	661	3108
印刷业、记录媒介的复制	Printing and Record Medium Reproduction	7	1	68	14	276
文教体育用品制造业	Stationery,Educational and Sports Goods					
石油加工及炼焦业	Petroleum Refining and Coking	75	25	541	155	2596
化学原料及化学制品制造业	Raw Chemical Materials and Chemical Products	270	100	2289	1015	15676
医药制造业	Medical and Pharmaceutical Products	68	48	451	213	2746
化学纤维制造业	Chemical Fiber	11	9	401	207	4391
橡胶制品业	Rubber Products	41	6	118	67	1473
塑料制品业	Plastic Products	17	11	93	33	261
非金属矿物制品业	Nonmetal Mineral Products	44	11	682	279	2547
黑色金属冶炼及压延加工业	Smelting and Pressing of Ferrous Metals	283	31	2213	1423	20259
有色金属冶炼及压延加工业	Smelting and Pressing of Nonferrous Metals	186	75	1527	775	7643
金属制品业	Metal Products	14	11	184	78	1324
普通机械制造业	Ordinary Machinery	222	97	1856	845	3849
专用设备制造业	Special Purposes Equipment	125	88	1317	692	6865
交通运输设备制造业	Transport Equipment	358	174	4486	2480	20523
电气机械及器材制造业	Electric Equipment and Machinery	183	121	2205	1069	9170
电子及通信设备制造业	Electric and Telecommunications Equipment	68	42	851	463	6350
仪器仪表及文化办公用机械制造业	Instruments,Meters,Cultural and Clerical Machinery	132	80	411	304	5620
其他制造业	Other Manufacturing	87	69	1308	414	3236
电力、蒸汽、热水的生产和供应业	Production and Supply of Power,Steam and Hot Water	151	22	1267	706	4759
煤气生产和供应业	Production and Supply of Gas					
自来水的生产和供应业	Production and Supply of Tap water	9		34	19	23

十五、文化、体育、卫生

CULTURE, SPORTS AND PUBLIC HEALTH

资料整理人员：陈洲艳

15-1 文化产业机构和人员(2001年)

Cultural Institutions and Personnel (2001)

类别	Item	合计 Total		文化部门 Culture Department		其他部门 Other Department	
		机构(个) Institutions (unit)	人员(人) Personnel (person)	机构(个) Institutions (unit)	人员(人) Personnel (person)	机构(个) Institutions (unit)	人员(人) Personnel (person)
总 计	Total	14457	87487	6025	30053	8035	32234
出版发行业	Publication and Distribution	397	25200				
艺术业	Art	232	6768	232	6768		
图书馆业	Libraries	115	1898	115	1898		
群众文化业	Mass Culture	2632	6125	2632	6125		
艺术教育业	Culture and Education	7	577	7	577		
娱乐业	Recreational Services	7306	32758	1821	8041	5485	24717
文艺科研业	Art Research Institutions	1	29	1	29		
文物业	Culture Relics	196	2339	191	2113	5	226
其他文化产业	Other Culture	3571	11793	1026	4502	2545	7291

15-2 艺术业机构和人员

Art Institutions and Personnel

类别	Item	2000		2001	
		机构(个) Institutions (unit)	人员(人) Personnel (person)	机构(个) Institutions (unit)	人员(人) Personnel (person)
总 计	**Total**	**214**	**6759**	**232**	**6768**
艺术表演团体	**Art Performance Troupes**	**91**	**4500**	**87**	**4372**
话剧团	Drama	1	95	1	102
歌剧、舞剧、歌舞剧团	Opera,Ballet and Dance Troupes	8	654	7	596
歌舞团、轻音乐团	Song and Dance Troupe, Light Music Troupes	3	157	4	181
文工团、文宣队	Culture and Performance Troupes	7	262	6	211
戏曲剧团	Local Opera Troupes	69	3108	67	3045
曲艺、杂技、木偶、皮影团	Recitation and Ballad Troupes,Acrobatics and Circus Troupes,Puppet Show Troupes and Shadow Play Troupes	3	224	2	237
艺术表演场所(剧场、影剧院)	**Art Centers (Theaters and Music Halls)**	**94**	**2018**	**96**	**2079**
艺术创作机构	**Art Creation Institutions**	**20**	**118**	**20**	**116**
艺术展览机构	**Art Exhibition Institutions**	**3**	**16**	**3**	**16**
其他	**Others**	**6**	**107**	**26**	**185**

15-3 出版发行、文物、图书馆、群众文化业机构人员（2001年）

Number of Institutions and Personnel in Publishing and Distribution, Cultural Relics, Library and Mass Culture (2001)

类别	Item	合计 Total		文化部门 Culture Department		其他部门 Other Department	
		机构(个) Institutions (unit)	人员(人) Personnel (person)	机构(个) Institutions (unit)	人员(人) Personnel (person)	机构(个) Institutions (unit)	人员(人) Personnel (person)
出版发行事业	**Publishing and Distribution**	**397**	**25200**				
图书	Books Published	14	1203				
报纸	Newspaper Published	104	5828				
杂志	Magazines Published	228	1754				
音像出版	Image to Publish	5	310				
音像电复制	Image to copy	2	120				
出版物印刷	Publication to Print	41	8991				
发行	Distribution	1	6779				
印刷物质供销	Print Materiat Supply and Marketing	2	280				
文物事业	**Cultural Relics**	196	2339	191	2113		
#文物保护管理机构	#Protection and Management Agencies	122	927	122	927		
博物馆	Museums	72	1329	67	1103	5	226
#综合性的	#Comprehensive Museum	32	812	32	812		
纪念性的	Memorial Museum	40	489	35	291	5	226
文物商店	Cultural Relics Agencies	2	83	2	83		
图书馆事业	**Libraries**	115	1898	115	1898		
群众文化事业	**Mass Culture**	2632	6125	2632	6125		
群众艺术馆	Mass Art Centers	15	476	15	476		
文化馆	Cultural Centers	124	1850	124	1850		
文化站	Cultural Stations	2493	3799	2493	3799		

注：文物保护管理机构的人员包含文物行政主管机关中文物事业编制的人员。

Protection and management agencies include administrative departments and other agencies.

15-4 图书、杂志、报纸出版情况

Statistics on Books, Magazines and Newspapers Published

年份 Year	图书 Books Published			杂志 Magazines Published			报纸 Newspaper Published		
	种数(种) Number of Publica-tions (kind)	总印数(万册) Printed Copies (10 000 copies)	总印张(亿印张) Printed Sheets (100 million sheets)	种数(种) Number of Publica-tions (kind)	总印数(万册) Printed Copies (10 000 copies)	总印张(亿印张) Printed Sheets (100 million sheets)	种数(种) Number of Publica-tions (kind)	总印数(万份) Printed Copies (10 000 copies)	总印张(亿印张) Printed Sheets (100 million sheets)
1995	2357	33677	14.9	208	7768	1.75	63	62425	6.9
1997	2856	37494	14.92	212	7686	1.83	61	68726	8.58
1998	3513	36582	15.41	202	8920	1.93	55	75879	9.28
1999	3367	30765	13.99	214	12437	2.35	62	84995	11.83
2000	3156	24844	12.37	244	10504	2.11	95	83467	12.75
2001	3346	23808	12.7	251	10050.6	2.27	109	92272.7	18.65

注：图书种数不包括租型图书。

The total collection books excludes the books for rental.

15-5 广播、电视事业情况

Statistics on Broadcasting and Television Stations

项 目	Item	1995	1999	2000	2001
广播电视系统全部职工（万人）	**Number of Staff and Workers in System of Broadcasting and Television (10000 persons)**	**1.88**	**2.19**	**2.32**	**2.39**
广播	**Broadcasting**				
广播电台数（座）	Number of Broadcasting Stations (set)	**10**	11	11	11
广播电台节目套数（套）	Number of Broadcasting Program (set)	15	51	53	53
平均每日播出时间（小时）	Broadcasting Hours per Day (hour)	161	458	483	486
中、短波发射台、转播台数（座）	Medium Wave and Short Wave Broadcast Transmission Station and Relaying Station (set)	27	25	25	25
中、短波发射机（部）	Medium Wave and Short Wave Broadcast Transmitters (set)	42	35	36	36
中、短波发射机功率（千瓦）	Power of Medium and Short Wave Broadcast Transmitters (kw)	582	581	579	579
覆盖率（%）	Listener-Coverage Rate (%)	54.8	81.09	81.46	81.62
电视	**Television**				
电视中心台数（座）	Number of Television Stations (set)	26	16	16	15
电视节目套数（套）	Number of Television Program (set)	29	32	33	101
平均每周播出时间（小时）	Broadcasting Hours per Week (hour)	1291	2170	2338	8224
电视发射台（座）	Television Transmission Stations (set)	803	614	542	534
#1千瓦以上（座）	#One KW and Over (set)	42	48	48	50
电视发射机（部）	Television Transmitters (set)	1105	806	720	709
电视发射机功率（千瓦）	Power of Television Transmitters (kw)	120	274	291	291
覆盖率（%）	Viewer-Coverage Rate (%)	86.9	90.38	91.38	91.7

注：广播电台数、电视中心台数从1998年起不包括县级台数。

Note: Number of Broadcasting Stations and Number of Television Stations Exclude County Level Stations Since 1998.

15-6 体育事业情况

Statistics on Sports

项 目	Item	1995	1999	2000	2001
体委系统职工人数(人)	**Number of Staff and Workers in Sports Commissions (person)**	**4571**	**5207**	**5303**	**5587**
#体育运动学校	#Sports Schools	341	376	387	372
业余体校	Popular Sparetime Sports Schools	1012	1199	1232	1241
训练基地	Training Bases	111	108	105	121
公共体育场、馆	Public Stadiums and Gymnasiums	404	519	682	566
优秀运动队	Excellent Sports Teams	1342	1298	1361	1367
体育场(个)	**Stadiums (unit)**	**21**	**37**	**37**	**311**
体育馆(个)	**Gymnasiums (unit)**	**37**	**55**	**55**	**36**
游泳池、馆(个)	**Swimming Pools and Natatorums (unit)**	**73**	**111**	**111**	**43**
举办县级以上运动会(次)	**Number of Sports Meets Above County Level (time)**	**1807**	**1998**	**1705**	**1658**
国家体育锻炼标准达标人数(万人)	**Number of Persons Who Have Come up to the State Physical Training Standards (10000 persons)**	**150**	**759.88**	**1155.04**	**811.82**
等级运动员发展人数(人)	**Number of Athletes in Grades (person)**	**7362**	**5711**	**5175**	**5571**
#国际级运动健将	#International Master of Sports	5	7	2	2
国家级运动健将	National Master of Sports	43	10	31	11
一 级	First Grade Sportsmen	84	110	13	43
二 级	Second Grade Sportsmen	464	654	890	1047
三 级	Third Grade Sportsmen	4860	2354	2191	2711
少年级	Juvenile Grade Sportsmen	1906	2576	2048	1757
等级裁判员发展人数(人)	**Number of Referees in Grades (person)**	**1818**	**3947**	**4173**	**3723**
#国家级裁判员	#National Referees	12	16	21	18
打破纪录情况(人/次/项)	**Basic Situation of Records Chalked Up (person/time/event)**				
世界纪录	#World Records		3/5/3	3/1/5	2/7/3
亚洲纪录	Asia Records	1/1/1			2/2/2
全国纪录	National Records	1/1/1		1/1/1	4/6/7
获奖情况	**Basic Situation of Medallion Won**				
参加全国比赛获奖	National Competitions				
金 牌(枚)	# Gold-plate (piece)	30.5	33.5	32	54.5
银 牌(枚)	Silver-plate (piece)	39	30	36	48
铜 牌(枚)	Copper-plate (piece)	16	35	36	44
参加国际比赛获奖	International Competitions				
金 牌(枚)	# Gold-plate (piece)	18	17	12	7
银 牌(枚)	Silver-plate (piece)	9	3	7	7
铜 牌(枚)	Copper-plate (piece)	10	4	6	6

注: 1. 体育场、体育馆、游泳池只包括体委系统的。

2. 参加全国比赛指参加全国性的成人竞技比赛。参加国际比赛指参加世界锦标赛、世界杯赛、奥运会、亚洲锦标赛和亚运会。

3. 奖牌数包括我省运动员参加国家队集体项目所得的奖牌。

a. Data of stadiums, gymnasiums and natatoriums only refer to those of sports commissions.

b. National games refer to nation-wide adult athletics. International games include the world championship, the world cup, the Olympics, the Asia championship and the Asian Games.

c. The number of medals includes that of medals won by athletes of our province in national collective events.

15-7 卫生机构

Health Care Institutions

单位：个 (unit)

项目	Item	1995	1999	2000	2001
总 计	**Total**	**9137**	**4259**	**4286**	**4205**
医院、卫生院	Hospitals	3879	3359	3339	3335
#县及县以上医院	#At the Above County Level	641	678	673	671
疗养院、所	Sanatoriums	12	10	10	10
门诊部	Clinics	4417	111	109	95
专科防治所、站	Specialized Prevention &Treatment Centers or Stations	115	117	118	116
卫生防疫站	Sanitation and Anti-epidemic Agencies	151	165	165	163
妇幼保健所、站	Maternity and Child Care Centers	125	125	125	123
药品检验所、室	Medicines and Chemical Reagent Test Labs	112	110	96	44
医学科学研究机构	Research Institutes of Medical Science	4	6	6	6
其他卫生机构	Other Institutions	322	256	318	313

注：从1998年起，卫生机构、人员数均未包括诊所、卫生保健所、医务室的机构、人员数。

The number of health institutions and persons engaged in health institutions did not include clinics, health care centres since 1998.

15-8 卫生机构床位

Number of Beds in Health Care Institutions

单位：万张 (10 000 unit)

项目	Item	1995	1999	2000	2001
卫生机构床位总计	Number of Beds in Health Institutions	14.95	14.54	14.34	14.62
医院、卫生院	Hospitals	13.52	13.46	13.21	13.43
#县及县以上医院	#Hospitals at and Above County Level	9.04	9.3	9.22	9.34
疗养院、所	Sanatoriums	0.28	0.25	0.28	0.3
其他卫生机构	Other Health Institutions	1.15	0.83	0.86	0.88
每万人口中拥有医院病床数（张）	Number of Hospital Beds per 10000 Population (unit)	21.28	20.6	20.13	20.36

15-9 各类卫生机构、床位和人员(2001年)

Health Care Institutions, Beds and Personnel by Type (2001)

类别	Item	机构(个) Number of Institutions (unit)	床位(张) Beds (unit)	卫生工作人员(人) Personnel (person)	#卫生技术人员 Medical Technical Personnel
总计	**Total**	**4205**	**146165**	**243706**	**198971**
医院、卫生院	Hospitals	3335	134259	207838	174851
县及县以上医院	At and Above County Level	671	93405	131486	104169
综合医院	General Hospitals	476	62985	88153	70140
中医院	Hospitals of Chinese Medicine	111	14455	22902	18995
医学院附属医院	Hospitals Attached to Medical Colleges	8	5756	8460	6302
传染病院	Hospitals for Infectious Diseases	4	618	731	484
精神病院	Mental Hospitals	18	3927	3017	2066
结核病院	Tuberculosis Hospitals	5	846	974	604
妇幼保健院	Hospitals for Maternity and Child Care	12	1092	2217	1684
儿童医院	Children's Hospitals	1	375	546	412
职业病院	Hospitals for Occupational Diseases	2	205	220	153
肿瘤医院	Tumor Hospitals	4	912	1370	996
康复医院	Rehabilitation Hospitals	5	500	484	357
口腔医院	Hospitals for Oral Cavity Diseases	2	36	272	194
骨科医院	Orthopaedics Hospitals	2	108	189	171
整形医院	Plastic Hospitals	1	100	154	115
中西医结合医院	Hospitals Which Integrate Traditional Chinese Therapeutics with Western Therapeutics	4	487	770	640
其他专科医院	Other Specialized Hospitals	16	1003	1027	856
其他医院	Other Hospitals	23	770	1199	1020
城市街道卫生院	Urban Township Hospitals	87	550	1176	1092
农村卫生院	Rural Township Hospitals	2554	39534	73977	68570
疗养院、所	Sanatoriums	10	3044	1679	1047
门诊部	Clinics	95	1543	2018	1726
专科防治所、站、	Specialized Prevention & Treatment Centers or Stations	116	3176	4006	3136
卫生防疫站	Sanitation and Anti-epidemic Agencies	163	160	10030	7916
妇幼保健所、站	Maternity and Child Care Centers	123	2298	5400	4526
药品检验所、室	Medicines and Chemical Reagent Test Labs	44		729	556
医学科学研究机构	Research Institutes of Medical Science	6	453	1120	638
高等医药院、校	Medical Institutions of Higher Education	7		4607	1082
中等医药学校	Secondary Schools of Medicines and Health	75	603	4130	1914
其他卫生事业机构	Other Health Care Institutions	231	629	2149	1579

15-10 卫生机构各类卫生人员

Personnel in Health Care Institutions by Type of Personnel

单位：人 (person)

类别	Item	1995	1999	2000	2001
卫生工作人员	**Personnel in Health Care Institutions**	**236447**	**239524**	**243384**	**243706**
#卫生技术人员	Medical Technical Personnel	192526	195254	198891	198971
中医师	Doctors of Traditional Chinese Medicine	13750	12649	12873	13110
西医师	Doctors of Western Medicine	49216	48622	50849	51280
中、西医结合高级医师	Senior Doctors Who Integrate Traditional Chinese Therapeutics with Western Therapeutics in Practice	349	277	321	481
护师	Senior Nurses	25445	33502	35794	36528
中药师	Pharmacists of Chinese Medicine	6087	7317	7445	7380
西药师	Pharmacists of Western Medicine	4827	5732	6089	6184
检验师	Laboratory Technicians	4432	5536	5802	6043
其他技师	Other Technicians	3765	4698	4656	4548
中医士	Paramedics of Chinese Medicine	4455	3904	3824	3808
西医士	Paramedics of Western Medicine	15603	18963	20611	20652
护士	Junior Nurses	23790	20160	19751	19064
助产士	Midwives	2100	2307	1989	1854
中药剂士	Junior Pharmacists of Chinese Medicine	5915	5827	5703	5336
西药剂士	Junior Pharmacists of Western Medicine	3581	3607	3757	3602
检验士	Junior Laboratory Technicians	2917	3109	3055	3062
其他技士	Other Junior Technicians	2308	2060	2055	2039
其他中医	Other Doctors of Chinese Medicine	1223	438	235	165
护理员	Assistant Nurses	3495	2159	1558	1380
中药剂员	Assistant Pharmacists of Chinese Medicine	3650	2181	1611	1462
西药剂员	Assistant Pharmacists of Western Medicine	1316	985	741	690
检验员	Assistant Laboratory Technicians	872	709	491	445
其他初级卫生技术人员	Other Junior Medical Technical Personnel	13763	10512	9681	9858
平均每万人口中卫生技术人员	**Number of Medical Technical Personnel Per 10000 Population**	**30.31**	**29.89**	**30.33**	**30.17**
#医生	Doctors	13.32	12.99	13.52	13.54
乡村医生和卫生员	**Doctors or Health Workers in Rural Areas**	**64121**	**66805**	**68135**	**64415**
#乡村医生	Doctors in Rural Areas	47571	48433	48415	64271
乡村接生员	**Number of Rural Midwives**	**40234**	**35568**	**32839**	**29591**

15-11 县及县以上医院病床使用情况

Utilization of Hospital beds of County and Above Level

指标	Item	1995	1999	2000	2001
病床周转率(次)	Turnover of Beds (time)	15.2	14.38	17.02	17.62
病床工作日数(日)	Days Per Bed in Use (day)	236.5	178.79	166.39	209.65
病床使用率(%)	Utilization Rate of Beds (%)	64.6	48.98	45.59	57.44
出院病人平均住院日数(日)	Average Hospitalization Period (day)	14.8	11.69	9.17	11.11

15-12 医院诊疗人次及入院人数(2001年)

Hospital Patients (2001)

类 别	Item	诊疗人次 (万人次) Number of Patients Treated (10 000 person-time)	#门诊、急诊人次 (万人次) Out-Patients and Emergency Patients	入院人数 (万人) Hospital Admissions (10 000 persons)	每百诊次的入院人数 (人) Hospital Admissions per 100 Patients-times (person)	每百门诊、急诊人次的入院人数 (人) Hospital Admissions per 100 Out-Patient times and Emergency Patient-times (person)
总 计	**Total**	**8969.52**	**7446.48**	**240.00**	**2.67**	**3.22**
县及县以上医院	Hospitals at and Above County Level	3667.04	3470.03	162.75	4.44	4.69
#卫生部门	Health Departments	2617.43	2538.41	137.99	5.28	5.44
工业及其他部门	Industrial and Other Departments	1028.79	911.23	24.42	2.37	2.68
集体所有制	Collective Owned Units	20.82	20.39	0.33	1.59	1.62
卫生院	Rural Township Hospitals	5270.69	3944.74	76.50	1.45	1.94
其他医院	Other Hospitals	31.79	31.71	0.75	2.36	2.37

15-13 城乡主要疾病死亡构成(2001年)

Death Rate of Major Disease of Urban and Rural Areas (2001)

单位：% (%)

类 别	Item	城市 Urban 合计 Total	城市 男 Male	城市 女 Female	农村 Rural 合计 Total	农村 男 Male	农村 女 Female
传染病和寄生虫病	Infectious Disease and Verminosis	1.86	2.14	1.51	3.72	4.05	3.29
#传染病	Infectious Disease	1.80	2.07	1.45	3.48	3.81	3.06
#肺结核	Pulmonary Tuberculosis	0.91	1.10	0.66	2.25	2.49	1.94
肿瘤	Tumor Disease	22.93	25.33	19.83	15.34	16.22	14.21
#恶性肿瘤	Malignant Tumor	22.82	25.33	19.68	15.24	16.13	14.08
内分泌、营养和代谢及免疫疾病	Internal System,Nutrition,Metabolite and Immunity Disease	2.45	1.79	3.30	0.78	0.66	0.93
循环系统	Circulative Disease	43.04	41.74	44.72	32.29	32.55	31.96
#心脏病	Heart Trouble	20.96	19.70	22.61	13.82	12.88	15.04
脑血管病	Cerebrovasular Disease	16.98	17.46	16.36	13.50	14.58	12.11
呼吸系统	Respiratory Disease	11.72	10.23	13.65	21.24	19.64	23.31
消化系统	Digestive Disease	2.68	3.24	1.95	4.71	5.03	4.30
泌尿生殖系统	Urinary Disease	1.65	1.79	1.46	1.49	1.53	1.44
新生儿病	Newborn Baby Disease	0.68	0.64	0.72	1.11	1.10	1.13
损伤和中毒	Trauma and Poisoning	7.50	8.19	6.59	13.19	13.88	12.31
其他	Others	5.51	4.92	6.27	6.12	5.35	7.12

十六、党群、政法和社会福利

PARTY AND MASS，POLITICS AND LAW，SOCIAL WELFARE

资料整理人员：陈洲艳

16-1 历届省人民代表大会的代表人数

Number of Deputies to All the Previous Provincial People's Congress

单位：人 (person)

指标	Item	代表总数 Total Number of All Deputies	#女性代表 Female Deputies	占代表总数% As Percentage to Total (%)	#少数民族代表 Deputies From National Minorities	占代表总数% As Percentage to Total (%)	#中青年代表 Midlife and Youth Deputies	占代表总数% As Percentage to Total (%)
第一届 (1954)	First Congress (1954)	552	36	6.5	9	1.6	399	72.3
第二届 (1958)	Second Congress (1958)	552	36	6.5	9	1.6	399	72.3
第三届 (1964)	Third Congress (1964)	662	148	22.4	57	8.6	409	61.8
省革命委员会 (1968)	The Provincial Revolutionary Committee (1968)	160						
第五届 (1977)	Fifth Congress (1977)	1252	274	21.9	72	5.8	966	77.2
第六届 (1983)	Sixth Congress (1983)	988	225	22.8	84	8.5	570	57.7
第七届 (1988)	Seventh Congress (1988)	874	210	24.0	78	8.9	529	60.5
第八届 (1993)	Eighth Congress (1993)	870	191	22.0	87	10.0	587	62.0
第九届 (1997)	Ninth Congress (1997)	763	175	22.9	85	11.1	488	64.0

注：1968年省革命委员会召开了全体委员会议，代表人数为委员人数。

The plenary meeting was held by the provincial revolutionary committee in 1968, and the number of delegates was that of committee members.

16-2 历届省政治协商会议的委员人数

Number of Deputies to All the Previous Chinese People's Political consultative Conferences

单位：人 (person)

指标	Item	委员总数 Total Number of All Deputies	#中国共产党代表 Deputies from the Communist Party of China	占代表总数% As Percentage to Total (%)	#少数民族代表 Deputies From National Minorities	占代表总数% As Percentage to Total (%)
第一届 (1955)	First Congress (1955)	175	39	22.3	6	3.4
第二届 (1959)	Second Congress (1959)	396	131	33.1	15	3.8
第三届 (1964)	Third Congress (1964)	398	134	33.7	20	5.0
第四届 (1977)	Fourth Congress (1977)	500	222	44.4	26	5.2
第五届 (1983)	Fifth Congress (1983)	732	270	36.9	38	5.2
第六届 (1988)	Sixth Congress (1988)	703	280	39.8	58	8.3
第七届 (1993)	Seventh Congress (1993)	724	288	39.8	61	8.4
第八届 (1997)	Eighth Congress (1997)	716	280	39.1	70	9.8

16-3 工 会 工 作 情 况

Labor Union Work

项　目	Item	1995	1999	2000	2001
工会基层组织个数（万个）	Number of Grassroots Unions (10 000 unit)	2.5	2.01	4.1	8.5
女职工委员会（万个）	Number of Women Workers Working Committees (10 000 units)		1.34	1.68	
已建工会组织的基层单位在岗职工人数（万人）	Number of Staff and Workers in Grassroots Unions (10 000 persons)	428.32	309	487	589.21
#在岗女职工	#Female	172	117	186	
工会专职干部数（万人）	Full-time Cadres (10 000 persons)	2.04	1.96	2.14	
已建立职代会制度的单位个数（万个）	Number of Units Established With Workers Delegating Congress System (10 000 units)	1.35	1.36	1.34	1.56
召开职代会的单位个数（万个）	Number of Units Convoked Staff Congress (10 000 units)	1.29	1.21	1.21	1.56
开展合理化建议活动的单位个数（个）	Number of Units Developing Rationalization Proposals (unit)		9337	9611	7000
本年度提出合理化建议（万件）	Advanced Rationalization Proposals This Year (10 000 piece)	56.31	79.71	66.6	100
开展民主评议领导干部的公有制单位个数（个）	Number of Units Developing Democratic Remark Public Owenrship on Leaders (unit)	9322	10400	9233	9417
建立工会劳动法律监督组织（个）	Number of Units Established With Labor Law Supervisional Organization (unit)	5700	5244	6295	8700
建立经费审查组织的单位个数（个）	Number of Units Established with Outlay Went Through (unit)		15057	17904	

16-4 其他社会福利事业单位机构和人员

Institution and Personnel in Social Welfare and Special Care

项　目	Item	机构数（个）Number of Institutions (unit)		职工人数（人）Staff and Workers (person)	
		2000	2001	2000	2001
福利企业单位总计	**Social Welfare Institutions and Enterprises**	**923**	**810**	**30324**	**28330**
福利工厂	Welfare Factories	910	769	30034	27029
假肢厂	Artificial Limb Factories	1	1	89	89
商业服务业	Commercial Services	12	40	201	1212
收容遣送安置单位总计	**Collecting and Repatriation Units**	**61**	**60**	**1912**	**1357**
收容遣送站	Collecting and Repatriation Stations	54	53	799	771
流浪儿童救助保护中心	The Centers of Salvation and Safeguard Children on the Tramp	1	1	4	5
安置农场	Settle Down Farm	6	6	1109	581
殡仪事业单位	**Funeral and Interment Institutions**	**63**	**68**	**1162**	**1237**

16-5 享受补助、救济人员情况(2001年)

Persons Accessing Subsidies or Relief Funds (2001)

类 别	Item	指标值 Volume
城镇传统救济情况	**Traditional Relief in Urban**	
救济退职老职工人数（万人）	Number of Laid-off, Retired, Elderly Staff and Workers Receiving Relief Funds (10 000 persons)	4.19
#享受40%救济人数	Persons Receiving 40% of Their Original Wages	1.43
享受定救人数	Persons Receiving Periodical and Fixed Relief Funds	3.48
农村传统救济情况	**Traditional Relief in Rural**	
困难户得到救济人次数（万人次）	Number of Person-times in Rural Poor Households Receiving Relief Funds (10 000 person-times)	100.64
临时救济人次数	Number of Person-times Receiving Temporarily Relief Funds	71.35
国家定救人次数	Number of Person-times Receiving Periodical and Fixed Government Relief Funds	29.29
五保户得到救济人数（万人）	Number of persons in Rural Households With Livelihood Guaranteed in Five Aspects (10 000 persons)	22.67

注: 1.本表中各类优抚救济人数,均不包括优抚、社会福利事业单位的在院收养人员数。

2.国家定救人次数=国家定期定量救济困难户人数x12。

a.Data on the members of martyrs and disabled veterans do not include those on people who live in convalescent homes and social welfare homes.

b.Number and times of persons receiving government relief funds= number of persons receiving periodical and fixed government relief funds * 12.

16-6 收养性社会福利、优抚事业单位基本情况(2001年)

Basic Statistics on Adoption Social Welfare and Special Care Units (2001)

项 目	Item	机 构（个） Institution (unit)	职 工（人） Staff and Workers (person)	床 位（张） Beds (unit)	年末在院人数(人) Number of Persons Housed (person)
总计	**Total**	**1609**	**6969**	**70210**	**28445**
国有收养性单位	Run by Government	358	4012	15609	11553
集体收养性单位	Run by Collective Units	1251	2957	54601	16892
在总计中:	**Among Total:**				
荣誉军人康复医院	Rehabilitation Hospitals for Glory Soldiers	1	123	100	86
复员军人疗养院	Convalescent Homes for Demobilized Soldiers	1	21	20	2
复退军人精神病院	Mental Hospitals for Veteran and Demobilized Soldiers	7	577	943	417
光荣院	Homes for Disabled Veterans	178	795	4401	3247
社会福利院	Social Welfare Homes	102	1153	6128	4654
儿童福利院	Baby Welfare Homes	13	163	1179	994
精神病人福利院	Psychopathic Welfare Homes	6	957	1400	1042
城镇老年福利机构	Urban Elderly Welfare Units	172	535	5339	4287
农村老年福利机构	Rural Elderly Welfare Units	1128	2537	50668	13731
其他福利机构	Other Adopting Units	3	122	162	110

16-7 社会救济和福利主要费用

Value of Major Social Relief and Welfare Funds

单位：万元 (10 000 yuan)

项 目	Item	1995	1999	2000	2001
总 计	**Total**	**63354.0**	**111434.8**	**120397.0**	**159271.6**
民政事业费支出	**Civil Administration Department Funds**	**42681.0**	**73272.0**	**80343.0**	**104818.1**
抚恤事业费	Commiserate	10896.0	19393.0	23214.0	26041.3
社会救济福利事业费	Subsidies of Welfare	8106.0	20215.0	27834.0	39123.2
离休、退休费	Pensions for Retired and Resigned Persons	6398.0	6119.0	11163.0	13443.0
社会残疾人福利事业费	Social Welfare Relief Funds for Handicapped		609.0	579.0	427.5
自然灾害救济费	Relief Funds for Natural Disasters	13030.0	18212.0	8010.0	13820.5
其他民政事业费	Others	4251.0	8724.0	9543.0	11962.6
集体供给	**Collective Funds**		**38162.8**	**40054.0**	**54453.5**
优抚对象优待总金额	Funds for Family Members of Martyrs and Disabled Veterans		11514.5	10534.0	11952.4
农村困难户集体补助金额	Funds for Poor Households in Rural		1322.3	1243.0	487.0
农村五保户集体供养金额	Funds for Households with Livelihood Guaranteed in Five Aspects in Rural		14161.7	13837.0	14467.5
城镇保障资金	Funds for Urban Social Security		10037.4	13535.0	26634.2
农村保障资金	Funds for Rural Social Security		1126.9	905.0	912.4

16-8 婚 姻 登 记 情 况

Basic Statistics on Marriage Registration

项 目	Item	1995	1999	2000	2001
准予登记结婚 (万对)	**Registered Marriages (10 000 couples)**	**43.77**	**40.52**	**38.31**	**36.57**
初 婚 (万人)	First Marriages (10 000 persons)	82.96	76.02	71.77	66.71
再 婚 (万人)	Remarriages (10 000 persons)	4.58	4.48	4.85	5.5
离婚人数 (万对)	**Number of Divorces (10 000 couples)**	**6.33**	**5.67**	**6.45**	**7.34**
离婚率 (‰)	Divorce Rate (‰)	1.99	1.74	1.97	2.23

16-9 律师、公证、调解工作基本情况

Basic Statistics on Lawyers,Notarization and Mediation

类 别	Item	1995	1999	2000	2001
律师工作	**Lawyers**				
律师事务所 (个)	Number of Law Offices (unit)	309	340	352	380
律师 (人)	Number of lawyers (persons)	3824	4816	4888	4859
专职律师	Full-time Lawyers	1731	2378	2471	3204
兼职律师	Part-time Lawyers	1554	1397	1439	919
特邀律师	Specially Invited Lawyers	539	341	295	
担任法律顾问工作 (家)	Number of Units with Permanent Legal Advisors (unit)	7713	7541	7899	7210
刑事案件代理及辩护 (件)	Agent & Defender of Criminal Cases (case)	10414	12761	13664	13219
民事案件诉讼代理 (件)	Agent of Civil Cases (case)	16271	22724	25820	23941
经济案件诉讼代理 (件)	Agent of Economic Cases (case)	14179	13297	13455	11690
非诉讼法律事务 (件)	Agent of Non-Litigious Legal Affairs (case)	30335	31172	25883	24088
行政案件诉讼代理 (件)	Agent of Administrative Action (case)	1441	1910	2156	1951
解答法律询问 (人次)	Agent of Legal Advisory Services (person-time)	93608	160476	236553	172749
代写法律事务文书 (件)	Agent of Legal Documents Written on Behalf of Clients (case)	21494	27105	35934	34854
公证工作	**Notarization**				
公证处 (个)	Number of Notary Offices (unit)	136	138	138	138
公证人员 (人)	Notarization Personnel (person)	613	622	604	619
受理公证文书 (件)	Number of Accept Notarized Documents (case)	462267	291054	319416	196827
出证公证文书 (件)	Number of Show Notarized Documents (case)	305904	288797	317705	195870
#国内经济合同公证 (件)	Number of Domestic Notarized Business Contracts (case)	105233	83182	81815	69417
人民调解工作	**Number of People's Mediation**				
专职司法助理员 (人)	Number of Full-time Judicial Assistants (person)	3952	3881	4114	3574
人民调解委员会 (个)	Number of People's Mediation Committees (person)	60358	58194	57231	59448
调解人员 (人)	Number of Mediators (person)	846129	798482	723389	275778
调解民间纠纷 (件)	Number of Civil Disputes Mediated (case)	353996	339387	340612	332876

16-10 交 通 事 故 发 生 情 况

Statistics on Traffic Accidents

指标	Item	合计 Total	按事故发生程度分 By Serious Degree of Traffic Accidents		
			特大 Extraordinarily Serious	重大 Serious	一般 Ordinary
发生次数	Number of Traffic Accidents (case)				
（起）	1995	10361	151	3082	7128
	1996	10994	148	3113	7733
	1997	10401	155	2981	7265
	1998	10128	122	2951	7055
	1999	15337	138	3278	11921
	2000	23938	149	3094	20695
	2001	32504	9	232	32263
死亡人数	Number of Deaths (person)				
（人）	1995	3428	440	2983	5
	1996	3368	346	3022	
	1997	3308	422	2882	4
	1998	3290	325	2921	44
	1999	3698	411	3239	48
	2000	3401	375	3026	
	2001	3316	24	229	3063
受伤人数	Number of Injuries (person)				
（人）	1995	9176	697	2200	6279
	1996	10448	518	2614	7316
	1997	9978	742	2336	6900
	1998	9963	472	2144	7347
	1999	14714	617	2548	11549
	2000	22028	521	2272	19235
	2001	29434	81	81	29272
损失折款	Losses Coverted into Cash (10 000 yuan)				
（万元）	1995	6202.99	1122.50	1660.69	3419.80
	1996	6967.38	1048.38	1961.14	3957.86
	1997	6586.39	1183.34	1795.00	3608.05
	1998	6458.15	899.64	1713.18	3845.33
	1999	8314.70	981.60	1847.96	5485.14
	2000	9662.20	939.54	1937.15	6785.60
	2001	8799.48	51.36	145.22	860.29
平均每起损失	Average Loss per Traffic Accident (yuan)				
（元）	1995	5986.86	74337.75	5388.36	4797.70
	1996	6337.44	70836.49	6299.84	5118.14
	1997	6332.46	76343.52	6021.47	4966.35
	1998	6376.53	73740.98	5805.42	5450.50
	1999	5421.33	71130.43	5673.46	4601.24
	2000	4036.38	63056.63	6261.00	3278.86
	2001	2707.22	5706.67	6259.48	2666.49

16-11 火灾发生情况

Statistics on Fires

指标	Item	合计 Total	按事故发生程度分 By Serious Degree of Fires		
			特大 Extraordinarily Serious	重大 Serious	一般 Ordinary
发生次数（起）	Number of Fires Accidents (case)				
	1995	1128	18	133	977
	1996	1087	19	127	941
	1997	2467	6	29	3432
	1998	2908	5	32	2871
	1999	2871	6	28	2837
	2000	3440	5	19	3416
	2001	3979	1	19	3959
死亡人数（人）	Number of Deaths (person)				
	1995	73	9	21	43
	1996	106	16	36	54
	1997	130	41	33	56
	1998	89	4	28	57
	1999	86	4	22	60
	2000	102	19	16	67
	2001	95	0	21	74
受伤人数（人）	Number of Injuries (person)				
	1995	266	41	70	155
	1996	195	21	84	90
	1997	328	96	45	187
	1998	188	11	7	170
	1999	145	1	2	142
	2000	165	20	11	134
	2001	121	0	10	111
损失折款	Losses Coverted into Cash (10 000 yuan)				
（万元）	1995	6824.18	3157.17	2490.81	1176.20
	1996	5271.00	1894.18	2179.35	1197.47
	1997	7666.43	2802.15	1186.95	3677.33
	1998	5975.11	858.40	1481.69	3635.02
	1999	6275.00	1620.00	1220.00	3435.00
	2000	4799.00	878.00	683.00	3238.86
	2001	4397.35	347.00	1020.00	3030.35
平均每起损失	Average Loss per Fire (10 000 yuan)				
（万元）	1995	6.05	175.40	18.73	1.20
	1996	4.85	99.69	17.16	1.27
	1997	3.11	467.03	40.93	1.51
	1998	2.05	171.68	46.30	0.79
	1999	2.19	270.00	43.56	1.21
	2000	1.40	175.63	35.93	0.95
	2001	1.10	347.00	53.68	0.77

十七、企业调查

ENTERPRISES SURVEY

资料整理人员：　刘于惠　夏普照　陈　梗

17-1 重点企业集团基本情况及主要经济指标(2001年)

Basic Conditions and Main Economic Indicators of Key Enterprises Group (2001)

分类	Item	单位数（个） Number of Enterprises (unit)	从业人员（人） Number of Employed Persons (person)	在岗职工 Number of Fully Employed Staff and Workers	其他人员 Others
总计	**Total**	**70**	**310838**	**294650**	**16188**
按集团审批部门分	**By Examining Department**				
国务院	The State Council	1	15321	15211	110
国务院主管部门	Governing Department of the State Council	1	3611	3437	174
省级人民政府	Provincial Government	25	164118	158581	5537
省级政府主管部门	Governing Department of the Provincial Government	16	59918	55876	4042
其他	Others	27	67870	61545	6325
按母公司控股情况分	**By Situation of Share Holding**				
国有绝对控股	Controlling Share Holding Absolutely by the State	46	229776	225519	4257
国有相对控股	Controlling Share Holding Comparatively by the State	8	24356	21951	2405
集体绝对控股	Controlling Share Holding Absolutely by the Collective	1	1848	1419	429
集体相对控股	Controlling Share Holding Comparatively by the Collective	1	4845	4210	635
其他	Others	14	50013	41551	8462
按企业规模分	**By Size of Enterprises**				
特大型	Extra Large	3	59654	59344	310
大型	Large	52	229721	214092	15629
中型	Medium	14	18863	18814	49
小型	Small	1	2600	2400	200
按主营行业分	**By Sector**				
农、林、牧、渔业	Farming, Forestry, Animal Husbandry and Fishery				
采掘业	Mining and Quarrying	2	28485	28485	
制造业	Manufacturing	43	187618	180025	7593
电气水的生产和供应业	Production and Supply of Electric Power, Gas and Water				
建筑业	Construction	5	35546	30013	5533
运输邮电业	Transportation, Post and Telecommunication	2	4611	4611	
批发零售贸易餐饮业	Wholesale and Retail Trade and Catering Services	15	40277	39507	770
金融保险业	Banking ang Insurance				
房地产业	Real Estate	1	315	295	20
其他	Others	2	13986	11714	2272
按母公司注册类型分	**By Type of Registration**				
国有企业	State-owned Enterprises	13	39480	38924	556
国有独资企业	State Funded Corporations	22	117340	114820	2520
其他有限责任公司	Others Limited Liability Corporations	15	75350	72692	2658
股份有限公司	Share Holding Co. Ltd.	18	71536	66409	5127
其他	Others	2	7132	1805	5327

17-1 续表 1 continued

分类	Item	从业人员劳动报酬（万元）Labor Reward of Employed Persons (10 000 yuan)	在岗职工 Number of Fully Employed Staff and Workers	其他人员 Others	固定资产投资完成额（万元）Actually Completed Investment in Fixed Assets (10 000 yuan)
总计	**Total**	**368697**	**350836**	**17861**	**373262**
按集团审批部门分	**By Examining Department**				
国务院	The State Council	17900	17445	455	28142
国务院主管部门	Governing Department of the State Council	7561	7397	164	10169
省级人民政府	Provincial Government	192193	189763	2430	243257
省级政府主管部门	Governing Department of the Provincial Government	71485	62902	8583	35724
其他	Others	79558	73329	6229	55970
按母公司控股情况分	**By Situation of Share Holding**				
国有绝对控股	Controlling Share Holding Absolutely by the State	282043	277072	4971	328314
国有相对控股	Controlling Share Holding Comparatively by the State	23731	22739	992	17462
集体绝对控股	Controlling Share Holding Absolutely by the Collective	1448	1025	423	5800
集体相对控股	Controlling Share Holding Comparatively by the Collective	4844	4313	531	
其他	Others	56631	45687	10944	21686
按企业规模分	**By Size of Enterprises**				
特大型	Extra Large	94890	94529	361	149052
大型	Large	256810	239462	17348	187654
中型	Medium	15125	15069	56	36556
小型	Small	1872	1776	96	
按主营行业分	**By Sector**				
农、林、牧、渔业	Farming, Forestry, Animal Husbandry and Fishery				
采掘业	Mining and Quarrying	21820	21820		4600
制造业	Manufacturing	229405	220940	8465	351936
电气水的生产和供应业	Production and Supply of Electric Power, Gas and Water				
建筑业	Construction	43147	37685	5462	982
运输邮电业	Transportation, Post and Telecommunication	3262	3262		
批发零售贸易餐饮业	Wholesale and Retail Trade and Catering Services	43956	43220	736	15744
金融保险业	Banking ang Insurance				
房地产业	Real Estate	318	308	10	
其他	Others	26789	23601	3188	
按母公司注册类型分	**By Type of Registration**				
国有企业	State-owned Enterprises	52751	49945	2806	79919
国有独资企业	State Funded Corporations	123982	122481	1501	75153
其他有限责任公司	Others Limited Liability Corporations	102313	101324	989	160816
股份有限公司	Share Holding Co. Ltd.	82807	75596	7211	50592
其他	Others	6844	1490	5354	6782

单位：万元　　　　17-1 续表 2　continued　　　　(10 000 yuan)

年末资产总计 Total Assets at the Year-end	固定资产原价合计 Original Value of Fixed Assets	累计折旧 Accumulated Deprecia-tion	#本年折旧 Deprecia-tion Charge of the Year	累计对外投资 Accumulated Value of Investing Abroad	#本年对外投资 Value of Investing Abroad of the Year	存货 Inventory	流动资产年均余额 Annual Average Balance of Circulation Funds	年末负债合计 Total Liabilities at the Year-end	流动负债 Liquid Liabilities
9394870	**5314827**	**1820620**	**243083**	**476733**	**96251**	**1229629**	**3714009**	**5439557**	**4110115**
442930	261419	79656	10499	26877	2871	61005	219172	251713	203199
347860	467486	233051	18003			35504	11040	273792	96317
5306275	3129451	1030645	145328	293773	63027	687325	1993496	3007533	2284298
1929717	774510	275236	44495	113817	22822	273842	967376	1134664	927140
1368088	681961	202032	24758	42266	7531	171953	522925	771855	599161
7907331	4688256	1650511	206229	416316	68809	997142	3029474	4643076	3441618
609538	309082	82419	14081	10694	1469	93313	256667	334559	287041
70150	48069	11915	1172			5059	19280	40779	16167
23943	8126	2613	551			5086	18246	12885	
783908	261294	73162	21050	49723	25973	129029	390342	408258	365289
2116153	1631324	554107	99678	68033		259069	773392	1134432	819023
6839285	3476051	1230826	136066	403515	95322	934682	2798587	4072684	3119087
412812	190611	33749	6630	5185	929	32280	131823	219789	162364
26620	16841	1938	709			3598	10207	12652	9641
258616	163337	60924	4963	3119	2160	12549	98131	108658	70736
6800757	4267480	1483688	203200	377215	90655	935903	2679352	3790635	2708424
192819	65737	17137	1292	1418	3	46765	72517	87675	64291
61535	48827	16909	1759	814	224	928	2228	33988	10497
1420002	500761	161784	22311	80923	105	161166	682402	1083746	944355
17205	5685	819	277	1380		6471	10846	9500	5914
643936	263000	79359	9281	11864	3104	65847	168533	325355	305898
1325517	777660	232126	26453	37077	4780	140109	501890	784447	609359
3519054	1817217	663850	67298	170574	42036	428785	1367235	2173273	1696688
2403726	1642124	524358	96740	141679	10526	343586	902499	1277783	914327
2054927	1026959	387847	51252	126038	38909	300915	908655	1152335	864384
91646	50867	12439	1340	1365		16234	33730	51719	25357

单位：万元　　17-1 续表 3　continued　　(10 000 yuan)

分类	Item	所有者权益 Creditors' Equity	股本 Share Capital	营业收入 Business Revenue	主营收入 Major Business Revenue
总计	**Total**	**3955313**	**1873839**	**5272697**	**5217219**
按集团审批部门分	**By Examining Department**				
国务院	The State Council	191217	72057	101600	99362
国务院主管部门	Governing Department of the State Council	74068	118700	115413	115413
省级人民政府	Provincial Government	2298742	886089	3235500	3207998
省级政府主管部门	Governing Department of the Provincial Government	795053	359482	1121792	1102339
其他	Others	596233	437511	698392	692107
按母公司控股情况分	**By Situation of Share Holding**				
国有绝对控股	Controlling Share Holding Absolutely by the State	3264255	1498506	4208503	4159321
国有相对控股	Controlling Share Holding Comparatively by the State	274979	151424	379519	377794
集体绝对控股	Controlling Share Holding Absolutely by the Collective	29371	24454	40525	40525
集体相对控股	Controlling Share Holding Comparatively by the Collective	11058	7680	24226	24226
其他	Others	375650	191775	619924	615353
按企业规模分	**By Size of Enterprises**				
特大型	Extra Large	981721	347686	1195654	1192804
大型	Large	2766601	1383841	3872137	3820969
中型	Medium	193023	130512	191087	189763
小型	Small	13968	11800	13819	13683
按主营行业分	**By Sector**				
农、林、牧、渔业	Farming, Forestry, Animal Husbandry and Fishery				
采掘业	Mining and Quarrying	149958	70571	79295	71821
制造业	Manufacturing	3010122	1417134	3552655	3513925
电气水的生产和供应业	Production and Supply of Electric Power, Gas and Water				
建筑业	Construction	105144	85585	143618	143114
运输邮电业	Transportation, Post and Telecommunication	27547	8654	29598	26114
批发零售贸易餐饮业	Wholesale and Retail Trade and Catering Services	336256	184498	968923	966073
金融保险业	Banking ang Insurance				
房地产业	Real Estate	7705	6325	2791	2695
其他	Others	318581	101072	495817	493477
按母公司注册类型分	**By Type of Registration**				
国有企业	State-owned Enterprises	541070	229121	551279	540586
国有独资企业	State Funded Corporations	1345781	732674	1976721	1946675
其他有限责任公司	Others Limited Liability Corporations	1125943	405068	1446609	1434881
股份有限公司	Share Holding Co. Ltd.	902592	473443	1234293	1231772
其他	Others	39927	33533	63795	63305

#出口额 Value of Exports	其他业务收入 Revenue of Others Business	主营业务成本 Accumulated Value of Investing Abroad	主营业务税金及附加 Pre-tax and Related Payment of Major Business	存货跌价损失及营业管理财务费用 Loss of Inventory Value-decrease and Expenditrue for Financial Management	#利息支出 Expenditrue for Interest	利润总额 Total Profits	应交所得税 Income Taxes Payable	应交增值税 Added Value Tax Payable	研究开发费用 Expenditrue for Research and Development
355433	**55478**	**4231080**	**67641**	**791223**	**108920**	**165443**	**60718**	**175524**	**87638**
27138	2238	91113	2317	35282	6838	-20122	293	2537	5816
1550		106320	156			-42868	92	1555	284
82831	27502	2615090	40166	442088	62340	157885	34461	121532	72917
213608	19453	853783	14573	187480	26532	61374	20425	34996	5837
30306	6285	564774	10429	126373	13210	9174	5447	14904	2784
258051	49182	3376395	58418	637066	88236	115012	45506	151108	76301
18577	1725	302346	2472	70857	11079	10141	3533	12873	5331
250		34898	1327	1982	1273	2318	766	393	1450
		21029	811	1317	48	1070	327		
78555	4571	496412	4613	80001	8284	36902	10586	11150	4556
2919	2850	993899	9017	155372	29293	49264	10789	77912	10388
344882	51168	3072229	55908	612741	75091	108251	47513	92502	76128
6352	1324	154425	2667	21638	4025	6156	1831	3876	909
1280	136	10527	49	1472	511	1772	585	1234	213
11667	7474	25851	16299	19447	615	109	3397	2160	500
184980	38730	2852499	35193	528888	89671	96399	37125	152093	84449
	504	122733	4681	6083	113	7615	2252		60
	3484	21179	706	22983	253	70	44	11	
155600	2850	820397	5953	126322	13899	21909	8253	18950	2629
	96	1596	91	1233		13		25	
3186	2340	386825	4718	86267	4369	39328	9647	2285	
136584	10693	433329	7788	128985	18633	3139	4049	7278	6170
83966	30046	1576134	34082	310695	30443	67091	22707	54158	13888
32499	11728	1209283	9492	157411	38997	69005	12878	82123	17105
102134	2521	956403	14200	191691	19516	23304	20125	31572	48965
250	490	55931	2079	2441	1331	2904	959	393	1510

17-2 建立现代企业制度的重点企业基本情况(2001年)

分类	Item	单位数（个）Number of Enterprises (unit)	注册资本合计（万元）Total Registered Capital (10 000 yuan)
总计	**Total**	**198**	**3813305**
按企业改制主管部门分	**By Department Responsible for Enterprises Restructure**		
国家重点企业	Key Enterprises in Contact with State	17	972338
重组集团的原512户企业	The Previous 512 Enterprises Rebuilding Groups	11	493989
中央企工委管理的企业	Enterprises Control by Enterprises Committee of the State	1	16169
省级重点企业	Key Enterprises in Contact with Province	81	2575155
原国家百户试点企业	Enterprises in Experiment of the State	5	144059
原省级试点企业	Enterprises in Experiment of the Province	67	1054519
企业集团母公司	Parent Company of Enterprises Group	2	41164
按母公司控股情况分	**By Situation of Share Holding**		
国有绝对控股	Controlling Share Holding Absolutely by the State	145	3241643
国有相对控股	Controlling Share Holding Comparatively by the State	16	134035
集体绝对控股	Controlling Share Holding Absolutely by the Collective	6	53377
集体相对控股	Controlling Share Holding Comparatively by the Collective	2	4594
其他	Others	28	372058
按企业规模分	**By Size of Enterprises**		
特大型	Extra Large	5	443169
大型	Large	127	3125376
中型	Medium	57	207375
小型	Small	8	27187
其他	Others	1	10198
按主营行业分	**By Sector**		
农、林、牧、渔业	Farming, Forestry, Animal Husbandry and Fishery	9	80336
采掘业	Mining and Quarrying	8	184929
制造业	Manufacturing	134	2709209
电气水的生产和供应业	Production and Supply of Electric Power, Gas and Water	9	351500
建筑业	Construction	6	135845
运输邮电业	Transportation, Post and Telecommunication	2	10322
批发零售贸易餐饮业	Wholesale and Retail Trade and Catering Services	25	206863
金融保险业	Banking ang Insurance	1	50534
房地产业	Real Estate	1	20480
其他	Others	3	63287
按母公司注册类型分	**By Type of Registration**		
国有企业	State-owned Enterprises	68	1129209
国有独资企业	State Funded Corporations	33	716961
其他有限责任公司	Others Limited Liability Corporations	31	493135
股份有限公司	Share Holding Co. Ltd.	55	1182410
其他	Others	10	291022

Basic Conditions of Key Enterprises Building Modern Eenterprises System (2001)

固定资产投资完成额（万元）Actually Completed Investment in Fixed Assets (10 000 yuan)	从业人员（人）Number of Employed Persons (person)	#在岗职工 Number of Fully Employed Staff and Workers	#其他人员 Others	从业人员劳动报酬（万元）Labor Reward of Employed Persons (10 000 yuan)	#在岗职工 Number of Fully Employed Staff and Workers	#其他人员 Others
537550	**452106**	**443069**	**6761**	**570663**	**549792**	**6686**
198184	117258	117039	157	184102	183993	109
166061	127252	126825	427	184080	183845	235
3226	3657	3657		2452	2452	
336763	257083	254221	1227	354281	349553	3388
57056	13048	12986	62	18859	18787	72
219367	153238	150389	2851	209004	192413	4120
4585	4141	4129	12	5764	5662	102
432294	392889	386851	5183	503240	484332	5540
57430	24056	22640	1416	27934	26959	975
26090	7082	7045	37	8061	8571	18
193	1612	1612		1199	1199	
18907	18106	16562	123	20659	19169	151
66052	91692	91382	310	148090	147729	361
449498	313277	307433	4361	372200	366158	5050
19396	43028	41142	1093	47254	33093	968
1504	3478	2481	997	2570	2263	307
1100	631	631		549	549	
1467	9460	7781	42	7408	5968	101
68504	69926	68751	1175	77513	77269	244
388367	319199	314862	3696	410344	394795	2703
52829	10376	10374	2	19972	19948	24
2929	18007	17195	812	20065	19204	861
3822	5314	5314		3732	3732	0
19522	16458	15820	640	18377	18004	373
110	19	19		48	48	
	514	514		402	402	
	2833	2439	398	12802	10422	2380
166721	130390	126782	3031	180484	165473	1637
183104	143566	143172	396	170969	170516	454
25526	90534	89233	1085	116706	116692	542
155559	80555	76832	2238	92253	86873	4040
6337	5511	5500	11	8221	8208	13

17-3 建立现代企业制度的重点企业主要经济指标(2001年)

单位：万元

分类	Item	年末资产总计 Total Assets at the Year-end	固定资产原价合计 Original Value of Fixed Assets	累计折旧 Accumulated Depreciation
总计	**Total**	**14871542**	**9360013**	**3599573**
按企业改制主管部门分	**By Department Responsible for Enterprises Restructure**			
国家重点企业	Key Enterprises in Contact with State	5252215	3904646	1646976
重组集团的原512户企业	The Previous 512 Enterprises Rebuilding Groups	4021738	3340379	1259650
中央企工委管理的企业	Enterprises Control by Enterprises Committee of the State	69789	47747	12755
省级重点企业	Key Enterprises in Contact with Province	9712178	5493077	2109290
原国家百户试点企业	Enterprises in Experiment of the State	886116	337763	137233
原省级试点企业	Enterprises in Experiment of the Province	4921971	2844256	1064256
企业集团母公司	Parent Company of Enterprises Group	345193	74902	26134
按母公司控股情况分	**By Situation of Share Holding**			
国有绝对控股	Controlling Share Holding Absolutely by the State	13207561	8101956	3059103
国有相对控股	Controlling Share Holding Comparatively by the State	586687	479180	117756
集体绝对控股	Controlling Share Holding Absolutely by the Collective	373110	249047	112900
集体相对控股	Controlling Share Holding Comparatively by the Collective	24819	16287	8151
其他	Others	588752	493418	293488
按企业规模分	**By Size of Enterprises**			
特大型	Extra Large	3226162	2620271	978905
大型	Large	10728130	6238556	2455705
中型	Medium	808119	460661	153356
小型	Small	74706	32956	9556
其他	Others	34425	7569	2051
按主营行业分	**By Sector**			
农、林、牧、渔业	Farming, Forestry, Animal Husbandry and Fishery	396800	97049	31910
采掘业	Mining and Quarrying	1019387	826455	333783
制造业	Manufacturing	10749008	6980820	2708583
电气水的生产和供应业	Production and Supply of Electric Power, Gas and Water	572283	725309	370166
建筑业	Construction	213255	72472	27709
运输邮电业	Transportation, Post and Telecommunication	47412	37635	13373
批发零售贸易餐饮业	Wholesale and Retail Trade and Catering Services	1459913	339783	70720
金融保险业	Banking ang Insurance	59512	126	6
房地产业	Real Estate	48240	26058	3759
其他	Others	305732	254306	39564
按母公司注册类型分	**By Type of Registration**			
国有企业	State-owned Enterprises	4283460	2261762	946833
国有独资企业	State Funded Corporations	4189945	2714450	1014793
其他有限责任公司	Others Limited Liability Corporations	2604599	1989713	747802
股份有限公司	Share Holding Co. Ltd.	3524217	2029893	632342
其他	Others	232410	345408	249726

Main Economic Indicators on Key Enterprises

Building Modern Eenterprises System (2001)

(10 000 yuan)

#本年折旧 Depreciation Charge of the Year	累计对外投资 Accumulated Value of Investing Abroad	#本年对外投资 Value of Investing Abroad of the Year	存货 Inventory	流动资产年均余额 Annual Average Balance of Circulation Funds	年末负债合计 Total Liabilities at the Year-end	流动负债 Liquid Liabilities	所有者权益 Creditors' Equity	股本 Share Capital
618620	**935383**	**163710**	**2184535**	**5486707**	**8717971**	**5969187**	**6084497**	**3934508**
232169	357366	43499	861537	1380531	2713910	1544466	2534674	725144
197944	149560	41909	515964	788702	2375240	1317634	1645121	575102
1572	4367	600	6698	21589	50876	31092	18913	12546
462886	768302	105810	1470427	3479054	5382683	3868130	4268784	3048377
19137	75853	6825	190095	432232	507610	465143	378506	127688
146002	311923	80783	596232	1952615	2989754	2205129	1846786	1448879
2194	26143	7	59011	202933	203290	158566	92624	41164
579041	888132	148137	2019530	4813920	7725857	5360537	5388179	3623397
12834	17501	6103	54052	230598	331223	210112	254801	134034
3081	4562	1389	44723	140806	230587	122830	142523	54799
718	726		3108	13690	18838	12861	5981	4565
21932	24462	8081	51645	226797	334895	191121	278971	110115
320588	83194	1855	438373	489036	1880050	1254572	1312647	546159
275995	824795	154822	1617955	4621039	6215066	4311443	4453005	3143442
20536	18428	917	100561	316662	547802	333621	284767	210333
969	16	16	25654	45254	62872	57370	11834	23111
532	8950	6100	1992	14716	12181	12181	22244	11463
5372	23515	7753	56290	249832	234351	172529	183299	86179
53391	19440	2180	118714	360273	597421	383131	421364	198919
508046	733043	130024	1720545	3748742	5877637	4003459	4782319	3266604
32652	335	43	5144	151866	369431	51976	202852	67428
2252	2486	2486	20171	91127	165920	158661	47335	35855
1754	7527	4752	297	5555	25339	18772	22073	10322
9255	79272	8756	229259	730048	1245311	1022373	214332	140901
6	56701	6875	9416	1613	5497	4497	54015	50534
496	4926	650	6319	12822	20049	1200	28191	20480
5396	8138	191	18380	134829	177015	152589	128717	57286
284856	465003	73100	821673	1821155	2489975	1719633	1740356	1414566
134547	160303	47059	537029	1663245	2639706	1976837	1513145	861858
101608	157679	10719	338844	290829	1431900	1005288	1172100	493619
82002	151885	3232742	464315	1600561	2003592	1184707	1542373	1141262
15135	513	90	2571	86779	126245	59323	106165	14635

分类	Item	营业收入 Business Revenue	主营收入 Major Business Revenue	#出口额 Value of Exports
总　计	**Total**	**9526378**	**9339476**	**372889**
按企业改制主管部门分	**By Department Responsible for Enterprises Restructure**			
国家重点企业	Key Enterprises in Contact with State	4080974	3973599	79372
重组集团的原512户企业	The Previous 512 Enterprises Rebuilding Groups	2916564	2806023	29256
中央企工委管理的企业	Enterprises Control by Enterprises Committee of the State	22272	22228	1204
省级重点企业	Key Enterprises in Contact with Province	5971122	5870924	251216
原国家百户试点企业	Enterprises in Experiment of the State	847970	845153	6523
原省级试点企业	Enterprises in Experiment of the Province	2388797	2333588	145333
企业集团母公司	Parent Company of Enterprises Group	56695	56302	1297
按母公司控股情况分	**By Situation of Share Holding**			
国有绝对控股	Controlling Share Holding Absolutely by the State	8480315	8311773	358467
国有相对控股	Controlling Share Holding Comparatively by the State	430637	428776	4513
集体绝对控股	Controlling Share Holding Absolutely by the Collective	157604	154480	96
集体相对控股	Controlling Share Holding Comparatively by the Collective	9199	8286	85
其他	Others	387145	380343	9728
按企业规模分	**By Size of Enterprises**			
特大型	Extra Large	2057165	2055080	21909
大型	Large	6983965	6809164	341418
中型	Medium	450489	444356	9552
小型	Small	23399	23376	10
其他	Others	11360	7500	
按主营行业分	**By Sector**			
农、林、牧、渔业	Farming, Forestry, Animal Husbandry and Fishery	185898	184570	1354
采掘业	Mining and Quarrying	724997	665118	37396
制造业	Manufacturing	6903287	6802150	243640
电气水的生产和供应业	Production and Supply of Electric Power, Gas and Water	266584	266332	4385
建筑业	Construction	266206	258162	
运输邮电业	Transportation, Post and Telecommunication	15815	14968	
批发零售贸易餐饮业	Wholesale and Retail Trade and Catering Services	936298	928981	69004
金融保险业	Banking ang Insurance	91832	86305	17110
房地产业	Real Estate	2165	1194	
其他	Others	133296	131696	
按母公司注册类型分	**By Type of Registration**			
国有企业	State-owned Enterprises	3075976	3056813	148775
国有独资企业	State Funded Corporations	2331964	2247463	98106
其他有限责任公司	Others Limited Liability Corporations	1446368	1435676	53164
股份有限公司	Share Holding Co. Ltd.	2490011	2417698	64171
其他	Others	165456	165223	4045

continued (10 000 yuan)

其他业务收入 Revenue of Others Business	主营业务成本 Accumulated Value of Investing Abroad	主营业务税金及附加 Pre-tax and Related Payment of Major Business	存货跌价损失及营业管理财务费用 Loss of Inventory Value-decrease and Expenditrue for Financial Management	#利息支出 Expenditrue for Interest	利润总额 Total Profits	应交所得税 Income Taxes Payable	应交增值税 Added Value tax Payable	研究开发费用 Expenditrue for Research and Development
186902	**8917979**	**703910**	**1406594**	**184261**	**346389**	**109999**	**533715**	**67567**
107375	2751520	631701	418005	65290	209077	65029	306266	18828
110541	2390125	59512	336978	62373	70455	22903	179426	14372
44	16936	142	6256	1057	50	194	1425	316
100198	5954739	634898	931822	114642	331008	87045	388535	59478
2817	2197150	244942	66337	8933	59495	18841	59905	1653
55209	1850169	28991	375123	56990	108838	27140	128093	13498
393	39226	7760	17476	5345	5866	5215	7059	220
168542	8112916	695887	1245271	166722	285329	97722	488672	60808
1861	336038	2843	67141	6236	29093	8238	19633	1690
3124	139723	458	19794	2601	919	901	4012	2694
913	5470	142	3167	311	133	33	695	42
6802	274517	2953	64547	7629	30404	3000	20653	2333
2085	1724991	30145	241286	53465	69878	15582	139573	13632
174801	6791344	668848	1087042	119767	279397	91469	379267	51240
6133	376610	4622	72529	10733	-4392	2580	13368	2295
23	19769	206	4710	285	119	160	1187	152
3860	5265	89	1027	11	1387	208	320	248
1328	134648	798	45026	4267	5847	1640	8921	2189
59879	543265	5223	105095	10361	27087	5259	45972	5345
101137	5060172	681111	1103572	146029	262222	96486	444079	57584
252	211800	1128	11733	865	25181	2346	24489	152
8044	241282	7119	14754	1168	-3167	142	50	20
847	8140	404	6619	333	407	127		
7317	2556119	4296	90238	11171	13004	3817	7527	2252
5527	76711		-1044	3821	2265	180	1557	25
971	520	311	2215	861	-1252			
1600	85322	3520	28386	5385	14795	2	1120	
19163	1992192	612283	489525	40973	167082	62610	232427	18587
84501	3574150	21708	351502	51768	70463	16218	119758	17580
10692	1204888	8681	173267	39937	53152	12852	88564	11884
72313	2010111	60504	378269	49035	42313	18181	79394	19276
233	125840	598	8339	1829	13297	72	11523	

17-4 企业景气指数

Business Climate Indics

单位：点 (point)

指标	Item	2000 一季度 1st. Quarter	2000 二季度 2nd. Quarter	2000 三季度 3rd. Quarter	2000 四季度 4th. Quarter
全省总计	**Total**	**90.04**	**90.73**	**91.29**	**93.54**
按行业门类分	**By Sector**				
工业	Industry	96.37	98.38	100.77	101.53
建筑业	Construction	60.03	64.56	71.83	81.27
交通邮电仓储业	Transportation, Storage, Postal and Telecommunication Service	105.44	78.91	87.61	79.52
商贸餐饮业	Wholesale and Retail Trade & Catering Trade	82.24	80.02	83.66	81.7
房地产业	Real Estate	89.88	78.79	96.93	100.41
社会服务业	Social Services	82.41	97.74	79.51	87.61
按注册类型分	**By Registration**				
国有企业	State-owned	85.84	83.17	90.25	89.38
集体企业	Colletive-owned	74.82	71.88	68.39	68.87
有限责任公司	Limited-liability Companies	89.63	95.43	92.66	93.17
股份有限公司	Share Holding Ltd. Companies	129.93	130.81	130.24	126.33
港澳台外商投资	Funded by Overseas Entrepreneurs	98.54	106.52	85.84	111.51
按企业规模分	**By Size of Enterprises**				
大型企业	Large	113.63	115.24	133.87	126.54
中型企业	Medium	84.29	82.41	79.41	81.29
小型企业	Small	79.57	77.41	79.62	81
上市公司	**Share Listed Companies**	**166.78**	**177.06**	**168.97**	**167.87**

指标	Item	2001 一季度 1st. Quarter	2001 二季度 2nd. Quarter	2001 三季度 3rd. Quarter	2001 四季度 4th. Quarter
全省总计	**Total**	**100.76**	**100.18**	**99.33**	**101.17**
按行业门类分	**By Sector**				
工业	Industry	107.31	106.41	98.56	101.9
建筑业	Construction	82.77	93.24	108.28	100.28
交通邮电仓储业	Transportation, Storage, Postal and Telecommunication Service	84.82	84.07	99.36	93.93
商贸餐饮业	Wholesale and Retail Trade & Catering Trade	93.22	87.44	91.65	95.66
房地产业	Real Estate	124.62	118.75	114.46	124.1
社会服务业	Social Services	98.34	96.67	100.5	105.44
按注册类型分	**By Registration**				
国有企业	State-owned	95.83	92.33	93.01	98.92
集体企业	Colletive-owned	82.98	80.35	75.06	83.29
有限责任公司	Limited-liability Companies	109.53	107.71	105.55	109.05
股份有限公司	Share Holding Ltd. Companies	120.37	125.07	121.35	113.02
港澳台外商投资	Funded by Overseas Entrepreneurs	115.77	111.45	112.85	114.62
按企业规模分	**By Size of Enterprises**				
大型企业	Large	129.8	132.68	120.83	121.48
中型企业	Medium	94.3	91.67	93.54	97.72
小型企业	Small	91.68	86.69	90.31	93.7
上市公司	**Share Listed Companies**	**137.31**	**134.44**	**133.69**	**121.25**

17-5 企业家信心指数

Enterprepreneur Expectation Indics

单位：点 (point)

指标	Item	2000 一季度 1st. Quarter	2000 二季度 2nd. Quarter	2000 三季度 3rd. Quarter	2000 四季度 4th. Quarter
全省总计	**Total**	**96.73**	**94.81**	**94.89**	**92.82**
按行业门类分	**By Sector**				
工业	Industry	94.64	95.25	98.23	100
建筑业	Construction	88.49	77.27	73.91	82.94
交通邮电仓储业	Transportation, Storage, Postal and Telecommunication Service	108.7	96.96	89.7	95.99
商贸餐饮业	Wholesale and Retail Trade & Catering Trade	88.62	81.28	83.49	77.81
房地产业	Real Estate	95.45	95.45	110.61	115.38
社会服务业	Social Services	106.41	110.74	103.41	102.14
按注册类型分	**By Registration**				
国有企业	State-owned	92.29	88.05	91.3	87.52
集体企业	Colletive-owned	82.85	75.25	73.8	77.95
有限责任公司	Limited-liability Companies	106.93	101.36	99.25	98.8
股份有限公司	Share Holding Ltd. Companies	104.58	113.2	113.88	110.03
港澳台外商投资	Funded by Overseas Entrepreneurs	107.77	115.77	99.8	114.32
按企业规模分	**By Size of Enterprises**				
大型企业	Large	100.72	106.74	115.76	107.63
中型企业	Medium	92.77	86.98	84.7	85.02
小型企业	Small	90.49	85.31	87.82	85.85
上市公司	**Share Listed Companies**	**111.94**	**123.53**	**126.78**	**121.34**

指标	Item	2001 一季度 1st. Quarter	2001 二季度 2nd. Quarter	2001 三季度 3rd. Quarter	2001 四季度 4th. Quarter
全省总计	**Total**	**108.41**	**106.4**	**103.48**	**102.57**
按行业门类分	**By Sector**				
工业	Industry	111.63	111.66	104.74	102.78
建筑业	Construction	104.81	97.55	103.68	105.24
交通邮电仓储业	Transportation, Storage, Postal and Telecommunication Service	101.94	96.52	96.47	94.27
商贸餐饮业	Wholesale and Retail Trade & Catering Trade	93.12	91.29	86.55	89.25
房地产业	Real Estate	132.31	131.25	133.22	132.01
社会服务业	Social Services	115.38	108.31	121.23	119.24
按注册类型分	**By Registration**				
国有企业	State-owned	102.3	98.37	97.51	97.47
集体企业	Colletive-owned	84.11	87.71	83.31	89.94
有限责任公司	Limited-liability Companies	127.8	126.72	114.71	117.86
股份有限公司	Share Holding Ltd. Companies	114.35	120.89	113.65	100.94
港澳台外商投资	Funded by Overseas Entrepreneurs	127.84	125.92	128.85	130.03
按企业规模分	**By Size of Enterprises**				
大型企业	Large	129.46	137.33	127.02	113.94
中型企业	Medium	99.27	95.56	94.24	97.19
小型企业	Small	99.63	95.38	94.73	96.76
上市公司	**Share Listed Companies**	**117.23**	**118.22**	**105.06**	**79.71**

17-6 工业景气指数

Business Survey of Industry

单位：点 (point)

指标	Item	2000 一季度 1st. Quarter	二季度 2nd. Quarter	三季度 3rd. Quarter	四季度 4th. Quarter
综合生产经营状况	**Comprehensive Conditions of Production and Management**	**96.57**	**98.38**	**100.77**	**101.53**
生产成本	Production Cost	104.23	97.96	91.74	89.57
生产总量	Total Production Quantity	96.26	127.48	116.05	110.01
产品订货	Production Order	96.17	98.5	96.09	97.01
产品销售量	Sales Volume of Products	101.17	122.01	111.3	123.36
产品销售价格	Selling Price of Products	76.86	89.83	80.67	80.13
产成品库存	Inventory of Products	113.97	110.2	108.5	113.75
税后利润	After-tax Profits	79.13	110.59	84.74	91.33
流动资金	Circulating Funds	43.74	44.48	47.41	49.31
货款拖欠	Payment Delinquent	103	98.09	106.38	116.86
设备利用	Utilization of Equipment	101.93	106.09	96.71	99.95
用工	Employment	66.23	85.35	84.52	75.58
固定资产投资	Investment in Fixed Assets	104.52	106.8	110.45	110
科技开发	Scientific and Technical Development	121.12	120.73	121.43	116.1
原材料能源进价	Bid of Raw Materials and Energy				
原材料能源供应	Supply of Raw Materials and Energy	128.59	117.77	122.94	117.86

指标	Item	2001 一季度 1st. Quarter	二季度 2nd. Quarter	三季度 3rd. Quarter	四季度 4th. Quarter
综合生产经营状况	**Comprehensive Conditions of Production and Management**	**107.31**	**106.41**	**98.56**	**101.9**
生产成本	Production Cost	103.97	100.51	90.9	96.34
生产总量	Total Production Quantity	110.33	126.22	118.19	119.08
产品订货	Production Order	102.39	97.31	92.07	95.14
产品销售量	Sales Volume of Products	108.81	122.85	107.72	110.57
产品销售价格	Selling Price of Products	88.12	87.27	82.53	78.39
产成品库存	Inventory of Products	123	117.59	108.86	110.19
税后利润	After-tax Profits	102.24	112.87	94.34	101.72
流动资金	Circulating Funds	48.61	50.85	52.83	50.25
货款拖欠	Payment Delinquent	101.42	100.45	98.72	105.28
设备利用	Utilization of Equipment	124.04	126.12	119.53	117.31
用工	Employment	84.7	88.38	83.79	85.24
固定资产投资	Investment in Fixed Assets	109.7	111.2	107.11	104.56
科技开发	Scientific and Technical Development	120.88	116.53	116.42	113.99
原材料能源进价	Bid of Raw Materials and Energy				
原材料能源供应	Supply of Raw Materials and Energy	122.6	120.97	113.83	117.33

17-7 建筑业景气指数

Business Survey of Construction

单位：点 (point)

指标	Item	2000 一季度 1st. Quarter	2000 二季度 2nd. Quarter	2000 三季度 3rd. Quarter	2000 四季度 4th. Quarter
综合生产经营状况	**Comprehensive Conditions of Production and Management**	**60.03**	**64.56**	**71.83**	**81.27**
工程合同签定	Signment of Project Contracts	84.65	78.45	78.36	100.77
建筑产品实物工程量	Volume of Projects in Physical Unit	62.15	94.71	109.33	116.11
施工产值	Output Value of Construction	65.23	91.42	105.08	121.14
竣工产值	Output Value of Completed Construction	80.34	56.52	98.67	131.71
工程结算收入	Income from Project Settlement	72.83	68.73	96.86	124.68
建筑材料进价	Bid of Construction Materials	92.72	42.24	46.41	47.86
工程结算成本	Cost of Project Settlement	95.87	53.06	64.42	62.68
税后利润	After-tax Profits	67.51	35.63	82.48	74.2
流动资金	Circulating Funds	33.61	36.08	29.93	37.54
货款拖欠	Payment Delinquent	78.72	76.25	64.93	54.75
用工	Employment	61.21	69.17	94.48	87.78
固定资产投资	Investment in Fixed Assets	63.66	83.5	107.38	93.3

指标	Item	2001 一季度 1st. Quarter	2001 二季度 2nd. Quarter	2001 三季度 3rd. Quarter	2001 四季度 4th. Quarter
综合生产经营状况	**Comprehensive Conditions of Production and Management**	**81.39**	**91.66**	**108.18**	**100.27**
工程合同签定	Signment of Project Contracts	95.13	132.81	123.59	107.02
建筑产品实物工程量	Volume of Projects in Physical Unit	95.37	109.84	100.18	128.89
施工产值	Output Value of Construction	78.38	109.79	139.15	135.32
竣工产值	Output Value of Completed Construction	57.78	92.45	148.38	145.58
工程结算收入	Income from Project Settlement	70.98	90.55	130.23	134.18
建筑材料进价	Bid of Construction Materials	83.6	90.42	88.41	83.74
工程结算成本	Cost of Project Settlement	73.91	87.11	76.09	72.11
税后利润	After-tax Profits	68.25	81.66	117.44	109.44
流动资金	Circulating Funds	35.68	45.03	42.71	42.59
货款拖欠	Payment Delinquent	86.55	65.29	57.24	65.04
用工	Employment	63.81	98.11	115.07	111.69
固定资产投资	Investment in Fixed Assets	75.05	111.78	108.83	83.38

17-8 交通邮电仓储业景气指数

Business Survey of Transportation, Storage, Postal and Telecommunication Services

单位：点 (point)

指标	Item	2000 一季度 1st. Quarter	2000 二季度 2nd. Quarter	2000 三季度 3rd. Quarter	2000 四季度 4th. Quarter
综合生产经营状况	**Comprehensive Conditions of Production and Management**	**105.44**	**78.91**	**87.61**	**79.52**
业务量	Business Volume	124.53	92.05	105.1	98.31
业务收入	Business Revenue	114.06	84.79	82.3	84.59
业务收费价格	Business Charges	90.27	84.97	71.16	97.51
营业成本	Business Cost	45.86	57.09	57.13	80.24
税后利润	After-tax Profits	108.36	68.58	63.28	61.44
流动资金	Circulating Funds	43.9	30.05	34.64	30
货款拖欠	Payment Delinquent	89.09	73.12	94.1	99.38
用工	Employment	71.23	72.23	67.77	59.35
固定资产投资	Investment in Fixed Assets	118.42	127.09	107.84	112.74

指标	Item	2001 一季度 1st. Quarter	2001 二季度 2nd. Quarter	2001 三季度 3rd. Quarter	2001 四季度 4th. Quarter
综合生产经营状况	**Comprehensive Conditions of Production and Management**	**84.82**	**84.07**	**99.36**	**93.93**
业务量	Business Volume	102.24	103.91	124.57	105.05
业务收入	Business Revenue	101.17	82.29	115.58	103.58
业务收费价格	Business Charges	69.52	80.83	87.72	90.08
营业成本	Business Cost	87.38	101.85	88.9	81.24
税后利润	After-tax Profits	88.7	84.85	101.57	101.34
流动资金	Circulating Funds	55.38	51.62	47.38	43.95
货款拖欠	Payment Delinquent	90.81	89.42	92.61	89.5
用工	Employment	75.79	73.6	74.56	75.1
固定资产投资	Investment in Fixed Assets	97.66	122.01	112.21	115.76

17-9 批发、零售贸易与餐饮业景气指数

Business Survey of Wholesales, Retail Trade and Catering Services

单位：点 (point)

指标	Item	2000 一季度 1st. Quarter	2000 二季度 2nd. Quarter	2000 三季度 3rd. Quarter	2000 四季度 4th. Quarter
综合生产经营状况	**Comprehensive Conditions of Production and Management**	**82.08**	**79.85**	**83.37**	**81.74**
商品购进额	Commodity Purchases	93.89	88.08	88.99	102.63
商品购进价格	Bid of Commodities	95.08	97.09	97.75	94.97
商品销售额	Sales of Commodities	92.58	85.91	88.43	91.61
# 出口销售额	#Export	79.59	89.48	103.6	106.31
商品销售价格	Selling Price of Commodities	84.5	76.75	81.9	83.09
商品库存	Inventory of Commodities	111.42	119.27	114.24	107.92
经营费用（营业费用）	Business Cost	94.49	89.99	90.76	87.98
税后利润	After-tax Profits	76.7	71.12	71.51	79.44
流动资金	Circulating Funds	44.68	48.32	46.5	45.24
货款拖欠	Payment Delinquent	115.17	118.54	114.66	109.54
用工	Employment	69.64	75.67	76.61	78.71
固定资产投资	Investment in Fixed Assets	91.27	100.88	104.34	93.71

指标	Item	2001 一季度 1st. Quarter	2001 二季度 2nd. Quarter	2001 三季度 3rd. Quarter	2001 四季度 4th. Quarter
综合生产经营状况	**Comprehensive Conditions of Production and Management**	**93.06**	**87.55**	**91.71**	**96.09**
商品购进额	Commodity Purchases	98.24	96.22	100.72	100.35
商品购进价格	Bid of Commodities	105.75	100.23	101.92	111.96
商品销售额	Sales of Commodities	99	93.87	97.89	95.01
# 出口销售额	#Export	103.66	105.29	101.03	95.76
商品销售价格	Selling Price of Commodities	76.14	81.57	75.95	78.45
商品库存	Inventory of Commodities	107.39	108.14	110.48	106.01
经营费用（营业费用）	Business Cost	101.03	92.96	92.91	89.42
税后利润	After-tax Profits	89.73	84.02	90.5	94.62
流动资金	Circulating Funds	64.03	60.6	66.09	66.27
货款拖欠	Payment Delinquent	110.71	115.16	116.32	113.22
用工	Employment	81.11	76.76	82.09	86.56
固定资产投资	Investment in Fixed Assets	96.96	104.73	106.77	98.82

17-10 房地产业景气指数

Business Survey of Real Estate Trade

单位：点 (point)

指标	Item	2000 一季度 1st. Quarter	二季度 2nd. Quarter	三季度 3rd. Quarter	四季度 4th. Quarter
综合生产经营状况	**Comprehensive Conditions of Production and Management**	**87.88**	**78.79**	**96.97**	**100.41**
土地开发面积	Area of Land Development	93.02	93.43	111.11	95.98
完成投资	Completed Investment	94.56	100.7	123.44	121.88
房屋施工面积	Floor Space under Construction	92.31	95.8	119.28	110.21
房屋竣工面积	Floor Space Completed	92.19	86.56	110.94	103.17
商品房预售面积	Presold Space of Commercial Buildings	78.36	90.91	96.92	109.79
商品房销售面积	Sold Space of Commercial Buildings	77.27	89.39	86.15	108.23
商品房销售价格	Selling Price of Commercial Buildings	78.99	76.092	75.38	79.69
空置商品房面积	Vacant Space of Commercial Buildings	130.3	137.5	136.1	133.96
税后利润	After-tax Profits	72.31	65.15	72.72	78.12
流动资金	Circulating Funds	47.58	54.55	57.58	63.49
货款拖欠	Payment Delinquent	109.38	109.64	102.01	105.19
用工	Employment	82.22	83.08	86.57	91.18
固定资产投资	Investment in Fixed Assets	111.85	102.25	120	121.54

指标	Item	2001 一季度 1st. Quarter	二季度 2nd. Quarter	三季度 3rd. Quarter	四季度 4th. Quarter
综合生产经营状况	**Comprehensive Conditions of Production and Management**	**124.62**	**118.75**	**114.46**	**124.1**
土地开发面积	Area of Land Development	104.76	108.2	102.5	105.82
完成投资	Completed Investment	109.38	118.75	118.29	127.02
房屋施工面积	Floor Space under Construction	101.59	108.06	103.75	110.98
房屋竣工面积	Floor Space Completed	98.39	100	105.06	100.89
商品房预售面积	Presold Space of Commercial Buildings	89.06	95.16	102.96	94.71
商品房销售面积	Sold Space of Commercial Buildings	104.69	103.17	106.62	102.2
商品房销售价格	Selling Price of Commercial Buildings	95.31	90.48	103.66	102.44
空置商品房面积	Vacant Space of Commercial Buildings	139.68	137.1	150.36	147.27
税后利润	After-tax Profits	100	90.32	98.77	104.94
流动资金	Circulating Funds	71.88	65.63	73.49	80.72
货款拖欠	Payment Delinquent	118.75	124.19	130.49	118.64
用工	Employment	98.46	93.75	103.27	101.2
固定资产投资	Investment in Fixed Assets	123.44	115.63	119.51	118.93

17-11 社会服务业景气指数

Business Survey of Social Services

单位：点 (point)

指标	Item	2000 一季度 1st. Quarter	2000 二季度 2nd. Quarter	2000 三季度 3rd. Quarter	2000 四季度 4th. Quarter
综合生产经营状况	**Comprehensive Conditions of Production and Management**	**82.41**	**97.74**	**79.51**	**87.61**
业务量	Business Volume	87.66	104.17	88.35	104.36
客房出租（限于旅馆业）	Rent of Guest Rooms(hotels)	55.23	75.05	57.89	63.89
旅游客源（限于旅游业）	Tourists(tourism)	78.8	130.67	95.22	105.02
业务收费（服务）价格	Business(services) Charges	79.26	80.82	76.39	79.52
营业收入	Business Revenue	85.42	103.85	80.72	87.65
营业成本	Business Cost	80.35	79.61	68.89	65.92
税后利润	After-tax Profits	70.44	92.62	67.88	69.89
流动资金	Circulating Funds	57.95	63.7	54.24	53.49
货款拖欠	Payment Delinquent	104.14	89.92	74.62	82.7
用工	Employment	88.8	98.38	95.23	99.83
固定资产投资	Investment in Fixed Assets	121.92	121.88	111.66	110.69

指标	Item	2001 一季度 1st. Quarter	2001 二季度 2nd. Quarter	2001 三季度 3rd. Quarter	2001 四季度 4th. Quarter
综合生产经营状况	**Comprehensive Conditions of Production and Management**	**98.34**	**96.67**	**100.5**	**105.44**
业务量	Business Volume	103.41	103.11	86.45	115.77
客房出租（限于旅馆业）	Rent of Guest Rooms(hotels)	81.63	89.06	100	92.31
旅游客源（限于旅游业）	Tourists(tourism)	98.86	111.42	89.57	111.12
业务收费（服务）价格	Business(services) Charges	82.95	91.34	87.8	83.67
营业收入	Business Revenue	92.71	102.72	87.68	112
营业成本	Business Cost	81.59	79.55	81.27	69.22
税后利润	After-tax Profits	84.72	91.01	82.09	83.55
流动资金	Circulating Funds	71.21	65.72	79.65	74.39
货款拖欠	Payment Delinquent	89.11	85.79	98.98	99.39
用工	Employment	98.05	100.3	95.29	99.77
固定资产投资	Investment in Fixed Assets	115.92	116.69	120.43	122.04

十八、各市、州、县主要经济和社会统计指标

MAIN ECONOMIC AND SOCIAL STATISTICS INDICATORS OF CITIES, PREFECTURE AND COUNTIES

资料整理人员：石　梅　欧阳普　肖首雄　刘昕毅
唐　颖　向延华　唐双全　顾　虹
陈洲艳　杨鸿雁　郑红梅

18-1 各市、州、县年末人口(2001年)

Population at the Year-end (2001)

市县名称	Cities and Counties	总人口 (万人) Total Population (10 000 persons)	男 Male	女 Female	城镇人口 Urban	乡村人口 Rural	城市化水平 (%) City Level (%)
长沙市	**Changsha City**	**587.09**	**303.06**	**284.03**	**262.42**	**324.67**	**44.70**
芙蓉区	Furong District	32.30	16.55	15.75	32.30		100.00
天心区	Tianxin District	36.91	19.15	17.76	36.91		100.00
岳麓区	Yuelu District	32.64	16.99	15.65	32.64		100.00
开福区	Kaifu District	38.13	19.12	19.01	38.13		100.00
雨花区	Yuhua District	40.78	21.08	19.70	40.78		100.00
长沙县	Changsha County	73.60	37.77	35.83	17.43	56.16	23.69
望城县	Wangcheng County	70.69	36.40	34.29	14.14	56.55	20.00
宁乡县	Ningxiang County	130.21	67.44	62.77	23.44	106.77	18.00
浏阳市	Liuyang City	131.83	68.56	63.27	26.64	105.19	20.21
株洲市	**Zhuzhou City**	**372.10**	**191.92**	**180.18**	**147.53**	**224.57**	**39.65**
荷塘区	Hetang District	23.11	12.02	11.09	23.11		100.00
芦淞区	Lousong District	20.46	10.49	9.97	20.46		100.00
石峰区	Shifeng District	26.12	13.70	12.42	26.12		100.00
天元区	Tianyuan District	11.06	5.52	5.54	5.17	5.89	46.75
株洲县	Zhuzhou County	44.49	23.04	21.45	21.01	23.48	47.23
攸县	You County	74.73	38.50	36.23	13.76	60.97	18.42
茶陵县	Chaling County	56.01	28.68	27.33	7.79	48.22	13.91
炎陵县	Yanling County	17.66	9.06	8.60	4.01	13.65	22.69
醴陵市	Liling City	98.46	50.91	47.55	26.10	72.36	26.50
湘潭市	**Xiangtan City**	**280.47**	**144.76**	**135.71**	**103.77**	**176.70**	**37.00**
雨湖区	Yuhu District	35.33	18.20	17.13	35.33		100.00
岳塘区	Yuetang District	32.82	16.99	15.83	32.82		100.00
湘潭县	Xiangtan County	112.89	58.32	54.57	11.39	101.50	10.09
湘乡市	Xiangxiang City	89.32	46.12	43.20	22.21	67.11	24.87
韶山市	Shaoshan City	10.11	5.13	4.98	2.02	8.09	20.00
衡阳市	**Hengyang City**	**708.93**	**373.99**	**334.94**	**190.69**	**518.24**	**26.90**
珠辉区	Zhuhui District	26.44	13.61	12.83	22.96	3.48	86.84
雁峰区	Yanfeng District	19.21	9.80	9.41	18.97	0.24	98.75
石鼓区	Shigu District	19.26	9.93	9.33	18.31	0.95	95.07
蒸湘区	Zhengxiang District	19.38	10.10	9.28	16.86	2.52	87.00
南岳区	Nanyue District	5.28	2.70	2.58	4.69	0.59	88.83
衡阳县	Hengyang County	111.78	59.20	52.58	16.92	94.86	15.14
衡南县	Hengnan County	100.20	52.92	47.28	12.92	87.28	12.89
衡山县	Hengshan County	40.46	20.96	19.50	5.17	35.29	12.78
衡东县	Hengdong County	66.37	34.37	32.00	8.67	57.70	13.06
祁东县	Qidong County	91.89	48.48	43.41	15.44	76.45	16.80
耒阳市	Leiyang City	123.95	66.29	57.66	27.03	96.92	21.81
常宁市	Changning City	84.71	45.63	39.08	22.75	61.96	26.86

18-1 续表1

市县名称	Cities and Counties	总人口（万人） Total Population (10 000 persons)	男 Male	女 Female	城镇人口 Urban	乡村人口 Rural	城市化水平(%) City Level (%)
邵阳市	**Shaoyang City**	**726.85**	**378.65**	**348.20**	**170.76**	**556.09**	**23.49**
双清区	Shuangqing District	25.12	13.05	12.07	25.12		100.00
大祥区	Daxiang District	28.32	14.27	14.05	28.32		100.00
北塔区	Beita District	7.42	3.69	3.73	7.42		100.00
邵东县	Shaodong County	117.63	61.62	56.01	13.25	104.39	11.26
新邵县	Xinshao County	72.35	38.03	34.32	6.42	65.93	8.87
邵阳县	Shaoyang County	95.17	48.83	46.34	9.10	86.08	9.56
隆回县	Longhui County	110.92	58.23	52.69	11.03	99.88	9.95
洞口县	Dongkou County	78.48	41.13	37.35	9.43	69.05	12.01
绥宁县	Shuining County	34.62	17.93	16.69	3.68	30.94	10.64
新宁县	Xinning County	58.70	30.99	27.71	5.94	52.76	10.12
城步县	Chengbu County	25.41	13.02	12.39	5.19	20.22	20.42
武冈市	Wugang City	72.69	37.86	34.83	45.86	26.83	63.09
岳阳市	**Yueyang City**	**523.65**	**273.93**	**249.72**	**172.80**	**350.85**	**33.00**
岳阳楼区	Yueyanglou District	52.70	27.60	25.10	42.23	10.47	80.13
云溪区	Yunxi District	16.02	8.31	7.71	10.73	5.29	66.98
君山区	Junshan District	22.18	12.00	10.18	7.32	14.86	33.00
岳阳县	Yueyang County	75.04	39.28	35.76	19.51	55.53	26.00
华容县	Huarong County	71.62	36.75	34.87	18.62	53.00	26.00
湘阴县	Xiangying County	68.95	36.03	32.92	17.93	51.02	26.00
平江县	Pingjiang County	99.18	52.35	46.83	25.79	73.39	26.00
汨罗市	Miluo City	70.34	36.65	33.69	18.29	52.05	26.00
临湘市	Linxiang City	47.62	24.96	22.66	12.38	35.24	26.00
常德市	**Changde City**	**596.04**	**306.36**	**289.68**	**167.73**	**428.31**	**28.14**
武陵区	Wuling District	44.25	22.51	21.74	40.38	3.87	91.25
鼎城区	Dingcheng District	90.45	46.18	44.27	15.25	75.20	16.86
安乡县	Anxiang County	57.78	29.18	28.60	16.76	41.02	29.01
汉寿县	Hanshou County	80.59	42.30	38.29	16.92	63.67	21.00
澧　县	Li County	87.81	45.01	42.80	20.95	66.86	23.86
临澧县	Linli County	43.55	22.39	21.16	9.72	33.83	22.32
桃源县	Taoyuan County	97.34	50.28	47.06	21.11	76.23	21.69
石门县	Shimen County	68.45	35.11	33.34	12.40	56.05	18.12
津市市	Jinshi City	25.82	13.40	12.42	14.24	11.58	55.15
张家界市	**Zhangjiajie City**	**156.29**	**80.78**	**75.51**	**40.08**	**116.20**	**25.65**
永定区	Yongding District	41.58	21.39	20.19	18.02	23.56	43.35
武陵源区	Wulingyuan District	4.47	2.32	2.15	2.12	2.34	47.51
慈利县	Cili County	67.41	34.86	32.55	12.21	55.20	18.11
桑植县	Sangzhi County	42.83	22.21	20.62	7.73	35.10	18.05
益阳市	**Yiyang City**	**453.16**	**232.75**	**220.41**	**127.32**	**325.84**	**28.10**
资阳区	Ziyang District	40.90	21.06	19.84	19.56	21.34	47.82
赫山区	Heshan District	85.69	44.24	41.45	41.25	44.44	48.14
南县	Nan County	74.37	38.11	36.26	16.98	57.39	22.83
桃江县	Taojiang County	82.15	42.00	40.15	12.32	69.83	15.00
安化县	Anhua County	95.11	49.75	45.36	12.76	82.35	13.42
沅江市	Yuanjiang City	74.94	37.59	37.35	24.45	50.49	32.63

18-1 续表2

市县名称	Cities and Counties	总人口（万人） Total Population (10 000 persons)	男 Male	女 Female	城镇人口 Urban	乡村人口 Rural	城市化水平(%) City Level (%)
郴州市	**Chenzhou City**	**455.46**	**238.48**	**216.98**	**121.59**	**333.87**	**26.70**
北湖区	Beihu District	28.84	15.13	13.71	18.49	10.35	64.11
苏仙区	Suxian District	34.17	17.89	16.28	14.98	19.19	43.84
桂阳县	Guiyang County	77.80	39.96	37.84	19.69	58.11	25.31
宜章县	Yizhang County	55.52	29.74	25.78	10.99	44.53	19.79
永兴县	Yongxing County	63.66	33.33	30.33	12.05	51.61	18.93
嘉禾县	Jiahe County	33.88	17.95	15.92	6.32	27.56	18.65
临武县	Linwu County	31.39	16.56	14.83	5.70	25.69	18.16
汝城县	Rucheng County	36.70	19.40	17.30	6.62	30.08	18.04
桂东县	Guidong County	17.09	9.07	8.02	3.05	14.04	17.85
安仁县	Anren County	39.82	20.77	19.05	7.12	32.70	17.88
资兴市	Zixing City	36.59	18.68	17.91	16.58	20.01	45.31
永州市	**Yongzhou City**	**566.47**	**297.31**	**269.16**	**121.65**	**444.82**	**21.48**
芝山区	Zhishan District	58.00	30.85	27.15	18.78	39.22	32.38
冷水滩区	Lengshuitan District	49.58	25.67	23.91	22.73	26.85	45.85
祁阳县	Qiyang County	98.14	51.46	46.68	20.98	77.16	21.37
东安县	Dongan County	58.26	30.23	28.03	8.62	49.65	14.79
双牌县	Shuangpai County	16.99	9.22	7.77	3.07	13.93	18.06
道县	Dao County	65.84	33.98	31.86	14.57	51.28	22.12
江永县	Jiangyong County	24.77	12.71	12.06	5.73	19.04	23.14
宁远县	Ningyuan County	77.42	41.53	35.89	9.85	67.57	12.72
蓝山县	Lanshan County	35.11	18.42	16.69	5.50	29.61	15.66
新田县	Xintian County	37.19	19.37	17.82	5.19	32.00	13.97
江华县	Jianghua County	45.16	23.87	21.29	6.64	38.52	14.70
怀化市	**Huaihua City**	**486.60**	**253.03**	**233.57**	**111.64**	**374.96**	**22.94**
鹤城区	Hecheng District	31.66	16.29	15.37	27.04	4.62	85.40
中方县	Zhongfang County	25.93	13.58	12.35	2.88	23.06	11.09
沅陵县	Yuanling County	64.04	33.31	30.73	9.65	54.39	15.07
辰溪县	Chenxi County	51.19	26.48	24.71	10.29	40.90	20.09
溆浦县	Xupu County	84.58	44.16	40.42	12.91	71.67	15.26
会同县	Huitong County	34.41	17.83	16.58	4.74	29.67	13.77
麻阳县	Mayang County	35.93	18.77	17.16	4.50	31.43	12.53
新晃县	Xinhuang County	25.36	13.66	11.70	4.00	21.36	15.77
芷江县	Zhijiang County	35.27	18.45	16.82	4.92	30.35	13.95
靖州县	Jingzhou County	25.66	13.24	12.42	8.97	16.69	34.97
通道县	Tongdao County	21.88	11.32	10.56	3.80	18.08	17.37
洪江市	Hongjiang City	43.26	22.15	21.11	12.38	30.88	28.62
洪江区	Hongjiang District	7.43	3.79	3.64	5.57	1.86	74.97
娄底市	**Loudi City**	**399.88**	**207.33**	**192.55**	**101.32**	**298.56**	**25.34**
娄星区	Louxing District	39.87	20.63	19.24	27.84	12.03	69.83
双峰县	Shuangfeng County	88.73	46.01	42.72	11.18	77.55	12.60
新化县	Xinhua County	128.86	67.08	61.78	16.88	111.98	13.10
冷水江市	Lengshuijiang District	35.33	18.23	17.10	17.67	17.66	50.01
涟源市	Liangyuan City	107.09	55.38	51.71	27.75	79.34	25.91
湘西自治州	**West Hunan A.P**	**262.43**	**135.86**	**126.57**	**57.92**	**204.51**	**22.07**
吉首市	Jishou City	27.85	14.43	13.42	15.12	12.74	54.28
泸溪县	Louxi County	27.99	14.43	13.56	5.85	22.15	20.89
凤凰县	Fenghuang County	36.92	19.06	17.86	5.63	31.29	15.25
花垣县	Huayuan County	27.08	13.80	13.28	3.61	23.47	13.33
保靖县	Baojing County	27.80	15.05	12.75	4.16	23.64	14.96
古丈县	Guzhang County	13.69	7.13	6.56	2.53	11.16	18.48
永顺县	Yongshun County	48.28	24.68	23.60	10.19	38.09	21.11
龙山县	Longshan County	52.81	27.28	25.53	10.83	41.98	20.51

18-2 各市、州、县计划生育指标(2001年)

Indicators of Family Plan (2001)

市县名称	City and County	出生率(‰) Birth Rate (‰)	死亡率(‰) Death Rate (‰)	自然增长率(‰) Natural Growth Rate (‰)	计划内生育率(%) Birth Within Plan Rate (%)	多孩率(%) More Childrens Rate (%)	已婚育龄妇女人数(万人) Married Women at Child-Bearing Age (10 000 persons)	节育率(%) Contra-ceptive Rate (%)	措施落实率(%) Contra-ception Using Rate (%)	节育手术(万例) Birth Control Opera-tion. (10 000 cases)
长沙市	**Changsha City**	**10.80**	**6.84**	**3.96**	**97.82**	**0.33**	**125.66**	**90.15**	**96.30**	**8.84**
芙蓉区	Furong District	9.37	5.82	3.56	98.98	0.10	6.95	86.68	92.59	0.22
天心区	Tianxin District	7.13	5.69	1.44	98.78	0.04	5.79	85.80	91.64	0.23
岳麓区	Yuelu District	8.96	5.11	3.85	99.12	0.07	6.18	83.69	89.40	0.32
开福区	Kaifu District	8.64	7.16	1.48	99.01	0.18	7.86	89.09	95.16	0.32
雨花区	Yuhua District	10.02	6.37	3.65	98.76	0.05	7.86	86.16	92.03	0.34
长沙县	Changsha County	10.60	7.36	3.25	97.98	0.14	16.81	90.94	97.14	1.33
望城县	Wangcheng County	10.61	6.75	3.86	97.33	0.38	16.10	90.93	97.13	1.15
浏阳市	Liuyang City	11.97	7.33	4.63	96.45	0.74	29.10	90.70	96.89	2.71
宁乡县	Ningxiang County	12.48	7.10	5.37	98.23	0.24	29.02	90.97	97.17	2.22
株洲市	**Zhuzhou City**	**11.06**	**6.96**	**4.10**	**97.32**	**0.30**	**85.16**	**90.66**	**96.84**	**5.82**
荷塘区	Hetang District	12.24	6.66	5.58	98.81	0.19	4.24	90.87	97.06	0.22
芦淞区	Lousong District	12.33	8.24	4.09	98.96	0.22	4.30	86.63	92.54	0.15
石峰区	Shifeng District	10.56	6.94	3.62	99.09	0.19	5.30	86.56	92.47	0.45
天元区	Tianyuan District	11.06	6.92	4.14	97.98	0.34	2.29	91.11	97.32	0.17
醴陵市	Liling City	10.33	7.05	3.28	97.24	0.37	22.56	90.83	97.02	1.33
株洲县	Zhuzhou County	9.52	6.86	2.67	97.72	0.49	10.99	90.95	97.15	0.80
攸 县	You County	11.30	6.80	4.50	96.79	0.21	18.62	90.97	97.17	1.48
茶陵县	Chaling County	12.49	6.54	5.95	95.68	0.32	12.88	90.85	97.04	0.93
炎陵县	Yanling County	11.19	7.62	3.57	97.96	0.15	3.98	91.24	97.46	0.29
湘潭市	**Xiangtan City**	**11.24**	**6.95**	**4.28**	**95.50**	**0.76**	**61.19**	**91.15**	**97.36**	**3.73**
雨湖区	Yuhu District	10.05	6.43	3.62	98.27	0.20	7.41	90.33	96.49	0.28
岳塘区	Yuetang District	10.92	6.66	4.26	97.01	0.22	8.07	90.76	96.95	0.31
韶山市	Shaoshan City	10.45	7.22	3.23	98.96	0.28	2.26	90.95	97.14	0.13
湘乡市	Xiangxiang City	12.07	7.32	4.75	95.01	1.14	19.05	90.96	97.16	1.26
湘潭县	Xiangtan County	11.10	6.89	4.22	94.42	0.78	24.39	91.41	97.64	1.75
衡阳市	**Hengyang City**	**13.16**	**7.14**	**6.02**	**91.15**	**1.24**	**155.20**	**90.02**	**96.24**	**12.02**
珠辉区	Zhuhui District	10.31	6.72	3.59	98.70	0.47	6.04	90.07	98.41	0.19
雁峰区	Yanfeng District	10.60	6.66	3.94	98.45	0.36	4.33	90.18	96.32	0.16
石鼓区	Shigu District	10.15	6.60	3.55	98.62	0.42	5.00	90.90	97.10	0.16
蒸湘区	Zhengxiang District	10.86	6.50	4.36	94.44	0.99	4.42	90.17	96.32	0.25
南岳区	Nanyue District	11.99	6.98	5.01	97.47	0.32	1.16	90.83	97.03	0.09

市县名称	City and County	出生率(‰) Birth Rate (‰)	死亡率(‰) Death Rate (‰)	自然增长率(‰) Natural Growth Rate (‰)	计划内生育率(%) Birth Within Plan Rate (%)	多孩率(%) More Childrens Rate (%)	已婚育龄妇女人数(万人) Married Women at Child-Bearing Age (10 000 persons)	节育率(%) Contra-ceptive Rate (%)	措施落实率(%) Contra-ception Using Rate (%)	节育手术(万例) Birth Control Opera-tion (10 000 cases)
耒阳市	Leiyang City	12.98	6.64	6.35	93.14	0.53	25.45	89.64	95.75	2.06
衡阳县	Hengyang County	13.90	7.73	6.17	92.87	0.46	25.83	89.08	95.15	2.26
衡南县	Hengnan County	13.55	7.51	6.04	91.91	2.89	22.57	90.59	96.76	1.74
衡山县	Hengshan County	13.66	7.20	6.47	85.75	1.85	8.65	90.98	97.18	0.75
衡东县	Hengdong County	13.31	7.55	5.76	91.45	0.64	14.58	88.77	94.83	1.26
常宁市	Changning City	14.38	6.89	7.49	80.83	2.52	17.46	88.80	94.85	1.53
祁东县	Qidong County	13.02	7.05	5.98	93.19	0.68	19.73	90.78	96.97	1.55
邵阳市	**Shaoyang City**	**12.84**	**6.78**	**6.06**	**91.67**	**1.20**	**153.30**	**90.87**	**97.07**	**10.64**
双清区	Shuangqing District	14.15	7.35	6.80	96.96	0.43	6.73	90.80	96.99	0.24
大祥区	Daxiang District	12.82	6.43	6.39	95.30	0.88	6.45	90.62	96.80	0.33
北塔区	Beita District	13.91	7.94	5.97	95.16	0.66	1.73	90.78	96.97	0.15
邵东县	Shaodong County	13.01	6.82	6.19	89.81	0.74	26.39	90.82	97.01	1.77
新邵县	Xinshao County	11.95	7.02	4.93	90.31	0.97	14.58	90.79	96.97	0.87
邵阳县	Shaoyang County	14.15	6.43	7.72	88.31	2.18	18.58	90.85	97.05	1.28
隆回县	Longhui County	13.14	6.87	6.27	92.71	2.21	22.61	90.85	97.04	1.88
洞口县	Dongkou County	13.30	6.61	6.68	89.49	0.79	16.54	90.45	96.61	1.37
武冈市	Wugang City	12.62	6.94	5.68	92.85	0.49	16.25	90.58	96.75	1.11
绥宁县	Shuining County	11.90	6.80	5.10	96.60	0.62	7.11	90.97	97.17	0.51
新宁县	Xinning County	10.75	6.50	4.25	93.90	0.90	11.48	90.89	97.09	0.82
城步县	Chengbu County	12.19	6.94	5.25	95.20	1.36	4.85	90.87	97.07	0.31
岳阳市	**Yueyang City**	**11.62**	**6.98**	**4.64**	**95.08**	**1.24**	**112.25**	**91.08**	**97.36**	**8.17**
岳阳楼区	Yueyanglou District	12.89	5.97	6.92	97.63	0.29	8.60	89.78	95.90	0.52
云溪区	Yunxi District	14.25	6.77	7.49	98.28	0.48	3.50	90.69	96.87	0.28
君山区	Junshan District	9.80	7.09	2.71	97.29	0.86	4.33	91.47	99.52	0.29
汨罗市	Miluo City	11.05	7.07	3.97	94.00	1.18	18.34	90.79	96.98	1.27
岳阳县	Yueyang County	11.79	7.17	4.61	97.52	0.71	15.86	91.01	97.21	1.21
临湘市	Linxiang City	11.28	6.93	4.36	96.31	0.81	10.22	90.96	97.16	0.77
华容县	Huarong County	11.57	6.99	4.58	97.47	0.50	16.14	91.42	97.65	1.28
湘阴县	Xiangyin County	11.87	7.52	4.35	92.45	1.83	15.13	90.91	97.11	1.09
平江县	Pingjiang County	11.29	6.98	4.31	90.92	2.83	20.14	90.87	97.07	1.45
常德市	**Changde City**	**9.65**	**7.07**	**2.58**	**96.31**	**0.13**	**136.48**	**91.08**	**97.29**	**8.75**
武陵区	Wuling District	9.96	6.95	3.01	98.58	0.07	9.78	90.83	97.02	0.43
鼎城区	Dingcheng District	8.31	6.95	1.36	92.33	0.08	21.01	90.90	97.09	1.16
津市市	Jinshi City	9.58	6.93	2.65	98.75	0.04	5.66	90.82	97.01	0.23
安乡县	Anxiang County	7.62	6.94	0.68	97.65	0.05	11.97	91.15	97.36	0.83

18-2 续表 2 continued

市县名称	City and County	出生率(‰) Birth Rate (‰)	死亡率(‰) Death Rate (‰)	自然增长率(‰) Natural Growth Rate (‰)	计划内生育率(%) Birth Within Plan Rate (%)	多孩率(%) More Childrens Rate (%)	已婚育龄妇女人数(万人) Married Women at Child-Bearing Age (10 000 persons)	节育率(%) Contra-ceptive Rate (%)	措施落实率(%) Contra-ception Using Rate (%)	节育手术(万例) Birth Control Opera-tion (10 000 cases)
汉寿县	Hanshou County	9.71	6.98	2.73	92.52	0.51	16.76	90.83	97.02	1.54
澧　县	Li County	10.94	7.50	3.44	97.18	0.10	22.55	91.28	97.50	1.83
临澧县	Linli County	9.44	7.18	2.26	98.68	0.05	9.52	90.95	97.15	0.56
桃源县	Taoyuan County	9.95	6.98	2.96	97.24	0.10	21.95	90.97	97.17	1.13
石门县	Shimen County	10.88	7.10	3.77	97.57	0.05	17.28	90.76	96.94	1.04
张家界市	**Zhangjiajie City**	**12.23**	**7.24**	**4.98**	**95.30**	**1.46**	**32.25**	**90.91**	**97.10**	**2.42**
永定区	Yongding District	13.96	6.95	7.01	96.73	0.93	8.30	90.90	97.09	0.68
武陵源区	Wulingyuan District	12.02	6.60	5.41	98.53	0.18	0.95	90.12	96.26	0.09
慈利县	Cili County	9.78	7.33	2.45	96.49	0.33	14.70	91.12	97.33	0.94
桑植县	Sangzhi County	14.44	7.47	6.97	92.41	3.29	8.29	90.63	96.81	0.71
益阳市	**Yiyang City**	**10.30**	**6.61**	**3.69**	**96.36**	**0.49**	**94.07**	**91.14**	**97.35**	**6.27**
资阳区	Ziyang District	11.47	6.92	4.55	96.90	1.57	9.05	91.04	97.24	0.56
赫山区	Heshan District	10.69	6.64	4.04	97.45	0.26	17.37	90.99	97.20	1.01
沅江市	Yuanjiang City	8.85	6.61	2.24	97.55	0.20	15.32	90.99	97.19	1.00
南县	Nan County	8.96	6.27	2.68	97.13	0.31	15.39	91.13	97.34	1.28
桃江县	Taojiang County	11.03	6.93	4.10	95.49	0.56	17.86	90.91	97.10	1.28
安化县	Anhua County	10.96	6.41	4.55	94.68	0.43	19.08	90.87	97.07	1.14
郴州市	**Chenzhou City**	**12.32**	**6.79**	**5.53**	**94.70**	**0.94**	**91.70**	**90.92**	**97.12**	**5.71**
北湖区	Beihu District	11.61	6.17	5.43	97.23	0.36	6.34	89.96	96.10	0.31
苏仙区	Suxian District	11.12	6.34	4.79	97.46	1.03	7.09	90.81	97.00	0.43
资兴市	Zixing City	10.72	7.04	3.67	97.92	0.31	7.97	90.84	97.04	0.49
桂阳县	Guiyang County	12.79	6.91	5.88	94.75	0.36	14.80	91.26	97.48	1.13
永兴县	Yongxing County	11.64	6.25	5.38	95.37	0.57	12.60	90.86	97.06	0.66
宜章县	Yizhang County	13.27	6.88	6.39	88.87	3.45	10.52	90.79	96.98	0.59
嘉禾县	Jiahe County	13.39	6.95	6.44	92.68	0.93	6.83	90.80	96.99	0.51
临武县	Linwu County	11.15	6.86	4.29	95.84	0.40	6.01	90.94	97.14	0.34
汝城县	Rucheng County	14.06	7.58	6.48	95.00	0.68	7.50	90.97	97.17	0.53
桂东县	Guidong County	11.53	7.87	3.67	96.24	0.86	3.33	91.32	97.55	0.24
安仁县	Anren County	12.93	6.53	6.40	96.02	0.41	8.71	90.89	97.09	0.48
永州市	**Yongzhou City**	**10.80**	**6.84**	**3.96**	**93.13**	**0.92**	**110.93**	**91.02**	**97.23**	**7.26**
芝山区	Zhishan District	10.69	6.82	3.86	96.37	0.36	11.40	90.85	97.04	0.61
冷水滩区	Lengshuitan District	11.38	6.61	4.78	96.66	0.29	9.91	90.89	97.08	0.71
东安县	Dongan County	10.63	6.93	3.70	94.59	0.54	11.51	90.81	97.00	0.62
道县	Dao County	10.41	7.24	3.17	91.94	1.64	12.62	90.88	97.08	0.75

18-2 续表3 continued

市县名称	City and County	出生率(‰) Birth Rate (‰)	死亡率(‰) Death Rate (‰)	自然增长率(‰) Natural Growth Rate (‰)	计划内生育率(%) Birth Within Plan Rate (%)	多孩率(%) More Childrens Rate (%)	已婚育龄妇女人数(万人) Married Women at Child-Bearing Age (10 000 persons)	节育率(%) Contraceptive Rate (%)	措施落实率(%) Contraception Using Rate (%)	节育手术(万例) Birth Control Operation (10 000 cases)
宁远县	Ningyuan County	9.66	6.53	3.12	92.65	0.59	14.50	91.16	97.38	1.10
江永县	Jiangyong County	10.47	6.62	3.85	96.41	0.46	4.77	90.91	97.11	0.33
江华县	Jianghua County	12.97	6.91	6.06	91.95	1.24	8.84	90.78	96.97	0.71
蓝山县	Lanshan County	11.86	6.85	5.01	86.27	1.33	6.86	90.85	97.04	0.42
新田县	Xintian County	7.85	7.05	0.80	95.06	0.27	7.32	90.47	96.64	0.45
双牌县	Shuangpai County	9.51	6.98	2.54	95.72	0.81	3.29	90.95	97.15	0.22
祁阳县	Qiyang County	11.90	6.82	5.08	91.44	1.50	19.91	90.52	96.69	1.34
怀化市	**Huaihua City**	**13.13**	**6.91**	**6.22**	**95.83**	**0.96**	**101.86**	**91.00**	**97.20**	**7.76**
鹤城区	Hecheng District	15.61	6.55	9.06	97.54	0.63	6.59	91.30	97.52	0.43
洪江市	Hongjiang City	12.20	6.95	5.25	96.49	0.42	9.71	90.80	96.99	0.64
洪江区	Hongjiang District	10.12	6.79	3.34	98.61	0.25	2.12	91.94	98.21	0.12
中方县	Zhongfang County	13.99	7.72	6.28	95.20	0.97	5.68	91.22	97.44	0.49
沅陵县	Yuanling County	10.82	7.35	3.47	97.04	0.49	12.38	91.25	97.47	0.99
辰溪县	Chenxi County	11.46	6.75	4.71	93.85	1.40	10.00	91.02	97.23	0.79
溆浦县	Xupu County	12.79	6.73	6.06	96.15	0.62	17.63	91.13	97.35	1.27
麻阳县	Mayang County	15.99	6.52	9.48	96.18	0.53	7.02	89.89	96.02	0.61
新晃县	Xinhuang County	12.67	7.27	5.40	97.19	0.87	5.39	89.39	95.49	0.50
芷江县	Zhijiang County	16.36	6.95	9.41	92.28	2.36	8.34	90.95	97.15	0.62
会同县	Huitong County	12.37	6.80	5.57	96.44	0.94	7.67	90.16	96.31	0.59
靖州县	Jingzhou County	13.02	6.74	6.28	97.05	1.14	5.07	89.94	96.07	0.33
通道县	Tongdao County	15.33	6.75	8.58	94.45	1.89	4.25	87.14	93.08	0.39
娄底市	**Loudi City**	**13.05**	**6.89**	**6.16**	**89.98**	**0.89**	**82.64**	**91.10**	**97.32**	**5.97**
娄星区	Louxing District	11.87	6.78	5.09	97.24	0.17	8.43	90.82	97.01	0.53
冷水江市	Lengshuijiang District	12.08	6.87	5.20	96.91	0.40	8.12	89.12	95.20	0.42
涟源市	Liangyuan City	13.13	6.95	6.18	85.10	0.88	22.46	91.02	97.23	1.65
双峰县	Shuangfeng County	13.08	6.75	6.33	95.36	0.61	19.29	91.19	97.41	1.33
新化县	Xinhua County	13.62	6.98	6.63	86.67	1.40	24.35	90.88	97.07	2.04
湘西自治州	**West Hunan A.P**	**13.82**	**6.79**	**7.02**	**89.81**	**2.46**	**48.62**	**90.18**	**97.30**	**4.90**
吉首市	Jishou City	11.73	6.59	5.14	93.88	1.17	5.08	90.85	97.04	0.47
泸溪县	Louxi County	12.80	6.73	6.07	91.62	1.98	5.12	90.80	96.99	0.48
凤凰县	Fenghuang County	12.99	6.77	6.21	89.82	1.81	6.43	90.82	97.01	0.62
花垣县	Huayuan County	12.94	6.99	5.95	87.76	2.98	4.98	90.84	97.04	0.47
保靖县	Baojing County	15.82	6.54	9.28	88.22	3.77	5.37	90.80	96.99	0.58
古丈县	Guzhang County	12.60	7.55	5.05	90.81	1.98	2.42	90.42	96.59	0.27
永顺县	Yongshun County	16.48	6.68	9.79	89.36	1.69	8.96	87.16	98.42	0.99
龙山县	Longshan County	13.27	6.89	6.38	89.33	3.63	10.27	89.53	95.64	1.02

18-3 各市、州、县从业人员年末人数(2001年)

Employment at the Year-end (2001)

单位：万人 (10 000 persons)

市县名称	City and County	从业人员人数 Number of Employed Persons	在岗职工 Staff and Workers on the Job	#国有经济 State-owned Units	#城镇集体经济 Urban Collective Owned Units	城镇个体从业人员 Employed Persons in Urban Self Employed Individuals	城镇私营企业从业人员 Employed Persons in Urban Private Enterprises	农村从业人员 Rural Employed Persons	其他从业人员 Other Employed Persons	离开本单位仍保留劳动关系的职工 Staff and Workers Left Self-Unit and Remind Labor Relations
长沙市	**Changsha City**	**347.23**	**59.40**	**42.43**	**4.99**	**23.80**	**11.35**	**232.91**	**3.09**	**16.67**
长沙市区	Urban District	97.59	44.49	31.26	3.41	13.57	9.08	14.67	2.86	12.93
长沙县	Changsha County	45.19	3.69	2.40	0.26	0.41	0.11	40.37	0.01	0.59
望城县	Wangcheng County	38.67	3.16	2.15	0.57	0.64	0.13	34.14	0.00	0.60
宁乡县	Ningxiang County	85.73	4.21	3.52	0.30	4.58	0.30	74.80	0.17	1.67
浏阳市	Liuyang City	80.05	3.85	3.10	0.45	4.60	1.74	68.94	0.05	0.88
株洲市	**Zhuzhou City**	**208.71**	**29.95**	**21.08**	**3.94**	**11.51**	**6.01**	**147.50**	**1.59**	**12.16**
株洲市区	Urban District	43.16	18.71	12.65	2.24	5.51	1.34	9.61	0.99	7.00
株洲县	Zhuzhou County	23.80	1.49	1.13	0.31	1.02	0.22	20.72	0.10	0.24
攸县	You County	43.76	2.80	2.41	0.32	1.21	0.24	37.96	0.11	1.45
茶陵县	Chaling County	29.46	2.05	1.74	0.22	0.92	0.12	25.09	0.09	1.19
炎陵县	Yanling County	10.02	1.01	0.83	0.12	0.19	0.01	8.19	0.04	0.58
醴陵市	Liling City	58.51	3.89	2.31	0.72	2.66	4.07	45.93	0.26	1.70
湘潭市	**Xiangtan City**	**167.00**	**24.33**	**18.14**	**3.03**	**9.88**	**2.92**	**119.74**	**0.80**	**9.32**
湘潭市区	Urban District	39.85	15.52	12.29	1.83	7.32	2.53	6.17	0.68	7.62
湘潭县	Xiangtan County	65.63	3.36	2.76	0.52	0.52	0.18	60.65	0.02	0.90
湘乡市	Xiangxiang City	55.31	4.73	2.51	0.63	1.48	0.18	48.18	0.10	0.64
韶山市	Shaoshan City	6.22	0.72	0.58	0.06	0.56	0.03	4.74	0.01	0.16
衡阳市	**Hengyang City**	**368.23**	**40.77**	**30.06**	**5.46**	**13.76**	**2.76**	**292.99**	**1.65**	**16.30**
衡阳市区	Urban District	40.91	15.83	10.71	2.00	4.56	2.09	8.61	0.72	9.11
#南岳区	Nanyue District	2.81	0.60	0.47	0.13	0.40	0.01	1.73	0.01	0.05
衡阳县	Hengyang County	63.34	3.86	2.99	0.84	1.35	0.04	57.21	0.07	0.81
衡南县	Hengnan County	50.41	4.20	3.44	0.66	1.15	0.08	43.98	0.16	0.84
衡山县	Hengshan County	23.63	1.77	1.48	0.13	1.30	0.12	19.91	0.10	0.43
衡东县	Hengdong County	34.77	2.33	1.83	0.38	0.63	0.11	30.80	0.14	0.78
祁东县	Qidong County	47.12	3.18	2.60	0.56	0.86	0.02	41.65	0.34	1.07
耒阳市	Leiyang City	62.87	5.46	3.40	0.38	2.39	0.26	52.99	0.05	1.72
常宁市	Changning City	45.18	4.15	3.60	0.51	1.52	0.05	37.84	0.07	1.54
邵阳市	**Shaoyang City**	**411.00**	**31.01**	**26.27**	**2.97**	**16.03**	**2.90**	**345.64**	**0.87**	**14.56**
邵阳市区	Urban District	35.58	9.34	7.53	1.29	1.67	0.74	16.50	0.34	7.00
邵东县	Shaodong County	56.87	3.85	3.48	0.28	2.27	0.50	48.99	0.00	1.25
新邵县	Xinshao County	42.48	2.36	1.96	0.20	2.97	1.13	34.79	0.11	1.12
邵阳县	Shaoyang County	53.38	2.29	2.08	0.10	0.60	0.04	50.01	0.02	0.43
隆回县	Longhui County	59.35	2.66	2.21	0.21	2.84	0.06	53.06	0.11	0.61
洞口县	Dongkou County	49.46	2.69	2.46	0.18	1.79	0.05	43.59	0.10	1.24
绥宁县	Shuining County	19.80	1.55	1.13	0.12	0.55	0.10	17.16	0.04	0.40
新宁县	Xinning County	34.05	2.01	1.68	0.20	0.72	0.04	30.45	0.04	0.80
城步县	Chengbu County	14.29	1.70	1.54	0.08	0.23	0.06	11.76	0.03	0.52
武冈市	Wugang City	45.74	2.56	2.20	0.30	2.40	0.18	39.34	0.08	1.19

单位：万人　　18-3 续表 1　continued　　(10 000 persons)

市县名称	City and County	从业人员人数 Number of Employed Persons	在岗职工 Staff and Workers on the Job	#国有经济 State-owned Units	#城镇集体经济 Urban Collective Owned Units	城镇个体从业人员 Employed Persons in Urban Self Employed Individuals	城镇私营企业从业人员 Employed Persons in Urban Private Enterprises	农村从业人员 Rural Employed Persons	其他从业人员 Other Employed Persons	离开本单位仍保留劳动关系的职工 Staff and Workers Left Self-Unit and Remind Labor Relations
岳阳市	**Yueyang City**	**256.57**	**34.14**	**29.09**	**3.15**	**13.55**	**2.82**	**196.34**	**1.13**	**8.60**
岳阳市区	Urban District	40.10	15.27	12.66	1.31	5.24	1.74	14.07	0.51	3.28
#岳阳楼区	Yueyanglou District	8.87	0.77	0.59	0.18	2.78	0.19	4.03	0.00	0.09
云溪区	Yunxi District	5.52	0.79	0.58	0.17	0.43	0.09	4.16	0.03	0.01
君山区	Junshan District	6.89	1.36	1.20	0.11	0.00	0.00	5.38	0.00	0.15
岳阳县	Yueyang County	33.76	2.10	1.84	0.15	1.61	0.19	29.37	0.03	0.46
华容县	Huarong County	36.59	2.40	2.03	0.29	1.04	0.16	31.63	0.11	1.26
湘阴县	Xiangyin County	37.63	2.75	2.16	0.46	1.10	0.08	32.50	0.06	1.14
平江县	Pingjiang County	50.55	2.94	2.48	0.24	0.93	0.03	45.88	0.10	0.67
汨罗市	Miluo City	34.63	6.25	5.76	0.47	1.58	0.38	25.52	0.19	0.72
临湘市	Linxiang City	23.30	2.42	2.15	0.23	2.06	0.23	17.37	0.14	1.08
常德市	**Changde City**	**300.48**	**26.03**	**21.18**	**2.02**	**9.42**	**3.25**	**253.15**	**0.44**	**8.19**
常德市区	Urban District	66.25	10.08	8.06	0.52	4.67	1.08	46.94	0.22	3.25
#武陵区	Wuling District	20.48	6.63	5.36	0.24	1.94	0.66	9.35	0.21	1.69
鼎城区	Dingchen District	45.77	3.46	2.69	0.28	2.73	0.42	37.59	0.01	1.56
安乡县	Anxiang County	27.54	2.05	1.57	0.22	0.51	0.27	23.73	0.00	0.99
汉寿县	Hanshou County	41.28	2.25	1.99	0.20	0.59	0.39	37.14	0.07	0.83
澧县	Li County	43.76	2.88	2.30	0.39	0.91	0.32	38.69	0.01	0.94
临澧县	Linli County	23.97	1.82	1.33	0.22	0.55	0.29	21.03	0.06	0.23
桃源县	Taoyuan County	51.22	2.50	2.32	0.14	0.80	0.31	46.91	0.04	0.67
石门县	Shimen County	35.68	2.64	2.07	0.23	0.87	0.32	31.20	0.03	0.62
津市市	Jinshi City	10.77	1.80	1.54	0.10	0.52	0.27	7.51	0.00	0.67
张家界市	**Zhangjiajie City**	**81.94**	**8.07**	**6.30**	**0.91**	**2.40**	**1.09**	**68.78**	**0.09**	**1.52**
市区	Urban District	24.40	3.59	2.82	0.24	1.58	0.71	17.66	0.05	0.83
#永定区	Yongding District	19.43	1.90	1.34	0.21	1.18	0.22	15.39	0.02	0.72
武陵源区	Wulingyuan District	2.95	0.47	0.38	0.01	0.10	0.06	2.27	0.02	0.03
慈利县	Cili County	35.42	2.89	2.06	0.62	0.70	0.26	31.07	0.01	0.50
桑植县	Sangzhi County	22.12	1.59	1.42	0.05	0.12	0.13	20.05	0.04	0.19
益阳市	**Yiyang City**	**252.05**	**25.44**	**21.46**	**2.31**	**7.26**	**2.67**	**203.55**	**1.56**	**11.56**
益阳市区	Urban District	82.06	13.26	10.95	1.06	3.81	2.18	57.03	0.63	5.14
#资阳区	Ziyang District	21.70	1.40	1.16	0.18	0.60	0.07	18.51	0.08	1.04
赫山区	Heshan District	40.38	2.54	2.09	0.44	2.44	0.25	34.24	0.01	0.90
南县	Nan County	36.20	2.51	1.98	0.46	0.78	0.08	31.45	0.01	1.37
桃江县	Taojiang County	45.62	2.87	2.33	0.32	0.81	0.15	40.19	0.10	1.49
安化县	Anhua County	47.75	2.52	2.27	0.26	0.95	0.10	42.93	0.08	1.18
沅江市	Yuanjiang City	40.42	4.28	3.94	0.21	0.91	0.15	31.95	0.75	2.37
郴州市	**Chenzhou City**	**256.98**	**25.52**	**21.39**	**2.09**	**14.66**	**1.57**	**207.89**	**0.87**	**6.46**
郴州市区	Urban District	34.97	8.84	7.10	0.51	3.20	0.80	18.84	0.41	2.85
#北湖区	Beihu District	10.79	1.41	0.92	0.24	0.56	0.03	7.80	0.04	0.94
苏仙区	Suxian District	12.98	1.10	0.95	0.10	0.48	0.02	11.04	0.07	0.26
桂阳县	Guiyang County	44.28	2.27	2.09	0.15	1.91	0.07	39.54	0.06	0.42
宜章县	Yizhang County	32.24	2.17	1.87	0.19	1.86	0.10	27.67	0.02	0.42
永兴县	Yongxing County	32.63	2.11	1.78	0.30	1.84	0.12	28.04	0.05	0.47
嘉禾县	Jiahe County	19.69	1.38	1.29	0.07	0.81	0.11	17.12	0.03	0.24
临武县	Linwu County	19.00	1.49	1.38	0.11	1.28	0.11	15.73	0.05	0.35
汝城县	Rucheng County	18.80	1.24	1.15	0.07	1.09	0.03	16.05	0.05	0.34

单位：万人　　18-3 续表 2 continued　　(10 000 persons)

市县名称	City and County	从业人员人数 Number of Em-polyed Persons	在岗职工 Staff and Workers on the Job	#国有经济 State-owned Units	#城镇集体经济 Urban Collec-tive Owned Units	城镇个体从业人员 Em-polyed Persons in Urban Self Em-polyed Indi-viduals	城镇私营企业从业人员 Em-polyed Persons in Urban Private Enter-prises	农村从业人员 Rural Em-polyed Persons	其他从业人员 Other Em-polyed Persons	离开本单位仍保留劳动关系的职工 Staff and Workers Left Self-Unit and Remind Labor Relations
桂东县	Guidong County	10.15	0.77	0.64	0.08	0.41	0.01	8.81	0.02	0.14
安仁县	Anren County	24.34	1.56	1.26	0.29	0.68	0.03	21.63	0.04	0.41
资兴市	Zixing City	20.88	3.68	2.81	0.34	1.57	0.19	14.47	0.15	0.83
永州市	**Yongzhou City**	**307.94**	**24.61**	**20.56**	**2.05**	**6.72**	**2.26**	**265.51**	**1.51**	**7.34**
永州市区	Urban District	57.53	8.17	6.04	0.58	2.42	0.78	42.74	0.34	1.63
#芝山区	Zhishan District	29.10	2.00	1.74	0.26	1.15	0.17	25.12	0.06	0.60
冷水滩区	Lengshuitan District	22.28	2.14	1.47	0.26	1.26	0.38	17.61	0.02	0.87
祁阳县	Qiyang County	51.59	3.93	3.38	0.31	0.61	0.58	44.82	0.29	1.36
东安县	Dongan County	27.51	1.96	1.73	0.20	1.59	0.11	23.38	0.04	0.42
双牌县	Shuangpai County	8.57	1.00	0.84	0.16	0.25	0.08	6.79	0.12	0.33
道县	Dao County	35.46	2.05	1.89	0.14	0.58	0.04	31.88	0.09	0.84
江永县	Jiangyong County	13.33	1.10	1.03	0.07	0.33	0.02	11.41	0.26	0.20
宁远县	Ningyuan Couny	46.88	2.11	1.75	0.30	0.37	0.04	43.98	0.05	0.32
蓝山县	Lanshan County	19.38	1.34	1.19	0.14	0.24	0.11	17.52	0.04	0.13
新田县	Xintian County	22.04	1.46	1.31	0.08	0.30	0.15	19.86	0.05	0.22
江华县	Jianghua County	25.66	1.49	1.41	0.07	0.02	0.35	23.14	0.23	0.42
怀化市	**Huaihua City**	**262.60**	**24.51**	**19.02**	**2.55**	**7.24**	**1.15**	**220.98**	**0.99**	**7.73**
鹤城区	Hecheng District	16.16	4.93	3.67	0.43	2.63	0.28	6.45	0.33	1.54
中方县	Zhongfang County	13.80	0.88	0.80	0.03	0.00	0.00	12.77	0.03	0.12
沅陵县	Yuanling County	34.31	2.73	2.07	0.29	1.11	0.08	29.42	0.05	0.92
辰溪县	Chenxi County	26.00	2.68	2.23	0.36	0.10	0.01	21.74	0.21	1.25
溆浦县	Xupu County	42.88	2.93	2.23	0.24	0.71	0.10	37.97	0.04	1.13
会同县	Huitong County	20.76	1.18	0.93	0.11	0.35	0.24	18.76	0.06	0.17
麻阳县	Mayang County	18.71	1.32	1.17	0.13	0.75	0.09	16.27	0.06	0.22
新晃县	Xinhuang County	15.14	1.13	0.96	0.13	0.20	0.08	13.41	0.02	0.28
芷江县	Zhijiang County	19.83	1.47	1.12	0.24	0.32	0.04	17.68	0.04	0.28
靖州县	Jingzhou County	14.23	1.25	0.97	0.16	0.21	0.07	12.43	0.03	0.23
通道县	Tongdao County	13.89	0.93	0.78	0.12	0.43	0.05	12.37	0.03	0.08
洪江市	Hongjiang City	26.90	3.07	2.08	0.30	0.43	0.11	21.70	0.07	1.52
娄底市	**Loudi City**	**221.08**	**23.57**	**19.69**	**3.04**	**7.53**	**1.87**	**179.34**	**0.93**	**7.82**
娄底市区	Urban District	22.32	6.82	5.76	0.75	2.46	0.99	9.34	0.39	1.68
#娄星区	Louxing District	14.34	1.30	0.98	0.30	2.47	0.58	9.35	0.03	0.62
冷水江市	Lengshuijiang City	51.91	2.78	2.49	0.28	0.76	0.15	47.12	0.05	1.04
涟源市	Lianyuan City	71.94	4.20	3.53	0.67	1.31	0.14	64.44	0.07	1.77
双峰县	Shuangfrng County	18.21	5.56	4.43	0.68	1.29	0.19	9.67	0.19	1.32
新化县	Xinhua County	56.69	4.21	3.48	0.66	1.71	0.40	48.77	0.22	1.38
湘西自治州	**West Hunan A.P**	**153.05**	**13.50**	**11.98**	**1.12**	**11.57**	**1.80**	**122.35**	**0.37**	**3.46**
吉首市	Jishou City	17.98	3.56	3.19	0.23	3.16	0.79	9.42	0.13	0.92
泸溪县	Luxi County	16.86	1.20	1.13	0.07	1.35	0.17	13.54	0.01	0.58
凤凰县	Fenghuang County	20.85	1.36	1.24	0.09	0.93	0.13	18.25	0.02	0.16
花垣县	Huayuan County	17.10	1.71	1.30	0.28	1.85	0.21	13.21	0.01	0.11
保靖县	Baojing County	16.73	1.12	0.98	0.10	1.63	0.12	13.50	0.03	0.33
古丈县	Guzhang County	8.85	0.66	0.58	0.08	0.90	0.00	7.04	0.03	0.22
永顺县	Yongsun County	25.65	1.92	1.75	0.14	0.11	0.06	23.05	0.05	0.45
龙山县	Longshan County	29.04	1.97	1.80	0.14	1.65	0.30	24.34	0.09	0.69
未列入地区的单位	**Not Classified by Region**	**13.10**	**10.94**	**10.94**					**1.40**	**0.76**

18-4 各市、州、县国有经济各行业在岗职工年末人数(2001年)

Employed Staff and Workers in State – Owned Units by Sector at the Year-end (2001)

单位：人 (person)

市县名称	Cities and Counties	农林牧渔业 Farming, Foresty, Animal Husbandry and Fishery	采掘业 Mining and Quarrying	制造业 Manufacturing	电力煤气及水的生产和供应 Production and Spply of Electricity Gas and Water	建筑业 Construction	地质勘查水利管理 Geological Prospecting and Water Conservancy	交通运输仓储及邮电通信业 Transport, Storage, Postal and Telecommunications	批发和零售贸易、餐饮业 Wholesale and Retail Trade, Catering Services
长沙市	**Changsha City**	**12623**	**6223**	**53242**	**7792**	**29677**	**5429**	**23982**	**25256**
长沙市区	Urban District	10286	17	40682	5354	29186	2567	17008	19877
长沙县	Changsha County	744		5525	758		963	3413	1306
望城县	Wangcheng County	318		4868	150		250	954	1575
宁乡县	Ningxiang County	975	4910	1373	482	321	1153	1633	1734
浏阳市	Liuyang City	300	1296	794	1048	170	496	974	764
株洲市	**Zhuzhou City**	**5731**	**4039**	**66215**	**6674**	**10060**	**1960**	**8607**	**11090**
株洲市区	Urban District	351	1416	57300	3654	9941	941	4497	5180
株洲县	Zhuzhou County	311	37	1625	322	8	98	494	790
攸县	You County	993	1414	4188	854		404	752	1649
茶陵县	Chaling County	2843	1031	594	450		180	765	1464
炎陵县	Yanling County	898	84	157	798		67	434	368
醴陵市	Liling City	335	57	2351	596	111	270	1665	1639
湘潭市	**Xiangtan City**	**986**	**6635**	**65050**	**2847**	**13432**	**1610**	**4565**	**7256**
湘潭市区	Urban District	346	2592	62680	1877	9530	1187	3115	3587
湘潭县	Xiangtan County	331	3993	852	87	2818	139	410	1561
湘乡市	Xiangxiang City	287	50	1387	836	19	284	969	1683
韶山市	Shaoshan City	22		131	47	1065		71	425
衡阳市	**Hengyang City**	**6570**	**12095**	**62227**	**8550**	**13053**	**4287**	**9631**	**16881**
衡阳市区	Urban District	1255	1869	33605	3484	7030	1367	4451	5148
#南岳区	Nanyue District	271			82	160	160	305	99
衡阳县	Hengyang County	1054	385	4620	245		487	962	2095
衡南县	Hengnan County	1559	2157	2195	4	5279	664	509	2731
衡山县	Hengshan County	534	755	2555	292		4	497	759
衡东县	Hengdong County	509		2224	1439	19	169	676	1545
祁东县	Qidong County	913	151	4127	158	20	126	945	1220
耒阳市	Leiyang City	284	3651	1783	2267	270	1323	980	2125
常宁市	Changning City	462	3127	11118	661	435	147	611	1258
邵阳市	**Shaoyang City**	**13019**	**13119**	**26634**	**11006**	**11220**	**3043**	**13037**	**16397**
邵阳市区	Urban District	764	930	16071	2614	8281	368	5836	5843
邵东县	Shaodong County	464	5684	1532	271	2713	175	1545	1582
新邵县	Xinshao County	683	2152	2167	470		226	747	1000
邵阳县	Shaoyang County	198	1333	795	771			828	992
隆回县	Longhui County	305	623	1879	538	8	313	924	1124
洞口县	Dongkou County	4668	843	561	1432		694	749	1627
绥宁县	Shuining County	301	302		722		144	502	596
新宁县	Xinning County	1265	255	635	1843			570	1210
城步县	Chengbu County	1954	9	2331	1007	218		703	1120
武冈市	Wugang City	2417	988	663	1338		1123	633	1303

单位：人　　　　18-4 续表 1　continued　　　　(person)

市县名称	Cities and Counties	农林牧渔业 Farming, Foresty, Animal Husbandry and Fishery	采掘业 Mining and Quarrying	制造业 Manufacturing	电力煤气及水的生产和供应 Production and Spply of Electricity Gas and Water	建筑业 Construction	地质勘查水利管理 Geological Prospecting and Water Conservancy	交通运输仓储及邮电通信业 Transport, Storage, Postal and Telecommunications	批发和零售贸易、餐饮业 Wholesale and Retail Trade, Catering Services
岳阳市	**Yueyang City**	**45849**	**1450**	**65168**	**4502**	**9202**	**3278**	**18323**	**15682**
岳阳市区	Urban District	6278		50075	2558	8408	440	12079	5649
#岳阳楼区	Yueyanglou District	20		228			35	191	25
云溪区	Yunxi District	1985		87	30	47		303	166
君山区	Junshan District	3422		519	200	146	189	220	322
岳阳县	Yueyang County	894	40	114	168	36	503	800	1669
华容县	Huarong County	2087	3	904	382	38	1007	914	1279
湘阴县	Xiangyin County	2029		480	398	38	853	1086	2795
平江县	Pingjiang County	510	403	1366	535	11	10	1903	790
汨罗市	Miluo City	32378	66	7776	275	474	36	800	2287
临湘市	Linxiang City	1673	938	4453	186	197	429	741	1213
常德市	**Changde City**	**10991**	**6168**	**20170**	**6144**	**2408**	**6246**	**8951**	**11944**
常德市区	Urban District	1850	4	12589	3315	1715	1770	6513	4594
#武陵区	Wuling District	158		12470	3165	1715	71	6094	2188
鼎城区	Dingchen District	1692	4	119	150		1699	419	2406
安乡县	Anxiang County	1084		823	178		386	333	1117
汉寿县	Hanshou County	3079		939	145	554	627	498	918
澧县	Li County	1529	1224	919	166	67	1769	270	1341
临澧县	Linli County	365		1198	204		331	393	1027
桃源县	Taoyuan County	1292	28	253	574		943	256	1499
石门县	Shimen County	1792	2936	15	1394	72	400	293	917
津市市	Jinshi City		1976	3434	168		20	395	531
张家界市	**Zhangjiajie City**	**1800**	**1766**	**2005**	**4098**	**563**	**382**	**3179**	**3476**
张家界市区	Urban District	230	508	871	1097	530	311	1545	1594
#永定区	Yongding District	222	508	992	694	398	268	442	522
武陵源区	Wulingyuan District	8					43	169	25
慈利县	Cili County	471	503	1134	1794	33	71	964	1445
桑植县	Sangzhi County	1099	755		1207			670	437
益阳市	**Yiyang City**	**61140**	**373**	**18669**	**4368**	**1357**	**3789**	**9152**	**9639**
益阳市区	Urban District	44202		9728	1955	1281	1048	6063	3850
#资阳区	Ziyang District	334		1196		22	527	26	891
赫山区	Heshan District	336		1938	85	73	225	198	1634
南县	Nan County	946	21	482	271		1285	766	1447
桃江县	Taojiang County	546	191	3085	666		323	682	1407
安化县	Anhua County	900	161	1378	1124		243	611	1535
沅江市	Yuanjiang City	14546		3996	352	76	890	1030	1400
郴州市	**Chenzhou City**	**5565**	**31416**	**19312**	**8857**	**4558**	**2924**	**6413**	**14565**
郴州市区	Urban District	521	6865	14593	2170	3561	1277	2351	5446
#北湖区	Beihu District	3		117		748	47	194	1003
苏仙区	Suxian District	509	304	22	387		22	41	271
桂阳县	Guiyang County	743	4424		679	116	397	509	1997
宜章县	Yizhang County	235	2633	757	559		132	648	986
永兴县	Yongxing County	253	1127	478	699	457	251	564	1497
嘉禾县	Jiahe County	739	1693	9	434	18	221	350	760
临武县	Linwu County	589	3317	353	710		101	394	1115
汝城县	Rucheng County	540	973	201	553		126	343	488

单位：人　　　　18-4 续表 2　continued　　　　(person)

市县名称	Cities and Counties	农林牧渔业 Farming, Foresty, Animal Husbandry and Fishery	采掘业 Mining and Quarrying	制造业 Manufacturing	电力煤气及水的生产和供应 Production and Spply of Electricity Gas and Water	建筑业 Construction	地质勘查水利管理 Geological Prospecting and Water Conservancy	交通运输仓储及邮电通信业 Transport, Storage, Postal and Telecommunications	批发和零售贸易、餐饮业 Wholesale and Retail Trade, Catering Services
桂东县	Guidong County	280			309			321	388
安仁县	Anren County	791		312	420	12	170	452	1018
资兴市	Zixing City	874	10384	2609	2324	394	249	481	870
永州市	**Yongzhou City**	**7572**	**4439**	**21988**	**8388**	**2158**	**1676**	**7690**	**12536**
永州市区	Urban District	1670	629	8669	2222	1542	797	3281	3098
#芝山区	Zhishan District	864	25	672	579	576	70	848	469
冷水滩区	Lengshuitan District	167	96	822	187	14	88	21	798
祁阳县	Qiyang County	1451	2820	3206	1542	448	67	755	1263
东安县	Dongan County	741		1637	859		264	593	1208
双牌县	Shuangpai County	69	23	1672	448	19		273	543
道县	Dao County	595	250	3312	221		115	241	1320
江水县	Jiangyong County	1303		771	462	2		402	710
宁远县	Ningyuan Couny	372		485	707	20	298	687	1752
蓝山县	Lanshan County	468		62	1081	127		298	569
新田县	Xintian County	264		1217	232		135	663	1151
江华县	Jianghua County	639	717	957	614			497	922
怀化市	**Huaihua City**	**7331**	**5520**	**15662**	**8726**	**2436**	**1213**	**7940**	**8808**
鹤城区	Hecheng District	589	107	6279	1119	901	423	1960	1594
中方县	Zhongfang County	355	228	357	24			289	130
沅陵县	Yuanling County	914	216	350	1987	120	21	1245	1083
辰溪县	Chenxi County	570	2255	4332	451	1261	220	638	1124
溆浦县	Xupu County	1101	651	1126	1338	45	225	449	981
会同县	Huitong County	546	99	9	154	25	40	424	359
麻阳县	Mayang County	573	914	211	844		117	371	417
新晃县	Xinhuang County	151	212	1060	499		43	428	457
芷江县	Zhijiang County	479		50	541			390	625
靖州县	Jingzhou County	1088	116	146	71	54	67	516	509
通道县	Tongdao County	391		327	313	7		531	297
洪江市	Hongjiang City	574	722	1415	1385	23	57	699	1232
娄底市	**Loudi City**	**4075**	**20367**	**43558**	**3616**	**8376**	**2803**	**6132**	**9008**
娄底市区	Urban District	605	97	21162	1058	5135	830	3791	2124
#娄星区	Louxing District	111		907		107	15	148	1043
冷水江市	Lengshuijiang City	1174	1949	248	278	81	100	398	1421
涟源市	Lianyuan City	641	1323	7170	274	278	1204	595	1757
双峰县	Shuangfrng County	109	15173	8612	1635	2440	14	576	2366
新化县	Xinhua County	1546	1825	6366	371	442	655	772	1340
湘西自治州	**West Hunan A.P**	**2947**	**1095**	**15850**	**8288**	**879**	**1273**	**5922**	**7428**
吉首市	Jishou City	344		5848	971	650	465	3266	1897
泸溪县	Luxi County	627		2316	1105	12	94	453	400
凤凰县	Fenghuang County	106	103	974	893	97	193	326	873
花垣县	Huayuan County	115	48	2764	1941		53	288	594
保靖县	Baojing County	240	125	698	628			304	648
古丈县	Guzhang County	356		495	353			247	240
永顺县	Yongsun County	750	296	1418	1139	112	235	461	1332
龙山县	Longshan County	409	523	1337	1258	8	233	577	1444
未列入地区的单位	**Not Classified by Region**		438	848		8440		84522	1972

单位：人　　18-4 续表 3　continued　　(person)

市县名称	City and County	金融保险业 Banking and Insurance	房地产业 Real Estate Trade	社会服务业 Social Services	卫生、体育和社会福利业 Health Care, Sports and Social Welfare	教育文化艺术及广播影视业 Education Culture and Arts, Radio, Film and Television	科学研究和综合技术服务业 Scientific Research and Poly-technical Services	国家机关政党机关社会团体 Government Party Agencies, Social Organizations	其他行业 Others
长沙市	**Changsha City**	**13829**	**4260**	**22939**	**28106**	**98279**	**22004**	**59487**	**11175**
长沙市区	Urban District	11786	3354	20140	20692	63159	21238	37253	10031
长沙县	Changsha County	300	17	405	826	5449	328	3917	
望城县	Wangcheng County	446		317	1575	6992	41	4057	
宁乡县	Ningxiang County	527	641	1161	2660	10682	202	6317	414
浏阳市	Liuyang City	770	248	916	2353	11997	195	7943	730
株洲市	**Zhuzhou City**	**4848**	**793**	**8975**	**9287**	**35944**	**4242**	**31774**	**520**
株洲市区	Urban District	3466	405	7162	4460	9410	3798	14324	215
株洲县	Zhuzhou County	129	77	104	606	4078	11	2608	
攸县	You County	351	67	498	989	7196	19	4684	123
茶陵县	Chaling County	298	31	214	939	5031	98	3352	19
炎陵县	Yanling County	104	42	277	570	2180	37	2302	9
醴陵市	Liling City	500	171	720	1715	8049	279	4504	154
湘潭市	**Xiangtan City**	**3760**	**1250**	**5785**	**8917**	**32352**	**1166**	**24185**	**1582**
湘潭市区	Urban District	2749	1054	3784	4784	12543	888	10719	1472
湘潭县	Xiangtan County	227		47	1159	9797	155	5921	72
湘乡市	Xiangxiang City	526	188	1231	2551	8787	85	6207	36
韶山市	Shaoshan City	258	8	723	423	1225	38	1338	2
衡阳市	**Hengyang City**	**6836**	**3154**	**9892**	**22838**	**72070**	**3468**	**47476**	**1586**
衡阳市区	Urban District	4050	1920	6484	7916	14438	1646	12044	435
#南岳区	Nanyue District	141	36	1048	558	861	117	998	7
衡阳县	Hengyang County	434	85	573	1716	9983	266	6876	166
衡南县	Hengnan County	200	76	160	2535	9778	988	5445	132
衡山县	Hengshan County	351	77	219	1242	4462	103	2912	80
衡东县	Hengdong County	357	74	308	1358	5799	110	3624	53
祁东县	Qidong County	408	463	448	2749	9410	83	4502	275
耒阳市	Leiyang City	593	313	1251	2477	10685	68	5895	61
常宁市	Changning City	443	146	449	2845	7515	204	6178	384
邵阳市	**Shaoyang City**	**5997**	**1714**	**6528**	**15296**	**57658**	**1511**	**62883**	**3627**
邵阳市区	Urban District	2018	898	3328	4162	8321	888	13237	1719
邵东县	Shaodong County	1107	100	739	1348	1486	50	15227	818
新邵县	Xinshao County	351	139	447	1153	6363	23	3590	96
邵阳县	Shaoyang County	274	78	150	901	7824	110	5913	670
隆回县	Longhui County	471	78	282	1025	8253	67	6155	46
洞口县	Dongkou County	523	167	340	1661	7059	33	4114	100
绥宁县	Shuining County	293	18	74	1220	3379	56	3633	27
新宁县	Xinning County	210	19	322	1506	4990	44	3836	105
城步县	Chengbu County	336	54	280	851	3417	25	3041	34
武冈市	Wugang City	414	163	566	1469	6566	215	4137	12

单位：人 18-4 续表 4 continued (person)

市县名称	City and County	金融保险业 Banking and Insurance	房地产业 Real Estate Trade	社会服务业 Social Services	卫生、体育和社会福利业 Health Care, Sports and Social Welfare	教育文化艺术及广播影视业 Education Culture and Arts, Radio, Film and Television	科学研究和综合技术服务业 Scientific Research and Poly-technical Services	国家机关政党机关社会团体 Government Party Agencies, Social Organizations	其他行业 Others
岳阳市	**Yueyang City**	**5337**	**1234**	**8912**	**12906**	**53980**	**2572**	**40093**	**2410**
岳阳市区	Urban District	3231	497	5831	3857	12227	1421	13844	233
#岳阳楼区	Yueyanglou District		65	153	555	2548	147	1877	60
云溪区	Yunxi District				51	1362		1810	
君山区	Junshan District	125	54	482	407	1944		3929	
岳阳县	Yueyang County	237	110	556	1547	6439	64	4565	687
华容县	Huarong County	411	143	804	1523	6906	81	3807	3
湘阴县	Xiangyin County	481	125	295	1260	7039	560	4136	
平江县	Pingjiang County	351	161	420	2512	9065	44	5713	1032
汨罗市	Miluo City	321	136	529	1014	6872		4569	102
临湘市	Linxiang City	305	62	477	1193	5432	402	3459	353
常德市	**Changde City**	**5841**	**1516**	**8685**	**16564**	**56932**	**1888**	**45560**	**1827**
常德市区	Urban District	2717	658	5254	5914	15332	883	16511	919
#武陵区	Wuling District	2166	496	4519	3505	7555	825	8177	528
鼎城区	Dingchen District	551	162	735	2409	7777	58	8364	391
安乡县	Anxiang County	305	176	472	1419	5285	144	3613	341
汉寿县	Hanshou County	328	106	363	1344	6616	418	3967	14
澧县	Li County	441	323	621	1748	7920	174	4452	48
临澧县	Linli County	384	68	470	841	4825	87	3063	62
桃源县	Taoyuan County	961	58	534	2481	8259	65	5920	91
石门县	Shimen County	349	127	297	2061	5731	97	3873	352
津市市	Jinshi City	356		674	756	2964	20	4131	
张家界市	**Zhangjiajie City**	**1834**	**489**	**3039**	**4061**	**14628**	**451**	**18150**	**246**
张家界市区	Urban District	1272	269	2032	1802	3582	212	8113	154
#永定区	Yongding District	167	132	190	1048	2510	88	2563	19
武陵源区	Wulingyuan District	66		936	94	41		2312	63
慈利县	Cili County	347	141	650	1060	6396	140	5567	73
桑植县	Sangzhi County	215	79	357	1199	4650	11	4470	19
益阳市	**Yiyang City**	**3809**	**1232**	**4695**	**13175**	**49044**	**1403**	**31296**	**1462**
益阳市区	Urban District	2260	592	3179	4645	17069	804	12639	226
#资阳区	Ziyang District	340		284	1250	4404		2170	113
赫山区	Heshan District	492	30	141	1954	8716	9	4952	95
南县	Nan County	434	247	372	2001	7500	68	3546	383
桃江县	Taojiang County	382	203	285	2113	8426	155	4626	192
安化县	Anhua County	355	170	198	2330	7751	136	5647	121
沅江市	Yuanjiang City	378	20	661	2086	8298	240	4838	540
郴州市	**Chenzhou City**	**4526**	**1246**	**6888**	**14128**	**45542**	**1300**	**44873**	**1807**
郴州市区	Urban District	2061	546	3904	4315	10537	890	10773	1235
#北湖区	Beihu District	733	54	100	856	2942	12	2368	62
苏仙区	Suxian District	441	55	91	759	3867	20	2674	47
桂阳县	Guiyang County	365	221	338	1889	3642	9	5438	88
宜章县	Yizhang County	393	115	459	1473	5283	65	4889	118
永兴县	Yongxing County	287	71	315	1191	5702	117	4791	39
嘉禾县	Jiahe County	215	92	313	849	3534	8	3532	158
临武县	Linwu County	285	40	338	758	3077	44	2699	24
汝城县	Rucheng County	201	21	224	563	3510	59	3649	87

单位：人　　　　　　　　18-4 续表 5 continued　　　　　　　　(person)

市县名称	City and County	金融保险业 Banking and Insurance	房地产业 Real Estate Trade	社会服务业 Social Services	卫生、体育和社会福利业 Health Care, Sports and Social Welfare	教育文化艺术及广播影视业 Education Culture and Arts, Radio, Film and Television	科学研究和综合技术服务业 Scientific Research and Poly-technical Services	国家机关政党机关社会团体 Government Party Agencies, Social Organizations	其他行业 Others
桂东县	Guidong County	99	23	184	498	1825	46	2443	16
安仁县	Anren County	185	33	150	1491	4357	5	3194	
资兴市	Zixing City	435	84	663	1101	4075	57	3465	42
永州市	**Yongzhou City**	**4861**	**966**	**6218**	**15196**	**49041**	**1201**	**60226**	**1459**
永州市区	Urban District	2035	113	2625	4933	13640	689	13748	718
#芝山区	Zhishan District	662	74	181	1485	6123	193	4583	
冷水滩区	Lengshuitan District	462	7	60	1425	5307	5	4942	328
祁阳县	Qiyang County	612	306	1221	2679	2207	176	14937	140
东安县	Dongan County	363	31	339	1615	5732	40	3862	
双牌县	Shuangpai County	135	45	107	352	1973	114	2629	
道县	Dao County	291	149	291	1261	6802	93	3915	
江水县	Jiangyong County	166	55	381	551	2813	14	2514	109
宁远县	Ningyuan Couny	351	150	434	800	6236	34	5139	5
蓝山县	Lanshan County	383	15	290	887	3643	19	3588	467
新田县	Xintian County	289	58	235	998	1592	11	6289	
江华县	Jianghua County	236	44	295	1120	4403	11	3605	20
怀化市	**Huaihua City**	**4932**	**1211**	**9138**	**14212**	**52795**	**1017**	**48348**	**925**
鹤城区	Hecheng District	1907	161	4992	2673	6156	436	7211	237
中方县	Zhongfang County	103	34	75	474	2962	37	2961	3
沅陵县	Yuanling County	398	174	535	1061	6926	138	5262	288
辰溪县	Chenxi County	272	52	355	883	5058	46	4778	12
溆浦县	Xupu County	408	414	613	2272	7096	53	5466	18
会同县	Huitong County	256	51	350	757	3634	18	2508	109
麻阳县	Mayang County	206	60	209	842	3665	63	3161	76
新晃县	Xinhuang County	226		282	774	2834	44	2538	7
芷江县	Zhijiang County	255	73	334	721	3767	16	3979	10
靖州县	Jingzhou County	300		282	721	3012	33	2733	70
通道县	Tongdao County	212	29	228	639	2345	100	2357	11
洪江市	Hongjiang City	389	163	883	2395	5340	33	5394	84
娄底市	**Loudi City**	**3492**	**1326**	**6526**	**11685**	**38535**	**1164**	**35070**	**1152**
娄底市区	Urban District	1831	779	2389	2195	6578	706	7662	668
#娄星区	Louxing District	14	45	359	520	3249	242	2882	157
冷水江市	Lengshuijiang City	372	63	538	1538	9021	105	7562	12
涟源市	Lianyuan City	514	148	532	3352	10553	128	6682	180
双峰县	Shuangfrng County	407	245	2371	1289	2404	143	6368	157
新化县	Xinhua County	368	91	696	3311	9979	82	6796	135
湘西自治州	**West Hunan A.P**	**2738**	**451**	**3639**	**9003**	**30355**	**1226**	**27923**	**545**
吉首市	Jishou City	1375	235	1481	2423	6016	691	6145	103
泸溪县	Luxi County	211	32	128	807	2891	90	2092	72
凤凰县	Fenghuang County	189	38	510	517	3498	88	3957	48
花垣县	Huayuan County	197	22	211	726	2982	70	2985	48
保靖县	Baojing County	168	10	162	908	2953	42	2893	24
古丈县	Guzhang County	56	7	189	506	1605	38	1487	222
永顺县	Yongsun County	239	39	388	1498	5164	126	4314	
龙山县	Longshan County	303	68	570	1618	5246	81	4050	28
未列入地区的单位	**Not Classified by Region**			1372	3464	3748			7616

18-5 各市、州、县城镇集体经济各行业在岗职工年末人数(2001年)

Employed Staff and Workers in Urban Collective-Owned Units by Sector at the Year-end (2001)

单位：人 (person)

市县名称	Cities and Counties	农林牧渔业 Farming, Foresty, Animal Husbandry and Fishery	采掘业 Mining and Quarrying	制造业 Manufacturing	电力煤气及水的生产和供应 Production and Spply of Electricity Gas and Water	建筑业 Construction	地质勘查水利管理 Geological Prospecting and Water Conservancy	交通运输仓储及邮电通信业 Transport, Storage, Postal and Telecommunications	批发和零售贸易、餐饮业 Wholesale and Retail Trade, Catering Services
长沙市	**Changsha City**	**26**	**880**	**20893**		**9986**	**6**	**1378**	**5389**
长沙市区	Urban District		384	16695		8634		548	3438
长沙县	Changsha County			549		525			123
望城县	Wangcheng County	8		3213				819	915
宁乡县	Ningxiang County	18		167		214		11	725
浏阳市	Liuyang City		496	269		613			188
株洲市	**Zhuzhou City**	**796**	**10**	**18305**		**4834**	**13**	**2706**	**5045**
株洲市区	Urban District			14330		2911	13	4723	2035
株洲县	Zhuzhou County	226		368		694		261	838
攸县	You County	291		272		692		128	429
茶陵县	Chaling County	254		164		408		439	174
炎陵县	Yanling County	10	10	4		129		600	95
醴陵市	Liling City	15		3167				555	1474
湘潭市	**Xiangtan City**	**62**	**151**	**11553**	**78**	**6189**	**93**	**2824**	**3917**
湘潭市区	Urban District	29	87	10158		3503	20	974	1135
湘潭县	Xiangtan County			101		766		509	1576
湘乡市	Xiangxiang City	33	64	1272	78	1782	41	1341	1023
韶山市	Shaoshan City			22		138	32		183
衡阳市	**Hengyang City**	**1216**	**254**	**15782**		**15539**	**161**	**2535**	**8153**
衡阳市区	Urban District		31	7346		7323		93	663
#南岳区	Nanyue District			10		1119			53
衡阳县	Hengyang County	415		2282		415		246	2503
衡南县	Hengnan County	450		832		2852		212	1253
衡山县	Hengshan County			622				71	397
衡东县	Hengdong County		223	599		1056		387	761
祁东县	Qidong County			254		3565	161	123	937
耒阳市	Leiyang City			924		231		1202	833
常宁市	Changning City	351		2923		97		201	806
邵阳市	**Shaoyang City**	**45**	**177**	**5777**		**10062**	**28**	**1200**	**4813**
邵阳市区	Urban District	21	66	2072		6900	22	10	1398
邵东县	Shaodong County	24	86	118		206		55	725
新邵县	Xinshao County		18	691		660	6	365	248
邵阳县	Shaoyang County			214		283			85
隆回县	Longhui County			347		810		13	332
洞口县	Dongkou County			683		8		196	78
绥宁县	Shuining County			511					518
新宁县	Xinning County			23		92		350	935
城步县	Chengbu County			183		174			211
武冈市	Wugang City			935		929		211	283

单位：人　　18-5 续表 1　continued　　(person)

市县名称	Cities and Counties	农林牧渔业 Farming, Foresty, Animal Husbandry and Fishery	采掘业 Mining and Quarrying	制造业 Manufacturing	电力煤气及水的生产和供应 Production and Spply of Electricity Gas and Water	建筑业 Construction	地质勘查水利管理 Geological Prospecting and Water Conservancy	交通运输仓储及邮电通信业 Transport, Storage, Postal and Telecommunications	批发和零售贸易、餐饮业 Wholesale and Retail Trade, Catering Services
岳阳市	**Yueyang City**	**2282**	**244**	**8308**		**2204**	**42**	**2374**	**10378**
岳阳市区	Urban District	505	115	6134		1410	12	427	3300
#岳阳楼区	Yueyanglou District	186	53	466		600	12	30	34
云溪区	Yunxi District			46		612		88	514
君山区	Junshan District		62	906					54
岳阳县	Yueyang County			56		250			704
华容县	Huarong County		29	35		106	30	194	1969
湘阴县	Xiangyin County			1009				602	1857
平江县	Pingjiang County			382		111			1331
汨罗市	Miluo City	1378		278		20		1030	896
临湘市	Linxiang City	399	100	414		307		121	321
常德市	**Changde City**	**804**	**27**	**4126**	**230**	**1633**	**314**	**1328**	**4531**
常德市区	Urban District	321		1780		406	105	402	872
#武陵区	Wuling District			787		163	105	241	548
鼎城区	Dingchen District	321		993		243		161	324
安乡县	Anxiang County		7	251		328		65	1231
汉寿县	Hanshou County	118		113		16	209		395
澧县	Li County	314		935		160		360	116
临澧县	Linli County	51		327	133			73	401
桃源县	Taoyuan County			416	47	17		179	474
石门县	Shimen County		20	99	50	705		25	837
津市市	Jinshi City			205		1		224	205
张家界市	**Zhangjiajie City**	**776**	**83**	**1544**	**61**	**2267**	**176**	**340**	**927**
张家界市区	Urban District		42	418		798		201	15
#永定区	Yongding District		42	418		798		201	117
武陵源区	Wulingyuan District								
慈利县	Cili County	586	41	1126	61	1469	176	126	782
桑植县	Sangzhi County	190						13	13
益阳市	**Yiyang City**	**114**		**7845**	**91**	**2724**	**426**	**2482**	**3410**
益阳市区	Urban District	17		5575	8	339		740	1734
#资阳区	Ziyang District			905					218
赫山区	Heshan District			2493					1219
南县	Nan County	65		1971		942	426	193	423
桃江县	Taojiang County	10		57		890		475	474
安化县	Anhua County			77	83	442		353	617
沅江市	Yuanjiang City	22		165		111		721	162
郴州市	**Chenzhou City**	**561**	**1687**	**4262**	**120**	**2516**	**325**	**1049**	**5075**
郴州市区	Urban District		127	885		901		506	1071
#北湖区	Beihu District		5	455		246		477	438
苏仙区	Suxian District			153		108			167
桂阳县	Guiyang County		666	229		48			50
宜章县	Yizhang County		516	154	120	385			413
永兴县	Yongxing County	219		547		10	22	474	490
嘉禾县	Jiahe County	86		27				29	199
临武县	Linwu County		272	4		325			286
汝城县	Rucheng County			37		15			101

市县名称	Cities and Counties	农林牧渔业 Farming, Foresty, Animal Husbandry and Fishery	采掘业 Mining and Quarrying	制造业 Manufacturing	电力煤气及水的生产和供应 Production and Spply of Electricity Gas and Water	建筑业 Construction	地质勘查水利管理 Geological Prospecting and Water Conservancy	交通运输仓储及邮电通信业 Transport, Storage, Postal and Telecommunications	批发和零售贸易、餐饮业 Wholesale and Retail Trade, Catering Services
桂东县	Guidong County	65	5	142		353			70
安仁县	Anren County		101	1305		479	303	40	404
资兴市	Zixing City	191		932					1991
永州市	**Yongzhou City**	**1111**	**106**	**3781**	**178**	**6794**		**503**	**3770**
永州市区	Urban District		79	1644		1513		254	1003
#芝山区	Zhishan District			1301		383		12	293
冷水滩区	Lengshuitan District		79	231		1130		242	297
祁阳县	Qiyang County		27	1065		806			550
东安县	Dongan County	284		399		737			395
双牌县	Shuangpai County	440		252		415			
道县	Dao County			313		552		12	477
江水县	Jiangyong County	66		24		423			
宁远县	Ningyuan Couny	300		22		930		224	819
蓝山县	Lanshan County					1036			45
新田县	Xintian County	21		41		312			323
江华县	Jianghua County			21	178	70		13	158
怀化市	**Huaihua City**	**114**		**4577**	**816**	**5595**		**2514**	**4887**
鹤城区	Hecheng District			264		1782		227	662
中方县	Zhongfang County								144
沅陵县	Yuanling County			239	443	67		96	1030
辰溪县	Chenxi County			1150	112	913		254	226
溆浦县	Xupu County			542	148	486		496	244
会同县	Huitong County	47				24			666
麻阳县	Mayang County			274		158		246	276
新晃县	Xinhuang County			180		382		259	104
芷江县	Zhijiang County			532	113	582		128	362
靖州县	Jingzhou County			378		190		378	169
通道县	Tongdao County	67		33		406		221	279
洪江市	Hongjiang City			985		605		209	725
娄底市	**Loudi City**		**1323**	**12497**		**2856**		**4555**	**6635**
娄底市区	Urban District		1087	3899		289		872	890
#娄星区	Louxing District		1087	67		114		872	538
冷水江市	Lengshuijiang City			99		865		389	611
涟源市	Lianyuan City		80	3121		618		942	1362
双峰县	Shuangfrng County		156	2716		990		1812	814
新化县	Xinhua County			2662		94		540	2958
湘西自治州	**West Hunan A.P**	**228**		**2799**	**85**	**2443**		**862**	**3118**
吉首市	Jishou City			271	42	665		441	532
泸溪县	Luxi County			196		187		93	57
凤凰县	Fenghuang County			100		252			355
花垣县	Huayuan County			1828	43	145			530
保靖县	Baojing County			18		393		25	401
古丈县	Guzhang County			82		90		227	279
永顺县	Yongsun County			78		571			518
龙山县	Longshan County	228		226		140		76	446

单位：人　　　　　　　　18-5 续表 3　continued　　　　　　　　(person)

市县名称	City and County	金融保险业 Banking and Insurance	房地产业 Real Estate Trade	社会服务业 Social Services	卫生、体育和社会福利业 Health Care, Sports and Social Welfare	教育文化艺术及广播影视业 Education Culture and Arts, Radio, Film and Television	科学研究和综合技术服务业 Scientific Research and Poly-technical Services	国家机关政党机关社会团体 Government Party Agencies, Social Organizations	其他行业 Others
长沙市	**Changsha City**	**2254**	**441**	**1718**	**5026**	**670**	**63**	**17**	**1170**
长沙市区	Urban District	197	424	1703	923	176	55		929
长沙县	Changsha County	361	17		1016	30	8	17	
望城县	Wangcheng County	365			200	128			20
宁乡县	Ningxiang County	646		15	1125				73
浏阳市	Liuyang City	685			1762	336			148
株洲市	**Zhuzhou City**	**2209**	**177**	**1275**	**3284**	**47**		**287**	**399**
株洲市区	Urban District	459	153	1003	339	17		287	149
株洲县	Zhuzhou County	217			521				
攸县	You County	309	19		1097				
茶陵县	Chaling County	317	5	100	330				15
炎陵县	Yanling County	183		46	116				25
醴陵市	Liling City	724		126	881	30			210
湘潭市	**Xiangtan City**	**1549**	**274**	**1207**	**2020**	**237**			**177**
湘潭市区	Urban District	295	274	1149	303	234			126
湘潭县	Xiangtan County	584			1601				17
湘乡市	Xiangxiang City	582		58		3			23
韶山市	Shaoshan City	88			116				11
衡阳市	**Hengyang City**	**4359**	**206**	**1998**	**3642**	**91**		**245**	**452**
衡阳市区	Urban District	1380	178	1663	915	69		130	249
#南岳区	Nanyue District	59			4			8	
衡阳县	Hengyang County	600			1914				
衡南县	Hengnan County	786	28		169	22			
衡山县	Hengshan County	207						18	
衡东县	Hengdong County	255			479				23
祁东县	Qidong County	401						97	100
耒阳市	Leiyang City	364		45	165				51
常宁市	Changning City	366		290					29
邵阳市	**Shaoyang City**	**3253**	**137**	**1266**	**2626**	**177**	**11**		**99**
邵阳市区	Urban District	851	79	75	1256	159	11		8
邵东县	Shaodong County	427		372	716	18			18
新邵县	Xinshao County	16							16
邵阳县	Shaoyang County	284		125					29
隆回县	Longhui County	409	15	203	11				
洞口县	Dongkou County	364	19	414					
绥宁县	Shuining County	185							
新宁县	Xinning County	260	24	17	327				8
城步县	Chengbu County	185							20
武冈市	Wugang City	262		60	316				

单位：人　　18-5 续表 4 continued　　(person)

市县名称	City and County	金融保险业 Banking and Insurance	房地产业 Real Estate Trade	社会服务业 Social Services	卫生、体育和社会福利业 Health Care, Sports and Social Welfare	教育文化艺术及广播影视业 Education Culture and Arts, Radio, Film and Television	科学研究和综合技术服务业 Scientific Research and Poly-technical Services	国家机关政党机关社会团体 Government Party Agencies, Social Organizations	其他行业 Others
岳阳市	**Yueyang City**	**2580**	**56**	**328**	**1978**	**42**	**29**	**255**	**414**
岳阳市区	Urban District	229	56	318	522	12	29	61	31
#岳阳楼区	Yueyanglou District		38	76	223	12	7	61	
云溪区	Yunxi District	159		78	249				
君山区	Junshan District	70			27				
岳阳县	Yueyang County	435				24			39
华容县	Huarong County	366				6		107	50
湘阴县	Xiangyin County	654			462			28	
平江县	Pingjiang County	351		10	12				154
汨罗市	Miluo City	261			826				45
临湘市	Linxiang City	284			156			59	95
常德市	**Changde City**	**2938**	**242**	**811**	**2337**	**209**	**20**	**78**	**582**
常德市区	Urban District	972	11	197		33			110
#武陵区	Wuling District	485	11						65
鼎城区	Dingchen District	487		197		33			45
安乡县	Anxiang County	275							47
汉寿县	Hanshou County	410		111	528	100		39	
澧县	Li County	395	231	234	1031	50			57
临澧县	Linli County	338		156	645	25	20	39	
桃源县	Taoyuan County	24		10		1			261
石门县	Shimen County	357		100					84
津市市	Jinshi City	167		3	133				23
张家界市	**Zhangjiajie City**	**879**	**7**	**675**	**845**	**124**			**60**
张家界市区	Urban District	357		376					37
#永定区	Yongding District	324		154					16
武陵源区	Wulingyuan District	33		67					
慈利县	Cili County	288		299	845	124			
桑植县	Sangzhi County	234	7						23
益阳市	**Yiyang City**	**2492**		**283**	**2162**	**291**	**1**	**83**	**652**
益阳市区	Urban District	891		121	685	270	1	83	68
#资阳区	Ziyang District	234		22	396	37		23	
赫山区	Heshan District	657				27			34
南县	Nan County			13	88	20			470
桃江县	Taojiang County	529		147	623				35
安化县	Anhua County	628			324	1			26
沅江市	Yuanjiang City	444		2	442				53
郴州市	**Chenzhou City**	**1907**	**124**	**228**	**1072**	**24**		**79**	**1883**
郴州市区	Urban District	321	124	228	254	24		37	632
#北湖区	Beihu District	42	77	19	13	7		37	564
苏仙区	Suxian District	279			241	17			24
桂阳县	Guiyang County				17				506
宜章县	Yizhang County	254						34	
永兴县	Yongxing County	237			337				621
嘉禾县	Jiahe County	148			153				27
临武县	Linwu County	153						8	24
汝城县	Rucheng County	170			311				24

单位：人　　　　18-5 续表 5　continued　　　　(person)

市县名称	City and County	金融保险业 Banking and Insurance	房地产业 Real Estate Trade	社会服务业 Social Services	卫生、体育和社会福利业 Health Care, Sports and Social Welfare	教育文化艺术及广播影视业 Education Culture and Arts, Radio, Film and Television	科学研究和综合技术服务业 Scientific Research and Poly-technical Services	国家机关政党机关社会团体 Govern-ment Party Agencies, Social Organiza-tions	其他行业 Others
桂东县	Guidong County	121							15
安仁县	Anren County	240							34
资兴市	Zixing City	263							
永州市	**Yongzhou City**	**2408**	**220**	**72**	**844**	**252**	**80**	**284**	**199**
永州市区	Urban District	750	8	36	86	209	80	149	31
#芝山区	Zhishan District	458	8			40			
冷水滩区	Lengshuitan District	266			86	169		115	31
祁阳县	Qiyang County	457	148	4					93
东安县	Dongan County	226							
双牌县	Shuangpai County	108		10	241			60	26
道县	Dao County							24	
江永县	Jiangyong County	123			40				25
宁远县	Ningyuan Couny	250			446			46	
蓝山县	Lanshan County	148	64	22	12	43			
新田县	Xintian County	127							
江华县	Jianghua County	219			19			5	24
怀化市	**Huaihua City**	**3175**	**54**	**653**	**2409**	**66**	**106**	**427**	**108**
鹤城区	Hecheng District	458	13	314	357			136	38
中方县	Zhongfang County	171						19	15
沅陵县	Yuanling County	356		40	381		10	83	
辰溪县	Chenxi County	264		141	534	26		22	
溆浦县	Xupu County	370		18		28		21	10
会同县	Huitong County	214			161			24	
麻阳县	Mayang County	186			107	12		10	
新晃县	Xinhuang County	193			154			24	
芷江县	Zhijiang County	198		55	400			17	38
靖州县	Jingzhou County	226		38	115		96	20	3
通道县	Tongdao County	155		45				22	
洪江市	Hongjiang City	384	41	2				29	4
娄底市	**Loudi City**	**1617**	**111**	**266**	**395**		**50**	**37**	**14**
娄底市区	Urban District	214		158			21	37	
#娄星区	Louxing District	214		98					
冷水江市	Lengshuijiang City	377	41		388				
涟源市	Lianyuan City	467	21	53					
双峰县	Shuangfrng County	191	49	55	7		29		
新化县	Xinhua County	368							14
湘西自治州	**West Hunan A.P**	**1355**		**36**	**124**	**22**			**127**
吉首市	Jishou City	261		11	15	22			38
泸溪县	Luxi County	134							
凤凰县	Fenghuang County	165							38
花垣县	Huayuan County	119			109				
保靖县	Baojing County	134							20
古丈县	Guzhang County	80							
永顺县	Yongsun County	234		19					
龙山县	Longshan County	228		6					31

18-6 各市、州、县在岗职工工资总额和年平均工资(2001年)

Total Wage Bill and Average Annual Wage of Employed Staff and Workers (2001)

市县名称	City and County	在岗职工工资总额(万元) Total Wages of Staff and Workers on the Job (10 000 yuan)	#国有经济 State-owned Units	#城镇集体经济 Urban Collective Owned Units	在岗职工年平均工资(元) Average Annual Wages of Staff and Workers on the Job (yuan)	#国有经济 State-owned Units	#城镇集体经济 Urban Collective Owned Units	在岗职工年平均工资为上年% Average Annual Wages as Percentage of Preceding Year (%)
长沙市	**Changsha City**	**733661**	**566626**	**38262**	**12303**	**13301**	**7608**	**121.4**
长沙市区	Urban District	583929	450598	27066	13058	11429	6799	122.2
长沙县	Changsha County	35876	21522	1926	9633	8896	7024	113.7
望城县	Wangcheng County	27415	20139	2907	8676	9331	5042	115.8
宁乡县	Ningxiang County	39925	34641	2484	9548	9832	8262	121.5
浏阳市	Liuyang City	46516	39725	3879	12096	12622	9254	128.7
株洲市	**Zhuzhou City**	**327981**	**244718**	**30152**	**10536**	**11264**	**7179**	**111.9**
株洲市区	Urban District	228878	164729	18167	11378	12528	7937	107.7
株洲县	Zhuzhou County	12764	10444	2051	8574	9221	6536	112.9
攸县	You County	25277	21596	3225	8195	8623	6332	105.5
茶陵县	Chaling County	18698	16733	1396	8781	9289	6309	113.0
炎陵县	Yanling County	9000	7579	1031	8485	8703	8271	115.5
醴陵市	Liling City	33364	23637	4282	8625	10424	5769	115.3
湘潭市	**Xiangtan City**	**243604**	**192043**	**22074**	**10064**	**10562**	**7324**	**119.5**
湘潭市区	Urban District	165989	137924	13930	10644	11131	7584	121.1
湘潭县	Xiangtan County	28344	24402	3456	8466	8862	6740	130.2
湘乡市	Xiangxiang City	43191	24605	4344	9523	9981	7150	108.8
韶山市	Shaoshan City	6080	5112	344	8515	8927	6051	120.2
衡阳市	**Hengyang City**	**362270**	**278400**	**36381**	**8994**	**9320**	**6828**	**118.6**
衡阳市区	Urban District	156967	111496	14175	9941	10427	7382	117.8
#南岳区	Nanyue District	6313	5031	1185	10611	10797	9816	111.1
衡阳县	Hengyang County	34994	28691	6099	9134	9747	7114	116.0
衡南县	Hengnan County	31157	25883	4755	7503	7611	7230	116.4
衡山县	Hengshan County	13078	11702	649	7669	7916	4967	115.2
衡东县	Hengdong County	18276	15555	1787	8117	8593	5598	120.7
祁东县	Qidong County	26946	23283	3559	8525	8983	6407	114.4
耒阳市	Leiyang City	44228	29014	1773	8407	8578	4639	135.9
常宁市	Changning City	36626	32775	3584	8880	9182	7085	123.7
邵阳市	**Shaoyang City**	**236884**	**204020**	**19823**	**8084**	**8223**	**7252**	**117.3**
邵阳市区	Urban District	68712	53966	8723	9182	8516	7947	130.5
邵东县	Shaodong County	33048	30576	1866	8629	8778	6622	126.4
新邵县	Xinshao County	17147	15004	1354	7334	7663	5754	117.6
邵阳县	Shaoyang County	17152	15999	557	7591	7776	5490	132.9
隆回县	Longhui County	22739	20118	1447	9046	9620	5392	115.2
洞口县	Dongkou County	20345	18969	1322	7639	7808	5943	109.5
绥宁县	Shuining County	13110	10398	919	8834	9371	7718	111.0
新宁县	Xinning County	13286	11202	1282	6628	6677	6447	112.6
城步县	Chengbu County	12157	10859	464	7226	7112	6036	111.6
武冈市	Wugang City	19189	16929	1889	7717	7909	6636	108.4

18-6 续表 1

continued

市县名称	City and County	在岗职工工资总额(万元) Total Wages of Staff and Workers on the Job (10 000 yuan)	#国有经济 State-owned Units	#城镇集体经济 Urban Collective Owned Units	在岗职工年平均工资(元) Average Annual Wages of Staff and Workers on the Job (yuan)	#国有经济 State-owned Units	#城镇集体经济 Urban Collective Owned Units	在岗职工年平均工资为上年% Average Annual Wages as Percentage of Preceding Year (%)
岳阳市	**Yueyang City**	**308281**	**269654**	**20281**	**9081**	**9317**	**6433**	**123.9**
岳阳市区	Urban District	157422	134428	9301	10308	10576	6945	128.5
#岳阳楼区	Yueyanglou District	7188	6142	1046	9360	10437	5826	135.3
云溪区	Yunxi District	5428	4268	971	6833	7295	5569	93.6
君山区	Junshan District	10597	9466	761	8046	8013	6770	165.1
岳阳县	Yueyang County	18370	16277	942	8862	9012	6401	137.7
华容县	Huarong County	18938	16427	1731	7780	8101	6015	112.9
湘阴县	Xiangyin County	20558	17625	2304	7580	8275	4810	125.6
平江县	Pingjiang County	24045	21086	1371	8207	8554	5803	111.8
汨罗市	Miluo City	48614	45577	2960	7885	7979	6686	128.3
临湘市	Linxiang City	20335	18234	1672	8612	8719	7574	118.5
常德市	**Changde City**	**258119**	**219010**	**15618**	**9634**	**10123**	**7440**	**125.8**
常德市区	Urban District	112257	94309	4368	10993	11564	8170	125.4
#武陵区	Wuling District	85350	73722	2211	12633	13548	8498	123.0
鼎城区	Dingchen District	27305	20587	2157	7820	7586	7524	119.4
安乡县	Anxiang County	15807	13107	1310	7654	8283	5945	115.1
汉寿县	Hanshou County	18092	16242	1500	8019	8128	7442	162.3
澧县	Li County	25734	21541	2919	8699	9109	7299	115.0
临澧县	Linli County	15415	11889	1692	8587	8913	8073	110.8
桃源县	Taoyuan County	25443	24211	953	9103	9383	5263	120.4
石门县	Shimen County	27342	21588	2133	9552	10419	8794	114.7
津市市	Jinshi City	18029	16123	743	9952	10421	7654	117.5
张家界市	**Zhangjiajie City**	**73698**	**62700**	**5812**	**9400**	**9983**	**6677**	**117.7**
张家界市区	Urban District	33532	31347	1656	9533	10350	7977	149.8
#永定区	Yongding District	16405	12875	1421	8438	9334	7897	115.9
武陵源区	Wulingyuan District	3986	3209	64	8588	8533	6430	108.6
慈利县	Cili County	25573	17960	3767	8945	9979	6258	108.6
桑植县	Sangzhi County	14594	13393	389	9270	9539	8246	132.0
益阳市	**Yiyang City**	**185270**	**160467**	**12657**	**7234**	**7404**	**5699**	**119.4**
益阳市区	Urban District	91944	77638	5476	6952	7108	5730	122.9
#资阳区	Ziyang District	10973	9579	1087	7872	8364	5909	110.6
赫山区	Heshan District	18749	16465	2154	7733	7969	6243	122.2
南县	Nan County	19546	16788	2227	7798	8505	4869	118.7
桃江县	Taojiang County	23768	20097	2099	8337	8690	6479	116.5
安化县	Anhua County	21542	19900	1640	7787	7980	6027	115.3
沅江市	Yuanjiang City	28470	26044	1215	6679	6645	5768	127.5
郴州市	**Chenzhou City**	**241330**	**209170**	**15972**	**9446**	**9779**	**7419**	**118.5**
郴州市区	Urban District	94267	80208	3667	10831	11532	7167	116.7
#北湖区	Beihu District	13331	9824	1706	9418	10643	6853	114.0
苏仙区	Suxian District	11148	9962	867	10117	10509	8976	123.2
桂阳县	Guiyang County	21560	19819	1377	9595	9614	8966	135.2
宜章县	Yizhang County	18380	16663	903	8508	8948	4931	127.8
永兴县	Yongxing County	16906	15006	1743	8051	8443	5907	116.5
嘉禾县	Jiahe County	12113	11434	555	8824	8870	8387	116.5
临武县	Linwu County	13455	12639	802	9126	9254	7537	111.2
汝城县	Rucheng County	10634	9962	505	8824	8902	7726	122.7

18-6 续表 2 continued

市县名称	City and County	在岗职工工资总额 (万元) Total Wages of Staff and Workers on the Job (10 000 yuan)	#国有经济 State-owned Units	#城镇集体经济 Urban Collective Owned Units	在岗职工年平均工资 (元) Average Annual Wages of Staff and Workers on the Job (yuan)	#国有经济 State-owned Units	#城镇集体经济 Urban Collective Owned Units	在岗职工年平均工资为上年% Average Annual Wages as Percentage of Preceding Year (%)
桂东县	Guidong County	5771	5091	474	7507	7927	6266	110.9
安仁县	Anren County	12260	10342	1774	7823	8210	6069	114.5
资兴市	Zixing City	35985	28007	4172	9113	9163	10337	115.9
永州市	**Yongzhou City**	**192096**	**166324**	**11609**	**8011**	**8211**	**6128**	**113.1**
永州市区	Urban District	71051	56479	3229	8817	9205	5996	110.8
#芝山区	Zhishan District	14759	13524	1235	7456	7857	4781	102.8
冷水滩区	Lengshuitan District	15265	12453	1458	7910	8446	6807	112.6
祁阳县	Qiyang County	28927	25947	1639	7591	7791	6409	111.4
东安县	Dongan County	16461	15038	1242	8693	8926	6868	117.1
双牌县	Shuangpai County	7138	6516	621	7334	7954	4034	123.9
道县	Dao County	14345	13567	461	7018	7196	3397	109.7
江水县	Jiangyong County	8307	7860	407	7585	7666	6444	131.6
宁远县	Ningyuan Couny	14555	12188	2066	6895	6990	6858	108.1
蓝山县	Lanshan County	7829	6935	772	5989	5972	5958	103.9
新田县	Xintian County	10384	9580	440	8701	8995	6672	131.9
江华县	Jianghua County	13099	12215	734	8767	8684	10386	106.4
怀化市	**Huaihua City**	**201623**	**158554**	**16768**	**8217**	**8313**	**6719**	**115.1**
鹤城区	Hecheng District	49235	37699	3203	10062	10294	8135	118.5
中方县	Zhongfang County	7298	6603	216	8270	8191	5388	115.5
沅陵县	Yuanling County	22177	15244	2582	8119	7342	8800	114.2
辰溪县	Chenxi County	17256	15061	1624	6419	6592	5065	121.8
溆浦县	Xupu County	22022	15965	1683	7445	7156	6611	114.7
会同县	Huitong County	9300	7588	529	7834	8103	4648	107.1
麻阳县	Mayang County	9590	8810	688	7300	7530	5462	111.7
新晃县	Xinhuang County	9624	8329	921	8702	8956	7113	109.7
芷江县	Zhijiang County	13160	10562	1636	8831	9278	6700	115.6
靖州县	Jingzhou County	10349	8177	1215	8254	8380	7608	111.3
通道县	Tongdao County	7712	6709	866	8310	8591	6900	116.1
洪江市	Hongjiang City	23900	17806	1606	7699	8557	5338	111.8
娄底市	**Loudi City**	**208679**	**185398**	**16232**	**8942**	**9440**	**5634**	**115.7**
娄底市区	Urban District	81045	73132	5018	11671	12431	6737	118.5
#娄星区	Louxing District	11847	9385	2244	9314	9742	7821	135.0
冷水江市	Lengshuijiang City	20209	18674	1362	7265	7522	4905	104.0
涟源市	Lianyuan City	31077	28117	2961	7651	8288	4424	114.1
双峰县	Shuangfrng County	45502	37132	4560	8204	8374	6834	118.5
新化县	Xinhua County	30847	28344	2330	7705	8223	4463	116.1
湘西自治州	**West Hunan A.P**	**113721**	**102880**	**7769**	**8446**	**8595**	**6919**	**114.5**
吉首市	Jishou City	32567	29841	1585	9005	9185	6822	112.7
泸溪县	Luxi County	9168	8866	307	7777	7972	4525	121.4
凤凰县	Fenghuang County	11809	10890	707	9007	9137	7943	105.6
花垣县	Huayuan County	13592	10612	2027	8013	8104	7351	110.8
保靖县	Baojing County	9564	8582	750	8141	8357	7090	122.0
古丈县	Guzhang County	5654	5095	541	8485	8655	7291	127.5
永顺县	Yongsun County	16077	14832	960	8443	8552	6827	115.6
龙山县	Longshan County	15290	14161	892	7974	8055	6475	114.3
未列入地区的单位	**Not Classified by Region**	**168070**	**168070**		**14829**	**14829**		**108**

18-7 离开本单位仍保留劳动关系的职工生活费和年平均生活费(2001年)

Living Income and Annual Average Living Income of Staff and Workers Left-Self Units and Remind Labor Relations (2001)

市县名称	City and County	离开本单位仍保留劳动关系的职工生活费 Living Income of Staff and Workers Left-Self Units and Remind Labor Relations 合计(万元) Total (10 000 yuan)	#国有经济 State- owned Units	城镇集体经济 Urban Collective Owned Units	年平均生活费 Annual Average Living Income 合计(元) Total (yuan)	#国有经济 State- owned Units	城镇集体经济 Urban Collective Owned Units
长沙市	**Changsha City**	**46050**	**29614**	**7073**	**2725**	**3071**	**1487**
长沙市区	Urban District	38578	23270	5978	2935	2959	1297
长沙县	Changsha County	1509	1429	77	2674	2782	1701
望城县	Wangcheng County	1137	558	677	2079	2422	1862
宁乡县	Ningxiang County	2359	2179	167	1400	1807	350
浏阳市	Liuyang City	2368	2177	175	2598	2898	1855
株洲市	**Zhuzhou City**	**20392**	**14970**	**2010**	**1792**	**2056**	**744**
株洲市区	Urban District	14810	10028	1626	2313	2455	1366
株洲县	Zhuzhou County	259	187	73	1069	1349	696
攸县	You County	1771	1646	119	1157	1496	284
茶陵县	Chaling County	1669	1587	68	1395	1852	241
炎陵县	Yanling County	374	351	14	1238	1653	198
醴陵市	Liling City	1509	1172	110	889	1324	174
湘潭市	**Xiangtan City**	**18965**	**14482**	**1948**	**2055**	**2338**	**852**
湘潭市区	Urban District	15866	13190	1500	2096	2483	849
湘潭县	Xiangtan County	829	668	161	941	1198	513
湘乡市	Xiangxiang City	2177	539	282	3557	2993	1433
韶山市	Shaoshan City	93	85	5	565	582	506
衡阳市	**Hengyang City**	**18219**	**12964**	**1219**	**1174**	**1257**	**347**
衡阳市区	Urban District	11156	8348	611	1247	1297	399
#南岳区	Nanyue District	88	86	2	1696	2000	174
衡阳县	Hengyang County	590	383	207	721	831	578
衡南县	Hengnan County	602	562	19	743	1055	73
衡山县	Hengshan County	442	405	18	1055	1329	175
衡东县	Hengdong County	466	418	23	959	2030	91
祁东县	Qidong County	1216	966	250	1178	1423	707
耒阳市	Leiyang City	2871	1020	89	1912	1325	434
常宁市	Changning City	875	862	3	581	932	7
邵阳市	**Shaoyang City**	**14964**	**12245**	**1561**	**1054**	**1282**	**465**
邵阳市区	Urban District	7330	6192	572	1096	1198	785
邵东县	Shaodong County	1150	968	94	981	1179	476
新邵县	Xinshao County	1014	934	33	928	1259	175
邵阳县	Shaoyang County	790	547	172	1374	2096	624
隆回县	Longhui County	1516	1274	170	2552	3949	752
洞口县	Dongkou County	611	568	43	489	825	77
绥宁县	Shuining County	596	327	75	1643	1950	781
新宁县	Xinning County	664	425	176	834	1099	483
城步县	Chengbu County	185	158	28	377	380	361
武冈市	Wugang City	1109	852	199	941	1597	425

市县名称	City and County	离开本单位仍保留劳动关系的职工生活费 Living Income of Staff and Workers Left-Self Units and Remind Labor Relations			年平均生活费 Annual Average Living Income		
		合计 (万元) Total (10 000 yuan)	#国有经济 State- owned Units	城镇集体经济 Urban Collective Owned Units	合计 (元) Total (yuan)	#国有经济 State- owned Units	城镇集体经济 Urban Collective Owned Units
岳阳市	**Yueyang City**	**18864**	**16096**	**1462**	**2293**	**2729**	**830**
岳阳市区	Urban District	12981	11135	652	3811	4059	1936
#岳阳楼区	Yueyanglou District	108	74	35	1139	2442	534
云溪区	Yunxi District	13	12	1	1300	1557	333
君山区	Junshan District	397	375	10	3194	3433	866
岳阳县	Yueyang County	858	688	158	2009	2511	1036
华容县	Huarong County	1334	1173	151	1060	1326	425
湘阴县	Xiangyin County	780	497	264	843	1155	625
平江县	Pingjiang County	759	638	66	1139	1560	400
汨罗市	Miluo City	899	807	86	1697	2259	640
临湘市	Linxiang City	1253	1159	84	1238	1448	436
常德市	**Changde City**	**14841**	**11231**	**1043**	**1738**	**2386**	**380**
常德市区	Urban District	7061	4922	569	2023	2773	512
#武陵区	Wuling District	5564	4056	258	2871	3352	727
鼎城区	Dingchen District	1497	865	311	964	1532	411
安乡县	Anxiang County	732	582	135	1151	1363	246
汉寿县	Hanshou County	651	606	44	773	1326	115
澧县	Li County	1161	1083	72	1318	1863	245
临澧县	Linli County	797	665	61	3637	3826	2139
桃源县	Taoyuan County	1717	1508	66	1947	2588	337
石门县	Shimen County	1209	619	34	2240	2362	557
津市市	Jinshi City	1514	1247	61	2299	2742	470
张家界市	**Zhangjiajie City**	**2325**	**1926**	**322**	**1593**	**1873**	**873**
张家界市区	Urban District	1414	1123	250	1786	2000	1149
#永定区	Yongding District	1094	827	247	1568	1752	1149
武陵源区	Wulingyuan District	105	98	4	3170	3053	
慈利县	Cili County	622	527	62	1383	1865	415
桑植县	Changzhi County	288	276	10	1327	1497	2182
益阳市	**Yiyang City**	**11150**	**9808**	**735**	**1008**	**1229**	**269**
益阳市区	Urban District	4590	3761	307	912	950	360
#资阳区	Ziyang District	255	143	81	249	246	196
赫山区	Heshan District	990	880	100	1137	1315	498
南县	Nan County	650	621	29	585	699	137
桃江县	Taojiang County	1565	1293	202	1060	1343	445
安化县	Anhua County	609	518	89	562	814	207
沅江市	Yuanjiang City	3737	3615	107	1583	2292	137
郴州市	**Chenzhou City**	**10927**	**8972**	**825**	**1803**	**2351**	**659**
郴州市区	Urban District	5482	4331	408	2118	2802	939
#北湖区	Beihu District	886	551	205	985	1494	742
苏仙区	Suxian District	234	177	38	936	2169	447
桂阳县	Guiyang County	890	728	9	2152	2418	754
宜章县	Yizhang County	651	579	28	1602	2445	190
永兴县	Yongxing County	380	312	50	992	1248	391
嘉禾县	Jiahe County	338	277	34	1781	2004	1003
临武县	Linwu County	667	511	156	1948	1950	1944
汝城县	Rucheng County	406	365	32	1202	1490	382

市县名称	City and County	离开本单位仍保留劳动关系的职工生活费 Living Income of Staff and Workers Left-Self Units and Remind Labor Relations			年平均生活费 Annual Average Living Income		
		合计 (万元) Total (10 000 yuan)	#国有经济 State- owned Units	城镇集体经济 Urban Collective Owned Units	合计 (元) Total (yuan)	#国有经济 State- owned Units	城镇集体经济 Urban Collective Owned Units
桂东县	Guidong County	115	74	19	892	1049	508
安仁县	Anren County	413	328	71	1045	1611	379
资兴市	Zixing City	1585	1466	19	1808	2605	177
永州市	**Yongzhou City**	**9940**	**7801**	**611**	**1441**	**1544**	**487**
永州市区	Urban District	4826	3353	176	1612	1567	849
#芝山区	Zhishan District	331	331		562	792	
冷水滩区	Lengshuitan District	763	679	84	957	1071	515
祁阳县	Qiyang County	1787	1424	207	1555	1684	841
东安县	Dongan County	631	536	81	1529	1979	638
双牌县	Shuangpai County	283	276	7	893	1199	81
道县	Dao County	685	682	3	830	1037	20
江永县	Jiangyong County	287	286	1	1480	1479	2000
宁远县	Ningyuan Couny	314	255	47	1119	1818	357
蓝山县	Lanshan County	177	157	19	1357	1359	1333
新田县	Xintian County	304	262	34	1659	2288	522
江华县	Jianghua County	645	569	38	1571	1703	718
怀化市	**Huaihua City**	**9100**	**6961**	**657**	**1192**	**1359**	**349**
鹤城区	Hecheng District	2317	1817	252	1437	1405	1563
中方县	Zhongfang County	197	186	1	1710	1855	80
沅陵县	Yuanling County	831	636	22	921	1098	74
辰溪县	Chenxi County	1589	1295	164	1368	1560	593
溆浦县	Xupu County	981	629	29	872	786	102
会同县	Huitong County	302	231	10	1905	2221	308
麻阳县	Mayang County	388	351	10	1754	1950	306
新晃县	Xinhuang County	681	623	28	2442	3297	376
芷江县	Zhijiang County	336	277	31	1416	2094	369
靖州县	Jingzhou County	257	204	24	1026	1512	236
通道县	Tongdao County	146	112	34	1619	2921	686
洪江市	Hongjiang City	1076	601	51	728	811	108
娄底市	**Loudi City**	**13397**	**11614**	**694**	**1807**	**2066**	**461**
娄底市区	Urban District	5852	5478	346	2592	2788	1726
#娄星区	Louxing District	594	520	74	1011	1102	642
冷水江市	Lengshuijiang City	708	630	72	683	1070	161
涟源市	Lianyuan City	1321	1199	122	904	1082	345
双峰县	Shuangfrng County	3917	2770	116	2917	2681	770
新化县	Xinhua County	1600	1538	37	1213	1655	105
湘西自治州	**West Hunan A.P**	**5419**	**4792**	**484**	**1589**	**1817**	**716**
吉首市	Jishou City	1945	1794	150	2136	2265	1280
泸溪县	Luxi County	330	325	6	568	706	46
凤凰县	Fenghuang County	524	452	65	3207	4030	1540
花垣县	Huayuan County	190	170	7	1809	2301	436
保靖县	Baojing County	454	354	87	1431	1329	2307
古丈县	Guzhang County	240	237	1	1083	1174	25
永顺县	Yongsun County	829	725	99	1835	2220	797
龙山县	Longshan County	908	736	70	1375	1815	353
未列入地区的单位	**Not Classified by Region**	5948	5948	-	9116	9116	-

18-8 各市、州、县国内生产总值(2001年)

Gross Domestic Products (2001)

市县	Cities and Counties	国内生产总值 (万元) GDP (10 000 yuan)	第一产业 Primary Industry	第二产业 Secondary Industry	#工业 Industry	第三产业 Tertiary Industry	GDP 为上年% Index (preceding year=100)	人均GDP (元) Per Capita GDP (yuan)
长沙市	**Changsha City**	**7280774**	**783636**	**2970933**	**2179077**	**3526205**	**112.1**	**12443**
长沙市区	Urban District	4688731	88015	1845957	1310662	2754759	113.4	26328
长沙县	Changsha County	966727	179300	524327	425457	263100	111.2	13108
望城县	Wangcheng County	548901	126067	237962	179881	184872	110.4	7726
宁乡县	Ningxiang County	680472	202950	241566	201276	235956	110.5	5215
浏阳市	Liuyang City	746008	188927	345631	274677	211450	110.2	5659
株洲市	**Zhuzhou City**	**3226716**	**515986**	**1530467**	**1315340**	**1180263**	**110.7**	**8805**
株洲市区	Urban District	1616171	42258	924532	807394	649381	112.1	21367
株洲县	Zhuzhou County	250532	70292	85806	56664	94434	108.3	5634
攸县	You County	443730	151850	129696	97787	162184	108.0	5967
茶陵县	Chaling County	217303	90681	61416	49565	65206	108.7	3889
炎陵县	Yanling County	85678	27934	21600	16954	36144	108.6	4841
醴陵市	Liling City	613302	132971	307417	286976	172914	111.0	6233
湘潭市	**Xiangtan City**	**2382813**	**341186**	**1034156**	**862177**	**1007471**	**110.7**	**8509**
湘潭市区	Urban District	1297993	26042	651687	552066	620264	111.1	19190
湘潭县	Xiangtan County	527316	172836	149482	129275	204998	110.0	4669
湘乡市	Xiangxiang City	484504	129814	207725	161723	146965	110.3	5423
韶山市	Shaoshan City	73000	12494	25262	19113	35244	110.6	7221
衡阳市	**Hengyang City**	**3862195**	**1089687**	**1363531**	**1135727**	**1408977**	**109.2**	**5483**
衡阳市区	Urban District	1007164	41206	381515	247238	584443	111.9	12639
衡阳县	Hengyang County	473363	226866	130601	115666	115896	105.3	4233
衡南县	Hengnan County	493460	204245	170281	149460	118934	107.9	4836
衡山县	Hengshan County	193199	64019	57478	42148	71702	106.3	4782
衡东县	Hengdong County	302695	117767	75039	53963	109889	107.4	4569
祁东县	Qidong County	430521	139893	140515	117969	150113	109.7	4719
耒阳市	Leiyang City	514017	156723	176463	154575	180831	109.5	4170
常宁市	Changning City	385588	119579	145868	111765	120141	109.0	4662
邵阳市	**Shaoyang City**	**2432092**	**931482**	**633868**	**490100**	**866742**	**107.1**	**3348**
双清区	Shuangqing District	73588	9171	27922	24835	36495	111.0	2902
大祥区	Daxiang District	76440	12653	39287	25942	24500	110.3	4034
北塔区	Beita District	22519	6455	10507	8925	5557	113.1	3055
邵东县	Shaodong County	711712	181812	219790	166990	310110	107.1	6128
新邵县	Xinshao County	209238	79006	52714	26578	77518	105.5	2899
邵阳县	Shaoyang County	187947	84523	33352	21726	70072	104.9	1978
隆回县	Longhui County	275362	92467	79015	31792	103880	109.1	2518
洞口县	Dongkou County	292779	138612	38509	26168	115658	108.0	3738
绥宁县	Shuining County	150914	70744	31781	26299	48389	106.5	4365
新宁县	Xinning County	144901	61913	21065	14731	61923	107.3	2469
城步县	Chengbu County	65954	25666	16710	12533	23578	107.3	2607
武冈市	Wugang City	229555	114796	32665	24212	82094	107.2	3158

注:总量指标按当年价格计算,指数按可比价格计算。

Aggregate data are calculated at current prices, while indices are calculated at comparable prices.

市县	Cities and Counties	国内生产总值 (万元) GDP (10 000 yuan)	第一产业 Primary Industry	第二产业 Secondary Industry	#工业 Industry	第三产业 Tertiary Industry	GDP 为上年% Index (preceding year=100)	人均GDP (元) Per Capita GDP (yuan)
岳阳市	**Yueyang City**	**4069650**	**982000**	**1663645**	**1437695**	**1424005**	**110.6**	**7777**
岳阳楼区	Yueyanglou District	271681	21325	74174	57937	176182	111.7	9533
云溪区	Yunxi District	108126	21965	47873	40885	38288	111.4	10447
君山区	Junshan District	125300	63200	24500	18460	37600	112.0	5637
岳阳县	Yueyang County	371951	156342	92132	78331	123477	110.6	4957
华容县	Huarong County	384983	181694	103836	89941	99453	110.0	5376
湘阴县	Xiangyin County	387309	165526	147865	126438	73918	110.5	5617
平江县	Pingjiang County	314011	118187	93809	75571	102015	110.6	3169
汨罗市	Miluo City	361978	120102	163919	145864	77957	111.0	5674
临湘市	Linxiang City	223799	77018	83781	74185	63000	110.8	4710
常德市	**Changde City**	**3985929**	**1100375**	**1548652**	**1277380**	**1336902**	**110.6**	**6692**
武陵区	Wuling District	1115579	30862	654261	553283	430456	162.5	18844
鼎城区	Dingchen District	541464	186800	167919	123348	186745	108.5	6108
安乡县	Anxiang County	260693	115526	61200	50884	83967	112.4	4513
汉寿县	Hanshou County	326520	134510	67610	46060	124400	110.3	4054
澧 县	Li County	442117	157320	98494	74322	186303	110.6	5036
临澧县	Linli County	250925	82353	90572	87715	78000	108.4	5762
桃源县	Taoyuan County	582317	224298	166371	108010	191648	109.0	5991
石门县	Shimen County	312701	103948	98767	75108	109986	110.9	4572
津市市	Jinshi City	139075	39440	54499	48508	45136	109.0	5386
张家界市	**Zhangjiajie City**	**667147**	**151481**	**141040**	**90982**	**374626**	**109.5**	**4273**
永定区	Yongding District	147748	46705	25301	17283	75742	111.5	3569
武陵源区	Wulingyuan District	45128	5098	2419	1675	37611	114.8	10164
慈利县	Cili County	198736	76750	42057	32385	79929	105.0	2949
桑植县	Sangzhi County	78155	32527	13972	10405	31656	108.0	1829
益阳市	**Yiyang City**	**2100108**	**563009**	**632717**	**489651**	**904382**	**108.5**	**4661**
资阳区	Ziyang District	150748	39895	43387	34042	67466	108.1	3699
赫山区	Heshan District	302800	99394	82599	49775	120807	108.3	4262
南县	Nan County	237634	107164	64680	47661	65790	108.5	3583
桃江县	Taojiang County	214285	84783	61719	49114	67783	108.6	2621
安化县	Anhua County	216851	86379	56238	45917	74234	106.3	2281
沅江市	Yuanjiang City	331287	125620	88063	74831	117604	108.7	4577
郴州市	**Chenzhou City**	**2571121**	**628999**	**863420**	**726035**	**1078702**	**110.6**	**5661**
北湖区	Beihu District	432461	31387	217272	185756	183802	112.5	15105
苏仙区	Suxian District	271706	44093	108912	87464	118701	113.3	8043
桂阳县	Guiyang County	383942	121328	118775	90241	143839	110.4	4949
宜章县	Yizhang County	236169	64325	54838	46842	117006	110.3	4322
永兴县	Yongxing County	296873	77654	101412	93087	117807	110.6	4675
嘉禾县	Jiahe County	168062	53024	44013	38411	71025	110.6	4978
临武县	Linwu County	157689	45532	60901	56648	51256	112.2	5118
汝城县	Rucheng County	143843	42182	49089	42727	52572	110.9	3987
桂东县	Guidong County	46116	16075	11205	7590	18836	111.7	2722
安仁县	Anren County	123375	65259	21196	16427	36920	104.7	3132
资兴市	Zixing City	296985	68621	119286	91124	109078	112.0	8193

市县	Cities and Counties	国内生产总值(万元) GDP (10 000 yuan)	第一产业 Primary Industry	第二产业 Secondary Industry	#工业 Industry	第三产业 Tertiary Industry	GDP为上年% Index (preceding year=100)	人均GDP(元) Per Capita GDP (yuan)
永州市	**Yongzhou City**	**2492887**	**838696**	**695239**	**567143**	**958952**	**108.9**	**4404**
芝山区	Zhishan District	401935	86783	203772	186948	111380	109.2	6944
冷水滩区	Lengshuitan District	326626	70452	145018	125479	111156	110.1	7305
祁阳县	Qiyang County	356612	131112	91532	60368	133968	104.3	3641
东安县	Dongan County	280492	108054	79692	47078	92746	109.3	4826
双牌县	Shuangpai County	66257	22944	22325	18534	20988	106.4	3904
道县	Dao County	255453	110039	52837	40181	92577	104.2	3886
江永县	Jiangyong County	109440	47375	22528	18572	39537	104.6	4433
宁远县	Ningyuan Couny	187480	81141	42307	31432	64032	103.1	2441
蓝山县	Lanshan County	131398	39934	49359	44993	42105	109.4	3801
新田县	Xintian County	109125	48617	29876	26188	30632	101.5	2937
江华县	Jianghua County	131845	56088	40104	37521	35653	109.7	2933
怀化市	**Huaihua City**	**2141565**	**584056**	**581120**	**464654**	**976389**	**108.7**	**4415**
鹤城区	Hecheng District	140655	23762	48720	47280	68173	110.2	5120
中方县	Zhongfang County	96828	40535	16785	12961	39508	106.7	3769
沅陵县	Yuanling County	279168	63860	153226	145776	62082	103.4	4375
辰溪县	Chenxi County	120463	43871	30548	25514	46044	103.9	2361
溆浦县	Xupu County	224639	120802	47943	34169	55894	107.0	2669
会同县	Huitong County	117401	48960	24956	20306	43485	107.8	3473
麻阳县	Mayang County	86211	39462	16120	12916	30629	107.0	2442
新晃县	Xinhuang County	79459	29923	21662	20049	27874	104.1	3185
芷江县	Zhijiang County	124539	48124	30345	24182	46070	109.0	3546
靖州县	Jingzhou County	120912	42223	23861	19554	54828	107.8	4721
通道县	Tongdao County	49096	22852	8307	7177	17937	105.5	2256
洪江市	Hongjiang City	141053	58724	37606	26245	44723	109.1	3320
娄底市	**Loudi City**	**1800628**	**400011**	**709035**	**558598**	**691582**	**108.2**	**4508**
娄星区	Louxing District	444128	29052	228369	187855	186707	108.5	11201
双峰县	Lengshuijiang City	340482	155991	88796	61876	95695	104.6	3839
新化县	Lianyuan City	279240	109600	54899	39495	114741	107.0	2170
冷水江市	Shuangfrng County	313705	18279	172915	162868	122511	107.7	8892
涟源市	Xinhua County	282408	87088	98520	72720	96800	101.1	2639
湘西自治州	**West Hunan A.P**	**718144**	**227940**	**251252**	**196698**	**238952**	**108.0**	**2745**
吉首市	Jishou City	191348	27513	89842	72520	73993	109.0	6928
泸溪县	Luxi County	62602	26032	16304	11821	20266	107.9	2255
凤凰县	Fenghuang County	83520	25070	22580	17659	35870	107.6	2267
花垣县	Huayuan County	66412	23329	25977	23179	17106	110.1	2462
保靖县	Baojing County	62410	21830	23532	13664	17048	111.1	2233
古丈县	Guzhang County	28584	11771	5861	3971	10952	107.6	2091
永顺县	Yongsun County	94518	43599	21814	14451	29105	106.9	1958
龙山县	Longshan County	128750	48796	45342	39433	34612	105.6	2451

18-9 各市、州、县耕地面积及播种面积(2001年)

Cultivated Area and Sown Area (2001)

单位：千公顷 (1 000 hectares)

市县名称	City and County	耕地面积 Cultivated Area	水田 Paddy Fields	旱地 Dry Fields	农作物播种面积 Total Sown Area	#粮食作物 Grain Crops	#经济作物 Economical Crops
长沙市	**Changsha City**	**285.62**	**255.47**	**30.15**	**609.91**	**384.5**	**28.49**
芙蓉区	Furong District	0.41	0.07	0.34	3.7	0.03	
天心区	Tianxin District	1.19	0.90	0.29	2.8	1.2	
岳麓区	Yuelu District	2.68	2.01	0.67	6.59	1.59	0.04
开福区	Kaifu District	4.72	4.37	0.35	10.08	5.05	0.18
雨花区	Yuhua District	2.82	2.15	0.67	7.64	1.41	0.01
长沙县	Changsha County	57.95	54.34	3.61	133.31	78.32	5.7
望城县	Wangcheng County	48.22	44.08	4.14	103.82	71.37	2.4
宁乡县	Ningxiang County	92.55	79.18	13.37	195.08	131.7	6.58
浏阳市	Liuyang City	75.08	68.37	6.71	146.89	93.83	13.58
株洲市	**Zhuzhou City**	**207.58**	**169.64**	**37.94**	**343.47**	**247.54**	**24.5**
荷塘区	Hetang District	4.28	3.47	0.81	6.96	4.9	0.17
芦淞区	Lousong District	1.25	0.95	0.30	1.88	0.93	0.01
石峰区	Shifeng District	4.48	3.54	0.94	8.8	4.74	0.46
天元区	Tianyuan District	4.22	3.49	0.73	7.27	5.57	0.13
株洲县	Zhuzhou County	32.25	28.06	4.19	55.31	42.55	1.65
攸县	You County	55.02	42.67	12.35	93.07	63.25	10.1
茶陵县	Chaling County	37.70	29.97	7.73	61.34	46.89	7.49
炎陵县	Yanling County	14.94	13.03	1.91	22.89	17.48	2.02
醴陵市	Liling City	53.44	44.46	8.98	85.95	61.23	2.47
湘潭市	**Xiangtan City**	**144.10**	**126.07**	**18.03**	**268.62**	**196.99**	**6.85**
雨湖区	Yuhu District	1.69	1.31	0.38	3.37	1.44	
岳塘区	Yuetang District	4.61	3.56	1.05	7.73	4.61	0.3
湘潭县	Xiangtan County	77.15	71.36	5.79	139.46	108.65	3.28
湘乡市	Xiangxiang City	54.62	44.48	10.14	106.02	73.57	2.48
韶山市	Shaoshan City	6.03	5.36	0.67	12.04	8.72	0.79
衡阳市	**Hengyang City**	**373.31**	**304.74**	**68.57**	**803.39**	**499.15**	**131.8**
郊区	Jiaoqu District	10.30	7.77	2.53	16.8	8.88	1.26
南岳区	Nanyue District	1.95	1.66	0.29	3.81	1.98	0.4
衡阳县	Hengyang County	69.33	61.06	8.27	168.58	97.18	47.92
衡南县	Hengnan County	61.58	56.20	5.38	158.3	93.7	32.74
衡山县	Hengshan County	23.75	19.61	4.14	41.24	29.78	2.82
衡东县	Hengdong County	43.32	34.87	8.45	90.24	57.08	10.89
祁东县	Qidong County	54.52	40.52	14.00	82.14	57	5.48
耒阳市	Leiyang City	61.33	43.59	17.74	137.63	82.91	18.72
常宁市	Changning City	47.23	39.46	7.77	104.65	70.64	11.57
邵阳市	**Shaoyang City**	**412.80**	**291.06**	**121.74**	**741.64**	**510.17**	**95.41**
双清区	Shuangqing District	4.90	3.29	1.61	7.22	5.12	0.24
大祥区	Daxiang District	8.09	5.17	2.92	13.26	9.14	1.13
北塔区	Beita District	2.69	1.81	0.88	4.92	3.03	0.37
邵东县	Shaodong County	58.62	35.96	22.66	100.9	67.9	11.75

市县名称	City and County	耕地面积 Cultivated Area	水田 Paddy Fields	旱地 Dry Fields	农作物播种面积 Total Sown Area	#粮食作物 Grain Crops	#经济作物 Economical Crops
新邵县	Xinshao County	37.54	25.41	12.13	65.27	51.48	4.04
邵阳县	Shaoyang County	62.88	41.39	21.49	96.85	66.51	14.03
隆回县	Longhui County	63.54	44.62	18.92	120.37	77.59	19.04
洞口县	Dongkou County	50.50	38.44	12.06	109.55	70.89	19.29
绥宁县	Suining County	23.93	20.77	3.16	38.6	22.29	5.74
新宁县	Xinning County	39.96	27.25	12.71	71.66	51.39	7.55
城步县	Chengbu County	16.21	12.23	3.98	25.6	17.4	4.57
武冈市	Wugang City	43.94	34.72	9.22	87.44	67.43	7.66
岳阳市	**Yueyang City**	**334.38**	**234.82**	**99.56**	**727.49**	**367.57**	**129.49**
岳阳楼区	Yueyanglou District	3.50	1.18	2.32	7.15	2.21	0.52
云溪区	Yunxi District	8.83	4.77	4.06	15.43	6.15	2.83
君山区	Junshan District	24.89	12.37	12.52	49.72	17	17.59
岳阳县	Yueyang County	50.32	29.87	20.45	114.53	65.96	14.86
华容县	Huarong County	68.83	43.32	25.51	130.18	42.44	48.61
湘阴县	Xiangyin County	41.10	35.69	5.41	123.74	58.73	13.31
平江县	Pingjiang County	55.84	45.42	10.42	105.45	69.5	10.94
汨罗市	Miluo City	45.52	35.90	9.62	101.14	63.73	9.02
临湘市	Linxiang City	35.55	26.30	9.25	80.15	41.85	11.81
常德市	**Changde City**	**468.18**	**345.31**	**122.87**	**1008.89**	**502.92**	**346.34**
武陵区	Wuling District	9.44	8.00	1.44	19.38	7.28	4.04
鼎城区	Dingcheng District	83.71	65.00	18.71	183.05	98.37	49.13
安乡县	Anxiang County	45.90	31.16	14.74	90.55	34.43	45.84
汉寿县	Hanshou County	58.43	45.86	12.57	130.22	66.18	34.13
澧县	Li County	72.09	50.02	22.07	145.56	62.08	63.58
临澧县	Linli County	41.45	31.14	10.30	83.69	44	31.41
桃源县	Taoyuan County	94.09	69.34	24.75	210.38	106.47	71.41
石门县	Shimen County	44.35	32.88	11.47	105.82	64.66	30.05
津市市	Jinshi City	18.72	11.91	6.81	40.24	19.45	16.75
张家界市	**Zhangjiajie City**	**108.52**	**69.10**	**39.42**	**228.57**	**138.98**	**62.19**
永定区	Yongding District	32.34	19.23	13.11	61.14	32.4	18.54
武陵源区	Wulingyuan District	3.69	2.12	1.57	5.67	3.36	1.74
慈利县	Chili County	48.72	31.10	17.62	100.3	61.01	28.13
桑植县	Sangzhi County	23.77	16.65	7.12	61.46	42.21	13.78
益阳市	**Yiyang City**	**276.92**	**209.43**	**67.49**	**570.4**	**313.25**	**132.07**
资阳区	Ziyang District	23.27	20.20	3.07	45.68	32.43	2.31
赫山区	Heshan District	45.96	39.88	6.08	91.3	63.66	3.31
南县	Nan County	58.76	39.75	19.01	139.78	50.41	55.29
桃江县	Taojiang County	44.26	38.34	5.92	77.51	55.23	2.09
安化县	Anhua County	42.05	29.91	12.14	99.41	59.93	25.23
沅江市	Yuanjiang City	62.62	41.35	21.27	116.72	51.59	43.84
郴州市	**Chenzhou City**	**283.08**	**202.97**	**80.11**	**522.75**	**336.21**	**56.39**
北湖区	Beihu District	8.12	6.54	1.58	22.15	10.46	1.79
苏仙区	Suxian District	16.37	13.75	2.62	30.26	21.94	1.64
桂阳县	Guiyang County	61.17	35.10	26.07	97.74	57.45	20.7
宜章县	Yizhang County	32.07	19.60	12.47	63.32	40.57	3.77
永兴县	Yongxing County	33.87	24.73	9.14	72.32	47.47	6.49

单位：千公顷　　18-9 续表 2　continued　　(1 000 hectares)

市县名称	City and County	耕地面积 Cultivated Area	水田 Paddy Fields	旱地 Dry Fields	农作物播种面积 Total Sown Area	#粮食作物 Grain Crops	#经济作物 Economical Crops
嘉禾县	Jiahe County	19.03	12.50	6.53	42.08	26.24	4.21
临武县	Linwu County	17.70	12.45	5.25	35.82	21.93	1.83
汝城县	Rucheng County	26.12	20.64	5.48	44.49	30.93	2.48
桂东县	Guidong County	11.65	10.35	1.30	14.16	10.21	1.25
安仁县	Anreng County	28.08	22.79	5.29	52.45	37.34	9.46
资兴市	Zixing City	22.29	19.38	2.91	47.96	31.67	2.77
永州市	**Yongzhou City**	**342.44**	**260.82**	**81.62**	**739.67**	**462.5**	**62.54**
芝山区	Zhishan District	38.63	33.39	5.24	92.76	57.01	6.12
冷水滩区	Lengshuitan District	32.90	24.73	8.17	60.98	43.95	3.9
祁阳县	Qiyang County	53.82	42.13	11.69	131.9	92.1	13.36
东安县	Dongan County	40.52	35.00	5.52	95.71	55.97	5.04
双牌县	Shuangpai County	8.32	7.18	1.14	18.44	12.19	0.89
道县	Dao County	45.30	30.79	14.51	101.23	56.09	5.94
江永县	Jiangyong County	21.42	15.72	5.70	36.22	19.67	5.81
宁远县	Ningyuan County	38.37	28.35	10.02	65.06	45.6	5.11
蓝山县	Lanshan County	18.69	13.30	5.39	33.25	20.28	3.83
新田县	Xintian County	18.54	11.85	6.69	46.36	24.91	4.82
江华县	Jianghua County	25.93	18.38	7.55	57.76	34.73	7.72
怀化市	**Huaihua City**	**306.31**	**260.66**	**45.65**	**606.35**	**340.6**	**101.71**
鹤城区	Hecheng District	11.06	9.90	1.16	21.32	9.93	3.04
中方县	Zhongfang County	19.59	17.29	2.30	39.05	19.88	5.3
沅陵县	Yuanling County	39.35	35.25	4.10	91.29	51.54	18.99
辰溪县	Chenxi County	28.37	22.74	5.63	54.16	30.99	8.61
溆浦县	Xupu County	49.39	35.93	13.46	104.75	66.86	18.96
会同县	Huitong County	22.17	19.96	2.21	43.61	21.91	7.42
麻阳县	Mayang County	19.15	17.49	1.66	47.01	24.51	9.18
新晃县	Xinhuang County	19.09	12.79	6.30	36.27	21.36	5.82
芷江县	Zhijiang County	30.09	27.38	2.71	54.21	31.46	8.42
靖州县	Jinzhou County	22.65	20.13	2.52	35.56	17.34	6.34
通道县	Tongdao County	17.87	15.84	2.03	27.8	14.26	3.83
洪江市	Hongjiang City	27.53	25.96	1.58	51.32	30.56	5.8
娄底市	**Loudi City**	**181.80**	**116.23**	**65.57**	**354.14**	**271.45**	**26.39**
娄星区	Louxing District	11.71	7.63	4.08	22.18	15.61	1.09
双峰县	Shuangfeng County	51.41	40.65	10.76	108.29	80.72	11.34
新化县	Xinhua County	56.88	31.70	25.18	107.28	83.56	9.91
冷水江市	Lenshuijiang City	7.79	4.70	3.09	13.12	9.45	0.43
涟源市	Lianyuan City	54.01	31.55	22.46	103.27	82.11	3.62
湘西自治州	**West Hunan A.P**	**187.51**	**113.58**	**73.93**	**406.42**	**230.98**	**101.21**
吉首市	Jishou City	11.79	7.36	4.43	27.43	11.07	7.92
泸溪县	Louxi County	17.87	13.18	4.69	40.57	19.07	10.21
凤凰县	Fenghuang County	33.75	20.66	13.09	66.76	30.16	19.62
花垣县	Huayuan County	25.59	12.25	13.34	34.9	23.47	6.86
保靖县	Baojin County	18.39	10.23	8.16	45.63	26.05	11.3
古丈县	Guzhang County	9.34	7.45	1.89	21.23	11.4	5.05
永顺县	Yongshun County	36.42	24.56	11.86	88.46	57.65	20.69
龙山县	Longshan County	34.36	17.89	16.47	81.44	52.11	19.56

18-10 各市、州、县机耕、灌溉面积及水库、塘坝和堤防(2001年)

Tractor-Ploughed Area and Irrigated Area,Reservoirs,Small Reservoirs and Dikes (2001)

市县名称	City and County	机耕面积(千公顷) Tractor Ploughed Area (1 000 hectares)	有效灌溉面积(千公顷) Irrigated Area (1 000 hectares)	水库(座) Number of Reservoirs (set)	水库容量(万立方米) Capacity (10 000 cu.m)	塘坝(座) Number of Small Reservoirs (set)	塘坝容量(万立方米) Capacity (10 000 cu.m)	堤防长度(公里) Total Length of Dikes (km)
长沙市	**Changsha City**	**163.33**	**219.29**	**762**	**115896**	**242276**	**104843**	**530**
芙蓉区	Furong District	0.50	0.41	1	80	200	60	15
天心区	Tianxin District	0.50	1.17	2	48	800	320	13
岳麓区	Yuelu District	1.14	2.12	16	610	1978	1400	37
开福区	Kaifu District	2.23	4.04	17	708	4080	4390	75
雨花区	Yuhua District	1.80	2.14	11	507	1850	4409	30
长沙县	Changsha County	33.96	44.79	173	18122	64556	23186	98
望城县	Wangcheng County	24.60	37.49	85	6494	37546	15610	201
宁乡县	Ningxiang County	49.70	66.83	277	32358	76094	39298	61
浏阳市	Liuyang City	48.90	60.30	180	56969	55172	16170	
株洲市	**Zhuzhou City**	**94.13**	**144.40**	**887**	**84319**	**97697**	**44846**	**171**
荷塘区	Hetang District	1.60	3.03	17	571	2389	1321	14
芦淞区	Lousong District	0.50	0.61	2	40	935	400	7
石峰区	Shifeng District	1.26	2.98	13	668	2641	1586	7
天元区	Tianyuan District	2.06	3.22	12	157	2022	1474	32
株洲县	Zhuzhou County	17.93	24.86	144	7936	17206	11700	111
攸 县	You County	24.67	40.06	299	38033	21987	16870	
茶陵县	Chaling County	19.03	24.68	196	9010	22439	4829	
炎陵县	Yanling County	4.33	10.81	11	630	2100	220	
醴陵市	Liling City	22.75	34.15	193	27274	25978	6446	
湘潭市	**Xiangtan City**	**90.20**	**115.65**	**383**	**94072**	**141662**	**69579**	**268**
雨湖区	Yuhu District	0.54	1.45	1	20	1760	1334	17
岳塘区	Yuetang District	2.70	3.03	6	362	2830	1950	30
湘潭县	Xiangtan County	58.00	63.39	146	19925	60041	46058	143
湘乡市	Xiangxiang City	26.00	43.35	181	71789	72600	18900	78
韶山市	Shaoshan City	2.96	4.43	49	1976	4431	1337	
衡阳市	**Hengyang City**	**226.84**	**252.18**	**1529**	**188333**	**428606**	**78305**	**422**
郊区	Jiaoqu District	4.76	5.71	24	900	9931	3654	92
南岳区	Nanyue District	0.76	0.88	8	568	1760	300	
衡阳县	Hengyang County	36.47	50.77	235	31000	109698	19990	31
衡南县	Hengnan County	67.58	51.71	348	24017	97250	15520	118
衡山县	Hengshan County	14.31	13.89	109	9915	22550	4550	72
衡东县	Hengdong County	27.20	29.70	189	20266	35468	10621	91
祁东县	Qidong County	31.70	30.53	161	22326	83136	9155	1
耒阳市	Leiyang City	18.06	39.01	275	60447	28000	7400	16
常宁市	Changning City	26.00	29.98	180	18894	40813	7115	1
邵阳市	**Shaoyang City**	**157.48**	**253.65**	**1245**	**139273**	**259648**	**61095**	
双清区	Shuangqing District	1.42	2.83	15	667	5267	1066	
大祥区	Daxiang District	1.21	4.28	27	2076	8310	1143	
北塔区	Beita District	0.45	1.89	13	367	2560	494	
邵东县	Shaodong County	25.12	38.76	126	19588	73900	12800	

注：有效灌溉面积、水库、塘坝、堤防长度数据由水利部门提供。

The date of irrigated area, reservoirs, small reservoirs and length of dikes are provided by the water conservancy department.

市县名称	City and County	机耕面积(千公顷) Tractor Ploughed Area (1 000 hectares)	有效灌溉面积(千公顷) Irrigated Area (1 000 hectares)	水库(座) Number of Reservoirs (set)	水库 容量(万立方米) Capacity (10 000 cu.m)	塘坝(座) Number of Small Reservoirs (set)	塘坝 容量(万立方米) Capacity (10 000 cu.m)	堤防长度(公里) Total Length of Dikes (km)
新邵县	Xinshao County	11.97	20.76	106	12486	30127	6959	
邵阳县	Shaoyang County	12.33	32.20	270	18077	44000	12000	
隆回县	Longhui County	23.96	36.90	245	32406	27518	5204	
洞口县	Dongkou County	29.09	36.08	151	16801	17400	3936	
绥宁县	Suining County	19.30	16.60	39	2808	5200	2980	
新宁县	Xinning County	10.64	25.05	107	17660	18020	8265	
城步县	Chengbu County	6.86	9.54	26	2039	2246	2398	
武冈市	Wugang City	15.13	28.76	120	14298	25100	3850	
岳阳市	**Yueyang City**	**224.4**	**245.93**	**1457**	**161514**	**99467**	**30789**	**1108**
岳阳楼区	Yueyanglou District	0.25	1.40	22	913	1685	379	8
云溪区	Yunxi District	2.75	4.25	47	2147	2500	2100	77
君山区	Junshan District	36.6	22.88	24	584	178	20	203
岳阳县	Yueyang County	29.94	37.78	357	83850	8001	3482	88
华容县	Huarong County	33.9	48.07	60	5617	6394	1720	323
湘阴县	Xiangyin County	38.47	35.30	75	4142	7980	2809	247
平江县	Pingjiang County	17.65	33.50	290	20184	26733	5931	
汨罗市	Miluo City	47.34	36.14	283	22113	28466	3380	111
临湘市	Linxiang City	17.5	26.61	299	21964	17530	10968	51
常德市	**Changde City**	**157.51**	**391.88**	**1201**	**243674**	**186981**	**76331**	**1287**
武陵区	Wuling District	5.5	7.35					14
鼎城区	Dingcheng District	46	73.94	189	30023	18704	7461	127
安乡县	Anxiang County	25	38.93					395
汉寿县	Hanshou County	33.21	45.60	211	11865	8602	4290	178
澧县	Li County	34.66	59.30	117	50784	42165	17089	301
临澧县	Linli County		35.25	138	27493	26430	9600	49
桃源县	Taoyuan County		81.60	352	96094	58990	14630	167
石门县	Shimen County	9.7	37.86	163	25000	23750	19501	
津市市	Jinshi City	3.44	12.05	31	2415	8340	3760	56
张家界市	**Zhangjiajie City**	**10.58**	**49.47**	**210**	**210051**	**17751**	**8767**	**61**
永定区	Yongding District	4.02	13.65	87	13087	2795	1507	22
武陵源区	Wulingyuan District		0.94	4	716	226	392	
慈利县	Chili County	4.41	26.67	102	193597	13619	6393	32
桑植县	Sangzhi County	2.15	8.21	17	2651	1111	475	7
益阳市	**Yiyang City**	**235.21**	**219.20**	**548**	**412303**	**50061**	**17980**	**999**
资阳区	Ziyang District	43.04	17.40	29	3998	2900	654	133
赫山区	Heshan District	38.82	34.50	138	10647	10978	6802	159
南县	Nan County	31.25	56.02					356
桃江县	Taojiang County	42.4	36.81	210	19264	13139	5045	42
安化县	Anhua County	5.1	21.13	168	369217	21635	5065	1
沅江市	Yuanjiang City	74.6	53.34	3	9177	1409	414	308
郴州市	**Chenzhou City**	**101.9**	**169.55**	**912**	**1023163**	**89414**	**23933**	**32**
北湖区	Beihu District	7.18	8.17	13	4211	2508	953	5
苏仙区	Suxian District	8.18	13.89	47	6927	6359	2243	8
桂阳县	Guiyang County	16.68	26.75	187	16834	23417	3330	
宜章县	Yizhang County	7.9	17.98	130	7770	4906	3426	
永兴县	Yongxing County	13.39	21.47	128	27073	13376	3658	8

18-10 续表 2 continued

市县名称	City and County	机耕面积(千公顷) Tractor Ploughed Area (1 000 hectares)	有效灌溉面积(千公顷) Irrigated Area (1 000 hectares)	水库(座) Number of Reservoirs (set)	容量(万立方米) Capacity (10 000 cu.m)	塘坝(座) Number of Small Reservoirs (set)	容量(万立方米) Capacity. (10 000 cu.m)	堤防长度(公里) Total Length of Dikes (km)
嘉禾县	Jiahe County	5.51	11.13	74	9660	8906	1113	
临武县	Linwu County	8.77	10.03	67	8232	5570	1175	3
汝城县	Rucheng County	9.51	19.22	63	6441	1434	1038	
桂东县	Guidong County	4.04	6.33	30	1120	2982	542	6
安仁县	Anreng County	13.36	19.22	112	14230	14993	3809	2
资兴市	Zixing City	7.38	15.36	61	920665	4963	2646	
永州市	**Yongzhou City**	**142.63**	**237.21**	**1262**	**177630**	**172192**	**58228**	
芝山区	Zhishan District	12.34	29.32	146	13393	10000	13212	
冷水滩区	Lengshuitan District	8.34	21.74	137	7073	19358	13202	
祁阳县	Qiyang County	47.87	38.44	206	15186	72250	12000	
东安县	Dongan County	19.9	30.50	262	11422	18133	3971	
双牌县	Shuangpai County	2.36	6.44	27	70080	1619	651	
道县	Dao County	9.2	29.95	100	9063	17106	5820	
江永县	Jiangyong County	5.48	14.44	101	9257	2008	1188	
宁远县	Ningyuan County	16.77	25.32	87	10714	11896	3500	
蓝山县	Lanshan County	7.63	12.31	33	2455	1237	561	
新田县	Xintian County	5.8	11.63	72	13252	16520	1833	
江华县	Jianghua County	6.94	17.12	91	15735	2065	2470	
怀化市	**Huaihua City**	**48.7**	**183.35**	**1579**	**702837**	**68314**	**40663**	**22**
鹤城区	Hecheng District	1.98	6.16	45	6132	1474	776	
中方县	Zhongfang County	2.33	10.97	138	7344	1576	1156	
沅陵县	Yuanling County	4.08	24.82	195	615513	4864	6449	
辰溪县	Chenxi County	3.12	18.00	238	9895	3100	2297	2
溆浦县	Xupu County	6.07	27.45	153	15458	21116	14520	5
会同县	Huitong County	3	14.84	129	5746	6302	1408	
麻阳县	Mayang County	0.9	13.03	258	13085	5947	1535	2
新晃县	Xinhuang County	1.94	7.76	66	3080	1198	422	4
芷江县	Zhijiang County	7.75	16.64	135	11600	5860	1566	5
靖州县	Jinzhou County	9.8	13.86	46	4300	7439	4590	2
通道县	Tongdao County	4.63	11.21	34	900	4378	3698	
洪江市	Hongjiang City	3.1	18.61	142	9784	5060	2246	2
娄底市	**Loudi City**	**68.66**	**112.52**	**711**	**61785**	**179469**	**33294**	**6**
娄星区	Louxing District	6.81	6.02	51	1351	15305	3164	
双峰县	Shuangfeng County	39.52	33.11	205	13015	71900	13880	
新化县	Xinhua County	9.98	35.02	271	28815	28760	8204	
冷水江市	Lenshuijiang City	1.55	5.31	30	2176	6057	1015	5
涟源市	Lianyuan City	10.8	33.06	154	16428	57447	7031	1
湘西自治州	**West Hunan A.P**	**20.16**	**82.07**	**612**	**42466**	**6036**	**4421**	
吉首市	Jishou City	0.89	4.87	23	3300	500	420	6
泸溪县	Louxi County	1.6	8.08	127	8047	1520	1860	
凤凰县	Fenghuang County	2.4	13.39	92	7860	792	631	6
花垣县	Huayuan County	2.33	10.12	55	3190	328	200	
保靖县	Baojin County	1.85	8.16	57	4900	518	320	
古丈县	Guzhang County	0.22	4.25	47	1800	338	220	
永顺县	Yongshun County	5.35	15.30	146	8129	1091	330	
龙山县	Longshan County	5.52	17.90	65	5240	949	440	

18-11 各市、州、县主要农业机械年末拥有量(2001年)

Year-End Possession of Major Agriculture Machinery (2001)

市县名称	City and County	农业机械总动力(千瓦) Power of Agricultural Machinery (kw)	大中型拖拉机 Large and Medium Tractors		小型及手扶拖拉机 Mini and Walking Tractors		排灌机械 Machinery for Agricultural Drainage and Irrigation		农用载重汽车(辆) Trucks for Agricultural Use (unit)
			台 (unit)	千瓦 (kw)	台 (unit)	千瓦 (kw)	台 (unit)	千瓦 (kw)	
长沙市	**Changsha City**	**2584651**	**1257**	**27486**	**19317**	**170031**	**140259**	**578414**	**8687**
芙蓉区	Furong District	36434	26	536	109	959	3991	16934	197
天心区	Tianxin District	26935	29	904	90	822	924	6206	143
岳麓区	Yuelu District	44003	10	180	68	598	1030	8651	346
开福区	Kaifu District	58908	27	550	246	2087	2591	23508	243
雨花区	Yuhua District	50072	9	242	103	909	1102	5894	367
长沙县	Changsha County	651997	22	859	2854	25501	52099	162293	2037
望城县	Wangcheng County	409344	75	4420	3300	29139	29870	158064	1096
宁乡县	Ningxiang County	687653	237	5595	6107	53916	29530	97301	2104
浏阳市	Liuyang City	619305	822	14200	6440	56100	19122	99563	2154
株洲市	**Zhuzhou City**	**1189283**	**594**	**11373**	**16634**	**153664**	**37055**	**212253**	**4406**
荷塘区	Hetang District	26555	47	1478	110	1169	2379	8327	145
芦淞区	Lousong District	10603			150	1325	220	1591	33
石峰区	Shifeng District	28365	1	37	157	1545	1132	4501	194
天元区	Tianyuan District	32600	1	37	231	2093	2257	7059	102
株洲县	Zhuzhou County	167233	13	471	1188	10475	10092	43943	625
攸县	You County	349113	480	8353	3884	35057	8192	43942	1909
茶陵县	Chaling County	195094			3185	31239	4491	33598	641
炎陵县	Yanling County	63965	52	997	1564	14072	987	5282	54
醴陵市	Liling City	315755			6165	56689	7305	64010	703
湘潭市	**Xiangtan City**	**987988**	**167**	**3142**	**10711**	**96454**	**104778**	**290882**	**2310**
雨湖区	Yuhu District	17664			179	1569	1027	3894	94
岳塘区	Yuetang District	53072	8	312	1035	9190	3678	10294	280
湘潭县	Xiangtan County	578268	92	1558	6200	55684	54842	182024	1308
湘乡市	Xiangxiang City	308551	42	832	2460	21782	43077	87132	628
韶山市	Shaoshan City	30433	25	440	837	8229	2154	7538	
衡阳市	**Hengyang City**	**1666949**	**3051**	**66372**	**11881**	**109651**	**85359**	**372514**	**6499**
郊区	Jiaoqu District	140460	413	12909	669	6246	8107	30891	267
南岳区	Nanyue District	8122			73	642	779	2198	14
衡阳县	Hengyang County	223636	983	21211	1687	15698	15288	41561	827
衡南县	Hengnan County	351602	562	9490	1387	12299	16336	84496	1787
衡山县	Hengshan County	176886			895	7902	5704	24089	796
衡东县	Hengdong County	218422	1	26	2426	21944	7748	36994	869
祁东县	Qidong County	177863	549	10883	452	4459	15127	53812	724
耒阳市	Leiyang City	205946	72	1676	2503	24031	7447	42092	919
常宁市	Changning City	164012	471	10177	1789	16430	8823	56381	296
邵阳市	**Shaoyang City**	**1935180**	**1884**	**39711**	**23195**	**216375**	**107423**	**405479**	**5754**
双清区	Shuangqing District	55575	54	1534	472	4168	2479	9973	255
大祥区	Daxiang District	30318	49	1318	300	2605	2771	11028	79
北塔区	Beita District	41529			93	822	1453	10181	99
邵东县	Shaodong County	363417	352	6765	3376	29964	27421	77240	1258

(continued)

市县名称	City and County	农业机械总动力(千瓦) Power of Agri-cultural Machinery (kw)	大中型拖拉机 Large and Medium Tractors		小型及手扶拖拉机 Mini and Walking Tractors		排灌机械 Machinery for Agricultural Drainage and Irrigation		农用载重汽车(辆) Trucks for Agri-cultural Use (unit)
			台 (unit)	千瓦 (kw)	台 (unit)	千瓦 (kw)	台 (unit)	千瓦 (kw)	
新邵县	Xinshao County	139095	106	2584	1987	22095	5988	28127	332
邵阳县	Shaoyang County	250257			2506	23902	21989	86871	478
隆回县	Longhui County	138217	392	8048	1705	15924	12790	55400	212
洞口县	Dongkou County	267397	483	10916	3449	31023	11502	37722	1398
绥宁县	Suining County	187044	129	2193	2556	21978	2395	20322	515
新宁县	Xinning County	130075			1231	12585	2947	13335	355
城步县	Chengbu County	99543	79	1423	1926	17796	2188	10738	300
武冈市	Wugang City	232713	240	4930	3594	33513	13500	44542	473
岳阳市	**Yueyang City**	**2991556**	**2035**	**79505**	**19783**	**178248**	**94847**	**715841**	**7617**
岳阳楼区	Yueyanglou District	47486	4	209	335	2958	528	4308	538
云溪区	Yunxi District	74759	17	935	310	2653	1422	15138	466
君山区	Junshan District	183884	702	31728	824	7852	2260	30514	530
岳阳县	Yueyang County	456957	72	3187	2028	17894	11949	83210	1297
华容县	Huarong County	434550	270	8201	2829	24958	24549	232753	334
湘阴县	Xiangyin County	482684	1	55	2312	20417	12995	70038	486
平江县	Pingjiang County	301416			3590	30515	8727	65354	808
汨罗市	Miluo City	577817	613	25053	4992	48501	14360	101910	1446
临湘市	Linxiang City	432003	356	10137	2563	22500	18057	112616	1712
常德市	**Changde City**	**2379233**	**1235**	**35064**	**23534**	**218641**	**167775**	**1039653**	**6122**
武陵区	Wuling District	138936	8	485	780	7163	5411	27826	434
鼎城区	Dingcheng District	449669	407	9127	4491	44358	27755	151302	1710
安乡县	Anxiang County	292202	183	9730	2412	21219	16238	109496	162
汉寿县	Hanshou County	332786	30	750	3250	35750	27424	303730	411
澧县	Li County	359058	37	639	2497	22562	39654	218344	968
临澧县	Linli County	204499			3450	26469	15606	71362	582
桃源县	Taoyuan County	277225	213	5634	2702	25350	18072	80624	977
石门县	Shimen County	229657	287	5703	2766	25253	10495	33865	695
津市市	Jinshi City	95201	70	2996	1186	10517	7120	43104	183
张家界市	**Zhangjiajie City**	**494207**	**138**	**2777**	**7399**	**66281**	**10983**	**59749**	**2215**
永定区	Yongding District	160992			2691	23735	2173	21253	760
武陵源区	Wulingyuan District	6789	2	37	285	2517	49	245	29
慈利县	Chili County	221913	100	1788	3049	27692	6764	31903	916
桑植县	Sangzhi County	104513	36	952	1374	12337	1997	6348	510
益阳市	**Yiyang City**	**2429016**	**1402**	**50921**	**19688**	**197129**	**145746**	**721414**	**4453**
资阳区	Ziyang District	308518	118	3264	2668	23571	20054	96827	552
赫山区	Heshan District	414317	199	8842	4841	44859	34172	154197	1187
南县	Nan County	511586	317	12169	4267	42515	35993	206526	220
桃江县	Taojiang County	470893	328	7534	2038	23288	16958	67051	902
安化县	Anhua County	271534	89	1660	2457	25167	7899	27055	1170
沅江市	Yuanjiang City	452168	351	17452	3417	37729	30670	169758	422
郴州市	**Chenzhou City**	**1774500**	**1051**	**24680**	**17576**	**161139**	**42549**	**201516**	**7887**
北湖区	Beihu District	90500			822	8916	749	5091	470
苏仙区	Suxian District	204057	20	352	879	7757	5151	21141	785
桂阳县	Guiyang County	224654	95	1986	2706	24157	7853	28398	826
宜章县	Yizhang County	341499	279	8355	1522	14776	10733	58760	1892
永兴县	Yongxing County	157076	57	1376	1689	15554	4179	22437	664

18-11 续表 2

(continued)

市县名称	City and County	农业机械总动力(千瓦) Power of Agricultural Machinery (kw)	大中型拖拉机 Large and Medium Tractors		小型及手扶拖拉机 Mini and Walking Tractors		排灌机械 Machinery for Agricultural Drainage and Irrigation		农用载重汽车(辆) Trucks for Agricultural Use (unit)
			台 (unit)	千瓦 (kw)	台 (unit)	千瓦 (kw)	台 (unit)	千瓦 (kw)	
嘉禾县	Jiahe County	172499	298	5929	1706	15080	5055	20989	988
临武县	Linwu County	202458	1	40	1895	17908	2542	12405	1166
汝城县	Rucheng County	123866	179	2862	2670	23692	2265	10016	259
桂东县	Guidong County	34129	10	233	987	9433	489	1798	58
安仁县	Anreng County	98532	14	1177	1357	11982	1295	8642	412
资兴市	Zixing City	125230	98	2370	1343	11884	2238	11839	367
永州市	**Yongzhou City**	**1842050**	**3179**	**55852**	**9113**	**79321**	**135467**	**627117**	**5413**
芝山区	Zhishan District	227443			572	6539	37677	141043	89
冷水滩区	Lengshuitan District	192998	543	9479	814	6954	20988	66499	277
祁阳县	Qiyang County	402000			708	5664	30600	183600	1230
东安县	Dongan County	184952	488	7174	565	5033	14791	54692	223
双牌县	Shuangpai County	49616	52	1072	191	1555	517	3707	13
道县	Dao County	90960	518	8127	484	4146	2400	22884	355
江永县	Jiangyong County	62036	25	1013	810	7152	3723	21146	204
宁远县	Ningyuan County	204580	505	7424	310	2737	10783	46568	423
蓝山县	Lanshan County	181436	150	5190	1040	7939	3553	19712	2040
新田县	Xintian County	122821	200	3000	2400	20000	3772	24600	477
江华县	Jianghua County	123208	698	13373	1219	11602	6663	42666	82
怀化市	**Huaihua City**	**1338996**	**1222**	**27321**	**8765**	**83536**	**51834**	**278912**	**3841**
鹤城区	Hecheng District	98809			715	6893	3568	13846	197
中方县	Zhongfang County	99172	170	3442	403	3562	1505	9233	379
沅陵县	Yuanling County	173082	39	733	599	5283	7137	30167	523
辰溪县	Chenxi County	129193	30	569	709	6684	5119	22507	434
溆浦县	Xupu County	216018	30	630	1451	15961	13576	82405	334
会同县	Huitong County	92362	133	4004	929	8721	2918	12659	192
麻阳县	Mayang County	61782	82	2603	248	2187	2652	24064	196
新晃县	Xinhuang County	55399	1	26	438	3826	1387	6830	125
芷江县	Zhijiang County	113449	222	4152	814	7188	6072	37688	252
靖州县	Jinzhou County	84751	108	2265	631	6310	3650	14235	369
通道县	Tongdao County	83461	344	7826	330	2915	1178	7599	360
洪江市	Hongjiang City	131518	63	1071	1498	14006	3072	17679	480
娄底市	**Loudi City**	**1284686**	**897**	**19946**	**8798**	**84382**	**81697**	**296797**	**6143**
娄星区	Louxing District	148234	33	1933	1738	16314	9794	25994	766
双峰县	Shuangfeng County	424960	314	7011	1630	15124	42637	111849	2170
新化县	Xinhua County	254370	538	10825	1559	17183	10520	67169	903
冷水江市	Lenshuijiang City	87805	12	177	252	2215	1924	16792	567
涟源市	Lianyuan City	369317			3619	33546	16822	74993	1737
湘西自治州	**West Hunan A.P**	**681928**	**283**	**6384**	**9191**	**84184**	**15107**	**91101**	**1681**
吉首市	Jishou City	72531			1050	9272	598	5026	244
泸溪县	Louxi County	74816	32	574	568	5015	3632	24814	224
凤凰县	Fenghuang County	83415	4	221	681	6595	3003	23994	95
花垣县	Huayuan County	72500			1230	12767	1365	6523	182
保靖县	Baojin County	53894	106	2343	907	8057	974	3606	117
古丈县	Guzhang County	38058			398	3502	549	2613	184
永顺县	Yongshun County	87307	67	1932	1803	16077	2768	10137	175
龙山县	Longshan County	199407	74	1314	2554	22899	2218	14388	460

18-12 各市、州、县农村用电及化肥农药施用量(2001年)

E1ectricity Consumed and Fertilizer，Pesticide Applied in Rural Areas (2001)

市县名称	City and County	农村小水电(个数) Small Hydropower Station in Rural Areas (unit)	装机容量(千瓦) Capacity of Power Generating Sets (kw)	农村用电量(万千瓦小时) Electricity Consumed in Rural Area (10 000 kw.h)	化肥施用实物量(吨) Consumption of Chemical Fertilizer (ton)	每公顷播种面积施用量(公斤) Consumption of Per Hectare Sown Area (kg)	农药施用量(吨) Consumption of Chemical Pesticide (ton)
长沙市	**Changsha City**	**129**	**6575**	**73563**	**513404**	**842**	**8554**
芙蓉区	Furong District			2635	963	260	36
天心区	Tianxin District			1629	2438	871	56
岳麓区	Yuelu District			5131	5218	792	81
开福区	Kaifu District			2598	5876	583	131
雨花区	Yuhua District			4321	6153	805	116
长沙县	Changsha County	2	750	18964	94914	712	1641
望城县	Wangcheng County	4	536	10417	81353	784	1194
宁乡县	Ningxiang County	27	2889	13153	185845	953	2987
浏阳市	Liuyang City	96	2400	14715	130644	889	2312
株洲市	**Zhuzhou City**	**169**	**40600**	**40571.3**	**316922**	**923**	**3446**
荷塘区	Hetang District			2030	2465	354	65
芦淞区	Lousong District			1750	1020	543	45
石峰区	Shifeng District			3592	2320	264	35
天元区	Tianyuan District			485	5777	795	102
株洲县	Zhuzhou County	9	337	2905	49460	894	540
攸 县	You County	45	12400	8664.3	105980	1139	681
茶陵县	Chaling County	7	2695	3065	67433	1099	675
炎陵县	Yanling County	25	17740	8108	11137	487	89
醴陵市	Liling City	83	7428	9972	71330	830	1214
湘潭市	**Xiangtan City**	**23**	**1715**	**26711**	**333309**	**1241**	**4347**
雨湖区	Yuhu District			1548	3116	925	31
岳塘区	Yuetang District			2475	7581	981	80
湘潭县	Xiangtan County	22	1675	12346	189467	1359	2652
湘乡市	Xiangxiang City	1	40	7744	124210	1172	1484
韶山市	Shaoshan City			2598	8935	742	100
衡阳市	**Hengyang City**	**135**	**9554**	**29473.2**	**693855**	**864**	**13397**
郊区	Jiaoqu District			2402	19436	1157	320
南岳区	Nanyue District	4	68	245	3278	860	57
衡阳县	Hengyang County	8	895	6220	126225	749	1551
衡南县	Hengnan County	10	849	5026	136276	861	2345
衡山县	Hengshan County	17	2510	2789	40941	993	811
衡东县	Hengdong County	12	690	2866	82596	915	1247
祁东县	Qidong County	8	99	3329	72402	881	1237
耒阳市	Leiyang City	26	880	4350	112833	820	1500
常宁市	Changning City	50	3563	2246.2	99868	954	4329
邵阳市	**Shaoyang City**	**236**	**31570**	**38325.03**	**629703**	**849**	**6722**
双清区	Shuangqing District	1	375	675	6077	842	52
大祥区	Daxiang District			691.97	9056	683	106
北塔区	Beita District			513.1	4559	927	50
邵东县	Shaodong County	5	895	7890	120488	1194	981

市县名称	City and County	农村小水电(个数) Small Hydropower Station in Rural Areas (unit)	装机容量(千瓦) Capacity of Power Generating Sets (kw)	农村用电量(万千瓦小时) Electricity Consumed in Rural Area (10 000 kw.h)	化肥施用实物量(吨) Consumption of Chemical Fertilizer (ton)	每公顷播种面积施用量(公斤) Consumption of Per Hectare Sown Area (kg)	农药施用量(吨) Consumption of Chemical Pesticide (ton)
新邵县	Xinshao County	10	2396	3529	53896	826	537
邵阳县	Shaoyang County	7	287	3569.33	79458	820	643
隆回县	Longhui County	13	2511	8274.83	100672	836	999
洞口县	Dongkou County	18	6375	4229.8	91735	837	1644
绥宁县	Suining County	34	7330	2380	26639	690	364
新宁县	Xinning County	70	2621	3172	54359	759	610
城步县	Chengbu County	58	6170	964	13289	519	128
武冈市	Wugang City	20	2610	2436	69475	795	608
岳阳市	**Yueyang City**	**66**	**13050**	**31161**	**721807**	**992**	**6057**
岳阳楼区	Yueyanglou District			1960	5333	746	28
云溪区	Yunxi District			1268	17525	1136	90
君山区	Junshan District			1870	58515	1177	740
岳阳县	Yueyang County	9	1504	2281	104732	914	722
华容县	Huarong County			3885	191516	1471	1325
湘阴县	Xiangyin County			4710	101147	817	635
平江县	Pingjiang County	42	8446	6038	97339	923	616
汨罗市	Miluo City	1	150	6220	91747	907	1530
临湘市	Linxiang City	14	2950	2929	53953	673	371
常德市	**Changde City**	**60**	**12964**	**59839.06**	**1074197**	**1065**	**7736**
武陵区	Wuling District			2973.98	20138	1039	104
鼎城区	Dingcheng District	3	250	10909	165350	903	1665
安乡县	Anxiang County			6259	155011	1712	901
汉寿县	Hanshou County			7723.14	172038	1321	1347
澧县	Li County	7	1156	6779.5	184744	1269	1598
临澧县	Linli County	2	660	11291	82466	985	317
桃源县	Taoyuan County	32	8595	8751.6	138873	660	717
石门县	Shimen County	16	2303	3925.84	114582	1083	745
津市市	Jinshi City			1226	40995	1019	342
张家界市	**Zhangjiajie City**	**68**	**13807**	**6255.42**	**144469**	**632**	**1782**
永定区	Yongding District	16	2786	1226	30085	492	562
武陵源区	Wulingyuan District			231	3739	659	32
慈利县	Chili County	42	7871	3325	73020	728	855
桑植县	Sangzhi County	10	3150	1473.42	37625	612	333
益阳市	**Yiyang City**	**276**	**20687**	**31775**	**615338**	**1079**	**8425**
资阳区	Ziyang District			2596	49707	1088	1119
赫山区	Heshan District	4	350	8214	95108	1042	2280
南县	Nan County			7007	195325	1397	2183
桃江县	Taojiang County	48	3559	6600	60003	774	460
安化县	Anhua County	224	16778	2216	53741	541	512
沅江市	Yuanjiang City			5142	161454	1383	1871
郴州市	**Chenzhou City**	**965**	**125345**	**30351.05**	**476505**	**912**	**5825**
北湖区	Beihu District	56	16457	1594.87	16635	751	284
苏仙区	Suxian District	120	17861	3767.7	29572	977	429
桂阳县	Guiyang County	326	18729	5719.87	92585	947	917
宜章县	Yizhang County	56	14418	3663.97	49651	784	579
永兴县	Yongxing County	127	3975	2425.16	68048	941	609

市县名称	City and County	农村小水电(个数) Small Hydropower Station in Rural Areas (unit)	装机容量(千瓦) Capacity of Power Generating Sets (kw)	农村用电量(万千瓦小时) Electricity Consumed in Rural Area (10000 kw.h)	化肥施用实物量(吨) Consumption of Chemical Fertilizer (ton)	每公顷播种面积施用量(公斤) Consumption of Per Hectare Sown Area (kg)	农药施用量(吨) Consumption of Chemical Pesticide (ton)
嘉禾县	Jiahe County	7	2760	1822.06	33349	793	333
临武县	Linwu County	31	7944	1935.21	30257	845	294
汝城县	Rucheng County	82	21581	1333.56	53617	1205	796
桂东县	Guidong County	46	4105	770	14321	1011	138
安仁县	Anreng County	11	2757	1851.65	44839	855	556
资兴市	Zixing City	103	14758	5467	43631	910	890
永州市	**Yongzhou City**	**1621**	**50750**	**31147.8**	**635723**	**859**	**7692**
芝山区	Zhishan District	113	4697	2664	58710	633	680
冷水滩区	Lengshuitan District	16	1580	2994.8	56201	922	581
祁阳县	Qiyang County	74	5079	7512	105945	803	1668
东安县	Dongan County	143	7213	3955	58394	610	826
双牌县	Shuangpai County	145	6283	1857	16279	883	170
道县	Dao County	155	1471	1278	97006	958	793
江永县	Jiangyong County	55	147	472	47692	1317	641
宁远县	Ningyuan County	479	3110	2582	70212	1079	847
蓝山县	Lanshan County	234	3283	1769	38469	1157	592
新田县	Xintian County	175	342	1394	43722	943	343
江华县	Jianghua County	32	17545	4670	43093	746	551
怀化市	**Huaihua City**	**239**	**49067**	**29661.91**	**306731**	**506**	**6093**
鹤城区	Hecheng District	7	2375	1620	7727	362	321
中方县	Zhongfang County	20	4815	1671	16668	427	413
沅陵县	Yuanling County	11	4800	6253.44	24409	267	551
辰溪县	Chenxi County	8	1452	1968	30561	564	650
溆浦县	Xupu County	75	2731	3134.37	79890	763	1352
会同县	Huitong County	23	6121	2201	16467	378	359
麻阳县	Mayang County	10	3035	1563	19854	422	415
新晃县	Xinhuang County	5	2200	1925.3	13278	366	184
芷江县	Zhijiang County	14	2808	2319	30186	557	598
靖州县	Jinzhou County	13	3400	1406	16254	457	275
通道县	Tongdao County	14	2435	1124.5	10211	367	134
洪江市	Hongjiang City	39	12895	4476.3	41226	803	841
娄底市	**Loudi City**	**83**	**18969**	**28047.28**	**300460**	**848**	**3617**
娄星区	Louxing District	8	3940	4302	18059	814	272
双峰县	Shuangfeng County			7039.28	120935	1117	1458
新化县	Xinhua County	50	7405	4496	75049	700	615
冷水江市	Lenshuijiang City	3	570	4850	9202	701	268
涟源市	Lianyuan City	22	7054	7360	77215	748	1004
湘西自治州	**West Hunan A.P**	**108**	**22888**	**10465.61**	**171464**	**422**	**1898**
吉首市	Jishou City	10	1740	1204	17473	637	284
泸溪县	Louxi County	10	1881	849.77	15091	372	307
凤凰县	Fenghuang County	14	3440	1219	19466	292	309
花垣县	Huayuan County	20	4838	1073	29910	857	64
保靖县	Baojin County	14	2424	2399	17606	386	149
古丈县	Guzhang County	11	1650	304.34	4703	222	59
永顺县	Yongshun County	14	2425	1257.02	31129	352	425
龙山县	Longshan County	15	4490	2159.48	36086	443	301

18-13 各市、州、县农林牧渔业总产值(2001年)

Gross Output Value of Farming,Forestry,Animal Husbandry and fishery (2001)

单位：万元 (10 000 yuan)

市县名称	City and County	农林牧渔业总产值 Gross Output Value of Farming, Forestry, Animal Husbandry and Fishery	指数(上年为100) Indices (preceding year=100)	农业产值 Gross Output Value of Farming	#种植业产值 Gross Output Value of Planting	林业产值 Gross Output Value of Forestry	牧业产值 Gross Output Value of Animal Husbandry	渔业产值 Gross Output Value of Fishery
长沙市	**Changsha City**	**1239985.2**	**5.91**	**672703.9**	**624720.7**	**47407.8**	**464640.8**	**55232.8**
芙蓉区	Furong District	19591.0	4.10	11222.1	10592.1	43.7	7430.7	894.5
天心区	Tianxin District	11963.3	7.94	7387.8	5567.8	162.7	3192.5	1220.3
岳麓区	Yuelu District	29215.7	4.98	15988.3	14834.1	276.7	11987.2	963.5
开福区	Kaifu District	35180.0	8.28	15680.9	13133.9	536.2	14986.9	3976.0
雨花区	Yuhua District	31738.2	4.93	19843.0	17189.0	59.6	10543.8	1291.9
长沙县	Changsha County	287751.1	5.57	155724.9	146236.2	4915.0	118980.0	8131.2
望城县	Wangcheng County	196662.7	4.99	96345.7	88951.7	4761.7	83249.4	12306.0
宁乡县	Ningxiang County	332998.3	5.59	188125.2	175515.8	11664.6	119690.6	13517.9
浏阳市	Liuyang City	294884.8	7.15	162385.9	152700.3	24987.6	94579.9	12931.4
株洲市	**Zhuzhou City**	**782113.8**	**4.07**	**396463.8**	**362129.4**	**46253.5**	**301762.7**	**37633.8**
荷塘区	Hetang District	15177.5	-11.03	7911.5	7476.5	689.2	5712.7	864.1
芦淞区	Lousong District	9876.6	12.40	3992.1	3825.8	965.7	3895.0	1023.7
石峰区	Shifeng District	21479.2	9.09	10254.8	10060.8	503.5	9280.7	1440.2
天元区	Tianyuan District	20255.7	7.35	10658.4	10084.1	442.0	8675.0	480.2
株洲县	Zhuzhou County	107150.4	3.23	57713.4	54896.4	4852.1	38806.5	5778.4
攸 县	You County	228342.7	4.20	118447.1	105715.7	12751.4	88287.4	8856.8
茶陵县	Chaling County	137390.1	3.76	63768.2	58370.7	8356.3	57973.5	7292.1
炎陵县	Yanling County	42213.5	3.56	18337.9	17366.2	10484.6	12877.3	513.7
醴陵市	Liling City	200228.2	4.92	105380.4	94333.4	7208.7	76254.6	11384.5
湘潭市	**Xiangtan City**	**556338.6**	**5.03**	**239035.1**	**224625.3**	**7253.4**	**274662.0**	**35388.1**
雨湖区	Yuhu District	21890.1	7.78	6484.5	6295.5	18.3	14410.1	977.2
岳塘区	Yuetang District	24626.5	6.02	9887.0	9034.5	178.0	13157.7	1403.8
湘潭县	Xiangtan County	287430.9	5.01	130750.4	122962.7	3558.0	135304.0	17818.6
湘乡市	Xiangxiang City	202283.9	4.67	83109.1	77869.4	3408.7	101919.8	13846.4
韶山市	Shaoshan City	20107.1	4.95	8804.2	8463.2	90.4	9870.4	1342.1
衡阳市	**Hengyang City**	**1647209.2**	**3.48**	**708380.8**	**645491.3**	**45666.4**	**765604.9**	**127557.1**
郊区	Jiaoqu District	52453.2	0.68	27664.8	26733.3	1006.6	18261.4	5520.4
南岳区	Nanyue District	11129.7	3.22	5971.2	5228.8	893.2	3984.4	281.0
衡阳县	Hengyang County	357014.2	3.22	135978.0	121481.7	6938.8	182950.9	31146.5
衡南县	Hengnan County	330626.1	3.08	155791.3	140434.6	3193.2	146211.5	25430.2
衡山县	Hengshan County	99517.2	3.53	44433.5	37284.0	2024.6	47980.0	5079.1
衡东县	Hengdong County	171688.9	4.11	70883.0	64973.2	6036.7	86402.1	8367.1
祁东县	Qidong County	210342.1	3.77	97192.0	86589.2	1164.6	86221.2	25764.4
耒阳市	Leiyang City	234364.7	4.23	94305.5	90909.7	14959.2	111632.4	13467.6
常宁市	Changning City	180073.2	3.63	76161.6	71856.8	9449.6	81961.0	12500.9
邵阳市	**Shaoyang City**	**1288123.1**	**2.77**	**673891.9**	**618013.1**	**62976.7**	**504143.9**	**47110.6**
双清区	Shuangqing District	16783.6	11.74	6857.5	6568.4	43.1	8867.3	1015.7
大祥区	Daxiang District	22246.2	9.56	12059.1	11476.1	106.9	9060.8	1019.2
北塔区	Beita District	10266.3	7.45	4920.7	4810.7	97.2	4441.6	806.8
邵东县	Shaodong County	240569.1	2.96	131364.7	117747.1	1836.7	89372.5	17995.2

单位：万元 18-13 续表 1 (10 000 yuan)

市县名称	City and County	农林牧渔业总产值 Gross Output Value of Farming, Forestry, Animal Husbandry and Fishery	指数(上年为100) Indices (preceding year=100)	农业产值 Gross Output Value of Farming	#种植业产值 Gross Output Value of Planting	林业产值 Gross Output Value of Forestry	牧业产值 Gross Output Value of Animal Husbandry	渔业产值 Gross Output Value of Fishery
新邵县	Xinshao County	113981.9	2.70	64107.3	56757.2	2280.5	44556.4	3037.7
邵阳县	Shaoyang County	120387.9	0.82	73884.9	69585.8	2345.9	39628.4	4528.6
隆回县	Longhui County	150859.4	1.37	89941.4	83052.4	4398.7	53513.4	3005.9
洞口县	Dongkou County	205643.1	4.50	91420.0	87540.7	5955.3	103228.1	5039.8
绥宁县	Suining County	105961.0	-1.59	44159.4	39118.6	35455.1	24894.2	1452.4
新宁县	Xinning County	88285.9	4.17	56635.7	50974.3	3443.8	25244.0	2962.4
城步县	Chengbu County	37783.5	2.39	19246.5	17503.9	5670.8	12487.6	378.7
武冈市	Wugang City	175355.1	3.80	79294.7	72877.8	1342.7	88849.6	5868.2
岳阳市	**Yueyang City**	**1508819.1**	**6.79**	**759185.4**	**721719.8**	**29464.7**	**549418.5**	**170750.5**
岳阳楼区	Yueyanglou District	38083.3	-0.42	10947.9	10077.3	26.6	18602.1	8506.7
云溪区	Yunxi District	40964.4	9.72	18016.2	17074.0	711.9	14040.1	8196.3
君山区	Junshan District	99084.3	8.36	57364.1	55224.8	692.5	26947.2	14080.5
岳阳县	Yueyang County	236586.0	8.00	122803.7	115884.6	4278.0	90396.5	19107.8
华容县	Huarong County	291674.6	7.79	160144.8	157071.7	2631.6	88381.4	40516.8
湘阴县	Xiangyin County	256531.0	3.68	123277.1	118721.0	635.8	81336.6	51281.6
平江县	Pingjiang County	182202.5	6.60	97430.6	89331.5	12286.5	70463.2	2022.2
汨罗市	Miluo City	246888.8	7.56	99817.9	94074.8	1283.7	129322.5	16464.7
临湘市	Linxiang City	116804.2	7.59	69383.2	64260.1	6918.1	29928.8	10574.0
常德市	**Changde City**	**1649031.0**	**4.88**	**738044.0**	**708891.0**	**27419.0**	**675437.0**	**208131.0**
武陵区	Wuling District	46085.0	6.02	20486.0	20201.0	101.0	15776.0	9722.0
鼎城区	Dingcheng District	275828.0	1.85	128337.0	124299.0	5801.0	99220.0	42470.0
安乡县	Anxiang County	170973.0	5.63	71163.0	69984.0	810.0	54834.0	44166.0
汉寿县	Hanshou County	197244.0	5.43	101281.0	97442.0	2666.0	52695.0	40602.0
澧县	Li County	236742.0	10.11	109899.0	108248.0	1849.0	102477.0	22517.0
临澧县	Linli County	156470.0	0.85	62860.0	55546.0	3948.0	78007.0	11655.0
桃源县	Taoyuan County	336800.0	5.82	145458.0	139501.0	9863.0	158733.0	22746.0
石门县	Shimen County	162073.0	2.79	70690.0	66594.0	1879.0	85454.0	4050.0
津市市	Jinshi City	66816.0	6.08	27870.0	27076.0	502.0	28241.0	10203.0
张家界市	**Zhangjiajie City**	**238286.1**	**2.53**	**140292.1**	**126247.8**	**17631.6**	**75882.0**	**4480.4**
永定区	Yongding District	74792.6	2.99	46183.8	42536.1	4486.5	22237.7	1884.7
武陵源区	Wulingyuan District	7390.3	6.78	4581.2	4199.6	841.4	1958.8	9.0
慈利县	Chili County	109642.5	2.71	60968.4	55028.2	7951.4	38509.0	2213.7
桑植县	Sangzhi County	46460.7	0.99	28558.8	24483.9	4352.4	13176.5	373.0
益阳市	**Yiyang City**	**881048.0**	**5.81**	**498780.0**	**433685.0**	**35489.0**	**246555.0**	**100224.0**
资阳区	Ziyang District	61567.0	6.26	36278.0	34959.0	641.0	16216.0	8432.0
赫山区	Heshan District	156223.0	5.21	89131.0	66253.0	3871.0	54312.0	8909.0
南县	Nan County	200421.0	11.19	121839.0	110818.0	930.0	43965.0	33687.0
桃江县	Taojiang County	134599.0	4.65	84028.0	62429.0	10926.0	37568.0	2077.0
安化县	Anhua County	134975.0	5.68	66286.0	60671.0	16130.0	46275.0	6284.0
沅江市	Yuanjiang City	193263.0	1.74	101218.0	98555.0	2991.0	48219.0	40835.0
郴州市	**Chenzhou City**	**981665.5**	**5.06**	**485064.0**	**445621.8**	**65217.8**	**385119.5**	**46264.2**
北湖区	Beihu District	50629.3	6.89	25178.3	23812.6	3311.7	20227.9	1911.4
苏仙区	Suxian District	71902.5	6.85	27547.9	25957.6	6524.3	33073.6	4756.8
桂阳县	Guiyang County	182091.8	3.96	115209.1	104533.1	8279.7	52072.5	6530.6
宜章县	Yizhang County	98051.7	6.49	47979.3	44203.6	3578.2	43017.6	3476.7
永兴县	Yongxing County	126145.9	5.99	56596.4	50849.5	6703.8	54460.2	8385.5

单位：万元

18-13 续表 2

(10 000 yuan)

市县名称	City and County	农林牧渔业总产值 Gross Output Value of Farming, Forestry, Animal Husbandry and Fishery	指数(上年=100) Indices (preceding year=100)	农业产值 Gross Output Value of Farming	#种植业产值 Gross Output Value of Planting	林业产值 Gross Output Value of Forestry	牧业产值 Gross Output Value of Animal Husbandry	渔业产值 Gross Output Value of Fishery
嘉禾县	Jiahe County	86641.0	5.73	40436.7	38130.0	3172.5	41335.8	1696.0
临武县	Linwu County	70045.0	5.22	37436.8	36050.5	3670.0	26889.7	2048.6
汝城县	Rucheng County	64017.3	3.74	30753.1	28646.7	7405.4	25181.6	677.1
桂东县	Guidong County	24036.3	4.08	12472.2	11192.4	2465.6	8669.8	428.6
安仁县	Anreng County	103123.6	1.66	52990.0	44977.0	4364.7	40791.4	4977.6
资兴市	Zixing City	104981.1	6.55	38464.2	37268.8	15741.9	39399.5	11375.4
永州市	**Yongzhou City**	**1327864.9**	**4.50**	**677969.4**	**607427.1**	**61019.3**	**519023.5**	**69852.7**
芝山区	Zhishan District	161173.2	3.48	90237.1	83134.4	2421.4	63454.2	5060.6
冷水滩区	Lengshuitan District	123806.1	5.60	59766.4	52820.1	3117.5	52405.3	8517.0
祁阳县	Qiyang County	228159.5	3.75	109942.8	106326.8	10221.8	88896.0	19098.9
东安县	Dongan County	161758.2	6.19	94004.3	76959.8	6420.3	52834.1	8499.5
双牌县	Shuangpai County	38748.5	1.36	18903.5	15569.9	6876.7	11341.2	1627.1
道县	Dao County	164252.0	2.82	79508.4	75057.3	6316.2	66490.8	11936.6
江永县	Jiangyong County	77028.0	9.53	45467.4	43454.6	2130.0	27444.9	1985.7
宁远县	Ningyuan County	128761.1	2.88	60727.0	54769.2	3901.8	56427.7	7704.6
蓝山县	Lanshan County	72491.6	2.02	31739.4	25426.9	4952.7	34600.9	1198.6
新田县	Xintian County	80818.3	2.00	42228.8	38792.6	1714.3	33983.9	2891.4
江华县	Jianghua County	90868.5	10.23	45444.3	35115.5	12946.6	31144.8	1332.9
怀化市	**Huaihua City**	**894045.0**	**3.46**	**491170.1**	**431299.7**	**75416.1**	**301335.8**	**26122.9**
鹤城区	Hecheng District	36415.0	3.30	18907.3	15836.6	3921.9	10982.4	2603.5
中方县	Zhongfang County	60035.8	4.10	30464.6	28740.2	6922.5	19906.3	2742.5
沅陵县	Yuanling County	98366.1	2.48	56114.0	46243.4	13305.8	26340.3	2606.1
辰溪县	Chenxi County	66179.4	2.99	39772.6	36282.5	2567.5	22827.1	1012.1
溆浦县	Xupu County	181851.3	4.26	99462.3	91270.9	7132.2	70764.1	4492.8
会同县	Huitong County	76396.1	2.14	40841.1	29743.0	8951.5	24812.5	1790.9
麻阳县	Mayang County	60738.3	3.33	39170.1	33147.4	2034.0	18056.8	1477.5
新晃县	Xinhuang County	34970.8	3.26	17153.9	15667.0	1608.2	15402.9	805.8
芷江县	Zhijiang County	80302.3	3.96	41677.2	38827.0	6105.0	30595.4	1924.7
靖州县	Jinzhou County	66108.5	2.52	32557.9	30529.5	9967.9	20639.0	2943.7
通道县	Tongdao County	38648.8	4.63	20435.5	17209.4	7073.5	10230.6	909.2
洪江市	Hongjiang City	94032.7	4.24	54613.7	47802.8	5826.2	30778.5	2814.3
娄底市	**Loudi City**	**611165.4**	**0.50**	**268435.3**	**253875.8**	**9785.4**	**303859.4**	**29085.3**
娄星区	Louxing District	44167.6	0.70	18929.0	18127.4	724.3	21555.4	2958.9
双峰县	Shuangfeng County	235590.7	1.48	99639.4	95746.3	4350.9	119575.1	12025.3
新化县	Xinhua County	169867.6	0.44	68813.2	63515.1	2606.1	91307.1	7141.1
冷水江市	Lenshuijiang City	28603.7	1.84	10854.8	10089.9	506.7	15727.0	1515.3
涟源市	Lianyuan City	132935.8	-1.44	70199.0	66397.1	1597.4	55694.8	5444.6
湘西自治州	**West Hunan A.P**	**355636.5**	**2.81**	**236042.1**	**207492.7**	**19538.6**	**88058.4**	**11997.4**
吉首市	Jishou City	43709.7	4.01	31525.1	28961.2	1423.0	9518.7	1243.0
泸溪县	Louxi County	38642.9	0.23	24416.7	22216.3	1452.8	11528.7	1244.7
凤凰县	Fenghuang County	37689.4	3.16	28643.7	24319.5	1425.0	6635.0	985.6
花垣县	Huayuan County	35893.0	2.65	21291.9	17709.2	949.8	11543.4	2107.9
保靖县	Baojin County	36636.6	3.18	24813.3	21904.7	1379.8	9619.1	824.4
古丈县	Guzhang County	17549.1	0.47	10941.7	8411.3	1794.0	3970.3	843.2
永顺县	Yongshun County	67203.7	4.36	43985.7	40627.3	3973.9	18035.4	1208.8
龙山县	Longshan County	78312.2	2.48	50424.0	43343.2	7140.4	17207.7	3540.0

18-14 各市州、县主要农产品产量(2001年)

Output of Major Farm Crops (2001)

单位：吨 (ton)

市县名称	City and County	粮食合计 Total Grain	稻谷 Rice	小麦 Wheat	薯类 Tubers	杂粮 Coarse Cereals	#玉米 Corn	大豆 Beans
长沙市	**Changsha City**	**2503041**	**2299943**	**6859**	**97099**	**73964**	**63284**	**13097**
芙蓉区	Furong District	84			60			24
天心区	Tianxin District	8489	8234		30			225
岳麓区	Yuelu District	11773	10113		1514	73	73	23
开福区	Kaifu District	37599	36110		635	525	525	317
雨花区	Yuhua District	10804	10736					38
长沙县	Changsha County	530937	492534	855	11390	21437	20241	2567
望城县	Wangcheng County	463012	425892	272	28135	6710	5471	965
宁乡县	Ningxiang County	826820	767340	2696	35514	11119	5369	6118
浏阳市	Liuyang City	613523	548984	3036	19821	34100	31605	2820
株洲市	**Zhuzhou City**	**1788599**	**1709320**	**18**	**40554**	**19276**	**18867**	**12519**
荷塘区	Hetang District	36741	35747		794	36	36	96
芦淞区	Lousong District	6758	6739					19
石峰区	Shifeng District	31731	28969		1107	368	368	764
天元区	Tianyuan District	40950	40200		510			64
株洲县	Zhuzhou County	306887	297195		5523	604	569	1308
攸 县	You County	469265	454312		9171	2308	2219	2661
茶陵县	Chaling County	331323	315723		9583	784	784	4380
炎陵县	Yanling County	107823	102344		3328	300	252	1462
醴陵市	Liling City	457121	428091	18	10538	14876	14639	1765
湘潭市	**Xiangtan City**	**1377917**	**1342510**	**1486**	**15579**	**12045**	**10846**	**2788**
雨湖区	Yuhu District	10442	10442					
岳塘区	Yuetang District	34386	33766		455	80	80	
湘潭县	Xiangtan County	765649	746722	438	7501	8262	8160	1192
湘乡市	Xiangxiang City	506374	491596	931	7048	3514	2417	1520
韶山市	Shaoshan City	61066	59984	117	575	189	189	76
衡阳市	**Hengyang City**	**3184796**	**2980558**	**12559**	**86598**	**42282**	**24444**	**37179**
郊区	Jiaoqu District	55221	51410		1691	1662	966	177
南岳区	Nanyue District	12455	11367		931	38	38	34
衡阳县	Hengyang County	674743	638439	990	18144	5474	910	5640
衡南县	Hengnan County	591718	553257	780	9332	11068	8701	9792
衡山县	Hengshan County	191587	185612		2121	2472	162	682
衡东县	Hengdong County	391754	366279		15948	3371	2541	3133
祁东县	Qidong County	398461	375489	2672	8700	1744	936	6793
耒阳市	Leiyang City	469684	430884	3564	15465	10866	8667	5153
常宁市	Changning City	399173	367821	4553	14266	5587	1523	5775
邵阳市	**Shaoyang City**	**2949837**	**2402797**	**45023**	**168817**	**269751**	**259350**	**55480**
双清区	Shuangqing District	27420	23685	77	2138	755	655	701
大祥区	Daxiang District	44498	37227	348	2495	2780	2743	1325
北塔区	Beita District	17847	14322	245	2121	402	317	596
邵东县	Shaodong County	410932	345071	5155	15095	34150	32627	9526

单位：吨　　18-14 续表 1　continued　　(ton)

市县名称	City and County	粮食合计 Total Grain	稻谷 Rice	小麦 Wheat	薯类 Tubers	杂粮 Coarse Cereals	#玉米 Corn	大豆 Beans
新邵县	Xinshao County	297160	228561	11177	38452	11364	9449	6736
邵阳县	Shaoyang County	335634	286739	3185	14577	20741	18515	9762
隆回县	Longhui County	402462	326401	10016	31986	25833	25202	7450
洞口县	Dongkou County	451377	378233	6941	18964	38059	35940	7319
绥宁县	Suining County	146865	129533	350	10101	4044	3345	2591
新宁县	Xinning County	283466	214388	1680	14843	48576	48576	3709
城步县	Chengbu County	91167	70062	812	2770	16451	16080	792
武冈市	Wugang City	441009	348575	5037	15275	66596	65901	4973
岳阳市	**Yueyang City**	**2246005**	**1981805**	**2830**	**101693**	**113206**	**110917**	**34105**
岳阳楼区	Yueyanglou District	11591	6575		2406	2119	1939	10
云溪区	Yunxi District	32359	26157	36	3775	1095	1095	813
君山区	Junshan District	93920	89604		551	2167	2147	825
岳阳县	Yueyang County	400445	325390	500	31578	27450	27450	11551
华容县	Huarong County	274211	259123		3500	6488	6368	4000
湘阴县	Xiangyin County	406853	365800	468	16050	20500	20500	2100
平江县	Pingjiang County	422663	386847	1640	19346	7498	5573	5992
汨罗市	Miluo City	392124	335748	25	9690	43368	43324	2156
临湘市	Linxiang City	211839	186561	161	14797	2521	2521	6658
常德市	**Changde City**	**2490389**	**2282948**	**9976**	**87016**	**62792**	**60136**	**30136**
武陵区	Wuling District	32211	31815		80	56	56	182
鼎城区	Dingcheng District	483225	473299		3678	464	464	4349
安乡县	Anxiang County	197912	189906	7	2065	2679	2297	1486
汉寿县	Hanshou County	372969	363603	10	5118	846	846	2174
澧县	Li County	327336	296555	3284	10595	10834	10141	2986
临澧县	Linli County	234298	225737	900	2593	975	496	2107
桃源县	Taoyuan County	511887	462157	61	25016	8871	8110	11238
石门县	Shimen County	226049	141624	5591	36244	35628	35502	3950
津市市	Jinshi City	104502	98252	123	1627	2439	2224	1664
张家界市	**Zhangjiajie City**	**581810**	**339906**	**18540**	**106088**	**97698**	**96733**	**15561**
永定区	Yongding District	159059	107644	1401	28389	17441	17083	3674
武陵源区	Wulingyuan District	13591	8651	330	1848	2181	2060	453
慈利县	Chili County	270981	162279	12450	38240	49592	49272	5840
桑植县	Sangzhi County	138179	61332	4359	37611	28484	28318	5594
益阳市	**Yiyang City**	**1735050**	**1577646**	**6052**	**86834**	**41226**	**37201**	**11550**
资阳区	Ziyang District	169138	156872		11106	91	91	191
赫山区	Heshan District	368365	357450	420	7411	1073	1035	985
南县	Nan County	315833	300177	354	6568	4292	3734	1164
桃江县	Taojiang County	302008	278212	221	16655	5093	4271	1013
安化县	Anhua County	264688	193265	5057	32381	23935	21328	7475
沅江市	Yuanjiang City	315018	291670		12713	6742	6742	722
郴州市	**Chenzhou City**	**1940989**	**1617506**	**4118**	**133321**	**145585**	**140654**	**34271**
北湖区	Beihu District	63095	52055		5887	3534	3393	1288
苏仙区	Suxian District	125590	110654		6321	6711	6585	1795
桂阳县	Guiyang County	320952	258675	837	34712	13267	12196	13148
宜章县	Yizhang County	232537	184077		16749	28816	28577	2787
永兴县	Yongxing County	258833	221224	1923	13343	18131	17050	2028

单位：吨　　18-14 续表 2　continued　　(ton)

市县名称	City and County	粮食合计 Total Grain	稻谷 Rice	小麦 Wheat	薯类 Tubers	杂粮 Coarse Cereals	#玉米 Corn	大豆 Beans
嘉禾县	Jiahe County	157056	107348	740	18079	26701	26261	3333
临武县	Linwu County	130647	96167	371	12994	18389	17652	2186
汝城县	Rucheng County	160418	145730	89	5795	7324	7158	1188
桂东县	Guidong County	56073	52683	30	1782	785	785	570
安仁县	Anreng County	261388	246858		9950	616	538	3579
资兴市	Zixing City	174400	142035	128	7709	21311	20459	2369
永州市	**Yongzhou City**	**2549867**	**2215874**	**15114**	**143511**	**87111**	**74270**	**68742**
芝山区	Zhishan District	324779	303356	1100	7857	5252	1949	4970
冷水滩区	Lengshuitan District	246337	221703		9023	9545	8799	5250
祁阳县	Qiyang County	567977	487058	11541	24714	18267	13376	17283
东安县	Dongan County	319842	286379	458	13006	10993	10738	8408
双牌县	Shuangpai County	60258	51322	19	4829	2394	1899	1378
道县	Dao County	271335	218309	756	27889	6692	6026	14427
江永县	Jiangyong County	98672	83128	54	9225	3972	3972	1963
宁远县	Ningyuan County	246813	218265	1096	20012	2697	1603	3627
蓝山县	Lanshan County	113275	102248		8579	1067	855	1100
新田县	Xintian County	141935	108838	70	7945	17913	16859	6416
江华县	Jianghua County	158644	135268	20	10432	8319	8194	3920
怀化市	**Huaihua City**	**1769932**	**1538395**	**19173**	**113847**	**66863**	**60337**	**24763**
鹤城区	Hecheng District	57600	53854	49	1928	748	650	600
中方县	Zhongfang County	117272	104643	332	5759	4190	3196	1800
沅陵县	Yuanling County	226685	185898	40	20295	9580	8465	10044
辰溪县	Chenxi County	163958	149006	1700	8765	1493	1383	2827
溆浦县	Xupu County	349752	289362	10035	21777	20634	18993	6420
会同县	Huitong County	113927	103638	1289	4799	3199	2865	541
麻阳县	Mayang County	126656	116330	1252	5883	2319	1518	372
新晃县	Xinhuang County	95749	59123	3442	16853	15723	14694	233
芷江县	Zhijiang County	163337	146459	913	9957	4464	4419	834
靖州县	Jinzhou County	109661	103685	40	4145	757	555	197
通道县	Tongdao County	80859	74023		4694	1604	1470	426
洪江市	Hongjiang City	164476	152374	81	8992	2152	2129	469
娄底市	**Loudi City**	**1509937**	**1231811**	**45103**	**111440**	**80007**	**59479**	**29955**
娄星区	Louxing District	91984	79523	1784	3610	3725	578	2649
双峰县	Shuangfeng County	516476	450451	3927	24210	20850	16882	11978
新化县	Xinhua County	441711	352687	12293	33758	36492	31751	4580
冷水江市	Lenshuijiang City	54052	44123	2781	5693	859	677	295
涟源市	Lianyuan City	405714	305027	24318	44169	18081	9591	10453
湘西自治州	**West Hunan A.P**	**856571**	**527378**	**27219**	**155298**	**121719**	**118355**	**19631**
吉首市	Jishou City	48438	35540	109	5179	5635	5431	1512
泸溪县	Louxi County	80416	69824	878	3924	2520	1962	2107
凤凰县	Fenghuang County	105503	77922	1590	13088	11053	10943	1792
花垣县	Huayuan County	102082	61592	2659	13100	22660	22660	2007
保靖县	Baojin County	89251	50847	3145	12589	19820	19618	2252
古丈县	Guzhang County	37042	28678	261	1660	5380	5257	804
永顺县	Yongshun County	209199	115896	7038	50913	28504	26351	4611
龙山县	Longshan County	184640	87079	11539	54845	26147	26133	4546

单位：吨　　　　18-14 续表 3 continued　　　　(ton)

市县名称	City and County	棉花 Cotton	油料 Oil-bearing	#油菜籽 Rapeseeds	黄红麻 Jute and Ambary Hemp	苎麻 Ramie	烤烟 Fluecured Tobacco	茶叶 Tea	柑桔 Citrus
长沙市	**Changsha City**	**958**	**27686**	**15418**	**15**	**73**	**11991**	**7928**	**53232**
芙蓉区	Furong District								50
天心区	Tianxin District								79
岳麓区	Yuelu District		60	60				45	422
开福区	Kaifu District		34	34				4	1217
雨花区	Yuhua District		12	12					206
长沙县	Changsha County	34	7314	6473		8	39	4475	9364
望城县	Wangcheng County		3536	2142				512	8947
宁乡县	Ningxiang County	602	9291	1341		36	2400	2207	24500
浏阳市	Liuyang City	322	7439	5356	15	29	9552	685	8447
株洲市	**Zhuzhou City**	**1392**	**30101**	**19136**		**894**	**993**	**1252**	**31127**
荷塘区	Hetang District		198	180				24	504
芦淞区	Lousong District		12	12				20	167
石峰区	Shifeng District		780	332				16	608
天元区	Tianyuan District	15	236	90				33	315
株洲县	Zhuzhou County	144	2690	735		24		225	3930
攸 县	You County	552	13266	8683		62	93	262	3555
茶陵县	Chaling County	420	8767	6127		788	900	262	14619
炎陵县	Yanling County	27	1707	1134				108	2419
醴陵市	Liling City	234	2445	1843		20		302	5010
湘潭市	**Xiangtan City**	**510**	**7880**	**1954**		**28**		**1139**	**8459**
雨湖区	Yuhu District							2	305
岳塘区	Yuetang District		482	88				44	428
湘潭县	Xiangtan County	170	4378	781		8		500	4500
湘乡市	Xiangxiang City	313	2182	391		20		538	3086
韶山市	Shaoshan City	27	838	694				55	140
衡阳市	**Hengyang City**	**19380**	**162231**	**125382**	**67**	**261**	**9916**	**1678**	**68008**
郊区	Jiaoqu District		1974	1404				20	4000
南岳区	Nanyue District		78	34				38	565
衡阳县	Hengyang County	12081	60715	53243	5	57	439	35	10715
衡南县	Hengnan County	4566	46371	36230			3277	363	10995
衡山县	Hengshan County	80	2331	1417		63		238	8152
衡东县	Hengdong County	299	10554	6962		5	15	291	9345
祁东县	Qidong County	168	8111	3675			1032	58	8747
耒阳市	Leiyang City	1879	18962	15660	51	30	4687	182	9200
常宁市	Changning City	307	13135	6757	11	106	466	453	6289
邵阳市	**Shaoyang City**	**807**	**106993**	**74702**		**356**	**6460**	**3192**	**208553**
双清区	Shuangqing District		373	203				3	8234
大祥区	Daxiang District	41	1437	641				9	13081
北塔区	Beita District		462	272				6	1364
邵东县	Shaodong County	40	11840	7063		20		375	20430

单位：吨　　　　18-14 续表 4 continued　　　　(ton)

市县名称	City and County	棉花 Cotton	油料 Oil-bearing	#油菜籽 Rapeseeds	黄红麻 Jute and Ambary Hemp	苎麻 Ramie	烤烟 Fluecured Tobacco	茶叶 Tea	柑桔 Citrus
新邵县	Xinshao County	157	3960	2102		57	1173	65	8975
邵阳县	Shaoyang County	154	19441	10099		160	1918	21	11374
隆回县	Longhui County	72	14063	10961			1620	150	6971
洞口县	Dongkou County	170	25087	21631		80	120	1600	61197
绥宁县	Suining County	1	5502	4301		8		74	31004
新宁县	Xinning County	70	8955	4900			1150	12	34447
城步县	Chengbu County		5641	4885				138	1751
武冈市	Wugang City	102	10232	7644		31	479	739	9725
岳阳市	**Yueyang City**	**47442**	**116988**	**93446**	**746**	**8180**		**12358**	**52071**
岳阳楼区	Yueyanglou District	3	966	273				100	1547
云溪区	Yunxi District	40	2563	2105				196	782
君山区	Junshan District	8736	9766	9058		248		5	8900
岳阳县	Yueyang County	1240	20637	11145		35		1603	5654
华容县	Huarong County	32915	39820	39420	488	4389		431	18158
湘阴县	Xiangyin County	1120	11052	7952	258	1575		1335	5740
平江县	Pingjiang County	920	9913	6997		63		2077	5708
汨罗市	Miluo City	1050	10643	6956				1351	4185
临湘市	Linxiang City	1418	11628	9540		1870		5260	1397
常德市	**Changde City**	**90774**	**389329**	**365034**	**434**	**23299**	**4142**	**7119**	**270050**
武陵区	Wuling District	919	4839	4143				75	15917
鼎城区	Dingcheng District	12816	48267	44510	20	143		201	34442
安乡县	Anxiang County	22269	46096	45884	39	1660		16	13565
汉寿县	Hanshou County	8198	32469	30252	375	5964	60	1442	17117
澧县	Li County	22615	76445	74738		64		71	9533
临澧县	Linli County	7675	42601	41315			963	107	3008
桃源县	Taoyuan County	8870	82489	73278		15156	1598	2586	68353
石门县	Shimen County	3528	36540	33561		300	1521	2532	103015
津市市	Jinshi City	3884	19583	17353		12		89	5100
张家界市	**Zhangjiajie City**	**2402**	**77597**	**58303**		**8070**	**6047**	**1445**	**88116**
永定区	Yongding District	217	24234	17317		3607	1438	165	19064
武陵源区	Wulingyuan District	100	2188	1608		100		6	1129
慈利县	Chili County	2080	33517	27557		3990	2750	1130	63250
桑植县	Sangzhi County	5	17658	11821		373	1859	144	4673
益阳市	**Yiyang City**	**31294**	**105799**	**95402**	**504**	**51616**	**3120**	**11314**	**109030**
资阳区	Ziyang District	203	2192	1819		660		355	7218
赫山区	Heshan District	72	3244	2300		430		1751	5542
南县	Nan County	19670	33465	33216	504	19252			18919
桃江县	Taojiang County	140	1898	781		30		3600	5100
安化县	Anhua County	324	31799	24553		228	3120	5300	9802
沅江市	Yuanjiang City	10885	33201	32733		31016		308	62449
郴州市	**Chenzhou City**	**486**	**42956**	**15723**		**99**	**62592**	**1509**	**76839**
北湖区	Beihu District		1445				2738	77	2352
苏仙区	Suxian District	62	1541	112			860	55	3659
桂阳县	Guiyang County	7	7039	20			40630	274	6777
宜章县	Yizhang County	10	3732	1145			3110	47	5059
永兴县	Yongxing County	76	3506	2178		78	6805	146	10041

单位：吨　　18-14 续表 5 continued　　(ton)

市县名称	City and County	棉花 Cotton	油料 Oil-bearing	#油菜籽 Rapeseeds	黄红麻 Jute and Ambary Hemp	苎麻 Ramie	烤烟 Fluecured Tobacco	茶叶 Tea	柑桔 Citrus
嘉禾县	Jiahe County	1	4378			12	5298	67	10209
临武县	Linwu County		2646				1556	28	7804
汝城县	Rucheng County	207	2630	1522			83	85	427
桂东县	Guidong County	16	684	335			451	122	565
安仁县	Anreng County	41	11967	9121		3	815	261	3768
资兴市	Zixing City	66	3388	1290		6	246	347	26178
永州市	**Yongzhou City**	**2810**	**59796**	**12502**	**57**	**41**	**26876**	**1622**	**194086**
芝山区	Zhishan District	540	5907	286	6		488	47	23617
冷水滩区	Lengshuitan District	831	3233	810			837	722	17580
祁阳县	Qiyang County	669	17331	6989	35		653	269	41232
东安县	Dongan County	315	6111	206	7		347	3	11925
双牌县	Shuangpai County	9	726					33	3989
道县	Dao County	35	7624	90			1360	16	28591
江永县	Jiangyong County		4435	1625			2815	86	28139
宁远县	Ningyuan County	411	4291	215	9	26	4094	116	23891
蓝山县	Lanshan County		1521				5895	65	7968
新田县	Xintian County		2849	144		15	6376	64	2829
江华县	Jianghua County		5768	2137			4011	201	4325
怀化市	**Huaihua City**	**2433**	**108051**	**89585**	**39**	**30**	**2469**	**1259**	**219868**
鹤城区	Hecheng District	4	4002	3100	2		4		3412
中方县	Zhongfang County	291	6604	4950			31	28	9541
沅陵县	Yuanling County	34	20126	15597			13	507	3410
辰溪县	Chenxi County	440	9328	6480			38	16	15976
溆浦县	Xupu County	1388	18439	17417			289	631	31736
会同县	Huitong County	80	8276	7805	31		196	28	29114
麻阳县	Mayang County	57	13296	8297		16		2	25795
新晃县	Xinhuang County	3	4205	3804	6	14	701	1	3330
芷江县	Zhijiang County	40	9238	8356			1001	8	27081
靖州县	Jinzhou County	56	6033	5609			76	2	12068
通道县	Tongdao County	35	3041	2943			2	1	2635
洪江市	Hongjiang City	5	5463	5227			118	35	55770
娄底市	**Loudi City**	**755**	**32629**	**14200**		**197**	**1665**	**5964**	**25379**
娄星区	Louxing District	12	1650	368		16		1235	4454
双峰县	Shuangfeng County	552	13549	7309		139	71	2678	5761
新化县	Xinhua County	45	11333	5452		6	1238	915	4033
冷水江市	Lenshuijiang City	9	478	64			2	34	5123
涟源市	Lianyuan City	137	5619	1007		36	354	1102	6008
湘西自治州	**West Hunan A.P**	**852**	**105903**	**83635**		**1034**	**14863**	**656**	**136685**
吉首市	Jishou City	51	8465	6744		608	763	1	26670
泸溪县	Louxi County	382	12978	10361		183	207	4	21710
凤凰县	Fenghuang County	34	13506	10677		180	2751	47	25126
花垣县	Huayuan County	36	8625	6236			881	4	3742
保靖县	Baojin County	200	9707	6000			1483	71	21292
古丈县	Guzhang County	74	4768	4490			118	342	7446
永顺县	Yongshun County	54	29630	23164		63	2293	127	16487
龙山县	Longshan County	21	18224	15963			6367	60	14212

18-15 各市、州、县主要林产品产量(2001年)

Output of Major Forest Products (2001)

市县名称	City and County	油茶籽(吨) Tea-oil Seeds (ton)	油桐籽(吨) Tung-oil Seeds (ton)	松脂(吨) Pine Resin (ton)	板栗(吨) Chestnuts (ton)	棕片(吨) Palm Leaf (ton)	竹笋干(吨) Bamboo Shoots (ton)	木材采伐量(万方) Woods Cuts (10 000 cu.m)	竹材采伐量(万根) Bamboo Cuts (10 000 roots)
长沙市	**Changsha City**	**48653**	**1573**	**1126**	**1402**	**865**	**3008**	**26.23**	**991.01**
芙蓉区	Furong District							0.1	1
天心区	Tianxin District	2						0.05	
岳麓区	Yuelu District			48	6		54	0.01	
开福区	Kaifu District	11	4	25	3	3	1	0.4	4
雨花区	Yuhua District	20	2	15	2			0.02	0.01
长沙县	Changsha County	2820	175	218	20	30	1	3.09	62
望城县	Wangcheng County	300	30	100	10	20	950	3	95
宁乡县	Ningxiang County	6500	462	200	161	452	552	8.76	373
浏阳市	Liuyang City	39000	900	520	1200	360	1450	10.8	456
株洲市	**Zhuzhou City**	**47647**	**915**	**1583**	**1412**	**491**	**3823**	**18.67**	**256.78**
荷塘区	Hetang District	1245				50	12	0.02	1.6
芦淞区	Lousong District	2100	3			2	4	0.04	0.8
石峰区	Shifeng District	1350		22	2	35	6	0.08	
天元区	Tianyuan District	886			2		2	0.02	1
株洲县	Zhuzhou County	5548	26	180	332	13	20	1.26	65
攸 县	You County	15000	100	20	90	170	600	3.22	31.35
茶陵县	Chaling County	11972	730	1000	748	161	820	1.6	55
炎陵县	Yanling County	1392	18	271	68	40	2319	8.61	81.03
醴陵市	Liling City	8154	38	90	170	20	40	3.82	21
湘潭市	**Xiangtan City**	**7816**	**326**	**797**	**267**	**111**	**526**	**5.11**	**66.22**
雨湖区	Yuhu District	2		5	2			0.03	0.02
岳塘区	Yuetang District	80		2	1	1		0.25	0.82
湘潭县	Xiangtan County	5099	105	650	115	85	60	2.89	36.5
湘乡市	Xiangxiang City	2600	220	120	149	25	465	1.84	26.5
韶山市	Shaoshan City	35	1	20			1	0.1	2.38
衡阳市	**Hengyang City**	**67059**	**2725**	**410**	**2928**	**574**	**1409**	**10.89**	**1751.2**
郊区	Jiaoqu District	830	3	29	9		3	0.3	1.2
南岳区	Nanyue District	365	10	4	15	2	60	0.25	84
衡阳县	Hengyang County	8900	70	50	120	70		2.8	152
衡南县	Hengnan County	4100	1450	68	280	60	30	1.4	64
衡山县	Hengshan County	3000	155	80	150	110	10	0.68	70
衡东县	Hengdong County	11264	582	64	308	33	16	1.76	84
祁东县	Qidong County	1800	50		30		30	0.8	15
耒阳市	Leiyang City	15800	380	100	1420	235	300	1.3	1210
常宁市	Changning City	21000	25	15	596	64	960	1.6	71
邵阳市	**Shaoyang City**	**5169**	**762**	**2525**	**721**	**441**	**2350**	**75.12**	**864.77**
双清区	Shuangqing District	10					2	0.02	0.8
大祥区	Daxiang District	165	18					0.04	2.21
北塔区	Beita District	180			1			0.06	0.2
邵东县	Shaodong County	135	42	25	30			2.35	22

18-15 续表 1 continued

市县名称	City and County	油茶籽(吨) Tea-oil Seeds (ton)	油桐籽(吨) Tung-oil Seeds (ton)	松脂(吨) Pine Resin (ton)	板栗(吨) Chestnuts (ton)	棕片(吨) Palm Leaf (ton)	竹笋干(吨) Bamboo Shoots (ton)	木材采伐量(万方) Woods Cuts (10 000 cu.m)	竹材采伐量(万根) Bamboo Cuts (10 000 roots)
新邵县	Xinshao County	20	5	1	11	40	11	2.07	23.3
邵阳县	Shaoyang County	3078	270	128	335	8		1.69	4.1
隆回县	Longhui County	324	64	8	42	42	453	3.66	21.16
洞口县	Dongkou County	20	30		20	2	10	9.84	213
绥宁县	Suining County	953	165	1640	106	184	1478	44	260
新宁县	Xinning County	80	30	610	51	45	210	3.32	110
城步县	Chengbu County	124	100	110	75	60	156	7.1	180
武冈市	Wugang City	80	38	3	50	60	30	0.97	28
岳阳市	**Yueyang City**	**8176**	**561**	**821**	**855**	**148**	**293**	**10.25**	**1395.1**
岳阳楼区	Yueyanglou District								
云溪区	Yunxi District		15		35			0.04	54
君山区	Junshan District			30				0.38	
岳阳县	Yueyang County	1273	72	418	165	2	19	0.93	68.1
华容县	Huarong County	20	25	3	117	2	10	1.54	75
湘阴县	Xiangyin County	170	60	50		2	8	0.9	10
平江县	Pingjiang County	6400	352		265	103	233	3.23	650
汨罗市	Miluo City	220	18	320	50	3	11	1.01	20
临湘市	Linxiang City	93	19		223	36	12	2.22	518
常德市	**Changde City**	**21248**	**1687**	**127**	**1022**	**332**	**33**	**7.55**	**1075.43**
武陵区	Wuling District	72						0.01	
鼎城区	Dingcheng District	6592	76		37	2	1	1.21	425.56
安乡县	Anxiang County							0.52	16
汉寿县	Hanshou County	1683	17					0.99	134.58
澧县	Li County	741	86	11	59	9		0.63	80.82
临澧县	Linli County	3483	53	50	117			1.08	0.2
桃源县	Taoyuan County	7437	787	61	293	166	32	2.47	392.76
石门县	Shimen County	1096	554		493	146		0.49	19.51
津市市	Jinshi City	144	114	5	23	9		0.15	6
张家界市	**Zhangjiajie City**	**2146**	**2970**	**228**	**1878**	**723**	**137**	**9.37**	**657.72**
永定区	Yongding District	370	492		400	113	5	3.68	36
武陵源区	Wulingyuan District	221	321		60			0.5	38
慈利县	Chili County	960	1600	220	1010	560	130	3.72	330
桑植县	Sangzhi County	595	557	8	408	50	2	1.47	253.72
益阳市	**Yiyang City**	**7954**	**543**	**242**	**584**	**1217**	**528**	**30.36**	**3148.8**
资阳区	Ziyang District	400	1		12	5	2	0.32	24.8
赫山区	Heshan District	2610	30	11	26	88	17	2.5	1777
南县	Nan County					23		1.14	
桃江县	Taojiang County	2100	150		200	300	200	6.89	623
安化县	Anhua County	2832	362	231	346	791	309	14.5	724
沅江市	Yuanjiang City	12				10		5.01	
郴州市	**Chenzhou City**	**35194**	**772**	**1799**	**1707**	**803**	**1681**	**53.79**	**494.4**
北湖区	Beihu District	2049	63	210	230		188	2.62	52
苏仙区	Suxian District	3077	30	40	56	7	102	4.22	118
桂阳县	Guiyang County	7960	89	650	75	130	138	4.2	15.4
宜章县	Yizhang County	1105	9	127	50	98	50	2.6	6
永兴县	Yongxing County	5650	8	74	42	96	34	3.02	81

18-15 续表 2 continued

市县名称	City and County	油茶籽(吨) Tea-oil Seeds (ton)	油桐籽(吨) Tung-oil Seeds (ton)	松脂(吨) Pine Resin (ton)	板栗(吨) Chestnuts (ton)	棕片(吨) Palm Leaf (ton)	竹笋干(吨) Bamboo Shoots (ton)	木材采伐量(万方) Woods Cuts (10 000 cu.m)	竹材采伐量(万根) Bamboo Cuts (10 000 roots)
嘉禾县	Jiahe County	3500	80	158	200	15	20	1.7	13
临武县	Linwu County	1600	120	125	150	60	100	2.22	11
汝城县	Rucheng County	3070	34	74	330	170	372	8	56
桂东县	Guidong County	220	30	6	20	35	205	2.05	32
安仁县	Anreng County	4864	70	224	140	42	50	2.73	10
资兴市	Zixing City	2099	239	111	414	150	422	20.43	100
永州市	**Yongzhou City**	**45445**	**1255**	**7001**	**1508**	**534**	**1516**	**51**	**204.04**
芝山区	Zhishan District	2180	44	75	89	68	110	1.4	15
冷水滩区	Lengshuitan District	5637	23	587	18	5	8	1.84	3
祁阳县	Qiyang County	9638	338	1	930	90	550	5.1	32
东安县	Dongan County	3313	12	5	30	140	24	2.41	4.18
双牌县	Shuangpai County	115	30	38	54	31	83	6.9	58.21
道县	Dao County	9680	156	138	138	26	65	3.5	6
江永县	Jiangyong County	576	15	330	20		10	3.6	0.68
宁远县	Ningyuan County	3720	19	135	30	30	11	5.1	5.3
蓝山县	Lanshan County	1360	29	80	21	41	49	7.15	55
新田县	Xintian County	1676	9	12	80	8	16	1.7	18
江华县	Jianghua County	7550	580	5600	98	95	590	12.3	6.67
怀化市	**Huaihua City**	**24930**	**13844**	**3161**	**3689**	**1546**	**731**	**85.33**	**485.56**
鹤城区	Hecheng District	2050	980	752	702	280	50	2.62	7
中方县	Zhongfang County	6200	2600		441	841	62	4.3	3
沅陵县	Yuanling County	562	387	3	818	150	58	19.7	40.5
辰溪县	Chenxi County	1743	165	2	108	32	29	3.04	12
溆浦县	Xupu County	1800	820	4	36	40	20	7.6	40
会同县	Huitong County	5990	4602	589	229	58	188	8.34	97.25
麻阳县	Mayang County	150	315		363			2.1	0.08
新晃县	Xinhuang County	79	1241		84	93	6	2.53	12.03
芷江县	Zhijiang County	1282	958	18	481	30	11	5.53	31.3
靖州县	Jinzhou County	609	74	760	55	1	51	12.11	48
通道县	Tongdao County	2300	540	902	69	1	51	10.01	56.4
洪江市	Hongjiang City	2165	1162	131	303	20	205	7.45	138
娄底市	**Loudi City**	**5518**	**407**	**125**	**126**	**132**	**402**	**5.88**	**176.4**
娄星区	Louxing District	320	6	2	10	5	5	0.54	3.5
双峰县	Shuangfeng County	4260	215	123	41	50	55	1.64	68.9
新化县	Xinhua County	250	160		50	33	310	2.5	75
冷水江市	Lenshuijiang City	48	18		13	19	11	0.3	12.2
涟源市	Lianyuan City	640	8		12	25	21	0.9	16.8
湘西自治州	**West Hunan A.P**	**9261**	**12276**	**26**	**3069**	**160**	**79**	**7.68**	**80.48**
吉首市	Jishou City	341	520		432	12		0.32	16.15
泸溪县	Louxi County	800	620		357	25	5	0.67	0.01
凤凰县	Fenghuang County	120	270		300	2		1.05	5
花垣县	Huayuan County	1139	636		87	22	38	0.04	7
保靖县	Baojin County	203	950	10	684	41	18	0.31	2.8
古丈县	Guzhang County	1018	533	1	96	4	1	2.1	
永顺县	Yongshun County	4041	2919	6	537	18	15	1.21	12.44
龙山县	Longshan County	1599	5828	9	576	36	2	1.98	37.08

18-16 各市、州、县牲畜头数、畜产品及水产品产量(2001年)

Number of Livestocks,Output of Livestock Products and Aquatic Products (2001)

市县名称	City and County	大牲畜年末存栏数(头) Large Animals (head)	#耕牛 Cattle and Buffaloes for Cultivation	猪牛羊肉产量(吨) Output of Pork, Beef and Mutton (ton)	生猪存栏头数(万头) Hogs (10 000 heads)	肉猪出栏头数(万头) Slaughtered Fattened Hogs (10 000 heads)	水产品(吨) Aquatic Products (ton)	#鱼 Fish
长沙市	**Changsha City**	**336065**	**272066**	**444431**	**364.91**	**655.78**	**89965**	**88334**
芙蓉区	Furong District	84		7562	4.54	11.25	938	898
天心区	Tianxin District	336	103	3493	4.27	5.26	2102	2099
岳麓区	Yuelu District	509	509	12685	7.7	19.37	1850	1850
开福区	Kaifu District	3200	2608	15451	12.2	24.2	6161	6143
雨花区	Yuhua District	600	531	11768	8.5	18	1591	1577
长沙县	Changsha County	131933	121800	122364	95.4	178.5	13228	13198
望城县	Wangcheng County	20108	19608	72690	71.3	113	17018	16144
宁乡县	Ningxiang County	94215	43465	104288	89.6	152	28077	28045
浏阳市	Liuyang City	85080	83442	94130	71.4	134.2	19000	18380
株洲市	**Zhuzhou City**	**179862**	**178380**	**226863**	**209.45**	**334.75**	**52822**	**51343**
荷塘区	Hetang District	800	710	4925	6.9	7.3	1500	1480
芦淞区	Lousong District	700	467	3128	2.53	4.54	1384	1358
石峰区	Shifeng District	2100	2100	8222	7.1	12.25	2102	2079
天元区	Tianyuan District	592	583	5209	4.8	7.83	844	835
株洲县	Zhuzhou County	9260	9205	31034	24.98	46.61	9432	8906
攸 县	You County	53200	53050	64689	55	96.48	12400	12147
茶陵县	Chaling County	64712	64312	43910	42.35	63.5	10500	10219
炎陵县	Yanling County	23098	23098	9482	10.43	14.2	700	660
醴陵市	Liling City	25400	24855	56264	55.36	82.04	13960	13659
湘潭市	**Xiangtan City**	**77065**	**72194**	**280211**	**203.13**	**416.82**	**57985**	**55700**
雨湖区	Yuhu District	259	113	19214	10.83	28.06	1915	1903
岳塘区	Yuetang District	633	355	15007	8.35	22.16	1879	1709
湘潭县	Xiangtan County	9051	8742	133669	90.89	197.8	29544	28620
湘乡市	Xiangxiang City	64819	60687	102187	79.88	152.8	22475	21302
韶山市	Shaoshan City	2303	2297	10134	13.18	16	2172	2166
衡阳市	**Hengyang City**	**239456**	**236043**	**556687**	**406.7**	**797.04**	**194071**	**183580**
郊区	Jiaoqu District	2600	2505	13197	8.32	20.5	9036	8817
南岳区	Nanyue District	5437	5437	3480	2.72	4.9	480	466
衡阳县	Hengyang County	52800	52550	121421	83	172	44603	41904
衡南县	Hengnan County	56000	56000	96533	60.53	139.5	38690	36275
衡山县	Hengshan County	8800	8800	36316	25.4	54.62	8913	8551
衡东县	Hengdong County	32800	30095	65554	59.33	93.4	13521	10698
祁东县	Qidong County	15000	14781	76701	43.5	101.05	38856	37642
耒阳市	Leiyang City	34505	34500	82386	61.9	118.3	22500	22075
常宁市	Changning City	31514	31375	61099	62	92.77	17472	17152
邵阳市	**Shaoyang City**	**896386**	**860700**	**492765**	**438.66**	**678.96**	**65738**	**63652**
双清区	Shuangqing District	3630	3186	9171	5.87	14.01	1785	1767
大祥区	Daxiang District	7006	6618	9110	6.9	12.29	1455	1413
北塔区	Beita District	4120	3960	3299	2.2	4.55	1100	1074
邵东县	Shaodong County	29063	28901	79296	59.27	113.86	22100	20649

市县名称	City and County	大牲畜年末存栏数(头) Large Animals (head)	#耕牛 Cattle and Buffaloes for Cultivation	猪牛羊肉产量(吨) Output of Pork, Beef and Mutton (ton)	生猪存栏头数(万头) Hogs (10 000 heads)	肉猪出栏头数(万头) Slaughtered Fattened Hogs (10 000 heads)	水产品(吨) Aquatic Products (ton)	#鱼 Fish
新邵县	Xinshao County	78873	77712	40443	45.17	58.02	4260	4194
邵阳县	Shaoyang County	85752	79491	41054	33.81	56.8	6568	6537
隆回县	Longhui County	147282	144261	50025	48.24	64.27	5874	5841
洞口县	Dongkou County	85918	84868	107044	89.55	150	8520	8405
绥宁县	Suining County	116535	110231	26015	29.5	31.5	1638	1573
新宁县	Xinning County	158846	154008	21268	32.1	23.25	4050	4034
城步县	Chengbu County	102259	92186	12855	15.3	16.3	528	528
武冈市	Wugang City	77102	75278	93185	70.75	134.11	7860	7637
岳阳市	**Yueyang City**	**219393**	**216110**	**439861**	**358.8**	**658.96**	**273920**	**258962**
岳阳楼区	Yueyanglou District	1612	1612	15525	8.2	23.8	17200	17074
云溪区	Yunxi District	4815	4672	11166	10.71	16.53	12568	11878
君山区	Junshan District	10900	10900	19544	20	29.8	26500	25848
岳阳县	Yueyang County	30000	30000	73077	70	110.23	35111	34333
华容县	Huarong County	22072	21493	44222	32.7	68.5	68901	65936
湘阴县	Xiangyin County	23600	22340	63455	54	96.9	68980	63013
平江县	Pingjiang County	54828	53884	70835	51.2	96.79	4318	4281
汨罗市	Miluo City	54300	54300	117169	89.6	180.2	22650	19646
临湘市	Linxiang City	17266	16909	24868	22.39	36.21	17692	16953
常德市	**Changde City**	**342051**	**325132**	**366483**	**260.13**	**456.66**	**242951**	**231139**
武陵区	Wuling District	2893	2639	10207	7.7	13.68	11459	11060
鼎城区	Dingcheng District	36264	33035	47138	39.86	62.69	52342	51141
安乡县	Anxiang County	10667	7146	25049	17.78	32.91	45132	43878
汉寿县	Hanshou County	21056	20351	34979	30.27	48.88	41426	36474
澧县	Li County	26086	24111	51763	30.06	68.11	31509	30848
临澧县	Linli County	29993	29698	33808	25.44	40.65	12191	11366
桃源县	Taoyuan County	120344	114983	90868	58.3	105.41	30530	28520
石门县	Shimen County	84644	84103	53617	37.98	60.3	6283	6265
津市市	Jinshi City	10104	9066	19054	12.74	24.03	12079	11587
张家界市	**Zhangjiajie City**	**183201**	**180892**	**87716**	**76.04**	**100.71**	**7202**	**7126**
永定区	Yongding District	55208	54998	24631	22.37	28.51	2605	2600
武陵源区	Wulingyuan District	3115	3115	2128	0.93	2.54	16	16
慈利县	Chili County	66700	65690	42330	33.29	48.5	3986	3944
桑植县	Sangzhi County	58178	57089	18627	19.45	21.16	595	566
益阳市	**Yiyang City**	**300293**	**238110**	**215830**	**191.54**	**289.34**	**157158**	**151114**
资阳区	Ziyang District	4003	3993	17205	14.01	25.5	13200	12964
赫山区	Heshan District	11500	10610	42400	33.2	55.45	15000	14642
南县	Nan County	11962	8438	38187	29.1	53.28	50860	49022
桃江县	Taojiang County	38396	31340	31555	39.5	45.8	3650	3576
安化县	Anhua County	219035	168332	45090	38.22	51	10401	10145
沅江市	Yuanjiang City	15397	15397	41393	37.51	58.31	64047	60765
郴州市	**Chenzhou City**	**393872**	**385553**	**366800**	**295.7**	**482.88**	**66805**	**64950**
北湖区	Beihu District	27535	27087	18019	12	22.75	2884	2806
苏仙区	Suxian District	66926	66926	31832	20.02	37.89	7000	6940
桂阳县	Guiyang County	47913	47814	50328	45.08	65.95	9765	9668
宜章县	Yizhang County	43751	43200	39900	37.21	54.72	4820	4749
永兴县	Yongxing County	62237	61516	48288	45.22	65.21	12472	12214

18-16 续表 2

continued

市县名称	City and County	大牲畜年末存栏数(头) Large Animals (head)	#耕牛 Cattle and Buffaloes for Cultivation	猪牛羊肉产量(吨) Output of Pork, Beef and Mutton (ton)	生猪存栏头数(万头) Hogs (10 000 heads)	肉猪出栏头数(万头) Slaughtered Fattened Hogs (10 000 heads)	水产品(吨) Aquatic Products (ton)	#鱼 Fish
嘉禾县	Jiahe County	16633	13477	43008	30.66	54.85	2295	2186
临武县	Linwu County	18563	18294	24242	22.18	31.54	2811	2288
汝城县	Rucheng County	28490	28482	24536	27.1	33.1	965	903
桂东县	Guidong County	22407	22400	8466	8.08	10.84	580	578
安仁县	Anreng County	30926	30005	40805	23.35	55.8	7111	6691
资兴市	Zixing City	28491	26352	37376	24.8	50.23	16102	15927
永州市	**Yongzhou City**	**650424**	**629810**	**421767**	**359.52**	**552.26**	**103433**	**99008**
芝山区	Zhishan District	63896	63595	41898	33.18	56.99	8249	7559
冷水滩区	Lengshuitan District	29251	29209	39470	32.84	53.86	13123	12821
祁阳县	Qiyang County	15725	15084	73013	48.45	99.02	30149	29113
东安县	Dongan County	78480	75660	37675	27.1	48.8	12385	11748
双牌县	Shuangpai County	22991	22931	9108	9.22	10.8	2410	2273
道县	Dao County	160429	147317	60422	57.98	70.6	15783	14969
江永县	Jiangyong County	109645	109042	23979	17.11	30.71	2879	2551
宁远县	Ningyuan County	46833	44140	48450	44.81	65.58	11169	10901
蓝山县	Lanshan County	28244	28150	31012	29.5	42.17	1638	1571
新田县	Xintian County	15800	15632	28136	26.33	37.68	3700	3636
江华县	Jianghua County	79130	79050	28604	33	36.05	1948	1866
怀化市	**Huaihua City**	**680713**	**675365**	**263584**	**241.53**	**312.01**	**31070**	**29892**
鹤城区	Hecheng District	12957	12895	9971	10.8	13.68	3195	3132
中方县	Zhongfang County	29050	29050	20858	16.1	26.8	2999	2862
沅陵县	Yuanling County	104708	104630	25473	23.21	29.57	4802	4523
辰溪县	Chenxi County	41545	41545	17845	21.21	26.25	1512	1477
溆浦县	Xupu County	64500	63776	50843	40.06	61.7	4702	4692
会同县	Huitong County	75296	73886	20798	22	20.29	1805	1740
麻阳县	Mayang County	46029	46029	13205	14.9	16.7	1917	1895
新晃县	Xinhuang County	102451	101706	26172	24.45	27.32	885	868
芷江县	Zhijiang County	46209	45990	27464	23.95	32.19	2430	2429
靖州县	Jinzhou County	59180	58200	16910	16.19	17.3	2424	2072
通道县	Tongdao County	53636	52869	8182	12.5	9.85	1157	1087
洪江市	Hongjiang City	45152	44789	25863	16.16	30.36	3242	3115
娄底市	**Loudi City**	**301428**	**300712**	**271461**	**256.71**	**413.07**	**49257**	**47627**
娄星区	Louxing District	20670	20500	15601	16.9	22.9	4612	4172
双峰县	Shuangfeng County	37014	37014	107338	93.2	169.35	20824	20305
新化县	Xinhua County	172907	172684	86820	78	127.4	12368	12129
冷水江市	Lenshuijiang City	17301	17185	12810	11.41	18.35	2502	2463
涟源市	Lianyuan City	53536	53329	48892	57.2	75.07	8951	8558
湘西自治州	**West Hunan A.P**	**460750**	**460138**	**86769**	**107.62**	**108.3**	**17271**	**16989**
吉首市	Jishou City	33167	32783	7036	6.44	9.13	1450	1418
泸溪县	Louxi County	48590	48590	8129	7.92	9.67	1558	1434
凤凰县	Fenghuang County	61382	61379	6808	11.75	8.69	2200	2166
花垣县	Huayuan County	53700	53700	11969	17.85	14.65	2750	2743
保靖县	Baojin County	55914	55914	11909	14.49	15.01	1200	1197
古丈县	Guzhang County	35280	35270	4168	5.04	5.67	1095	1095
永顺县	Yongshun County	115392	115200	16969	24.71	21.23	1450	1417
龙山县	Longshan County	57325	57302	19781	19.42	24.25	5568	5519

18-17 各市、州、县规模以上工业总产值(2001年)

Gross Output Vale of Industrial Enterprises Above Designated Size (2001)

单位：万元 (10 000 yuan)

市县名称	City and County	工业总产值 Gross Industrial Output Value	轻工业 Light Industry	重工业 Heavy Industry	#国有经济 State-owned Economic	#集体经济 Collective Owned Economic	指数(上年为100) Indices (precending year=100)
长沙市	**Changsha City**	**3251518**	**1244975**	**2006543**	**686256**	**284404**	**10.3**
市直	Directly Under City	2174571	680740	1493831	632413	26695	7.2
芙蓉区	Furong District	79733	3183	76550		1671	28.8
天心区	Tianxin District	43728	14642	29086		11911	34.6
岳麓区	Yuelu District	54571	29571	25000		7931	20.5
开福区	Kaifu District	38355	16072	22283		8565	0.5
雨花区	Yuhua District	27687	22102	5586		14848	4.6
长沙县	Changsha County	465811	233821	231991	7116	113103	23
望城县	Wangcheng County	120280	87925	32355	5735	29559	10.2
宁乡县	Ningxiang County	131431	77006	54425	21234	33635	12.2
浏阳市	Liuyang City	115350	79914	35437	19758	36487	-1.7
株洲市	**Zhuzhou City**	**1961096**	**385461**	**1575635**	**791714**	**182632**	**13.6**
市直	Directly Under City	1536348	192857	1343491	728101	61326	13.5
荷塘区	Hetang District	10181	1697	8483		818	33.8
芦淞区	Lusong District	16823	10800	6024		1923	-24.9
石峰区	Shifeng District	90656	2164	88492		13533	19.9
天元区	Tianyuan District	1569	647	921			13.9
株洲县	Zhuzhou County	21116	8184	12931	9203	4842	25.9
攸　县	You County	61045	20687	40357	24626	14648	13.4
茶陵县	Chaling County	23316	6209	17107	10397	9443	4.8
炎陵县	Yanling County	3616	622	2994	3156		-9.6
醴陵市	Liling City	196426	141592	54833	16231	76099	17.3
湘潭市	**Xiangtan City**	**1161739**	**326981**	**834758**	**642158**	**106966**	**16.5**
市直	Directly Under City	812324	196487	615838	547712	25497	19.4
雨湖区	Yuhu District	35719	14977	20743		16082	21.5
岳塘区	Yuetang District	52319	18648	33672		22605	15.9
湘潭县	Xiangtan County	56747	19538	37208	9714	24228	17.1
湘乡市	Xiangxiang City	185552	65389	120163	78440	13665	5.1
韶山市	Shaoshan City	19078	11943	7134	6292	4890	14.6

注:本表统计范围为全部国有及年销售收入500万元及以上的非国有工业企业。资料来源为2001年12月份快报累计数。

表中所列相对数按同口径可比价计算。

The statistical coverage was to cover all state-owned and the non-state-owned enterprises with an annual sales income of above 5 million yuan.

Data were obtained from the bulletin in December, 2001. The relative figures were calculated at comparable prices within the same coverage.

单位：万元 18-17 续表 1 continued (10 000 yuan)

市县名称	City and County	工业总产值 Gross Industrial Output Value	轻工业 Light Industry	重工业 Heavy Industry	#国有经济 State-owned Economic	#集体经济 Collective Owned Economic	指数(上年为100) Indices (precending year=100)
衡阳市	**Hengyang City**	**1130199**	**322633**	**807566**	**599702**	**241120**	**14.5**
市直	Directly Under City	531748	127021	404727	340604	10370	15.8
珠晖区	Zhuhui District	307		307			
雁峰区	Yanfeng District	4204		4204		1812	
石鼓区	Shigu District	6937	5850	1087		6937	
蒸湘区	Zhengxiang District	17173	10919	6254	72	13350	
南岳区	Nanyue District	664	162	502	162	502	15.7
衡阳县	Hengyang County	91255	55501	35754	22163	62721	14.5
衡南县	Hengnan County	70088	20538	49549	15848	29445	6.7
衡山县	Hengshan County	24610	10033	14576	14435	557	23.6
衡东县	Hengdong County	52273	12561	39711	15674	32789	1.9
祁东县	Qidong County	97311	76952	20359	24178	33045	16.1
耒阳市	Leiyang City	77878	2887	74991	40805	20310	35.4
常宁市	Changning City	155046	209	154837	125763	29283	11.2
邵阳市	**Shaoyang City**	**500167**	**228971**	**271195**	**217888**	**80926**	**14.3**
市直	Directly Under City	166622	75027	91595	109105	3329	6.8
双清区	Shuangqing District	20942	9811	11131		5839	18
大祥区	Daxiang District	8783	5380	3403		6992	14.5
北塔区	Beita District	9716	6165	3551		3551	46.5
邵东县	Shaodong County	71064	34711	36353	14340	17801	13.9
新邵县	Xinshao County	30259	6199	24059	13393	1473	9.9
邵阳县	Shaoyang County	16505	7602	8903	3378	7141	7
隆回县	Longhui County	38989	21041	17948	26764	7374	15.6
洞口县	Dongkou County	23370	8218	15152	12238	8483	25.3
绥宁县	Suining County	54046	30051	23995	971	1955	25.6
新宁县	Xinning County	20108	4814	15294	10893	7940	9.2
城步县	Chengbu County	24844	16431	8413	22103		26.4
武冈市	Wugang City	14920	3520	11400	4704	9048	21.7
岳阳市	**Yueyang City**	**2125056**	**876469**	**1248587**	**391040**	**553496**	**7.4**
市直	Directly Under City	246808	30	246778			-14.2
岳阳楼区	Yueyanglou District	1159559	451601	707958	217146	150191	13.1
云溪区	Yunxi District	15579	6639	8941	644	14936	30.2
君山区	Junshan District	30920	19838	11083	11089		26
岳阳县	Yueyang County	52002	39572	12430	18731	20575	32.1
华容县	Huarong County	121125	69811	51313	9539	109715	25.3
湘阴县	Xiangyin County	143058	81654	61404	25299	116026	23.9
平江县	Pingjiang City	43217	3708	39509	29045	8092	16.7
汨罗市	Miluo City	222295	171161	51134	33431	92449	20.9
临湘市	Linxiang County	90493	32456	58038	46116	41513	54.5

单位：万元　　18-17 续表 2　continued　　(10 000 yuan)

市县名称	City and County	工业总产值 Gross Industrial Output Value	轻工业 Light Industry	重工业 Heavy Industry	#国有经济 State-owned Economic	#集体经济 Collective Owned Economic	指数（上年为100）Indices (precending year=100)
常德市	**Changde City**	**1006156**	**669480**	**336676**	**461460**	**189808**	**12.8**
市直	Directly Under City	14813	8543	6271		7144	10.2
武陵区	Wuling District	362877	305569	57308	255420		13.2
鼎城区	Dingcheng District	110881	39745	71136	575	42704	2.7
安乡县	Anxiang County	58504	54803	3701	9648	25805	10.3
汉寿县	Hanshou County	54011	38391	15619	16672	11321	15
澧　县	Li County	80480	53708	26772	28341	13719	15.8
临澧县	Linli County	79042	53265	25778	14302	36700	17.9
桃源县	Taoyuan County	91043	53544	37499	38435	31993	15.8
石门县	Shimen County	62231	16895	45336	28430	11874	18.5
津市市	Jinshi City	92274	45017	47257	69639	8549	8.6
张家界市	**Zhangjiajie City**	**64756**	**19126**	**45630**	**37968**	**7491**	**11.4**
市直	Directly Under City	5625	2315	3310	5625		-2.5
永定区	Yongdi District	18002	6907	11095	11740	2895	29.3
武陵源区	Wulingyuan District	922	347	575	922		72
慈利县	Cili County	29772	6967	22805	9849	4596	8.9
桑植县	Sangzhi County	10435	2590	7845	9833		9.5
益阳市	**Yiyang City**	**514622**	**263621**	**251001**	**225995**	**129477**	**12.4**
市直	Directly Under City	149027	78331	70697	73279	474	20
资阳区	Ziyang District	33160	20553	12607	15024	8977	1.5
赫山区	Heshan District	61081	9646	51435	8473	25167	6
南　县	Nan County	77312	64676	12636	28409	43471	16.2
桃江县	Taojiang County	59979	15691	44288	33469	10281	9.6
安化县	Anhua County	47265	8905	38359	26652	15270	6.7
沅江市	Yuanjiang City	86798	65819	20979	40690	25837	10.9
郴州市	**Chenzhou City**	**707574**	**188481**	**519093**	**309694**	**195184**	**13.6**
市直	Directly Under City	248877	105681	143196	201900	1235	4.2
北湖区	Beihu District	71082	26906	44176	2702	45430	16.5
苏仙区	Suxian District	37751		37751	3244	29196	28.7
桂阳县	Guiyang County	63021	10049	52971	20512	17396	9.7
宜章县	Yizhang County	51210	11730	39480	9481	41730	24.8
永兴县	Yongxing County	38168	5340	32829	965	14368	27.3
嘉禾县	Jiahe County	22727	3966	18761	3313	1126	18.5
临武县	Linwu County	35227	1645	33582	11032	1984	11.2
汝城县	Rucheng County	33898	500	33398	6714	1208	27.5
桂东县	Guidong County	3680	19	3661	523	3157	16.2
安仁县	Anren County	22608	12180	10428	3933	18675	7.5
资兴市	Zixing City	79325	10465	68860	45375	19680	18.2

市县名称	City and County	工业总产值 Gross Industrial Output Value	轻工业 Light Industry	重工业 Heavy Industry	#国有经济 State-owned Economic	#集体经济 Collective Owned Economic	指数(上年为100) Indices (precending year=100)
永州市	**Yongzhou City**	**651722**	**181058**	**470664**	**229719**	**64221**	**13.9**
市直	Directly Under City	373937	89654	284284	115785	388	15
芝山区	Zhishan District	17541	2208	15333	2584	5696	25.9
冷水滩区	Lengshuitan District	35465	21373	14092	4083	8529	17
祁阳县	Qiyang County	70593	18718	51875	20475	25358	10
东安县	DonganCounty	26934	1761	25173	8331	8102	15.3
双牌县	Shuangpai County	23261	724	22538	10340	2468	31.4
道　县	Dao County	28168	14414	13755	22401	5359	2.7
江永县	Jiangyong County	13563	871	12691	7409	2475	13.5
宁远县	Ningyuan County	13384	5823	7561	6683	2393	25.2
蓝山县	Lanshan County	9388	2934	6453	4037	1012	36.8
新田县	Xintian County	17129	10836	6293	10910	1836	-17.6
江华县	Jianghua County	22358	11742	10616	16682	605	8
怀化市	**Huaihua City**	**516886**	**202040**	**314846**	**272740**	**63037**	**11.6**
市直	Directly Under City	78944	50826	28119	47519		0.2
鹤城区	Hecheng District	56498	24365	32133	13260	13235	14.9
中方县	Zhongfang County	15755	1430	14325	2593	10442	18.5
沅陵县	Yuanling County	76514	8096	68417	68609	7002	-5
辰溪县	Chenxi County	33129	3393	29736	26570	4059	14.4
溆浦县	Xupu County	57584	33319	24265	26679	2005	28.4
会同县	Huitong County	17791	3993	13798		1915	18.6
麻阳县	Mayang County	11958	2949	9008	9369	1399	14.9
新晃县	Xinhuang County	28381	15145	13236	16673	9518	19.9
芷江县	Zhijiang County	25442	10645	14796	6194	4641	39.5
靖州县	Jingzhou County	23467	4224	19243	19797	3299	32
通道县	Tongdao County	9745	4531	5214	5646		43.1
洪江市	Hongjiang City	81680	39123	42556	29831	5524	22.5
娄底市	**Loudi City**	**635877**	**47283**	**588594**	**493926**	**80139**	**12.7**
娄星区	Louxing District	339666	4720	334946	296285	37702	14.6
双峰县	Shuangfeng County	35445	10458	24987	8813	14246	14.5
新化县	Xinhua County	35874	6695	29179	22363	8561	-2
冷水江市	Lengshuijiang County	155482	9037	146445	121184	14268	12.1
涟源市	Lianyuan County	69411	16374	53037	45283	5362	11.9
湘西自治州	**West Hunan A.P**	**322067**	**119213**	**202854**	**242346**	**31394**	**19.5**
吉首市	Jishou County	116730	65420	51310	93257	13890	15.2
泸溪县	Luxi County	30280	230	30051	22541	1541	30.1
凤凰县	Fenghuang County	17191	5269	11922	13304	1123	14.3
花垣县	Huayuan County	74227	1535	72693	52108	13160	34.1
保靖县	Baojing County	24430	6884	17546	9580		15.2
古丈县	Guzhang County	4522	254	4269	2910		32.9
永顺县	Yongshun County	7189	3452	3737	6412	778	1.5
龙山县	Longshan County	47496	36170	11326	42234	903	11.5

18-18 各市、州、县国有经济固定资产投资

新增固定资产及房屋竣工面积(2001年)

Investment in Fixed Assets,Newly Increased Fixed Assets and Completed Building Floor Space of State-Owned Units (2001)

市县名称	Cities and Counties	固定资产投资(万元) Total Investment in Fixed Assets (10 000 yuan)	基本建设 Investment in Capital Construction	更新改造 Investment in Innovation	其他投资 Others Investment	房地产开发 Real Estate Development	新增固定资产(万元) Newly Increased Fixed Assets (10 000 yuan)	房屋建筑竣工面积(平方米) Floor Space of Buildings Completed (sq.m)	#住宅 Residential Buildings
长沙市	**Changsha City**	**1377977**	**1066976**	**152386**	**24958**	**133657**	**663177**	**2552618**	**1311768**
芙蓉区	Furong District	203811	132167	25906	10464	35274	158020	571324	321943
天心区	Tianxin District	125998	92945	6661	7761	18631	47347	293451	156409
岳麓区	Yuelu District	212171	189609	5482		17080	85452	371133	191274
开福区	Kaifu District	277591	223485	18749		35357	109776	472874	253477
雨花区	Yuhua District	297461	203629	75715	83	18034	134157	427479	215733
长沙县	Changsha County	58932	45660	8931	4341		32620	53099	7890
望城县	Wangcheng County	33784	29266	3985	533		9864	101725	44920
宁乡县	Ningxiang County	102694	88588	5850	1776	6480	62940	153935	54008
浏阳市	Liuyang City	65535	61627	1107		2801	23001	107598	66114
株洲市	**Zhuzhou City**	**382256**	**175672**	**184823**	**11780**	**9981**	**258820**	**684628**	**347363**
荷塘区	Hetang District	58381	31799	25405	210	967	57610	88976	63898
芦淞区	Lousong District	92554	21739	60918	7962	1935	72633	126963	52454
石峰区	Shifeng District	116882	41582	73542		1758	48674	173744	103721
天元区	Tianyuan District	47909	20852	24259	58	2740	46230	83827	43512
株洲县	Zhuzhou County	7987	7502	120	365		6349	19593	12140
攸 县	You County	24466	22670		1283	513	6590	53704	9986
茶陵县	Chaling County	14332	13244	277	716	95	6438	48647	13697
炎陵县	Yanling County	3575	2066		1186	323	5033	24844	10540
醴陵市	Liling County	16170	14218	302		1650	9263	64330	37415
湘潭市	**Xiangtan City**	**220189**	**103721**	**92174**	**11673**	**12621**	**247987**	**646933**	**299645**
雨湖区	Yuhu District	91930	52920	27858	2655	8497	110020	237020	113618
岳塘区	Yuetang District	81255	26238	50642	1750	2625	100127	207071	69635
湘潭县	Xiangtan County	14380	9994	3994	62	330	9753	60395	17913
湘乡市	Xiangxiang City	28744	10689	9680	7206	1169	24306	129037	96199
韶山市	Shaoshan City	3880	3880				3781	13410	2280

市县名称	Cities and Counties	固定资产投资(万元) Total Investment in Fixed Assets (10 000 yuan)	基本建设 Investment in Capital Construction	更新改造 Investment in Innovation	其他投资 Others Investment	房地产开发 Real Estate Development	新增固定资产(万元) Newly Increased Fixed Assets (10 000 yuan)	房屋建筑竣工面积(平方米) Floor Space of Buildings Completed (sq.m)	#住宅 Residential Buildings
衡阳市	**Hengyang City**	**319104**	**201730**	**91598**	**14698**	**11078**	**201479**	**799700**	**462070**
江东区	Jiangdong District	6957	2851	3871	202	33	7254	42694	34343
城南区	Chengnan District	38062	19565	12672	3945	1880	32118	193567	128866
城北区	Chengbei District	104806	76169	19234	8902	501	63874	191839	80672
郊　区	Jiaoqu District	10137	4720			5417	9796	65848	55444
南岳区	Nanyue District	5410	3992	1275	143		2224	14739	2990
衡阳县	Hengyang County	39332	26375	12700	257		16562	78355	63485
衡南县	Hengnan County	13427	9100	3977		350	14424	29927	22210
衡山县	Hengshan County	7703	4912	2791			7038	46983	19240
衡东县	Hengdong County	9272	6867	2004	269	132	5238	20947	9449
祁东县	Qidong County	18543	7502	10640	401		14615	35592	22931
耒阳市	Leiyang City	43714	31859	10860	158	837	16350	35293	13240
常宁市	Changning City	21741	7818	11574	421	1928	11986	43916	9200
邵阳市	**Shaoyang City**	**173656**	**132498**	**34682**	**242**	**6234**	**147215**	**666078**	**335878**
双清区	Shuangqing District	22100	8854	10254		3221	15086	119568	85214
大祥区	Daxiang District	33520	30078	3242		200	11414	73162	50512
北塔区	Beita District	5816	5716	100			387	2235	
邵东县	Shaodong County	13820	10500	3078	242		12371	94726	70378
新邵县	Xinshao County	9429	7898	1531			6994	24360	9046
邵阳县	Shaoyang County	5196	4666	530			3369	2880	2480
隆回县	Longhui County	24857	19033	4174		1650	24765	57435	15600
洞口县	Dongkou County	13622	10521	3101			10662	44416	4300
绥宁县	Suining County	8295	7830	465			3081	44794	16880
新宁县	Xinning County	10333	8232	2101			5140	36150	18649
城步县	Chengbu County	14669	10574	4015		80	43764	46633	2778
武冈市	Wugang City	11770	8596	2091		1083	10182	119719	60041
岳阳市	**Yueyang City**	**475274**	**258699**	**188182**	**3801**	**24592**	**271725**	**1166832**	**827550**
岳阳楼区	Yueyanglou District	290330	112475	157207	2844	17804	180513	510629	343174
云溪区	Yunxi District	17266	6957	9512	797		6526	3030	
君山区	Junshan District	12707	11971	736			236		
岳阳县	Yueyang County	23380	20542	2149		689	20533	253746	237736
华容县	Huarong County	20805	16799	2876		1130	16135	105222	68739
湘阴县	Xiangyin County	44922	37414	2908		4600	18860	45618	18208
平江县	Pingjiang County	20196	15434	4762			10520	93593	57369
汨罗市	Miluo City	19542	16861	2592		89	5707	47636	25571
临湘市	Linxiang City	26126	20246	5440	160	280	12695	107358	76753

市县名称	Cities and Counties	固定资产投资(万元) Total Investment in Fixed Assets (10 000 yuan)	基本建设 Investment in Capital Construction	更新改造 Investment in Innovation	其他投资 Others Investment	房地产开发 Real Estate Development	新增固定资产(万元) Newly Increased Fixed Assets (10 000 yuan)	房屋建筑竣工面积(平方米) Floor Space of Buildings Completed (sq.m)	#住宅 Residential Buildings
常德市	**Changde City**	**428197**	**299992**	**102312**	**7363**	**18530**	**143060**	**588026**	**365153**
武陵区	Wuling District	260280	152920	85464	6600	15296	95966	295796	218442
鼎城区	Dingcheng District	18202	3314	14888			1503	19812	16690
安乡县	Anxiang County	17214	15000	650	610	954	10090	63654	26500
汉寿县	Hanshou County	10327	9607			720	5356	41336	18616
澧县	Li County	54682	54522			160	10462	59948	36019
临澧县	Linli County	5405	5105			300	3865	14969	2023
桃源县	Taoyuan County	29018	29018				7910	31424	19074
石门县	Shimen County	24295	22912	300	153	930	4461	57117	24429
津市市	Jinshi City	8774	7594	1010		170	3447	3970	3360
张家界市	**Zhangjiajie City**	**88490**	**53285**	**18395**	**11057**	**5753**	**51849**	**211310**	**110169**
永定区	Yongding District	44989	27142	12642	40	5165	10094	71228	46074
武陵源区	Wulingyuan District	16221	9485	1968	4768		16221	14500	
慈利县	Chili County	8778	7362	808	488	120	11762	32293	9895
桑植县	Sangzhi County	18502	9296	2977	5761	468	13772	93289	54200
益阳市	**Yiyang City**	**277269**	**234318**	**30935**	**4967**	**7049**	**135758**	**547789**	**293373**
资阳区	Ziyang District	18674	18161	313		200	18018	50155	16566
赫山区	Heshan District	178806	154581	16186	2424	5615	56279	305303	192094
南县	Nan County	18705	15714	2917		74	11240	19648	6800
桃江县	Taojiang County	24102	18109	4963	300	730	13916	73289	29758
安化县	Anhua County	17557	13099	1928	2100	430	22879	62710	29930
沅江市	Yuanjiang City	19425	14654	4628	143		13426	36684	18225
郴州市	**Chenzhou City**	**342519**	**234744**	**85462**	**15438**	**6875**	**258316**	**927926**	**572083**
北湖区	Beihu District	118824	53472	54990	9641	721	72720	224104	153095
苏仙区	Suxian District	60018	50434	6433	489	2662	69915	161332	102840
桂阳县	Guiyang County	26638	20637	3394	1123	1484	23951	110267	69807
宜章县	Yizhang County	9651	6684	1959	808	200	6462	39494	18111
永兴县	Yongxing County	20342	19422	770		150	24326	80963	35842
嘉禾县	Jiahe County	9802	6722	3080			10472	47688	38640
临武县	Linwu County	13177	9764	1822	1591		11846	78484	36892
汝城县	Rucheng County	12716	11762	240	536	178	7888	18289	11559
桂东县	Guidong County	5567	5409	158			6172	46664	24738
安仁县	Anreng County	10639	8463	2176			8474	25152	3130
资兴市	Zixing City	55145	41975	10440	1250	1480	16090	95489	77429

市县名称	Cities and Counties	固定资产投资 (万元) Total Investment in Fixed Assets (10 000 yuan)	基本建设 Investment in Capital Construction	更新改造 Investment in Innovation	其他投资 Others Investment	房地产开发 Real Estate Development	新增固定资产 (万元) Newly Increased Fixed Assets (10 000 yuan)	房屋建筑竣工面积 (平方米) Floor Space of Buildings Completed (sq.m)	#住宅 Residential Buildings
永州市	**Yongzhou City**	**195189**	**139301**	**40485**	**14043**	**1360**	**114954**	**501491**	**244655**
芝山区	Zhishan District	47592	37404	7090	3048	50	20599	94657	57412
冷水滩区	Lengshuitan District	56552	33589	21420	843	700	35730	169220	92274
祁阳县	Qiyang County	34233	26575	6148	900	610	20057	10295	5899
东安县	Dongan County	9661	8227	846	588		5306	72336	32841
双牌县	Shuangpai County	6193	4433	560	1200		4512	17250	12900
道县	Dao County	9225	3830	855	4540		7013	23065	4200
江永县	Jiangyong County	5691	4403	1106	182		3582	31590	11189
宁远县	Ningyuan County	9715	9272	443			2685	13424	2000
蓝山县	Lanshan County	2078	1518	140	420		2649	11258	5880
新田县	Xintian County	3897	2910	175	812		2700	15156	8400
江华县	Jianghua County	10352	7140	1702	1510		10121	43240	11660
怀化市	**Huaihua City**	**169284**	**98624**	**63862**	**337**	**6461**	**107261**	**687120**	**410365**
鹤城区	Hecheng District	66332	36985	23405	337	5605	38694	191981	144087
中方县	Zhongfang County	787	787				186		
沅陵县	Yuanling County	8804	6380	2424			6368	33853	23806
辰溪县	Chenxi County	9074	6213	2861			5025	39313	21728
溆浦县	Xupu County	9059	6812	2247			4233	42475	36730
会同县	Huitong County	11470	8228	3242			11470	150195	51135
麻阳县	Mayang County	9547	4808	4739			10567	51900	8850
新晃县	Xinhuang County	7111	3765	3285		61	3709	29604	12410
芷江县	Zhijiang County	7865	7700			165	2939	9857	9857
靖州县	Jinzhou County	9699	7245	2454			5295	60156	47156
通道县	Tongdao County	4549	2667	1732		150	4774	25559	11373
洪江市	Hongjiang City	24987	7034	17473		480	14001	52227	43233
娄底市	**Loudi City**	**206196**	**97388**	**98090**	**2756**	**7962**	**176967**	**518819**	**266003**
娄星区	Louxing District	119500	40286	73173		6041	125525	234525	119143
双峰县	Shuangfeng County	30899	24060	4052	993	1794	8935	70670	27288
新化县	Xinhua County	15071	11010	3759	302		14911	53559	38156
冷水江市	Lengshuijian City	19213	8172	10516	525		16085	116782	66241
涟源市	Lianyuan City	21513	13860	6590	936	127	11511	43283	15175
湘西自治州	**West Hunan A.P**	**167913**	**124422**	**41204**	**1992**	**295**	**101258**	**402002**	**194862**
吉首市	Jishou City	67312	41579	24565	1168		55174	162502	92910
泸溪县	Louxi County	8061	4591	3470			8483	36111	12700
凤凰县	Fenghuang County	7037	5104	1422	511		4302	29736	13560
花垣县	Huayuan County	18020	9015	9005			17475	33228	3182
保靖县	Baojin County	26388	25671	717			2532	30952	23589
古丈县	Guzhang County	3939	2979	647	313		2965	23607	5196
永顺县	Yongshun County	24613	24115	203		295	7100	66305	37375
龙山县	Longshan County	12543	11368	1175			3227	19561	6350
不分地区	**Not Classified by Region**	**1361893**	**1117669**	**244224**			**617735**	**40104**	**24850**

18-19 各市、州、县社会消费品零售总额(2001年)

Total Value of Retail Sales of Consumer Goods (2001)

单位：万元 (10 000 yuan)

市县名称	City and County	社会消费品零售总额 Total Retial Sales of Consumer Goods	公有经济 Public-owned	#国有及国有控股 State-owned & Controlling Share Hold by the State	非公有经济 Non-Public Owned
长沙市	**Changsha City**	**3449742.0**	**1365588.3**	**818515.9**	**2084153.7**
长沙市区	Urban District	2699311.0	1163008.3	722432.9	1536302.7
长沙县	Changsha County	183041.0	50267.0	13727.0	132774.0
望城县	Wangcheng County	137724.0	51923.0	21924.0	85801.0
宁乡县	Ningxiang County	174600.0	51808.0	33413.0	122792.0
浏阳市	Liuyang City	255066.0	48582.0	27019.0	206484.0
株洲市	**Zhuzhou City**	**1235633.0**	**257680.0**	**145549.0**	**977953.0**
株洲市区	Urban District	676698.0	132149.0	75455.0	544549.0
醴陵市	Liling City	244277.0	51705.0	33563.0	192572.0
株洲县	Zhuzhou County	83181.0	17618.0	5423.0	65563.0
攸 县	You County	138485.0	30395.0	14300.0	108090.0
茶陵县	Chaling County	67824.0	18600.0	12073.0	49224.0
炎陵县	Yanling County	25168.0	7213.0	4735.0	17955.0
湘潭市	**Xiangtan City**	**770180.0**	**164899.0**	**66496.0**	**605281.0**
湘潭市区	Urban District	434679.0	78682.0	32099.0	355997.0
湘乡市	Xiangxiang City	154621.0	34763.0	15323.0	119858.0
韶山市	Shaoshan City	26597.0	5456.0	3262.0	21141.0
湘潭县	Xiangtan County	154283.0	45998.0	15812.0	108285.0
衡阳市	**Hengyang City**	**1303394.0**	**304602.0**	**197797.0**	**998792.0**
衡阳市区	Urban District	497760.0	14141.0	5312.0	483619.0
#南岳区	Nanyue District	25268.0	5466.0	3896.0	19802.0
耒阳市	Leiyang City	134474.0	49047.0	31806.0	85427.0
常宁市	Changning City	102568.0	28790.0	13268.0	73778.0
衡阳县	Hengyang County	112028.0	36115.0	23951.0	75913.0
衡南县	Hengnan County	94212.0	22168.0	11058.0	72044.0
衡山县	Hengshan County	45618.0	11344.0	9094.0	34274.0
衡东县	Hengdong County	78530.0	14510.0	7767.0	64020.0
祁东县	Qidong County	96453.0	32315.0	14502.0	64138.0
邵阳市	**Shaoyang City**	**944399.0**	**310650.0**	**142624.0**	**633749.0**
邵阳市区	Urban District	216192.0	114572.0	39834.0	101620.0
武冈市	Wugang City	77808.0	18471.0	8704.0	59337.0
邵东县	Shaodong County	240250.0	12491.0	12491.0	227759.0
新邵县	Xinshao County	84997.0	31606.0	15048.0	53391.0
邵阳县	Shaoyang County	78519.0	37016.0	17221.0	41503.0
隆回县	Longhui County	73567.0	31555.0	12869.0	42012.0
洞口县	Dongkou County	72207.0	32647.0	14127.0	39560.0
绥宁县	Shuining County	43494.0	13043.0	7731.0	30451.0
新宁县	Xinning County	28516.0	9441.0	7217.0	19075.0
城步县	Chengbu County	28849.0	9808.0	7382.0	19041.0

单位：万元 18-19 续表 1 continued (10 000 yuan)

市县名称	City and County	社会消费品零售总额 Total Retial Sales of Consumer Goods	公有经济 Public-owned	#国有及国有控股 State-owned & Controlling Share Hold by the State	非公有经济 Non-Public Owned
岳阳市	**Yueyang City**	**1426812.0**	**229787.0**	**152764.0**	**1197025.0**
岳阳市区	Urban District	794777.0	110259.0	72392.0	684518.0
汨罗市	Miluo City	92754.0	30969.0	20811.0	61785.0
临湘市	Linxiang City	90180.0	15945.0	10292.0	74235.0
岳阳县	Yueyang County	137600.0	7119.0	6049.0	130481.0
华容县	Huarong County	129527.0	26021.0	15818.0	103506.0
湘阴县	Xiangyin County	91285.0	17135.0	11480.0	74150.0
平江县	Pingjiang County	90689.0	22339.0	15922.0	68350.0
常德市	**Changde City**	**1288316.0**	**249685.0**	**134689.0**	**1038631.0**
常德市区	Urban District	437820.0	61812.0	52896.0	376008.0
#武陵区	Wuling District	218621.0	49498.0	47217.0	169123.0
鼎城区	Dingchen District	219199.0	12314.0	5679.0	206885.0
津市市	Jinshi City	81921.0	6210.0	5602.0	75711.0
安乡县	Anxiang County	87654.0	20735.0	10845.0	66919.0
汉寿县	Hanshou County	101579.0	10220.0	6914.0	91359.0
澧县	Li County	146443.0	16011.0	9012.0	130432.0
临澧县	Linli County	86843.0	19328.0	6831.0	67515.0
桃源县	Taoyuan County	211806.0	90290.0	31032.0	121516.0
石门县	Shimen County	134250.0	25079.0	11557.0	109171.0
张家界市	**Zhangjiajie City**	**236599.4**	**55894.9**	**49248.5**	**180704.5**
张家界市区	Urban District	117342.6	30766.6	30766.6	86576.0
#永定区	Yongding District	93382.0	15333.0	15333.0	78049.0
武陵源区	Wulingyuan District	15408.0	6881.0	6881.0	8527.0
慈利县	Cili County	78691.0	16110.0	11480.0	62581.0
桑植县	Sangzhi County	41565.8	7177.4	6864.0	34388.4
益阳市	**Yiyang City**	**768104.0**	**240955.0**	**137981.0**	**527149.0**
益阳市区	Urban District	346035.0	62817.0	40658.0	283218.0
#资阳区	Ziyang District	130332.0	3495.0	3033.0	126837.0
赫山区	Heshan District	183775.0	41968.0	19271.0	141807.0
沅江市	Yuanjiang City	95682.0	16629.0	11858.0	79053.0
南县	Nan County	107873.0	35375.0	10882.0	72498.0
桃江县	Taojiang County	102750.0	42645.0	23539.0	60105.0
安化县	Anhua County	115764.0	83489.0	51044.0	32275.0
郴州市	**Chenzhou City**	**1183300.0**	**293855.0**	**197441.0**	**889445.0**
郴州市区	Urban District	490828.0	156501.0	106068.0	334327.0
#北湖区	Beihu District	135268.0	37119.0	8954.0	98149.0
苏仙区	Suxian District	70263.0	10432.0	5886.0	59831.0
资兴市	Zixing City	137071.0	17974.0	13700.0	119097.0
桂阳县	Guiyang County	120290.0	13528.0	10133.0	106762.0
永兴县	Yizhang County	125994.0	29198.0	20325.0	96796.0
宜章县	Yongxing County	133694.0	27665.0	7803.0	106029.0
嘉禾县	Jiahe County	53079.0	14405.0	14405.0	38674.0
临武县	Linwu County	33124.0	13714.0	9497.0	19410.0
汝城县	Rucheng County	34218.0	5555.0	5515.0	28663.0
桂东县	Guidong County	12617.0	3971.0	3023.0	8646.0
安仁县	Anren County	42385.0	11344.0	6972.0	31041.0

单位：万元 18-19 续表 2 continued (10 000 yuan)

市县名称	City and County	社会消费品零售总额 Total Retial Sales of Consumer Goods	公有经济 Public-owned	#国有及国有控股 State-owned & Controlling Share Hold by the State	非公有经济 Non-Public Owned
永州市	**Yongzhou City**	**760924.5**	**183293.0**	**125574.7**	**577631.5**
永州市区	Urban District	295437.5	47855.0	24724.7	247582.5
#芝山区	Zhishan District	114625.0	15408.0	6689.0	99217.0
冷水滩区	Lengshuitan District	102880.0	14896.0	10296.0	87983.0
东安县	Dongan County	69704.0	13332.0	9416.0	56372.0
道县	Dao County	63811.0	28577.0	19979.0	35234.0
宁远县	Ningyuan Couny	81810.0	24872.0	13998.0	56938.0
江永县	Jiangyong County	32779.0	3804.0	3281.0	28975.0
江华县	Jianghua Couny	40329.0	8849.0	6210.0	31480.0
蓝山县	Lanshan County	30601.0	10072.0	8702.0	20529.0
新田县	Xintian County	25112.0	10568.0	7209.0	14544.0
双牌县	Shuangpai County	17760.0	6498.0	4787.0	11262.0
祁阳县	Qiyang County	103581.0	28866.0	27268.0	74715.0
怀化市	**Huaihua City**	**731695.0**	**208153.0**	**132743.0**	**523542.0**
怀化市区	Urban District	209567.0	65777.0	36719.0	143790.0
#鹤城区	Hecheng District	74930.0	23760.0	12144.0	51170.0
洪江区	Hongjiang District	35647.0	11056.0	6742.0	24591.0
中方县	Zhongfang County	26408.0	3777.0	3777.0	22631.0
洪江市	Hongjiang City	60830.0	7422.0	3587.0	53408.0
沅陵县	Yuanling County	73754.0	26383.0	15042.0	47371.0
辰溪县	Chenxi County	57035.0	10553.0	8339.0	46482.0
溆浦县	Xupu County	101654.0	28682.0	13960.0	72972.0
麻阳县	Mayang County	35928.0	12433.0	6899.0	23495.0
新晃县	Xinhuang County	24822.0	6338.0	5228.0	18484.0
芷江县	Zhijiang County	42986.0	15196.0	13479.0	27790.0
会同县	Huitong County	32278.0	12511.0	10527.0	19767.0
靖州县	Jingzhou County	39001.0	5447.0	4991.0	33554.0
通道县	Tongdao County	27432.0	13634.0	10195.0	13798.0
娄底市	**Loudi City**	**729933.6**	**202888.9**	**137279.8**	**527044.7**
娄星区	Louxing District	160046.6	60517.9	45752.1	99528.7
冷水江市	Lengshuijiang City	130904.0	30553.0	22065.0	100351.0
涟源市	Lianyuan City	175962.0	43343.0	24332.0	132619.0
双峰县	Shuangfrng County	130010.0	34263.0	19938.0	95747.0
新化县	Xinhua County	133011.0	34212.0	20768.0	98799.0
湘西自治州	**West Hunan A.P**	**362495.5**	**59745.2**	**41942.3**	**302750.3**
吉首市	Jishou City	121743.8	19564.7	16872.9	102179.1
泸溪县	Luxi County	26703.6	3613.9	2393.8	23089.7
凤凰县	Fenghuang County	47416.9	7136.9	4040.0	40280.0
花垣县	Huayuan County	24614.5	4744.8	2770.0	19869.7
保靖县	Baojing County	21335.8	6049.3	4408.6	15286.5
古丈县	Guzhang County	13274.6	1727.8	1244.5	11546.8
永顺县	Yongsun County	56149.0	8111.0	4078.7	48038.0
龙山县	Longshan County	51257.3	8796.8	6133.8	42460.5

18-20 各市、州、县财政收入与支出(2001年)

Government Revenue and Expenditures (2001)

单位：万元 (10 000 yuan)

市县名称	City and County	财政收入 Total Revenue	财政支出 Total Expenditures
长沙市	**Changsha City**	**421620**	**523252**
本级	City Level	237664	260824
芙蓉区	Furong District	17765	19878
天心区	Tianxin District	14428	18255
岳麓区	Yuelu District	11010	16089
开福区	Kaifu District	16988	21996
雨花区	Yuhua District	15583	22299
长沙县	Changsha County	38382	51732
望城县	Wangcheng County	18724	26984
宁乡县	Ningxiang County	19318	35466
浏阳市	Liuyang City	31758	49729
株洲市	**Zhuzhou City**	**145092**	**209950**
本级	City Level	55191	93416
荷塘区	Hetang District	6647	6629
芦淞区	Lousong District	9893	7395
石峰区	Shifeng District	9689	6658
天元区	Tianyuan District	12449	12855
株洲县	Zhuzhou County	6500	11668
攸县	You County	12282	19550
茶陵县	Chaling County	9156	14984
炎陵县	Yanling County	4409	8394
醴陵市	Liling City	18876	28401
湘潭市	**Xiangtan City**	**79698**	**142801**
本级	City Level	37028	73135
雨湖区	Yuhu District	7390	8962
岳塘区	Yuetang District	5769	6518
湘潭县	Xiangtan County	12530	23116
湘乡市	Xiangxiang City	14360	25730
韶山市	Shaoshan City	2621	5340
衡阳市	**Hengyang City**	**140208**	**236880**
本级	City Level	42469	77181
珠晖区	Zhuhui District	2367	3809
雁峰区	Yanfeng District	2902	3940
石鼓区	Shigu District	2399	4165
蒸湘区	Zhengxiang District	1891	4255
南岳区	Nanyue District	2482	5062
耒阳市	Leiyang City	13846	24200
常宁市	Changning City	13189	19782
衡阳县	Hengyang County	13166	21812
衡南县	Hengnan County	15479	24418
衡山县	Hengshan County	5938	9293
衡东县	Hengdong County	10120	14982
祁东县	Qidong County	13960	23981
邵阳市	**Shaoyang City**	**106774**	**233049**
本级	City Level	9244	53200
双清区	Shuangqing District	5700	6501
大祥区	Daxiang District	5162	6627
北塔区	Beita District	1310	2483
邵东县	Shaodong County	14758	25587
新邵县	Xinshao County	6292	15098
邵阳县	Shaoyang County	8677	18463
隆回县	Longhui County	14122	25970
洞口县	Dongkou County	9206	17954
绥宁县	Suining County	9028	15172
新宁县	Xinning County	7565	15695
城步县	Chengbu County	4827	11711
武冈市	Wugang City	10919	18588
岳阳市	**Yueyang City**	**150950**	**248131**
本级	City Level	56100	90896
岳阳楼区	Yueyanglou District	13604	14303
云溪区	Yunxi District	7828	8048
君山区	Junshan District	2607	6875
岳阳县	Yueyang County	8261	20029
华容县	Huarong County	10936	19816
湘阴县	Xiangyin County	8357	17366
平江县	Pingjiang County	13336	25783
汨罗市	Miluo City	17676	27403
临湘市	Linxiang City	12245	17612
常德市	**Changde City**	**145591**	**233514**
本级	City Level	42835	71207
武陵区	Wuling District	8636	12920
鼎城区	Dingcheng District	14843	23093
安乡县	Anxiang County	8862	15278
汉寿县	Hanshou County	10590	17911
澧县	Li County	14530	23102
临澧县	Linli County	9068	13579

单位：万元 18-20 续表 continued (10 000 yuan)

市县名称	City and County	财政收入 Total Revenue	财政支出 Total Expenditures	市县名称	City and County	财政收入 Total Revenue	财政支出 Total Expenditures
桃源县	Taoyuan County	16813	22496	道县	Dao County	9683	16691
石门县	Shimen County	11906	20686	江永县	Jiangyong County	5533	8762
津市市	Jinshi City	7508	13242	宁远县	Ningyuan County	6863	15799
张家界市	**Zhangjiajie City**	**30115**	**76003**	蓝山县	Lanshan County	6013	10027
本级	City Level	6596	17217	新田县	Xintian County	3877	10904
永定区	Yongding District	6245	14267	江华县	Jianghua County	5616	13440
武陵源区	Wulingyuan District	6508	8521	**怀化市**	**Huaihua City**	**86158**	**182514**
慈利县	Cili County	6866	17431	本级	City Level	18233	35030
桑植县	Sangzhi County	3900	18567	鹤城区	Hecheng District	4087	8611
益阳市	**Yiyang City**	**67975**	**147346**	中方县	Zhongfang County	1830	8430
本级	City Level	17845	43834	沅陵县	Yuanling County	9575	19655
资阳区	Ziyang District	4964	13107	辰溪县	Chenxi County	6640	13904
赫山区	Heshan District	10648	16047	溆浦县	Xupu County	8310	16460
南县	Nan County	7360	15752	会同县	Huitong County	6372	11753
桃江县	Taojiang County	8241	18272	麻阳县	Mayang County	3817	11413
安化县	Anhua County	10273	20945	新晃县	Xinhuang County	3440	9752
沅江市	Yuanjiang City	8644	19389	芷江县	Zhijiang County	5544	10670
郴州市	**Chenzhou City**	**152350**	**237560**	靖州县	Jinzhou County	6299	10687
本级	City Level	30998	50491	通道县	Tongdao County	3320	8180
北湖区	Beihu District	10709	17758	洪江市	Hongjiang City	8691	17969
苏仙区	Suxian District	11239	16082	**娄底市**	**Loudi City**	**80421**	**145474**
桂阳县	Guiyang County	17855	23711	本级	City Level	17789	38407
宜章县	Yizhang County	13607	20541	娄星区	Louxing District	7672	15989
永兴县	Yongxing County	14306	23129	双峰县	Shuangfeng County	12703	22502
嘉禾县	Jiahe County	11353	15825	新化县	Xinhua County	13553	28629
临武县	Linwu County	10449	14347	冷水江市	Lenshuijiang City	14605	17367
汝城县	Rucheng County	7967	13120	涟源市	Lianyuan City	14099	22580
桂东县	Guidong County	2928	8664	**湘西自治州**	**West Hunan A.P**	**35183**	**158701**
安仁县	Anreng County	7439	12186	本级	City Level	9304	43725
资兴市	Zixing City	13500	21706	吉首市	Jishou City	8425	17050
永州市	**Yongzhou**	**92405**	**188228**	泸溪县	Louxi County	1446	10505
本级	City Level	19909	38467	凤凰县	Fenghuang County	2838	17967
芝山区	Zhishan District	5414	15397	花垣县	Huayuan County	3750	13522
冷水滩区	Lengshuitan District	5925	13403	保靖县	Baojin County	2272	11310
祁阳县	Qiyang County	12754	23464	古丈县	Guzhang County	756	8792
东安县	Dongan County	7093	14651	永顺县	Yongshun County	2655	17476
双牌县	Shuangpai County	3725	7223	龙山县	Longshan County	3737	18354

18-21 各市、州、县各级学校(2001年)

Schools by Level (2001)

单位：所 (unit)

市县名称	City and County	普通高等学校 Regular Institutions of Higher Education	中等学校 Secondary Schools	普通中等专业学校 Specialized Secondary Schools	职业中学 Vocational Secondary Schools	普通中学 Regular Secondary Schools	普通小学 Primary Schools
长沙市	**Changsha City**	**29**	**496**	**32**	**96**	**368**	**1830**
长沙市区	Urban District	29	158	28	39	91	246
浏阳市	Liuyang City		127	1	44	82	505
长沙县	Changsha County		58	1	6	51	359
望城县	Wangcheng County		48	1	2	45	243
宁乡县	Ningxiang County		105	1	5	99	477
株洲市	**Zhuzhou City**	**5**	**276**	**10**	**33**	**233**	**1386**
株洲市区	Urban District	5	70	8	12	50	137
醴陵市	Liling City		71		9	62	379
株洲县	Zhuzhou County		32		1	31	206
攸县	You County		51	2	9	40	299
茶陵县	Chaling County		31		1	30	274
炎陵县	Yanling County		21		1	20	91
湘潭市	**Xiangtan City**	**5**	**283**	**11**	**33**	**239**	**961**
湘潭市区	Urban District	5	75	9	20	46	110
湘乡市	Xiangxiang City		101	1	8	92	342
韶山市	Shaoshan City		11		2	9	40
湘潭县	Xiangtan County		96	1	3	92	469
衡阳市	**Hengyang City**	**4**	**500**	**11**	**20**	**469**	**2789**
衡阳市区	Urban District	4	75	8	8	59	208
耒阳市	Leiyang City		70	1	2	67	539
常宁市	Changning City		66		2	64	319
衡阳县	Hengyang County		77		1	76	379
衡南县	Hengnan County		66	2	2	62	395
衡山县	Hengshan County		32		1	31	171
衡东县	Hengdong County		46		3	43	362
祁东县	Qidong County		68		1	67	416
邵阳市	**Shaoyang City**	**2**	**608**	**10**	**35**	**563**	**2785**
邵阳市区	Urban District	2	72	9	14	49	121
武冈市	Wugang City		57	1	1	55	266
邵东县	Shaodong County		95		10	85	329
新邵县	Xinshao County		62		1	61	201
邵阳县	Shaoyang County		64		1	63	395
隆回县	Longhui County		97		1	96	456
洞口县	Dongkou County		63		3	60	337
绥宁县	Shuining County		40		2	38	245
新宁县	Xinning County		39		1	38	215
城步县	Chengbu County		19		1	18	220

单位：所 18-21 续表 1 continued (unit)

市县名称	City and County	普通高等学校 Regular Institutions of Higher Education	中等学校 Secondary Schools	普通中等专业学校 Specialized Secondary Schools	职业中学 Vocational Secondary Schools	普通中学 Regular Secondary Schools	普通小学 Primary Schools
岳阳市	**Yueyang City**	**1**	**448**	**9**	**33**	**406**	**2216**
岳阳市区	Urban District	1	89	7	10	72	183
汨罗市	Miluo City		67	1	7	59	300
临湘市	Linxiang City		40	1	3	36	260
岳阳县	Yueyang County		56		1	55	480
华容县	Huarong County		58		2	56	201
湘阴县	Xiangyin County		59		2	57	331
平江县	Pingjiang County		79		8	71	461
常德市	**Changde City**	**1**	**378**	**10**	**35**	**333**	**1908**
常德市区	Urban District	1	105	8	16	81	392
津市市	Jinshi City		14	1	1	12	69
安乡县	Anxiang County		27		1	26	173
汉寿县	Hanshou County		45		4	41	358
澧县	Li County		52		7	45	246
临澧县	Linli County		24		1	23	153
桃源县	Taoyuan County		60	1	3	56	240
石门县	Shimen County		51		2	49	277
张家界市	**Zhangjiajie City**	**2**	**123**		**8**	**115**	**939**
张家界市区	Urban District	2	46		5	41	230
慈利县	Cili County		44		2	42	449
桑植县	Sangzhi County		33		1	32	260
益阳市	**Yiyang City**	**2**	**348**	**6**	**23**	**319**	**1688**
益阳市区	Urban District	2	92	5	8	79	487
沅江市	Yuanjiang City		70	1	3	66	297
南县	Nan County		55		2	53	233
桃江县	Taojiang County		63		2	61	329
安化县	Anhua County		68		8	60	342
郴州市	**Chenzhou City**	**3**	**391**	**5**	**24**	**362**	**2597**
郴州市区	Urban District	3	80	3	13	64	273
资兴市	Zixing City		41	1	1	39	267
桂阳县	Guiyang County		49		2	47	494
永兴县	Yongxing County		38	1	1	36	298
宜章县	Yizhang County		46		2	44	294
嘉禾县	Jiahe County		24		1	23	209
临武县	Linwu County		29		1	28	128
汝城县	Rucheng County		32		1	31	306
桂东县	Guidong County		15		1	14	117
安仁县	Anren County		37		1	36	211

单位：所　　18-21 续表 2 continued　　(unit)

市县名称	City and County	普通高等学校 Regular Institutions of Higher Education	中等学校 Secondary Schools	普通中等专业学校 Specialized Secondary Schools	职业中学 Vocational Secondary Schools	普通中学 Regular Secondary Schools	普通小学 Primary Schools
永州市	**Yongzhou City**	**2**	**432**	**6**	**19**	**407**	**3332**
永州市区	Urban District	2	107	4	9	94	581
东安县	Dongan County		48		1	47	295
道县	Dao County		46	1	1	44	417
宁远县	Ningyuan County		50		2	48	458
江永县	Jiangyong County		18		1	17	103
江华县	Jianghua County		28		1	27	317
蓝山县	Lanshan County		27		1	26	324
新田县	Xintian County		23		1	22	314
双牌县	Shuanpai County		19		1	18	154
祁阳县	Qiyang County		66	1	1	64	369
怀化市	**Huaihua City**	**2**	**414**	**5**	**22**	**387**	**3262**
怀化市区	Urban District	2	41	4	4	33	85
洪江市	Hongjiang City		37		5	32	219
中方县	Zhongfang County		24		1	23	81
沅陵县	Yuanling County		64		3	61	623
辰溪县	Chenxi County		40		2	38	341
溆浦县	Xupu County		63		1	62	520
麻阳县	Mayang County		27		1	26	276
新晃县	Xinhuang County		24		1	23	243
芷江县	Zhijiang County		33	1	1	31	276
会同县	Huitong County		28		1	27	261
靖州县	Jinzhou County		21		1	20	150
通道县	Tongdao County		12		1	11	187
娄底市	**Loudi City**	**2**	**354**	**4**	**37**	**313**	**1531**
娄底市区	Urban District	2	36	2	11	23	84
冷水江市	Lengshuijiang City		43	2	5	36	98
涟源市	Lianyuan City		89		13	76	438
双峰县	Shangfeng County		78		4	74	312
新化县	Xinhua County		108		4	104	599
湘西自治州	**West Hunan A.P**	**1**	**203**	**6**	**16**	**181**	**2116**
吉首市	Jishou City	1	30	5	4	21	176
泸溪县	Louxi County		20		1	19	198
凤凰县	Fenghuang County		30		2	28	336
花垣县	Huayuan County		22		1	21	193
保靖县	Baojing County		20		1	19	228
古丈县	Guzhang County		12		0	12	160
永顺县	Yongshun County		40	1	5	34	459
龙山县	Longshan County		29		2	27	366

18-22 各市、州、县各级学校教职工(2001年)

School Staff and workers by Level (2001)

单位：人 (person)

市县名称	City and County	普通高等学校 Regular Institutions of Higher Education	中等学校 Secondary Schools	普通中等专业学校 Specialized Secondary Schools	职业中学 Vocational Secondary Schools	普通中学 Regular Secondary Schools	普通小学 Primary Schools
长沙市	**Changsha City**	**29438**	**34806**	**3607**	**3869**	**27330**	**22187**
长沙市区	Urban District	29438	13663	3402	2034	8227	7987
浏阳市	Liuyang City		6776	90	656	6030	4088
长沙县	Changsha County		3979	115	370	3494	3072
望城县	Wangcheng County		3709		277	3432	2702
宁乡县	Ningxiang County		6679		532	6147	4338
株洲市	**Zhuzhou City**	**4336**	**20232**	**1613**	**1626**	**16993**	**14499**
株洲市区	Urban District	4336	5899	1336	841	3722	3195
醴陵市	Liling City		4466		374	4092	3143
株洲县	Zhuzhou County		2155		126	2029	1730
攸县	You County		4112	277	223	3612	3063
茶陵县	Chaling County		2529		37	2492	2375
炎陵县	Yanling County		1071		25	1046	993
湘潭市	**Xiangtan City**	**5813**	**15442**	**1404**	**1359**	**12679**	**11675**
湘潭市区	Urban District	5813	5235	1345	833	3057	2976
湘乡市	Xiangxiang City		4386	59	284	4043	3872
韶山市	Shaoshan City		509		58	451	483
湘潭县	Xiangtan County		5312		184	5128	4344
衡阳市	**Hengyang City**	**3444**	**31346**	**1796**	**1533**	**28017**	**34530**
衡阳市区	Urban District	3444	6091	1371	452	4268	4212
耒阳市	Leiyang City		4514	140	129	4245	6540
常宁市	Changning City		3235		183	3052	4155
衡阳县	Hengyang County		4556		211	4345	5343
衡南县	Hengnan County		4236	285	66	3885	5153
衡山县	Hengshan County		1948		143	1805	2072
衡东县	Hengdong County		2632		179	2453	2843
祁东县	Qidong County		4134		170	3964	4212
邵阳市	**Shaoyang City**	**957**	**30740**	**1315**	**1488**	**27937**	**29978**
邵阳市区	Urban District	957	4583	1179	386	3018	2803
武冈市	Wugang City		2733	136	185	2412	3029
邵东县	Shaodong County		5054		230	4824	4449
新邵县	Xinshao County		2960		103	2857	2908
邵阳县	Shaoyang County		2861		101	2760	3767
隆回县	Longhui County		4190		124	4066	4404
洞口县	Dongkou County		3001		126	2875	3084
绥宁县	Shuining County		1831		98	1733	1983
新宁县	Xinning County		2292		85	2207	1980
城步县	Chengbu County		1235		50	1185	1571

单位：人 18-22 续表 1 continued (person)

市县名称	City and County	普通高等学校 Regular Institutions of Higher Education	中等学校 Secondary Schools	普通中等专业学校 Specialized Secondary Schools	职业中学 Vocational Secondary Schools	普通中学 Regular Secondary Schools	普通小学 Primary Schools
岳阳市	**Yueyang City**	**1196**	**27079**	**1546**	**1763**	**23770**	**24551**
岳阳市区	Urban District	1196	7228	1303	608	5317	4764
汨罗市	Miluo City		3901	243	414	3244	3001
临湘市	Linxiang City		2367		179	2188	2602
岳阳县	Yueyang County		2972		86	2886	3173
华容县	Huarong County		3539		123	3416	3186
湘阴县	Xiangyin County		3136		159	2977	3430
平江县	Pingjiang County		3936		194	3742	4395
常德市	**Changde City**	**966**	**26585**	**1449**	**1827**	**23309**	**25819**
常德市区	Urban District	966	7628	1050	750	5828	6183
津市市	Jinshi City		1451	263	84	1104	1142
安乡县	Anxiang County		2557		46	2511	2210
汉寿县	Hanshou County		3056		168	2888	3666
澧县	Li County		3489		344	3145	3809
临澧县	Linli County		2010		57	1953	2133
桃源县	Taoyuan County		3837	136	229	3472	3856
石门县	Shimen County		2557		149	2408	2820
张家界市	**Zhangjiajie City**	**803**	**6271**		**514**	**5757**	**8730**
张家界市区	Urban District	803	1944		172	1772	2862
慈利县	Cili County		2643		218	2425	3199
桑植县	Sangzhi County		1684		124	1560	2669
益阳市	**Yiyang City**	**861**	**23092**	**686**	**1369**	**21037**	**21599**
益阳市区	Urban District	861	7564	686	404	6474	6638
沅江市	Yuanjiang City		3894		271	3623	3451
南县	Nan County		4019		186	3833	3898
桃江县	Taojiang County		4144		208	3936	4022
安化县	Anhua County		3471		300	3171	3590
郴州市	**Chenzhou City**	**1078**	**22015**	**655**	**1270**	**20090**	**24186**
郴州市区	Urban District	1078	4911	469	627	3815	3864
资兴市	Zixing City		2470	136	141	2193	2168
桂阳县	Guiyang County		2968		102	2866	3915
永兴县	Yongxing County		2816	50	94	2672	2879
宜章县	Yizhang County		2325		86	2239	2879
嘉禾县	Jiahe County		1272		49	1223	1770
临武县	Linwu County		1225		35	1190	1705
汝城县	Rucheng County		1506		45	1461	1799
桂东县	Guidong County		703		28	675	890
安仁县	Anren County		1819		63	1756	2317

市县名称	City and County	普通高等学校 Regular Institutions of Higher Education	中等学校 Secondary Schools	普通中等专业学校 Specialized Secondary Schools	职业中学 Vocational Secondary Schools	普通中学 Regular Secondary Schools	普通小学 Primary Schools
永州市	**Yongzhou City**	**954**	**26058**	**814**	**1133**	**24111**	**29596**
永州市市区	Urban District	954	6599	416	330	5853	5744
东安县	Dongan County		2710		71	2639	2734
道县	Dao County		2789	303	105	2381	3612
宁远县	Ningyuan County		2600		122	2478	3662
江永县	Jiangyong County		1162		97	1065	1396
江华县	Jianghua County		1433		96	1337	2362
蓝山县	Lanshan County		1313		58	1255	1873
新田县	Xintian County		1556		86	1470	1798
双牌县	Shuanpai County		752		50	702	1083
祁阳县	Qiyang County		5144	95	118	4931	5332
怀化市	**Huaihua City**	**886**	**21225**	**761**	**1411**	**19053**	**27263**
怀化市区	Urban District	886	2932	585	509	1838	2042
洪江市	Hongjiang City		2347		229	2118	2826
中方县	Zhongfang County		1253		99	1154	1515
沅陵县	Yuanling County		2483		120	2363	3871
辰溪县	Chenxi County		1850		61	1789	3344
溆浦县	Xupu County		2876		97	2779	4186
麻阳县	Mayang County		1238		8	1230	2055
新晃县	Xinhuang County		1015		43	972	1229
芷江县	Zhijiang County		1659	176	125	1358	1793
会同县	Huitong County		1435		49	1386	1779
靖州县	Jinzhou County		1151		61	1090	1462
通道县	Tongdao County		986		10	976	1161
娄底市	**Loudi City**	**1091**	**20291**	**910**	**1585**	**17796**	**18733**
娄底市区	Urban District	1091	3343	533	567	2243	2327
冷水江市	Lengshuijiang City		2737	377	288	2072	2184
涟源市	Lianyuan City		5109		368	4741	4994
双峰县	Shangfeng County		4239		119	4120	4036
新化县	Xinhua County		4863		243	4620	5192
湘西自治州	**West Hunan A.P**	**1296**	**10169**	**581**	**795**	**8793**	**15760**
吉首市	Jishou City	1296	1834	461	155	1218	1765
泸溪县	Louxi County		1033		33	1000	1659
凤凰县	Fenghuang County		1288		138	1150	2148
花垣县	Huayuan County		826		37	789	1636
保靖县	Baojing County		990		63	927	1691
古丈县	Guzhang County		522			522	933
永顺县	Yongshun County		1908	120	248	1540	2968
龙山县	Longshan County		1768		121	1647	2960

18-23 各市、州、县各级学校在校学生(2001年)

Students Enrollment by Level (2001)

单位：人 (person)

市县名称	City and County	普通高等学校 Regular Institutions of Higher Education	中等学校 Secondary Schools	普通中等专业学校 Specialized Secondary Schools	职业学校 Vocational Secondary Schools	普通中学 Regular Secondary Schools	高中 Senior Secondary Schools	初中 Junior Secondary Schools	普通小学 Primary Schools
长沙市	**Changsha City**	**172567**	**526043**	**74473**	**38527**	**413043**	**83352**	**329691**	**399513**
长沙市区	Urban District	172526	185440	68088	17873	99479	28608	70871	114678
浏阳市	Liuyang City		110930	1368	8253	101309	18045	83264	93326
长沙县	Changsha County		57298	963	2720	53615	9472	44143	52287
望城县	Wangcheng County		61580	2283	2985	56312	9229	47083	49507
宁乡县	Ningxiang County		110795	1771	6696	102328	17998	84330	89715
株洲市	**Zhuzhou City**	**23025**	**300148**	**23687**	**13786**	**262675**	**47092**	**215583**	**312963**
株洲市区	Urban District	23025	78747	22142	7089	49516	13431	36085	61096
醴陵市	Liling City		77692		3255	74437	11238	63199	93449
株洲县	Zhuzhou County		32020		935	31085	3815	27270	36883
攸县	You County		53871	1545	2042	50284	8316	41968	59486
茶陵县	Chaling County		44119		231	43888	7991	35897	48053
炎陵县	Yanling County		13699		234	13465	2301	11164	13996
湘潭市	**Xiangtan City**	**41072**	**234262**	**13247**	**17089**	**203926**	**41128**	**162798**	**234662**
湘潭市区	Urban District	41072	63790	13044	10552	40194	12176	28018	46711
湘乡市	Xiangxiang City		75044	203	3322	71519	14431	57088	80558
韶山市	Shaoshan City		6682		985	5697	1021	4676	8577
湘潭县	Xiangtan County		88746		2230	86516	13500	73016	98816
衡阳市	**Hengyang City**	**27592**	**452475**	**18751**	**12009**	**421715**	**70919**	**350796**	**660555**
衡阳市区	Urban District	27592	75929	15534	3657	56738	14287	42451	80596
耒阳市	Leiyang City		62542	969	840	60733	8826	51907	124454
常宁市	Changning City		50043		847	49196	7671	41525	77084
衡阳县	Hengyang County		66103		2270	63833	10598	53235	98450
衡南县	Hengnan County		61518	2248	548	58722	8979	49743	91709
衡山县	Hengshan County		27492		1193	26299	3939	22360	37957
衡东县	Hengdong County		42099		945	41154	5833	35321	63248
祁东县	Qidong County		66749		1709	65040	10786	54254	87057
邵阳市	**Shaoyang City**	**7788**	**514688**	**13120**	**11534**	**490034**	**91896**	**398138**	**681325**
邵阳市区	Urban District	7788	57024	11963	3506	41555	10805	30750	48502
武冈市	Wugang City		46231	1157	971	44103	7060	37043	68938
邵东县	Shaodong County		86465		2100	84365	17375	66990	112353
新邵县	Xinshao County		46220		596	45624	8352	37272	67980
邵阳县	Shaoyang County		47599		713	46886	7070	39866	88348
隆回县	Longhui County		83750		1013	82737	16113	66624	104435
洞口县	Dongkou County		57203		834	56369	12209	44160	74677
绥宁县	Shuining County		27523		394	27129	4705	22424	37257
新宁县	Xinning County		45386		1305	44081	5971	38110	53774
城步县	Chengbu County		17287		102	17185	2286	14899	25061

市县名称	City and County	普通高等学校 Regular Institutions of Higher Education	中等学校 Secondary Schools	普通中等专业学校 Specialized Secondary Schools	职业学校 Vocational Secondary Schools	普通中学 Regular Secondary Schools	高中 Senior Secondary Schools	初中 Junior Secondary Schools	普通小学 Primary Schools
岳阳市	**Yueyang City**	**9257**	**380740**	**12178**	**19694**	**348868**	**62020**	**286848**	**512671**
岳阳市区	Urban District	9257	82181	10816	5889	65476	18725	46751	87310
汨罗市	Miluo City		52789	873	5446	46470	7179	39291	72172
临湘市	Linxiang City		33537	489	1849	31199	5522	25677	48766
岳阳县	Yueyang County		50309		1072	49237	7156	42081	72980
华容县	Huarong County		52120		1883	50237	8087	42150	65080
湘阴县	Xiangyin County		48301		1801	46500	6717	39783	71104
平江县	Pingjiang County		61503		1754	59749	8634	51115	95259
常德市	**Changde City**	**8631**	**384395**	**15286**	**18812**	**350297**	**66119**	**284178**	**466723**
常德市区	Urban District	8631	110900	10979	8512	91409	19090	72319	121904
津市市	Jinshi City		18329	3107	695	14527	2944	11583	20497
安乡县	Anxiang County		38754		455	38299	6855	31444	40515
汉寿县	Hanshou County		50148		1066	49082	7707	41375	74473
澧县	Li County		49233		3809	45424	7514	37910	64722
临澧县	Linli County		25237		458	24779	5679	19100	29700
桃源县	Taoyuan County		53695	1200	2460	50035	9286	40749	65998
石门县	Shimen County		38099		1357	36742	7044	29698	48914
张家界市	**Zhangjiajie City**	**2327**	**92125**	**2660**	**4944**	**84521**	**12579**	**71942**	**140890**
张家界市区	Urban District	2327	31199	2660	2218	26321	3528	22793	44380
慈利县	Cili County		36544		2416	34128	6113	28015	55067
桑植县	Sangzhi County		24382		310	24072	2938	21134	41443
益阳市	**Yiyang City**	**7664**	**328375**	**9212**	**12613**	**306550**	**51837**	**254713**	**397678**
益阳市区	Urban District	7664	97786	9212	2709	85865	17364	68501	110523
沅江市	Yuanjiang City		58735		3272	55463	9237	46226	66816
南县	Nan County		43963		1503	48163	7705	40458	63040
桃江县	Taojiang County		59723		1459	58264	10754	47510	69489
安化县	Anhua County		62465		3670	58795	6777	52018	87810
郴州市	**Chenzhou City**	**7327**	**316504**	**9690**	**6986**	**299828**	**49628**	**250200**	**462811**
郴州市区	Urban District	7327	61437	8677	3916	48844	13505	35339	57434
资兴市	Zixing City		23631	788	291	22552	4344	18208	28876
桂阳县	Guiyang County		43900		480	43420	5546	37874	78540
永兴县	Yongxing County		43082	225	424	42433	6127	36306	62305
宜章县	Yizhang County		39657		422	39235	5147	34088	66557
嘉禾县	Jiahe County		21318		117	21201	2342	18859	41223
临武县	Linwu County		19385		147	19238	2882	16356	33953
汝城县	Rucheng County		23123		368	22755	3520	19235	38740
桂东县	Guidong County		11524		226	11298	1482	9816	18142
安仁县	Anren County		29447		595	28852	4733	24119	37041

单位：人　　18-23 续表 2 continued　　(person)

市县名称	City and County	普通高等学校 Regular Institutions of Higher Education	中等学校 Secondary Schools	普通中等专业学校 Specialized Secondary Schools	职业学校 Vocational Secondary Schools	普通中学 Regular Secondary Schools	高中 Senior Secondary Schools	初中 Junior Secondary Schools	普通小学 Primary Schools
永州市	**Yongzhou City**	**5053**	**382525**	**13818**	**9202**	**359505**	**65892**	**293613**	**559377**
永州市市区	Urban District	5053	93106	9918	2149	81039	18146	62893	84538
东安县	Dongan County		44006		525	43481	8427	35054	50888
道县	Dao County		39326	2929	972	35425	5170	30255	72872
宁远县	Ningyuan County		41160		1115	40045	6469	33576	82953
江永县	Jiangyong County		15246		731	14515	2426	12089	25451
江华县	Jianghua County		23767		829	22938	2756	20182	59608
蓝山县	Lanshan County		21505		567	20938	2899	18039	39563
新田县	Xintian County		26068		402	25666	3520	22146	48007
双牌县	Shuanpai County		11451		371	11080	1868	9212	15470
祁阳县	Qiyang County		66890	971	1541	64378	14211	50167	80027
怀化市	**Huaihua City**	**6334**	**314286**	**11089**	**13148**	**290049**	**38681**	**251368**	**447553**
怀化市区	Urban District	6334	40827	9745	5178	25904	5073	20831	38192
洪江市	Hongjiang City		31759		2354	29405	4381	25024	39998
中方县	Zhongfang County		17352		837	16515	1660	14855	22511
沅陵县	Yuanling County		31857		243	31614	4742	26872	53399
辰溪县	Chenxi County		31432		513	30919	4881	26038	51960
溆浦县	Xupu County		50281		1077	49204	6116	43088	72275
麻阳县	Mayang County		18927		48	18879	2454	16425	37983
新晃县	Xinhuang County		15429		234	15195	1462	13733	20287
芷江县	Zhijiang County		22236	1344	1487	19405	2101	17304	33082
会同县	Huitong County		22298		520	21778	2614	19164	29723
靖州县	Jinzhou County		18704		581	18123	1881	16242	25090
通道县	Tongdao County		13184		76	13108	1316	11792	23053
娄底市	**Loudi City**	**4823**	**313976**	**15756**	**13433**	**284787**	**54598**	**230189**	**414751**
娄底市区	Urban District	4823	47733	12117	5939	29677	7989	21688	37743
冷水江市	Lengshuijiang City		32224	3639	1682	26903	5790	21113	32646
涟源市	Lianyuan City		79905		2976	76929	14024	62905	120570
双峰县	Shangfeng County		69949		1340	68609	14050	54559	84687
新化县	Xinhua County		84165		1496	82669	12745	69924	139105
湘西自治州	**West Hunan A.P**	**7841**	**155039**	**7943**	**7036**	**140060**	**16838**	**123222**	**321107**
吉首市	Jishou City	7841	26017	7298	1868	16851	3197	13654	30715
泸溪县	Louxi County		15123		184	14939	1990	12949	36461
凤凰县	Fenghuang County		19302		1080	18222	1565	16657	45551
花垣县	Huayuan County		13992		300	13692	1367	12325	32169
保靖县	Baojing County		15920		161	15759	1644	14115	32892
古丈县	Guzhang County		6618		0	6618	701	5917	15046
永顺县	Yongshun County		26548	645	2624	23279	3827	19452	59092
龙山县	Longshan County		31519		819	30700	2547	28153	69181

18-24 各市、州、县卫生机构、人员与床位(2001年)

Health Care Institutions, Personnel and Beds (2001)

市县名称	City and County	机构(个) Health Care Institutions (unit)	医院卫生院 Hospital	卫生工作人员(人) Personnel in Health Care Institutions (person)	#卫生技术人员 Medical Technical Personnel	#医生 Doctors	床位(张) Beds (unit)	#医院、卫生院床位 Number of Hospital Beds
长沙市	**Changsha City**	**365**	**265**	**35976**	**25766**	**10841**	**22538**	**18906**
长沙市区	Urban District	174	100	25173	16815	6735	14744	12744
浏阳市	Liuyang City	52	46	3098	2638	1247	2138	2045
长沙县	Changsha County	41	37	1771	1443	733	1293	1273
望城县	Wangcheng County	45	39	1946	1572	689	1492	1120
宁乡县	Ningxiang County	53	43	3988	3298	1437	2871	1724
株洲市	**Zhuzhou City**	**198**	**175**	**14925**	**12402**	**5367**	**9739**	**9645**
株洲市区	Urban District	34	24	6641	5206	2085	4830	4800
醴陵市	Liling City	45	44	2662	2255	1138	1788	1788
株洲县	Zhuzhou County	27	25	1009	907	385	500	485
攸县	You County	40	37	2319	2032	954	1189	1180
茶陵县	Chaling County	31	28	1565	1355	533	997	957
炎陵县	Yanling County	21	17	729	647	272	435	435
湘潭市	**Xiangtan City**	**157**	**117**	**12192**	**9897**	**4079**	**7782**	**7350**
湘潭市区	Urban District	53	44	6554	4961	1903	4463	4100
湘乡市	Xiangxiang City	36	33	2703	2375	1058	1726	1706
韶山市	Shaoshan City	11	8	535	436	190	355	340
湘潭县	Xiangtan County	57	32	2400	2125	928	1238	1204
衡阳市	**Hengyang City**	**404**	**354**	**29696**	**23617**	**10844**	**14611**	**13951**
衡阳市区	Urban District	95	74	11123	7767	3404	6883	6452
耒阳市	Leiyang City	55	49	3407	2895	1305	1785	1657
常宁市	Changning City	72	68	3171	2662	1163	1350	1320
衡阳县	Hengyang County	34	30	3369	2857	1375	797	777
衡南县	Hengnan County	35	30	3041	2623	1482	983	978
衡山县	Hengshan County	33	31	1152	1028	445	625	618
衡东县	Hengdong County	37	32	1907	1597	656	824	785
祁东县	Qidong County	43	40	2526	2188	1014	1364	1364
邵阳市	**Shaoyang City**	**308**	**264**	**19343**	**16074**	**7057**	**11883**	**11067**
邵阳市区	Urban District	48	40	4472	3453	1345	2966	2786
武冈市	Wugang City	27	23	1599	1386	623	963	953
邵东县	Shaodong County	43	40	2345	2018	982	1581	1581
新邵县	Xinshao County	21	18	1644	1381	594	1494	1072
邵阳县	Shaoyang County	34	28	2035	1715	781	965	848
隆回县	Longhui County	33	29	2105	1826	935	1129	1089
洞口县	Dongkou County	29	25	1872	1539	709	831	822
绥宁县	Shuining County	31	27	839	730	396	561	541
新宁县	Xinning County	26	22	1675	1387	405	890	872
城步县	Chengbu County	16	12	757	639	287	503	503

注:本表资料未含医务室、卫生保健所、诊所。

The clinics, health care centres were excluded.

市县名称	City and County	机构(个) Health Care Institutions (unit)	医院卫生院 Hospital	卫生工作人员(人) Personnel in Health Care Institutions (person)	#卫生技术人员 Medical Technical Personnel	#医生 Doctors	床位(张) Beds (unit)	#医院、卫生院床位 Number of Hospital Beds
岳阳市	**Yueyang City**	**304**	**214**	**16536**	**14069**	**6362**	**10195**	**8407**
岳阳市区	Urban District	74	36	5361	4333	2006	3885	3296
汨罗市	Miluo City	43	33	1881	1635	759	1174	939
临湘市	Linxiang City	33	26	1483	1256	585	983	874
岳阳县	Yueyang County	34	25	1686	1527	745	813	705
华容县	Huarong County	35	24	1840	1576	619	1194	914
湘阴县	Xiangyin County	53	41	1818	1543	729	1328	921
平江县	Pingjiang County	32	29	2467	2199	919	818	758
常德市	**Changde City**	**367**	**270**	**19781**	**16610**	**7155**	**12086**	**10856**
常德市区	Urban District	94	61	6420	5178	2085	3877	3434
津市市	Jinshi City	21	16	1117	929	365	773	683
安乡县	Anxiang County	34	26	1703	1463	598	1212	1080
汉寿县	Hanshou County	60	37	2235	1879	825	1561	1261
澧县	Li County	50	39	2449	2123	949	1445	1280
临澧县	Linli County	25	20	1397	1223	467	713	658
桃源县	Taoyuan County	49	45	2450	2111	1045	1456	1426
石门县	Shimen County	34	26	2010	1704	821	1049	1034
张家界市	**Zhangjiajie City**	**134**	**112**	**5288**	**4506**	**2108**	**3439**	**3249**
张家界市区	Urban District	47	36	2094	1735	875	1475	1425
慈利县	Cili County	41	36	2008	1746	744	1196	1086
桑植县	Sangzhi County	46	40	1186	1025	485	768	738
益阳市	**Yiyang City**	**227**	**180**	**16017**	**13692**	**6257**	**8722**	**7525**
益阳市区	Urban District	65	48	5311	4339	1996	3085	2522
沅江市	Yuanjiang City	54	40	2897	2519	1129	1600	1195
南县	Nan County	40	31	2487	2126	899	1443	1279
桃江县	Taojiang County	34	31	2764	2471	1208	1238	1223
安化县	Anhua County	34	30	2558	2237	1025	1356	1306
郴州市	**Chenzhou City**	**340**	**293**	**16532**	**13584**	**6120**	**10323**	**9879**
郴州市区	Urban District	57	44	4984	3823	1796	3280	3014
资兴市	Zixing City	45	40	1830	1560	707	981	971
桂阳县	Guiyang County	47	44	1906	1551	738	1239	1207
永兴县	Yongxing County	32	28	1812	1542	628	998	986
宜章县	Yizhang County	33	30	1608	1375	509	1147	1095
嘉禾县	Jiahe County	22	19	978	840	337	508	496
临武县	Linwu County	25	20	778	641	290	555	545
汝城县	Rucheng County	28	24	957	829	438	627	597
桂东县	Guidong County	23	20	452	389	195	325	315
安仁县	Anren County	28	24	1227	1034	482	663	653

市县名称	City and County	机构(个) Health Care Institutions (unit)	医院卫生院 Hospital	卫生工作人员(人) Personnel in Health Care Institutions (person)	#卫生技术人员 Medical Technical Personnel	#医生 Doctors	床位(张) Beds (unit)	#医院、卫生院床位 Number of Hospital Beds
永州市	**Yongzhou City**	**362**	**299**	**16755**	**14427**	**7361**	**9003**	**8354**
永州市市区	Urban District	57	45	5137	4227	2160	3052	2689
东安县	Dongan County	40	38	1553	1362	828	566	532
道县	Dao County	30	25	1406	1252	526	830	750
宁远县	Ningyuan County	52	49	1661	1452	660	826	826
江永县	Jiangyong County	18	16	571	503	233	435	401
江华县	Jianghua County	32	28	1222	1043	470	865	817
蓝山县	Lanshan County	30	28	849	735	339	466	436
新田县	Xintian County	26	23	857	785	345	558	538
双牌县	Shuanpai County	17	14	500	424	213	312	312
祁阳县	Qiyang County	60	33	2999	2644	1587	1093	1053
怀化市	**Huaihua City**	**466**	**405**	**16849**	**14201**	**6633**	**11650**	**11322**
怀化市区	Urban District	54	42	4799	3804	1617	2889	2824
中方县	Hongjiang City	25	23	441	414	199	315	307
洪江市	Zhongfang County	36	31	1500	1297	570	1021	981
沅陵县	Yuanling County	74	62	1783	1522	793	1469	1419
辰溪县	Chenxi County	42	38	1569	1378	717	1163	1143
溆浦县	Xupu County	62	57	1926	1640	786	1429	1401
麻阳县	Mayang County	33	28	925	793	332	628	596
新晃县	Xinhuang County	27	24	745	619	262	635	615
芷江县	Zhijiang County	35	31	1086	932	469	599	599
会同县	Huitong County	32	29	748	660	349	626	611
靖州县	Jinzhou County	20	17	719	622	299	474	444
通道县	Tongdao County	26	23	608	520	240	402	382
娄底市	**Loudi City**	**171**	**144**	**14833**	**12623**	**5708**	**8131**	**7882**
娄底市区	Urban District	35	26	3532	2642	1093	2021	1971
冷水江市	Lengshuijiang City	33	28	2248	1894	779	1507	1457
涟源市	Lianyuan City	35	30	3590	3213	1478	2228	2112
双峰县	Shangfeng County	26	23	2357	2203	1137	1133	1113
新化县	Xinhua County	42	37	3106	2671	1221	1242	1229
湘西自治州	**West Hunan A.P**	**402**	**243**	**8983**	**7503**	**3604**	**6063**	**5866**
吉首市	Jishou City	34	21	2299	1748	764	1454	1390
泸溪县	Louxi County	25	21	766	658	308	486	480
凤凰县	Fenghuang County	72	34	945	808	438	636	616
花垣县	Huayuan County	33	22	783	661	342	578	548
保靖县	Baojing County	56	27	869	755	305	607	593
古丈县	Guzhang County	20	16	402	343	170	317	312
永顺县	Yongshun County	97	49	1394	1217	626	1072	1038
龙山县	Longshan County	65	53	1525	1313	651	913	889

18-25 各市、州、县农民平均每人纯收入(2001年)

Annual Per Capita Net Income of Rural Residents (2001)

市县名称	City and County	调查户数(户) Number of Households Surveyed (household)	调查户常住人口(人) Number of Residents Surveyed (person)	平均每人全年纯收入(元) Per Capita Annual Net Income (yuan)	工资性收入 Laborers' Remuneration	家庭经营收入 Income from Household Business	转移性收入 Transfer Income	财产性收入 Property Income
长沙市	**Changsha City**	**560**	**2255**	**3218.07**	**1273.12**	**1501.27**	**401.18**	**42.50**
芙蓉区	Furong District	30	117	4854.98	985.15	3183.35	300.11	386.37
天心区	Tianxin District	30	121	4577.21	1563.78	2174.62	491.56	347.25
岳麓区	Yuelu District	30	109	4635.31	1588.76	2493.53	413.06	139.96
开福区	Kaifu District	30	122	4388.17	1181.48	2836.47	285.67	84.55
雨花区	Yuhua District	30	130	4539.30	986.99	2668.43	367.65	516.23
长沙县	Changsha County	100	414	3485.19	1078.51	1908.70	476.69	21.29
望城县	Wangcheng County	100	385	3147.93	993.45	1751.97	389.01	13.50
宁乡县	Ningxiang County	100	393	2784.55	866.71	1504.51	377.66	35.67
浏阳市	Liuyang City	110	464	3320.10	1946.25	941.13	396.67	36.05
株洲市	**Zhuzhou City**	**670**	**2730**	**2795.68**	**1001.78**	**1436.36**	**291.44**	**66.10**
荷塘区	Hetang District	30	121	3505.71	1347.68	1529.34	230.73	397.96
芦淞区	Lousong District	30	109	3516.96	1915.12	1095.42	377.10	129.32
石峰区	Shifeng District	40	161	3488.71	1582.78	1302.86	438.24	164.83
天元区	Tianyuan District	40	169	3211.70	330.25	2458.40	221.92	201.13
株洲县	Zhuzhou County	100	403	2753.03	730.21	1861.19	150.27	11.36
攸县	You County	110	428	2976.82	1335.31	1384.76	243.54	13.21
茶陵县	Chaling County	100	417	1816.95	502.69	1017.00	276.40	20.86
炎陵县	Yanling County	100	418	1705.40	517.20	1098.65	83.26	6.29
醴陵市	Liling City	120	502	3091.47	1329.95	1289.62	427.28	44.62
湘潭市	**Xiangtan City**	**310**	**1189**	**2825.36**	**944.21**	**1610.67**	**238.30**	**32.18**
雨湖区	Yuhu District	30	108	4037.33	1123.31	2261.09	299.20	353.73
岳塘区	Yuetang District	40	163	3730.84	1337.91	2017.27	276.60	99.06
湘潭县	Xiangtan County	100	395	2785.92	915.41	1646.33	210.07	14.11
湘乡市	Xiangxiang City	110	424	2665.24	950.96	1436.25	252.63	25.40
韶山市	Shaoshan City	30	99	3179.32	729.91	2005.96	377.31	66.14
衡阳市	**Hengyang City**	**800**	**3175**	**2743.20**	**1098.98**	**1448.35**	**157.08**	**38.79**
衡阳市郊区	Jiaoqu District	60	251	3408.87	1397.94	1857.97	146.59	6.37
南岳区	Nanyue District	50	185	3024.19	809.79	1944.48	235.78	34.14
衡阳县	Hengyang County	100	347	2702.76	808.32	1623.18	173.12	98.14
衡南县	Hengnan County	100	390	2719.21	1063.14	1491.52	124.64	39.91
衡山县	Hengshan County	80	340	2804.52	1000.44	1575.08	220.53	8.47
衡东县	Hengdong County	100	395	2783.29	912.22	1774.98	95.44	0.65
祁东县	Qidong County	100	399	2685.81	1242.36	1122.52	270.90	50.03
耒阳市	Leiyang City	100	433	2713.18	1284.59	1272.14	129.37	27.08
常宁市	Changning City	110	435	2720.84	1297.54	1313.54	101.80	7.96
邵阳市	**Shaoyang City**	**1140**	**4541**	**1862.72**	**738.39**	**917.46**	**186.53**	**20.34**
双清区	Shuangqing District	60	203	2899.83	1309.13	1360.07	221.25	9.38
大祥区	Daxiang District	60	235	2713.01	575.03	1769.56	274.56	93.86
北塔区	Beita District	40	151	2563.2	741.58	1587.66	224.2	9.76

18 - 25 续表 1 continued

市县名称	City and County	调查户数(户) Number of Households Surveyed (household)	调查户常住人口(人) Number of Residents Surveyed (person)	平均每人全年纯收入(元) Per Capita Annual Net Income (yuan)	工资性收入 Laborers' Remuneration	家庭经营收入 Income from Household Business	转移性收入 Transfer Income	财产性收入 Property Income
邵东县	Shaodong County	100	402	2960.88	1299.87	1247.64	353.19	60.18
新邵县	Xinshao County	120	513	1448.46	860.80	400.95	165.52	21.19
邵阳县	Shaoyang County	120	467	1072.58	450.33	551.46	69.97	0.82
隆回县	Longhui County	100	396	1129.06	522.20	562.79	37.98	6.09
洞口县	Dongkou County	90	335	2188.52	822.36	1181.05	176.64	8.47
绥宁县	Suining County	80	344	2305.74	823.67	1175.66	275.76	30.65
新宁县	Xinning County	120	513	1064.99	348.45	600.90	110.21	5.43
城步县	Chengbu County	100	444	1141.99	271.08	800.20	69.75	0.96
武冈市	Wugang City	170	654	1954.66	538.55	1138.64	275.81	1.66
岳阳市	**Yueyang City**	**760**	**2867**	**2506.93**	**766.97**	**1377.17**	**323.56**	**39.23**
岳阳楼区	Yueyanglou District	30	113	3850.96	1795.09	1370.03	551.77	134.07
云溪区	YungXi District	50	198	3316.21	956.23	2119.04	195.40	45.54
君山区	JungShang District	80	318	2634.08	472.00	1903.21	245.10	13.77
岳阳县	Yueyang County	100	390	2575.26	446.34	1800.19	297.76	30.97
华容县	Huarong County	100	394	2532.50	600.12	1482.66	437.37	12.35
湘阴县	Xiangyin County	100	410	2505.60	1135.93	1031.55	294.48	43.64
平江县	Pingjiang County	100	416	1297.15	454.90	770.36	70.60	1.29
汨罗市	Miluo City	100	374	2834.76	584.92	1724.08	465.36	60.40
临湘市	Linxiang City	100	407	2569.65	746.37	1427.37	278.16	117.75
常德市	**Changde City**	**870**	**3052**	**2211.08**	**745.40**	**1148.66**	**285.57**	**31.45**
武陵区	Wuling District	70	272	3239.68	889.64	1812.89	282.64	254.51
鼎城区	Dingcheng District	100	337	2248.55	742.57	1213.28	205.40	87.30
安乡县	Anxiang County	100	352	2125.06	602.81	1247.46	238.74	36.05
汉寿县	Hanshou County	100	381	2092.88	869.64	933.28	283.62	6.34
澧县	Li County	110	380	2196.08	837.98	1023.85	332.31	1.94
临澧县	Linli County	100	327	2356.59	607.43	1403.73	311.96	33.47
桃源县	Taoyuan County	100	363	2402.82	883.77	1152.19	362.61	4.25
石门县	Shimen County	110	369	1739.62	518.93	963.21	250.96	6.52
津市市	Jinshi City	80	271	2075.41	445.89	1418.33	210.25	0.94
张家界市	**Zhangjiajie City**	**340**	**1273**	**1770.70**	**534.46**	**966.12**	**257.21**	**12.91**
永定区	Yongding District	100	391	1586.95	650.34	751.18	179.30	6.13
武陵源区	Wulingyuan District	30	120	1758.23	503.28	857.96	284.91	12.08
慈利县	Cili County	100	359	1636.35	722.09	810.22	94.20	9.84
桑植县	Sangzhi County	100	396	1198.48	92.40	817.95	287.63	0.50
益阳市	**Yiyang City**	**600**	**2350**	**2106.67**	**787.31**	**1005.79**	**297.60**	**15.97**
资阳区	Ziyang District	100	414	2186.07	671.62	1216.68	289.17	8.60
赫山区	Heshan District	100	365	2344.77	869.79	1141.80	298.18	35.00
南县	Nan County	100	394	2075.32	755.80	974.88	331.82	12.82
桃江县	Taojiang County	100	378	2260.50	1108.72	654.56	487.41	9.81
安化县	Anhua County	100	416	1344.98	516.45	735.19	87.18	6.16
沅江市	Yuanjiang City	100	383	2384.95	599.33	1446.42	309.90	29.30
郴州市	**Chenzhou City**	**950**	**3926**	**2531.03**	**752.58**	**1597.67**	**135.37**	**45.41**
北湖区	Beihu District	80	332	3084.91	651.61	2069.83	197.76	165.71
苏仙区	Suxian District	60	233	3035.01	850.26	1910.68	259.70	14.37
桂阳县	Guiyang County	90	348	2742.99	632.51	1909.15	172.43	28.90
宜章县	Yizhang County	100	449	1991.41	416.36	1450.64	56.11	68.30
永兴县	Yongxing County	100	423	2787.15	1059.03	1626.00	81.90	20.22

市县名称	City and County	调查户数(户) Number of Households Surveyed (household)	调查户常住人口(人) Number of Residents Surveyed (person)	平均每人全年纯收入(元) Per Capita Annual Net Income (yuan)	工资性收入 Laborers' Remuneration	家庭经营收入 Income from Household Business	转移性收入 Transfer Income	财产性收入 Property Income
嘉禾县	Jiahe County	80	325	2820.57	1188.24	1550.88	62.67	18.78
临武县	Linwu County	100	396	2686.74	846.44	1532.60	189.68	118.02
汝城县	Rucheng County	80	367	1445.64	396.72	943.64	85.44	19.82
桂东县	Guidong County	70	297	1282.29	314.13	928.85	25.72	13.59
安仁县	Anreng County	90	371	1853.32	778.75	965.48	104.37	4.72
资兴市	Zixing City	100	385	3088.35	916.79	1963.82	187.96	19.78
永州市	**Yongzhou City**	**1030**	**4326**	**1966.94**	**616.22**	**1249.75**	**76.19**	**24.78**
芝山区	Zhishan District	100	412	2311.71	642.03	1538.67	41.09	89.92
冷水滩区	Lengshuitan District	110	394	2340.21	656.69	1526.92	49.98	106.62
祁阳县	Qiyang County	100	422	2305.69	760.57	1382.20	132.33	30.59
东安县	Dongan County	100	383	2242.59	530.45	1643.48	61.79	6.87
双牌县	Shuangpai County	80	339	1676.22	423.29	1145.04	97.25	10.64
道县	Dao County	100	446	2358.35	750.48	1566.08	35.15	6.64
江永县	Jiangyong County	80	342	2337.98	603.75	1678.45	46.58	9.20
宁远县	Ningyuan County	120	507	1308.69	599.77	634.92	69.17	4.83
蓝山县	Lanshan County	70	328	2042.81	632.35	1262.73	143.59	4.14
新田县	Xintian County	80	332	1290.16	319.43	873.51	97.22	
江华县	Jianghua County	90	421	1253.07	520.61	625.86	98.90	7.70
怀化市	**Huaihua City**	**1000**	**4041**	**1884.02**	**478.83**	**1239.40**	**149.35**	**16.44**
鹤城区	Hecheng District	30	120	2408.02	453.01	1580.00	332.83	42.18
中方县	Zhongfang County	60	216	1810.35	265.06	1156.64	236.39	152.26
沅陵县	Yuanling County	100	450	1359.42	358.45	878.90	113.86	8.21
辰溪县	Chenxi County	90	380	1731.26	373.24	1225.49	131.90	0.63
溆浦县	Xupu County	100	371	2361.37	615.94	1532.35	207.68	5.40
会同县	Huitong County	100	371	1951.78	941.88	915.32	92.81	1.77
麻阳县	Mayang County	90	413	1338.98	351.88	968.49	17.07	1.54
新晃县	Xinhuang County	100	452	1290.87	229.71	972.64	77.10	11.42
芷江县	Zhijiang County	100	367	1672.56	476.25	1035.67	139.13	21.51
靖州县	Jinzhou County	70	282	2191.35	367.89	1723.73	98.81	0.92
通道县	Tongdao County	70	313	1272.40	474.67	672.95	123.32	1.46
洪江市	Hongjiang City	80	278	2321.76	526.35	1681.79	101.95	11.67
娄底市	**Loudi City**	**480**	**1891**	**1979.05**	**888.25**	**869.93**	**216.34**	**4.53**
娄星区	Louxing District	100	366	2802.82	974.46	1580.63	238.73	9.00
双峰县	Shuangfeng County	100	382	2367.03	967.10	1064.25	331.68	4.00
新化县	Xinhua County	100	427	1223.59	491.78	659.64	71.49	0.68
冷水江市	Lenshuijiang City	80	315	2344.48	1054.31	933.40	329.18	27.59
涟源市	Lianyuan City	120	515	1638.91	935.98	552.39	147.78	2.76
湘西自治州	**West Hunan A.P**	**690**	**3131**	**1292.90**	**264.38**	**927.37**	**91.94**	**9.22**
吉首市	Jishou City	70	312	1867.43	359.97	1316.46	182.14	8.86
泸溪县	Louxi County	80	379	1129.10	199.94	820.42	80.19	28.55
凤凰县	Fenghuang County	100	504	1254.12	251.70	971.36	29.82	1.24
花垣县	Huayuan County	70	324	1150.33	244.57	821.60	82.93	1.23
保靖县	Baojin County	100	444	1117.39	205.83	887.57	22.09	1.90
古丈县	Guzhang County	70	294	1120.57	147.15	826.48	135.44	11.50
永顺县	Yongshun County	100	420	1203.94	162.09	985.41	37.73	18.71
龙山县	Longshan County	100	455	1298.38	365.62	774.95	153.70	4.11

18-26 农村小康县(市、区)综合评价情况(2001年)

Basic Indicators of Counties(Cities. Districts) of Being Fairly Well of Rural (2001)

市县	City and County	综合分值 Evaluate Results	收入分配 Income		物资生活 Physical Life				精神生活 Spiritual Life	
			人均纯收入(元) Per Capita Net Income (yuan)	基尼系数 Geni Index	恩格尔系数 Engel Index	每日人均蛋白质摄入量(克) Per Day Per Capita Amount of Protein Englobe (g)	人均衣着消费支出(元) Per Capita Expenditure for Clothing (yuan)	钢木结构住房比重(%) Rate of Reinforced Concrete and Brick &Wood Structure (%)	电视机普及率(台/百户) Popularity Rate of TV Set (unit/100 households)	服务消费支出比重(%) Proportion of Service Expenditure (%)
芙蓉区	Furong District	100.00	4854.98	0.30	44.00	95.00	173.98	100.00	130.00	13.00
天心区	Tianxin District	99.00	4577.21	0.26	45.00	90.00	177.70	98.00	123.00	10.00
岳麓区	Yuelu District	99.00	4635.31	0.26	41.00	101.00	226.01	94.00	110.00	10.00
开福区	Kaifu District	99.00	4388.17	0.28	47.00	90.00	147.19	97.00	123.00	12.00
雨花区	Yuhua District	98.00	4539.30	0.22	39.00	99.00	142.01	96.00	103.00	10.00
长沙县	Changsha County	96.80	3485.19	0.24	48.00	105.00	85.17	96.00	127.00	13.00
望城县	Wangcheng County	96.60	3147.93	0.21	49.00	98.00	147.56	100.00	112.00	10.00
宁乡县	Ningxiang County	96.70	2784.55	0.20	43.00	90.00	96.50	99.00	114.00	14.00
浏阳市	Liuyang City	99.70	3320.10	0.30	46.00	85.00	133.81	97.00	128.00	10.00
荷塘区	Hetang District	98.50	3505.71	0.27	37.00	95.00	133.71	93.50	120.00	28.90
芦淞区	Lousong District	97.40	3516.96	0.26	42.80	91.00	169.92	95.00	110.00	12.80
石峰区	Shifeng District	98.00	3488.71	0.27	44.30	94.00	168.82	94.00	110.00	13.40
天元区	Tianyuan District	97.60	3211.70	0.27	37.00	95.00	82.17	93.00	110.00	11.80
株洲县	Zhuzhou County	95.47	2573.03	0.22	51.00	92.00	91.73	95.10	100.00	28.80
攸县	You County	99.57	2976.82	0.28	47.90	84.50	150.49	99.40	115.00	30.70
醴陵市	Liling City	93.60	3091.47	0.29	53.30	79.01	133.81	88.20	104.00	15.10
雨湖区	Yuhu District	100.00	4037.33	0.30	40.00	80.19	112.07	100.00	100.00	23.86
岳塘区	Yuetang District	99.49	3730.84	0.38	49.00	86.17	111.98	91.62	100.00	21.34
湘潭县	Xiangtan County	95.09	2785.92	0.29	55.00	89.35	103.00	100.00	99.02	24.05
湘乡市	Xiangxiang City	96.08	2665.24	0.27	51.00	76.41	91.00	94.15	99.19	24.19
韶山市	Shaoshan City	98.72	3179.32	0.36	47.00	84.98	107.00	91.19	100.00	21.78
蒸湘区	Jiaoqu District	98.85	3408.87	0.23	41.90	76.00	172.85	94.00	100.00	12.60
珠晖区	Zhuhui District	98.85	3408.87	0.23	41.90	76.00	172.85	94.00	100.00	12.60
雁峰区	Yanfeng District	98.85	3408.87	0.23	41.90	76.00	172.85	94.00	100.00	12.60
石鼓区	Shigu District	98.85	3408.87	0.23	41.90	76.00	172.85	94.00	100.00	12.60
南岳区	Nanyue District	91.47	3024.19	0.23	44.18	80.00	75.62	92.00	96.00	17.00
衡阳县	Hengyang County	94.82	2702.76	0.27	49.20	63.70	130.01	100.00	119.00	11.70
衡南县	Hengnan County	93.23	2719.21	0.24	62.25	72.00	130.41	100.00	100.00	10.20
衡山县	Hengshan County	96.57	2804.52	0.28	43.12	83.14	99.74	89.90	99.00	13.70
衡东县	Hengdong County	95.00	2783.29	0.26	53.68	88.41	69.97	99.00	100.00	15.87
祁东县	Qidong County	94.03	2685.81	0.27	51.00	72.00	85.06	80.00	67.00	13.00
耒阳市	Leiyang City	96.79	2713.18	0.26	60.49	62.40	86.00	100.00	100.00	14.40
常宁市	Changning City	91.50	2720.84	0.27	53.61	78.52	80.22	90.27	100.00	8.00

18-26 续表 1 continued

市县	City and County	综合分值 Evaluate Results	收入分配 Income 人均纯收入（元）Per Capita Net Income (yuan)	基尼系数 Geni Index	物资生活 Physical Life 恩格尔系数 Engel Index	每日人均蛋白质摄入量（克）Per Day Per Capita Amount of Protein Englobe (g)	人均衣着消费支出（元）Per Capita Expenditure for Clothing (yuan)	钢木结构住房比重（%）Rate of Reinforced Concrete and Brick &Wood Structure (%)	精神生活 Spiritual Life 电视机普及率（台/百户）Popularity Rate of TV Set (unit/100 households)	服务消费支出比重（%）Proportion of Service Expenditure (%)
双清区	Shuangqing District	96.28	2899.83	0.27	49.00	71.00	153.83	97.00	106.00	58.00
大祥区	Daxiang District	92.79	2713.00	0.23	56.00	73.00	97.53	99.00	95.00	6.04
北塔区	Beita District	90.66	2563.00	0.16	55.60	78.00	107.38	97.30	100.00	10.00
邵东县	Shaodong County	93.23	2960.88	0.31	51.00	88.10	101.73	85.00	79.80	4.50
岳阳楼区	Yueyanglou District	95.83	3850.96	0.24	33.70	121.00	195.00	99.90	101.00	8.30
云溪区	Yunxi District	97.77	3316.21	0.26	35.50	75.00	135.38	99.00	100.00	13.90
君山区	Junshan District	94.56	2634.08	0.27	49.40	120.00	157.32	98.00	106.00	13.10
岳阳县	Yueyang County	90.11	2575.26	0.25	48.90	107.30	158.73	89.40	95.00	14.36
华容县	Huarong County	91.33	2532.50	0.23	47.30	73.00	122.34	82.00	101.00	13.00
湘阴县	Xiangyin County	90.36	2505.60	0.25	51.00	79.00	81.97	83.00	108.00	11.00
汨罗市	Miluo City	97.86	2834.76	0.30	45.50	82.50	96.26	90.00	95.00	29.70
临湘市	Linxiang City	93.36	2569.65	0.20	49.70	79.00	95.43	89.00	109.00	13.60
武陵区	Wuling District	99.20	3239.68	0.26	46.00	78.00	162.80	98.00	136.00	30.00
临澧县	Linli County	90.13	2356.59	0.30	52.00	79.00	86.50	100.00	100.00	13.00
桃源县	Taoyuan County	90.39	2402.82	0.27	53.00	77.00	79.00	80.00	106.00	10.00
赫山区	Heshan District	91.10	2344.77	0.29	49.60	78.10	114.00	99.20	106.00	17.20
桃江县	Taojiang County	90.40	2260.50	0.24	50.90	82.00	101.00	94.30	90.00	17.90
沅江市	Yuanjiang City	93.50	2385.00	0.31	50.10	64.00	229.00	99.50	100.00	14.30
北湖区	Beihu District	93.60	3084.91	0.29	52.80	72.03	113.23	91.90	106.00	29.70
苏仙区	Suxian District	94.67	3035.00	0.19	48.30	74.00	154.63	99.60	132.00	23.10
桂阳县	Guiyang County	93.45	2743.00	0.26	51.30	82.20	77.63	99.40	103.00	29.90
永兴县	Yongxing County	95.72	2787.00	0.25	44.20	73.90	137.45	100.00	108.00	34.60
嘉禾县	Jiahe County	93.97	2821.00	0.15	48.40	71.80	169.95	97.10	110.00	24.30
临武县	Linwu County	94.52	2687.00	0.30	51.80	78.00	85.91	99.50	112.00	28.10
资兴市	Zixing City	94.56	3088.00	0.28	48.30	77.50	85.28	98.00	106.00	26.50
芝山区	Zhishan District	90.25	2311.71	0.27	52.10	70.00	107.06	98.87	99.00	15.70
冷水滩区	Lengshuitan District	90.37	2340.21	0.29	51.40	75.00	143.29	94.50	97.30	13.29
祁阳县	Qiyang County	90.06	2305.69	0.27	54.19	105.40	99.90	98.23	113.00	19.67
道县	Dao County	90.06	2358.35	0.21	52.97	86.00	117.99	100.00	114.00	20.00
娄星区	Louxing District	96.30	2802.82	0.23	56.00	79.40	95.00	100.00	110.00	11.30
双峰县	Shuangfeng County	90.72	2367.03	0.27	54.56	71.00	123.47	76.94	92.00	13.03
冷水江市	Lenshuijiang City	90.00	2344.48	0.30	53.00	89.00	95.22	98.00	97.00	18.00

continued

市县	City and County	劳动力平均寿教育年限（年） Labor Force Education Level (year)	农村人口平均预期寿命（岁） Average Rural Popular Anticipate Life (year-old)	安全卫生水普及率（%） Popularity Rate of Safe and Hygienic Drinking Water (%)	用电户比重（%） Proportion of Household Using Electric Power (%)	已通公路的行政村比重（%） Proportion of Villages Having Highway (%)	已通电话的行政村比重（%） Proportion of Villages Having Telephone (%)	五保户生活有保障比重（%） Proportion of Five-guaranteed Indemnitee (%)	万人刑事案件立案件数（件） Registered Criminal Case Per 10 000 Persons (case)
		人口素质 Population Anlage		生活环境 Living Environment				社会保障与安全 Social Security	
芙蓉区	Furong District	9.90	71.60	100.00	100.00	100.00	100.00	100.00	3.20
天心区	Tianxin District	9.92	71.30	100.00	100.00	100.00	100.00	100.00	3.20
岳麓区	Yuelu District	9.99	71.20	100.00	100.00	100.00	100.00	100.00	3.80
开福区	Kaifu District	9.13	71.30	100.00	100.00	100.00	100.00	100.00	2.50
雨花区	Yuhua District	9.48	71.80	100.00	100.00	100.00	100.00	100.00	4.60
长沙县	Changsha County	8.94	71.65	98.20	100.00	100.00	100.00	100.00	4.80
望城县	Wangcheng County	8.74	71.50	99.50	100.00	100.00	100.00	100.00	6.00
宁乡县	Ningxiang County	8.89	71.30	100.00	100.00	100.00	100.00	100.00	6.00
浏阳市	Liuyang City	8.78	72.00	99.10	100.00	100.00	100.00	100.00	4.00
荷塘区	Hetang District	8.38	73.14	95.00	100.00	100.00	100.00	100.00	15.50
芦淞区	Lousong District	8.40	73.20	91.00	100.00	100.00	100.00	91.00	16.90
石峰区	Shifeng District	8.40	73.40	95.00	100.00	100.00	100.00	98.00	18.50
天元区	Tianyuan District	8.30	73.10	95.00	100.00	100.00	100.00	93.00	15.50
株洲县	Zhuzhou County	8.58	73.04	99.00	100.00	97.90	98.00	100.00	14.50
攸县	You County	7.92	69.80	98.20	100.00	100.00	100.00	91.40	18.80
醴陵市	Liling City	8.50	70.06	95.80	100.00	100.00	98.00	77.30	16.00
雨湖区	Yuhu District	9.12	71.30	99.80	100.00	100.00	100.00	100.00	4.20
岳塘区	Yuetang District	8.69	73.40	99.69	100.00	100.00	100.00	99.20	7.70
湘潭县	Xiangtan County	8.70	72.40	99.10	100.00	100.00	98.02	98.57	7.90
湘乡市	Xiangxiang City	8.69	74.15	99.15	100.00	100.00	100.00	95.30	8.13
韶山市	Shaoshan City	9.10	72.35	99.39	100.00	100.00	100.00	100.00	5.30
蒸湘区	Jiaoqu District	8.80	71.00	100.00	100.00	100.00	100.00	100.00	3.00
珠晖区	Zhuhui District	8.80	71.00	100.00	100.00	100.00	100.00	100.00	3.00
雁峰区	Yanfeng District	8.80	71.00	100.00	100.00	100.00	100.00	100.00	3.00
石鼓区	Shigu District	8.80	71.00	100.00	100.00	100.00	100.00	100.00	3.00
南岳区	Nanyue District	8.00	72.50	100.00	100.00	100.00	100.00	100.00	4.00
衡阳县	Hengyang County	7.81	71.30	95.00	96.00	90.00	92.00	100.00	4.00
衡南县	Hengnan County	8.00	70.14	100.00	100.00	100.00	100.00	100.00	6.00
衡山县	Hengshan County	8.70	69.20	98.00	99.00	99.00	94.00	100.00	1.00
衡东县	Hengdong County	8.16	70.10	100.00	100.00	100.00	100.00	100.00	7.64
祁东县	Qidong County	7.70	71.00	85.00	97.00	90.00	90.00	95.00	11.00
耒阳市	Leiyang City	8.00	70.00	100.00	100.00	100.00	100.00	90.00	7.00
常宁市	Changning City	7.00	69.00	100.00	100.00	98.00	78.00	93.20	6.00

continued

市县	City and County	人口素质 Population Anlage		生活环境 Living Environment				社会保障与安全 Social Security	
		劳动力平均寿教育年限（年）Labor Force Education Level (year)	农村人口平均预期寿命（岁）Average Rural Popular Anticipate Life (year-old)	安全卫生水普及率（%）Popularity Rate of Safe and Hygienic Drinking Water (%)	用电户比重（%）Proportion of Household Using Electric Power (%)	已通公路的行政村比重（%）Proportion of Villages Having Highway (%)	已通电话的行政村比重（%）Proportion of Villages Having Telephone (%)	五保户生活有保障比重（%）Proportion of Five-guaranteed Indemnitee (%)	万人刑事案件立案件数（件）Registered Criminal Case Per 10 000 Persons (case)
双清区	Shuangqing District	8.83	71.00	80.00	100.00	100.00	100.00	100.00	13.00
大祥区	Daxiang District	11.00	73.00	98.00	100.00	100.00	92.00	100.00	6.00
北塔区	Beita District	11.94	71.00	52.50	100.00	100.00	98.00	90.00	17.50
邵东县	Shaodong County	8.60	71.00	62.00	100.00	98.99	90.00	100.00	4.00
岳阳楼区	Yueyanglou District	8.90	71.00	100.00	100.00	100.00	100.00	100.00	5.00
云溪区	Yunxi District	8.80	71.80	99.80	100.00	100.00	100.00	100.00	3.80
君山区	Junshan District	8.60	71.00	100.00	100.00	100.00	100.00	100.00	55.00
岳阳县	Yueyang County	8.55	71.00	100.00	100.00	100.00	98.10	76.40	20.00
华容县	Huarong County	8.00	68.00	100.00	100.00	100.00	100.00	100.00	9.00
湘阴县	Xiangyin County	7.60	69.00	95.00	100.00	99.10	100.00	88.80	11.60
汨罗市	Miluo City	7.80	71.00	98.90	100.00	100.00	98.50	100.00	10.30
临湘市	Linxiang City	8.30	72.50	98.00	100.00	100.00	100.00	100.00	15.30
武陵区	Wuling District	9.30	70.80	100.00	100.00	100.00	100.00	100.00	5.00
临澧县	Linli County	7.80	70.00	55.00	100.00	100.00	100.00	100.00	13.00
桃源县	Taoyuan County	8.00	70.00	92.00	100.00	100.00	95.00	100.00	6.00
赫山区	Heshan District	8.84	59.90	88.00	100.00	100.00	100.00	100.00	32.50
桃江县	Taojiang County	8.46	72.00	98.10	87.80	97.00	99.50	100.00	13.00
沅江市	Yuanjiang City	8.00	71.00	80.00	100.00	100.00	100.00	100.00	1.00
北湖区	Beihu District	8.50	71.50	100.00	100.00	100.00	100.00	100.00	6.30
苏仙区	Suxian District	8.50	71.10	100.00	100.00	100.00	100.00	100.00	14.30
桂阳县	Guiyang County	8.10	70.10	100.00	100.00	100.00	100.00	99.20	7.00
永兴县	Yongxing County	8.40	69.90	99.80	100.00	99.20	100.00	100.00	4.00
嘉禾县	Jiahe County	8.70	70.10	100.00	100.00	100.00	100.00	100.00	11.00
临武县	Linwu County	8.70	71.00	100.00	100.00	100.00	100.00	100.00	3.70
资兴市	Zixing City	8.70	70.80	99.00	100.00	90.00	90.00	85.00	10.90
芝山区	Zhishan District	8.40	71.82	95.00	100.00	98.00	96.00	100.00	6.90
冷水滩区	Lengshuitan District	8.00	69.20	95.00	100.00	97.00	100.00	100.00	3.50
祁阳县	Qiyang County	8.00	70.00	96.00	92.00	93.00	97.00	100.00	12.00
道县	Dao County	7.85	70.00	98.50	96.70	94.80	81.30	93.40	11.00
娄星区	Louxing District	8.74	73.00	100.00	100.00	100.00	100.00	100.00	7.40
双峰县	Shuangfeng County	8.51	71.00	92.15	99.50	99.77	93.63	100.00	11.86
冷水江市	Lenshuijiang City	8.00	69.00	100.00	100.00	100.00	100.00	100.00	2.50

十九、各省、市、自治区
主要经济社会统计指标

MAIN ECONOMIC AND SOCIAL STATISTICS INDICATORS BY PROVINCES, MUNICIPALITIES AND AUTONOMOUS REGIONS

资料整理人员：　李生春

19-1 各省(市、区)国内生产总值(2001年)

Gross Domestic Product (2001)

地区	Region	国内生产总值 (亿元) Gross Domestic Product (100 million yuan)	第一产业 Primary Industry	第二产业 Secondry Industry		
					工业 Industry	建筑业 Construction
全国	**Total National**	**95933.3**	**14609.9**	**49069.1**	**42607.1**	**6462**
北京	Beijing	2817.6	93.0	1063.7	845.7	218.1
天津	Tianjin	1826.7	78.6	891.5	807.3	84.2
河北	Hebei	5577.7	914.1	2744.3	2415.4	328.9
山西	Shanxi	1774.6	160.4	917.2	779.0	138.2
内蒙古	Inner Mongolia	1545.5	361.3	624.4	507.0	117.4
辽宁	Liaoning	5033.1	545.0	2444.2	2188.9	255.3
吉林	Jilin	2032.5	409.6	880.8	711.8	169.1
黑龙江	Heilongjiang	3561.0	408.9	1998.7	1767.8	231.0
上海	Shanghai	4950.8	85.5	2355.5	2128.3	227.3
江苏	Jiangsu	9514.6	1088.4	4913.7	4269.1	644.6
浙江	Zhejiang	6700.0	690.0	3440.0	3105.0	335.0
安徽	Anhui	3290.1	754.2	1415.2	1191.6	223.7
福建	Fujian	4258.4	652.4	1904.2	1645.3	258.9
江西	Jiangxi	2173.8	506.0	784.8	595.0	189.8
山东	Shandong	9438.3	1359.5	4654.5	4094.9	559.6
河南	Henan	5645.0	1234.0	2662.3	2287.6	374.7
湖北	Hubei	4662.3	692.2	2313.7	2066.5	247.2
湖南	Hunan	3983.0	825.7	1573.0	1584.3	260.5
广东	Guangdong	10556.5	1008.5	5301.9	4716.9	585.0
广西	Guangxi	2231.2	556.2	816.9	671.2	145.7
海南	Hainan	545.3	200.3	110.4	70.3	40.1
重庆	Chongqi	1749.8	293.0	726.6	576.6	150.1
四川	Sichuan	4421.8	981.7	1756.9	1407.8	349.0
贵州	Guizhu	1082.2	274.3	421.6	335.0	86.6
云南	Yunnan	2077.5	450.5	880.5	722.1	158.4
西藏	Tibet	-	-	-	-	-
陕西	Shanxi	1841.2	280.5	815.7	604.9	210.8
甘肃	Gansu	1074.9	207.0	482.5	356.3	126.2
青海	Qinghai	300.8	41.1	132.6	89.2	43.4
宁夏	Ningxia	298.1	49.5	134.8	102.0	32.8
新疆	Xinjiang	1483.5	287.4	638.8	450.0	188.8

注: 1.本表绝对数按当年价格计算,增长速度按可比价格计算。

2.以下各表均为国家统计局为确保时效,反馈较早的初步统计数,正式数据以即将出版的《中国统计年鉴(2002)》为准。

a. Absolute figures in this table are calculated at current prices, and the growth rate is calculated at comparable prices.

b. Data were initial from the National Bureau of Statistics. Please refer to the China Statistical Yearbook(2002) for official data.

19-1 续表 continued

地区	Region	第三产业 Tertiary Industry (100 million yuan)	#交通运输仓储邮电通信业 Transportation, Storage,Postal and Telecom-munications	#批发和零售贸易餐饮业 Wholesale and Retail, Catering Trade	国内生产总值比上年增长(%) Increase Rate of GDP in 2001 over 2000 (%)	人均国内生产总值(元/人) Per Capita GDP (yuan/person)
全国	**Total National**	**32254.3**	**5222.1**	**7823.5**	**7.0**	**7543**
北京	Beijing	1660.9	218.6	230.5	11.0	25300
天津	Tianjin	856.6	205.3	176.3	12.0	19986
河北	Hebei	1919.3	504.1	502.6	8.7	8337
山西	Shanxi	697.0	162.2	146.0	8.3	5444
内蒙古	Inner Mongolia	559.7	163.7	148.3	9.6	6458
辽宁	Liaoning	2043.8	398.3	697.3	9.0	12070
吉林	Jilin	742.0	128.5	266.1	9.3	7640
黑龙江	Heilongjiang	1153.4	239.2	350.2	9.3	9349
上海	Shanghai	2509.8	343.2	524.6	10.2	37382
江苏	Jiangsu	3512.6	633.9	945.5	10.2	12925
浙江	Zhejiang	2570.0	495.6	948.3	10.5	14550
安徽	Anhui	1120.7	195.3	340.8	8.6	5221
福建	Fujian	1701.8	468.5	411.5	9.0	12375
江西	Jiangxi	883.0	199.9	193.2	8.8	5217
山东	Shandong	3424.3	643.2	873.2	10.1	10465
河南	Henan	1748.7	451.1	421.4	9.1	5929
湖北	Hubei	1656.5	282.5	473.4	9.1	7813
湖南	Hunan	1587.0	294.9	382.4	9.0	6054
广东	Guangdong	4246.1	1028.5	1061.1	9.5	13612
广西	Guangxi	858.1	178.0	301.3	8.2	4697
海南	Hainan	234.6	51.3	73.1	8.9	7110
重庆	Chongqi	730.1	109.7	168.1	9.0	5655
四川	Sichuan	1683.2	313.8	474.8	9.2	5250
贵州	Guizhu	386.3	70.1	82.0	8.8	2865
云南	Yunnan	746.4	136.8	214.3	6.5	4872
西藏	Tibet	-	-	-	-	-
陕西	Shanxi	745.0	183.5	124.9	9.1	5015
甘肃	Gansu	385.3	56.6	123.0	9.4	4173
青海	Qinghai	127.1	22.8	23.1	12.0	5732
宁夏	Ningxia	113.8	21.0	23.6	10.1	5338
新疆	Xinjiang	557.4	131.3	128.2	8.0	7898

19-2 各省(市、区)国内生产总值构成(2000年)

Constrcture of Gross Domestic Product(2000)

(国内生产总值=100) (GDP=100)

地区	Region	国内生产总值 Gross Domestic Product	第一产业 Primary Industry	第二产业 Secondary Industry	工业 Industry	建筑业 Construction	第三产业 Tertiary Industry	#交通运输仓储邮电通信业 Transportation, Storage, Postal and Telecommunications	#批发和零售贸易餐饮业 Wholesale, and Retial, Catering Trade
全国	**Total National**	100.0	15.2	51.2	44.4	6.7	33.6	5.4	8.2
北京	Beijing	100.0	3.3	37.8	30.0	7.7	58.9	7.8	8.2
天津	Tianjin	100.0	4.3	48.8	44.2	4.6	46.9	11.2	9.7
河北	Hebei	100.0	16.4	49.2	43.3	5.9	34.4	9.0	9.0
山西	Shanxi	100.0	9.0	51.7	43.9	7.8	39.3	9.1	8.2
内蒙古	Inner Mongolia	100.0	23.4	40.4	32.8	7.6	36.2	10.6	9.6
辽宁	Liaoning	100.0	10.8	48.6	43.5	5.1	40.6	7.9	13.9
吉林	Jilin	100.0	20.2	43.3	35.0	8.3	36.5	6.3	13.1
黑龙江	Heilongjiang	100.0	11.5	56.1	49.6	6.5	32.4	6.7	9.8
上海	Shanghai	100.0	1.7	47.6	43.0	4.6	50.7	6.9	10.6
江苏	Jiangsu	100.0	11.4	51.6	44.9	6.8	36.9	6.7	9.9
浙江	Zhejiang	100.0	10.3	51.3	46.3	5.0	38.4	7.4	14.2
安徽	Anhui	100.0	22.9	43.0	36.2	6.8	34.1	5.9	10.4
福建	Fujian	100.0	15.3	44.7	38.6	6.1	40.0	11.0	9.7
江西	Jiangxi	100.0	23.3	36.1	27.4	8.7	40.6	9.2	8.9
山东	Shandong	100.0	14.4	49.3	43.4	5.9	36.3	6.8	9.3
河南	Henan	100.0	21.9	47.2	40.5	6.6	31.0	8.0	7.5
湖北	Hubei	100.0	14.8	49.6	44.3	5.3	35.5	6.1	10.2
湖南	Hunan	100.0	20.7	39.5	32.9	6.5	39.8	7.4	9.6
广东	Guangdong	100.0	9.6	50.2	44.7	5.5	40.2	9.7	10.1
广西	Guangxi	100.0	24.9	36.6	30.1	6.5	38.5	8.0	13.5
海南	Hainan	100.0	36.7	20.2	12.9	7.4	43.0	9.4	13.4
重庆	Chongqi	100.0	16.7	41.5	33.0	8.6	41.7	6.3	9.6
四川	Sichuan	100.0	22.2	39.7	31.8	7.9	38.1	7.1	10.7
贵州	Guizhu	100.0	25.3	39.0	31.0	8.0	35.7	6.5	7.6
云南	Yunnan	100.0	21.7	42.4	34.8	7.6	35.9	6.6	10.3
西藏	Tibet	-	-	-	-	-	-	-	-
陕西	Shanxi	100.0	15.2	44.3	32.9	11.4	40.5	10.0	6.8
甘肃	Gansu	100.0	19.3	44.9	33.2	11.7	35.8	5.3	11.4
青海	Qinghai	100.0	13.7	44.1	29.7	14.4	42.3	7.6	7.7
宁夏	Ningxia	100.0	16.6	45.2	34.2	11.0	38.2	7.0	7.9
新疆	Xinjiang	100.0	19.4	43.1	30.3	12.7	37.6	8.9	8.6

注:本表按当年价格计算。

Data in value terms in this table are calculated at current prices.

19-3 各省(市、区)总人口和从业人员(2001年)

Total Poputation and Employed Persons (2001)

地 区	Region	总人口 (万人) Total Population (10 000 persons)	出生率 Birth Rate ‰	死亡率 Death Rate ‰	自然增长率 Natural Growth Rate ‰	从业人员 (万人) Number of Employed Persons (10 000 persons)
全 国	**National Total**	**127627**	**13.38**	**6.43**	**6.95**	**73025**
北 京	Beijing	1383	6.1	5.3	0.80	630
天 津	Tianjin	1004	7.58	5.94	1.64	411
河 北	Hebei	6699	11.16	6.18	4.98	3380
山 西	Shanxi	3272	13.06	5.9	7.16	1413
内蒙古	Inner Mongolia	2377	10.77	5.79	4.98	1013
辽 宁	Liaoning	4194	7.74	6.1	1.64	1833
吉 林	Jilin	2691	8.76	5.38	3.38	1057
黑龙江	Heilongjiang	3811	8.48	5.49	2.99	1631
上 海	Shanghai	1614	5.02	5.97	-0.95	692
江 苏	Jiangsu	7355	9.03	6.62	2.41	3565
浙 江	Zhejiang	4613	10.02	6.25	3.77	2772
安 徽	Anhui	6328	12.46	5.85	6.61	3390
福 建	Fujian	3440	11.56	5.52	6.04	1678
江 西	Jiangxi	4186	15.44	6.06	9.38	1933
山 东	Shandong	9041	11.12	6.24	4.88	4672
河 南	Henan	9555	13.2	6.26	6.94	5517
湖 北	Hubei	5975	8.51	6.07	2.44	2452
湖 南	Hunan	6596	11.8	6.72	5.08	3608
广 东	Guangdong	7783	13.95	5.12	8.83	3963
广 西	Guangxi	4788	13.8	6.07	7.73	2543
海 南	Hainan	796	15.23	5.76	9.47	340
重 庆	Chongqi	3097	9.7	6.9	2.80	1624
四 川	Sichuan	8640	11.16	6.79	4.37	4415
贵 州	Guizhu	3799	18.56	7.23	11.33	2068
云 南	Yunnan	4287	18.51	7.57	10.94	2323
西 藏	Tibet	263	18.6	6.5	12.10	125
陕 西	Shanxi	3659	10.5	6.34	4.16	1785
甘 肃	Gansu	2575	13.58	6.43	7.15	1187
青 海	Qinghai	523	19.06	6.44	12.62	240
宁 夏	Ningxia	563	16.55	4.84	11.71	278
新 疆	Xinjiang	1876	16.82	5.69	11.13	685

19-4 各省(市、区)职工人数(2001年底)

Namber of Staff and Workers (2001)

单位：万人 (10 000 persons)

地区	Region	年末人数 Number of Staff and Workers at the Year-end	国有经济单位 State-owned Units	集体经济单位 Collective Owned Units	股份合作单位 Share Holding Units	联营单位 Joint-owned Units	有限责任公司 Limited Liability Corpra-tions	股份有限公司 Share Holding Corpra-tions Ltd.	港澳台商投资单位 Funded by Enter-preneurs from HongKong Macro and Taiwan	外商投资单位 Foreign Funded Economic Units
全　国	**National Total**	**10791.79**	**7409.03**	**1240.82**	**147.30**	**43.02**	**809.64**	**461.69**	**315.30**	**328.21**
北　京	Beijing	400.32	235.88	39.99	8.43	4.09	42.05	15.10	12.89	22.39
天　津	Tianjin	183.96	103.27	18.00	1.10	0.72	17.76	5.90	11.23	25.93
河　北	Hebei	519.22	402.78	52.44	6.25	0.42	29.70	14.66	5.36	7.30
山　西	Shanxi	362.96	267.21	45.79	4.32	0.29	33.99	8.40	1.74	1.18
内蒙古	Inner Mongolia	250.99	186.27	20.25	2.21	0.51	29.03	9.33	1.63	1.73
辽　宁	Liaoning	545.35	372.76	73.69	5.33	0.35	41.59	22.54	8.06	20.66
吉　林	Jilin	313.26	230.24	38.41	2.28	0.29	15.84	17.33	2.43	6.07
黑龙江	Heilongjiang	510.91	369.00	67.97	7.80	0.94	25.91	31.99	3.64	3.57
上　海	Shanghai	289.97	163.68	21.53	4.49	2.49	24.61	21.65	17.61	33.21
江　苏	Jiangsu	625.83	377.40	90.34	15.58	4.20	52.17	32.01	20.82	32.43
浙　江	Zhejiang	353.19	177.50	37.27	15.40	1.39	68.42	22.08	16.83	13.97
安　徽	Anhui	372.01	252.80	58.15	5.62	1.09	29.88	17.71	1.83	4.05
福　建	Fujian	314.27	158.27	28.91	3.50	4.01	13.92	8.63	61.33	35.00
江　西	Jiangxi	279.28	222.16	27.93	2.70	0.23	17.12	3.54	3.47	1.36
山　东	Shandong	770.52	519.51	91.97	11.74	2.54	53.98	36.03	12.64	41.70
河　南	Henan	704.35	447.72	134.35	6.49	1.77	68.36	32.30	7.60	5.39
湖　北	Hubei	501.59	379.53	52.36	4.30	1.45	15.88	31.47	4.18	5.54
湖　南	Hunan	397.90	316.41	39.11	3.22	0.81	19.93	12.94	2.79	2.30
广　东	Guangdong	724.58	391.75	90.00	11.82	6.08	44.37	28.45	104.92	46.03
广　西	Guangxi	274.32	218.70	23.66	1.21	0.31	15.72	8.24	2.76	3.68
海　南	Hainan	74.69	62.00	4.32	0.24	0.68	1.77	2.32	1.49	1.65
重　庆	Chongqi	201.23	134.79	23.77	3.56	3.87	20.32	9.90	2.11	2.64
四　川	Sichuan	486.70	350.45	58.39	5.62	1.07	35.24	29.11	2.32	3.01
贵　州	Guizhu	189.17	148.87	15.73	1.37	0.48	16.81	4.13	0.74	0.99
云　南	Yunnan	261.61	207.31	20.03	4.36	0.30	16.22	10.20	1.61	1.26
西　藏	Tibet	15.97	14.46	0.85	0.02	0.01	0.28	0.33		0.02
陕　西	Shanxi	323.79	257.90	26.49	3.15	0.32	21.79	10.36	1.46	2.24
甘　肃	Gansu	192.98	158.81	19.84	2.86	1.74	4.34	3.23	0.58	1.43
青　海	Qinghai	43.55	36.19	3.71	0.43	0.02	2.04	1.11	0.03	
宁　夏	Ningxia	60.38	47.92	3.92	1.00	0.14	4.48	1.87	0.25	0.81
新　疆	Xinjiang	246.95	197.47	11.65	0.92	0.40	26.12	8.83	0.94	0.55

19-5 各省(市、区)职工平均工资(2001年)

Averge Wage of Staff and Workers by Region (2001)

单位：元 (yuan)

地 区	Region	全部职工年平均工资 Annual Average Wages of All Staff and Workers	国有经济单位 State-owned Units	集体经济单位 Collective Owned Units	股份合作单位 Share Holding Units	联营单位 Joint-owned Units	有限责任公司 Limited Liability Corpra-tions	股份有限公司 Share Holding Corpra-tions Ltd.	港澳台商投资单位 Funded by Enter-preneurs from HongKong Macro and Taiwan	外商投资单位 Foreign Funded Economic Units
全 国	**National Total**	**10870**	**11178**	**6867**	**8398**	**11887**	**10993**	**12385**	**12544**	**16101**
北 京	Beijing	19155	19776	11063	11003	14312	18487	20836	21210	34481
天 津	Tianjin	14308	15110	8345	12791	13809	13874	17512	13042	15564
河 北	Hebei	8730	9139	5746	6551	9787	9360	7272	10283	9166
山 西	Shanxi	8122	8618	4927	5795	7559	9092	6780	7796	8072
内蒙古	Inner Mongolia	8250	8737	5525	4900	6353	7896	7706	5936	6882
辽 宁	Liaoning	10145	10609	6354	6584	8877	10826	11441	12505	12766
吉 林	Jilin	8771	9043	5765	8169	6174	8975	10044	9625	13550
黑龙江	Heilongjiang	8910	8924	4917	10321	9235	7819	17468	10135	8628
上 海	Shanghai	21781	21961	13693	15290	17396	19564	24520	19625	28787
江 苏	Jiangsu	11842	12917	7543	8272	10414	11257	12227	11460	14483
浙 江	Zhejiang	16385	19514	12208	10633	14147	13127	15851	14099	14105
安 徽	Anhui	7908	8501	5106	5443	7807	7246	10048	7369	10130
福 建	Fujian	12013	13313	9098	10292	12594	12007	14133	10334	11015
江 西	Jiangxi	8026	8346	5149	6463	6818	8604	10281	6721	8331
山 东	Shandong	10008	11067	6235	6435	8494	8863	8705	7914	9526
河 南	Henan	7916	8573	5726	5712	5717	7808	8074	9558	8924
湖 北	Hubei	8619	9133	5677	6240	8423	8936	7541	8592	10959
湖 南	Hunan	9623	9991	6877	8165	8123	9112	9904	9489	9769
广 东	Guangdong	15682	16779	9040	10830	18104	20282	19860	13601	18192
广 西	Guangxi	9075	9209	6388	6926	7093	10763	10759	6637	10309
海 南	Hainan	8321	8102	6207	9944	8386	11100	12729	10088	11296
重 庆	Chongqi	9523	10035	6614	7572	9247	8581	11033	10694	12903
四 川	Sichuan	9934	10783	6575	7862	7568	8172	9124	10167	10408
贵 州	Guizhu	8991	9308	6218	7231	7059	8777	9631	9695	8871
云 南	Yunnan	10537	10880	7203	7927	10960	10016	11700	10965	13611
西 藏	Tibet	19144	20112	6236	12833	7868	13546	12564	-	17877
陕 西	Shanxi	9120	9440	5293	5582	8015	9450	10479	9788	13524
甘 肃	Gansu	9949	10442	6728	5762	14133	7038	10647	9822	11911
青 海	Qinghai	12906	14028	6101	6257	3203	9662	8490	5727	-
宁 夏	Ningxia	10442	11112	7166	7922	8807	8260	8449	6469	10797
新 疆	Xinjiang	10278	10145	8197	8335	9132	10569	15617	10873	10153

19-6 各省(市、区)国有及国有控股企业从业人员和劳动报酬(2001年)

Number of Empolyed Persons and Their Labor Payment in State-Owned and State-Owned Share-Holding Enterprises (2001)

地 区	Region	从业人员(万人) Number of Empolyed Persons (10 000 persons)	#女性 #Female	在岗职工(万人) Staff and Workers on the Job (10 000 persons)	#专业技术人员 Specialized Technical Personnel	从业人员劳动报酬(万元) Earnings of Empolyed (10 000 yuan)	#在岗职工工资总额 Wages of Staff and Workers on the Job	在岗职工平均工资(元) Average Wages of Staff and Workers on the Job (yuan)
全 国	**National Total**	**5332.94**	**1893.32**	**5141.44**	**1124.85**	**59368597**	**57663579**	**11014**
北 京	Beijing	196.42	65.51	182.37	50.46	3894637	3639244	19242
天 津	Tianjin	93.04	31.57	89.82	21.35	1401672	1369785	14794
河 北	Hebei	232.21	81.28	227.82	46.09	2224695	2190372	9439
山 西	Shanxi	196.83	61.02	191.96	35.72	1665546	1634762	8468
内蒙古	Inner Mongolia	122.25	42.71	120.41	22.72	1004843	992137	8112
辽 宁	Liaoning	438.68	156.03	428.74	125.99	4767701	4687448	10759
吉 林	Jilin	159.55	54.82	156.83	33.24	1462867	1439844	9031
黑龙江	Heilongjiang	302.31	99.12	281.24	50.29	2616541	2505395	8858
上 海	Shanghai	180.40	58.49	155.40	34.61	3842866	3556153	21993
江 苏	Jiangsu	285.01	104.37	273.75	54.96	3490615	3383998	11937
浙 江	Zhejiang	104.30	39.63	99.02	26.19	1827661	1765073	17512
安 徽	Anhui	178.25	61.74	173.76	33.34	1463503	1438632	8166
福 建	Fujian	88.20	31.28	84.31	18.37	1216505	1172551	13675
江 西	Jiangxi	149.67	54.82	145.04	33.38	1172062	1144749	7779
山 东	Shandong	333.93	121.39	327.07	64.24	3568217	3512753	10610
河 南	Henan	329.83	118.88	321.65	54.05	2724081	2673618	8317
湖 北	Hubei	255.63	97.96	249.58	40.46	2250218	2214107	8647
湖 南	Hunan	221.44	81.84	209.64	48.29	2133978	2055256	9725
广 东	Guangdong	230.40	83.95	225.58	53.47	4191189	4115966	17838
广 西	Guangxi	117.17	43.60	113.68	23.20	1091165	1071984	9390
海 南	Hainan	45.06	18.77	44.01	6.78	310479	305429	6879
重 庆	Chongqi	148.24	51.70	146.28	50.36	1520420	1505392	10073
四 川	Sichuan	220.63	77.82	212.12	47.24	2308981	2226439	10237
贵 州	Guizhu	94.40	30.27	87.92	18.21	865726	821348	9226
云 南	Yunnan	108.00	39.67	105.70	23.57	1163563	1152700	10751
西 藏	Tibet	16.83	5.78	15.50	3.85	301075	291116	19453
陕 西	Shanxi	164.55	57.62	160.35	35.91	1530962	1501032	9286
甘 肃	Gansu	117.82	41.99	114.84	28.60	1205488	1189970	10251
青 海	Qinghai	19.93	6.95	19.32	4.32	275423	271716	13506
宁 夏	Ningxia	30.89	11.17	30.18	6.23	330862	324154	10615
新 疆	Xinjiang	151.08	61.58	147.56	29.34	1545058	1510457	9589

19-7 各省(市、区)固定资产投资

Investment in Fixed Assets

地区	Region	固定资产投资 (亿元) Investment in Fixed Assets (100 million yuan)		基本建设投资 Capital Construction		更新改造 Investment in Innotation	
		2000	2001	2000	2001	2000	2001
全国	**National Total**	**32917.7**	**36898.4**	**13427.3**	**14567.0**	**5107.6**	**5889.2**
北京	Beijing	1186.3	1410.3	447.0	387.3	185.9	186.51
天津	Tianjin	526.2	612.5	280.4	309.4	111.9	141.85
河北	Hebei	1047.8	1085.4	624.5	591.8	305.9	339.59
山西	Shanxi	456.5	549.8	278.5	325.9	110.8	145.16
内蒙古	Inner Mongolia	347.3	418.3	229.4	268.8	58.6	69.58
辽宁	Liaoning	1028.2	1166.6	451.4	490.8	283.4	329.87
吉林	Jilin	484.9	580.2	276.7	317.8	114.5	127.4
黑龙江	Heilongjiang	740.7	845.5	379.8	481.7	239.7	201.92
上海	Shanghai	1678.8	1793.6	703.5	710.5	396.3	432.03
江苏	Jiangsu	1645.3	1837.0	751.3	838.0	338.0	402.15
浙江	Zhejiang	1444.6	1879.1	821.0	979.4	242.6	319.06
安徽	Anhui	573.8	659.4	318.0	347.8	152.8	185.33
福建	Fujian	810.5	881.7	334.6	341.7	175.4	201.7
江西	Jiangxi	321.9	415.4	198.6	235.0	75.4	103.13
山东	Shandong	1563.9	1801.0	762.2	848.9	398.6	517.67
河南	Henan	884.6	977.3	586.2	633.4	163.4	198.53
湖北	Hubei	988.2	1108.4	600.4	657.2	245.2	282.74
湖南	Hunan	684.5	799.5	404.0	476.7	175.2	198.31
广东	Guangdong	2535.7	2786.0	1133.3	1201.4	435.4	480.79
广西	Guangxi	397.7	458.4	267.5	307.6	80.2	86.6
海南	Hainan	150.3	171.9	132.0	137.0	9.8	14.03
重庆	Chongqi	458.4	568.5	215.6	258.5	89.9	105.61
四川	Sichuan	1016.4	1169.4	636.9	696.1	173.9	196.35
贵州	Guizhu	288.3	413.4	148.0	230.9	93.3	102.68
云南	Yunnan	504.1	513.6	341.9	321.0	81.1	97.03
西藏	Tibet	48.6	85.0	54.7	75.3	4.5	5.52
陕西	Shanxi	529.1	632.3	303.6	372.7	135.2	133.08
甘肃	Gansu	322.1	383.6	208.3	232.1	89.0	112.09
青海	Qinghai	131.9	178.0	99.0	133.8	17.1	20.65
宁夏	Ningxia	123.9	151.9	86.2	102.1	22.7	25.28
新疆	Xinjiang	519.9	608.6	392.8	389.0	77.5	108.57

注:各地区数据不包括城乡集体和个人投资。

The regional data on the collective and individual investment were not included.

19-8 各省(市、区)房地产开发企业完成投资额及住宅竣工、销售面积

Investment Completed in Real Estate Development and Floor Space Completed of Residential Buildings and Floor Space of Selling Houses

地区	Region	完成投资额(亿元) Investment Completed (100 million yuan)		住宅竣工面积(万平方米) Floor Space Completed (10 000 sq.m)		住宅销售面积(万平方米) Floor Space of Selling Houses (10 000 sq.m)	
		2000	2001	2000	2001	2000	2001
全　国	**National Total**	**4984.1**	**6245.5**	**25104.9**	**27303.2**	**18637.1**	**20779.2**
北　京	Beijing	522.1	783.8	1365.6	1707.4	956.9	1205.0
天　津	Tianjin	133.9	161.3	583.5	690.2	391.8	537.4
河　北	Hebei	108.4	141.0	771.3	758.3	489.4	490.4
山　西	Shanxi	39.5	45.2	306.4	383.1	190.6	201.0
内蒙古	Inner Mongolia	45.2	65.8	412.9	448.7	293.8	309.8
辽　宁	Liaoning	264.9	321.6	1619.0	1616.4	948.7	1048.0
吉　林	Jilin	63.5	93.0	464.8	502.3	309.3	278.5
黑龙江	Heilongjiang	104.1	147.0	827.9	987.8	499.8	607.6
上　海	Shanghai	566.2	620.3	1643.6	1758.0	1557.9	1767.4
江　苏	Jiangsu	358.7	411.8	2143.2	2116.6	1740.9	1794.0
浙　江	Zhejiang	362.2	536.3	1676.9	2004.5	1502.2	1736.5
安　徽	Anhui	87.9	111.0	759.3	963.8	535.9	682.1
福　建	Fujian	207.4	214.5	1009.4	998.5	810.7	813.7
江　西	Jiangxi	42.4	54.9	402.8	344.6	286.7	313.7
山　东	Shandong	223.3	291.6	1426.5	1556.5	1078.4	1210.0
河　南	Henan	77.9	102.0	597.5	664.2	509.2	497.7
湖　北	Hubei	134.6	151.2	843.5	1049.5	612.1	744.2
湖　南	Hunan	74.8	106.3	577.6	654.3	377.8	444.4
广　东	Guangdong	858.6	943.0	3161.6	2755.2	2259.9	2144.3
广　西	Guangxi	38.7	55.6	226.7	330.7	191.4	296.7
海　南	Hainan	10.3	17.0	36.0	57.1	42.2	56.1
重　庆	Chongqi	139.6	196.7	849.4	1020.6	580.0	746.1
四　川	Sichuan	196.0	266.2	1285.3	1713.2	945.6	1307.1
贵　州	Guizhu	46.6	60.9	349.2	310.0	251.7	257.4
云　南	Yunnan	83.2	80.6	426.0	337.9	343.2	287.6
西　藏	Tibet	1.0	1.6	6.7		4.8	
陕　西	Shanxi	78.9	99.2	585.3	578.8	396.4	390.7
甘　肃	Gansu	27.7	31.4	187.1	188.9	123.0	110.5
青　海	Qinghai	13.5	15.2	74.3	87.9	39.9	23.6
宁　夏	Ningxia	15.6	22.2	155.5	150.5	104.5	113.5
新　疆	Xinjiang	57.4	97.3	330.1	567.7	262.5	364.3

19-9 各省(市、区)财政收入决算情况(2001年)

Final Statement of Government Revenue (2001)

单位：万元 (10 000 yuan)

地区	Region	收入合计 Total Revenue	增值税 Value-Added Tax	营业税 Operation Tax	企业所得税 Income Income Tax of Enterprises	企业所得税退税 Return for Income Tax of Enterprises	个人所得税 Individual Income Tax	资源税 Resources Tax	城市建设维护税 Tax on Town Maintenance and Construction	房产税 Tax on Real Estates
地方合计	**Total**	**78033015**	**13416584**	**18490999**	**16361250**	**-77597**	**7160142**	**671084**	**3806212**	**2284249**
北京	Beijing	4541676	589957	1813472	899075	-38354	795167	2431	205316	214340
天津	Tianjin	1636350	348737	429946	393829	-66	165772	3851	76875	50835
河北	Hebei	2835023	488480	500222	541367	-26	233082	49876	122231	70590
山西	Shanxi	1327618	308705	261131	221608	-2143	90615	59428	75565	44549
内蒙古	Inner Mongolia	994313	148386	196127	151985	-123	66710	20247	48921	42363
辽宁	Liaoning	3704403	665132	878545	636167	-1159	294413	87004	192641	157925
吉林	Jilin	1211015	242028	280301	206802	-709	87726	10198	73527	45424
黑龙江	Heilongjiang	2136398	525551	363088	219392	-75	126149	129349	161032	66158
上海	Shanghai	6094719	1119511	1911225	1498156	-678	784443	0	247477	146551
江苏	Jiangsu	5721473	1319931	1094859	1408127	0	445417	9645	304506	142038
浙江	Zhejiang	5006948	1024086	1248934	1756406	-3618	516942	2769	284890	113013
安徽	Anhui	1921813	282788	326479	382527	-1602	113132	19327	98111	48121
福建	Fujian	2742846	407776	614213	563513	-2815	364543	7140	97508	98497
江西	Jiangxi	1319790	172324	266187	226096	-10	79102	8674	57160	28788
山东	Shandong	5731793	1002918	926921	1491110	0	369925	64405	290458	165321
河南	Henan	2677459	443548	528903	608462	-70	192469	24343	137300	70309
湖北	Hubei	2319410	371308	446806	365089	-51	166625	15010	114028	58800
湖南	Hunan	2054078	293807	364410	227791	-2831	186663	6663	118145	44161
广东	Guangdong	11605126	1724793	3181606	2678119	-9	1178630	9603	354286	287375
广西	Guangxi	1786706	238650	328720	373009	-106	167500	8041	64830	43449
海南	Hainan	437656	35186	127383	43037	0	43721	4173	17113	24356
重庆	Chongqi	1061243	177603	278403	118737	-601	106138	10944	54482	28870
四川	Sichuan	2711245	380085	628085	457425	-15	159951	31185	136019	78044
贵州	Guizhu	997494	142622	220764	123437	-2775	66684	7291	63307	30002
云南	Yunnan	1912799	336212	366782	262891	-5815	114532	9390	190847	56863
西藏	Tibet	61108						1906	2410	0
陕西	Shanxi	1358109	233318	334989	207586	-540	73119	13592	80401	50512
甘肃	Gansu	699485	133758	173483	104045	-417	38788	8448	48963	27210
青海	Qinghai	198241	38500	48664	28928	-10400	9387	4273	12490	6330
宁夏	Ningxia	275745	38530	75194	60084	-852	19764	740	14399	9314
新疆	Xinjiang	950933	173861	252540	93439	-1732	98407	41138	60974	34141

单位：万元　　19-9 续表 continued　　(10 000 yuan)

地区	Region	印花税 Stamp Tax	农业税 Agricultural Tax	农业特产税 Tax on Special Agricultural Products	契税 Contract Tax	国有企业计划亏损补贴 Planning Subsidies to Loss-suffering State-owned Enterprises	行政性收费收入 Income From Adiministrative Fees	罚没收入 Penalty and Confiscatory Income	专项收入 Expert Project Income	其它收入 Other Income
地方合计	**Total**	**711235**	**1639218**	**1219726**	**1570773**	**-2617594**	**3711484**	**3566919**	**2510648**	**1198538**
北京	Beijing	67447	5880	2222	126297	-532229	84182	86547	136227	5802
天津	Tianjin	13325	3227	482	34989	-40000	43444	49850	39989	3486
河北	Hebei	13591	64057	24857	27813	-35354	263414	215931	126067	43822
山西	Shanxi	10685	29677	5538	7587	-48418	59683	81490	59673	21719
内蒙古	Inner Mongolia	7731	44169	28209	10728	-14436	82459	47363	33623	14071
辽宁	Liaoning	34533	36809	29705	83131	-47195	185029	165620	141908	18146
吉林	Jilin	7872	29219	19843	24500	-62176	60550	74412	51123	13249
黑龙江	Heilongjiang	8322	102352	31627	35848	-24646	96518	85151	123281	27459
上海	Shanghai	158268	16746	1692	189180	-362320	84653	121974	128095	2612
江苏	Jiangsu	43558	239778	14220	137505	-75366	54587	275463	179664	37927
浙江	Zhejiang	30295	49784	18688	181319	-766221	75757	185879	177034	10692
安徽	Anhui	10267	256903	28703	25655	-68275	180850	76109	55147	27668
福建	Fujian	19935	11879	70103	65059	-4260	101137	114643	66175	69731
江西	Jiangxi	5959	47011	58868	20739	-2286	123165	88035	34891	33645
山东	Shandong	26963	97073	181590	51423	-88303	403697	200800	216762	56075
河南	Henan	11436	67304	93672	30070	-114599	140060	199806	106848	36722
湖北	Hubei	15688	78291	83428	33488	-47861	179925	192236	56474	88764
湖南	Hunan	13521	77836	51579	21302	-59121	215082	212715	71671	116187
广东	Guangdong	147806	70604	33333	282855	-52048	488865	474892	257016	217520
广西	Guangxi	4817	41849	56017	19149	-17988	148998	103231	51845	65267
海南	Hainan	3587	4890	25676	10036	-3129	43688	19282	9580	2840
重庆	Chongqi	6758	36811	12073	19029	-27670	85956	67969	36678	8309
四川	Sichuan	12405	85858	47599	64276	-27937	239235	143421	70976	49339
贵州	Guizhu	3644	30313	41132	8995	-5242	76754	48793	36019	49743
云南	Yunnan	12338	34519	150541	20964	-28677	40262	74567	76120	109697
西藏	Tibet	396	0	0	0	-9703	4908	2405	1833	7218
陕西	Shanxi	7994	25010	71794	13538	-21169	48210	70609	69084	28413
甘肃	Gansu	3617	15621	22593	7801	-11942	24837	25602	37178	17844
青海	Qinghai	878	3313	2734	1701	-121	11040	6180	8786	7453
宁夏	Ningxia	1603	9381	397	3932	-557	14005	8785	9680	1462
新疆	Xinjiang	5996	23054	10811	11864	-18345	50534	47159	41201	5656

19-10 各省(市、区)财政支出决算情况(2001年)

Final Statement of Government Expenditure (2001)

单位：万元

(10 000 yuan)

地区	Region	支出合计 Total Expenditure	基本建设支出 Expenditure for Capital Construction	挖潜改造支出 Expenditure for Innovation Enterprises	地质勘探费 Expenditure for Geological Prospecting	科技三项费用 Expenditure for Science and Technology Promotion	流动资金 Expenditure for Circulating Funds	支援农村生产支出 Expenditure Supporting for Agriculture Production	农林综合开发支出 Expenditure for Comprehensive of Development Agriculture
地方合计	**Total**	**131345699**	**16475818**	**6021182**	**692722**	**1424909**	**92130**	**2466588**	**1094815**
北京	Beijing	5591063	929621	354651	5655	48664	11903	117269	28924
天津	Tianjin	2346673	374269	282510	9720	60570		23658	15117
河北	Hebei	5146312	381937	193931	15140	56248		72459	39113
山西	Shanxi	2895027	254447	22943	13710	23617	25586	63476	28721
内蒙古	Inner Mongolia	3192620	513916	97638	29985	23568		60815	35087
辽宁	Liaoning	6343995	656019	263525	32492	117582		140001	61578
吉林	Jilin	3264343	298628	115681	26723	30641	610	25817	24891
黑龙江	Heilongjiang	4782724	475613	175765	32854	53186		78026	42179
上海	Shanghai	7081382	1443460	952702	1082	12850		101364	30216
江苏	Jiangsu	7296421	609976	605365	15999	93892	1788	212622	62588
浙江	Zhejiang	5972991	446356	434321	21237	124034		130794	65687
安徽	Anhui	4037998	435524	233515	27104	20769	34	64385	44339
福建	Fujian	3743122	395657	125743	10995	48266	541	91072	33102
江西	Jiangxi	2837144	279192	116647	48387	12096		48401	42759
山东	Shandong	7537781	409608	523941	16791	115257	2970	146001	86253
河南	Henan	5085795	332591	201082	28106	41388	1935	86490	46223
湖北	Hubei	4844034	770397	101112	17548	46217	29111	74223	34712
湖南	Hunan	4316953	394040	97654	46502	51541		65467	41131
广东	Guangdong	13213314	1924571	209739	22376	236139	2659	281956	48075
广西	Guangxi	3516498	418730	135480	24323	19102	1000	84841	32178
海南	Hainan	780049	101716	1416	2505	2028		18985	11659
重庆	Chongqi	2375486	406801	48466	5212	24158		30195	25368
四川	Sichuan	5940981	783327	303298	45688	46290	11390	81710	66857
贵州	Guizhu	2751875	431347	44494	26865	14869	600	49582	18684
云南	Yunnan	4964302	830696	123494	27287	40526	40	165271	31848
西藏	Tibet	1045690	348096	3261	11134	2616		12663	8557
陕西	Shanxi	3500506	503090	82158	39993	22773	1505	69432	28685
甘肃	Gansu	2358650	391787	86179	35304	11963	158	38791	14937
青海	Qinghai	1012951	262317	11252	10894	4985		16645	9857
宁夏	Ningxia	935787	242952	45265	9963	7079	300	14177	12652
新疆	Xinjiang	2633232	429137	27954	31148	11995		24568	22838

单位：万元　　　　19-10 续表1 continued　　　　(10 000 yuan)

地 区	Region	农林水利气象等部门的事业费 Operating Expenses of Agriculture, Forestry, Water Conservancy and Meteorology	工业交通等部门的事业费 Operating Expenses of Departments of Industry and Transportation	文体广播事业费 Operating Expenses of Departments of Culture, Sport and Broadcasting	教育事业费 Expenditure for Operating Expenses of Education	科学事业费 Operating Expenses of Department of Science	卫生经费 Expenditure for Public Health	税务等部门的事业费 Operating Expenses for Departments of Revenue, Statistic, Finance and Audit	抚恤和社会福利救济费 Expenditure for Pensions and Relief Funds for Social Welfare
地方合计	**Total**	**4603378**	**1174688**	**3199877**	**20356888**	**876291**	**5575476**	**6218926**	**2647673**
北 京	Beijing	49621	28369	114758	722553	72723	330792	215650	143878
天 津	Tianjin	18584	12910	52892	362565	14171	100050	56028	36034
河 北	Hebei	137557	72971	128254	895642	23647	216635	411079	119193
山 西	Shanxi	108627	27714	82401	503801	12371	134067	147682	64974
内蒙古	Inner Mongolia	252747	24555	79883	397389	14025	112207	175245	54278
辽 宁	Liaoning	128146	45125	113528	749956	33031	175897	345806	183113
吉 林	Jilin	170492	38460	71078	442732	20690	110660	149321	66976
黑龙江	Heilongjiang	337399	59902	103141	649654	34646	162448	313225	83448
上 海	Shanghai	51102	38057	132593	997392	84740	345677	223031	96650
江 苏	Jiangsu	157771	48688	189299	1446083	50603	374021	223608	161603
浙 江	Zhejiang	205713	105887	174502	1082977	51223	327563	373691	97112
安 徽	Anhui	116685	24240	94125	666783	16136	127771	151343	98785
福 建	Fujian	118027	42237	111936	724541	30692	169701	208544	65305
江 西	Jiangxi	82951	28198	66674	484329	14891	117642	159303	56558
山 东	Shandong	246679	79048	206502	1377529	45428	306587	400182	175993
河 南	Henan	158427	51123	134691	960043	24464	194296	261678	112879
湖 北	Hubei	134230	41455	112788	704577	16902	215028	191577	134987
湖 南	Hunan	148858	48570	107482	650949	22641	135138	193434	100905
广 东	Guangdong	365486	64833	334967	1802758	116525	539932	682427	178904
广 西	Guangxi	119189	20867	95446	620103	23844	156254	240504	59385
海 南	Hainan	24815	3041	19223	111558	4124	29414	60859	15354
重 庆	Chongqi	71396	4823	46779	332065	8306	87254	70395	69191
四 川	Sichuan	346587	44312	130951	852367	32088	248216	191158	130249
贵 州	Guizhu	131595	27254	78148	444172	17406	135517	106913	47842
云 南	Yunnan	255474	61707	118315	762797	34435	251325	236861	102327
西 藏	Tibet	41952	26948	22775	89461	2263	39037	13316	12787
陕 西	Shanxi	247371	51524	92392	523579	16892	114542	174329	71961
甘 肃	Gansu	142562	16404	67527	359355	14319	98829	80610	38780
青 海	Qinghai	47579	9821	21812	101814	3581	41538	33370	16770
宁 夏	Ningxia	47982	7542	22720	108879	5263	39445	29515	13726
新 疆	Xinjiang	137774	18103	72295	428485	14221	137993	98242	37726

单位：万元 19-10 续表2 continued (10 000 yuan)

地 区	Region	行政事业单位离退休经费 Expenditure for Retired Persons in Administrative Department	社会保障补助支出 Expenditure on Subsidies to Social Security Programs	行 政管理费 Expenditure on Government Administration	城 市维护费 Expenditure for City Maintenance	政策性补贴支出 Expenditure for Price Subsidies	支援不发达地区支出 Expenditure for Supporting Undeveloped Areas	其他支出 Others Expenditure
地方合计	**Total**	**5690559**	**7473548**	**11794662**	**5681078**	**4426290**	**1335679**	**10432681**
北 京	Beijing	228974	63285	273574	273217	68509	138	997575
天 津	Tianjin	8520	192219	111505	160929	66099	39	187838
河 北	Hebei	265491	376836	462856	151459	252425	45880	289024
山 西	Shanxi	204139	269267	333116	84896	90276	33492	106224
内蒙古	Inner Mongolia	206464	161678	317590	112129	178707	55007	66953
辽 宁	Liaoning	287506	1045161	458875	390228	274884	27218	278714
吉 林	Jilin	228199	289193	223773	94261	478561	22386	77384
黑龙江	Heilongjiang	63822	514943	344677	194422	473188	28476	133341
上 海	Shanghai	56364	99019	287628	277483	65396		1213306
江 苏	Jiangsu	263378	171506	681694	645405	115694	4987	501741
浙 江	Zhejiang	51092	91514	598098	438197	72790	20164	395725
安 徽	Anhui	239604	318657	424417	123004	242335	41793	243106
福 建	Fujian	209303	73753	297452	125166	83161	27558	413750
江 西	Jiangxi	107184	212844	259773	95860	186548	38574	141238
山 东	Shandong	312186	302506	743144	485770	212299	12492	670031
河 南	Henan	317948	328837	582800	166034	247330	64202	272233
湖 北	Hubei	175653	314381	446872	135336	190273	40389	554935
湖 南	Hunan	243306	387483	414152	170653	205900	51379	330502
广 东	Guangdong	546047	299266	1203021	638734	187703	51159	1992198
广 西	Guangxi	131989	112846	353041	101776	72732	75850	288866
海 南	Hainan	37617	53479	79080	25167	7396	18332	85268
重 庆	Chongqi	166297	214719	247521	114276	60966	34479	85068
四 川	Sichuan	312709	441005	677156	167466	208969	99322	253199
贵 州	Guizhu	22378	162362	321894	79706	50967	96380	214396
云 南	Yunnan	313455	262296	447596	158702	58005	140124	155658
西 藏	Tibet	15784	14824	143065	4837	13782	22131	146545
陕 西	Shanxi	152091	314003	353754	115985	78456	84455	102805
甘 肃	Gansu	131616	100898	258285	50815	76945	78194	106883
青 海	Qinghai	106144	86538	92096	9127	13701	36953	18999
宁 夏	Ningxia	34662	73194	60773	19018	21747	26153	42512
新 疆	Xinjiang	250637	125036	295384	71020	70546	57973	66664

19-11 各省(市、区)居民消费价格分类指数(2001年)

General Consumer Price Indices by Category (2001)

(上年=100) (precending year=100)

地区	Region	居民消费价格指数 General Consumer Price Indices	食品 Foods	烟酒及用品 Beverages Tobacco and Liquor	衣着 Clothing	家庭设备用品服务 Household Facilities Articles and Services	医疗保健 Medcine and Medical Services	交通和通信 Transportation and Communications	娱乐教育文化 Recreation Education and Cultural Services	居住 Residence
全国	**National Total**	**100.7**	**100.0**	**99.7**	**98.1**	**97.7**	**100.0**	**99.0**	**106.6**	**101.2**
北京	Beijing	103.1	101.5	101.5	100.4	97.0	98.7	100.8	114.2	104.2
天津	Tianjin	101.2	100.8	99.2	93.5	95.9	100.7	106.7	104.3	106.4
河北	Hebei	100.5	100.8	99.1	97.4	98.2	98.2	99.5	103.6	102.4
山西	Shanxi	99.8	99.4	98.1	96.0	98.2	97.8	99.1	98.3	104.3
内蒙古	Inner Mongolia	100.6	101.8	99.2	97.7	99.0	98.1	98.4	102.0	103.7
辽宁	Liaoning	100.0	101.8	98.0	96.8	96.4	92.7	99.6	101.3	103.4
吉林	Jilin	101.3	101.3	98.4	98.2	99.4	103.7	98.7	101.4	105.3
黑龙江	Heilongjiang	100.8	101.9	99.9	100.0	98.4	96.9	102.7	100.3	102.3
上海	Shanghai	100.0	100.3	98.9	98.9	97.2	97.4	98.1	102.1	102.3
江苏	Jiangsu	100.8	99.3	99.3	97.7	97.6	101.1	96.8	110.1	100.4
浙江	Zhejiang	99.8	98.7	99.4	98.4	97.0	99.6	95.6	107.2	99.8
安徽	Anhui	100.5	99.7	101.2	97.7	98.0	99.3	97.3	104.1	102.7
福建	Fujian	98.7	97.6	100.5	96.5	97.6	102.5	97.2	100.6	99.9
江西	Jiangxi	99.5	98.0	99.0	98.4	97.1	100.5	101.4	103.0	99.9
山东	Shandong	101.8	101.1	101.5	98.6	98.7	102.4	96.9	108.2	101.7
河南	Henan	100.7	100.4	99.5	98.6	98.0	100.7	99.4	102.4	103.3
湖北	Hubei	100.3	99.3	99.5	96.9	94.0	98.1	99.7	109.0	99.2
湖南	Hunan	99.1	98.6	99.3	97.4	96.4	99.8	97.4	102.1	100.0
广东	Guangdong	99.3	98.2	100.0	98.2	99.4	99.3	99.7	101.5	99.9
广西	Guangxi	100.6	98.5	99.2	96.3	97.0	97.7	98.7	112.6	100.4
海南	Hainan	98.5	98.4	100.7	99.2	98.1	100.2	98.0	98.2	97.8
重庆	Chongqi	101.7	99.2	96.8	97.4	95.7	98.9	102.4	114.8	102.6
四川	Sichuan	102.1	101.3	99.3	97.9	99.2	98.8	105.4	111.9	99.9
贵州	Guizhu	101.8	98.5	100.2	97.8	94.6	102.4	107.0	115.0	99.5
云南	Yunnan	99.1	98.3	98.9	96.3	98.5	106.2	92.5	98.6	101.6
西藏	Tibet	100.1	99.3	99.6	101.1	99.4	100.1	103.6	98.7	101.3
陕西	Shanxi	101.0	99.2	100.0	97.3	96.2	99.7	98.2	112.6	100.5
甘肃	Gansu	104.0	100.0	100.0	99.9	98.2	98.3	103.6	123.2	102.8
青海	Qinghai	102.6	102.2	98.6	99.4	96.2	98.6	102.4	115.3	101.2
宁夏	Ningxia	101.6	100.1	97.9	99.4	97.4	99.8	100.6	112.4	102.5
新疆	Xinjiang	104.0	104.3	98.8	98.7	100.2	116.1	105.2	101.6	102.6

19-12 各省(市、区)城镇居民家庭人均收支情况(2001年)

Per Capita Annual Income and Expenditure of Urban Households (2001)

地区	Region	全部收入 (元) Total Income (yuan)	#可支配收入 Disposable Income	实际支出 (元) Real Expenditure (yuan)	消费性支出 Living Expenditure	非消费性支出 Non-living Expenditure	恩格尔系数 (%) Engler Quotiety (%)
全　国	**National Total**	**6907.1**	**6859.6**	**6553.6**	**5309.0**	**1240.8**	**37.94**
北　京	Beijing	11659.0	11577.8	10676.5	8922.7	1753.5	36.19
天　津	Tianjin	8999.4	8958.7	8367.0	6987.2	1379.7	37.04
河　北	Hebei	6027.8	5984.8	5749.7	4479.8	1267.7	35.35
山　西	Shanxi	5416.3	5391.1	5284.9	4123.0	1160.1	34.27
内蒙古	Inner Mongolia	5561.1	5535.9	5246.7	4195.6	1044.9	33.92
辽　宁	Liaoning	5832.6	5797.0	5998.2	4654.4	1340.9	39.66
吉　林	Jilin	5361.4	5340.5	5371.6	4337.2	1033.9	38.06
黑龙江	Heilongjiang	5461.7	5425.9	5128.4	4192.4	931.5	37.23
上　海	Shanghai	12981.5	12883.5	11977.4	9336.1	2641.3	43.08
江　苏	Jiangsu	7427.5	7375.1	6967.8	5532.7	1434.9	39.66
浙　江	Zhejiang	10540.4	10464.7	10073.9	7952.4	2121.2	36.32
安　徽	Anhui	5715.5	5668.8	5757.0	4517.7	1236.8	44.25
福　建	Fujian	8384.6	8313.1	7603.6	6015.1	1583.9	44.07
江　西	Jiangxi	5545.7	5506.0	4684.1	3894.5	777.5	40.76
山　东	Shandong	7141.2	7101.1	6386.1	5252.4	1132.9	34.30
河　南	Henan	5292.1	5267.4	4894.7	4110.2	784.1	34.67
湖　北	Hubei	5888.7	5856.0	5774.8	4804.8	961.5	37.45
湖　南	Hunan	6832.6	6780.6	6925.5	5546.2	1377.6	35.04
广　东	Guangdong	10534.7	10415.2	9607.3	8099.6	1498.8	38.15
广　西	Guangxi	6722.8	6665.7	6531.7	5224.7	1302.2	37.67
海　南	Hainan	5927.4	5838.8	5397.9	4367.9	976.6	46.30
重　庆	Chongqi	6755.5	6721.1	6668.7	5873.7	794.4	39.80
四　川	Sichuan	6406.6	6360.5	6114.0	5176.2	927.2	40.23
贵　州	Guizhu	5467.2	5451.9	5098.6	4273.9	822.1	40.92
云　南	Yunnan	6849.7	6797.7	6485.5	5252.6	1228.4	40.09
西　藏	Tibet	7912.4	7869.2	8431.7	5994.4	2435.3	43.82
陕　西	Shanxi	5513.8	5483.7	5647.7	4637.7	1008.6	34.27
甘　肃	Gansu	5413.7	5382.9	5174.5	4420.3	754.0	37.08
青　海	Qinghai	5883.8	5853.7	5664.6	4698.6	961.8	38.10
宁　夏	Ningxia	5582.2	5544.2	6064.2	4595.4	1466.6	34.00
新　疆	Xinjiang	6456.9	6395.0	5940.0	4931.4	1003.3	34.81

19-13 各省(市、区)农民家庭收支情况(2001年)

Per Capita Annual Income and Expendture of Rural Households (2001)

地区	Region	总收入 (元) Total Income (yuan)	#纯收入 Net Income	总支出 (元) Total Expenditure (yuan)	#生活消费 Living Expenditure	现金收入 (元) Cash Income (yuan)	现金支出 (元) Cash Expenditure (yuan)	恩格尔系数 (%) Engler Quotiety (%)
全 国	**National Total**	**3306.92**	**2366.40**	**2779.96**	**1741.09**	**2534.70**	**2284.62**	**47.7**
北 京	Beijing	6027.10	5025.50	4762.44	3552.07	5815.25	4686.29	35.2
天 津	Tianjin	5081.71	3947.72	3273.78	2050.89	4404.58	3044.17	42.8
河 北	Hebei	3478.42	2603.60	2389.20	1429.81	2788.67	2100.03	39.7
山 西	Shanxi	2500.89	1956.05	1834.03	1221.58	1957.30	1540.20	47.6
内蒙古	Inner Mongolia	3404.59	1973.37	3109.45	1554.59	2452.17	2529.21	43.7
辽 宁	Liaoning	3912.87	2557.93	3349.60	1786.28	3041.75	2837.83	45.6
吉 林	Jilin	3473.85	2182.22	3241.84	1661.69	2468.22	2775.31	45.6
黑龙江	Heilongjiang	4059.85	2280.28	3695.66	1604.53	3077.14	3224.82	42.7
上 海	Shanghai	6827.29	5870.87	6352.96	4753.23	6417.83	5961.79	40.3
江 苏	Jiangsu	4732.22	3784.71	3502.81	2374.66	3879.75	3067.06	42.6
浙 江	Zhejiang	5804.06	4582.34	4890.33	3479.17	5325.68	4544.52	41.6
安 徽	Anhui	2735.83	2020.04	2188.78	1412.41	2064.26	1747.87	49.8
福 建	Fujian	4291.44	3380.72	3571.40	2503.07	3709.35	3226.75	47.5
江 西	Jiangxi	2942.17	2231.60	2502.46	1720.01	2161.59	1956.99	51.5
山 东	Shandong	4161.97	2804.51	3326.79	1904.95	3362.19	2885.42	42.1
河 南	Henan	2916.28	2097.86	2251.59	1375.60	1967.64	1732.85	48.6
湖 北	Hubei	3124.10	2352.16	2597.86	1649.18	2189.22	1994.45	51.9
湖 南	Hunan	3305.64	2299.46	3030.13	1990.33	2550.02	2424.31	52.9
广 东	Guangdong	4742.76	3769.79	3682.98	2703.36	3945.53	3139.07	49.9
广 西	Guangxi	2753.79	1944.33	2424.20	1550.62	2076.02	1881.19	52.3
海 南	Hainan	2854.74	2226.47	1983.49	1357.43	2243.11	1500.92	59.0
重 庆	Chongqi	2709.49	1971.18	2250.39	1475.16	1752.07	1583.16	54.1
四 川	Sichuan	2946.30	1986.99	2494.07	1497.52	1983.26	1762.92	54.7
贵 州	Guizhu	1987.53	1411.73	1709.92	1098.39	1216.46	1096.59	60.0
云 南	Yunnan	2330.95	1533.74	2178.00	1336.25	1473.06	1420.09	57.5
西 藏	Tibet	1809.13	1404.01	1532.88	1123.71	1113.63	907.15	66.7
陕 西	Shanxi	2131.48	1490.80	2030.46	1331.03	1669.74	1711.71	41.9
甘 肃	Gansu	2080.05	1508.61	1759.16	1127.37	1413.24	1394.71	46.1
青 海	Qinghai	2157.65	1557.32	2055.53	1330.45	1470.60	1512.66	51.8
宁 夏	Ningxia	2987.70	1823.05	2680.15	1388.79	2295.15	2167.72	46.9
新 疆	Xinjiang	3129.68	1710.44	2879.17	1350.23	2316.72	2387.22	50.4

注:现金收支为已经扣除储蓄借贷后的现金收支。

Data on the cash income and expenditure are calculated with removing the factor of debit and credit.

19-14 各省(市、区)农林牧渔业总产值和指数(2001年)

Gross Output Value and the Related Indices of Farming, Forestry, Animal Husbandry and Fishery (2001)

地区	Region	农林牧渔业总产值（亿元） Gross Output Value (100 million yuan)	农业 Framing	林业 Forestry	牧业 Animal Husbandry	渔业 Fishery	指数（上年=100） Related Indices (precending year=100)
全 国	**National Total**	**26179.6**	**14462.8**	**938.8**	**7963.1**	**2815.0**	**104.2**
北 京	Beijing	214.1	89.7	9.5	105.2	9.6	107.5
天 津	Tianjin	169.5	86.7	1.5	60.8	20.6	108.0
河 北	Hebei	1680.5	899.4	34.0	685.9	61.2	105.3
山 西	Shanxi	301.5	191.3	12.3	96.3	1.7	93.0
内蒙古	Inner Mongolia	555.9	307.6	26.1	216.2	6.0	102.0
辽 宁	Liaoning	1045.7	503.1	21.8	332.3	188.5	106.6
吉 林	Jilin	659.3	405.9	11.3	236.4	5.8	106.9
黑龙江	Heilongjiang	711.0	450.6	15.7	224.6	20.1	106.4
上 海	Shanghai	227.6	95.5	3.5	88.4	40.1	107.5
江 苏	Jiangsu	1956.1	1142.7	30.8	448.5	334.2	104.5
浙 江	Zhejiang	1108.0	529.5	73.7	195.9	308.8	103.2
安 徽	Anhui	1258.1	688.0	66.2	371.6	132.3	102.8
福 建	Fujian	1061.6	433.2	82.3	215.5	330.5	103.9
江 西	Jiangxi	790.3	405.9	54.0	226.1	104.3	103.0
山 东	Shandong	2454.0	1401.3	47.2	654.7	350.7	104.0
河 南	Henan	2102.8	1331.6	57.0	693.8	20.4	105.6
湖 北	Hubei	1172.8	658.3	27.1	352.6	134.8	103.0
湖 南	Hunan	1313.2	665.7	51.9	51.4	85.2	104.0
广 东	Guangdong	1688.0	817.9	56.8	423.2	390.1	104.3
广 西	Guangxi	872.9	439.9	39.4	292.3	101.2	104.9
海 南	Hainan	325.1	141.3	43.3	58.2	82.3	113.5
重 庆	Chongqi	431.2	250.4	11.2	154.4	15.2	102.1
四 川	Sichuan	1466.8	769.9	50.9	605.0	41.0	102.6
贵 州	Guizhu	418.6	279.9	15.1	118.5	5.1	101.2
云 南	Yunnan	703.5	431.3	47.2	210.6	14.4	103.6
西 藏	Tibet	52.8	27.6	1.3	23.9	0.0	105.4
陕 西	Shanxi	478.8	337.4	23.6	114.1	3.8	102.5
甘 肃	Gansu	344.6	254.0	8.6	80.9	1.1	107.8
青 海	Qinghai	63.3	28.9	1.8	32.5	0.1	105.2
宁 夏	Ningxia	85.3	49.4	3.5	30.3	2.1	108.0
新 疆	Xinjiang	496.8	348.8	10.1	134.0	3.9	104.5

注:本表绝对数按当年价格计算,指数按可比价格计算。

Absolute data were calculated at current prices while the indices were calculated at comparable prices.

19-15 各省(市、区)主要农产品产量(2001年)

Output of Major Farm Production (2001)

单位：万吨 (10 000 tons)

地区	Region	粮食 Grain	#谷物 Cereal	油料 Oil-bearing Crops	棉花 Cotton	糖料 Sugar Crops	水果 Friutage
全国	**National Total**	**45263.7**	**39648.2**	**2864.8**	**532.4**	**8655.1**	**6658.0**
北京	Beijing	104.9	96.3	4.3	0.3		61.8
天津	Tianjin	143.3	134.0	3.9	6.4		29.3
河北	Hebei	2491.8	2309.0	153.8	41.9	9.9	669.8
山西	Shanxi	692.1	602.1	18.1	8.4	9.0	196.6
内蒙古	Inner Mongolia	1239.1	1016.5	80.6	0.3	133.1	19.5
辽宁	Liaoning	1394.4	1283.3	46.3	0.8	35.7	241.7
吉林	Jilin	1953.4	1775.6	34.3		69.4	34.7
黑龙江	Heilongjiang	2651.7	1989.1	36.3		329.8	21.3
上海	Shanghai	151.4	148.0	12.8	0.1	8.5	26.7
江苏	Jiangsu	2942.1	2745.1	232.5	46.1	32.0	195.3
浙江	Zhejiang	1072.7	952.1	58.2	3.2	106.0	250.6
安徽	Anhui	2500.3	2247.5	298.8	35.7	29.3	147.1
福建	Fujian	817.3	631.6	26.1		95.5	401.2
江西	Jiangxi	1600.0	1505.3	90.5	8.1	123.7	57.7
山东	Shandong	3720.6	3323.1	377.3	78.1	0.1	971.4
河南	Henan	4119.9	3724.7	362.5	82.8	26.2	399.1
湖北	Hubei	2138.5	1875.5	279.4	37.4	78.4	233.6
湖南	Hunan	2700.3	2476.2	137.4	19.0	166.4	185.1
广东	Guangdong	1600.1	1373.1	80.9		1213.0	686.2
广西	Guangxi	1511.4	1404.3	57.2	0.1	3653.3	406.3
海南	Hainan	195.8	157.0	10.3		320.8	143.6
重庆	Chongqi	1023.5	766.1	30.0		10.1	82.6
四川	Sichuan	2926.5	2400.3	181.0	3.0	155.8	272.9
贵州	Guizhu	1100.3	878.2	71.3	0.1	65.1	36.4
云南	Yunnan	1486.3	1246.7	27.7		1481.5	98.4
西藏	Tibet	98.3	95.0	4.4			0.7
陕西	Shanxi	976.6	865.9	37.5	5.0	1.9	493.7
甘肃	Gansu	753.2	568.4	38.4	9.9	45.1	121.7
青海	Qinghai	103.2	70.0	23.0			1.7
宁夏	Ningxia	274.8	249.0	7.3		0.3	16.9
新疆	Xinjiang	780.0	739.5	42.6	145.8	455.1	154.2

单位：万吨 19-15 续表 Continued (10 000 tons)

地 区	Region	肉类总产量 Total Output of Meat	猪肉 Pork	牛肉 Beef	羊肉 Mutton	奶类 Milk	水产品 Aquatic Products
全 国	**National Total**	**6333.92**	**4184.5**	**548.8**	**292.7**	**1122.9**	**4381.3**
北 京	Beijing	69.14	31.2	4.0	3.0	42.9	7.4
天 津	Tianjin	36.40	21.9	3.5	2.4	24.1	26.5
河 北	Hebei	445.68	260.3	68.5	25.6	119.3	84.9
山 西	Shanxi	63.53	44.2	6.6	6.9	40.4	2.8
内蒙古	Inner Mongolia	149.58	79.0	23.2	32.6	109.0	7.6
辽 宁	Liaoning	234.73	123.8	27.3	3.7	26.6	350.8
吉 林	Jilin	192.93	68.6	35.3	3.4	16.4	11.0
黑龙江	Heilongjiang	137.54	73.1	23.6	3.9	192.4	40.2
上 海	Shanghai	56.14	26.3	0.0	0.9	26.0	29.8
江 苏	Jiangsu	343.09	216.7	5.0	16.3	36.0	320.9
浙 江	Zhejiang	136.12	107.4	1.0	2.9	17.6	472.9
安 徽	Anhui	306.75	199.9	28.7	10.9	5.5	159.9
福 建	Fujian	139.99	107.2	2.2	1.5	11.4	542.5
江 西	Jiangxi	193.83	151.7	5.3	0.9	5.9	132.3
山 东	Shandong	595.44	298.7	73.0	27.6	90.4	686.1
河 南	Henan	537.93	343.8	89.2	34.5	30.0	31.5
湖 北	Hubei	264.28	205.1	13.4	3.6	8.8	242.2
湖 南	Hunan	456.85	389.8	13.2	6.7	1.8	141.0
广 东	Guangdong	333.33	213.7	5.2	0.5	10.4	609.7
广 西	Guangxi	266.14	208.1	10.4	2.6	2.1	247.8
海 南	Hainan	39.68	22.9	2.4	1.1	0.0	95.6
重 庆	Chongqi	146.28	122.6	4.7	2.1	6.8	19.7
四 川	Sichuan	541.34	441.2	22.3	16.3	33.3	57.1
贵 州	Guizhu	131.66	110.9	7.6	4.3	2.0	6.9
云 南	Yunnan	219.54	183.7	13.8	6.3	17.1	18.0
西 藏	Tibet	16.01	0.8	8.9	6.2	23.1	0.0
陕 西	Shanxi	85.53	61.8	8.2	5.8	69.5	6.3
甘 肃	Gansu	65.13	43.4	8.7	8.4	15.6	1.5
青 海	Qinghai	22.19	7.0	7.0	7.6	22.8	0.2
宁 夏	Ningxia	16.31	7.6	2.5	3.7	27.6	4.1
新 疆	Xinjiang	90.84	12.2	24.0	40.5	87.8	6.1

19-16 各省(市、区)规模工业增加值和指数(2001年)

Added Value of Industry and It's Indices (2001)

地区	Region	工业增加值（亿元） Added Value of Industry (100 million yuan)				2001年比上年增长% Increase Rate in 2001 Over 2000
		1998	1999	2000	2001	
全国	**National Total**	**19421.9**	**21564.7**	**25394.8**	**26950.0**	**9.9**
北京	Beijing	525.0	584.5	722.7	817.2	13.8
天津	Tianjin	451.3	490.1	630.1	689.6	13.0
河北	Hebei	889.1	976.6	1132.7	1215.9	10.6
山西	Shanxi	399.2	400.7	428.7	490.2	10.8
内蒙古	Inner Mongolia	222.6	235.7	279.5	307.2	12.9
辽宁	Liaoning	858.0	935.8	1194.0	1236.7	10.6
吉林	Jilin	355.3	412.2	496.2	557.3	15.1
黑龙江	Heilongjiang	777.3	933.8	1213.1	1253.5	10.6
上海	Shanghai	1333.2	1541.7	1687.2	1924.3	14.9
江苏	Jiangsu	1916.9	2234.6	2604.4	2920.7	12.0
浙江	Zhejiang	1098.4	1267.8	1560.1	1781.2	12.5
安徽	Anhui	445.0	494.5	507.4	550.1	11.6
福建	Fujian	601.5	665.0	797.1	813.6	11.8
江西	Jiangxi	232.8	249.0	269.7	286.0	10.9
山东	Shandong	1888.4	2098.8	2549.4	2908.4	14.8
河南	Henan	970.2	993.6	1116.4	1270.0	10.0
湖北	Hubei	898.2	946.4	1011.8	1096.8	12.8
湖南	Hunan	436.3	461.8	528.1	606.5	13.8
广东	Guangdong	2444.1	2788.2	3423.9	3553.8	12.8
广西	Guangxi	276.7	281.8	323.9	339.1	8.6
海南	Hainan	48.7	54.6	63.3	55.1	11.5
重庆	Chongqi	209.8	239.5	283.7	333.0	11.7
四川	Sichuan	593.0	634.3	662.4	776.1	13.0
贵州	Guizhu	181.8	196.0	217.0	235.9	9.8
云南	Yunnan	517.5	491.1	531.5	553.3	3.9
西藏	Tibet	7.1	8.4	9.3	9.5	5.8
陕西	Shanxi	286.2	346.0	411.2	455.0	9.7
甘肃	Gansu	207.9	225.6	244.7	296.5	11.5
青海	Qinghai	51.1	58.3	65.3	71.6	11.2
宁夏	Ningxia	57.7	61.6	73.7	82.6	9.2
新疆	Xinjiang	242.0	256.7	356.6	358.3	7.4

注:1.本表绝对数按当年价格计算;指数按可比价格计算。

2.本表综合范围是全部国有和年产品销售收入500万元以上的非国有企业。(下四表同)

a. Absolute data were calculated at current prices while the indices were calculated at comparable prices.

b. The coverage of this table was to cover all state-owned enterprises and the non-state-owned enterprises with an annual sales income of over 5 million yuan. (The same as in the following four tables.)

19-17 各省(市、区)工业主要经济指标(2001年)

Main Indicators of Industrial Economy (2001)

单位：亿元 (100 million yuan)

地区	Region	产品销售收入 Sales Revenue	#产品销售成本 Cost of Sales	#产品销售费用 Fees of Sales	#产品销售税金及附加 Sales Tax and Extra Charges	税金总额 Total Tax	利润总额 Total Profits
全　国	**National Total**	**92277.99**	**75690.00**	**3401.76**	**1554.50**	**5428.98**	**4657.19**
北　京	Beijing	2762.86	2328.89	128.67	25.01	120.57	126.96
天　津	Tianjin	2826.20	2325.39	118.10	27.72	134.36	184.07
河　北	Hebei	3709.26	3069.40	111.78	47.74	211.90	194.26
山　西	Shanxi	1275.22	965.87	93.01	18.83	105.77	39.14
内蒙古	Inner Mongolia	797.52	644.65	39.51	12.73	58.75	20.41
辽　宁	Liaoning	4425.63	3752.47	110.23	63.02	247.39	133.19
吉　林	Jilin	1790.12	1462.93	50.53	41.66	132.17	85.62
黑龙江	Heilongjiang	2406.33	1587.18	58.74	63.64	258.22	493.54
上　海	Shanghai	7191.48	5872.62	289.06	95.10	380.67	447.32
江　苏	Jiangsu	11269.45	9694.03	373.06	99.27	523.24	420.76
浙　江	Zhejiang	7472.16	6295.42	242.31	93.72	363.96	451.77
安　徽	Anhui	1798.52	1486.03	69.57	50.05	140.96	52.55
福　建	Fujian	2729.95	2282.74	94.39	49.17	138.36	113.67
江　西	Jiangxi	958.08	783.40	39.05	25.68	75.96	14.19
山　东	Shandong	9146.02	7550.32	304.34	107.02	487.85	571.48
河　南	Henan	3620.62	2990.29	129.72	64.72	217.87	138.49
湖　北	Hubei	3198.87	2569.80	123.96	70.88	213.96	119.26
湖　南	Hunan	1778.80	1422.19	65.13	87.09	182.36	51.67
广　东	Guangdong	13461.95	11200.71	555.71	122.25	493.55	583.53
广　西	Guangxi	1016.71	808.75	40.85	19.37	84.47	37.25
海　南	Hainan	164.77	125.73	16.68	3.65	12.18	6.35
重　庆	Chongqi	1057.94	859.20	53.08	23.06	75.28	21.79
四　川	Sichuan	2273.95	1774.98	121.71	52.08	166.67	84.60
贵　州	Guizhu	630.38	475.55	29.09	33.28	72.89	16.88
云　南	Yunnan	1123.23	722.78	35.35	172.24	262.97	81.10
西　藏	Tibet	11.66	8.06	1.11	0.27	1.25	0.91
陕　西	Shanxi	1256.09	957.47	52.16	33.29	98.92	60.40
甘　肃	Gansu	818.79	674.82	21.35	23.15	64.44	7.12
青　海	Qinghai	189.77	146.32	5.17	2.79	15.62	4.80
宁　夏	Ningxia	266.84	227.49	7.74	3.33	15.52	3.79
新　疆	Xinjiang	848.84	624.52	20.56	22.70	70.91	90.34

单位：亿元　　　　19-17 续表 continued　　　　(100 million yuan)

地 区	Region	亏损企业亏损额 Loss Value of Loss-making Enterprises	应收帐款净额 Net Value Receivables	产成品 Finished Goods	资产总计 Total Capital	负债总计 Total Liabilities	职工平均人数(万人) Average Staff and Workers (10000 persons)
全 国	**National Total**	**1112.41**	**14780.63**	**7037.59**	**134183.88**	**79647.67**	**5431.12**
北 京	Beijing	44.91	572.55	189.82	4291.70	2371.12	104.06
天 津	Tianjin	50.12	532.35	183.01	4004.94	2355.96	118.27
河 北	Hebei	43.00	495.61	334.94	5598.05	3480.67	264.50
山 西	Shanxi	22.00	298.12	152.17	3347.54	2247.41	175.51
内蒙古	Inner Mongolia	15.14	128.61	81.97	1946.45	1139.73	81.69
辽 宁	Liaoning	69.52	819.53	361.79	8285.97	4857.45	262.88
吉 林	Jilin	38.54	352.97	141.11	3302.61	2068.27	124.48
黑龙江	Heilongjiang	34.51	418.87	186.59	4217.17	2519.62	180.42
上 海	Shanghai	96.05	1277.04	392.98	10374.13	4826.17	204.65
江 苏	Jiangsu	82.07	1607.34	718.71	12107.70	7342.52	516.97
浙 江	Zhejiang	27.80	992.16	476.09	7222.46	3999.97	373.21
安 徽	Anhui	22.29	277.42	172.74	3150.52	1953.90	153.42
福 建	Fujian	36.36	427.29	186.19	3683.22	1997.91	155.75
江 西	Jiangxi	17.60	151.98	90.96	1898.41	1275.16	99.73
山 东	Shandong	46.08	916.13	634.27	10602.21	6452.86	522.61
河 南	Henan	41.43	538.77	323.42	5639.17	3632.47	335.63
湖 北	Hubei	40.46	543.44	212.43	5061.00	3112.33	223.38
湖 南	Hunan	30.11	287.24	144.74	3075.24	1958.40	154.42
广 东	Guangdong	152.04	2164.68	1026.44	14927.18	8571.75	572.32
广 西	Guangxi	21.45	158.33	105.72	1994.89	1317.85	89.57
海 南	Hainan	4.36	32.10	16.49	364.46	219.01	9.69
重 庆	Chongqi	22.36	233.20	87.07	1976.39	1269.14	84.92
四 川	Sichuan	36.48	465.19	230.68	4864.37	3045.82	202.20
贵 州	Guizhu	13.50	202.43	92.29	1670.04	1076.08	67.46
云 南	Yunnan	20.60	182.31	91.97	2553.05	1369.93	69.01
西 藏	Tibet	0.61	6.74	1.07	69.09	16.21	1.88
陕 西	Shanxi	30.56	290.23	156.31	2957.67	1933.32	118.64
甘 肃	Gansu	17.05	174.88	111.62	1887.37	1232.44	85.98
青 海	Qinghai	7.94	55.62	15.98	707.31	502.41	13.38
宁 夏	Ningxia	6.27	63.59	31.30	564.33	335.28	22.10
新 疆	Xinjiang	21.19	113.91	86.71	1839.26	1166.54	42.39

19-18 各省(市、区)工业经济效益指标(2001年)

Indicators on Industrial Economic Benefit (2001)

地区	Region	综合指数(%) Index of Synthesis (%)	总资产贡献率(%) Ratio of Ratio of Total Assets to Industrial Output Value(%)	资本保值增值率(%) Ratio of Assets Keeping Value and Increment (%)	资产负债率(%) Assets Liability Ratio (%)	流动资产周转次数(次/年) Number of Times of Annual of Turnover Circulating Funds (times/year)	成本费用利润率(%) Ratio of Pprofits to Industrial Cost (%)	全员劳动生产率(元/人) Overall Labor Productivity (yuan/ person-year)	产品销售率(%) Proportion of Products Sold (%)
全 国	**National Total**	**122.09**	**9.28**	**112.96**	**59.36**	**1.63**	**5.38**	**46315**	**97.72**
北 京	Beijing	131.57	6.81	112.44	55.25	1.42	4.68	76879	100.10
天 津	Tianjin	134.19	9.34	125.36	58.83	1.64	6.95	53182	98.45
河 北	Hebei	117.45	9.12	106.44	62.18	1.74	5.58	38492	98.10
山 西	Shanxi	84.77	6.00	113.74	67.14	1.06	3.22	21168	96.94
内蒙古	Inner Mongolia	90.61	5.95	113.57	58.55	1.28	2.63	27296	97.87
辽 宁	Liaoning	100.59	6.04	113.08	58.62	1.44	3.13	38021	97.35
吉 林	Jilin	111.06	8.01	114.12	62.63	1.38	4.96	39898	96.94
黑龙江	Heilongjiang	213.06	19.30	104.03	59.75	1.49	26.77	36531	97.67
上 海	Shanghai	157.15	9.61	120.31	46.52	1.56	6.59	94803	98.83
江 苏	Jiangsu	122.34	9.55	110.57	60.64	1.92	3.89	51384	97.14
浙 江	Zhejiang	143.64	13.65	118.51	55.38	2.10	6.45	53044	97.07
安 徽	Anhui	98.62	7.78	109.48	62.02	1.38	3.06	32342	98.00
福 建	Fujian	124.76	8.99	112.13	54.24	1.79	4.43	55198	97.29
江 西	Jiangxi	82.41	6.64	108.15	67.17	1.27	1.53	23527	97.26
山 东	Shandong	134.48	11.95	115.45	60.86	2.13	6.71	41895	97.77
河 南	Henan	101.43	8.50	110.53	64.41	1.51	4.03	27645	97.89
湖 北	Hubei	112.22	8.20	112.70	61.50	1.54	3.98	44281	97.73
湖 南	Hunan	102.25	9.62	110.82	63.68	1.51	3.11	30566	99.33
广 东	Guangdong	133.15	8.84	108.05	57.42	1.89	4.63	67585	97.33
广 西	Guangxi	102.19	7.87	111.38	66.06	1.43	3.87	34016	96.93
海 南	Hainan	113.88	6.54	105.19	60.09	1.14	3.96	60373	95.03
重 庆	Chongqi	94.58	6.66	115.13	64.22	1.18	2.12	37905	99.16
四 川	Sichuan	99.52	7.17	111.92	62.61	1.17	3.90	33755	98.04
贵 州	Guizhu	92.37	7.08	131.93	64.43	0.89	2.91	30060	95.10
云 南	Yunnan	150.14	16.24	115.40	53.66	1.22	9.16	53332	99.65
西 藏	Tibet	113.38	6.74	162.95	23.46	0.67	8.20	28994	88.32
陕 西	Shanxi	102.24	7.50	116.08	65.37	1.09	5.19	31193	96.98
甘 肃	Gansu	75.35	5.32	110.71	65.30	1.13	0.91	20703	96.99
青 海	Qinghai	80.73	4.88	106.97	71.03	0.81	2.72	28766	96.09
宁 夏	Ningxia	81.82	5.16	110.28	59.41	1.20	1.45	24869	96.98
新 疆	Xinjiang	143.29	10.44	105.74	63.42	1.36	12.44	41041	99.01

19-19 各省(市、区)主要工业产品产量(2001年)

Output of Major Industrial Production (2001)

地区	Region	钢(万吨) Steels (10 000 tons)	发电量(亿千瓦时) Electricity Hydropower (100 million kw.h)	原煤(万吨) Coal (10 000 tons)	水泥(万吨) Cement (10 000 tons)	农用化肥(万吨) Chemical Fertilizer (10 000 tons)	汽车(万辆) Motor Vehicle (10 000 units)
全国总计	**National Total**	**15266.1**	**14780.0**	**110700.0**	**64000.0**	**3396.5**	**233.4**
北京	Beijing	824.9	132.7	690.2	809.0	3.8	14.3
天津	Tianjin	395.3	217.4		339.0	14.9	5.9
河北	Hebei	1759.5	901.6	5865.7	4878.0	183.1	1.9
山西	Shanxi	603.8	707.4	21897.6	1309.3	159.9	0.1
内蒙古	Inner Mongolia	453.6	463.7	7422.2	636.2	35.0	0.1
辽宁	Liaoning	1660.7	662.1	4468.2	2100.5	159.6	7.9
吉林	Jilin	200.6	329.0	1632.1	895.5	3.1	39.1
黑龙江	Heilongjiang	92.1	438.1	5120.7	910.0	44.8	15.5
上海	Shanghai	1874.7	572.9		334.8	13.1	29.0
江苏	Jiangsu	836.1	986.6	2451.1	5135.7	187.6	9.8
浙江	Zhejiang	182.5	713.5	72.0	4762.8	62.5	3.6
安徽	Anhui	553.6	387.5	5347.5	2133.3	167.1	15.3
福建	Fujian	155.3	446.3	512.3	1525.5	57.4	3.3
江西	Jiangxi	399.4	216.2	1517.5	1606.7	48.1	16.0
山东	Shandong	722.6	1069.1	10687.8	6924.8	423.9	7.0
河南	Henan	531.0	791.1	8448.4	4200.8	280.1	0.9
湖北	Hubei	1003.9	587.3	333.9	2603.7	283.4	22.2
湖南	Hunan	441.9	384.4	1546.1	2496.0	146.1	2.1
广东	Guangdong	352.5	1351.7	123.6	5804.7	21.3	5.7
广西	Guangxi	128.5	292.3	613.5	2140.5	73.8	14.2
海南	Hainan	0.2	42.6	2.0	312.6	24.9	1.0
重庆	Chongqi	185.0	170.4	1154.7	1511.2	77.6	24.4
四川	Sichuan	690.8	583.6	2159.8	2816.6	282.8	2.7
贵州	Guizhu	147.0	480.3	3731.4	920.0	86.8	0.1
云南	Yunnan	219.6	340.4	1111.8	1534.0	194.8	2.7
西藏	Tibet		7.0	2.5	49.6		
陕西	Shanxi	69.4	303.5	4531.9	1110.2	97.3	1.9
甘肃	Gansu	236.6	285.7	1795.4	885.1	45.0	
青海	Qinghai	44.3	137.8	169.0	166.0	79.4	
宁夏	Ningxia		150.3	1551.1	311.2	69.2	
新疆	Xinjiang	127.5	180.4	1458.2	930.6	70.2	0.3

19-20 各省(市、区)建筑业总产值和房屋建筑面积

Total Output Value of Construction and Floor Space of Building Constrution

地 区	Region	总产值(亿元) Total Output Value of Construction (100 million yuan)		施工面积(万平方米) Floor Space of Buildings under Construction (10 000 sq.m)		竣工面积(万平方米) Floor Space of Buildings Completed (10 000 sq.m)	
		2000	2001	2000	2001	2000	2001
全 国	**National Total**	**12497.6**	**14000.2**	**160141.1**	**178757.5**	**80714.9**	**83778.1**
北 京	Beijing	727.5	887.9	7246.8	8919.4	2808.7	3197.6
天 津	Tianjin	238.1	277.9	2254.0	2122.9	1056.4	824.3
河 北	Hebei	492.1	522.7	6260.1	6714.2	3481.4	3530.3
山 西	Shanxi	239.4	280.5	2008.4	2079.5	946.7	930.4
内蒙古	Inner Mongolia	136.7	163.3	1804.9	2005.5	1119.5	1115.0
辽 宁	Liaoning	598.1	634.0	6334.9	7290.0	3547.9	3134.3
吉 林	Jilin	239.2	302.0	2209.5	2735.7	1439.7	1254.0
黑龙江	Heilongjiang	334.1	304.8	2962.6	3042.9	1886.9	1422.5
上 海	Shanghai	622.4	661.4	4625.8	4928.5	1710.0	1476.6
江 苏	Jiangsu	1538.8	1716.3	21190.2	22138.0	12237.6	12947.0
浙 江	Zhejiang	1383.8	1647.6	16570.1	20825.7	7145.3	9221.3
安 徽	Anhui	302.8	371.0	4631.3	6040.6	2595.3	3604.7
福 建	Fujian	271.1	299.2	4085.4	4495.1	1729.0	1757.1
江 西	Jiangxi	116.4	130.7	2572.3	2527.6	1359.8	1486.0
山 东	Shandong	817.1	876.4	11392.2	11967.4	5924.2	5632.1
河 南	Henan	357.3	448.0	5308.3	6164.7	2629.3	3060.4
湖 北	Hubei	454.2	454.0	6255.5	6784.0	3149.1	3872.0
湖 南	Hunan	354.4	398.4	5088.1	5016.7	2603.3	2483.2
广 东	Guangdong	892.0	998.2	15168.7	18444.7	6029.7	5972.0
广 西	Guangxi	150.9	170.7	2327.5	2408.7	1188.7	1124.7
海 南	Hainan	30.2	28.8	359.4	390.8	167.5	133.1
重 庆	Chongqi	348.7	409.4	6088.5	7710.8	3083.7	3441.5
四 川	Sichuan	713.8	776.8	10592.0	11350.9	5839.3	6047.5
贵 州	Guizhu	109.1	126.7	1792.5	1750.7	824.0	674.3
云 南	Yunnan	309.3	313.9	3479.2	3044.0	2189.7	1767.6
西 藏	Tibet	16.8		87.0		81.1	
陕 西	Shanxi	242.3	276.0	2396.5	2343.1	1087.2	919.7
甘 肃	Gansu	125.1	160.0	1905.4	1826.2	1058.8	981.3
青 海	Qinghai	44.7	45.5	339.4	375.3	192.9	138.8
宁 夏	Ningxia	56.2	64.8	563.1	656.9	340.7	393.1
新 疆	Xinjiang	235.0	253.9	2241.5	2657.0	1261.4	1235.7

19-21 各省(市、区)建筑业主要效益指标(2001年)

Main Value Indicators of Construction (2001)

地区	Region	企业个数(个) Number of Construction Enterprises (unit)	计算劳动生产率的平均人数(万人) Average Persons Calculated Overall Labor Productivity (10 000 persons)	按建筑业总产值计算的劳动生产率(元/人) Overall Labor Productivity in Terms of Total Output Value (yuan/person)	人均竣工产值(元/人) Per Capita Output Value of Completed (yuan/person)	人均施工面积(平方米) Per Capita Floor Space of Buildings under Construction (sq.m)	人均竣工面积(平方米) Per Capita Floor Space of Buildings Completed (sq.m)
全 国	**National Total**	**48639**	**2001.91**	**69934**	**43809**	**83.4**	**39.1**
北 京	Beijing	1893	58.04	152988	73791	106	38.0
天 津	Tianjin	468	18.39	151088	68881	82.4	32
河 北	Hebei	1753	87.86	59494	36105	69	36.3
山 西	Shanxi	832	34.43	81475	35318	54.2	24.2
内蒙古	Inner Mongolia	955	27.99	58357	26306	40.2	22.3
辽 宁	Liaoning	2517	97.66	64916	39029	68.0	29.2
吉 林	Jilin	673	29.97	100754	44110	75.3	34.5
黑龙江	Heilongjiang	1399	46.45	65610	30857	49.9	23.3
上 海	Shanghai	1481	28.10	235356	98113	126.7	38
江 苏	Jiangsu	3940	241	71214	53947	95	55.6
浙 江	Zhejiang	3454	170.43	96671	64604	125.1	55.4
安 徽	Anhui	1581	73.96	50162	41793	81.4	48.5
福 建	Fujian	1730	36.38	82229	53338	122.4	47.9
江 西	Jiangxi	1049	32.15	40638	22416	80.7	47.5
山 东	Shandong	4460	169.56	51686	28755	59.2	27.9
河 南	Henan	2497	82.5	54299	35445	71.7	35.6
湖 北	Hubei	1947	90.01	50438	42664	79.8	45.5
湖 南	Hunan	1657	77.11	51669	40919	69.2	34.3
广 东	Guangdong	3062	135.3	73775	40178	117.8	38.1
广 西	Guangxi	1179	34.00	50203	35735	72.8	34
海 南	Hainan	247	7.27	39560	22560	53.7	18.3
重 庆	Chongqi	1767	78.5	52148	32448	96.4	43
四 川	Sichuan	3122	157.29	49383	36273	73.8	39.3
贵 州	Guizhu	684	24.36	52016	27627	79.4	30.6
云 南	Yunnan	1487	52.98	59241	48168	70.2	40.7
西 藏	Tibet	-	-	-	-	-	-
陕 西	Shanxi	829	37.16	74265	39540	59.8	23.5
甘 肃	Gansu	550	31.49	50800	34393	55.3	29.7
青 海	Qinghai	248	8.34	54520	18829	37.9	14
宁 夏	Ningxia	501	8.13	79680	46917	56.7	33.9
新 疆	Xinjiang	677	25.10	101167	64285	93.0	43.24

19-22 各省(市、区)旅客周转量和货物周转量(2001年)

Passenger-Kilometers and Freight Ton-Kilometers (2001)

地区	Regions	旅客周转量(亿人公里) Total Passenger-Kilometers (100 million passenger-km)	铁路 Railways	公路 Highways	水运 Waterways	货物周转量(亿吨公里) Total Freight Ton-kilometers (100 million ton-km)	铁路 Railways	公路 Highways	水运 Waterways
全国	**National Total**	**13155.2**	**4766.8**	**7207.1**	**89.9**	**47590.3**	**14575.1**	**6330.4**	**25988.9**
北京	Beijing	121.2	68.2	53.0		393.6	311.0	82.6	
天津	Tianjin	94.1	72.0	22.0	…	5158.2	273.4	64.8	4820.1
河北	Hebei	860.9	415.6	445.3		2757.7	1637.0	608.0	512.7
山西	Shanxi	240.0	90.6	149.3	…	988.2	690.7	297.5	…
内蒙古	Inner Mongolia	209.3	87.4	121.9		985.0	764.6	220.4	
辽宁	Liaoning	513.1	337.6	167.1	8.4	1801.8	978.1	215.8	607.9
吉林	Jilin	212.2	132.6	79.5	0.1	500.1	413.7	86.0	…
黑龙江	Heilongjiang	382.5	163.3	219.1	0.1	937.9	761.6	161.2	15.2
上海	Shanghai	84.6	37.8	42.3	4.5	6721.7	39.4	60.3	6621.9
江苏	Jiangsu	860.0	176.7	682.2	1.1	1473.0	374.7	340.7	757.6
浙江	Zhejiang	653.3	166.0	479.5	7.8	1372.1	207.3	282.5	882.3
安徽	Anhui	542.0	217.6	323.4	0.9	1066.6	672.2	252.6	141.8
福建	Fujian	330.3	74.8	254.4	1.1	984.4	164.8	187.0	632.6
江西	Jiangxi	446.4	273.3	172.0	1.1	653.6	468.1	146.0	39.4
山东	Shandong	600.6	234.1	361.7	4.9	4693.1	848.2	429.0	3415.9
河南	Henan	799.8	430.1	369.4	0.3	1651.3	1263.5	375.8	12.0
湖北	Hubei	518.8	215.0	293.7	10.1	1069.3	546.4	224.5	298.4
湖南	Hunan	710.7	369.6	337.9	3.2	1111.6	654.4	316.0	141.2
广东	Guangdong	1130.3	280.0	841.3	9.1	3147.7	296.2	505.9	2345.5
广西	Guangxi	475.2	100.5	372.1	2.6	736.0	440.8	212.1	83.2
海南	Hainan	65.2	0.1	62.4	2.6	247.8	1.8	40.1	205.9
重庆	Chongqi	250.0	40.5	183.7	25.8	322.2	110.7	76.5	135.0
四川	Sichuan	530.5	143.2	383.5	3.8	675.1	471.8	191.1	12.2
贵州	Guizhu	251.1	124.2	125.8	1.1	439.3	364.7	70.4	4.2
云南	Yunnan	269.2	35.6	232.8	0.8	515.8	196.3	318.5	1.0
西藏	Tibet	5.3		5.3		17.2		17.2	
陕西	Shanxi	358.6	192.6	165.6	0.4	676.3	515.9	160.2	…
甘肃	Gansu	249.5	171.6	77.8	0.2	679.3	565.2	114.0	…
青海	Qinghai	33.0	13.4	19.6		97.5	59.0	38.4	
宁夏	Ningxia	51.4	18.0	33.4		223.4	164.9	58.5	
新疆	Xinjiang	215.0	85.0	130.0		495.4	318.7	176.8	
不分地区	Not Classified by Region	1091.0				4998.4			4301.9

注:不分地区合计中,包括公路和水运部门的直属企业、民航、管道完成数。

The total includes the quantities transported by highways, waterways, civil aviation and pipelines.

19-23 各省(市、区)社会消费品零售总额(2001年)

Total Retail Sales of Consumer Goods (2001)

(按销售单位所在地分) (By Location of Retailers)

地区	Region	社会消费品零售总额 (亿元) Total Retail Sales of Consumer Goods (100 million yuan)	市 City	县 County	县以下 Under County Level	比上年增长(%) Increase Rate in 2001 over 2000 (%)
全国	**National Total**	**37595.2**	**23543.4**	**4583.2**	**9468.6**	**10.1**
北京	Beijing	1593.5	1251.9	102.0	239.6	10.4
天津	Tianjin	832.7	651.2	62.4	119.1	13.0
河北	Hebei	1778.3	837.3	346.3	594.7	10.2
山西	Shanxi	679.9	408.3	135.7	135.9	8.1
内蒙古	Inner Mongolia	537.3	324.3	128.9	84.1	11.0
辽宁	Liaoning	2034.9	1683.6	114.2	237.1	10.1
吉林	Jilin	909.1	678.0	63.9	167.2	12.1
黑龙江	Heilongjiang	1198.9	867.4	171.8	159.7	9.6
上海	Shanghai	1861.3	1531.9	73.5	255.9	8.1
江苏	Jiangsu	2869.0	1898.9	198.6	771.5	10.2
浙江	Zhejiang	2555.5	1434.8	247.6	873.1	11.2
安徽	Anhui	1142.8	546.7	254.0	342.1	8.4
福建	Fujian	1499.5	844.9	198.6	456.0	9.2
江西	Jiangxi	763.3	368.9	171.2	223.2	8.3
山东	Shandong	2834.9	1758.4	273.7	802.8	11.4
河南	Henan	1979.8	976.7	416.6	586.5	10.8
湖北	Hubei	1975.2	1267.1	194.2	513.9	10.4
湖南	Hunan	1511.1	800.1	278.0	433.0	10.7
广东	Guangdong	4515.3	2974.4	239.5	1301.4	10.9
广西	Guangxi	935.9	463.1	194.6	278.2	8.9
海南	Hainan	187.5	124.1	16.0	47.4	8.7
重庆	Chongqi	699.3	397.4	96.1	205.8	8.7
四川	Sichuan	1680.4	790.7	292.0	597.7	10.3
贵州	Guizhu	378.0	220.0	72.3	85.7	10.0
云南	Yunnan	655.4	351.2	153.7	150.5	12.4
西藏	Tibet	49.0	21.7	21.6	5.7	14.2
陕西	Shanxi	665.1	443.5	110.5	111.1	9.5
甘肃	Gansu	395.4	255.9	62.8	76.7	9.0
青海	Qinghai	90.4	56.5	21.5	12.4	10.1
宁夏	Ningxia	98.9	64.8	18.1	16.0	9.6
新疆	Xinjiang	406.3	256.6	69.7	80.0	8.5

注: 1. 社会消费品零售总额及其增长速度均按当年价格计算。

2. 全国总计数字有调整,不等于各省合计(下两表同)。

a、Total retial sales of consumer goods and increase rate are calculated at current prices.

b、The national total was adjusted, The sum of provincial figures do not add up to the national total. Similarly in following two tables.

(按行业分组) (by sector)

continued

地 区	Regions	批发零售贸易业 Wholesale and Retail Sale Trade (100 million yuan)	餐饮业 Catering Trade (100 million yuan)	其他行业 Others (100 million yuan)		
					制造业 Manufacturing	农业生产者 Agriculture
全 国	**National Total**	**25510.8**	**4368.9**	**7715.5**	**2304.7**	**4191.7**
北 京	Beijing	1128.3	96.6	368.5	96.5	8.1
天 津	Tianjin	441.8	91.0	299.9	34.0	65.9
河 北	Hebei	1240	189.1	349.1	151.7	153.1
山 西	Shanxi	458.7	65.7	155.5	38.7	94.5
内蒙古	Inner Mongolia	349.1	56.5	131.7	37.9	71.5
辽 宁	Liaoning	1500.3	259.3	275.3	57.5	176.1
吉 林	Jilin	759.2	120.5	29.3	11.3	11.8
黑龙江	Heilongjiang	929.1	115.9	154	46	85.3
上 海	Shanghai	1482.8	141.6	236.8	46.9	175.6
江 苏	Jiangsu	2117.5	289.9	461.6	187.9	219.8
浙 江	Zhejiang	1792.5	250.2	512.9	165.5	272.1
安 徽	Anhui	735.4	131.2	276.2	85.9	166.3
福 建	Fujian	1086.9	171.1	241.5	74.5	93.5
江 西	Jiangxi	472	66.9	224.5	50.6	147.7
山 东	Shandong	1825	312.8	697.1	283.7	277.7
河 南	Henan	1235.9	246.4	497.6	251.9	178.5
湖 北	Hubei	1221.6	225.7	527.9	99.5	317.5
湖 南	Hunan	985.1	161.1	364.8	77.9	257.6
广 东	Guangdong	3234.3	739.5	541.5	183.9	287.4
广 西	Guangxi	628.8	112.7	194.3	47	125.2
海 南	Hainan	113.2	26	48.2	4.9	36.3
重 庆	Chongqi	427.3	60.6	211.5	41.2	161.3
四 川	Sichuan	976.4	262	442.0	97.2	296.2
贵 州	Guizhu	253.5	52.4	72.1	18.9	45.4
云 南	Yunnan	416	92.8	146.6	29.7	100.1
西 藏	Tibet	38.1	5.6	5.3	2.2	2.4
陕 西	Shanxi	418.2	72.2	174.7	56	104.1
甘 肃	Gansu	259	51.9	84.6	17.6	48.8
青 海	Qinghai	63	12.8	14.6	3.8	8.5
宁 夏	Ningxia	59.7	13.8	25.3	3.7	19.3
新 疆	Xinjiang	266.4	44.6	95.4	22.0	52.3

19-24 各省(市、区)海关进出口总额

Total Value of Import and Export (Customs Statistics)

单位：亿美元 (USD 100 million)

地区	Region	2000			2001		
		进出口总额 Imports and Exports	出口额 Exports	进口额 Imports	进出口总额 Imports and Exports	出口额 Exports	进口额 Imports
全　国	**National Total**	**4743.1**	**2492.1**	**2251**	**5097.7**	**2661.6**	**2436.1**
北　京	Beijing	242.4	76.6	165.8	515.4	117.9	397.5
天　津	Tianjin	171.6	76.8	94.8	181.7	94.9	86.8
河　北	Hebei	54.9	32.8	22.1	57.4	39.6	17.8
山　西	Shanxi	27.9	20.9	7	19.4	14.7	4.7
内蒙古	Inner Mongolia	23.9	11.2	12.7	20.4	6.3	14.1
辽　宁	Liaoning	200.7	105.9	94.8	198.1	110.1	88.0
吉　林	Jilin	29.9	14.9	15	32.1	14.6	17.5
黑龙江	Heilongjiang	39.9	24.2	15.7	33.8	16.1	17.7
上　海	Shanghai	547	246.4	300.6	608.9	276.2	332.7
江　苏	Jiangsu	492	263.8	228.2	513.5	288.7	224.8
浙　江	Zhejiang	315.2	204.8	110.4	328.0	229.8	98.2
安　徽	Anhui	36.9	21.2	15.7	36.2	22.8	13.4
福　建	Fujian	229.6	136.3	93.3	226.3	139.3	87.0
江　西	Jiangxi	20.5	11.9	8.6	15.3	10.4	4.9
山　东	Shandong	282.5	160.9	121.6	289.5	181.2	108.3
河　南	Henan	31.2	15.8	15.4	27.8	17.0	10.8
湖　北	Hubei	38.9	19	19.9	35.8	18.0	17.8
湖　南	Hunan	25.1	16.5	8.6	27.6	17.5	10.1
广　东	Guangdong	1754.9	934.3	820.6	1765.0	954.3	810.7
广　西	Guangxi	22.9	16.4	6.5	18.0	12.4	5.6
海　南	Hainan	10.9	6.1	4.8	17.5	8.0	9.5
重　庆	Chongqi	18.5	10.6	7.9	18.3	11.0	7.3
四　川	Sichuan	27.8	14.3	13.5	31.0	15.8	15.2
贵　州	Guizhu	8.6	4.8	3.8	6.5	4.2	2.3
云　南	Yunnan	18.8	10.9	7.9	19.9	12.4	7.5
西　藏	Tibet	1.5	1.1	0.4	0.9	0.8	0.1
陕　西	Shanxi	23.9	13.3	10.6	20.6	11.1	9.5
甘　肃	Gansu	6.9	4.2	2.7	7.8	4.8	3.0
青　海	Qinghai	2.3	1.4	0.9	2.0	1.5	0.5
宁　夏	Ningxia	5.3	3.5	1.8	5.3	3.5	1.8
新　疆	Xinjiang	25.9	11.5	14.4	17.7	6.7	11.0

19-25 各省(市、区)外商直接投资额

Actually Used Foreign Direct Investment

单位：万美元　　　　(USD 10 000)

		1996	1997	1998	1999	2000	2001
全　国	**National Total**	**4172552**	**4525704**	**4546275**	**4031871**	**4071481**	**4687759**
北　京	Beijing	155290	159286	216800	197525	168368	176818
天　津	Tianjin	200637	251135	211361	176399	116601	213348
河　北	Hebei	82587	110064	142868	104202	67923	66989
山　西	Shanxi	13802	26592	24451	39129	22472	23393
内蒙古	Inner Mongolia	7186	7325	9082	6456	10568	10703
辽　宁	Liaoning	173768	220470	219045	106173	204446	251612
吉　林	Jilin	45155	40227	40917	30120	33701	33766
黑龙江	Heilongjiang	54841	73485	52639	31828	30086	34114
上　海	Shanghai	394094	422536	360150	283665	316014	429159
江　苏	Jiangsu	521009	543511	663179	607756	642550	691482
浙　江	Zhejiang	152050	150345	131802	123262	161266	221162
安　徽	Anhui	50661	43443	27673	26131	31847	33672
福　建	Fujian	408451	419666	421211	402403	343191	391804
江　西	Jiangxi	30068	47768	46496	32080	22724	39575
山　东	Shandong	259041	249294	220274	225878	297119	352093
河　南	Henan	52356	69204	61654	52135	56403	45729
湖　北	Hubei	68004	79019	97294	91488	94368	118860
湖　南	Hunan	70344	91702	81816	65374	67833	81011
广　东	Guangdong	1162362	1171083	1201994	1165750	1128091	1193203
广　西	Guangxi	65618	87986	88613	63512	52466	38416
海　南	Hainan	78908	70554	71715	48449	43080	46691
重　庆	Chongqi	19412	38675	43107	23893	24436	25649
四　川	Sichuan	23132	24846	37248	34101	43694	58188
贵　州	Guizhu	3138	4977	4535	4090	2501	2829
云　南	Yunnan	6537	16566	14568	15385	12812	6457
西　藏	Tibet						
陕　西	Shanxi	32509	62816	30010	24197	28842	35174
甘　肃	Gansu	9002	4144	3864	4104	6235	7439
青　海	Qinghai	100	247		459		3649
宁　夏	Ningxia	555	671	1856	5134	1741	1680
新　疆	Xinjiang	6390	2472	2167	2404	1911	2035

19-26 各省(市、区)外商投资企业进出口商品总值

Total Value of Import and Export Goods of Foreign – Funded Enterprises

单位：万美元 (USD 10 000)

地区	Region	2000			2001		
		进出口总额 Imports and Exports	出口额 Exports	进口额 Imports	进出口总额 Imports and Exports	出口额 Exports	进口额 Imports
全 国	**National Total**	**23671390**	**11944121**	**11727269**	**25909797**	**13323506**	**12586290**
北 京	Beijing	776847	287108	489739	864474	323871	540603
天 津	Tianjin	1369289	637925	731364	1434185	710297	723888
河 北	Hebei	158147	101240	56907	180345	114229	66116
山 西	Shanxi	41876	15209	26667	26214	15445	10769
内蒙古	Inner Mongolia	18156	13798	4358	17852	12894	4958
辽 宁	Liaoning	1229697	624463	605234	1220577	629968	590609
吉 林	Jilin	112274	39197	73077	149260	42787	106473
黑龙江	Heilongjiang	47353	26679	20674	45231	25935	19296
上 海	Shanghai	3341054	1426102	1914952	3679700	1595857	2083843
江 苏	Jiangsu	3018081	1445340	1572741	3419131	1664217	1754914
浙 江	Zhejiang	938993	534851	404142	1187147	709930	477217
安 徽	Anhui	94779	39993	54786	99142	43112	56030
福 建	Fujian	1405740	759713	646027	1503478	828809	674669
江 西	Jiangxi	31814	16298	15516	28054	11233	16821
山 东	Shandong	1392568	792766	599802	1626503	923578	702925
河 南	Henan	57696	30889	26807	59699	31396	28303
湖 北	Hubei	104685	42956	61729	131725	50064	81661
湖 南	Hunan	47717	18250	29467	55962	21256	34706
广 东	Guangdong	9203696	4951011	4252685	9863228	5437384	4425844
广 西	Guangxi	55340	34112	21228	46242	24353	21889
海 南	Hainan	45993	30464	15529	80961	30039	50922
重 庆	Chongqi	32389	9666	22723	31346	9228	22118
四 川	Sichuan	61524	24517	37007	66734	23997	42737
贵 州	Guizhu	5690	4012	1678	6325	4423	1902
云 南	Yunnan	19658	8113	11545	21190	10952	10238
西 藏	Tibet	634	389	245	236	217	19
陕 西	Shanxi	35435	11612	23823	36600	10808	25792
甘 肃	Gansu	5657	3833	1824	8910	5294	3616
青 海	Qinghai	925	202	723	2328	154	2174
宁 夏	Ningxia	6125	4294	1831	7443	5904	1539
新 疆	Xinjiang	11559	9120	2439	9579	5877	3702

19-27 各省(市、区)国际旅游业接待情况

Basic Indicators of International Tourisn

地区	Region	2000 旅游人数(万人次) Number of Tourists (10 000 person-times)	2000 #外国人 Foreigners	2000 旅游创汇总额(亿美元) Foreign Exchange Earnings from Tourisn (USD 100 million)	2001 旅游人数(万人次) Number of Tourists (10 000 person-times)	2001 #外国人 Foreigners	2001 旅游创汇总额(亿美元) Foreign Exchange Earnings from Tourisn (USD 100 million)
北京	Beijing	282.09	237.96	27.68	285.8	239.9	29.5
天津	Tianjin	35.62	32.14	2.32	42.1	37.5	2.8
河北	Hebei	41.43	35.90	1.42	44.5	39.10	1.6
山西	Shanxi	16.53	11.66	0.50	19.8	12.9	0.60
内蒙古	Inner Mongolia	39.19	38.74	1.26	40	39.6	1.4
辽宁	Liaoning	61.22	50.05	3.82	72.4	60.7	4.6
吉林	Jilin	22.27	19.19	0.58	27.2	23.7	0.8
黑龙江	Heilongjiang	55.17	50.47	1.89	61.2	56.5	2.5
上海	Shanghai	181.40	143.90	16.13	204.30	151.60	18.1
江苏	Jiangsu	160.95	98.15	7.24	183.7	108.6	8.2
浙江	Zhejiang	112.59	64.75	5.14	147	82	7
安徽	Anhui	31.84	16.79	0.86	38.1	18.6	1.1
福建	Fujian	161.33	49.70	8.94	163.5	46.5	9.4
江西	Jiangxi	16.31	5.54	0.62	19.6	5.5	0.7
山东	Shandong	72.31	48.01	3.15	82.9	59.2	3.8
河南	Henan	32.50	18.21	1.24	36.60	24.9	1.3
湖北	Hubei	45.08	35.73	1.46	66.8	54.3	2
湖南	Hunan	45.40	15.79	2.21	50.50	18.8	2.7
广东	Guangdong	1198.94	212.85	41.12	1292.4	240.4	44.8
广西	Guangxi	122.91	50.80	3.07	126.7	55.00	3
海南	Hainan	48.68	9.37	1.09	45.7	13	1
重庆	Chongqi	26.61	19.29	1.38	31.3	21.9	1.6
四川	Sichuan	46.20	19.97	1.22	57.50	28.1	1.7
贵州	Guizhu	18.39	7.12	0.61	20.5	7.9	0.7
云南	Yunnan	100.11	66.59	3.39	113.1	69.6	3.7
西藏	Tibet	15.00	13.58	0.52	12.70	11.6	0.5
陕西	Shanxi	71.28	58.48	2.80	75.9	63.8	3.10
甘肃	Gansu	21.31	14.34	0.50	22.3	14.6	0.4
青海	Qinghai	3.26	1.46	0.07	4	1.8	0.1
宁夏	Ningxia	0.78	0.58	0.03	0.9	0.6	0.03
新疆	Xinjiang	25.61	20.84	0.94	27.3	21.9	1

中国统计出版社

最新资料书简目

中国统计年鉴-2002
中国统计摘要-2002
2002中国发展报告
中国城市统计年鉴-2001
中国农村统计年鉴-2002
中国劳动统计年鉴-2002
中国人口统计年鉴-2002
中国社会统计资料-2001
中国工业经济统计年鉴-2001
中国市场统计年鉴-2002
2001中国城市发展报告
中国建筑业统计年鉴-2001
中国固定资产投资统计年鉴-2002
中国价格及城镇居民家庭收支调查统计年鉴-2002
国际统计年鉴-2002
中国西部统计年鉴-2001
中国对外经济贸易统计年鉴-2001
中国商品交易市场统计年鉴-2001
中国基本单位统计年鉴-2001
中国食品工业年鉴-2001
中国民政统计年鉴-2002
如何使用统计年鉴
中国市民的经济观
北京统计年鉴-2002
天津统计年鉴-2002
河北经济年鉴-2002
山西统计年鉴-2002
内蒙古统计年鉴-2002
辽宁统计年鉴-2002
吉林统计年鉴-2002
黑龙江统计年鉴-2002
上海统计年鉴-2002
江苏统计年鉴-2002
浙江统计年鉴-2002
安徽统计年鉴-2002
福建统计年鉴-2002
江西统计年鉴-2002
山东统计年鉴-2002
河南统计年鉴-2002
湖北统计年鉴-2002
湖南统计年鉴-2002
广东统计年鉴-2002
广西统计年鉴-2002
贵州统计年鉴-2002

云南统计年鉴-2002
海南统计年鉴-2002
四川统计年鉴-2002
重庆统计年鉴-2002
西藏统计年鉴-2002
陕西统计年鉴-2002
甘肃年鉴-2002
青海统计年鉴-2002
宁夏统计年鉴-2002
甘肃年鉴-2002
新疆统计年鉴-2002
新疆生产建设兵团统计年鉴-2002
石家庄统计年鉴-2002
唐山统计年鉴-2002
保定统计年鉴-2002
邯郸统计年鉴-2002
张家口统计年鉴-2002
伊克昭盟统计年鉴-2002
太原统计年鉴-2002
临汾年鉴-2002
呼和浩特经济统计年鉴-2002
沈阳年鉴-2002
大连统计年鉴-2002
吉林省社会经济统计年鉴-2002
四平统计年鉴-2002
延吉统计年鉴-2002
哈尔滨统计年鉴-2002
齐齐哈尔经济统计年鉴-2002
黑龙江垦区统计年鉴-2002
牡丹江统计年鉴-2002
上海浦东新区统计年鉴-2002
连云港统计年鉴-2002
南京统计年鉴-2002
苏州统计年鉴-2002
无锡统计年鉴-2002
常州统计年鉴-2002
徐州统计年鉴-2002
南通统计年鉴-2002
盐城统计年鉴-2002
杭州统计年鉴-2002
宁波统计年鉴-2002
绍兴统计年鉴-2002
台州统计年鉴-2002
舟山统计年鉴-2002
温州统计年鉴-2002

福州年鉴-2002
厦门经济特区年鉴-2002
福州经济技术开发区年鉴-2002
南昌统计年鉴-2002
九江统计年鉴-2002
河池地区年鉴-2002
青岛统计年鉴-2002
天水统计年鉴-2002
泰安统计年鉴-2002
昆明统计年鉴-2002
济南统计年鉴-2001
郑州统计年鉴-2002
洛阳统计年鉴-2002
十堰统计年鉴-2002
三门峡统计年鉴-2002
平顶山统计年鉴-2002
南阳经济统计年鉴-2002
武汉统计年鉴-2002
宜昌统计年鉴-2002
广州统计年鉴-2002
深圳统计信息年鉴-2002
惠州统计年鉴-2002
珠海统计年鉴-2002
东莞统计年鉴-2002
南宁统计年鉴-2002
南宁地区统计年鉴-2002
桂林经济社会统计年鉴-2002
柳州经济统计年鉴-2002
柳州地区统计年鉴-2002
贵阳统计年鉴-2002
海口统计年鉴-2002
成都统计年鉴-2002
广安统计年鉴-2002
攀枝花统计年鉴-2002
西安统计年鉴-2002
兰州年鉴-2001
西宁统计年鉴-2002
乌鲁木齐统计年鉴-2002
巴音郭楞统计年鉴-2002
吐鲁番统计年鉴-2002
石河子统计年鉴-2002
庆阳年鉴-2002
银川统计年鉴-2002

编辑部电话：（010）63262276 63266600-30607

欲购以上图书请与中国统计出版社发行部联系。 电话：（010）63459084 同椙行书店电话：68585978

通讯地址：北京市西城区三里河月坛南街75号。 邮政编码：100826

求真